JavaScript & jQuery

the missing manual®

The book that should have been in the box®

JavaScript & jQuery

2nd Edition

the missing manual®

The book that should have been in the box®

David Sawyer McFarland

O'REILLY®

Beijing | Cambridge | Farnham | Köln | Sebastopol | Tokyo

JavaScript & jQuery: The Missing Manual, Second Edition

by David Sawyer McFarland

Copyright © 2012 David Sawyer McFarland. All rights reserved.

Printed in the United States of America.

Published by O'Reilly Media, Inc., 1005 Gravenstein Highway North, Sebastopol, CA 95472.

O'Reilly Media books may be purchased for educational, business, or sales promotional use. Online editions are also available for most titles: *safari.oreilly.com*. For more information, contact our corporate/institutional sales department: 800-998-9938 or *corporate@oreilly.com*.

Printing History:

July 2008:	First Edition.
October 2011:	Second Edition.

ISBN: 978-1-449-3-9902-3

[M]

Table of Contents

The Missing Credits. xiii

Introduction 1

Part One: Getting Started with JavaScript

Chapter 1: Writing Your First JavaScript Program 21
Introducing Programming 22
    What's a Computer Program? 24
How to Add JavaScript to a Page 25
    External JavaScript Files 27
Your First JavaScript Program 29
Writing Text on a Web Page 31
Attaching an External JavaScript File 33
Tracking Down Errors 34
    The Firefox JavaScript Console 35
    Displaying the Internet Explorer 9 Console 37
    Opening the Chrome JavaScript Console 38
    Accessing the Safari Error Console 39

Chapter 2: The Grammar of JavaScript 41
Statements 41
Built-In Functions 42
Types of Data 42
    Numbers 43
    Strings 43
    Booleans 44
Variables 45
    Creating a Variable 45
    Using Variables 48
Working with Data Types and Variables 50
    Basic Math 50
    The Order of Operations 51

Combining Strings 51
Combining Numbers and Strings 52
Changing the Values in Variables 53
Tutorial: Using Variables to Create Messages 55
Tutorial: Asking for Information 57
Arrays 59
Creating an Array 60
Accessing Items in an Array 62
Adding Items to an Array 63
Deleting Items from an Array 66
Tutorial: Writing to a Web Page Using Arrays 66
A Quick Object Lesson 70
Comments 72
When to Use Comments 73
Comments in This Book 74

Chapter 3: Adding Logic and Control to Your Programs 77
Making Programs React Intelligently 77
Conditional Statement Basics 79
Adding a Backup Plan 82
Testing More Than One Condition 83
More Complex Conditions 86
Nesting Conditional Statements 88
Tips for Writing Conditional Statements 88
Tutorial: Using Conditional Statements 89
Handling Repetitive Tasks with Loops 93
While Loops 93
Loops and Arrays 95
For Loops 97
Do/While Loops 98
Functions: Turn Useful Code Into Reusable Commands 100
Mini-Tutorial 101
Giving Information to Your Functions 102
Retrieving Information from Functions 104
Keeping Variables from Colliding 105
Tutorial: A Simple Quiz 108

Part Two: Getting Started with jQuery

Chapter 4: Introducing jQuery 117
About JavaScript Libraries 117
Getting jQuery 119
Adding jQuery to a Page 122
Modifying Web Pages: An Overview 124
Understanding the Document Object Model 127

Selecting Page Elements: The jQuery Way 129
    Basic Selectors 130
    Advanced Selectors 133
    jQuery Filters 135
    Understanding jQuery Selections 136
Adding Content to a Page 138
    Replacing and Removing Selections 140
Setting and Reading Tag Attributes 141
    Classes 142
    Reading and Changing CSS Properties 143
    Changing Multiple CSS Properties at Once 144
Reading, Setting, and Removing HTML Attributes 146
Acting on Each Element in a Selection 147
    Anonymous Functions 148
    this and *$(this)* 149
Automatic Pull Quotes 150
    Overview 151
    Programming 152

Chapter 5: Action/Reaction: Making Pages Come Alive with Events 157

What Are Events? 157
    Mouse Events 159
    Document/Window Events 160
    Form Events 161
    Keyboard Events 162
Using Events the jQuery Way 162
Tutorial: Introducing Events 165
More jQuery Event Concepts 169
    Waiting for the HTML to Load 169
    jQuery Events 171
    The Event Object 173
    Stopping an Event's Normal Behavior 175
    Removing Events 175
Advanced Event Management 177
    Other Ways to Use the *bind()* Function 179
Tutorial: A One-Page FAQ 180
    Overview of the Task 180
    The Programming 180

Chapter 6: Animations and Effects 185

jQuery Effects 185
    Basic Showing and Hiding 187
    Fading Elements In and Out 187
    Sliding Elements 188

Tutorial: Login Slider 190
    The Programming 191
Animations 192
    Easing 194
Performing an Action After an Effect Is Completed 196
Tutorial: Animated Dashboard 198
    The Programming 200

Part Three: Building Web Page Features

Chapter 7: Improving Your Images 207
Swapping Images 207
    Changing an Image's src Attribute 208
    Preloading Images 209
    Rollover Images 210
Tutorial: Adding Rollover Images 211
    Overview of the Task 212
    The Programming 213
Tutorial: Photo Gallery with Effects 216
    Overview of Task 217
    The Programming 218
Advanced Gallery with jQuery FancyBox 222
    The Basics 223
    Creating a Gallery of Images 225
    Customizing FancyBox 226
Tutorial: FancyBox Photo Gallery 231

Chapter 8: Improving Navigation 235
Some Link Basics 235
    Selecting Links with JavaScript 235
    Determining a Link's Destination 236
    Don't Follow That Link 237
Opening External Links in a New Window 238
Creating New Windows 240
    Window Properties 241
Opening Pages in a Window on the Page 245
    Tutorial: Opening a Page Within a Page 248
Basic, Animated Navigation Bar 249
    The HTML 250
    The CSS 252
    The JavaScript 253
    The Tutorial 254

Chapter 9: Enhancing Web Forms. **257**

Understanding Forms. 257

    Selecting Form Elements 259

    Getting and Setting the Value of a Form Element 261

    Determining Whether Buttons and Boxes Are Checked. 262

    Form Events. 263

Adding Smarts to Your Forms. 268

    Focusing the First Field in a Form 268

    Disabling and Enabling Fields 269

    Hiding and Showing Form Options 271

Tutorial: Basic Form Enhancements 272

    Focusing a Field 273

    Disabling Form Fields 273

    Hiding Form Fields 276

Form Validation 278

    jQuery Validation Plug-in. 280

    Basic Validation. 281

    Advanced Validation 284

    Styling Error Messages 290

Validation Tutorial. 291

    Basic Validation. 292

    Advanced Validation 294

    Validating Checkboxes and Radio Buttons 297

    Formatting the Error Messages 299

Chapter 10: Expanding Your Interface **301**

Organizing Information in Tabbed Panels 301

    The HTML. 302

    The CSS. 304

    The JavaScript 306

    Tabbed Panels Tutorial 307

Adding a Content Slider to Your Site 312

    Using AnythingSlider 313

    AnythingSlider Tutorial 314

    Customizing the Slider Appearance 316

    Customizing the Slider Behavior 318

Determining the Size and Position of Page Elements 319

    Determining the Height and Width of Elements. 319

    Determining the Position of Elements on a Page 322

    Determining a Page's Scrolling Position 324

Adding Tooltips 326

    The HTML. 326

    The CSS. 328

    The JavaScript 328

    Tooltips Tutorial. 329

Part Four: Ajax: Communication with the Web Server

Chapter 11: Introducing Ajax **341**
What Is Ajax? 342
Ajax: The Basics 343
Pieces of the Puzzle 344
Talking to the Web Server 346
Ajax the jQuery Way 349
Using the *load()* Function 349
Tutorial: The *load()* Function 352
The *get()* and *post()* Functions 356
Formatting Data to Send to the Server 357
Processing Data from the Server 360
Handling Errors 364
Tutorial: Using the *get()* Function 365
JSON 370
Accessing JSON Data 372
Complex JSON Objects 373

Chapter 12: Flickr and Google Maps **377**
Introducing JSONP 377
Adding a Flickr Feed to Your Site 378
Constructing the URL 379
Using the *$.getJSON()* Function 381
Understanding the Flickr JSON Feed 381
Tutorial: Adding Flickr Images to Your Site 383
Adding Google Maps to Your Site 387
Setting a Location for the Map 390
Other GoMap Options 391
Adding Markers 393
Adding Information Windows to Markers 397
GoMap Tutorial 397

Part Five: Tips, Tricks, and Troubleshooting

Chapter 13: Getting the Most from jQuery **403**
Useful jQuery Tips and Information 403
$() Is the Same as *jQuery()* 403
Saving Selections Into Variables 404
Adding Content as Few Times as Possible 405
Optimizing Your Selectors 406
Using the jQuery Docs 407
Reading a Page on the jQuery Docs Site 411
Traversing the DOM 413
More Functions For Manipulating HTML 419
Advanced Event Handling 421

Chapter 14: Going Further with JavaScript 425

Working with Strings 425
    Determining the Length of a String 425
    Changing the Case of a String 426
    Searching a String: *indexOf()* Technique 427
    Extracting Part of a String with *slice()* 428
Finding Patterns in Strings 430
    Creating and Using a Basic Regular Expression 431
    Building a Regular Expression 432
    Grouping Parts of a Pattern 435
    Useful Regular Expressions 436
    Matching a Pattern 441
    Replacing Text 443
    Trying Out Regular Expressions 444
Working with Numbers 445
    Changing a String to a Number 445
    Testing for Numbers 447
    Rounding Numbers 448
    Formatting Currency Values 448
    Creating a Random Number 449
Dates and Times 450
    Getting the Month 451
    Getting the Day of the Week 452
    Getting the Time 452
    Creating a Date Other Than Today 456
Putting It All Together 457
    Using External JavaScript Files 457
Writing More Efficient JavaScript 459
    Putting Preferences in Variables 460
    Ternary Operator 461
    The Switch Statement 462
Creating Fast-Loading JavaScript 465

Chapter 15: Troubleshooting and Debugging 467

Top JavaScript Programming Mistakes 467
    Non-Closed Pairs 467
    Quotation Marks 472
    Using Reserved Words 472
    Single Equals in Conditional Statements 473
    Case-Sensitivity 473
    Incorrect Path to External JavaScript File 474
    Incorrect Paths Within External JavaScript Files 474
    Disappearing Variables and Functions 476
Debugging with Firebug 477
    Installing and Turning On Firebug 477
    Viewing Errors with Firebug 478

Using *console.log()* to Track Script Progress 479
Tutorial: Using the Firebug Console 481
More Powerful Debugging 485
Debugging Tutorial 489

Appendix A: JavaScript Resources 497

Index 503

TABLE OF CONTENTS

The Missing Credits

About the Author

 **David Sawyer McFarland** is president of Sawyer McFarland Media, Inc., a web development and training company in Portland, Oregon. He's been building websites since 1995, when he designed his first site—an online magazine for communication professionals. He's served as webmaster at the University of California at Berkeley and the Berkeley Multimedia Research Center, and oversaw a complete CSS-driven redesign of Macworld.com.

In addition to building websites, David is also a writer, trainer, and instructor. He's taught web design at UC Berkeley Graduate School of Journalism, the Center for Electronic Art, the Academy of Art College, Ex'Pressions Center for New Media, and Portland State University. He's written articles about the web for *Practical Web Design, MX Developer's Journal, Macworld* magazine, and CreativePro.com.

He welcomes feedback about this book by email: *missing@sawmac.com*. (If you're seeking technical help, however, please refer to the sources listed in Appendix A.)

About the Creative Team

Nan Barber (editor) has worked with the Missing Manual series since its inception—long enough to remember HyperCard stacks.

Holly Bauer (production editor) lives in Ye Olde Cambridge, MA. She's a production editor by day and an avid home cook, prolific DIYer, and mid-century modern design enthusiast by evening/weekend. Email: *holly@oreilly.com*.

Carla Spoon (proofreader) is a freelance writer and copy editor. An avid runner, she works and feeds her tech gadget addiction from her home office in the shadow of Mount Rainier. Email: *carla_spoon@comcast.net*.

Angela Howard (indexer) has been indexing for more than 10 years, mostly for computer books, but occasionally for books on other topics, such as travel, alternative medicine, and leopard geckos. She lives in California with her husband, daughter, and two cats.

Acknowledgements

Many thanks to all those who helped with this book, including Shelley Powers and Steve Suehring, whose watchful eyes saved me from potentially embarrassing mistakes. Thanks also to my many students at Portland State University who have sat through my long JavaScript lectures and struggled through my programming assignments—especially the members of Team Futzbit (Combination Pizza Hut and Taco Bell) for testing the tutorials: Julia Hall, Amber Brucker, Kevin Brown, Josh Elliott, Tracy O'Connor, and Blake Womack. Also, we all owe a big debt of gratitude to John Resig and the jQuery team for creating the best tool yet for making JavaScript fun.

Finally, thanks to David Pogue for getting me started; Nan Barber for making my writing sharper and clearer; my wife, Scholle, for putting up with an author's crankiness; and thanks to my kids, Graham and Kate, because they're just awesome.

The Missing Manual Series

Missing Manuals are witty, superbly written guides to computer products that don't come with printed manuals (which is just about all of them). Each book features a handcrafted index and cross-references to specific page numbers (not just "see Chapter 14").

Recent and upcoming titles include:

- *Access 2010: The Missing Manual* by Matthew MacDonald
- *Buying a Home: The Missing Manual* by Nancy Conner
- *CSS: The Missing Manual*, Second Edition, by David Sawyer McFarland
- *Creating a Website: The Missing Manual*, Third Edition, by Matthew MacDonald
- *David Pogue's Digital Photography: The Missing Manual* by David Pogue
- *Dreamweaver CS5.5: The Missing Manual* by David Sawyer McFarland
- *Droid X2: The Missing Manual* by Preston Gralla
- *Droid 2: The Missing Manual* by Preston Gralla
- *Excel 2010: The Missing Manual* by Matthew MacDonald

- *Facebook: The Missing Manual*, Third Edition, by E.A. Vander Veer
- *FileMaker Pro 11: The Missing Manual* by Susan Prosser and Stuart Gripman
- *Flash CS5.5: The Missing Manual* by Chris Grover
- *Galaxy Tab: The Missing Manual* by Preston Gralla
- *Google Apps: The Missing Manual* by Nancy Conner
- *Google SketchUp: The Missing Manual* by Chris Grover
- *The Internet: The Missing Manual* by David Pogue and J.D. Biersdorfer
- *iMovie '11 & iDVD: The Missing Manual* by David Pogue and Aaron Miller
- *iPad 2: The Missing Manual* by J.D. Biersdorfer
- *iPhone: The Missing Manual*, Fourth Edition, by David Pogue
- *iPhone App Development: The Missing Manual* by Craig Hockenberry
- *iPhoto '11: The Missing Manual* by David Pogue and Lesa Snider
- *iPod: The Missing Manual*, Ninth Edition, by J.D. Biersdorfer and David Pogue
- *Living Green: The Missing Manual* by Nancy Conner
- *Mac OS X Snow Leopard: The Missing Manual* by David Pogue
- *Mac OS X Lion: The Missing Manual* by David Pogue
- *Microsoft Project 2010: The Missing Manual* by Bonnie Biafore
- *Motorola Xoom: The Missing Manual* by Preston Gralla
- *Netbooks: The Missing Manual* by J.D. Biersdorfer
- *Office 2010: The Missing Manual* by Nancy Connor, Chris Grover, and Matthew MacDonald
- *Office 2011 for Macintosh: The Missing Manual* by Chris Grover
- *Palm Pre: The Missing Manual* by Ed Baig
- *Personal Investing: The Missing Manual* by Bonnie Biafore
- *Photoshop CS5.5: The Missing Manual* by Lesa Snider
- *Photoshop Elements 10: The Missing Manual* by Barbara Brundage
- *PowerPoint 2007: The Missing Manual* by E.A. Vander Veer
- *Premiere Elements 8: The Missing Manual* by Chris Grover
- *QuickBase: The Missing Manual* by Nancy Conner
- *QuickBooks 2011: The Missing Manual* by Bonnie Biafore
- *QuickBooks 2012: The Missing Manual* by Bonnie Biafore

- *Switching to the Mac: The Missing Manual,* Snow Leopard Edition, by David Pogue
- *Switching to the Mac: The Missing Manual,* Lion Edition, by David Pogue
- *Wikipedia: The Missing Manual* by John Broughton
- *Windows Vista: The Missing Manual* by David Pogue
- *Windows 7: The Missing Manual* by David Pogue
- *Word 2007: The Missing Manual* by Chris Grover
- *Your Body: The Missing Manual* by Matthew MacDonald
- *Your Brain: The Missing Manual* by Matthew MacDonald
- *Your Money: The Missing Manual* by J. D. Roth

THE MISSING CREDITS

Introduction

The Web was a pretty boring place in its early days. Web pages were constructed from plain old HTML, so they could display information, and that was about all. Folks would click a link and then wait for a new web page to load. That was about as interactive as it got.

These days, most websites are almost as responsive as the programs on a desktop computer, reacting immediately to every mouse click. And it's all thanks to the subjects of this book—JavaScript and its sidekick, jQuery.

What Is JavaScript?

JavaScript is a programming language that lets you supercharge your HTML with animation, interactivity, and dynamic visual effects.

JavaScript can make web pages more useful by supplying immediate feedback. For example, a JavaScript-powered shopping cart page can instantly display a total cost, with tax and shipping, the moment a visitor selects a product to buy. JavaScript can produce an error message immediately after someone attempts to submit a web form that's missing necessary information.

JavaScript also lets you create fun, dynamic, and interactive interfaces. For example, with JavaScript, you can transform a static page of thumbnail images into an animated slideshow (as you'll learn how to do on page 314). Or you can do something more subtle like stuff more information on a page without making it seem crowded by organizing content into bite-size panels that visitors can access with a simple click of the mouse (page 301). Or add something useful and attractive, like pop-up tooltips that provide supplemental information for items on your web page (page 326).

Another one of JavaScript's main selling points is its immediacy. It lets web pages respond instantly to actions like clicking a link, filling out a form, or merely moving the mouse around the screen. JavaScript doesn't suffer from the frustrating delay associated with server-side programming languages like PHP, which rely on communication between the web browser and the web server. Because it doesn't rely on constantly loading and reloading web pages, JavaScript lets you create web pages that feel and act more like desktop programs than web pages.

If you've visited Google Maps (*http://maps.google.com*), you've seen JavaScript in action. Google Maps lets you view a map of your town (or pretty much anywhere else for that matter), zoom in to get a detailed view of streets and bus stops, or zoom out to get a birds-eye view of how to get across town, the state, or the nation. While there were plenty of map sites before Google, they always required reloading multiple web pages (usually a slow process) to get to the information you wanted. Google Maps, on the other hand, works without page refreshes—it responds immediately to your choices.

The programs you create with JavaScript can range from the really simple (like popping up a new browser window with a web page in it) to full-blown web applications like Google Docs (*http://docs.google.com*), which let you create presentations, edit documents, and create spreadsheets using your web browser with the feel of a program running directly on your computer.

A Bit of History

Invented by Netscape back in 1995, JavaScript is nearly as old as the web itself. While JavaScript is well respected today, it has a somewhat checkered past. It used to be considered a hobbyist's programming language, used for adding less-than-useful effects such as messages that scroll across the bottom of a web browser's status bar like a stock-ticker, or animated butterflies following mouse movements around the page. In the early days of JavaScript, it was easy to find thousands of free JavaScript programs (also called *scripts*) online, but many of those scripts didn't work in all web browsers, and at times even crashed browsers.

Note: JavaScript has nothing to do with the Java programming language. JavaScript was originally named LiveScript, but the marketing folks at Netscape decided they'd get more publicity if they tried to associate the language with the then-hot Java. Don't make the mistake of confusing the two…especially at a job interview!

In the early days, JavaScript also suffered from incompatibilities between the two prominent browsers, Netscape Navigator and Internet Explorer. Because Netscape and Microsoft tried to outdo each other's browsers by adding newer and (ostensibly) better features, the two browsers often acted in very different ways, making it difficult to create JavaScript programs that worked well in both.

Note: After Netscape introduced JavaScript, Microsoft introduced jScript, their own version of JavaScript included with Internet Explorer.

Fortunately the worst of those days is nearly gone and contemporary browsers like Firefox, Safari, Chrome, Opera, and Internet Explorer 9 have standardized much of the way they handle JavaScript, making it easier to write JavaScript programs that work for most everyone. (There are still a few incompatibilities among current web browsers, so you'll need to learn a few tricks for dealing with cross-browser problems. You'll learn how to overcome browser incompatibilities in this book.)

In the past several years, JavaScript has undergone a rebirth, fueled by high-profile websites like Google, Yahoo, and Flickr, which use JavaScript extensively to create interactive web applications. There's never been a better time to learn JavaScript. With the wealth of knowledge and the quality of scripts being written, you can add sophisticated interaction to your website—even if you're a beginner.

Note: JavaScript is also known by the name ECMAScript. ECMAScript is the "official" JavaScript specification, which is developed and maintained by an international standards organization called Ecma International: *http://www.ecmascript.org/*

JavaScript Is Everywhere

JavaScript isn't just for web pages, either. It's proven to be such a useful programming language that if you learn JavaScript you can create Yahoo Widgets and Apple's Dashboard Widgets, write programs for the iPhone, and tap into the scriptable features of many Adobe programs like Acrobat, Photoshop, Illustrator, and Dreamweaver. In fact, Dreamweaver has always offered clever JavaScript programmers a way to add their own commands to the program.

In addition, the programming language for Flash—ActionScript—is based on JavaScript, so if you learn the basics of JavaScript, you'll be well prepared to learn Flash programming.

What Is jQuery?

JavaScript has one embarrassing little secret: writing it is hard. While it's simpler than many other programming languages, JavaScript is still a programming language. And many people, including web designers, find programming difficult. To complicate matters further, different web browsers understand JavaScript differently, so a program that works in, say, Chrome may be completely unresponsive in Internet Explorer 9. This common situation can cost many hours of testing on different machines and different browsers to make sure a program works correctly for your site's entire audience.

That's where jQuery comes in. jQuery is a JavaScript library intended to make JavaScript programming easier and more fun. A JavaScript library is a complex JavaScript program that both simplifies difficult tasks and solves cross-browser problems. In other words, jQuery solves the two biggest headaches with JavaScript—complexity and the finicky nature of different web browsers.

jQuery is a web designer's secret weapon in the battle of JavaScript programming. With jQuery, you can accomplish tasks in a single line of code that would otherwise take hundreds of lines of programming and many hours of browser testing to achieve with your own JavaScript code. In fact, an in-depth book solely about JavaScript would be at least twice as thick as the one you're holding; and, when you were done reading it (if you could manage to finish it), you wouldn't be able to do half of the things you can accomplish with just a little bit of jQuery knowledge.

That's why most of this book is about jQuery. It lets you do so much, so easily. Another great thing about jQuery is that you can add advanced features to your website with thousands of easy-to-use jQuery plug-ins. For example, the FancyBox plug-in (which you'll meet on page 222) lets you take a simple page of thumbnail graphics and turn it into an interactive slideshow—all with a single line of programming!

Unsurprisingly, jQuery is used on millions of websites (*http://trends.builtwith.com/javascript/JQuery*). It's baked right into popular content management systems like Drupal and WordPress. You can even find job listings for "jQuery Programmers" with no mention of JavaScript. When you learn jQuery, you join a large community of fellow web designers and programmers who use a simpler and more powerful approach to creating interactive, powerful web pages.

HTML: The Barebones Structure

JavaScript isn't much good without the two other pillars of web design—HTML and CSS. Many programmers talk about the three languages as forming the "layers" of a web page: HTML provides the *structural* layer, organizing content like pictures and words in a meaningful way; CSS (Cascading Style Sheets) provides the *presentational* layer, making the content in the HTML look good; and JavaScript adds a *behavioral* layer, bringing a web page to life so it interacts with web visitors.

In other words, to master JavaScript, you need to have a good understanding of both HTML and CSS.

Note: For a full-fledged introduction to HTML and CSS, check out *Head First HTML with CSS and XHTML* by Elisabeth Freeman and Eric Freeman. For an in-depth presentation of the tricky subject of Cascading Style Sheets, pick up a copy of *CSS: The Missing Manual* by David Sawyer McFarland (both O'Reilly).

HTML (Hypertext Markup Language) uses simple commands called *tags* to define the various parts of a web page. For example, this HTML code creates a simple web page:

```
<!DOCTYPE html>
<html>
<head>
<meta charset=utf-8>
<title>Hey, I am the title of this web page.</title>
</head>
<body>
Hey, I am some body text on this web page.
</body>
</html>
```

It may not be exciting, but this example has all the basic elements a web page needs. This page begins with a single line—the document type declaration, or *doctype* for short—that states what type of document the page is and which standards it conforms to. HTML actually comes in different versions, and you use a different doctype with each. In this example, the doctype is for HTML5; the doctype for an HTML 4.01 or XHTML document is longer and also includes a URL that points the web browser to a file on the Internet that contains definitions for that type of file.

In essence, the doctype tells the web browser how to display the page. The doctype can even affect how CSS and JavaScript work. With an incorrect or missing doctype, you may end up banging your head against a wall as you discover lots of cross-browser differences with your scripts. If for no other reason, always include a doctype in your HTML.

There are five types of HTML commonly used today: HTML 4.01 Transitional, HTML 4.01 Strict, XHTML 1.0 Transitional, XHTML 1.0 Strict, and HTML5 (the new kid on the block). All five are very much alike, with just slight differences in how tags are written and which tags and attributes are allowed. Most web page editing programs add an appropriate doctype when you create a new web page, but if you want examples of how each is written, you can find templates for the different types of pages at *www.webstandards.org/learn/reference/templates*.

It doesn't really matter which type of HTML you use. All current web browsers understand each of the five common doctypes and can display web pages using any of the four document types without problem. Which doctype you use isn't nearly as important as making sure you've correctly written your HTML tags—a task that's helped by validating the page, as described in the box on page 7.

Note: XHTML was once heralded as the next big thing for web designers. Although you'll still find people who think you should only use XHTML, the winds of change have turned. The World Wide Web Consortium (W3C) has stopped development of XHTML in favor of HTML5. You can learn more about HTML5 by picking up a copy of *HTML5: The Missing Manual* by Matthew MacDonald or *HTML5: Up and Running* by Mark Pilgrim (both from O'Reilly).

How HTML Tags Work

In the example on the previous page, as in the HTML code of any web page, you'll notice that most commands appear in pairs that surround a block of text or other commands. Sandwiched between brackets, these *tags* are instructions that tell a web browser how to display the web page. Tags are the "markup" part of the Hypertext Markup Language.

The starting (*opening*) tag of each pair tells the browser where the instruction begins, and the ending tag tells it where the instruction ends. Ending or *closing* tags always include a forward slash (/) after the first bracket symbol (<). For example, the tag <p> marks the start of a paragraph, while </p> marks its end.

For a web page to work correctly, you must include at least these three tags:

- The **<html>** tag appears once at the beginning of a web page (after the doctype) and again (with an added slash) at the end. This tag tells a web browser that the information contained in this document is written in HTML, as opposed to some other language. All of the contents of a page, including other tags, appear between the opening and closing <html> tags.

  If you were to think of a web page as a tree, the <html> tag would be its trunk. Springing from the trunk are two branches that represent the two main parts of any web page—the *head* and the *body*.

- The *head* of a web page, surrounded by **<head>** tags, contains the title of the page. It may also provide other, invisible information (such as search keywords) that browsers and web search engines can exploit.

  In addition, the head can contain information that's used by the web browser for displaying the web page and for adding interactivity. You put Cascading Style Sheets, for example, in the head of the document. The head of the document is also where you often include JavaScript programming and links to JavaScript files.

- The *body* of a web page, as set apart by its surrounding **<body>** tags, contains all the information that appears inside a browser window: headlines, text, pictures, and so on.

Within the <body> tag, you commonly find tags like the following:

- You tell a web browser where a paragraph of text begins with a **<p>** (opening paragraph tag), and where it ends with a **</p>** (closing paragraph tag).

- The **** tag emphasizes text. If you surround some text with it and its partner tag, , you get boldface type. The HTML snippet Warning! tells a web browser to display the word "Warning!" in bold type.

- The **<a>** tag, or anchor tag, creates a *hyperlink* in a web page. When clicked, a hyperlink—or *link*—can lead anywhere on the web. You tell the browser where the link points by putting a web address inside the <a> tags. For instance, you might type *<a href="http://www.missingmanuals.com">Click here!</a>*.

  The browser knows that when your visitor clicks the words "Click here!" it should go to the Missing Manual website. The *href* part of the tag is called an *attribute* and the URL (the Uniform Resource Locator or web address) is the *value*. In this example, *http://www.missingmanuals.com* is the *value* of the *href* attribute.

Validating Web Pages

As mentioned on page 5, a web page's doctype identifies which type of HTML or XHTML you used to create the web page. The rules differ subtly depending on type: For example, unlike HTML 4.01, XHTML doesn't let you have an unclosed <p> tag, and requires that all tag names and attributes be lowercase (<a> *not* <A>, for example). HTML5 includes new tags and lets you use either HTML or XHTML syntax. Because different rules apply to each variant of HTML, you should always *validate* your web pages.

An HTML validator is a program that makes sure a web page is written correctly. It checks the page's doctype and then analyzes the code in the page to see whether it matches the rules defined by that doctype. For example, the validator flags mistakes like a misspelled tag name or an unclosed tag. The World Wide Web Consortium (W3C), the organization that's responsible for many of the technologies used on the web, has a free online validator at *http:// validator.w3.org*. You can copy your HTML and paste it into a web form, upload a web page, or point the validator to an already existing page on the web; the validator then analyzes the HTML and reports back whether the page is valid

or not. If there are any errors, the validator tells you what the error is and on which line of the HTML file it occurs.

If you use Firefox, you can download the HTML Validator plug-in from *http://users.skynet.be/mgueury/mozilla*. This plug-in lets you validate a page directly in your web browser; just open a page (even a page directly off of your computer) and the validator will point out any errors in your HTML. There's a similar plug-in for Safari, called Safari Validator, which you can find at *http://zappatic.net/projects/ safarivalidator*.

Valid HTML isn't just good form, it also helps to make sure your JavaScript programs work correctly. A lot of JavaScript involves manipulating a web page's HTML: identifying a particular form field, for example, or placing new HTML (like an error message) in a particular spot. In order for JavaScript to access and manipulate a web page, the HTML must be in proper working order. Forgetting to close a tag, using the same ID name more than once, or improperly nesting your HTML tags can make your JavaScript code behave erratically or not at all.

CSS: Adding Style to Web Pages

At the beginning of the Web, HTML was the only language you needed to know. You could build pages with colorful text and graphics and make words jump out using different sizes, fonts, and colors. But today, web designers turn to Cascading Style Sheets to add visual sophistication to their pages. CSS is a formatting language that lets you make text look good, build complex page layouts, and generally add style to your site.

Think of HTML as merely the language you use to structure a page. It helps identify the stuff you want the world to know about. Tags like <h1> and <h2> denote headlines and assign them relative importance: A *heading 1* is more important than a *heading 2*. The <p> tag indicates a basic paragraph of information. Other tags provide further structural clues: for example, a <ul> tag identifies a bulleted list (to make a list of recipe ingredients more intelligible, for example).

CSS, on the other hand, adds design flair to well-organized HTML content, making it more beautiful and easier to read. Essentially, a CSS *style* is just a rule that tells a web browser how to display a particular element on a page. For example, you can create a CSS rule to make all <h1> tags appear 36 pixels tall, in the Verdana font, and in orange. CSS can do more powerful stuff, too, like add borders, change margins, and even control the exact placement of a page element.

When it comes to JavaScript, some of the most valuable changes you make to a page involve CSS. You can use JavaScript to add or remove a CSS style from an HTML tag, or dynamically change CSS properties based on a visitor's input or mouse clicks. You can even animate from the properties of one style to the properties of another (say, animating a background color changing from yellow to red). For example, you can make a page element appear or disappear simply by changing the CSS *display* property. To animate an item across the screen, you can change the CSS position properties dynamically using JavaScript.

Anatomy of a Style

A single style that defines the look of one element is a pretty basic beast. It's essentially a rule that tells a web browser how to format something—turn a headline blue, draw a red border around a photo, or create a 150-pixel-wide sidebar box to hold a list of links. If a style could talk, it would say something like, "Hey, Browser, make *this* look like *that*." A style is, in fact, made up of two elements: the web page element that the browser formats (the *selector*) and the actual formatting instructions (the *declaration block*). For example, a selector can be a headline, a paragraph of text, a photo, and so on. Declaration blocks can turn that text blue, add a red border around a paragraph, position the photo in the center of the page—the possibilities are endless.

Note: Technical types often follow the lead of the W3C and call CSS styles *rules*. This book uses the terms "style" and "rule" interchangeably.

Of course, CSS styles can't communicate in nice, clear English. They have their own language. For example, to set a standard font color and font size for all paragraphs on a web page, you'd write the following:

```
p { color: red; font-size: 1.5em; }
```

This style simply says, "Make the text in all paragraphs—marked with <p> tags—red and 1.5 ems tall." (An *em* is a unit or measurement that's based on a browser's normal text size.) As Figure I-1 illustrates, even a simple style like this example contains several elements:

- **Selector**. The selector tells a web browser which element or elements on a page to style—like a headline, paragraph, image, or link. In Figure I-1, the selector (p) refers to the <p> tag, which makes web browsers format all <p> tags using the formatting directions in this style. With the wide range of selectors that CSS offers and a little creativity, you can gain fine control of your pages' formatting. (Selectors are an important part of using jQuery, so you'll find a detailed discussion of them starting on page 129.)

- **Declaration Block**. The code following the selector includes all the formatting options you want to apply to the selector. The block begins with an opening brace ({) and ends with a closing brace (}).

- **Declaration**. Between the opening and closing braces of a declaration, you add one or more *declarations*, or formatting instructions. Every declaration has two parts, a *property* and a *value*, and ends with a semicolon.

- **Property**. CSS offers a wide range of formatting options, called *properties*. A property is a word—or a few hyphenated words—indicating a certain style effect. Most properties have straightforward names like *font-size, margin-top*, and *background-color*. For example, the *background-color* property sets—you guessed it—a background color.

Note: If you need to brush up on your CSS, grab a copy of *CSS: The Missing Manual*.

- **Value**. Finally, you get to express your creative genius by assigning a *value* to a CSS property—by making a background blue, red, purple, or chartreuse, for example. Different CSS properties require specific types of values—a color (like *red*, or *#FF0000*), a length (like *18px, 2in,* or *5em*), a URL (like images/background.gif), or a specific keyword (like *top, center,* or *bottom*).

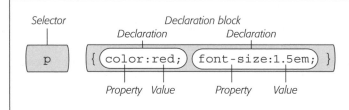

Figure I-1: *A style (or rule) is made of two main parts: a selector, which tells web browsers what to format, and a declaration block, which lists the formatting instructions that the browsers use to style the selector.*

You don't need to write a style on a single line as pictured in Figure I-1. Many styles have multiple formatting properties, so you can make them easier to read by breaking them up into multiple lines. For example, you may want to put the selector and opening brace on the first line, each declaration on its own line, and the closing brace by itself on the last line, like so:

```
p {
    color: red;
    font-size: 1.5em;
}
```

It's also helpful to indent properties, with either a tab or a couple of spaces, to visibly separate the selector from the declarations, making it easy to tell which is which. And finally, putting one space between the colon and the property value is optional, but adds to the readability of the style. In fact, you can put as much white space between the two as you want. For example *color:red, color: red,* and *color : red* all work.

Software for JavaScript Programming

To create web pages made up of HTML, CSS, and JavaScript, you need nothing more than a basic text editor like Notepad (Windows) or TextEdit (Mac). But after typing a few hundred lines of JavaScript code, you may want to try a program better suited to working with web pages. This section lists some common programs, some free and some you can buy.

Note: There are literally hundreds of tools that can help you create web pages and write JavaScript programs, so the following is by no means a complete list. Think of it as a greatest-hits tour of the most popular programs that JavaScript fans are using today.

Free Programs

There are plenty of free programs out there for editing web pages and style sheets. If you're still using Notepad or TextEdit, give one of these a try. Here's a short list to get you started:

- **Notepad++** (Windows, *http://notepad-plus-plus.org*) is a coder's friend. It highlights the syntax of JavaScript and HTML code, and lets you save macros and assign keyboard shortcuts to them so you can automate the process of inserting the code snippets you use most.

- **HTML-Kit** (Windows, *www.chami.com/html-kit*) is a powerful HTML/XHTML editor that includes lots of useful features, like the ability to preview a web page directly in the program (so you don't have to switch back and forth between browser and editor), shortcuts for adding HTML tags, and a lot more.

- **CoffeeCup Free HTML Editor** (Windows, *www.coffeecup.com/free-editor*) is the free version of the commercial ($49) CoffeeCup HTML editor.

- **TextWrangler** (Mac, *www.barebones.com/products/textwrangler*) is free software that's actually a pared-down version of BBEdit, the sophisticated, well-known text editor for the Mac. TextWrangler doesn't have all of BBEdit's built-in HTML tools, but it does include syntax-coloring (highlighting tags and properties in different colors so it's easy to scan a page and identify its parts), FTP support (so you can upload files to a web server), and more.

- **Eclipse** (Windows, Linux, Mac; *www.eclipse.org*) is a free, popular choice amongst Java Developers, but includes tools for working with HTML, CSS, and JavaScript. A version specifically for JavaScript developers is also available (*www.eclipse.org/downloads/packages/eclipse-ide-javascript-web-developers/indigor*), as well as Eclipse plug-ins to add autocomplete for jQuery (*http://marketplace.eclipse.org/category/free-tagging/jquery*).

- **Aptana Studio** (Windows, Linux, Mac; *www.aptana.org*) is a powerful, free coding environment with tools for working with HTML, CSS, JavaScript, PHP, and Ruby on Rails.

Commercial Software

Commercial website development programs range from inexpensive text editors to complete website construction tools with all the bells and whistles:

- **EditPlus** (Windows, *www.editplus.com*) is an inexpensive ($35) text editor that includes syntax-coloring, FTP, auto-completion, and other wrist-saving features.

- **CoffeeCup** (Windows, *www.coffeecup.com*) is a combination text and visual editor ($49). You can either write straight HTML code or use a visual interface to build your pages.

- **textMate** (Mac, *http://macromates.com*) is a darling of Mac programmers. This text editor ($57) includes many timesaving features for JavaScript programmers, like "auto-paired characters," which automatically plops in the second character of a pair of punctuation marks (for example, the program automatically inserts a closing parenthesis after you type an opening parenthesis).

- **BBEdit** (Mac, *www.barebones.com/products/bbedit*). This much-loved Mac text editor ($99.99) has plenty of tools for working with HTML, XHTML, CSS, JavaScript, and more. It includes many useful web building tools and shortcuts.

- **Dreamweaver** (Mac and Windows, *www.adobe.com/products/dreamweaver.html*) is a visual web page editor ($399.) It lets you see how your page looks in a web browser. The program also includes a powerful text editor for writing JavaScript programs and excellent CSS creation and management tools. Check out *Dreamweaver CS5.5: The Missing Manual* for the full skinny on how to use this powerful program.

- **Expression Web Designer** (Windows, *www.microsoft.com/expression/products/ StudioWebPro_Overview.aspx*) is Microsoft's entry in the web design field ($149). It includes many professional web design tools, including excellent CSS features.

About This Book

Unlike a piece of software such as Microsoft Word or Dreamweaver, JavaScript isn't a single product developed by a single company. There's no support department at JavaScript headquarters writing an easy-to-read manual for the average web developer. While you'll find plenty of information on sites like Mozilla.org (see, for example, *https://developer.mozilla.org/en/JavaScript/Reference*) or Ecmascript.org (*www.ecmascript.org/docs.php*), there's no definitive source of information on the JavaScript programming language.

Because there's no manual for JavaScript, people just learning JavaScript often don't know where to begin. And the finer points regarding JavaScript can trip up even seasoned web pros. The purpose of this book, then, is to serve as the manual that should have come with JavaScript. In this book's pages, you'll find step-by-step instructions for using JavaScript to create highly interactive web pages.

Likewise, you'll find good documentation on jQuery at *http://docs.jquery.com/Main_Page*. But it's written by programmers for programmers, and so the explanations are mostly brief and technical. And while jQuery is generally more straightforward than regular JavaScript programming, this book will teach you fundamental jQuery principles and techniques so you can start off on the right path when enhancing your websites with jQuery.

JavaScript & jQuery: The Missing Manual is designed to accommodate readers who have some experience building web pages. You'll need to feel comfortable with HTML and CSS to get the most from this book, since JavaScript often works closely with HTML and CSS to achieve its magic. The primary discussions are written for advanced-beginner or intermediate computer users. But if you're new to building web pages, special boxes called Up to Speed provide the introductory information you need to understand the topic at hand. If you're an advanced web page jockey, on the other hand, keep your eye out for similar shaded boxes called Power Users' Clinic. They offer more technical tips, tricks, and shortcuts for the experienced computer fan.

Note: This book periodically recommends *other* books, covering topics that are too specialized or tangential for a manual about using JavaScript. Sometimes the recommended titles are from Missing Manual series publisher O'Reilly Media—but not always. If there's a great book out there that's not part of the O'Reilly family, we'll let you know about it.

This Book's Approach to JavaScript

JavaScript is a real programming language: It doesn't work like HTML or CSS, and it has its own set of (often complicated) rules. It's not always easy for web designers to switch gears and start thinking like computer programmers, and there's no *one* book that can teach you everything there is to know about JavaScript.

The goal of *JavaScript & jQuery: The Missing Manual* isn't to turn you into the next great programmer (though it might start you on your way). This book is meant to familiarize web designers with the ins and outs of JavaScript and then move on to jQuery so that you can add really useful interactivity to a website as quickly and easily as possible.

In this book, you'll learn the basics of JavaScript and programming; but just the basics won't make for very exciting web pages. It's not possible in 500 pages to teach you everything about JavaScript that you need to know to build sophisticated, interactive web pages. Instead, much of this book will cover the wildly popular jQuery JavaScript library, which, as you'll soon learn, will liberate you from all of the minute, time-consuming details of creating JavaScript programs that run well across different browsers.

You'll learn the basics of JavaScript, and then jump immediately to advanced web page interactivity with a little help—OK, a *lot* of help—from jQuery. Think of it this

way: You could build a house by cutting down and milling your own lumber, constructing your own windows, doors, and doorframes, manufacturing your own tile,
and so on. That "do it yourself" approach is common to a lot of JavaScript books.
But who has that kind of time? This book's approach is more like building a house by
taking advantage of already-built pieces and putting them together using basic skills.
The end result will be a beautiful and functional house built in a fraction of the time
it would take you to learn every step of the process.

About the Outline

JavaScript & jQuery: The Missing Manual is divided into five parts, each containing
several chapters:

- **Part 1, Getting Started with JavaScript**, starts at the very beginning. You'll learn
the basic building blocks of JavaScript as well as get some helpful tips on computer programming in general. This section teaches you how to add a script to
a web page, store and manipulate information, and add smarts to a program
so it can respond to different situations. You'll also learn how to communicate
with the browser window, store and read cookies, respond to various events like
mouse clicks and form submissions, and modify the HTML of a web page.

- **Part 2, Getting Started with jQuery**, introduces the Web's most popular Java-
Script library, jQuery. Here you'll learn the basics of this amazing programming
tool that will make you a more productive and capable JavaScript programmer.
You'll learn how to select and manipulate page elements, add interaction by
making page elements respond to your visitors, and add flashy visual effects
and animations.

- **Part 3, Building Web Page Features**, provides many real-world examples of
JavaScript in action. You'll learn how to create pop-up navigation bars and build
an interactive photo gallery. You'll make your web forms more usable by adding form validation (so visitors can't submit forms missing information), add a
calendar widget to make selecting dates easy, and change form options based on
selections a web visitor makes. Finally, you'll create interesting user interfaces
with content sliders, tooltips, and pop-up dialog boxes that look great and function flawlessly.

- **Part 4, Ajax: Communicating with the Web Server**, covers the technology that
single-handedly made JavaScript one of the most glamorous web languages to
learn. In this section, you'll learn how to use JavaScript to communicate with a
web server so your pages can receive information and update themselves based on
information provided by a web server—without having to load a new web page.

Note: You'll find step-by-step instructions for setting up a web server on your computer so you can take
advantage of the cool technology (discussed in Part 3) on this book's companion web page. See "Living
Examples" on page 16 for details.

- **Part 5, Troubleshooting, Tips, and Tricks,** takes you past the basics, covering more complex concepts. You'll learn more about how to use jQuery effectively, as well as delve into advanced jQuery functions. This part of the book also helps you when nothing seems to be working: when your perfectly crafted JavaScript program just doesn't seem to do what you want (or worse, it doesn't work at all!). You'll learn the most common errors new programmers make as well as techniques for discovering and fixing bugs in your programs.

At the end of the book, an appendix provides a detailed list of references to aid you in your further exploration of the JavaScript programming language.

The Very Basics

To use this book, and indeed to use a computer, you need to know a few basics. This book assumes that you're familiar with a few terms and concepts:

- **Clicking**. This book gives you three kinds of instructions that require you to use your computer's mouse or trackpad. To *click* means to point the arrow cursor at something on the screen and then—without moving the cursor at all—to press and release the clicker button on the mouse (or laptop trackpad). To *right-click* means to do the same thing with the right mouse button. To *double-click*, of course, means to click twice in rapid succession, again without moving the cursor at all. And to *drag* means to move the cursor *while* pressing the button.

Tip: If you're on a Mac and don't have a right mouse button, you can accomplish the same thing by pressing the Control key as you click with the one mouse button.

When you're told to ⌘- *click* something on the Mac, or *Ctrl-click* something on a PC, you click while pressing the ⌘ or Ctrl key (both of which are near the space bar).

- **Menus**. The *menus* are the words at the top of your screen or window: File, Edit, and so on. Click one to make a list of commands appear, as though they're written on a window shade you've just pulled down.

- **Keyboard shortcuts**. If you're typing along in a burst of creative energy, it's sometimes disruptive to have to take your hand off the keyboard, grab the mouse, and then use a menu (for example, to use the Bold command). That's why many experienced computer mavens prefer to trigger menu commands by pressing certain combinations on the keyboard. For example, in the Firefox web browser, you can press Ctrl-+ (Windows) or ⌘-+ (Mac) to make text on a web page get larger (and more readable). When you read an instruction like "press ⌘-B," start by pressing the ⌘-key; while it's down, type the letter B, and then release both keys.

- **Operating-system basics.** This book assumes that you know how to open a program, surf the web, and download files. You should know how to use the Start menu (Windows) and the Dock or Apple menu (Macintosh), as well as the Control Panel (Windows), or System Preferences (Mac OS X).

If you've mastered this much information, you have all the technical background you need to enjoy *JavaScript & jQuery: The Missing Manual*.

About→These→Arrows

Throughout this book, and throughout the Missing Manual series, you'll find sentences like this one: "Open the System→Library→Fonts folder." That's shorthand for a much longer instruction that directs you to open three nested folders in sequence, like this: "On your hard drive, you'll find a folder called System. Open that. Inside the System folder window is a folder called Library; double-click it to open it. Inside *that* folder is yet another one called Fonts. Double-click to open it, too."

Similarly, this kind of arrow shorthand helps to simplify the business of choosing commands in menus, as shown in Figure I-2.

Figure I-2:
In this book, arrow notations help simplify menu instructions. For example, View→Text Size→Increase is a more compact way of saying, "From the View menu, choose Text Size; from the submenu that then appears, choose Increase."

About the Online Resources

This book is designed to get your work onto the web faster and more professionally; it's only natural, then, that much of the value of this book also lies on the web. Online, you'll find example files so you can get some hands-on experience. You can also communicate with the Missing Manual team and tell us what you love (or hate) about the book. Head over to *www.missingmanuals.com*, or go directly to one of the following sections.

Living Examples

As you read the book's chapters, you'll encounter a number of *living examples*—step-by-step tutorials that you can build yourself, using raw materials (like graphics and half-completed web pages) that you can download from either *www.sawmac.com/js2e* or from this book's Missing CD page at *www.missingmanuals.com/cds*. You might not gain very much from simply reading these step-by-step lessons while relaxing in your porch hammock, but if you take the time to work through them at the computer, you'll discover that these tutorials give you unprecedented insight into the way professional designers build web pages.

You'll also find, in this book's lessons, the URLs of the finished pages, so that you can compare your work with the final result. In other words, you won't just see pictures of JavaScript code in the pages of the book; you'll find the actual, working web pages on the Internet.

Registration

If you register this book at oreilly.com, you'll be eligible for special offers—like discounts on future editions of *JavaScript & jQuery: The Missing Manual*. Registering takes only a few clicks. To get started, type *www.oreilly.com/register* into your browser to hop directly to the Registration page.

Feedback

Got questions? Need more information? Fancy yourself a book reviewer? On our Feedback page, you can get expert answers to questions that come to you while reading, share your thoughts on this Missing Manual, and find groups for folks who share your interest in JavaScript and jQuery. To have your say, go to *www.missingmanuals.com/feedback*.

Errata

In an effort to keep this book as up to date and accurate as possible, each time we print more copies, we'll make any confirmed corrections you've suggested. We also note such changes on the book's website, so you can mark important corrections into your own copy of the book, if you like. Go to *http://tinyurl.com/jsjqtmm* to report an error and view existing corrections.

Safari® Books Online

 Safari® Books Online is an on-demand digital library that lets you easily search over 7,500 technology and creative reference books and videos to find the answers you need quickly.

With a subscription, you can read any page and watch any video from our library online. Read books on your cellphone and mobile devices. Access new titles before they're available for print, and get exclusive access to manuscripts in development and post feedback for the authors. Copy and paste code samples, organize your favorites, download chapters, bookmark key sections, create notes, print out pages, and benefit from tons of other time-saving features.

Part One: Getting Started with JavaScript

Chapter 1: Writing Your First JavaScript Program

Chapter 2: The Grammar of JavaScript

Chapter 3: Adding Logic and Control to Your Programs

1

Writing Your First JavaScript Program

By itself, HTML doesn't have any smarts: It can't do math, it can't figure out if someone has correctly filled out a form, and it can't make decisions based on how a web visitor interacts with it. Basically, HTML lets people read text, look at pictures, and click links to move to other web pages with more text and pictures. In order to add intelligence to your web pages so they can respond to your site's visitors, you need JavaScript.

JavaScript lets a web page react intelligently. With it, you can create *smart* web forms that let visitors know when they've forgotten to include necessary information; you can make elements appear, disappear, or move around a web page (see Figure 1-1); you can even update the contents of a web page with information retrieved from a web server—without having to load a new web page. In short, JavaScript lets you make your websites more engaging and effective.

Figure 1-1: *JavaScript lets web pages respond to visitors. On Amazon.com, mousing over the "Gifts & Wish Lists" link opens a tab that floats above the other content on the page and offers additional options.*

Note: Actually, HTML5 *does* add some smarts to HTML—including basic form validation. But since not all browsers support these nifty additions (and because you can do a whole lot more with forms and JavaScript), you still need JavaScript to build the best, most user-friendly and interactive forms. You can learn more about HTML5 and web forms in Mark Pilgrim's *HTML5: Up and Running* (O'Reilly).

Introducing Programming

For a lot of people, the term "computer programming" conjures up visions of super-intelligent nerds hunched over keyboards, typing nearly unintelligible gibberish for hours on end. And, honestly, some programming is like that. Programming can seem like complex magic that's well beyond the average mortal. But many programming concepts aren't difficult to grasp, and as programming languages go, JavaScript is relatively friendly to nonprogrammers.

Still, JavaScript is more complex than either HTML or CSS, and programming often is a foreign world to web designers; so one goal of this book is to help you think more like a programmer. Throughout this book, you'll learn fundamental programming concepts that apply whether you're writing JavaScript, ActionScript, or even writing a desktop program using C++. More importantly, you'll learn how to approach a programming task so you'll know exactly what you want to do before you start adding JavaScript to a web page.

Many web designers are immediately struck by the strange symbols and words used in JavaScript. An average JavaScript program is sprinkled with symbols ({ } [ ] ; , ()

!=) and full of unfamiliar words (var, null, else if). It's like staring at a foreign language, and in many ways, learning a programming language is a lot like learning another language. You need to learn new words, new punctuation, and understand how to put them together so you can communicate successfully.

In fact, every programming language has its own set of key words and characters, and its own set of rules for putting those words and characters together—the language's *syntax*. Learning JavaScript's syntax is like learning the vocabulary and grammar of another language. You'll need to memorize the words and rules of the language (or at least keep this book handy as a reference). When learning to speak a new language, you quickly realize that placing an accent on the wrong syllable can make a word unintelligible. Likewise, a simple typo or even a missing punctuation mark can prevent a JavaScript program from working, or trigger an error in a web browser. You'll make plenty of mistakes as you start to learn to program—that's just the nature of programming.

UP TO SPEED

The Client Side vs. the Server Side

JavaScript is a *client-side* language, which (in English) means that it works inside a web browser. The alternative type of web programming language is called a *server-side* language, which you'll find in pages built around PHP, .NET, ASP, ColdFusion, Ruby on Rails, and other web server technologies. Server-side programming languages, as the name suggests, run on a web server. They can exhibit a lot of intelligence by accessing databases, processing credit cards, and sending email around the globe. The problem with server-side languages is that they require the web browser to send requests to the web server, forcing visitors to wait until a new page arrives with new information.

Client-side languages, on the other hand, can react immediately and change what a visitor sees in his web browser without the need to download a new page. Content can appear or disappear, move around the screen, or automatically update based on how a visitor interacts with the page. This responsiveness lets you create websites that feel more like desktop programs than static web pages. But JavaScript isn't the only client-side technology in town. You can also use plug-ins to add programming smarts to a web page. Java applets are one example. These are small programs, written in the Java programming language, that run in a web browser. They also tend to start up slowly and have been known to crash the browser.

Flash is another plug-in based technology that offers sophisticated animation, video, sound, and lots of interactive potential. In fact, it's sometimes hard to tell if an interactive web page is using JavaScript or Flash. For example, Google Maps could also be created in Flash (in fact, Yahoo Maps was at one time a Flash application, until Yahoo recreated it using JavaScript). A quick way to tell the difference: Right-click on the part of the page that you think might be Flash (the map itself, in this case); if it is, you'll see a pop-up menu that includes "About the Flash Player."

Ajax, which you'll learn about in Part 4 of this book, brings both client-side and server-side together. Ajax is a method for using JavaScript to talk to a server, retrieve information from the server, and update the web page without the need to load a new web page. Google Maps uses this technique to let you move around a map without forcing you to load a new web page.

In truth, JavaScript can also be a server-side programming language. For example, the node.js web server (*http://nodejs.org/*) uses JavaScript as a server-side programming language to connect to a database, access the web server's file system, and perform many other tasks on a web server. This book doesn't discuss that aspect of JavaScript programming, however.

At first, you'll probably find JavaScript programming frustrating—you'll spend a lot of your time tracking down errors you made when typing the script. Also, you might find some of the concepts related to programming a bit hard to follow at first. But don't worry: If you've tried to learn JavaScript in the past and gave up because you thought it was too hard, this book will help you get past the hurdles that often trip up folks new to programming. (And if you do have programming experience, this book will teach you JavaScript's idiosyncrasies and the unique concepts involved in programming for web browsers.)

In addition, this book isn't just about JavaScript—it's also about jQuery, the world's most popular JavaScript library. jQuery makes complex JavaScript programming easier…much easier. So with a little bit of JavaScript knowledge and the help of jQuery, you'll be creating sophisticated, interactive websites in no time.

What's a Computer Program?

When you add JavaScript to a web page, you're writing a computer program. Granted, most JavaScript programs are much simpler than the programs you use to read email, retouch photographs, and build web pages. But even though JavaScript programs (also called *scripts*) are simpler and shorter, they share many of the same properties of more complicated programs.

In a nutshell, any computer program is a series of steps that are completed in a designated order. Say you want to display a welcome message using the name of the person viewing a web page: "Welcome, Bob!" There are several things you'd need to do to accomplish this task:

1. **Ask the visitor's name.**

2. **Get the visitor's response.**

3. **Print (that is, display) the message on the web page.**

While you may never want to print a welcome message on a web page, this example demonstrates the fundamental process of programming: Determine what you want to do, then break that task down into each step that's necessary to get it done. Every time you want to create a JavaScript program, you must go through the process of determining the steps needed to achieve your goal. Once you know the steps, you're ready to write your program. In other words, you'll translate your ideas into programming *code*—the words and characters that make the web browser behave how you want it to.

Compiled vs. Scripting Languages

JavaScript is called a scripting language. *I've heard this term used for other languages like PHP and ColdFusion as well. What's a scripting language?*

Most of the programs running on your computer are written using languages that are *compiled*. Compiling is the process of creating a file that will run on a computer by translating the code a programmer writes into instructions that a computer can understand. Once a program is compiled, you can run it on your computer, and since a compiled program has been converted directly to instructions a computer understands, it will run faster than a program written with a scripting language. Unfortunately, compiling a program is a time-consuming process: You have to write the program, compile it, and then test it. If the program doesn't work, you have to go through the whole process again.

A scripting language, on the other hand, is only compiled when an *interpreter* (another program that can convert the script into something a computer can understand) reads it. In the case of JavaScript, the interpreter is built into the web browser. So when your web browser reads a web page with a JavaScript program in it, the web browser translates the JavaScript into something the computer understands. As a result, a scripting language operates more slowly than a compiled language, since every time it runs, the program must be translated for the computer. Scripting languages are great for web developers: Scripts are generally much smaller and less complex than desktop programs, so the lack of speed isn't as important. In addition, since they don't require compiling, creating and testing programs that use a scripting language is a much faster process.

How to Add JavaScript to a Page

Web browsers are built to understand HTML and CSS and convert those languages into a visual display on the screen. The part of the web browser that understands HTML and CSS is called the *layout* or *rendering* engine. But most browsers also have something called a *JavaScript interpreter*. That's the part of the browser that understands JavaScript and can execute the steps of a JavaScript program. Since the web browser is usually expecting HTML, you must specifically tell the browser when JavaScript is coming by using the <script> tag.

The <script> tag is regular HTML. It acts like a switch that in effect says "Hey, web browser, here comes some JavaScript code; you don't know what to do with it, so hand it off to the JavaScript interpreter." When the web browser encounters the closing </script> tag, it knows it's reached the end of the JavaScript program and can get back to its normal duties.

Much of the time, you'll add the <script> tag in the <head> portion of the web page like this:

```
<!DOCTYPE HTML PUBLIC "-//W3C//DTD HTML 4.01//EN" "http://www.w3.org/TR/
html4/strict.dtd">
<html>
<head>
<title>My Web Page</title>
<script type="text/javascript">

</script>
</head>
```

The <script> tag's *type* attribute indicates the format and the type of script that follows. In this case, *type="text/javascript"* means the script is regular text (just like
HTML) and that it's written in JavaScript.

If you're using HTML5, life is even simpler. You can skip the type attribute entirely:

```
<!doctype html>
<html>
<head>
<meta charset="UTF-8">
<title>My Web Page</title>
<script>

</script>
</head>
```

In fact, web browsers let you leave out the type attribute in HTML 4.01 and XHTML
1.0 files as well—the script will run the same; however, your page won't validate
correctly without the type attribute (see the box on page 7 for more on validation).
This book uses HTML5 for the doctype, but the JavaScript code will be the same and
work the same for HTML 4.01, and XHTML 1.

You then add your JavaScript code between the opening and closing <script> tags:

```
<!doctype html>
<html>
<head>
<meta charset="UTF-8">
<head>
<title>My Web Page</title>
<script>
alert('hello world!');
</script>
</head>
```

You'll find out what this JavaScript actually does in a moment. For now, turn your
attention to the opening and closing <script> tags. To add a script to your page,
start by inserting these tags. In many cases, you'll put the <script> tags in the page's
<head> in order to keep your JavaScript code neatly organized in one area of the
web page.

However, it's perfectly valid to put <script> tags anywhere inside the HTML of the
page. In fact, as you'll see later in this chapter, there's a JavaScript command that lets
you write information directly into a web page. Using that command, you place the
<script> tags in the location on the page (somewhere inside the body) where you
want the script to write its message. It's even common to put <script> tags just below

the closing </body> tag—this approach makes sure the page is loaded and the visitor sees it before running any JavaScript.

External JavaScript Files

Using the <script> tag as discussed in the previous section lets you add JavaScript to a single page. But many times you'll create scripts that you want to share with all of the pages on your site. For example, you might use a JavaScript program to add animated, drop-down navigation menus to a web page. You'll want that same fancy navigation bar on every page of your site, but copying and pasting the same Java-Script code into each page of your site is a really bad idea for several reasons.

First, it's a lot of work copying and pasting the same code over and over again, especially if you have a site with hundreds of pages. Second, if you ever decide to change or enhance the JavaScript code, you'll need to locate every page using that Java-Script and update the code. Finally, since all of the code for the JavaScript program would be located in every web page, each page will be that much larger and slower to download.

A better approach is to use an external JavaScript file. If you've used external CSS files for your web pages, this technique should feel familiar. An external JavaScript file is simply a text file that ends with the file extension .js—*navigation.js*, for example. The file only includes JavaScript code and is linked to a web page using the <script> tag. For example, to add a JavaScript file named *navigation.js* to your home page, you might write the following:

```
<!doctype html>
<html>
<head>
<meta charset="UTF-8">
<title>My Web Page</title>
<script src="navigation.js"></script>
</head>
```

The src attribute of the <script> tag works just like the src attribute of an <img> tag, or an <a> tag's href attribute. In other words, it points to a file either in your website or on another website (see the box on the next page).

Note: When adding the src attribute to link to an external JavaScript file, don't add any JavaScript code between the opening and closing <script> tags. If you want to link to an external JavaScript file and add custom JavaScript code to a page, use a second set of <script> tags. For example:

```
<script src="navigation.js"></script>
<script >
  alert('Hello world!');
</script>
```

URL Types

When attaching an external JavaScript file to a web page, you need to specify a *URL* for the src attribute of the <script> tag. A URL or *Uniform Resource Locator* is a path to a file located on the web. There are three types of paths: *absolute path*, *root-relative path*, and *document-relative path*. All three indicate where a web browser can find a particular file (like another web page, a graphic, or a JavaScript file).

An *absolute path* is like a postal address—it contains all the information needed for a web browser located anywhere in the world to find the file. An absolute path includes http://, the hostname, and the folder and name of the file. For example: *http://www.cosmofarmer.com/scripts/site.js*.

A *root-relative* path indicates where a file is located relative to a site's top-level folder—the site's root folder. A root-relative path doesn't include http:// or the domain name. It begins with a / (slash) indicating the site's root folder—the folder the home page is in. For example, */scripts/site.js* indicates that the file site.js is located inside a folder named *scripts*, which is itself located in the site's top-level folder. An easy way to create a root-relative path is to take an absolute path and strip off the http:// and the host name. For example, *http://www.sawmac.com/index.html* written as a root-relative URL is */index.html*.

A *document-relative* path specifies the path from the web page to the JavaScript file. If you have multiple levels of folders on your website, you'll need to use different paths to point to the same JavaScript file. For example, suppose you have a JavaScript file named *site.js* located in a folder named *scripts* in your website's main directory. The document-relative path to that file will look one way for the home page—*scripts/site.js*—but for a page located inside a folder named *about*, the path to the same file would be different; *../scripts/site.js*—the *../* means climb up *out* of

the *about* folder, while the */scripts/site.js* means go to the *scripts* folder and get the file *site.js*.

Here are some tips on which URL type to use:

- If you're pointing to a file that's not on the same server as the web page, you *must* use an absolute path. It's the only type that can point to another website.

- Root-relative paths are good for JavaScript files stored on your own site. Since they always start at the root folder, the URL for a JavaScript file will be the same for every page on your website, even when web pages are located in folders and subfolders on your site. However, root-relative paths don't work unless you're viewing your web pages through a web server—either your web server out on the Internet, or a web server you've set up on your own computer for testing purposes. In other words, if you're just opening a web page off your computer using the browser's File→Open command, the web browser won't be able to locate, load, or run JavaScript files that are attached using a root-relative path.

- Document-relative paths are the best when you're designing on your own computer without the aid of a web server. You can create an external JavaScript file, attach it to a web page, and then check the JavaScript in a web browser simply by opening the web page off your hard drive. Document-relative paths work fine when moved to your actual, living, breathing website on the Internet, but you'll have to rewrite the URLs to the JavaScript file if you move the web page to another location on the server. In this book, we'll be using document-relative paths, since they will let you follow along and test the tutorials on your own computer without a web server.

You can (and often will) attach multiple external JavaScript files to a single web page. For example, you might have created one external JavaScript file that controls a drop-down navigation bar, and another that lets you add a nifty slideshow to a page of photos (you'll learn how to do that on page 222). On your photo gallery page, you'd want to have both JavaScript programs, so you'd attach both files.

In addition, you can attach external JavaScript files and add a JavaScript program to the same page like this:

```
<!doctype html>
<html>
<head>
<meta charset="UTF-8">
<title>My Web Page</title>
<script src="navigation.js"></script>
<script src="slideshow.js"></script>
<script>
  alert('hello world!');
</script>
</head>
```

Just remember that you must use one set of opening and closing <script> tags for each external JavaScript file. You'll create an external JavaScript file in the tutorial that starts on page 33.

You can keep external JavaScript files anywhere inside your website's root folder (or any subfolder inside the root). Many web developers create a special directory for external JavaScript files in the site's root folder: common names are *js* (meaning JavaScript) or *libs* (meaning libraries).

Note: Sometimes the order in which you attach external JavaScript files matters. As you'll see later in this book, sometimes scripts you write depend upon code that comes from an external file. That's often the case when using JavaScript libraries (JavaScript code that simplifies complex programming tasks). You'll see an example of a JavaScript library in action in the tutorial on page 33.

Your First JavaScript Program

The best way to learn JavaScript programming is by actually programming. Throughout this book, you'll find hands-on tutorials that take you step-by-step through the process of creating JavaScript programs. To get started, you'll need a text editor (see page 10 for recommendations), a web browser, and the exercise files located at *www.sawmac.com/js2e* (see the following Note for complete instructions).

Note: The tutorials in this chapter require the example files from this book's website, www.*sawmac.com/js2e/*. Click the "Download tutorials" link to download them. (The tutorial files are stored as a single Zip file.)

Windows users should download the Zip file and double-click it to open the archive. Click the Extract All Files option, and then follow the instructions of the Extraction Wizard to unzip the files and place them on your computer. Mac users, just double-click the file to decompress it. After you've downloaded and decompressed the files, you should have a folder named MM_JAVASCRIPT2E on your computer, containing all of the tutorial files for this book.

To get your feet wet and provide a gentle introduction to JavaScript, your first program will be very simple:

1. **In your favorite text editor, open the file *hello.html*.**

   This file is located in the *chapter01* folder in the MM_JAVASCRIPT2E folder you downloaded from *www.sawmac.com/js2e*. It's a very simple HTML page, with an external cascading style sheet to add a little visual excitement.

2. **Click in the empty line just *before* the closing </head> tag and type:**

   ```
   <script>
   ```

   This code is actually HTML, not JavaScript. It informs the web browser that the stuff following this tag is JavaScript.

3. **Press the Return key to create a new blank line, and type:**

   ```
   alert('hello world');
   ```

   You've just typed your first line of JavaScript code. The JavaScript *alert()* function is a command that pops open an Alert box and displays the message that appears inside the parentheses—in this case, *hello world*. Don't worry about all of the punctuation (the parentheses, quotes, and semicolon) just yet. You'll learn what they do in the next chapter.

4. **Press the Return key once more, and type *</script>*. The code should now look like this:**

   ```
   <link href="../_css/site.css" rel="stylesheet">
   <script>
   alert('hello world');
   </script>
   </head>
   ```

   In this example, the stuff you just typed is shown in boldface. The two HTML tags are already in the file; make sure you type the code exactly where shown.

5. **Launch a web browser and open the *hello.html* file to preview it.**

   A JavaScript Alert box appears (see Figure 1-2). Notice that the page is blank when the alert appears. (If you don't see the Alert box pictured in Figure 1-2, you probably mistyped the code listed in the previous steps. Double-check your typing and read the following Note.)

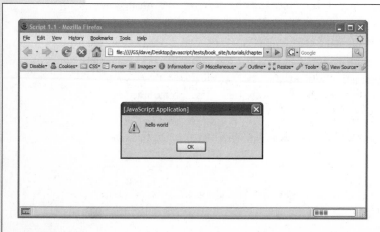

Figure 1-2: *The JavaScript Alert box is a quick way to grab someone's attention. It's one of the simplest JavaScript commands to learn and use.*

6. **Click the Alert box's OK button to close it.**

When the Alert box disappears, the web page appears in the browser window.

Tip: When you first start programming, you'll be shocked at how often your JavaScript programs don't seem to work…at all. For new programmers, the most common cause of nonfunctioning programs is simple typing mistakes. Always double-check to make sure you spelled commands (like *alert* in the first script) correctly. Also, notice that punctuation frequently comes in pairs (the opening and closing parentheses, and single-quote marks from your first script, for example). Make sure you include both opening and closing punctuation marks when they're required.

Although this first program isn't earth-shatteringly complex (or even that interesting), it does demonstrate an important concept: A web browser will run a JavaScript program the moment it reads in the JavaScript code. In this example, the *alert()* command appeared *before* the web browser displayed the web page, because the JavaScript code appeared *before* the HTML in the <body> tag. This concept comes into play when you start writing programs that manipulate the HTML of the web page—as you'll learn in Chapter 3.

Note: Internet Explorer (IE) doesn't like to run JavaScript programs contained in web pages that you open directly off your hard drive, for fear that the JavaScript program might do something harmful. So when you try to preview the tutorial files for this book in Internet Explorer, you'll see a message saying that IE has blocked the script. Click "Allow blocked content" to see the program run. This annoying behavior only applies to web pages you preview from your computer, not from files you put up on a web server. When following along with the tutorials in this book, it's better to preview pages in a different web browser like Firefox, Chrome, or Safari, so you can avoid having to hit the "Allow blocked content" button each time you view your pages.

Writing Text on a Web Page

The last script popped up a dialog box in the middle of your monitor. What if you want to print a message directly onto a web page using JavaScript? There are many ways to do so, and you'll learn some sophisticated techniques later in this book. However, you can achieve this simple goal with a built-in JavaScript command, and that's what you'll do in your second script:

1. **In your text editor, open the file *hello2.html*.**

While <script> tags usually appear in the <head> of a web page, you can put them and JavaScript programs directly in the body of the web page.

2. **Directly below <h1>Writing to the document window</h1>, type the following code:**

```
<script>
document.write('<p>Hello world!</p>');
</script>
```

Like the *alert()* function, *document.write()* is a JavaScript command that literally writes out whatever you place between the opening and closing parentheses. In this case, the HTML *<p>Hello world!</p>* is added to the page: a paragraph tag and two words.

3. **Save the page, and open it in a web browser.**

   The page opens and the words "Hello world!" appear below the red headline (see Figure 1-3).

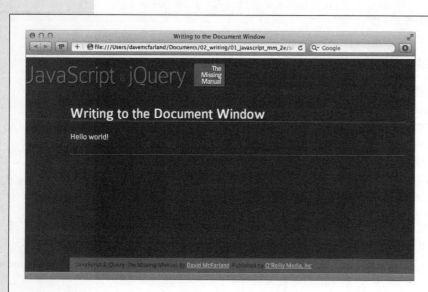

Figure 1-3:
Wow. This script may not be something to "document.write" home about–ha, ha, JavaScript humor–but it does demonstrate that you can use JavaScript to add content to a web page, a trick that comes in handy when you want to display messages (like "Welcome back to the site, Dave") after a web page has downloaded.

Note: The tutorial files you downloaded also include the completed version of each tutorial. If you can't seem to get your JavaScript working, compare your work with the file that begins with *complete_* in the same folder as the tutorial file. For example, the file *complete_hello2.html* contains a working version of the script you added to file *hello2.html*.

The two scripts you just created may leave you feeling a little underwhelmed with JavaScript…or this book. Don't worry. It's important to start out with a full understanding of the basics. You'll be doing some very useful and complicated things using JavaScript in just a few chapters. In fact, in the remainder of this chapter you'll get a taste of some of the advanced features you'll be able to add to your web pages after you've worked your way through the first two parts of this book.

Attaching an External JavaScript File

As discussed on page 27, you'll usually put JavaScript code in a separate file if you want to use the same scripts on more than one web page. You can then instruct a web page to load that file and use the JavaScript inside it. External JavaScript files also come in handy when you're using someone else's JavaScript code. In particular, there are collections of JavaScript code called *libraries*, which provide useful JavaScript programming: Usually, these libraries make it easy for you to do something that's normally quite difficult to do. You'll learn more about JavaScript libraries on page 117, and, in particular, the JavaScript library this book uses—jQuery.

But for now, you'll get experience attaching an external JavaScript file to a page, and writing a short program that does some amazing things:

1. **In your text editor, open the file *fadeIn.html*.**

   This page contains just some simple HTML—a few <div> tags, a headline, and a couple of paragraphs. You'll be adding a simple visual effect to the page, which causes all of the content to slowly fade into view.

2. **Click in the blank line between the <link> and closing </head> tags near the top of the page, and type:**

   ```
   <script src="../_js/jquery-1.6.3.min.js"></script>
   ```

   This code links a file named *jquery-1.6.3.min.js*, which is contained in a folder named *_js*, to this web page. When a web browser loads this web page, it also downloads the *jquery-1.6.3.min.js* JavaScript file and runs the code inside it.

   Next, you'll add your own JavaScript programming to this page.

Note: It's common to include a version number in the name of a JavaScript file. In this example, the filename is *jquery-1.6.3.min.js*. The 1.6.3 indicates the version 1.6.3 of jQuery. The min part means that the file is *minimized*—which makes the file smaller so that it downloads faster.

---

3. **Press Return to create a new blank line, and then type:**

   ```
   <script>
   ```

   HTML tags usually travel in pairs—an opening and closing tag. To make sure you don't forget to close a tag, it helps to close the tag immediately after typing the opening tag, and then fill in the stuff that goes between the tags.

4. **Press Return twice to create two blank lines, and then type:**

   ```
   </script>
   ```

   This ends the block of JavaScript code. Now you'll add some programming.

5. **Click the empty line between the opening and closing script tags and type:**

   ```
   $(document).ready(function() {
   ```

   You're probably wondering what the heck that is. You'll find out all the details of this code on page 169, but in a nutshell, this line takes advantage of the programming that's inside the *jquery-1.6.3.min.js* file to make sure that the browser executes the next line of code at the right time.

6. **Hit return to create a new line, and then type:**

```
$('body').hide().fadeIn(3000);
```

This line does something magical: It makes the page's content first disappear and then slowly fade into view over the course of 3 seconds (or 3000 milliseconds). How does it do that? Well, that's part of the magic of jQuery, which makes complex effects possible with just a single line of code.

7. **Hit Return one last time, and then type:**

```
});
```

This code closes up the JavaScript code, much as a closing </script> tag indicates the end of a JavaScript program. Don't worry too much about all those weird punctuation marks—you'll learn how they work in detail later in the book. The main thing you need to make sure of is to type the code exactly as it's listed here. One typo, and the program may not work.

The final code you added to the page should look like the bolded text below:

```
<link href="../_css/site.css" rel="stylesheet">
<script src="../_js/jquery-1.6.3.min.js"></script>
<script>
$(function() {
$('body').hide().fadeIn(3000);
});
</script>
</head>
```

8. **Save the HTML file, and open it in a web browser.**

You should now see the page slowly fade into view. Change the number 3000 to different values (like 250 and 10000) to see how that changes the way the page works.

Note: If you try to preview this page in Internet Explorer and it doesn't seem to do anything, you'll need to click the "Enable blocked content" box that appears at the bottom of the page (see the Note on page 31).

As you can see, it doesn't take a whole lot of JavaScript to do some amazing things to your web pages. Thanks to JavaScript libraries like jQuery, you'll be able to create sophisticated, interactive websites without being a programming wizard yourself. However, it does help to know the basics of JavaScript and programming. In the next three chapters, we'll cover the very basics of JavaScript so that you're comfortable with the fundamental concepts and syntax that make up the language.

Tracking Down Errors

The most frustrating moment in JavaScript programming comes when you try to view your JavaScript-powered page in a web browser...and nothing happens. It's one of the most common experiences for programmers. Even very experienced programmers don't always get it right the first time they write a program, so figuring out what went wrong is just part of the game.

Most web browsers are set up to silently ignore JavaScript errors, so you usually won't even see a "Hey this program doesn't work!" dialog box. (Generally, that's a good thing, since you don't want a JavaScript error to interrupt the experience of viewing your web pages.)

So how do you figure out what's gone wrong? There are many ways to track errors in a JavaScript program. You'll learn some advanced *debugging* techniques in Chapter 15, but the most basic method is to consult the web browser. Most web browsers keep track of JavaScript errors and record them in a separate window called an *error console*. When you load a web page that contains an error, you can then view the console to get helpful information about the error, like which line of the web page it occurred in and a description of the error.

Often, you can find the answer to the problem in the error console, fix the JavaScript, and then the page will work. The console helps you weed out the basic typos you make when you first start programming, like forgetting closing punctuation, or mistyping the name of a JavaScript command. You can use the error console in your favorite browser, but since scripts sometimes work in one browser and not another, this section shows you how to turn on the JavaScript console in all major browsers, so you can track down problems in each.

The Firefox JavaScript Console

Firefox's JavaScript console is a great place to begin tracking down errors in your code. Not only does the console provide fairly clear descriptions of errors (no descriptions are ever *that* clear when it comes to programming), it also identifies the line in your code where the error occurred.

For example, in Figure 1-4, the console identifies the error as an "unterminated string literal," meaning that there's an opening single quote mark before "slow" but no final quote mark. The console also identifies the name of the file the error is in (*fadeIn .html* in this case) and the line number the error occurs (line 11). Best of all, it even indicates the source of the error with an arrow—in this case, highlighting the opening quote mark.

Warning: Although the error console draws an arrow pointing to the location where Firefox encountered the error, that's not always where you made the mistake. Sometimes you need to fix your code before or after that arrow.

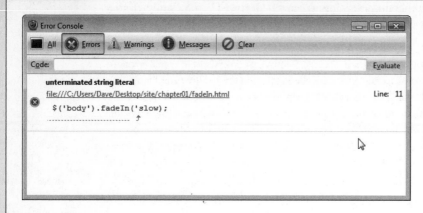

Figure 1-4:
Firefox's JavaScript console identifies errors in your programs. The console keeps a list of errors for previous pages as well, so pretty soon the list can get very long. Just click the Clear button to erase all the errors listed in the console.

To show the JavaScript console, click the Firefox menu and choose Web Developer→Error Console (on Windows) or Tools→Error Console (on Macs). The console is a free-floating window that you can move around. It not only displays JavaScript errors, but CSS errors as well, so if you've made any mistakes in your Cascading Styles Sheets, you'll find out about those as well. (Make sure you select the Errors button at the top of the console; otherwise, you might see warnings and messages that aren't related to your JavaScript error.)

Tip: Since the error console displays the line number where the error occurred, you may want to use a text editor that can show line numbers. That way, you can easily jump from the error console to your text editor and identify the line of code you need to fix.

Unfortunately, there's a long list of things that can go wrong in a script, from simple typos to complex errors in logic. When you're just starting out with JavaScript programming, many of your errors will be the simple typographic sort. For example, you might forget a semicolon, quote mark, or parenthesis, or misspell a JavaScript command. You're especially prone to typos when following examples from a book (like this one). Here are a few errors you may see a lot of when you first start typing the code from this book:

- **Missing) after argument list**. You forgot to type a closing parenthesis at the end of a command. For example, in this code—*alert('hello';*—the parenthesis is missing after *'hello'*.

- **Unterminated string literal**. A *string* is a series of characters enclosed by quote marks (you'll learn about these in greater detail on page 43). For example, *'hello'* is a string in the code *alert('hello');*. It's easy to forget either the opening or closing quote mark.

- **XXX is not defined**. If you misspell a JavaScript command—*aler('hello');*—you'll get an error saying that the (misspelled) command isn't defined: for example, "aler is not defined."

- **Syntax error**. Occasionally, Firefox has no idea what you were trying to do and provides this generic error message. A syntax error represents some mistake in your code. It may not be a typo, but you may have put together one or more statements of JavaScript in a way that isn't allowed. In this case, you need to look closely at the line where the error was found and try to figure out what mistake you made. Unfortunately, these types of errors often require experience with and understanding of the JavaScript language to fix.

As you can see from the list above, many errors you'll make simply involve forgetting to type one of a pair of punctuation marks—like quote marks or parentheses. Fortunately, these are easy to fix, and as you get more experience programming, you'll eventually stop making them almost completely (no programmer is perfect).

Note: The Firebug plug-in for Firefox (*http://getfirebug.com/*) greatly expands on Firefox's Error Console. In fact, it provided the model for the other developer tools you'll find in IE9, Chrome, and Safari (discussed next). You'll learn about Firebug in Chapter 15.

Displaying the Internet Explorer 9 Console

Internet Explorer 9 provides a sophisticated set of developer tools for viewing not only JavaScript errors, but also analyzing CSS, HTML, and transfers of information over the network. When open, the developer tool window appears in the bottom half of the browser window (see Figure 1-5). Press the F12 key to open the developer tools, and press it again to close them. You'll find JavaScript errors listed under the Console tab (circled in Figure 1-5). Unlike the Firefox Error Console, which keeps a running total of JavaScript errors for all of the pages you visit, you need to open the IE 9 Console, then reload the page to see an error.

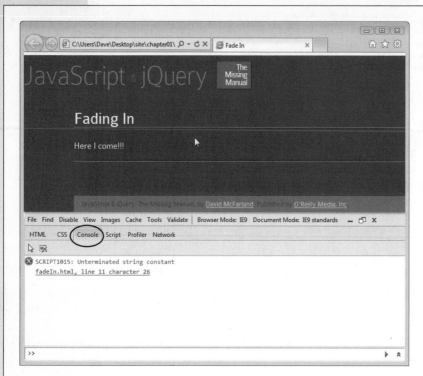

Figure 1-5:
The Internet Explorer Developer Tools provide access to JavaScript errors that occur on a page, as well as a whole lot of other information.

IE9's Console displays error messages similar to those described for Firefox above. For example, "Unterminated string constant" is the same as Firefox's "Unterminated string literal" message—meaning there's a missing quote mark. In addition, Internet Explorer identifies the line of code in the HTML file where the error occurred.

Opening the Chrome JavaScript Console

Google's Chrome browser also lets you view JavaScript errors from its JavaScript console. To open the console, click the tools icon (circled in Figure 1-6), select the Tools menu, and choose JavaScript console from the pop-out menu. Once the console opens, click the Errors button to see just the JavaScript errors you're after. Unfortunately, Chrome's error messages tend to be a little more cryptic. For example, the error message for leaving out a closing quote mark is "Uncaught SyntaxError: Unexpected token ILLEGAL." Not exactly clear or friendly. In fact, it kind of makes you feel as if you make one more mistake like that Chrome will scream, "Release the robotic hounds!"

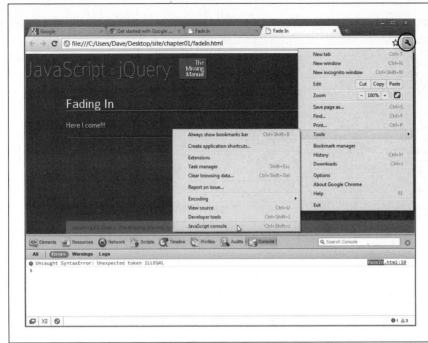

Figure 1-6:
*Chrome sports a
powerful set of
developer tools that
looks a lot like the
ones you'll find in
Internet Explorer 9
and Safari.*

Accessing the Safari Error Console

Safari's error console is available from the Develop menu: Develop→Show Error Console (on the Mac, you can use the keyboard shortcut Option-⌘-C, and on Windows, the shortcut is Ctrl+Alt+C). However, the Develop menu isn't normally turned on when Safari is installed, so there are a couple of steps to get to the JavaScript console.

To turn on the Develop menu, you need to first access the Preferences window. On a Mac, choose Safari→Preferences. On Windows, click the gear icon in the top right of the browser, and choose Preferences. Once the Preferences window opens, click the Advanced button. Check the "Show Develop menu in menu bar" box and close the Preferences window.

When you restart Safari, the Develop menu will appear between the Bookmarks and Window menus in the menu bar at the top of the screen on Macs; and on Windows, you'll find it under the page icon in the top right of the browser. Select Develop→Show Error Console to open the console (see Figure 1-7).

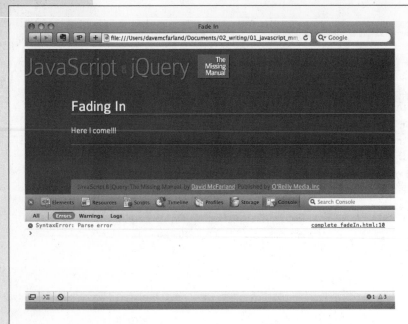

Figure 1-7:
The Safari Error Console displays the name of the JavaScript error, the file name (and location), and the line on which Safari encountered the error. Each tab or browser window has its own error console, so if you've already opened the console for one tab, you need to choose Develop→Error Console if you wish to see an error for another tab or window.

The Grammar of JavaScript

Learning a programming language is a lot like learning any new language: There are words to learn, punctuation to understand, and a new set of rules to master. And just as you need to learn the grammar of French to speak French, you must become familiar with the grammar of JavaScript to program JavaScript. This chapter covers the concepts that all JavaScript programs rely on.

If you've had any experience with JavaScript programming, many of these concepts may be old hat, so you might just skim this chapter. But if you're new to JavaScript, or you're still not sure about the fundamentals, this chapter introduces you to basic (but crucial) topics.

Statements

A JavaScript *statement* is a basic programming unit, usually representing a single step in a JavaScript program. Think of a statement as a sentence: Just as you string sentences together to create a paragraph (or a chapter, or a book), you combine statements to create a JavaScript program. In the last chapter you saw several examples of statements. For example:

```
alert('Hello World!');
```

This single statement opens an alert window with the message "Hello World!" in it. In many cases, a statement is a single line of code. Each statement ends with a semicolon—it's like a period at the end of a sentence. The semicolon makes it clear that the step is over and that the JavaScript interpreter should move on to the next action.

Note: Officially, putting a semicolon at the end of a statement is optional, and some programmers leave them out to make their code shorter. Don't be one of them. Leaving off the semicolon makes reading your code more difficult and, in some cases, causes JavaScript errors. If you want to make your JavaScript code more compact so that it downloads more quickly, see page 465.

The general process of writing a JavaScript program is to type a statement, enter a semicolon, press Return to create a new, blank line, type another statement, followed by a semicolon, and so on and so on until the program is complete.

Built-In Functions

JavaScript and web browsers let you use various commands to make things happen in your programs and on your web pages. These commands, called functions, are like verbs in a sentence. They get things done. For example, the *alert()* function you encountered earlier makes the web browser open a dialog box and display a message.

Some functions, like *alert()* or *document.write()*, which you encountered on page 31, are specific to web browsers. In other words, they only work with web pages, so you won't find them when programming in other environments that use JavaScript (like, for example, when scripting Adobe applications like Acrobat or Dreamweaver or in Flash's JavaScript-based ActionScript).

Other functions are universal to JavaScript and work anywhere JavaScript works. For example, *isNaN()* is a function that checks to see if a particular value is a number or not—this function comes in handy when you want to check if a visitor has correctly supplied a number for a question that requires a numerical answer (for example, "How many widgets would you like?"). You'll learn about *isNaN()* and how to use it on page 447.

JavaScript has many different functions, which you'll learn about throughout this book. One quick way to identify a function in a program is by the use of parentheses. For example, you can tell *isNaN()* is a function because of the parentheses following *isNaN*.

In addition, JavaScript lets you create your own functions, so you can make your scripts do things beyond what the standard JavaScript commands offer. You'll learn about functions in Chapter 3, starting on page 100.

Types of Data

You deal with different types of information every day. Your name, the price of food, the address of your doctor's office, and the date of your next birthday are all information that is important to you. You make decisions about what to do and how to live your life based on the information you have. Computer programs are no different. They also rely on information to get things done. For example, to calculate the total for a shopping cart, you need to know the price and quantity of each item ordered. To customize a web page with a visitor's name ("Welcome Back, *Kotter*"), you need to know her name.

Programming languages usually categorize information into different types, and treat each type in a different way. In JavaScript, the three most basic types of data are *number*, *string*, and *Boolean*.

Numbers

Numbers are used for counting and calculating; you can keep track of the number of days until summer vacation, or calculate the cost of buying two tickets to a movie. Numbers are very important in JavaScript programming: You can use numbers to keep track of how many times a visitor has visited a web page, to specify the exact pixel position of an item on a web page, or to determine how many products a visitor wants to order.

In JavaScript, a number is represented by a numeric character; 5, for example, is the number five. You can also use fractional numbers with decimals, like 5.25 or 10.3333333. JavaScript even lets you use negative numbers, like –130.

Since numbers are frequently used for calculations, your programs will often include mathematical operations. You'll learn about *operators* on page 50, but just to provide an example of using JavaScript with numbers, say you wanted to print the total value of 5 plus 15 on a web page; you could do that with this line of code:

```
document.write(5 + 15);
```

This snippet of JavaScript adds the two numbers together and prints the total (20) onto a web page. There are many different ways to work with numbers, and you'll learn more about them starting on page 445.

Strings

To display a name, a sentence, or any series of letters, you use strings. A *string* is just a series of letters and other symbols enclosed inside of quote marks. For example, '*Welcome Hal*', and "*You are here*" are both examples of strings. You used a string in the last chapter with the alert command—*alert('Hello World!');*.

A string's opening quote mark signals to the JavaScript interpreter that what follows is a string—just a series of symbols. The interpreter accepts the symbols literally, rather than trying to interpret the string as anything special to JavaScript like a command. When the interpreter encounters the final quote mark, it understands that it has reached the end of the string and continues onto the next part of the program.

You can use either double quote marks ("*hello world*") or single quote marks ('*hello world*') to enclose the string, but you must make sure to use the *same type* of quote mark at the beginning and end of the string (for example, "*this is not right*' isn't a valid string because it begins with a double-quote mark but ends with a single-quote).

Note: You'll notice that in the main body of this book, we use curly quotes—" "and ' '—but when coding JavaScript, you just use regular straight quote marks: " " and ' '. The code examples (like *alert('Warning, warning!');* below) use the proper quote mark style. Blame it in on Gutenberg—he didn't know how to program.

So, to pop-up an alert box with the message *Warning, warning!* you could write:

```
alert('Warning, warning!');
```

or

```
alert("Warning, warning!");
```

You'll use strings frequently in your programming—when adding alert messages, when dealing with user input on web forms, and when manipulating the contents of a web page. They're so important that you'll learn a lot more about using strings starting on page 425.

Putting Quotes into Strings

When I try to create a string with a quote mark in it, my program doesn't work. Why is that?

In JavaScript, quote marks indicate the beginning and end of a string, even when you don't want them to. When the JavaScript interpreter encounters the first quote mark, it says to itself, "Ahh, here comes a string." When it reaches a matching quote mark, it figures it has come to the end of the string. That's why you can't create a string like this: "He said, "Hello."". In this case, the first quote mark (before the word "He") marks the start of the string, but as soon as the JavaScript interpreter encounters the second quote mark (before the word "Hello"), it figures that the string is over, so you then end up with the string *"He said, "* and the *"Hello."* part, which creates a JavaScript error.

There are a couple of ways to get around this conundrum. The easiest method is to use single quotes to enclose a string that has one or more double quotes inside it. For example, *'He said, "Hello."'* is a valid string—the single quotes create the string, and the double quotes inside are a *part* of the string. Likewise, you can use double quotes to enclose

a string that has a single quote inside it: "This isn't fair," for example.

Another method is to tell the JavaScript interpreter to just treat the quote mark inside the string literally—that is, treat the quote mark as part of the string, not the end of the string. You do this using something called an *escape character*. If you precede the quote mark with a backward slash (\), the quote is treated as part of the string. You could rewrite the above example like this: *"He said, \"Hello.\""*. In some cases, an escape character is the only choice. For example: *'He said, "This isn\'t fair."'* Because the string is enclosed by single quotes, the lone single quote in the word "isn't" has to have a backward slash before it: *isn\'t*.

You can even escape quote marks when you don't necessarily have to—as a way to make it clear that the quote mark should be taken literally. For example. *'He said, "Hello."'*. Even though you don't need to escape the double quotes (since single quotes surround the entire string), some programmers do it anyway so that it's clear to them that the quote mark is just a quote mark.

Booleans

Whereas numbers and strings offer infinite possibilities, the Boolean data type is simple. It is either one of two values: *true* or *false*. You'll encounter Boolean data types when you create JavaScript programs that respond intelligently to user input and actions. For example, if you want to make sure a visitor supplied an email address before submitting a form, you can add logic to your page by asking the simple question: "Did the user type in a valid email address?" The answer to this question is a Boolean value: Either the email address is valid (true) or it's not (false). Depending on the answer to the question, the page could respond in different ways. For example, if the email address is valid (true), then submit the form; if it is not valid (false), then display an error message and prevent the form from being submitted.

In fact, Boolean values are so important that JavaScript includes two special keywords to represent those values:

```
true
```

and

```
false
```

You'll learn how Boolean values come into play when adding logic to your programs in the box on page 82.

Variables

You can type a number, string, or Boolean value directly into your JavaScript program, but these data types work only when you already have the information you need. For example, you can make the string "Hi Bob" appear in an alert box like this:

```
alert('Hi Bob');
```

But that statement only makes sense if everyone who visits the page is named Bob. If you want to present a personalized message for different visitors, the name needs to be different depending on who is viewing the page: 'Hi Mary,' 'Hi Joseph,' 'Hi Ezra,' and so on. Fortunately, all programming languages provide something known as a *variable* to deal with just this kind of situation.

A variable is a way to store information so that you can later use and manipulate it. For example, imagine a JavaScript-based pinball game where the goal is to get the highest score. When a player first starts the game, her score will be zero, but as she knocks the pinball into targets, the score will get bigger. In this case, the *score* is a variable since it starts at 0 but changes as the game progresses—in other words, a variable holds information that can *vary*. See Figure 2-1 for an example of another game that uses variables.

Think of a variable as a kind of basket: You can put an item into a basket, look inside the basket, dump out the contents of a basket, or even replace what's inside the basket with something else. However, even though you might change what's inside the basket, it still remains the same basket.

Creating a Variable

Creating a variable is a two-step process that involves *declaring* the variable and naming it. In JavaScript, to create a variable named *score,* you would type:

```
var score;
```

The first part, *var*, is a JavaScript keyword that creates, or, in programming-speak, *declares* the variable. The second part of the statement, *score*, is the variable's name.

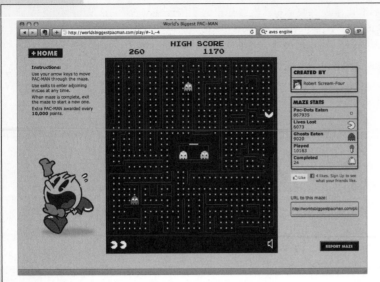

Figure 2-1:
*The World's Biggest Pac-Man
(http://worldsbiggestpacman
.com/) uses JavaScript to
create a Pac-Man game with
thousands of mazes. The game
tracks your current score and
your high score (top) as well
as the total number of Pac-dots
eaten and other game statistics
(right). These are all examples
of variables since they change
value as the game goes on.*

What you name your variables is up to you, but there are a few rules you must follow when naming variables:

- **Variable names must begin with a letter, $, or _.** In other words, you can't begin a variable name with a number or punctuation: so *1thing*, and *&thing* won't work, but *score*, *$score*, and *_score* are fine.

- **Variable names can only contain letters, numbers, $, and _.** You can't use spaces or any other special characters anywhere in the variable name: *fish&chips* and *fish and chips* aren't legal, but *fish_n_chips* and *plan9* are.

- **Variable names are case-sensitive.** The JavaScript interpreter sees uppercase and lowercase letters as distinct, so a variable named *SCORE* is different from a variable named *score*, which is also different from variables named *sCoRE* and *Score*.

- **Avoid keywords.** Some words in JavaScript are specific to the language itself: *var*, for example, is used to create a variable, so you can't name a variable *var*. In addition, some words, like *alert, document*, and *window*, are considered special properties of the web browser. You'll end up with a JavaScript error if you try to use those words as variable names. You can find a list of some reserved words in Table 2-1. Not all of these reserved words will cause problems in all browsers, but it's best to steer clear of these names when naming variables.

Table 2-1. *Some words are reserved for use by JavaScript and the web browser. Avoid using them as variable names*

JavaScript keywords	Reserved for future use	Reserved for browser
break	abstract	alert
case	boolean	blur
catch	byte	closed
continue	char	document
debugger	class	focus
default	const	frames
delete	double	history
do	enum	innerHeight
else	export	innerWidth
false	extends	length
finally	final	location
for	float	navigator
function	goto	open
if	implements	outerHeight
in	import	outerWidth
instanceof	int	parent
new	interface	screen
null	let	screenX
return	long	screenY
switch	native	statusbar
this	package	window
throw	private	
true	protected	
try	public	
typeof	short	
var	static	
void	super	
while	synchronized	
with	throws	
	transient	
	volatile	
	yield	

In addition to these rules, aim to make your variable names clear and meaningful. Naming variables according to what type of data you'll be storing in them makes it much easier to look at your programming code and immediately understand what's going on. For example, *score* is a great name for a variable used to track a player's game score. The variable name *s* would also work, but the single letter "s" doesn't give you any idea about what's stored in the variable.

Likewise, make your variable names easy to read. When you use more than one word in a variable name, either use an underscore between words or capitalize the first letter of each word after the first. For example, *imagepath* isn't as easy to read and understand as *image_path* or *imagePath*.

Using Variables

Once a variable is created, you can store any type of data that you'd like in it. To do so, you use the = sign. For example, to store the number 0 in a variable named *score*, you could type this code:

```
var score;
score = 0;
```

The first line of code above creates the variable; the second line stores the number 0 in the variable. The equal sign is called an *assignment operator*, because it's used to assign a value to a variable. You can also create a variable and store a value in it with just a single JavaScript statement like this:

```
var score = 0;
```

You can store strings, numbers, and Boolean values in a variable:

```
var firstName = 'Peter';
var lastName = 'Parker';
var age = 22;
var isSuperHero = true;
```

Tip: To save typing, you can declare multiple variables with a single *var* keyword, like this:

```
var x, y, z;
```

You can even declare and store values into multiple variables in one JavaScript statement:

```
var isSuperHero=true, isAfraidOfHeights=false;
```

Once you've stored a value in a variable, you can access that value simply by using the variable's name. For example, to open an alert dialog box and display the value stored in the variable *score*, you'd type this:

```
alert(score);
```

Notice that you don't use quotes with a variable—that's just for strings, so the code *alert('score')* will display the word "score" and not the value stored in the variable *score*. Now you can see why strings have to be enclosed in quote marks: The Java-Script interpreter treats words without quotes as either special JavaScript objects (like the *alert()* command) or as variable names.

Spaces, Tabs, and Carriage Returns in JavaScript

JavaScript seems so sensitive about typos. How do I know when I'm supposed to use space characters, and when I'm not allowed to?

In general, JavaScript is pretty relaxed about spaces, carriage returns, and tabs. You can often leave out spaces or even add extra spaces and carriage returns without a problem. JavaScript interpreters ignore extra spaces, so you're free to insert extra spaces, tabs, and carriage returns to format your code. For example, you don't need a space on either side of an assignment operator, but you can add them if you find it easier to read. Both of the lines of code below work:

```
var formName='signup';
var formRegistration = 'newsletter' ;
```

In fact, you can insert as many spaces as you'd like, and even insert carriage returns within a statement. So both of the following statements also work:

```
var formName      =      'signup';
var formRegistration

            =

      'newsletter';
```

Of course, just because you can insert extra space, doesn't mean you should. The last two examples are actually harder to read and understand because of the extra space. So the general rule of thumb is to add extra space if it makes your code easier to understand. For example, extra carriage returns help make code easier to read when declaring and setting the value of multiple variables at once. The following code is a single line:

```
var score=0, highScore=0, player='';
```

However, some programmers find it easier to read if each variable is on its own line:

```
var score=0,
    highScore=0,
    player='';
```

Whether you find this spacing easier to read is up to you; the JavaScript interpreter just ignores those line breaks. You'll see examples of how space can make code easier to read with JavaScript Object Literals (page 145) and with arrays (page 59).

There are a couple of important exceptions to the above rules. For example, you can't insert a carriage return inside a string; in other words, you can't split a string over two lines in your code like this:

```
var name = 'Bob
            Smith';
```

Inserting a carriage return (pressing the Enter or Return key) like this produces a JavaScript error and your program won't run.

In addition, you must put a space between keywords: *varscore=0*, for example, is not the same as var score=0. The latter example creates a new variable named score, while the former stores the value 0 in a variable named varscore. The JavaScript interpreter needs the space between *var* and *score* to identify the *var* keyword: *var score=0*. However, a space isn't necessary between keywords and symbols like the assignment operator (=) or the semicolon that ends a statement.

Note: You should only use the *var* keyword once for each variable—when you first create the variable. After that, you're free to assign new values to the variable without using *var*.

Working with Data Types and Variables

Storing a particular piece of information like a number or string in a variable is usually just a first step in a program. Most programs also manipulate data to get new results. For example, add a number to a score to increase it, multiply the number of items ordered by the cost of the item to get a grand total, or personalize a generic message by adding a name to the end: "Good to see you again, Igor." JavaScript provides various *operators* to modify data. An operator is simply a symbol or word that can change one or more values into something else. For example, you use the + symbol—the addition operator—to add numbers together. There are different types of operators for the different data types.

Basic Math

JavaScript supports basic mathematical operations such as addition, division, subtraction, and so on. Table 2-2 shows the most basic math operators and how to use them.

Table 2-2. Basic math with JavaScript

Operator	What it does	How to use it
+	Adds two numbers	5 + 25
-	Subtracts one number from another	25 - 5
*	Multiplies two numbers	5 * 10
/	Divides one number by another	15/5

You may be used to using an × for multiplication (4 × 5, for example), but in JavaScript, you use the * symbol to multiply two numbers.

You can also use variables in mathematical operations. Since a variable is only a container for some other value like a number or string, using a variable is the same as using the contents of that variable.

```
var price = 10;
var itemsOrdered = 15;
var totalCost = price * itemsOrdered;
```

The first two lines of code create two variables (*price* and *itemsOrdered*) and store a number in each. The third line of code creates another variable (*totalCost*) and stores the results of multiplying the value stored in the *price* variable (10) and the value stored in the *itemsOrdered* variable. In this case, the total (150) is stored in the variable *totalCost*.

This sample code also demonstrates the usefulness of variables. Suppose you write a program as part of a shopping cart system for an e-commerce website. Throughout the program, you need to use the price of a particular product to make various calculations. You could code the actual price throughout the program (for example, say the product cost 10 dollars, so you type 10 in each place in the program that price is used). However, if the price ever changes, you'd have to locate and change each line of code that uses the price. By using a variable, on the other hand, you can set the price of the product somewhere near the beginning of the program. Then, if the price ever changes, you only need to modify the one line of code that defines the product's price to update the price throughout the program:

```
var price = 20;
var itemsOrdered = 15;
var totalCost = price * itemsOrdered;
```

There are lots of other ways to work with numbers (you'll learn a bunch starting on page 445), but you'll find that you most frequently use the basic math operators listed in Table 2-2.

The Order of Operations

If you perform several mathematical operations at once—for example, you total up several numbers then multiply them all by 10—you need to keep in mind the order in which the JavaScript interpreter performs its calculations. Some operators take precedence over other operators, so they're calculated first. This fact can cause some unwanted results if you're not careful. Take this example:

```
4 + 5 * 10
```

You might think this simply is calculated from left to right: 4 + 5 is 9 and 9 * 10 is 90. It's not. The multiplication actually goes first, so this equation works out to 5 * 10 is 50, plus 4 is 54. Multiplication (the * symbol) and division (the / symbol) take precedence over addition (+) and subtraction (–).

To make sure that the math works out the way you want it, use parentheses to group operations. For example, you could rewrite the equation above like this:

```
(4 + 5) * 10
```

Any math that's performed inside parentheses happens first, so in this case the 4 is added to 5 first and the result, 9, is then multiplied by 10. If you want the multiplication to occur first, it would be clearer to write that code like this:

```
4 + (5*10);
```

Combining Strings

Combining two or more strings to make a single string is a common programming task. For example, if a web page has a form that collects a person's first name in one form field and his last name in a different field, you need to combine the two fields to get his complete name. What's more, if you want to display a message letting the user know his form information was submitted, you need to combine the generic message with the person's name: "John Smith, thanks for your order."

Combining strings is called *concatenation*, and you accomplish it with the + operator. Yes, that's the same + operator you use to add number values, but with strings it behaves a little differently. Here's an example:

```
var firstName = 'John';
var lastName = 'Smith';
var fullName = firstName + lastName;
```

In the last line of code above, the contents of the variable *firstName* are combined (or concatenated) with the contents of the variable *lastName*—the two are literally joined together and the result is placed in the variable *fullName*. In this example, the resulting string is "JohnSmith"—there isn't a space between the two names, since concatenating just fuses the strings together. In many cases (like this one), you need to add an empty space between strings that you intend to combine:

```
var firstName = 'John';
var lastName = 'Smith';
var fullName = firstName + ' ' + lastName;
```

The '' in the last line of this code is a single quote, followed by a space, followed by a final single quote. This code is simply a string that contains an empty space. When placed between the two variables in this example, it creates the string "John Smith". This last example also demonstrates that you can combine more than two strings at a time; in this case, three strings.

Note: Remember that a variable is just a container that can hold any type of data, like a string or number. So when you combine two variables with strings (firstName + lastName), it's the same as joining two strings like this: 'John' + 'Smith'.

Combining Numbers and Strings

Most of the mathematical operators only make sense for numbers. For example, it doesn't make any sense to multiply 2 and the string "eggs". If you try this example, you'll end up with a special JavaScript value *NaN*, which stands for "not a number." However, there are times when you may want to combine a string with a number. For example, say you want to present a message on a web page that specifies how many times a visitor has been to your website. The number of times she's visited is a *number*, but the message is a *string*. In this case, you use the + operator to do two things: convert the number to a string and concatenate it with the other string. Here's an example:

```
var numOfVisits = 101;
var message = 'You have visited this site ' + numOfVisits + ' times.';
```

In this case, *message* contains the string "You have visited this site 101 times." The JavaScript interpreter recognizes that there is a string involved, so it realizes it won't be doing any math (no addition). Instead, it treats the + as the concatenation operator, and at the same time realizes that the number should be converted to a string as well.

This example may seem like a good way to print words and numbers in the same message. In this case, it's obvious that the number is part of a string of letters that makes up a complete sentence, and whenever you use the + operator with a string value and a number, the JavaScript interpreter converts the number to a string.

That feature, known as *automatic type conversion*, can cause problems, however. For example, if a visitor answers a question on a form ("How many pairs of shoes would you like?") by typing a number (*2*, for example), that input is treated like a string—'*2*'. So you can run into a situation like this:

```
var numOfShoes = '2';
var numOfSocks = 4;
var totalItems = numOfShoes + numOfSocks;
```

You'd expect the value stored in *totalItems* to be 6 (2 shoes + 4 pairs of socks). Instead, because the value in *numOfShoes* is a string, the JavaScript interpreter converts the value in the variable *numOfSocks* to a string as well, and you end up with the string "24" in the *totalItems* variable. There are a couple of ways to prevent this error.

First, you add + to the beginning of the *string* that contains a number like this:

```
var numOfShoes = '2';
var numOfSocks = 4;
var totalItems = +numOfShoes + numOfSocks;
```

Adding a + sign before a variable (make sure there's no space between the two) tells the JavaScript interpreter to try to convert the string to a number value—if the string only contains numbers like "2", you'll end up with the string converted to a number. In this example, you end up with 6 (2 + 4). Another technique is to use the *Number()* command like this:

```
var numOfShoes = '2';
var numOfSocks = 4;
var totalItems = Number(numOfShoes) + numOfSocks;
```

Number() converts a string to a number if possible. (If the string is just letters and not numbers, you get the *NaN* value to indicate that you can't turn letters into a number.)

In general, you'll most often encounter numbers as strings when getting input from a visitor to the page; for example, when retrieving a value a visitor entered into a form field. So, if you need to do any addition using input collected from a form or other source of visitor input, make sure you run it through the *Number()* command first.

Note: This problem only occurs when adding a number with a string that contains a number. If you try to multiply the *numOfShoes* variable with a variable containing a number–*shoePrice*, for example–the JavaScript interpreter will convert the string in *numOfShoes* to a number and then multiply it with the *showPrice* variable.

Changing the Values in Variables

Variables are useful because they can hold values that change as the program runs—a score that changes as a game is played, for example. So how do you change a variable's value? If you just want to replace what's contained inside a variable, assign a new value to the variable. For example:

```
var score = 0;
score = 100;
```

However, you'll frequently want to keep the value that's in the variable and just add something to it or change it in some way. For example, with a game score, you never just give a new score—you always add or subtract from the current score. To add to the value of a variable, you use the variable's name as part of the operation like this:

```
var score = 0;
score = score + 100;
```

That last line of code may appear confusing at first, but it uses a very common technique. Here's how it works: All of the action happens to the right of the = sign first; that is, the *score + 100* part. Translated, it means "take what's currently stored in *score* (0) and then add 100 to it." The result of that operation is *then* stored back into the variable *score*. The final outcome of these two lines of code is that the variable score now has the value of 100.

The same logic applies to other mathematical operations like subtraction, division, or multiplication:

```
score = score - 10;
score = score * 10;
score = score / 10;
```

In fact, performing math on the value in a variable and then storing the result back into the variable is so common that there are shortcuts for doing so with the main mathematical operations, as pictured in Table 2-3.

Table 2-3. *Shortcuts for performing math on a variable*

Operator	What it does	How to use it	The same as
+=	Adds value on the right side of equal sign to the variable on the left.	score += 10	score = score + 10
-=	Subtracts value on the right side of the equal sign from the variable on the left.	score -= 10	score = score - 10
*=	Multiplies the variable on the left side of the equal sign and the value on the right side of the equal sign.	score *= 10	score = score * 10
/=	Divides the value in the variable by the value on the right side of the equal sign.	score /= 10	score = score / 10
++	Placed directly after a variable name, ++ adds 1 to the variable.	score++	score = score + 1
--	Placed directly after a variable name, -- subtracts 1 from the variable.	score--	score = score - 1

The same rules apply when concatenating a string to a variable. For example, say you have a variable with a string in it and want to add another couple of strings onto that variable:

```
var name = 'Franklin';
var message = 'Hello';
message = message + ' ' + name;
```

As with numbers, there's a shortcut operator for concatenating a string to a variable. The += operator adds the string value to the right of the = sign to the end of the variable's string. So the last line of the above code could be rewritten like this:

```
message += ' ' + name;
```

You'll see the += operator frequently when working with strings, and throughout this book.

Tutorial: Using Variables to Create Messages

In this tutorial, you'll use variables to print (that is, write) a message onto a web page.

Note: To follow along with the tutorials in this chapter, you need to download the tutorial files from this book's companion website: *http://sawmac.com/js2e/*. See the Note on page 29 for details.

---

1. **In a text editor, open the file *use_variable.html* in the *chapter02* folder.**

   This page is just a basic HTML file with a simple CSS-enhanced design. It doesn't yet have any JavaScript. You'll use variables to write a message onto a web page.

2. **Locate the <h1> tag (a little over half way down the file) and add the opening and closing <script> tags, so that the code looks like this:**

   ```
   <h1>Using a Variable</h1>
   <script>

   </script>
   ```

   This HTML should be familiar by now: It simply sets the page up for the script you're about to write.

Note: This page uses the HTML5 doctype. If you're using XHTML 1.0 or HTML 4.01, add type="javascript" to the <script> tag like this: <script type="text/javascript">. This step isn't needed for the script to work, only for the page to pass the W3C Validator (see page7 for more on validation).

---

3. **In between the <script> tags, type:**

   ```
   var firstName = 'Cookie';
   var lastName = 'Monster';
   ```

   You've just created your first two variables—*firstName* and *lastName*—and stored two string values into them. Next you'll add the two strings together, and print the results to the web page.

4. **Below the two variable declarations, type:**

```
document.write('<p>');
```

As you saw in Chapter 1, the *document.write()* command adds text directly to a web page. In this case, you're using it to write HTML tags to your page. You supply the command a string—'<p>'—and it outputs that string just as if you had typed it into your HTML code. It's perfectly OK to supply HTML tags as part of the *document.write()* command. In this case, the JavaScript is adding the opening tag for a paragraph to hold the text you're going to print on the page.

Note: There are more efficient methods than *document.write()* to add HTML to a web page. You'll learn about them on page 138.

---

5. **Press Return and type the following JavaScript:**

```
document.write(firstName + ' ' + lastName);
```

Here you use the values stored in the variables you created in step 3. The + operator lets you put several strings together to create one longer string, which the *document.write()* command then writes to the HTML of the page. In this case, the value stored in firstName—'*Cookie*'—is added to a space character, and then added to the value of lastName—'*Monster*'. The results are one string: 'Cookie Monster'.

6. **Press Return again and type** *document.write('</p>');.*

The finished script should look like this:

```
<script type="text/javascript">
var firstName = 'Cookie';
var lastName = 'Monster';
document.write('<p>');
document.write(firstName + ' ' + lastName);
document.write('</p>');
</script>
```

7. **Preview the page in a web browser to enjoy the fruits of your labor (see Figure 2-2).**

The words "Cookie Monster" should appear below the headline "Using a Variable." If you don't see anything, there's probably a typo in your code. Compare the script above with what you typed and check page 34 for tips on debugging a script using Firefox, Safari, Chrome, or IE 9.

8. **Return to your text editor and change the second line of the script to read:**

```
var lastName = 'Jar';
```

Save the page and preview it in a web browser. Voila, the message now reads: Cookie Jar. (The file *complete_use_variable.html* has a working copy of this script.)

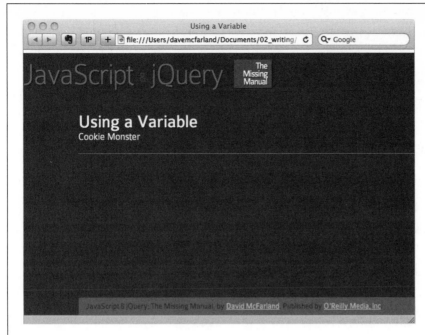

Figure 2-2:
While writing "Cookie Monster" may not be the reason you picked up a book on JavaScript, this script does demonstrate an important concept: how to create and use variables in JavaScript.

Tutorial: Asking for Information

In the last script, you saw how to create variables, but you didn't get to experience how variables can respond to the user and produce unique, customized content. In this next tutorial, you'll learn how to use the *prompt()* command to gather input from a user and change the display of the page based on that input.

1. **In a text editor, open the file *prompt.html* in the *chapter02* folder.**

   To make your programming go faster, the <script> tags have already been added to this file. You'll notice that there are two sets of <script> tags: one in the head and one in the body. The JavaScript you're about to add will do two things. First, it will open up a dialog box that asks the user to type in an answer to a question; second, in the body of the web page, a customized message using the user's response will appear.

2. **Between the first set of <script> tags in the document head, type the bolded code:**
   ```
   <script>
   var name = prompt('What is your name?', '');
   </script>
   ```
   The *prompt()* function produces a dialog box similar to the *alert()* function. However, instead of just displaying a message, the *prompt()* function can also retrieve an answer (see Figure 2-3). In addition, to use the *prompt()* function,

you supply two strings separated by a comma between the parentheses. Figure 2-3 shows what happens to those two strings: The first string appears as the dialog box's question ("What is your name?" in this example).

Note: IE7 won't let you use the *prompt()* method without enabling it in the browser's settings. Fortunately, IE7 is quickly disappearing from use.

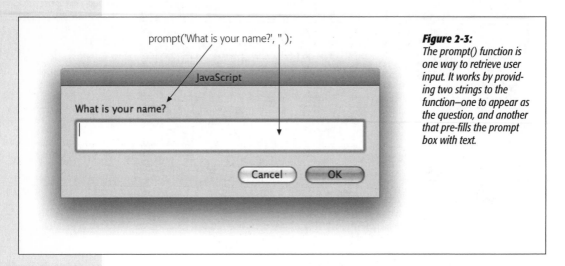

Figure 2-3:
The prompt() function is one way to retrieve user input. It works by providing two strings to the function—one to appear as the question, and another that pre-fills the prompt box with text.

The second string appears in the field the visitor types into. This example uses what's called an *empty string*, which is just two single quote marks (") and results in a blank text field. However, you can supply a useful instruction like "Please type both your first and last names" for the second string, and it will appear in the field. Unfortunately, a visitor will need to first delete that text from the text field before entering his own information.

The *prompt()* function returns a string containing whatever the visitor typed into the dialog box. In this line of JavaScript code, that result is stored into a new variable named *name*.

Note: Many functions *return* a value. In plain English, that just means the function supplies some information after it's done. You can choose to ignore this information or store it into a variable for later use. In this example, the *prompt()* function returns a string that you store in the variable *name*.

3. **Save the page and preview it in a web browser.**

When the page loads, you'll see a dialog box. Notice that nothing else happens—you don't even see the web page—until you fill out the dialog box and click OK. You'll also notice that nothing much happens after you click OK—that's because, at this point, you've merely collected and stored the response; you haven't used that response on the page. You'll do that next.

4. **Return to your text editor. Locate the second set of <script> tags and add the code in bold:**

```
<script>
document.write('<p>Welcome ' + name + '</p>');
</script>
```

Here you take advantage of the information supplied by the visitor. As with the script on page 55, you're combining several strings—an opening paragraph tag and text, the value of the variable, and a closing paragraph tag—and printing the results to the web page.

5. **Save the page and preview it in a web browser.**

When the Prompt dialog box appears, type in a name and click OK. Notice that the name you type appears in the web page (Figure 2-4). Reload the web page and type a new name—it changes! Just like a good variable should.

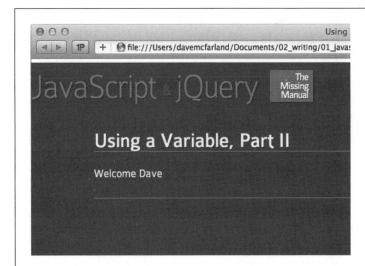

Figure 2-4:
The power of variables: This page customizes its message based on a visitor's response.

Arrays

Simple variables, like the ones you learned about in the previous section, only hold one piece of information, such as a number or a string value. They're perfect when you only need to keep track of a single thing like a score, an age, or a total cost. However, if you need to keep track of a bunch of related items—like the names of all of the days in a week, or a list of all of the images on a web page—simple variables aren't very convenient.

For example, say you've created a JavaScript shopping cart system that tracks items a visitor intends to buy. If you wanted to keep track of all of the items the visitor adds to her cart using simple variables, you'd have to write code like this:

```
var item1 = 'Xbox 360';
var item2 = 'Tennis shoes';
var item3 = 'Gift certificate';
```

But what if she wanted to add more items than that? You'd have to create more variables—*item4*, *item5*, and so on. And, because you don't know how many items the visitor might want to buy, you really don't know how many variables you'll have to create.

Fortunately, JavaScript provides a better method of tracking a list of items, called an *array*. An array is a way of storing more than one value in a single place. Think of an array like a shopping list. When you need to go to the grocery store, you sit down and write a list of items to buy. If you just went shopping a few days earlier, the list might only contain a few items; but if your cupboard is bare, your shopping list might be quite long. Regardless of how many items are on the list, though, there's still just a single list.

Without an array, you have to create a new variable for each item in the list. Imagine, for example, that you couldn't make a list of groceries on a single sheet of paper, but had to carry around individual slips of paper—one for each item that you're shopping for. If you wanted to add another item to buy, you'd need a new slip of paper; then you'd need to keep track of each slip as you shopped (see Figure 2-5). That's how simple variables work. But with an array, you can create a single list of items, and even add, remove, or change items at any time.

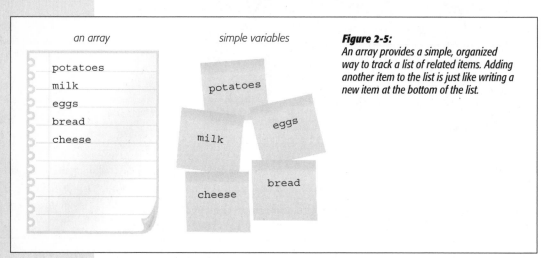

an array   *simple variables*

Figure 2-5:
An array provides a simple, organized way to track a list of related items. Adding another item to the list is just like writing a new item at the bottom of the list.

Creating an Array

To create and store items in an array, you first declare the array's name (just as you would a variable) and then supply a list of comma-separated values: Each value represents one item in the list. As with variables, what you name your array is up to you, but you need to follow the same naming rules listed on page 46. To create an array, you put the list of items between opening and closing brackets—[ ]. For example, to create an array containing abbreviations for the seven days of the week, you could write this code:

```
var days = ['Mon', 'Tues', 'Wed', 'Thurs', 'Fri', 'Sat', 'Sun'];
```

The brackets—[ ]—are very important; they tell the JavaScript interpreter that it's dealing with an array. You can create an empty array without any elements like this:

```
var playList = [];
```

Creating an empty array is the equivalent of declaring a variable as described on page 45. You'll create an empty array when you don't add items to the array until the program is running. For example, the above array might be used to track songs that someone selects from a list on a web page—you don't know ahead of time which songs the person will choose, so you declare an empty array and later fill it with items as the person selects music. (Adding items to an array is described on page 63.)

Note: When looking through other people's JavaScript programs (or other JavaScript books), you may encounter another way to create an array using the *Array* keyword, like this:

```
var days = new Array('Mon', 'Tues', 'Wed');
```

This method is valid, but the method used in this book (called an *array literal*) is preferred by the pros because it requires less typing, less code, and is considered more "elegant."

You can store any mix of values in an array. In other words, numbers, strings, and Boolean values can all appear in the same array:

```
var prefs = [1, 223, 'www.oreilly.com', false];
```

Note: You can even store arrays and other objects as elements inside an array. This technique can help store complex data.

The array examples above show the array created on a single line. However, if you've got a lot of items to add, or the items are long strings, trying to type all of that on a single line can make your program difficult to read. Another option many programmers use is to create an array over several lines, like this:

```
var authors = [ 'Ernest Hemingway',
                'Charlotte Bronte',
                'Dante Alighieri',
                'Emily Dickinson'
              ];
```

As mentioned in the box on page 49, a JavaScript interpreter skips extra space and line breaks, so even though this code is displayed on five lines, it's still just a single statement, as indicated by the final semicolon on the last line.

Tip: To make the names line up as above, you'd type the first line—*var authors = ['Ernest Hemingway',*—hit Return, then press the space key as many times as it takes to line up the next value, *'Charlotte Bronte',*.

Accessing Items in an Array

You can access the contents of a simple variable just by using the variable's name. For example, *alert(lastName)* opens an alert box with the value stored in the variable *lastName*. However, because an array can hold more than one value, you can't just use its name alone to access the items it contains. A unique number, called an *index*, indicates the position of each item in an array. To access a particular item in an array, you use that item's index number. For example, say you've created an array with abbreviations for the days of the week, and want to open an alert box that displayed the first item. You could write this:

```
var days = ['Mon', 'Tues', 'Wed', 'Thurs', 'Fri', 'Sat', 'Sun'];
alert(days[0]);
```

This code opens an alert box with 'Mon' in it. Arrays are *zero-indexed*, meaning that the *first* item in an array has an index value of 0, and the *second* item has an index value of 1: In other words, subtract one from the item's spot in the list to get its index value—the fifth item's index is 5 minus 1; that is, 4. Zero-indexing is pretty confusing when you first get started with programming, so Table 2-4 shows how the array *days* (from the above example) is indexed, as well as the values it contains and how to access each value.

Table 2-4. Items in an array must be accessed using an index number that's the equivalent to their place in the list minus 1

Index value	Item	To access item
0	Mon	days[0]
1	Tues	days[1]
2	Wed	days[2]
3	Thurs	days[3]
4	Fri	days[4]
5	Sat	days[5]
6	Sun	days[6]

You can change the value of an item in an array by assigning a new value to the index position. For example, to put a new value into the first item in the array *days*, you could write this:

```
days[0] = 'Monday';
```

Because the index number of the last item in an array is always one less than the total number of items in an array, you only need to know how many items are in an array to access the last item. Fortunately, this is an easy task since every array has a length property, which contains the total number of items in the array. To access the length property, add a period followed by *length* after the array's name: For example, *days.length* returns the number of items in the array named *days* (if you created a different array, *playList*, for example, you'd get its length like this: *playList. length*). So you can use this tricky bit of JavaScript to access the value stored in the last item in the array:

```
days[days.length-1]
```

This last snippet of code demonstrates that you don't have to supply a literal number for an index (for example, the 0 in *days[0]*). You can also supply an equation that returns a valid number. In this case, *days.length – 1* is a short equation: It first retrieves the number of items in the *days* array (that's 7 in this example) and subtracts 1 from it. So, in this case, *days[days.length-1]* translates to *days[6]*.

You can also use a variable containing a number as the index:

```
var i = 0;
alert(days[i]);
```

The last line of code is the equivalent of *alert(days[0]);*. You'll find this technique particularly useful when working with loops, as described in the next chapter (page 93).

Adding Items to an Array

Say you've created an array to track items that a user clicks on a web page. Each time the user clicks the page, an item is added to the array. JavaScript supplies several ways to add contents to an array.

Adding an item to the end of an array

To add an item to the end of an array, you can use the index notation from page 62, using an index value that's one greater than the last item in the list. For example, say you've have created an array named *properties*:

```
var properties = ['red', '14px', 'Arial'];
```

At this point, the array has three items. Remember that the last item is accessed using an index that's one less than the total number of items, so in this case, the last item in this array is properties[2]. To add another item, you could do this:

```
properties[3] = 'bold';
```

This line of code inserts *'bold'* into the fourth spot in the array, which creates an array with four elements: *['red', '14px', 'Arial', 'bold']*. Notice that when you add the new item, you use an index value that's equal to the total number of elements currently in the array, so you can be sure you're always adding an item to the end of an array by using the array's *length* property as the index. For example, you can rewrite the last line of code like this:

```
properties[properties.length] = 'bold';
```

You can also use an array's *push()* command, which adds whatever you supply between the parentheses to the end of the array. As with the *length* property, you apply *push()* by adding a period to the array's name followed by *push()*. For example, here's another way to add an item to the end of the *properties* array:

```
properties.push('bold');
```

Whatever you supply inside the parentheses (in this example, the string *'bold'*) is added as a new item at the end of the array. You can use any type of value, like a string, number, Boolean, or even a variable.

One advantage of the *push()* command is that it lets you add more than one item to the array. For example, say you want to add three values to the end of an array named *properties*, you could do that like this:

```
properties.push('bold', 'italic', 'underlined');
```

Adding an item to the beginning of an array

If you want to add an item to the beginning of an array, use the *unshift()* command. Here's an example of adding the *bold* value to the beginning of the *properties* array:

```
var properties = ['red', '14px', 'Arial'];
properties.unshift('bold');
```

After this code runs, the array *properties* contains four elements: *['bold', 'red', '14px', 'Arial']*. As with *push()*, you can use *unshift()* to insert multiple items at the beginning of an array:

```
properties.unshift('bold', 'italic', 'underlined');
```

Note: Make sure you use the *name* of the array followed by a period and the method you wish to use. In other words, *push('new item')* won't work. You must first use the array's name (whatever name you gave the array when you created it) followed by a period, and then the method, like this: *authors .push('Stephen King');*.

Choosing how to add items to an array

So far, this chapter has shown you three ways to add items to an array. Table 2-5 compares these techniques. Each of these commands accomplishes similar tasks, so the one you choose depends on the circumstances of your program. If the order that the items are stored in the array doesn't matter, then any of these methods work. For example, say you have a page of product pictures, and clicking one picture adds the product to a shopping cart. You use an array to store the cart items. The order the items appear in the cart (or the array) doesn't matter, so you can use any of these techniques.

However, if you create an array that keeps track of the order in which something happens, then the method you choose does matter. For example, say you've created a page that lets visitors create a playlist of songs by clicking song names on the page. Since a playlist lists songs in the order they should be played, the order is important.

So if each time the visitor clicks a song, the song's name should go at the end of the playlist (so it will be the last song played), then use the *push()* method.

Table 2-5. *Various ways of adding elements to an array*

Method	Original array	Example code	Resulting array	Explanation
.length property	`var p = [0,1,2,3]`	`p[p.length]=4`	[0,1,2,3,4]	Adds one value to the end of an array.
push()	`var p = [0,1,2,3]`	`p.push(4,5,6)`	[0,1,2,3,4,5,6]	Adds one or more items to the end of an array.
unshift()	`var p = [0,1,2,3]`	`p.unshift(4,5)`	[4,5,0,1,2,3]	Adds one or more items to the beginning of an array.

The *push()* and *unshift()* commands return a value. To be specific, once *push()* and *unshift()* complete their tasks, they supply the number of items that are in the array. Here's an example:

```
var p = [0,1,2,3];
var totalItems = p.push(4,5);
```

After this code runs, the value stored in *totalItems* is 6, because there are six items in the *p* array.

POWER USERS' CLINIC

Creating a Queue

The methods used to add items to an array–*push()* and *unshift()*–and the methods used to remove items from an array–*pop()* and *shift()*–are often used together to provide a way of accessing items in the order they were created. A classic example is a musical playlist. You create the list by adding songs to it; then, as you play each song, it's removed from the list. The songs are played in the order they appear in the list, so the first song is played and then removed from the list. This arrangement is similar to a line at the movies. When you arrive at the movie theater, you take your place at the end of the line; when the movie's about to begin, the doors open and the first person in line is the first to get in.

In programming circles, this concept is called FIFO for "First In, First Out." You can simulate this arrangement using arrays and the *push()* and *shift()* commands. For example, say you had an array named *playlist*. To add a new song to the end of the list, you'd use *push()*, like this:

```
playlist.push('Yellow Submarine');
```

To get the song that's supposed to play next, you get the first item in the list like this:

```
nowPlaying = playlist.shift();
```

This code removes the first item from the array and stores it in a variable named *nowPlaying*. The FIFO concept is useful for creating and managing queues such as a playlist, a to-do list, or a slideshow of images.

Deleting Items from an Array

If you want to remove an item from the end or beginning of an array, use the *pop()* or *shift()* commands. Both commands remove one item from the array: The *pop()* command removes the item from the end of the array, while *shift()* removes one item from the beginning. Table 2-6 compares the two methods.

Table 2-6. *Two ways of removing an item from an array*

Method	Original array	Example code	Resulting array	Explanation
pop()	var p = [0,1,2,3]	p.pop()	[0,1,2]	Removes the last item from the array.
shift()	var p = [0,1,2,3]	p.shift()	[1,2,3]	Removes the first item from the array.

As with *push()* and *unshift()*, *pop()* and *shift()* return a value once they've completed their tasks of removing an item from an array. In fact, they return the value that they just removed. So, for example, this code removes a value and stores it in the variable *removedItem*:

```
var p = [0,1,2,3];
var removedItem = p.pop();
```

The value of *removedItem* after this code runs is 3 and the array *p* now contains [0,1,2].

Note: This chapter's files include a web page that lets you interactively test out the different array commands. It's named *array_methods.html* and it's in the *testbed* folder. Open the file in a web browser and click the various buttons on the web page to see how the array methods work. (By the way, all the cool interactivity of that page is thanks to JavaScript.)

Tutorial: Writing to a Web Page Using Arrays

You'll use arrays in many of the scripts in this book, but to get a quick taste of creating and using arrays, try this short tutorial.

Note: See the note on page 29 for information on how to download the tutorial files.

1. **In a text editor, open the file *arrays.html* in the *chapter02* folder.**

    You'll start by simply creating an array containing four strings. As with the previous tutorial, this file already contains <script> tags in both the head and body regions.

2. **Between the first set of <script> tags, type the bolded code:**

```
<script>
var authors = [ 'Ernest Hemingway',
        'Charlotte Bronte',
        'Dante Alighieri',
        'Emily Dickinson'
      ];
</script>
```

This code comprises a single JavaScript statement, but it's broken over five lines. To create it, type the first line—*var authors = ['Ernest Hemingway',*—hit Return, then press the Space bar until you line up under the ' (about 16 spaces), and then type *'Charlotte Bronte',*.

Note: Most HTML editors use a *monospaced* font like Courier or Courier New for your HTML and JavaScript code. In a monospaced font, each character is the same width as every other character, so it's easy to line up columns (like all the author names in this example). If your text editor doesn't use Courier or something similar, you may not be able to line up the names perfectly.

As mentioned on page 61, when you create an array with lots of elements, you can make your code easier to read if you break it over several lines. You can tell it's a single statement since there's no semicolon until the end of line 5.

This line of code creates an array named *authors* and stores the names of four authors (four string values) into the array. Next, you'll access an element of the array.

3. **Locate the second set of <script> tags, and add the code in bold:**

```
<script>
document.write('<p>The first author is <strong>');
document.write(authors[0] + '</strong></p>');
</script>
```

The first line starts a new paragraph with some text and an opening <strong> tag—just plain HTML. The next line prints the value stored in the first item of the authors array and prints the closing </strong> and </p> tags to create a complete HTML paragraph. To access the first item in an array, you use a 0 as the index—*authors[0]*—instead of 1.

At this point, it's a good idea to save your file and preview it in a web browser. You should see "The first author is **Ernest Hemingway**" printed on the screen. If you don't, you may have made a typo when you created the array in either step 2 or 3.

Note: Remember to use the error console in your browser (described on page 34) to help you locate the source of any JavaScript errors.

---

4. **Return to your text editor and add these two lines of code below to your script:**

```
document.write('<p>The last author is <strong>');
document.write(authors[4] + '</strong></p>');
```

This step is pretty much the same as the previous one, except that you're printing a different array item. Save the page and preview it in a browser. You'll see "undefined" in place of an author's name (see Figure 2-6). Don't worry; that's intentional. Remember that an array's index values begin at 0, so the last item is actually the total number of items in the array minus 1. In this case, there are four strings stored in the authors array, so that last item would actually be accessed with *authors[3]*.

Note: If you try to read the value of an item using an index value that doesn't exist, you'll end up with the JavaScript "undefined" value. All that means is that there's no value stored in that index position.

Fortunately, there's an easy technique for retrieving the last item in an array no matter how many items are stored in the array.

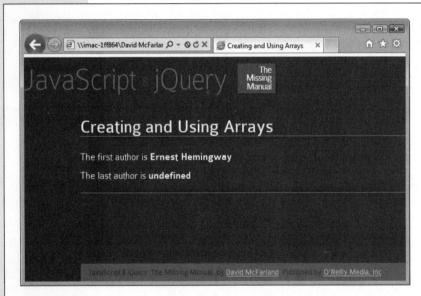

Figure 2-6:
If you try to access an array element that doesn't exist, then you'll end up with the value "undefined."

5. **Return to your text editor and edit the code you just entered. Erase the 4 and add the bolded code in its place:**

```
document.write('<p>The last author is <strong>');
document.write(authors[authors.length-1] + '</strong></p>');
```

As you'll recall from "Adding Items to an Array," an array's length property stores the number of items in the array. So the total number of items in the *authors* array can be found with this code: *authors.length*. At this point in the script, that turns out to be 4.

Knowing that the index value of the last item in an array is always 1 less than the total number of items in an array, you just subtract one from the total to get the index number of the last item: *authors.length-1*. You can provide that little equation as the index value when accessing the last item in an array: *authors[authors.length-1]*.

You'll finish up by adding one more item to the beginning of the array.

6. **Add another line of code after the ones you added in step 5:**

```
authors.unshift('Stan Lee');
```

As you read on page 64, the *unshift()* method adds one or more items to the beginning of an array. After this line of code runs, the authors array will now be *['Stan Lee', 'Ernest Hemingway', 'Charlotte Bronte', 'Dante Alighieri', 'Emily Dickinson']*.

Finally, you'll print out the newly added item on the page.

7. **Add three more lines (bolded below) so that your final code looks like this:**

```
document.write('<p>The first author is <strong>');
document.write(authors[0] + '</strong></p>');
document.write('<p>The last author is <strong>');
document.write(authors[authors.length-1] + '</strong></p>');
authors.unshift('Stan Lee');
document.write('<p>I almost forgot <strong>');
document.write(authors[0]);
document.write('</strong></p>');
```

Save the file and preview it in a web browser. You should see something like Figure 2-7. If you don't, remember that the error console in your web browser can help you locate the error (page 34).

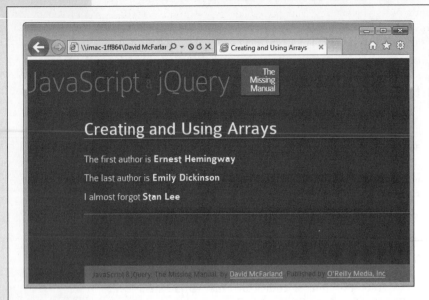

Figure 2-7:
*OK, Stan Lee may
not be your idea of
a literary giant, but
at least he's helping
you learn how arrays
work.*

A Quick Object Lesson

So far in this book, you've learned that you can write something to a web page with the *document.write()* command, and to determine how many items are in an array, you type the name of the array followed by a period and the word "length," like so: *days.length*. You're probably wondering what those periods are about. You've made it through three chapters without learning the particulars of this feature of JavaScript syntax, and it's time to address them.

You can conceptualize many of the elements of the JavaScript language, as well as elements of a web page, as *objects*. The real world, of course, is filled with objects too, such as a dog or a car. Most objects are made up of different parts: A dog has a tail, a head, and four legs; a car has doors, wheels, headlights, a horn; and so on. An object might also do something—a car can transport passengers, a dog can bark. In fact, even a part of an object can do something: For example, a tail can wag, and a horn can honk. Table 2-7 illustrates one way to show the relationships between objects, their parts, and actions.

Table 2-7. A simplified view of the world

Object	Parts	Actions
dog		bark
	tail	wag
car		transport
	horn	honk

The world of JavaScript is also filled with objects: a browser window, a document, a string, a number, and a date are just a few examples. Like real-world objects, Java-Script objects are also made up of different parts. In programming-speak, the parts of an object are called *properties*. The actions an object can perform are called *methods*, which are functions (like the built-in *alert()* function) that are specific to an object (see Table 2-8).

Note: You can always tell a method from a property because methods end in parentheses: *write()*, for example.

Each object in JavaScript has its own set of properties and methods. For example, the array object has a property named *length*, and the document object has a method named *write()*. To access an object's property or execute one of its methods, you use *dot-syntax*—those periods! The dot (period) connects the object with its property or method. For example, *document.write()* means "run the *write()* method of the document object." If the real world worked like that, you'd have a dog wag his tail like this: *dog.tail.wag()*. (Of course, in the real world, a doggy treat works a lot better.)

Table 2-8. *Some methods and properties of two JavaScript objects: the document object and an array.*

Object	Property	Method
document	title	
	url	
		write()
['Kate','Graham','Sam']	length	
		push()
		pop()
		unshift()

And just as you might own several dogs in the real world, your JavaScript programs can have multiple versions of the same kind of object. For example, say you create two simple variables like this:

```
var first_name = 'Jack';
var last_name = 'Hearts';
```

You've actually created two different *string* objects. Strings have their own set of properties and methods, which are different from the methods and properties of other objects, like dates (you'll learn some of these properties and methods on page 450). When you create an object (also called creating an *instance* of that object), you can access all of the properties and methods for that object.

Note: You've already encountered another object—called the window object—which represents the browser window itself. It's basically the container object for a web page and everything else on the page. For example, *alert()* and *prompt()* are both methods of the window object and can be written like this: *window.alert()* and *window.prompt()*. However, since the window object is always present in a web page, you can leave its name out, so *alert('hello')* and *window.alert('hello')* do the same thing.

Whenever you create a new variable and store a value into it, you're really creating a new instance of a particular type of object. So each of these lines of JavaScript create different types of JavaScript objects:

```
var first_name = 'Bob'; // a string object
var age = 32; // a number object
var valid = false; // a Boolean object
```

In fact, when you change the type of information stored in a variable, you change the type of object it is as well. For example, if you create a variable named *data* that stores an array, then store a number in the variable, you've changed that variable's type from an array to a number object:

```
var data = false; // an Boolean object
data = 32; //changes to number object
```

The concepts of objects, properties, methods, and dot-syntax may seem a little weird at first glance. However, since they are fundamental parts of how JavaScript works, and integral to using jQuery as well, you'll get used to them pretty quickly.

Tip: JavaScript includes a special keyword for determining the type of an object (string, number, Boolean, and so on.) It's called the *typeof* operator and is placed before a variable to determine the type of object inside that variable. For example:

```
var data = 32;
alert(typeof data); // "number" appears in alert window
```

As you continue reading this book, keep these few facts in mind:

- The world of JavaScript is populated with lots of different types of objects.
- Each object has its own properties and methods.
- You access an object's property or activate an object's method using dot-syntax: *document.write()*, for example.

Comments

There are times when you're in the midst of programming and you feel like you understand everything that's going on in your program. Every line of code makes sense, and better yet, it works! But a month or two later, when your boss or a client asks you to make a change or add a new feature to that cool script you wrote, you might find yourself scratching your head the moment you look at your once-familiar JavaScript: What's that variable for? Why'd I program it like that? What's going on in this section of the program?

It's easy to forget how a program works and why you wrote your code the way you did. Fortunately, most programming languages provide a way for programmers to leave notes for themselves or other programmers who might look through their code. JavaScript lets you leave *comments* throughout your code. If you've used HTML or CSS comments, these should feel familiar. A comment is simply a line or more worth of notes: The JavaScript interpreter ignores them, but they can provide valuable information on how your program works.

To create a single line comment, precede the comment with double forward slashes:

```
// this is a comment
```

You can also add a comment after a JavaScript statement:

```
var price = 10; // set the initial cost of the widget
```

The JavaScript interpreter executes everything on this line until it reaches the //, and then it skips to the beginning of the next line.

You can also add several lines worth of comments by beginning the comments with /* and ending them with */. (These are the same type of comments CSS uses.) The JavaScript interpreter ignores all of the text between these two sets of symbols. For example, say you want to give a description of how a program works at the beginning of your code. You can do that like this:

```
/*
    JavaScript Slideshow:
    This program automates the display of
    images in a pop-up window.
*/
```

You don't need to leave the /* and */ on their own lines, either. In fact, you can create a single line JavaScript comment with them:

```
/* this is a single line comment */
```

In general, if you want to just write a short, one-line comment, use //. For several lines of comments, use the /* and */ combination.

When to Use Comments

Comments are an invaluable tool for a program that's moderately long or complex and that you want to keep using (and perhaps changing) in the future. While the simple scripts you've learned so far are only a line or two of code, you'll eventually be creating longer and much more complex programs. To make sure you can quickly figure out what's going on in a script, it's a good idea to add comments to help you understand the overall logic of the program and to explain any particularly confusing or complex bits.

Note: Adding lots of comments to a script makes the script larger (and slower to download). In general, the amount of comments you'll add to a script won't add significantly to the size of the file. But, if you want to squeeze every unnecessary byte out of your files, page 465 shows you ways to make JavaScript files smaller and faster.

Many programmers add a block of comments at the beginning of an external Java-Script file. These comments can explain what the script is supposed to do, identify the date the script was created, include a version number for frequently updated scripts, and provide copyright information.

For example, at the beginning of the jQuery library's JavaScript file, you'll find this comment:

```
/*!
 * jQuery JavaScript Library v1.6.3
 * http://jquery.com/
 *
 * Copyright 2011, John Resig
 * Dual licensed under the MIT or GPL Version 2 licenses.
 * http://jquery.org/license
 *
 * Includes Sizzle.js
 * http://sizzlejs.com/
 * Copyright 2011, The Dojo Foundation
 * Released under the MIT, BSD, and GPL Licenses.
 *
 * Date: Wed Aug 31 10:35:15 2011 -0400
 */
```

At the beginning of the script, you might also include instructions on how to use the script: variables that might need to be set, anything special you might need to do to your HTML to make the script work, and so on.

You should also add a comment before a series of complex programming steps. For example, say you write a script that animates an image across a visitor's browser window. One part of that script is determining the image's current position in the browser window. This can take several lines of programming; it's a good idea to place a comment before that section of the program, so when you look at the script later, you'll know exactly what that part of the program does:

```
// determine x and y positions of image in window
```

The basic rule of thumb is to add comments anywhere you'll find them helpful later. If a line of code is painfully obvious, you probably don't need a comment. For example, there's no reason to add a comment for simple code like *alert('hello')*, because it's pretty obvious what it does (opens an alert box with the word "hello" in it).

Comments in This Book

Comments are also very helpful when explaining JavaScript. In this book, comments frequently explain what a line of programming does or indicate the results of a particular statement. For example, you might see a comment like the following to show the results of an alert statement:

```
var a = 'Bob';
var b = 'Smith';
alert( a + ' ' + b); // 'Bob Smith';
```

The third line ends with a comment that indicates what you should see when you preview this code in a web browser. If you want to test the code that you read in this book by adding it to a web page and viewing it in a web browser, you can leave out comments like these when typing the code into a web page. These types of comments are intended simply to help you understand what's happening in the code as you read along with the book.

Likewise, as you start to learn some of the more complex commands available in JavaScript, you'll begin to manipulate the data in variables. You'll often see comments in this book's code to display what should be stored in the variable after the command is run. For example, the *charAt()* command lets you select a character at a specific point in a string. When you read about how to use that command in this book, you might see code like this:

```
var x = "Now is the time for all good programmers.";
alert(x.charAt(2)); // 'w'
```

The comment // *'w'* that appears at the end of the second line indicates what you should see in an alert dialog box if this code were actually run in a web browser. (And, yes, 'w' is correct. When counting the letters in a string, the first letter is counted as character 0. So *charAt(2)* retrieves the *third* character from the string. Sometimes programming just hurts your brain.)

Adding Logic and Control to Your Programs

S o far you've learned about some of JavaScript's basic building blocks. But simply creating a variable and storing a string or number in it doesn't accomplish much. And building an array with a long list of items won't be very useful unless there's an easy way to work your way through the items in the array. In this chapter, you'll learn how to make your programs react intelligently and work more efficiently by using conditional statements, loops, and functions.

Making Programs React Intelligently

Our lives are filled with choices: "What should I wear today?", "What should I eat for lunch?", "What should I do Friday night?", and so on. Many choices you make depend on other circumstances. For example, say you decide you want to go to the movies on Friday night. You'll probably ask yourself a bunch of questions like "Are there any good movies out?", "Is there a movie playing at the right time?", "Do I have enough money to go to the movies (and buy a $17 bag of popcorn)?"

Suppose there *is* a movie that's playing at just the time you want to go. You then ask yourself a simple question: "Do I have enough money?" If the answer is yes, you'll head out to the movie. If the answer is no, you won't go. But on another Friday, you do have enough money, so you go to the movies. This scenario is just a simple example of how the circumstances around us affect the decisions we make.

JavaScript has the same kind of decision-making feature called *conditional statements*. At its most basic, a conditional statement is a simple yes or no question. If the answer to the question is yes, your program does one thing; if the answer is no, it does something else. Conditional statements are one of the most important programming concepts: They let your programs react to different situations and behave intelligently. You'll use them countless times in your programming, but just to get a clear picture of their usefulness, here are a few examples of how they can come in handy:

- **Form validation**. When you want to make sure someone filled out all of the required fields in a form ("Name," "Address," "Email," and so on), you'll use conditional statements. For example, if the Name field is empty, don't submit the form.

- **Drag and drop**. If you add the ability to drag elements around your web page, you might want to check where the visitor drops the element on the page. For example, if he drops a picture onto an image of a trash can, you make the photo disappear from the page.

- **Evaluating input**. Suppose you pop-up a window to ask a visitor a question like, "Would you like to answer a few questions about how great this website is?" You'll want your script to react differently depending on how the visitor answers the question.

Figure 3-1 shows an example of an application that uses conditional statements.

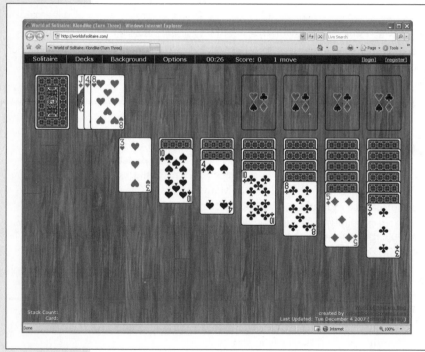

Figure 3-1:
It takes a lot of work to have fun. A JavaScript-based game like Solitaire (http://worldofsolitaire .com) demonstrates how a program has to react differently based on the conditions of the program. For example, when a player drags and drops a card, the program has to decide if the player dropped the card in a valid location or not, and then perform different actions in each case.

Conditional Statement Basics

Conditional statements are also called "if/then" statements, because they perform a task only if the answer to a question is true: "*If* I have enough money, *then* I'll go to the movies." The basic structure of a conditional statement looks like this:

```
if ( condition ) {
    // some action happens here
}
```

There are three parts to the statement: *if* indicates that the programming that follows is a conditional statement; the parentheses enclose the yes or no question, called the *condition* (more on that in a moment); and the curly braces ({ }) mark the beginning and end of the JavaScript code that should execute if the condition is true.

Note: In the code listed above, the "// some action happens here" is a JavaScript comment. It's not code that actually runs; it's just a note left in the program, and, in this case, points out to you, the reader, what's supposed to go in that part of the code. See page 72 for more on comments.

In many cases, the condition is a comparison between two values. For example, say you create a game that the player wins when the score is over 100. In this program, you'll need a variable to track the player's score and, at some point, you need to check to see if that score is more than 100 points. In JavaScript, the code to check if the player won could look like this:

```
if (score > 100) {
 alert('You won!');
}
```

The important part is *score > 100*. That phrase is the condition, and it simply tests whether the value stored in the *score* variable is greater than 100. If it is, then a "You won!" dialog box appears; if the player's score is less than or equal to 100, then the JavaScript interpreter skips the alert and moves onto the next part of the program. Figure 3-2 provides a visualization of this process.

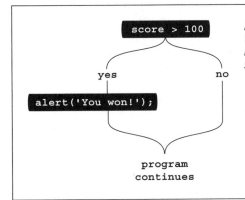

Figure 3-2:
With a basic conditional statement, the code inside the braces only runs if the condition is true. If the condition is false, that code is skipped and the program continues.

In addition to > (greater than), there are several other operators used to compare numbers (see Table 3-1).

Tip: Type two spaces (or press the Tab key once) before each line of JavaScript code contained within a pair of braces. The spaces (or tab) indent those lines and make it easier to see the beginning and ending brace, and to figure out what code belongs inside the conditional statement. Two spaces is a common technique, but if four spaces make your code easier for you to read, then use four spaces. The examples in this book always indent code inside braces.

Table 3-1. Use these comparison operators to test values as part of a conditional statement

Comparison operator	What it means
==	**Equal to**. Compares two values to see if they're the same. Can be used to compare numbers or strings.
!=	**Not equal to**. Compares two values to see if they're not the same. Can be used to compare numbers or strings.
===	**Strict equal to**. Compares not only the values but also the type of the value. In other words, the two values must also share the same type—string, number, or Boolean—in order for the condition to be true. For example, while '2'==2 is true, '2' === 2 is not true, because the first value is inside quote marks (a string) and the second is a number. You should be careful with this operator, since values in forms—even numbers—are always strings, so using strict equality to compare a number retrieved from a form field to a number using strict equality ('2' === 2) will be false.
!==	**Strict not equal to**. Like strict equal to compare values and type. For example, while '2' != 2 is false, '2' !== 2 is true, because although the values are the same, the types are not.
>	**Greater than**. Compares two numbers and checks if the number on the left side is greater than the number on the right. For example, 2 > 1 is true, since 2 is a bigger number than 1, but 2 > 3 is false, since 2 isn't bigger than 3.
<	**Less than**. Compares two numbers and checks if the number on the left side is less than the number on the right. For example, 2 < 3 is true, since 2 is a smaller number than 3, but 2 < 1 is false, since 2 isn't less than 1.
>=	**Greater than or equal to**. Compares two numbers and checks if the number on the left side is greater than or the same value as the number on the right. For example, 2 >= 2 is true, since 2 is the same as 2, but 2 >= 3 is false, since 2 isn't a bigger number 3, nor is it equal to 3.
<=	**Less than or equal to**. Compares two numbers and checks if the number on the left side is less than or the same value as the number on the right. For example, 2 <= 2 is true, since 2 is the same as 2, but 2 <= 1 is false, since 2 isn't a smaller number than 1, nor is 2 equal to 1.

More frequently, you'll test to see if two values are equal or not. For example, say you create a JavaScript-based quiz, and one of the questions asks, "How many moons does Saturn have?" The person's answer is stored in a variable named *answer*. You might then write a conditional statement like this:

```
if (answer == 31) {
  alert('Correct. Saturn has 31 moons.');
}
```

The double set of equal signs (==) isn't a typo; it instructs the JavaScript interpreter to compare two values and decide whether they're equal. As you learned in the last chapter, in JavaScript, a single equal sign is the *assignment operator* that you use to store a value into a variable:

```
var score = 0; //stores 0 into the variable score
```

Because the JavaScript interpreter already assigns a special meaning to a single equal sign, you need to use two equal signs whenever you want to compare two values to determine if they're equal or not.

You can also use the == (called the *equality operator*) to check to see if two strings are the same. For example, say you let the user type a color into a form, and if he types *red*, then you change the background color of the page to red. You could use the conditional operator for that:

```
if (enteredColor == 'red') {
  document.body.style.backgroundColor='red';
}
```

Note: In the code above, don't worry right now about how the page color is changed. You'll learn how to dynamically control CSS properties using JavaScript on page 143.

You can also test to see if two values aren't the same using the *inequality* operator:

```
if (answer != 31) {
  alert("Wrong! That's not how many moons Saturn has.");
}
```

The exclamation mark translates to "not", so != means "not equal to." In this example, if the value stored in *answer* is not 31, then the poor test taker would see the insulting alert message.

The code that runs if the condition is true isn't limited to just a single line of code as in the previous examples. You can have as many lines of JavaScript between the opening and closing curly braces as you'd like. For example, as part of the JavaScript quiz example, you might keep a running tally of how many correct answers the test-taker gets. So, when the Saturn question is answered correctly, you also want to add 1 to the test-taker's total. You would do that as part of the conditional statement:

```
if (answer == 31) {
  alert('Correct. Saturn has 31 moons.');
  numCorrect += 1;
}
```

Note: As described on page 54, the line of code above—*numCorrect += 1*—simply adds 1 to the value currently in the variable *numCorrect.*

And you could add additional lines of JavaScript code between the braces as well—any code that should run if the condition is true.

Adding a Backup Plan

But what if the condition is false? The basic conditional statement in the previous section doesn't have a backup plan for a condition that turns out to be false. In the real world, as you're deciding what to do Friday night and you don't have enough money for the movies, you'd want to do something *else*. An *if* statement has its own kind of backup plan, called an *else clause*. For example, say as part of the JavaScript testing script, you want to notify the test-taker if he gets the answer right, or if he gets it wrong. Here's how you can do that:

The Return of the Boolean

On page 44, you learned about the Boolean values—*true* and *false*. Booleans may not seem very useful at first, but you'll find out they're essential when you start using conditional statements. In fact, since a condition is really just a yes or no question, the answer to that question is a Boolean value. For example, check out the following code:

```
var x = 4;
if ( x == 4 ) {
    //do something
}
```

The first line of code stores the number 4 into the variable *x*. The condition on the next line is a simple question: Is the value stored in *x* equal to 4? In this case, it is, so the JavaScript between the curly braces runs. But here's what really happens in between the parentheses: The JavaScript interpreter converts the condition into a Boolean value; in programming-speak, the interpreter *evaluates* the condition. If the condition evaluates to *true* (meaning the answer to the question is yes), then the code between the braces runs. However, if the condition evaluates to *false*, then the code in the braces is skipped.

One common use of Booleans is to create what's called a *flag*—a variable that marks whether something is true. For example, when validating a form full of visitor-submitted information, you might start by creating a *valid* variable with a Boolean value of *true*—this means you're assuming, at first, that they filled out the form correctly. Then, you'd run through each form field, and if any field is missing information or has the wrong type of information, you change the value in *valid* to *false*. After checking all of the form fields, you test what's stored in *valid*, and if it's still true, you submit the form. If it's not true (meaning one or more form fields were left blank), you display some error messages and prevent the form from submitting:

```
var valid = true;
// lot of other programming gunk happens
in here
// if a field has a problem then you set
valid to false
if (valid) {
 //submit form
} else {
 //print lots of error messages
}
```

```
if (answer == 31) {
  alert('Correct. Saturn has 31 moons.');
  numCorrect = numCorrect + 1;
} else {
  alert("Wrong! That's not how many moons Saturn has.");
}
```

This code sets up an either/or situation; only one of the two messages will appear (see Figure 3-3). If the number 31 is stored in the variable *answer*, then the "correct" alert appears; otherwise, the "wrong" alert appears.

To create an *else* clause, just add "else" after the closing brace for the conditional statement followed by another pair of braces. You add the code that should execute if the condition turns out to be false in between the braces. Again, you can have as many lines of code as you'd like as part of the *else* clause.

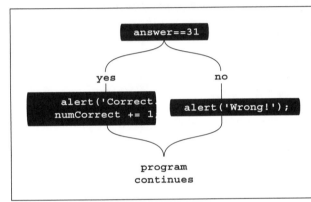

Figure 3-3:
When using an if else condition, you include two sets of code, but only one set will ever run. If the condition is true, then the code in the braces immediately following the condition runs (left); however, of the condition is false, then the code in the braces following the "else" runs (right).

Testing More Than One Condition

Sometimes you'll want to test several conditions and have several possible outcomes: Think of it like a game show where the host says, "Would you like the prize behind door #1, door #2, or door #3?" You can only pick one. In your day-to-day activities, you also are often faced with multiple choices like this one.

For example, return to the "What should I do Friday night?" question. You could expand your entertainment options based on how much money you have and are willing to spend. For example, you could start off by saying, "If I have more than $50, I'll go out to a nice dinner and a movie (and have some popcorn too)." If you don't have $50, you might try another test: "If I have $35 or more, I'll go to a nice dinner." If you don't have $35, then you'd say, "If I have $12 or more, I'll go to the movies." And finally, if you don't have $12, you might say, "Then I'll just stay at home and watch TV." What a Friday night!

JavaScript lets you perform the same kind of cascading logic using *else if* statements. It works like this: You start with an *if* statement, which is option number 1; you then add one or more *else if* statements to provide additional questions that can trigger additional options; and finally, you use the *else* clause as the fallback position. Here's the basic structure in JavaScript:

```
if (condition) {
  // door #1
} else if (condition2) {
  // door #2
} else {
  // door #3
}
```

This structure is all you need to create a JavaScript "Friday night planner" program. It asks visitors how much money they have, and then determines what they should do on Friday (sound familiar?). You can use the *prompt()* command that you learned about on page 57 to collect the visitor's response and a series of if/else if statements to determine what he should do:

```
var fridayCash = prompt('How much money can you spend?', '');
if (fridayCash >= 50) {
  alert('You should go out to a dinner and a movie.');
} else if (fridayCash >= 35) {
  alert('You should go out to a fine meal.');
} else if (fridayCash >= 12) {
  alert('You should go see a movie.');
} else {
  alert('Looks like you will be watching TV.');
}
```

Here's how this program breaks down step-by-step: The first line opens a prompt dialog box asking the visitor how much he can spend. Whatever the visitor types is stored in a variable named *fridayCash*. The next line is a test: Is the value the visitor typed 50 or more? If the answer is yes, then an alert appears, telling him to go get a meal and see a movie. At this point, the entire conditional statement is done. The JavaScript interpreter skips the next *else if* statement, the following *else if* statement, and the final *else* clause. With a conditional statement, only one of the outcomes can happen, so once the JavaScript interpreter encounters a condition that evaluates to *true*, it runs the JavaScript code between the braces for that condition and skips everything else within the conditional statement (see Figure 3-4).

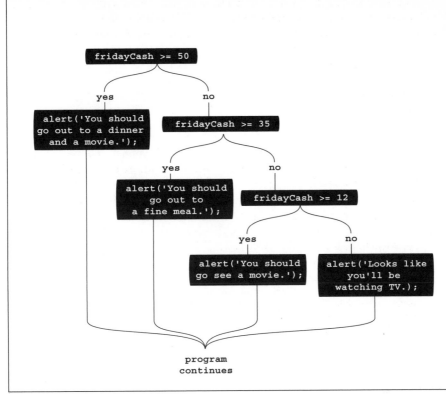

Figure 3-4:
*With a basic
conditional state-
ment, the code
inside the braces
only runs if the
condition is true.
If the condition is
false, that code
is skipped and
the program
continues*

Suppose the visitor typed 25. The first condition, in this case, wouldn't be true, since 25 is a smaller number than 50. So the JavaScript interpreter skips the code within the braces for that first condition and continues to the *else if* statement: "Is 25 greater than or equal to 35?" Since the answer is no, it skips the code associated with that condition and encounters the next *else if*. At this point, the condition asks if 25 is greater than or equal to 12; the answer is yes, so an alert box with the message, "You should go see a movie" appears and the program ends, skipping the final *else* clause.

Tip: There's another way to create a series of conditional statements that all test the same variable, as in the *fridayCash* example. *Switch* statements do the same thing, and you'll learn about them on page 462.

More Complex Conditions

When you're dealing with many different variables, you'll often need even more complex conditional statements. For example, when validating a required email address field in a form, you'll want to make sure both that the field isn't empty and that the field contains an email address (and not just random typed letters). Fortunately, JavaScript lets you do these kinds of checks as well.

Making sure more than one condition is true

You'll often need to make decisions based on a combination of factors. For example, you may only want to go to a movie if you have enough money *and* there's a movie you want to see. In this case, you'll go only if two conditions are true; if either one is false, then you won't go to the movie. In JavaScript, you can combine conditions using what's called the *logical AND operator,* which is represented by two ampersands (&&). You can use it between the two conditions within a single conditional statement. For example, if you want to check if a number is between 1 and 10, you can do this:

```
if (a < 10 && a > 1) {
//the value in a is between 1 and 10
alert("The value " + a + " is between 1 and 10");
}
```

In this example, there are two conditions: *a < 10* asks if the value stored in the variable *a* is less than 10; the second condition, *a > 1*, is the same as "Is the value in *a* greater than 1?" The JavaScript contained between the braces will run only if *both* conditions are true. So if the variable *a* has the number 0 stored in it, the first condition (*a < 10*) is true (0 is less than 10), but the second condition is false (0 is not greater than 1).

You're not limited to just two conditions. You can connect as many conditions as you need with the && operator:

```
if (b>0 && a>0 && c>0) {
// all three variables are greater than 0
}
```

This code checks three variables to make sure all three have a value greater than 0. If just one has a value of 0 or less, then the code between the braces won't run.

Making sure at least one condition is true

Other times you'll want to check a series of conditions, but you only need one to be true. For example, say you've added a keyboard control for visitors to jump from picture to picture in a photo gallery. When the visitor presses the N key, the next photo appears. In this case, you want her to go to the next picture when she types either *n* (lowercase), or if she has the Caps Lock key pressed, *N* (uppercase). You're looking for a kind of either/or logic: Either this key *or* that key was pressed. The *logical OR operator*, represented by two pipe characters (||), comes in handy:

```
if (key == 'n' || key == 'N') {
//move to the next photo
}
```

Note: To type a pipe character, press Shift-\. The key that types both backslashes and pipe characters is usually located just above the Return key.

With the OR operator, only one condition needs to be true for the JavaScript that follows between the braces to run.

As with the AND operator, you can compare more than two conditions. For example, say you've created a JavaScript racing game. The player has a limited amount of time, a limited amount of gas, and a limited number of cars (each time he crashes, he loses one car). To make the game more challenging, you want it to come to an end when any of these three things runs out:

```
if (gas <= 0 || time <= 0 || cars <= 0) {
//game is over
}
```

When testing multiple conditions, it's sometimes difficult to figure out the logic of the conditional statement. Some programmers group each condition in a set of parentheses to make the logic easier to grasp:

```
if ((key == 'n') || (key == 'N')) {
//move to the next photo
}
```

To read this code, simply treat each grouping as a separate test; the results of the operation between parentheses will always turn out to be either true or false.

Negating a condition

If you're a Superman fan, you probably know about Bizarro, an anti-hero who lived on a cubical planet named Htrae (Earth spelled backwards), had a uniform with a backwards S, and was generally the opposite of Superman in every way. When Bizarro said "Yes," he really meant "No," and when he said "No," he really meant "Yes."

JavaScript programming has an equivalent type of character called the *NOT* operator, which is represented by an exclamation mark (!). You've already seen the NOT operator used along with the equal sign to indicate "not equal to": !=. But the NOT operator can be used by itself to completely reverse the results of a conditional statement; in other words, it can make false mean true, and true mean false.

You use the NOT operator when you want to run some code based on a negative condition. For example, say you've created a variable named *valid* that contains a Boolean value of either *true* or *false* (see the box on page 82). You use this variable to track whether a visitor correctly filled out a form. When the visitor tries to submit the form, your JavaScript checks each form field to make sure it passes the requirements you set up (for example, the field can't be empty and it has to have an email address in it). If there's a problem, like the field is empty, you could then set *valid* to false (*valid = false*).

Now if you want to do something like print out an error and prevent the form from being submitted, you can write a conditional statement like this:

```
if (! valid) {
  //print errors and don't submit form
}
```

The condition *! valid* can be translated as "if not valid," which means if *valid* is false, then the *condition* is *true*. To figure out the results of a condition that uses the NOT operator, just evaluate the condition without the NOT operator, then reverse it. In other words, if the condition results to *true*, the ! operator changes it to *false*, so the conditional statement doesn't run.

As you can see, the NOT operator is very simple to understand (translated from Bizarro-speak: It's very confusing, but if you use it long enough, you'll get used to it).

Nesting Conditional Statements

In large part, computer programming entails making decisions based on information the visitor has supplied or on current conditions inside a program. The more decisions a program makes, the more possible outcomes and the "smarter" the program seems. In fact, you might find you need to make further decisions *after* you've gone through one conditional statement.

Suppose, in the "What to do on Friday night?" example, you want to expand the program to include every night of the week. In that case, you need to first determine what day of the week it is, and then figure out what to do on that day. So you might have a conditional statement asking if it's Friday, and if it is, you'd have another series of conditional statements to determine what to do on that day:

```
if (dayOfWeek == 'Friday') {
  var fridayCash = prompt('How much money can you spend?', '');
  if (fridayCash >= 50) {
   alert('You should go out to a dinner and a movie.');
  } else if (fridayCash >= 35) {
   alert('You should go out to a fine meal.');
  } else if (fridayCash >= 12) {
   alert('You should go see a movie.');
  } else {
   alert('Looks like you will be watching TV.');
  }
}
```

In this example, the first condition asks if the value stored in the variable *dayOfWeek* is the string *'Friday'*. If the answer is yes, then a prompt dialog box appears, gets some information from the visitor, and another conditional statement is run. In other words, the first condition (*dayOfWeek == 'Friday'*) is the doorway to another series of conditional statements. However, if *dayOfWeek* isn't 'Friday', then the condition is false and the nested conditional statements are skipped.

Tips for Writing Conditional Statements

The example of a nested conditional statement in the last section may look a little scary. There are lots of (), {}, elses, and ifs. And if you happen to mistype one of the crucial pieces of a conditional statement, your script won't work. There are a few things you can do as you type your JavaScript that can make it easier to work with conditional statements.

- **Type both of the curly braces before you type the code inside them.** One of the most common mistakes programmers make is forgetting to add a final brace to a conditional statement. To avoid this mistake, type the condition and the braces first, then type the JavaScript code that executes when the condition is true. For example, start a conditional like this:

```
if (dayOfWeek=='Friday') {

}
```

  In other words, type the *if* clause and the first brace, hit Return twice, and then type the last brace. Now that the basic syntax is correct, you can click in the empty line between the braces and add JavaScript.

- **Indent code within braces.** You can better visualize the structure of a conditional statement if you indent all of the JavaScript between a pair of braces:

```
if (a < 10 && a > 1) {
  alert("The value " + a + " is between 1 and 10");
}
```

  By using several spaces (or pressing the Tab key) to indent lines within braces, it's easier to identify which code will run as part of the conditional statement. If you have nested conditional statements, indent each nested statement:

```
if (a < 10 && a > 1) {
  //first level indenting for first conditional
  alert("The value " + a + " is between 1 and 10");
  if (a==5) {
    //second level indenting for 2nd conditional
    alert(a + " is half of ten.");
  }
}
```

- **Use == for comparing equals.** When checking whether two values are equal, don't forget to use the equality operator, like this:

```
if (name == 'Bob') {
```

  A common mistake is to use a single equal sign, like this:

```
if (name = 'Bob') {
```

  A single equal sign stores a value into a variable, so in this case, the string "Bob" would be stored in the variable *name*. The JavaScript interpreter treats this step as true, so the code following the condition will always run.

Tutorial: Using Conditional Statements

Conditional statements will become part of your day-to-day JavaScript toolkit. In this tutorial, you'll try out conditional statements to control how a script runs.

Note: See the note on page 29 for information on how to download the tutorial files.

---

1. **In a text editor, open the file *conditional.html* in the *chapter03* folder.**

   You'll start by simply prompting the visitor for a number. This file already contains <script> tags in both the head and body regions.

2. **Between the first set of <script> tags, in the page's <head> section, type the code in bold:**

   ```
   <script>
   var luckyNumber = prompt('What is your lucky number?','');
   </script>
   ```

   This line of code opens a JavaScript prompt dialog box, asks a question, and stores whatever the visitor typed into the *luckyNumber* variable. Next, you'll add a conditional statement to check what the visitor typed into the prompt dialog box.

3. **Locate the second set of <script> tags down in the body of the page, and add the code in bold:**

   ```
   <script>
   if (luckyNumber == 7 ) {
   </script>
   ```

   Here's the beginning of the conditional statement; it simply checks to see if the visitor typed 7.

4. **Press Return twice and type the closing brace, so that the code looks like this:**

   ```
   <script>
   if (luckyNumber == 7 ) {

   }
   </script>
   ```

   The closing brace ends the conditional statement. Any JavaScript you add between the two braces will only run if the condition is true.

   Note: As mentioned on page 89, it's a good idea to add the closing brace before writing the code that runs as part of the conditional statement.

   ---

5. **Click into the empty line above the closing brace. Hit the Space bar twice and type:**

   ```
   document.write("<p>Hey, 7 is my lucky number too!</p>");
   ```

   The two spaces before the code indent the line so you can easily see that this code is part of the conditional statement. The actual JavaScript here should feel familiar by now—it simply writes a message to the page.

6. **Save the file and preview it in a web browser. Type *7* when the prompt dialog box appears.**

   You should see the message "Hey, 7 is my lucky number too!" below the headline when the page loads. If you don't, go over your code and make sure you typed it correctly (see page 34 for tips on dealing with a broken script). Reload the page, but this time type a different number. This time, nothing appears underneath the headline. You'll add an *else clause* to print another message.

Note: Why two sets of script tags? When using the *document.write()* method to add content to a page, you have to place the *document.write()* code in the exact position on the page you want the message to appear—in this case, in the body below the <h1> tag. The first set of script tags appears in the head, because you want the prompt window to appear earlier. If you move the *prompt()* method down in the body (go ahead and try it), you'll see that when the page loads, only a part of the page gets displayed when the prompt appears. Because the JavaScript at that point runs immediately, before any of the other parts of the pages displays, the web browser has to wait until the visitor fills out the prompt window before it can display the rest of the page. In other words, the page looks weird. However, by putting the prompt up in the <head> section, the page starts off blank, when the prompt window appears—it just looks a little better. In the next chapter, you'll learn how to add content to any spot on a page without using the *document.write()* method. Once you know that technique, you can keep all of your JavaScript code together in one location on the page.

7. **Return to your text editor, and add the bolded text to your page:**

```
<script>
if (luckyNumber == 7 ) {
 document.write("<p>Hey, 7 is my lucky number too!</p>");
} else {
 document.write("<p>The number " + luckyNumber + " is lucky for you!</p>");
}
</script>
```

The *else* clause provides a backup message, so that if the visitor doesn't type 7, she'll see a different message that includes her lucky number. To round out this exercise, you'll add an *else if* statement to test more values and provide another message.

8. **Add the two bolded lines below to your script:**

```
<script>
if (luckyNumber == 7 ) {
 document.write("<p>Hey, 7 is my lucky number too!</p>");
} else if (luckyNumber == 13 || luckyNumber == 24) {
 document.write("<p>Wooh. " + luckyNumber + "? That's an unlucky number!</p>");
} else {
 document.write("<p>The number " + luckyNumber + " is lucky for you!</p>");
}
</script>
```

At this point, the script first checks to see if 7 is stored in the variable *luckyNumber*; if *luckyNumber* holds a value other than 7, then the *else if* kicks in. This conditional statement is made up of two conditions, *luckyNumber == 13* and *luckyNumber == 24*. The ||, called the logical OR operator, makes the entire conditional statement turn out to be true if either of the conditions are true. So if the visitor types in 13 *or* 24, a "That's an unlucky number" message is printed to the page.

Note: You add the logical OR operator by typing Shift-\ twice to get ||.

Preview the page in a web browser, and type *13* when the prompt dialog box appears. Press the browser's reload button, and try different numbers as well as letters or other characters. You'll notice that if you type a word or other non-number character, the final *else* clause kicks in, printing a message like, "The number asdfg is lucky for you!" Since that doesn't make a lot of sense, you'll pop up another prompt dialog box if your visitor enters a non-number the first time.

9. **Return to your text editor, and locate the first set of <script> tags in the <head> of the page. Add the code in bold:**

    ```
    <script>
    var luckyNumber = prompt('What is your lucky number?','');
    luckyNumber = parseInt(luckyNumber, 10);
    </script>
    ```

    This line of code runs the value of *luckyNumber* through a function named *parseInt()*. This JavaScript command takes a value and tries to convert it to an integer, which is a whole number like 1, 5, or 100. You can learn about this command on page 464, but for now just realize that if the visitor types in text like "ha ha," the *parseInt()* command won't be able to convert that to a number; instead, the command will provide a special JavaScript value, *NaN*, which stands for "not a number." You can use that information to pop up another prompt dialog box if a number isn't entered the first time.

10. **Add the bolded code to your script:**

     ```
     <script>
     var luckyNumber = prompt('What is your lucky number?','');
     luckyNumber = parseInt(luckyNumber);
     if (isNaN(luckyNumber)) {
      luckyNumber = prompt('Please, tell me your lucky number.','');
     }
     </script>
     ```

     Here again, a conditional statement comes in handy. The condition *isNaN(luckyNumber)* uses another JavaScript command that checks to see if something is a number. Specifically, it checks to see if the value in *luckyNumber* is *not* a number. If the value isn't a number (for example, the visitor types *askls-dkl*), a second prompt appears and asks the question again. If the visitor did type a number, the second prompt is skipped.

Save the page and preview it in a web browser again. This time, type a word and click OK when the prompt dialog box appears. You should then see a second prompt. Type a number this time. Of course, this script assumes the visitor made an honest mistake by typing a word the first time, but won't make the same mistake twice. Unfortunately, if the visitor types a word in the second prompt, you end up with the same problem—you'll learn how to fix that in the next section.

Note: You'll find a completed version of this tutorial in the *chapter03* tutorial folder: *complete_conditional.html*.

Handling Repetitive Tasks with Loops

Sometimes a script needs to repeat the same series of steps over and over again. For example, say you have a web form with 30 text fields. When the user submits the form, you want to make sure that none of the fields are empty. In other words, you need to perform the same set of actions—check to see if a form field is empty—30 times. Since computers are good at performing repetitive tasks, it makes sense that JavaScript includes the tools to quickly do the same thing repeatedly.

In programming-speak, performing the same task over and over is called a *loop*, and because loops are so common in programming, JavaScript offers several different types. All do the same thing, just in slightly different ways.

While Loops

A *while loop* repeats a chunk of code as long as a particular condition is true; in other words, *while* the condition is true. The basic structure of a while loop is this:

```
while (condition) {
  // javascript to repeat
}
```

The first line introduces the *while* statement. As with a conditional statement, you place a condition between the set of parentheses that follow the keyword *while*. The condition is any test you'd use in a conditional statement, such as *x > 10* or *answer == 'yes'*. And just like a conditional statement, the JavaScript interpreter runs all of the code that appears between the opening and closing braces *if* the condition is true.

However, unlike a conditional statement, when the JavaScript interpreter reaches the closing brace of a *while* statement, instead of continuing to the next line of the program, it jumps back to the top of the *while* statement and tests the condition a second time. If the condition is again true, the interpreter runs the JavaScript between the braces a second time. This process continues until the condition is no longer true; then the program continues to the next statement following the loop (see Figure 3-5).

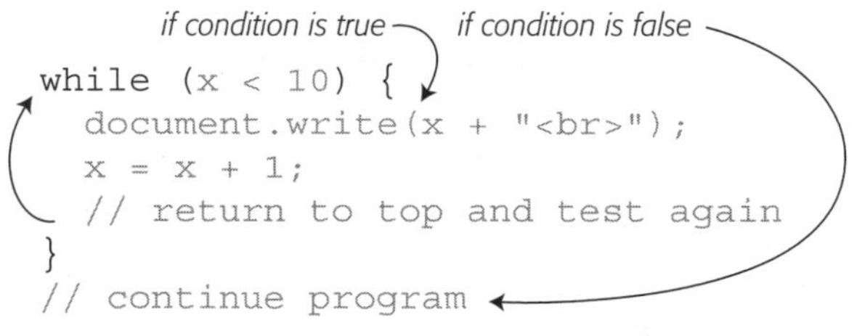

```
          if condition is true      if condition is false
  while (x < 10) {
    document.write(x + "<br>");
    x = x + 1;
    // return to top and test again
  }
  // continue program
```

Figure 3-5:
A while loop runs the JavaScript code between curly braces as long as the test condition (x < 10 in this case) is true.

Say you want to print the numbers 1 to 5 on a page. One possible way to do that is like this:

```
document.write('Number 1 <br>');
document.write('Number 2 <br>');
document.write('Number 3 <br>');
document.write('Number 4 <br>');
document.write('Number 5 <br>');
```

Notice that each line of code is nearly identical—only the number changes from line to line. In this situation, a loop provides a more efficient way to achieve the same goal:

```
var num = 1;
while (num <= 5) {
  document.write('Number ' + num + '<br>');
  num += 1;
}
```

The first line of code—*var num = 1;*—isn't part of the while loop: Instead, it sets up a variable to hold the number to be printed to the page. The second line is the start of the loop. It sets up the test condition. As long as the number stored in the variable *num* is less than or equal to 5, the code between the braces runs. When the test condition is encountered for the first time, the value of num is 1, so the test is true (1 is less than 5), and the *document.write()* command executes, writing "Number 1
" to the page (the <br> is just an HTML line break to make sure each line prints onto a separate line on the web page).

Tip: A more compact way to write *num + = 1* (which just adds one to the current number stored in the variable num) is like this:

```
num++
```

This shorthand method also adds one to the variable *num* (see Table 2-3 on page 54 for more information.)

The last line of the loop—*num += 1*—is very important. Not only does it increase the value of *num* by 1 so the next number (2, for example) will print, but it also makes it possible for the test condition to eventually turn out to be false (if the += thingy looks weird, turn back to page 54 for an explanation of how it works). Because the JavaScript code within a *while* statement repeats as long as the condition is true, you must change one of the elements of the condition so that the condition eventually becomes false in order to stop the loop and move onto the next part of the script. If the test condition never turns out to be false, you end up with what's called an *infinite loop*—a program that never ends. Notice what would happen if you left that line out of the loop:

```
var num = 1;
while (num <= 5) { // this is an endless loop
  document.write('Number ' + num + '<br>');
}
```

The first time through this loop, the test would ask: Is 1 less than or equal to 5? The answer is yes, so *document.write()* runs. At the end of the loop (the last brace), the JavaScript interpreter goes back to the beginning of the loop and tests the condition again. At this point, *num* is still 1, so the condition is true again and the *document .write()* executes. Again, the JavaScript interpreter returns to the beginning of the loop and tests the condition a third time. You can see where this goes: an endless number of lines that say "Number 1."

This simple example also shows some of the flexibility offered by loops. Say, for example, you wanted to write the numbers 1–100, instead of just 1–5. Instead of adding lots of additional lines of *document.write()* commands, you just alter the test condition like this:

```
var num = 1;
while (num <= 100) {
  document.write('Number ' + num + '<br>');
  num = num + 1;
}
```

Now the loop will execute 100 times, writing 100 lines to the web page.

Loops and Arrays

You'll find loops come in handy when dealing with a common JavaScript element—an array. As you recall from page 59, an array is a collection of data. You can think of an array as a kind of shopping list. When you go shopping, you actually perform a kind of loop: You walk around the store looking for an item on your list and, when you find it, you put it into your cart; then you look for the next item on your list, put it into the cart, and so on, until you've gone through the entire list. Then you're done (this is the same as exiting the loop) and you can go to the checkout counter (in other words, move to the next step of your "program").

You can use loops in JavaScript to go through items in an array and perform a task on each item. For example, say you're building a program that generates a calendar. The calendar is completely generated using JavaScript, and you want to print the name of each day of the week on the calendar. You might start by storing the names of the weeks into an array like this:

```
var days = ['Monday', 'Tuesday', 'Wednesday', 'Thursday', ↵
      'Friday', 'Saturday', 'Sunday'];
```

Note: The ↵ symbol that appears in the code above indicates that this line of JavaScript code belongs on a single line. Since the width of this book's pages sometimes prevents a single line of code from fitting on a single printed line, this book uses the ↵ symbol to indicate code that should appear together on a single line. If you were going to type this code into a text editor, you'd type it as one long line (and leave out the ↵).

You can then loop through each item in the array and print it to the page. Remember that you access one item in an array using the item's index value. For example, the first item in the *days* array above (Monday) is retrieved with *days[0]*. The second item is *days[1]*, and so on.

Here's how you can use a *while* loop to print each item in this array:

```
var counter = 0;
while (counter < days.length) {
    document.write(days[counter] + ', ');
    counter++;
}
```

The first line—*var counter = 0*—sets up (or *initializes* in programmer-speak) a counter variable that's used both as part of the test condition, and as the index for accessing array items. The condition—*counter < days.length*—just asks if the current value stored in the counter variable is less than the number of items in the array (remember, as described on page 63, the number of items in an array is stored in the array's *length* property). In this case, the condition checks if the counter is less than 7 (the number of days in the week). If *counter* is less than 7, then the loop begins: The day of the week is written to the page (followed by a comma and a period), and the counter is incremented by 1 (*counter++* is the same as *counter += 1, or counter = counter + 1* [see the Tip on page 94]). After the loop runs, it tries the test again; the loop continues to run until the test turns out to be false. This process is diagrammed in Figure 3-6.

```
var counter = 0;
while (counter < days.length) {
    document.write(days[counter] + ', ');
    counter++;
}
```

counter *value* before test	condition	loop?	days[counter]	counter *value* after counter++
0	0 < 7	yes	days[0]	1
1	1 < 7	yes	days[1]	2
2	2 < 7	yes	days[2]	3
3	3 < 7	yes	days[3]	4
4	4 < 7	yes	days[4]	5
5	5 < 7	yes	days[5]	6
6	6 < 7	yes	days[6]	7
7	7 < 7	no		

Figure 3-6:
For this loop, the condition is tested 8 times. The last test asks if 7 is less than 7. It isn't, so the while statement is completed, and the JavaScript interpreter skips the loop and continues with the next part of the script. The final result of this script will be "Monday, Tuesday, Wednesday, Thursday, Friday, Saturday, Sunday".

For Loops

JavaScript offers another type of loop, called a *for loop*, that's a little more compact (and a little more confusing). *For* loops are usually used for repeating a series of steps a certain number of times, so they often involve some kind of counter variable, a conditional test, and a way of changing the counter variable. In many cases, a *for* loop can achieve the same thing as a *while* loop, with fewer lines of code. For example, here's the *while* loop shown on page 96:

```
var num = 1;
while (num <= 100) {
 document.write('Number ' + num + '<br>');
 num += 1;
}
```

You can achieve the same effect using a *for* loop with only three lines of code:

```
for (var num=1; num<=100; num++) {
 document.write('Number ' + num + '<br>');
}
```

At first, *for* loops might look a little confusing, but once you figure out the different parts of the *for* statement, they aren't hard. Each *for* loop begins with the keyword *for*, followed by a set of parentheses containing three parts, and a pair of curly braces. As with *while* loops, the stuff inside curly braces (*document.write('Number ' + num + '<br>');* in this example) is the JavaScript code that executes as part of the loop.

Table 3-2 explains the three parts inside the parentheses, but in a nutshell, the first part (*var num=1;*) initializes a counter variable. This step only happens once at the very beginning of the statement. The second part is the condition, which is tested to see if the loop is run; the third part is an action that happens at the end of each loop—it usually changes the value of the counter, so that the test condition eventually turns out to be false and the loop ends.

Table 3-2. *Understanding the parts of a* for *loop*

Parts of loop	What it means	When it's applied
for	Introduces the for loop.	
var num = 1;	Set variable num to 1.	Only once; at the very beginning of the statement.
num <= 100;	Is num less than or equal to 100? If yes, then loop again. If not, then skip loop and continue script.	At beginning of the statement and before each time through the loop.
num++	Add 1 to variable num. Same as num=num + 1 and num+=1.	At end of each time through loop.

Since *for* loops provide an easy way to repeat a series of steps a set number of times, they work really well for working through the elements of an array. The *while* loop in Figure 3-5, which writes each item in an array to the page, can be rewritten using a *for* loop, like this:

```
var days = ['Monday', 'Tuesday', 'Wednesday', 'Thursday', ↵
    'Friday', 'Saturday', 'Sunday'];
for (var i=0; i<days.length; i++) {
    document.write(days[i] + ', ');
}
```

Tip: Seasoned programmers often use a very short name for counter variables in *for* loops. In the code above, the letter *i* acts as the name of the counter. A one-letter name (i, j, and z are common) is fast to type; and since the variable isn't used for anything except running the loop, there's no need to provide a more descriptive name like *counter*.

The examples so far have counted up to a certain number and then stopped the loop, but you can also count backwards. For example, say you want to print the items in an array in reverse order (in other words, the last item in the array prints first). You can do this:

```
var example = ['first','second','third','last'];
for (var j = example.length ; j > 0; j--) {
    document.write(example[j-1] + '<br>');
}
```

In this example, the counter variable *j* starts with the total number of items in the array (4). Each time through the loop, you test to see if the value in *j* is greater than 0; if it is, the code between the curly braces is run. Then, 1 is subtracted from *j* (*j--*), and the test is run again. The only tricky part is the way the program accesses the array item (*example[j-1]*). Since arrays start with an index of 0, the last item in an array is one less than the total number of items in the array (as explained on page 62). Here, *j* starts with the total number of items in the array, so in order to access the last item, you must subtract 1 from *j* to get the proper item.

Do/While Loops

There's another, less common type of loop, known as a *do/while loop*. This type of loop works nearly identically to a *while* loop. Its basic structure looks like this:

```
do {
// javascript to repeat
} while (condition) ;
```

In this type of loop, the conditional test happens at the *end*, after the loop has run. As a result, the JavaScript code within the curly braces always run *at least once*. Even if the condition isn't ever true, the test isn't run until after the code runs once.

There aren't too many cases where this comes in handy, but it's very useful when you want to prompt the user for input. The tutorial you did earlier in this chapter (page 89) is a good example. That script asks visitors to type in a number. It includes a bit of a fail-safe system, so that if they don't type a number, the script asks them one more time to type a number. Unfortunately, if someone's really stubborn and types something other than a number the second time, a nonsensical message is printed to the page.

However, with a *do/while loop*, you can continually prompt the visitor for a number until she types one in. To see how this works, you'll edit the page you completed on page 92:

1. **In a text editor, open the *conditional.html* page you completed on page 92.**

   (If you didn't complete that tutorial, you can just open the file *complete_conditional.html*.) You'll replace the code near the top of the page with a *do/while* loop.

2. **Locate the code between the <script> tags in the <head> of the page, and delete the code in bold below:**

   ```
   var luckyNumber = prompt('What is your lucky number?','');
   luckyNumber = parseInt(luckyNumber, 10);
   if (isNaN(luckyNumber)) {
    luckyNumber = prompt('Please, tell me your lucky number.','');
   }
   ```

   The code you deleted provided the second prompt dialog box. You won't need that anymore. Instead, you'll wrap the code that's left inside a *do/while* loop.

3. **Place the cursor before the first line of code (the line that begins with var *luckyNumber*) and type:**

   ```
   do {
   ```

   This code creates the beginning of the loop. Next, you'll finish the loop and add the test condition.

4. **Click at the end of the last line of JavaScript code in that section and type: }** *while (isNaN(luckyNumber));*. **The completed code block should look like this:**

   ```
   do {
    var luckyNumber = prompt('What is your lucky number?','');
    luckyNumber = parseInt(luckyNumber, 10);
   } while (isNaN(luckyNumber));
   ```

   Save this file and preview it in a web browser. Try typing text and other non-numeric symbols in the prompt dialog box. That annoying dialog box continues to appear until you actually type a number.

   Here's how it works: The *do* keyword tells the JavaScript interpreter that it's about to enter a *do/while* loop. The next two lines are then run, so the prompt appears and the visitor's answer is converted to a whole number. It's only at this point that the condition is tested. It's the same condition as the script on page 92: It just checks to see if the input retrieved from the visitor is "not a number." If the input isn't a number, the loop repeats. In other words, the prompt will keep reappearing as long as a non-number is entered. The good thing about this approach is that it guarantees that the prompt appears at least once, so if the visitor does type a number in response to the question, there is no loop.

   You can find the completed, functioning tutorial in the file *complete_do-while.html* in the Chapter03 folder.

Functions: Turn Useful Code Into Reusable Commands

Imagine that at work you've just gotten a new assistant to help you with your every task (time to file this book under "fantasy fiction"). Suppose you got hungry for a piece of pizza, but since the assistant was new to the building and the area, you had to give him detailed directions: "Go out this door, turn right, go to the elevator, take the elevator to the first floor, walk out of the building…" and so on. The assistant follows your directions and brings you a slice. A couple hours later, you're hungry again, and you want more pizza. Now, you don't have to go through the whole set of directions again—"Go out this door, turn right, go to the elevator…" By this time, your assistant knows where the pizza joint is, so you just say, "Get me a slice of pizza," and he goes to the pizza place and returns with a slice.

In other words, you only need to provide detailed directions a *single time*; your assistant memorizes those steps and with the simple phrase "Get me a slice," he instantly leaves and reappears a little while later with a piece of pizza. JavaScript has an equivalent mechanism called a *function*. A function is a series of programming steps that you set up at the beginning of your script—the equivalent of providing detailed directions to your assistant. Those steps aren't actually run when you create the function; instead, they're stored in the web browser's memory, where you can call upon them whenever you need those steps performed.

Functions are invaluable for efficiently performing multiple programming steps repeatedly. For example, say you create a photo gallery web page filled with 50 small thumbnail images. When someone clicks one of the small photos, you might want the page to dim, a caption to appear, and a larger version of that image to fill the screen (you'll learn to do just that on page 222). Each time someone clicks an image, the process repeats; so on a web page with 50 small photos, your script might have to do the same series of steps 50 times. Fortunately, you don't have to write the same code 50 times to make this photo gallery work. Instead, you can write a function with all the necessary steps, and then, with each click of the thumbnail, you run the function. You write the code once, but you run it any time you like.

The basic structure of a function looks like this:

```
function functionName() {
  // the JavaScript you want to run
}
```

The keyword *function* lets the JavaScript interpreter know you're creating a function—it's similar to how you use *if* to begin an *if/else* statement or *var* to create a variable. Next, you provide a function name; as with a variable, you get to choose your own function name. Follow the same rules listed on page 46 for naming variables. In addition, it's common to include a verb in a function name like *calculateTax, getScreenHeight, updatePage,* or *fadeImage.* An active name makes it clear that it does something and makes it easier to distinguish between function and variable names.

Directly following the name, you add a pair of parentheses, which are another characteristic of functions. After the parentheses, there's a space followed by a curly brace, one or more lines of JavaScript and a final, closing curly brace. As with *if* statements, the curly braces mark the beginning and end of the JavaScript code that makes up the function.

> **Note:** As with *if/else* statements, functions are more easily read if you indent the JavaScript code between the curly braces. Two spaces (or a tab) at the beginning of each line are common.

Here's a very simple function to print out the current date in a format like "Sun May 12 2008":

```
function printToday() {
  var today = new Date();
  document.write(today.toDateString());
}
```

The function's name is *printToday*. It has just two lines of JavaScript code that retrieve the current date, convert the date to a format we can understand (that's the *toDateString()* part), and then print the results to the page using our old friend the *document.write()* command. Don't worry about how all of the date stuff works—you'll find out about dates later in this book, on page 450.

Programmers usually put their functions at the beginning of a script, which sets up the various functions that the rest of the script will use later. Remember that a function doesn't run when it's first created—it's like telling your assistant how to get to the pizza place without actually sending him there. The JavaScript code is merely stored in the browser's memory, waiting to be run later, when you need it.

But how do you run a function? In programming-speak you *call* the function whenever you want the function to perform its task. Calling the function is just a matter of writing the function's name, followed by a pair of parentheses. For example, to make our *printToday* function run, you'd simply type:

```
printToday();
```

As you can see, making a function run doesn't take a lot of typing—that's the beauty of functions. Once they're created, you don't have to add much code to get results.

> **Note:** When calling a function, don't forget the parentheses following the function. That's the part that makes the function run. For example, *printToday* won't do anything, but *printToday()* executes the function.

Mini-Tutorial

Because functions are such an important concept, here's a series of steps for you to practice creating and using a function on a real web page:

1. **In a text editor, open the file *print_date.html*.**

   You'll start by adding a function in the head of the document.

2. **Locate the code between the <script> tags in the <head> of the page, and type the following code:**

```
function printToday() {
 var today = new Date();
 document.write(today.toDateString());
}
```

The basic function is in place, but it doesn't do anything yet.

3. **Save the file and preview it in a web browser.**

Nothing happens. Well, actually something does happen; you just don't see it. The web browser read the function statements into memory, and was waiting for you to actually call the function, which you'll do next.

4. **Return to your text editor and the *print_date.html* file. Locate the <p> tag that begins with "Today is", and between the two <strong> tags, add the following bolded code:**

```
<p>Today is <strong>
<script>printToday();</script>
</strong></p>
```

Save the page and preview it in a web browser. The current date is printed to the page. If you wanted to print the date at the bottom of the web page as well, all you'd need to do is call the function a second time.

Giving Information to Your Functions

Functions are even more useful when they receive information. Think back to your assistant—the fellow who fetches you slices of pizza. The original "function" described on page 100 was simply directions to the pizza parlor and instructions to buy a slice and return to the office. When you wanted some pizza, you "called" the function by telling your assistant "Get me a slice!" Of course, depending on how you're feeling, you might want a slice of pepperoni, cheese, or olive pizza. To make your instructions more flexible, you can tell your assistant what type of slice you'd like. Each time you request some pizza, you can specify a different type.

JavaScript functions can also accept information, called *parameters*, which the function uses to carry out its actions. For example, if you want to create a function that calculates the total cost of a person's shopping cart, then the function needs to know how much each item costs, and how many of each item was ordered.

To start, when you create the function, place the name of a new variable inside the parentheses—this is the *parameter*. The basic structure looks like this:

```
function functionName(parameter) {
 // the JavaScript you want to run
}
```

The parameter is just a variable, so you supply any valid variable name (see page 46 for tips on naming variables). For example, let's say you want to save a few keystrokes each time you print something to a web page. You create a simple function that lets you replace the web browser's *document.write()* function with a shorter name:

```
function print(message) {
  document.write(message);
}
```

The name of this function is *print* and it has one parameter, named *message*. When this function is called, it receives some information (the message to be printed) and then it uses the *document.write()* function to write the message to the page. Of course, a function doesn't do anything until it's called, so somewhere else on your web page, you can call the function like this:

```
print('Hello world.');
```

When this code is run, the print function is called and some text—the string 'Hello world.'—is sent to the function, which then prints "Hello World." to the page. Technically, the process of sending information to a function is called "passing an argument." In this example, the text—'Hello world.'—is the *argument*.

Even with a really simple function like this, the logic of when and how things work can be a little confusing if you're new to programming. Here's how each step breaks down, as shown in the diagram in Figure 3-7:

1. **The function is read by the JavaScript interpreter and stored in memory. This step just prepares the web browser to run the function later.**

2. **The function is called and information—"Hello world."—is passed to the function.**

3. **The information passed to the function is stored in a new variable named** *message*. **This step is equivalent to** *var message = 'Hello World.';*.

4. **Finally, the function runs, printing the value stored in the variable** *message* **to the web page.**

Figure 3-7:
When working with functions, you usually create the function before you use it. The print() function here is created in the first three lines of code, but the code inside the function doesn't actually run until the last line.

A function isn't limited to a single parameter, either. You can pass any number of arguments to a function. You just need to specify each parameter in the function, like this:

```
function functionName(parameter1, parameter2, parameter3) {
  // the JavaScript you want to run
}
```

And then call the function with the same number of arguments in the same order:

```
functionName(argument1, argument2, argument3);
```

In this example, when *functionName* is called, *argument1* is stored in *parameter1*, *argument2* in *parameter2*, and so on. Expanding on the print function from above, suppose in addition to printing a message to the web page, you want to specify an HTML tag to wrap around the message. This way, you can print the message as a headline or a paragraph. Here's what the new function would look like:

```
function print(message,tag) {
  document.write('<' + tag + '>' + message +'</' + tag + '>');
}
```

The function call would look like this:

```
print('Hello world.', 'p');
```

In this example, you're passing two arguments—'Hello world.' and 'p'—to the function. Those values are stored in the function's two variables—*message* and *tag*. The result is a new paragraph—*<p>Hello world.</p>*—printed to the page.

You're not limited to passing just strings to a function either: You can send any type of JavaScript variable or value to a function. For example, you can send an array, a variable, a number, or a Boolean value as an argument.

Retrieving Information from Functions

Sometimes a function simply does something like write a message to a page, move an object across the screen, or validate the form fields on a page. Other times, you'll want to get something back from a function: after all, the "Get me a slice of pizza" function wouldn't be much good if you didn't end up with some tasty pizza at the end. Likewise, a function that calculates the total cost of items in a shopping cart isn't very useful unless the function lets you know the final total.

Some of the built-in JavaScript functions we've already seen return values. For example, the *prompt()* command (see page 57) pops up a dialog box with a text field, and whatever the user types into the box is returned. As you've seen, you can then store that return value into a variable and do something with it:

```
var answer = prompt('What month were you born?', '');
```

The visitor's response to the prompt dialog box is stored in the variable *answer*; you can then test the value inside that variable using conditional comments or do any of the many other things JavaScript lets you do with variables.

To return a value from your own functions, you use *return* followed by the value you wish to return:

```
function functionName(parameter1, parameter2) {
  // the JavaScript you want to run
  return value;
}
```

For example, say you want to calculate the total cost of a sale including sales tax. You might create a script like this:

```
var TAX = .08; // 8% sales tax
function calculateTotal(quantity, price) {
  var total = quantity * price * (1 + TAX);
```

```
var formattedTotal = total.toFixed(2);
return formattedTotal;
}
```

The first line stores the tax rate into a variable named *TAX* (which lets you easily change the rate simply by updating this line of code). The next three lines define the function. Don't worry too much about what's happening inside the function—you'll learn more about working with numbers on page 445. The important part is the fourth line of the function—the return statement. It returns the value stored in the variable *formattedTotal*.

To make use of the return value, you usually store it inside a variable. So in this example, you could call the function like this:

```
var saleTotal = calculateTotal(2, 16.95);
document.write('Total cost is: $' + saleTotal);
```

In this case, the values 2 and 16.95 are passed to the function. The first number represents the number of items purchased, and the second their individual cost. The function determines the total cost plus tax and returns the total: That result is then stored into a new variable—*saleTotal*—which is then used as part of a *document .write()* command to print the total cost of the sale including tax.

Note: The return keyword should be the last statement in a function, since as soon as a browser's JavaScript interpreter encounters the return statement, it exits the function. Any lines of code following the return statement in the function are never executed.

You don't have to store the return value into a variable, however. You can use the return value directly within another statement like this:

```
document.write('Total: $' + calculateTotal(2, 16.95));
```

In this case, the function is called and its return value is added to the string '*Total: $*', which is then printed to the document. At first, this way of using a function may be hard to read, so you might want to take the extra step of just storing the function's results into a variable and then using that variable in your script.

Note: A function can only return one value. If you want to return multiple items, store the results in an array, and return the array.

Keeping Variables from Colliding

One great advantage of functions is that they can cut down the amount of programming you have to do. You'll probably find yourself using a really useful function time and time again on different projects. For example, a function that helps calculate shipping and sales tax could come in handy on every order form you create, so you might copy and paste that function into other scripts on your site or on other projects.

One potential problem arises when you just plop a function down into an already-created script. What happens if the script uses the same variable names as the function? Will the function overwrite the variable from the script, or vice versa? For example:

```
var message = 'Outside the function';
function warning(message) {
    alert(message);
}
warning('Inside the function'); // 'Inside the function'
alert(message); // 'Outside the function'
```

Notice that the variable *message* appears both outside the function (the first line of the script) and as a parameter in the function. A parameter is really just a variable that's filled with data when the function's called. In this case, the function call—*warning('Inside the function');*—passes a string to the function and the function stores that string in the variable *message*. It looks like there are now two versions of the variable *message*. So what happens to the value in the original *message* variable that's created in the first line of the script?

You might think that the original value stored in *message* is overwritten with a new value, the string 'Outside the function'; it's not. When you run this script, you'll see two alert dialog boxes: The first will say "Inside the function" and the second "Outside the function." There are actually two variables named *message*, but they exist in separate places (see Figure 3-8).

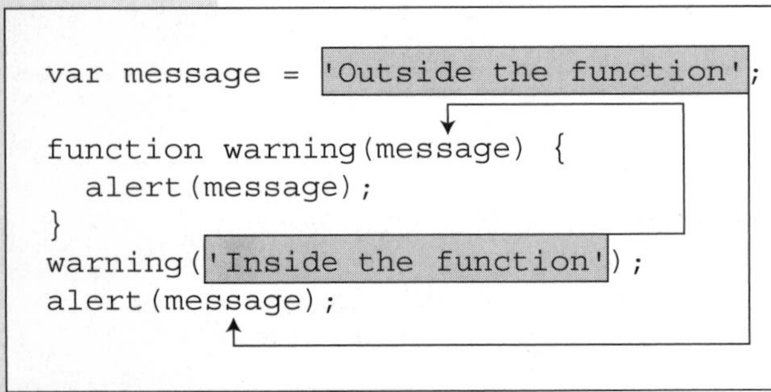

```
var message = 'Outside the function';

function warning(message) {
   alert(message);
}
warning('Inside the function');
alert(message);
```

Figure 3-8:
A function parameter is only visible inside the function, so the first line of this function—function warning(message)—creates a new variable named message that can only be accessed inside the function. Once the function is done, that variable disappears.

The JavaScript interpreter treats variables inside of a function differently than variables declared and created outside of a function. In programming-speak, each function has its own *scope*. A function's scope is like a wall that surrounds the function—variables inside the wall aren't visible to the rest of the script outside the wall. Scope is a pretty confusing concept when you first learn about it, but it's very useful. Because a function has its own scope, you don't have to be afraid that the names you use for parameters in your function will overwrite or conflict with variables used in another part of the script.

So far, the only situation we've discussed is the use of variables as parameters. But what about a variable that's created inside the function, but not as a parameter, like this:

```
var message = 'Outside the function';
function warning() {
 var message ='Inside the function';
 alert( message );
}
warning(); // 'Inside the function'
alert( message ); //'Outside the function'
```

Here, the code creates a *message* variable twice—in the first line of the script, and again in the first line inside the function. This situation is the same as with parameters—by typing *var message* inside the function, you've created a new variable inside the function's scope. This type of variable is called a *local variable*, since it's only visible within the walls of the function—the main script and other functions can't see or access this variable.

However, variables created in the main part of a script (outside a function) exist in *global scope*. All functions in a script can access variables that are created in its main body. For example, in the code below, the variable message is created on the first line of the script—it's a *global variable*, and it can be accessed by the function.

```
var message = 'Global variable';
function warning() {
 alert( message );
}
warning(); // 'Global variable'
```

This function doesn't have any parameters and doesn't define a *message* variable, so when the *alert(message)* part is run, the function looks for a global variable named *message*. In this case, that variable exists, so an alert dialog with the text "Global variable" appears.

There's one potential gotcha with local and global variables—a variable only exists within the function's scope if it's a parameter, or if the variable is created inside the function with the *var* keyword. Figure 3-9 demonstrates this situation. The top chunk of code demonstrates how both a global variable named *message* and a function's local variable named *message* can exist side-by-side. The key is the first line inside the function—*var message =‘Inside the function’;*. By using *var*, you create a local variable.

Compare that to the code in the bottom half of Figure 3-9. In this case, the function doesn't use the *var* keyword. Instead, the line of code *message=‘Inside the function’;* doesn't create a new local variable; it simply stores a new value inside the global variable *message*. The result? The function clobbers the global variable, replacing its initial value.

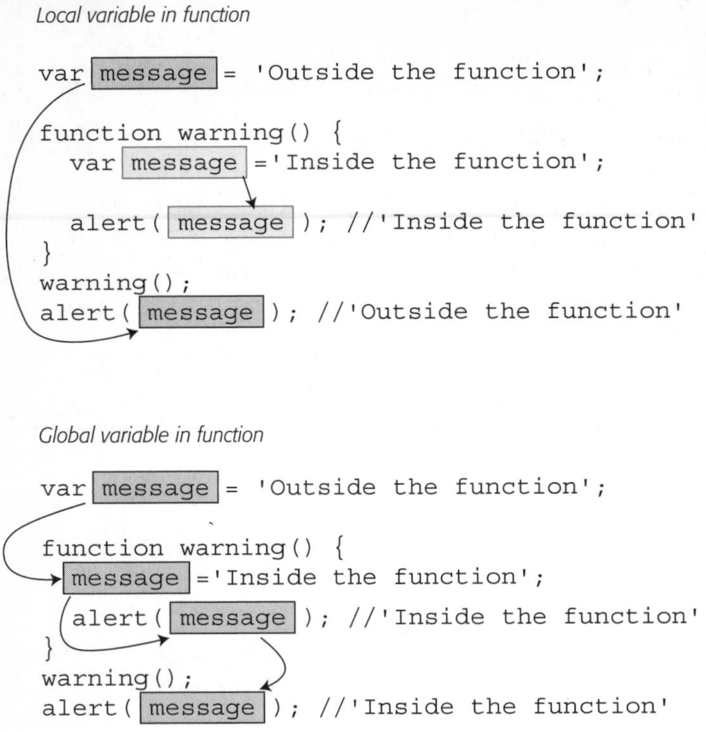

Local variable in function

```
var message = 'Outside the function';

function warning() {
  var message ='Inside the function';

  alert( message ); //'Inside the function'
}
warning();
alert( message ); //'Outside the function'
```

Figure 3-9:
There's a subtle yet crucial difference when assigning values to variables within a function. If you want the variable to only be accessible to the code inside the function, make sure to use the var keyword to create the variable inside the function (top). If you don't use var, you're just storing a new value inside the global variable (bottom).

Global variable in function

```
var message = 'Outside the function';

function warning() {
  message ='Inside the function';

  alert( message ); //'Inside the function'
}
warning();
alert( message ); //'Inside the function'
```

The notion of variable scope is pretty confusing, so the preceding discussion may not make a lot of sense for you right now. But just keep one thing in mind: If the variables you create in your scripts don't seem to be holding the values you expect, you might be running into a scope problem. If that happens, come back and reread this section.

Tutorial: A Simple Quiz

Now it's time to bring together the lessons from this chapter and create a complete program. In this tutorial, you'll create a simple quiz system for asking questions and evaluating the quiz-taker's performance. First, this section will look at a couple of ways you could solve this problem, and discuss efficient techniques for programming.

As always, the first step is to figure out what exactly the program should do. There are a few things you want the program to accomplish:

- **Ask questions.** If you're going to quiz people, you need a way to ask them questions. At this point, you know one simple way to get feedback on a web page:

the *prompt()* command. In addition, you'll need a list of questions; since arrays are good for storing lists of information, you'll use an array to store your quiz questions.

- **Let quiz-taker know if she's right or wrong**. First, you need to determine if the quiz-taker gave the right answer: A conditional statement can take care of that. Then, to let the quiz taker know if she's right or wrong, you can use the *alert()*command.

- **Print the results of the quiz**. You need a way to track how well the quiz-taker's doing—a variable that keeps track of the number of correct responses will work. Then, to announce the final results of the quiz, you can either use the *alert()* command or the *document.write()* method.

There are many ways to solve this problem. Some beginning programmers might take a blunt-force approach and repeat the same code to ask each question. For example, the JavaScript to ask the first two questions in the quiz might look like this:

```
var answer1=prompt('How many moons does Earth have?','');
if (answer1 == 1 ) {
 alert('Correct!');
} else {
 alert('Sorry. The correct answer is 1');
}
var answer2=prompt('How many moons does Saturn have?','');
if (answer2 == 31) {
 alert('Correct!');
} else {
 alert('Sorry. The correct answer is 31');
}
```

This kind of approach seems logical, since the goal of the program is to ask one question after another. However, it's not an efficient way to program. Whenever you see the same steps written multiple times in a program, it's time to consider using a loop or a function instead. We'll create a program that does both: uses a loop to go through each question in the quiz, and a function that performs the question asking tasks:

1. **In a text editor, open the file *quiz.html*.**

   You'll start by setting up a few variables that can track the number of correct answers and the questions for the quiz.

2. **Locate the code between the <script> tags in the <head> of the page, and type the following code:**

   ```
   var score = 0;
   ```

   This variable stores the number of answers the quiz-taker gets right. At the beginning of the quiz, before any questions have been answered, you set the variable to 0. Next, you'll create a list of questions and their answers.

3. **Hit Return to add a new line and type *var questions = [*.**

   You'll be storing all of the questions inside an array, which is really just a variable that can hold multiple items. The code you just typed is the first part of an array statement. You'll be typing the array over multiple lines as described on page 61.

4. **Press Return twice to add two new lines and type *];*. Your code should now look like this:**

```
var score = 0;
var questions = [

];
```

Since the quiz is made up of a bunch of questions, it makes sense to store each question as one item in an array. Then, when you want to ask the quiz questions, you simply go through each item in the list and ask the question. However, every question also has an answer, so you need a way to keep track of the answers as well.

One solution is to create another array—*answers[]*, for example—that holds all of the answers. To ask the first question, look for the first item in the questions array, and to see if the answer is correct, look in the first item of the answers array. However, this has the potential drawback that the two lists might get out of sync: For example, you add a question in the middle of the questions array, but mistakenly put the answer at the beginning of the answers array. At that point, the first item in the questions array no longer matches the first item in the answers array.

A better alternative is to use a *nested array* or (if you really want to sound scary and out-of-this-world) a *multidimensional array*. All this really means is that you create an array that includes the question *and* the answer, and you store that array as one item in the questions array. In other words, you create a list where each item in the list is another list.

5. **Click in the empty line between the *[* and *];* and add the code in bold below:**

```
var questions = [
 ['How many moons does Earth have?', 1],
];
```

The code *['How many moons does Earth have?', 1]* is an array of two items. The first item is a question, and the second item is the answer. This array is the first item in the array *questions*. You don't give this new array a name, since it's nested inside another array. The comma at the end of the line marks the end of the first item in the questions array and indicates that another array item will follow.

6. **Hit Return to create a new, empty line and add the following two bolded lines to the script:**

```
var questions = [
 ['How many moons does Earth have?', 1],
 ['How many moons does Saturn have?',31],
 ['How many moons does Venus have?', 0]
];
```

These are two more questions for the quiz. Note that after the last item in an array, you *don't* type a comma. Setting up all of your questions in a single array provides for a lot of flexibility. If you want to add another question to the list, just add another nested array containing a new question and answer.

Now that the basic variables for the quiz are set up, it's time to figure out how to ask each question. The questions are stored in an array, and you want to ask each question in the list. As you'll recall from page 95, a loop is a perfect way to go through each item in an array.

7. **Click after the *];* (the end of the *answers* array) and hit Return to create a new, empty line. Then add the following code:**

```
for (var i=0; i<questions.length; i++) {
```

This line is the first part of a *for* loop (page 97). It does three things: First, it creates a new variable named *i* and stores the number 0 in it. This variable is the counter that keeps track of the number of times through the loop. The second part—*i<questions.length*—is a condition, as in an *if/else* statement. It tests to see if the value in *i* is less than the number of items in the *questions* array—if that's true, the loop runs again. As soon as *i* is equal to or greater than the total number of items in the array, the loop is over. Finally, *i++* changes the value of *i* each time through the loop—it adds 1 to the value of *i*.

Now it's time for the core of the loop—the actual JavaScript that's performed each time through the loop.

8. **Hit Return to create a new, empty line and add the following line of code:**

```
askQuestion(questions[i]);
```

Instead of putting all of the programming code for asking the question in the loop, you'll merely run a function that asks the questions. The function (which you'll create in a moment) is named *askQuestion()*. Each time through the loop, you'll send one item from the questions array to the function—that's the *questions[i]* part. Remember that you access an item in an array using an index value, so *questions[0]* is the first item in the array, *questions[1]* is the second item, and so on.

By creating a function that asks the questions, you make a more flexible program. You can move and reuse the function to another program if you want. Finally, you'll finish the loop code.

9. **Hit Return to create a new, empty line and type } to indicate the end of the loop. The finished loop code should look like this:**

```
for (var i=0; i<questions.length; i++) {
 askQuestion(questions[i]);
}
```

Yes, that's all there is to it—just a simple loop that calls a function with every question in the quiz. Now, you'll create the heart of the quiz, the *askQuestion()* function.

10. **Create an empty line before the for loop you just added.**

In other words, you'll add the function between the two statements that define the basic variables at the beginning of the script and the loop you just added. It's OK to define functions anywhere in your script, but most programmers place functions near the beginning of the program. In many scripts, global variables—like *score* and *questions* in this script—are defined first, so that you can see and change those easily; functions appear next, since they usually form the core of most scripts; and finally, the step-by-step actions (like the loop) appear last.

11. **Add the following code:**

```
function askQuestion(question) {


}
```

This code indicates the body of the function—it's always a good idea to type both the beginning and ending curly braces of a function and then add the script within them. That way, you won't accidentally forget to add the closing curly brace.

This function receives a single argument and stores it in a variable named *question*. Note that this isn't the same as the *questions[]* array you created in step 6. In this case, the *question* variable will actually be filled by one item from the *questions[]* array. As you saw in step 8, one item from that array is actually another array containing two items, the question and the answer.

12. **Add the line in bold below:**

```
function askQuestion(question) {
 var answer = prompt(question[0],'');
}
```

This should look familiar—your old friend the *prompt()* command. The only part that might feel new is *question[0]*. That's how you access the first element in the array *question*. In this example, the function receives one array, which includes a question and answer. For example, the first array will be *['How many moons does Earth have?', 1]*. So *question[0]* accesses the first item—'How many moons does Earth have'—which is passed to the *prompt()* command as the question that will appear in the prompt dialog box.

Your program stores whatever the quiz-taker types into the prompt dialog box in the variable *answer*. Next, you'll compare the quiz-taker's response with the question's actual answer.

13. **Complete the function by adding the code in bold below:**

```
function askQuestion(question) {
 var answer = prompt(question[0],'');
    if (answer == question[1]) {
        alert('Correct!');
        score++;
    } else {
        alert('Sorry. The correct answer is ' + question[1]);
    }
}
```

This code is just a basic *if/else* statement. The condition—*answer == question[1]*—checks to see if what the user entered (*answer*) is the same as the answer, which is stored as the second item in the array (*question[1]*). If they match, then the quiz-taker was right: An alert appears to let her know she got it right, and her score is increased by one (*score++*). Of course, if she doesn't answer correctly, an alert appears displaying the correct answer.

At this point, the quiz is fully functional. If you save the file and load it into a web browser, you'll be able to take the quiz. However, you haven't yet provided the results to the quiz-taker so she can see how many she got correct. You'll add a script in the <body> of the web page to print out the results.

14. **Locate the second pair of <script> tags near the bottom of the web page and type:**

```
var message = 'You got ' + score;
```

Here, you create a new variable and store the string 'You got ' plus the quiz-taker's score. So if she got all three right, the variable *message* would be 'You got 3'. To make the script easier to read, you'll build up a longer message over several lines.

15. **Press Return and type:**

```
message += ' out of ' + questions.length;
```

This adds ' out of ' and the total number of questions to the message string, so at this point, the message will be something like "You got 3 out of 3". Now to finish up the message and print it to the screen.

16. **Add the bolded lines of code to your script:**

```
var message = 'You got ' + score;
message += ' out of ' + questions.length;
message += ' questions correct.';
document.write('<p>' + message + '</p>');
```

Save the page, and open it in a web browser. Take the quiz and see how well you do (see Figure 3-10). If the script doesn't work, remember to try some of the troubleshooting techniques mentioned on page 34. You can also compare your script with a completed, functional version in the file *complete_quiz.html*.

Try adding additional questions to the *questions[]* array at the beginning of the script to make the quiz even longer.

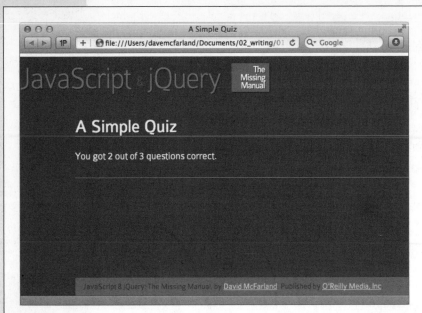

Figure 3-10:
The results of your simple quiz program. After you learn more about how to manipulate a web page on page 138, respond to events on page 157, and work with web forms on page 257, try to rewrite this quiz program so the questions appear directly within the web page, and the score is dynamically updated after each answer. In other words, you'll soon learn how to ditch that clunky prompt() command.

Now that you've grasped some of the not-so-exciting, brain-stretching details of JavaScript, it's time to turn your attention to the real fun. In the next section, you'll learn about jQuery, what it is, how to use it, and, most importantly, how to have a lot of fun and get a lot done with JavaScript programming.

Part Two: Getting Started with jQuery

Chapter 4: Introducing jQuery

Chapter 5: Action/Reaction: Making Pages Come Alive with Events

Chapter 6: Animations and Effects

2

Introducing jQuery

The first chapters of this book covered many of the fundamentals of the JavaScript programming language—the keywords, concepts, and syntax of JavaScript. Many of these concepts were fairly straightforward ("a variable is like a box in which you put a value"), but some topics may have had you scratching your head or reaching for a bottle of aspirin (like the "for" loops discussed on page 97). The truth is, for most people, JavaScript programming is difficult. In fact, a 1,000-page book on JavaScript programming won't cover everything there is to know about JavaScript and how it works in the many different web browsers out in the wild.

Programming is hard: That's why this books covers both JavaScript and jQuery. As you'll see in the first section of this chapter, jQuery is a JavaScript library that lets you jump-start your programming by handling many of the messy details of JavaScript programming for you. jQuery—whose motto is "write less, do more"—makes programming fun, fast, and rewarding. With jQuery, you can achieve in a single line of code what could take 100 lines of pure JavaScript programming. After you go through this and the following chapter, you'll be able to achieve more with your web pages than if you studied that 1,000-page book on JavaScript alone.

About JavaScript Libraries

Many JavaScript programs have to deal with the same set of web page tasks again and again: selecting an element, adding new content, hiding and showing content, modifying a tag's attributes, determining the value of form fields, and making programs react to different user interactions. The details of these basic actions can be quite complicated—especially if you want the program to work in all major browsers.

Fortunately, JavaScript *libraries* offer a way to leap-frog past many time-consuming programming details.

A JavaScript library is a collection of JavaScript code that provides simple solutions to many of the mundane, day-to-day details of JavaScript. Think of it as a collection of prewritten JavaScript functions that you add to your web page. These functions make it easy to complete common tasks. In many cases, you can replace many lines of your own JavaScript programming (and the hours required to test them) with a single function from a JavaScript library. There are lots of JavaScript libraries out there, and many of them help create major websites like Yahoo, Amazon, CNN, Apple, and Twitter.

This book uses the popular jQuery library (*www.jquery.com*). There are other JavaScript libraries (see the box on the opposite page), but jQuery has many advantages:

- **Relatively small file size**. A compressed version of the library is only around 90 k. (If your web server uses "gzip" compression, you can bring the file size down to just 30 k!)

- **Friendly to web designers**. jQuery doesn't assume you're a computer scientist. It takes advantage of CSS knowledge that most web designers already have.

- **It's tried and true**. jQuery is used on millions of sites, including many popular, highly-trafficked websites like Digg, Dell, the Onion, and NBC. Even Google uses it in some places, and it's built into the number one blogging software, WordPress. The fact that jQuery is so popular is a testament to how good it is.

- **It's free**. Hey, you can't beat that!

- **Large developer community**. As you read this, scores of people are working on the jQuery project—writing code, fixing bugs, adding new features, and updating the website with documentation and tutorials. A JavaScript library created by a single programmer (or one supplied by a single author) can easily disappear if the programmer (or author) grows tired of the project. jQuery, on the other hand, should be around for a long time, supported by the efforts of programmers around the world. Even big companies like Microsoft and Adobe are pitching in and supplying engineers and programming code. It's like having a bunch of JavaScript programmers working for you for free.

- **Plug-ins, plug-ins, plug-ins**. jQuery lets other programmers create *plug-ins*— add-on JavaScript programs that work in conjunction with jQuery to make certain tasks, effects, or features incredibly easy to add to a web page. In this book, you'll learn about plug-ins that make validating forms, adding drop-down navigation menus, and building interactive slideshows a half-hour's worth of work, instead of a two-week project. There are literally thousands of other plug-ins available for jQuery.

You've actually used jQuery in this book already. In the tutorial for Chapter 1 (page 33), you added just a few lines of JavaScript code to create a page fade-in effect.

Other Libraries

jQuery isn't the only JavaScript library in town. There are many, many others. Some are designed to perform specific tasks, and others are all-purpose libraries aimed at solving every JavaScript task under the sun. Here are a few of the most popular:

- **Yahoo User Interface Library** (*http://developer.yahoo.com/yui/*) is a project of Yahoo, and indeed the company uses it throughout its site. Yahoo programmers are constantly adding to and improving the library, and they provide very good documentation on the YUI site.

- **Dojo Toolkit** (*http://dojotoolkit.org/*) is another library that has been around a long time. It's a very

powerful and very large collection of JavaScript files that tackle nearly every JavaScript task around.

- **Mootools** (*http://mootools.net/*) is another popular library geared toward slick animation and visual effects. It has good documentation and a great-looking website.

- **Prototype** (*www.prototypejs.org/*) was one of the first JavaScript libraries available. It's often used in combination with a visual effects library named *scriptaculous* (*http://script.aculo.us/*), which adds animation and other user interface goodies.

Getting jQuery

jQuery is simply a bunch of JavaScript programming in an external JavaScript file. Like any external JavaScript file (page 27), you need to link it to your web page. However, because jQuery is so popular, you have a few choices when it comes to adding it to a web page: You can either use a version hosted at Google, Microsoft, or jQuery.com, or you can download the jQuery file to your own computer and add it to your website.

The first method uses a *CDN* or content distribution network—that is, another website hosts the jQuery file and sends it out to anyone who requests it. There are a couple of benefits to this approach: First, you can save your web server a few milliseconds by letting Google, Microsoft, or jQuery handle distributing the file to your site's visitors. In addition, CDNs have the added benefit of having servers located around the globe. So if someone in Singapore, for example, visits your site, he'll receive the jQuery file from a server that's probably a lot closer to him than your web server, which means he'll get the file faster and your site will appear to run more quickly. Lastly, and most importantly, because other designers use these CDNs as well, there's a pretty good chance that someone visiting your site already has the jQuery file saved in their browser's cache. Since he's already downloaded the jQuery file from Google while visiting another site, he doesn't need to download it again when visiting your site, resulting in a substantial speed increase.

There are a couple of downsides to using a CDN: First, visitors need to be connected to the Internet for this method to work. That becomes an issue if you need to make sure your site works offline, for example, in a kiosk at a museum or during a programming demonstration in a classroom. In that case, you need to download the jQuery file from jQuery.com (you'll learn how below) and add it to your website. Adding your own jQuery file also ensures that your website will continue to work if the CDN servers go down. (Of course, if Google's servers ever go down, then there may be bigger problems in the world than whether your website works.)

Linking to the jQuery file on a CDN server

Microsoft, jQuery, and Google all let you include the jQuery file on one of your web pages using their servers. For example, to link to version 1.6.3 of jQuery using Microsoft's CDN, you would add this line of code in the <head> of your web page (just before the closing </head> tag), like this:

```
<script src="http://ajax.aspnetcdn.com/ajax/jQuery/jquery-1.6.3.min.js">
</script>
```

Using the jQuery CDN, you'd use this code:

```
<script src="http://code.jquery.com/jquery-1.6.3.min.js"></script>
```

And the code using Google's CDN looks like this:

```
<script src="http://ajax.googleapis.com/ajax/libs/jquery/1.6.3/jquery.min.
js"></script>
```

You only need to use one of these lines on your page, based on the CDN you prefer to use. The Google CDN seems to be the most popular, so if you're unsure of which to use, use the Google servers.

Downloading your own jQuery file

You can easily download the jQuery file and add it to your site along with all your other web pages and files. The tutorial files you downloaded for this book at *www .sawmac.com/js2e/* include the jQuery library file, but since the jQuery team updates the library on a regular basis, you can find the latest version at *http://docs.jquery .com/Downloading_jQuery*, listed under the Current Release headline.

To download the latest version of jQuery:

1. Visit *http://docs.jquery.com/Downloading_jQuery*.

   This page has information about the code, a list of the CDNs mentioned above, and previous versions of jQuery. You're looking for the "Current Release."

2. **Click the "Current Release" link near the top of the page, or scroll down until you see the Current Release headline.**

The jQuery file comes in two versions on the download site—minified and uncompressed. The uncompressed file is very large (over 200 k), and is only provided so you can learn more about jQuery by looking at its code. The code includes lots of comments (page 72) that help make clear what the different parts of the file do. (But in order to understand the comments, you need to know *a lot* about JavaScript.)

You should use the minified version for your websites. A minified file is much smaller than a regular JavaScript file: All JavaScript comments and unnecessary spaces are removed (tabs, linebreaks, and so on), making the file hard-to-read, but faster to download.

Note: You can usually identify a minified JavaScript file by the appearance of .min in the file name; for example, *jquery-1.6.3.min.js* indicates that this file contains the minified version of version 1.6.3 of jQuery.

---

3. **Right-click (Control-click on Mac) the Minified link and from the contextual menu that appears, choose Save Link As.**

If you just click the link, you won't download the file: Instead, the web browser displays all the code in a browser window; so you need to use this "Save as" method.

4. **Navigate to the folder on your computer where you keep your website and save the file.**

You can save the jQuery file anywhere you want on your site, but many web designers keep their external JavaScript files in a folder that's dedicated to the purpose. Usually the folder has a name like *scripts, libs, js,* or *_js.*

FREQUENTLY ASKED QUESTION

jQuery Versions

I see that this book uses version 1.6.3 of jQuery, but the current version on the jQuery site is 1.X. Is this a problem?

jQuery is always evolving. New bugs are often discovered, and the jQuery team works diligently to fix them. In addition, as new web browsers come out with new capabilities and better support for current standards, the jQuery team updates jQuery to work most efficiently with those browsers. Finally, new features are sometimes added to jQuery to make it more useful for web programmers. For these reasons, it's likely that you can find a newer version of jQuery than the one that's used in this book. If there is a newer version, then by all means use it.

jQuery has matured over the years and its core functionality changes very little. While the jQuery programmers are often tinkering under the hood to make jQuery faster, work better across browsers, and fix bugs, the way you use jQuery doesn't usually change that much. In other words, while programmers might alter a jQuery function to perform better, the way you *use* that function—the function name, the arguments you give it, and the values it returns—don't often change. This means that what you learn in this book will most probably work with a newer version of jQuery, but only faster and better.

You can often tell how much different one version of jQuery is from another by the numbering scheme. The first number points to a very significant new version. Currently jQuery is in version 1, so we've seen version 1, 1.2, 1.3, 1.4, and so on. Version 2 (which probably won't arrive for quite some time) will undoubtedly offer some significant new capabilities. Then there are the dot releases like the .6 in jQuery 1.6. Each of those numbers usually offers new functions, rewriting of older functions to work better, and so on. Finally, the last number, like the final 3 in jQuery 1.6.3, usually refers to some sort of bug fix for the 1.6 branch of jQuery. So if you're using version 1.6.3 of jQuery and version 1.6.8 comes out, it's usually a good idea to upgrade, as this will probably include fixes from problems discovered in 1.6.3.

To find out what's changed in a new version, just visit the "Current release" section of the Downloads page at *http:// docs.jquery.com/Downloading_jQuery#Current_Release*. There you'll find a link to "Release notes." Click that link to visit a page listing changes made to that version. After reading the list of changes, you can decide for yourself if it seems worthwhile to upgrade (for example, if the changes relate to features you don't use on your site, you can probably skip this upgrade; however, if the changes are bug fixes related to features you do use, it's a good idea to upgrade. (If you use jQuery plug-ins on your site, you'll need to be a bit more cautious about upgrading to the latest version of jQuery, unless you're sure the plug-in works with the new version of jQuery.)

Adding jQuery to a Page

If you're using one of the CDN versions of jQuery (page 120), you can point to it using one of the code snippets listed on page 120. For example, to use the Google CDN version of jQuery, you'd add <script> tags to the head of the page like this:

```
<script src="http://ajax.googleapis.com/ajax/libs/jquery/1.6.3/jquery.min.
js"></script>
```

Tip: When using the Google CDN, you can leave off parts of the version number. If you use 1.6 instead of 1.6.1 in the link (*<script src="http://ajax.googleapis.com/ajax/libs/jquery/1.6/jquery.min.js"></script>*), then Google loads the latest version in the 1.6 family—1.6.3, for example. If jQuery is updated to 1.6.9, then Google loads that version. This technique is smart since (as mentioned in the box on page 122) the minor version changes 1.6.1 to 1.6.9 are often bug fixes that will improve the functioning of your site.

Once you've downloaded jQuery to your computer, you must attach it to the web page you wish to use it on. The jQuery file is simply an external .js file, so you attach it just like any external JavaScript file, as described on page 27. For example, say you've stored the *jquery.js* file in a folder named *js* in your site's root folder. To attach the file to your home page, you'd add the following script tag to the head of the page:

```
<script src="js/jquery-1.6.3.min.js"></script>
```

Once you've attached the jQuery file, you're ready to add your own scripts that take advantage of jQuery's advanced functions. The next step is to add a second set of <script> tags with a little bit of jQuery programming in it:

```
<script src="js/jquery-1.6.3.min.js"></script>
<script>
$(document).ready(function() {
  // your programming goes here
});
</script>
```

The second set of <script> tags holds any programming you want to add to the particular web page; however, you're probably wondering what that *$(document) .ready()* business is all about. The *$(document).ready()* function is a built-in jQuery function that waits until the HTML for a page loads before it runs your script.

Why would you want to do that? Because a lot of JavaScript programming is about manipulating the contents of a web page: for example, animating a div, fading an image into view, making a menu drop down when a visitor moves over a link, and so on. To do something fun and interactive with a page element, JavaScript needs to select it. However, JavaScript can't select an HTML tag until the web browser downloads it. Since a web browser immediately runs any JavaScript it encounters, the rest of the page doesn't download immediately. (You can see this effect in the quiz tutorial from the last chapter. When you load that quiz, the page is blank. Only after you finish the quiz does the content appear—that's because the JavaScript for the quiz runs first, before the web browser displays the HTML tags.)

In other words, in order to do cool stuff to the HTML on your page, you need to wait until the page loads. That's what the *$(document).ready()* function does: It simply waits until the HTML is finished loading and then it runs the JavaScript code. If all that seems super confusing, just keep in mind that you should always include a *.ready()* function and that you need to put your code inside it between *$(document) .ready(function() {* and the final *});*.

In addition, here are a few things to keep in mind:

- The link to the jQuery file must precede any programming that relies on jQuery. In other words, don't put any other script tags before the <script> tag that loads jQuery.

- Put your JavaScript programming *after* any CSS stylesheets (both linked, external stylesheets and internal stylesheets). Because jQuery programming often references styles from a stylesheet, you should put your JavaScript programming after the web browser has loaded any styles. A good rule of thumb is to put your JavaScript programming (all your <script> tags) after any other content inside the <head> tag, but before the closing </head> tag.

- Add a JavaScript comment—for example, *//end ready*—after the *});* that marks the end of the *ready()* function. For example:

```
$(document).ready(function() {
  // your programming goes here
}); // end ready
```

Putting a comment at the end of the function makes it easy to identify the end of the program. As you'll see later, jQuery often requires lots of little collections of this brace, parenthesis, and semicolon trio. By adding a comment after them, it'll be much easier to identify which group of punctuation belongs to which part of your program.

Tip: jQuery provides a shortcut method for writing *$(document).ready(function() { }*:

```
$(function() {
  // your programming goes here
}); // end ready
```

Modifying Web Pages: An Overview

JavaScript gives you the power to change a web page before your very eyes. Using JavaScript, you can add pictures and text, remove content, or change the appearance of an element on a page instantly. In fact, dynamically changing a web page is the hallmark of the newest breed of JavaScript-powered websites. For example, Google Maps (*http://maps.google.com/*) provides access to a map of the world; when you zoom into the map or scroll across it, the page gets updated without the need to load a new web page. Similarly, when you mouse over a movie title at Netflix (*www.netflix.com*), an information bubble appears on top of the page providing more detail about the movie (see Figure 4-1). In both of these examples, JavaScript is changing the HTML that the web browser originally downloaded.

In this chapter, you'll learn how to alter a web page using JavaScript. You'll add new content, HTML tags and HTML attributes, and also alter content and tags that are already on the page. In other words, you'll use JavaScript to generate new HTML and change the HTML that's already on the page.

Figure 4-1:
JavaScript can make web pages simpler to scan and read by only showing content when it's needed. At Netflix.com, movie descriptions are hidden from view, but revealed when the mouse travels over the movie title or thumbnail image.

It may seem hard to believe, but, if you know how to create web pages with HTML and CSS, you already know a lot of what you need to effectively use JavaScript to create interactive websites. For example, the popular Datepicker plug-in for the jQuery UI project makes it easy for visitors to select a date on a form (for instance, as part of a flight or event scheduler). When a visitor clicks into a specially marked text field, a calendar pops up (see Figure 4-2). While the effect is really cool, and the calendar makes it especially easy to pick a date, JavaScript provides only the interactivity—the actual calendar is created with the same old HTML and CSS that you're familiar with.

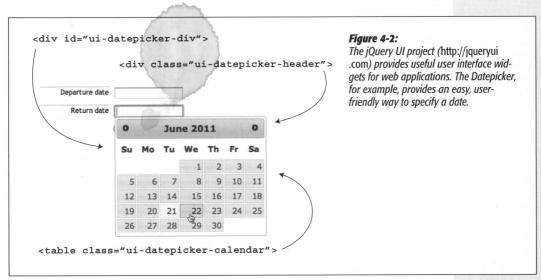

Figure 4-2:
The jQuery UI project (http://jqueryui .com) provides useful user interface widgets for web applications. The Datepicker, for example, provides an easy, user-friendly way to specify a date.

If you look under the hood of the calendar, you'll find a series of HTML tags such as divs, a table, and <td> tags, with special classes and IDs (ui-datepicker-month, ui-datepicker-div, and so on) applied to them. A style sheet with class and ID styles adds color, typography, and formatting. In other words, you could create this same calendar yourself with HTML and CSS. JavaScript just makes the presentation interactive by making the calendar appear when a visitor clicks on a form field and disappear when the visitor selects a date.

So one way of thinking about modern JavaScript programming—especially as it applies to user interface design—is as a way to automate the creation of HTML and the application of CSS. In the Netflix example in Figure 4-1, JavaScript makes the pop-up information bubble appear when a visitor mouses over a movie, but the really fun part (the design of that info bubble) is simply a good use of HTML and CSS...stuff you already know how to do!

So a lot of what you'll use JavaScript for is manipulating a web page by adding new content, changing the HTML of a page, or applying CSS to an element. Whenever you change the content, HTML, or CSS on a page—whether you're adding a navigation bar complete with pop-up menus, creating a JavaScript-driven slide show, or simply making a page fade into view (as you did in the tutorial in Chapter 1)—you'll perform two main steps.

1. **Select an element on a page.**

   An element is any existing tag, and before you can do anything with that element, you need to *select* it using JavaScript (which you'll learn how to do in this chapter). For example, to make a page fade into view, you first must select the page's content (the <body> tag); to make a pop-up menu appear when you mouse over a button, you need to select that button. Even if you simply want to use JavaScript to add text to the bottom of a web page, you need to select a tag to insert the text inside, before, or after that tag.

2. **Do something with the element.**

   OK, "do something" isn't a very specific instruction. That's because there's nearly an endless number of things you can *do* with an element to alter the way your web page looks or acts. In fact, most of this book is devoted to teaching you different things to do to page elements. Here are a few examples:

   - **Change a property of the element**. When animating a <div> across a page, for example, you change that element's position on the page.

   - **Add new content**. If, while filling out a web form, a visitor incorrectly fills out a field, it's common to make an error message appear—"Please supply an email address," for example. In this case, you're adding content somewhere in relation to that form field.

- **Remove the element**. In the Netflix example pictured in Figure 4-1, the pop-up bubble disappears when you mouse off the movie title. In this case, JavaScript removes that pop-up bubble from the page.

- **Extract information from the element**. Other times, you'll want to know something about the tag you've selected. For example, to validate a text field, you need to select that text field, then find out what text was typed into that field—in other words, you need to get the value of that field.

- **Add/remove a class attribute**. Sometimes you'll want an element on a page to change appearance: the text in a paragraph to turn blue, or the background color of a text field to turn red to indicate an error. While JavaScript can make these visual changes, often the easiest way is to simply apply a class and let a web browser make those visual changes based on a CSS style from a style sheet. To change the text of a paragraph to blue, for example, you can simply create a class style with blue text color, and use JavaScript to apply the class to the paragraph dynamically.

Many times, you'll do several of the things listed above at the same time. For example, say you want to make sure a visitor doesn't forget to type her email address into a form field. If she tries to submit the form without her email address, you can notify her. This task might involve first finding out if she's typed anything into that text field (extracting information from the element), printing an error message ("adding new content") if she doesn't, and highlighting that form field (by adding a class to the text field).

Selecting a page element is the first step. To understand how to identify and modify a part of a page using JavaScript, you first need to get to know the Document Object Model.

Understanding the Document Object Model

When a web browser loads an HTML file, it displays the contents of that file on the screen (appropriately styled with CSS, of course). But that's not all the web browser does with the tags, attributes, and contents of the file: It also creates and memorizes a "model" of that page's HTML. In other words, the web browser remembers the HTML tags, their attributes, and the order in which they appear in the file—this representation of the page is called the *Document Object Model*, or DOM for short.

The DOM provides the information needed for JavaScript to communicate with the elements on the web page. The DOM also provides the tools necessary to navigate through, change, and add to the HTML on the page. The DOM itself isn't actually JavaScript—it's a standard from the World Wide Web Consortium (W3C) that most browser manufacturers have adopted and added to their browsers. The DOM lets JavaScript communicate with and change a page's HTML.

To see how the DOM works, take look at this very simple web page:

```
<!DOCTYPE HTML>
<html>
<head>
<meta charset="UTF-8">
<title>A web page</title>
</head>
<body class="home">
<h1 id="header">A headline</h1>
<p>Some <strong>important</strong> text</p>
</body>
</html>
```

On this and all other websites, some tags wrap around other tags—like the <html> tag, which surrounds all other tags, or the <body> tag, which wraps around the tags and contents that appear in the browser window. You can represent the relationship between tags with a kind of family tree (see Figure 4-3). The <html> tag is the "root" of the tree—like the great-great-great granddaddy of all of the other tags on the page—while other tags represent different "branches" of the family tree; for example, the <head> and <body> tags, which each contain their own set of tags.

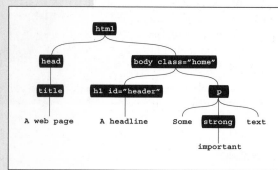

Figure 4-3:
The basic nested structure of an HTML page, where tags wrap around other tags, is often represented in the form of a family tree. Tags that wrap around other tags are called ancestors, *and tags inside other tags are called* descendents.

In addition to HTML tags, web browsers also keep track of the text that appears inside a tag (for example, "A headline" inside the <h1> tag in Figure 4-3), as well as the *attributes* that are assigned to each tag (the class attribute applied to the <body> and <h1> tags in Figure 4-3). In fact, the DOM treats each of these—tags (also called *elements*), attributes, and text—as individual units called *nodes*.

JavaScript provides several ways to select elements on a page so you can do something to them—like make them fade out of view or animate across the page. The *document.getElementById()* method lets you select an element with a particular ID applied to its HTML. So if you have a <div> tag with the ID banner applied to it—<div id="banner">—you could select that div like this:

```
document.getElementById('banner');
```

Likewise, the *document.getElementsByTagName()* method selects every instance of a particular tag *(document.getElementsByTagName('a'),* for example, selects all anchor tags (links) on a page); and some browsers support methods for selecting all elements with a particular class or using a CSS selector to select page elements.

The Problem with the DOM

Unfortunately, the major browsers have tranditionally interpreted the DOM differently. For example, versions of Internet Explorer prior to 9 handle events differently from other browsers; the same HTML can produce more text nodes in Firefox and Safari than in Internet Explorer; and IE doesn't always retrieve HTML tag attributes in the same way as Firefox, Safari, or Opera. Also, different browsers treat white space (like tabs and spaces) in HTML differently—in some cases treating white space like additional text nodes (Firefox and Safari) and in other cases ignoring that white space (IE). And those are just a few of the differences between how the most common web browsers handle the DOM.

Overcoming cross-browser JavaScript problems is such a huge task for JavaScript programmers that an entire (very boring) book could be dedicated to the subject. In fact, many JavaScript books spend a lot of time showing you the code needed to make the various browsers behave themselves. But life is too short—you'd rather be building interactive user interfaces and adding cool effects to your websites, instead of worrying about how to get your script to work identically in Internet Explorer, Firefox, Safari, and Opera.

In addition, the traditional DOM methods for selecting page elements aren't very intuitive for web designers, especially since you already have an excellent method of selecting page elements—CSS selectors. Fortunately, jQuery solves these problems and provides easy-to-use, cross-browser compatible ways of selecting and working with page elements.

Selecting Page Elements: The jQuery Way

As you read on the opposite page, web browsers provide two primary methods for selecting an element on a web page—*document.getElementById()* and *document .getElementsByTagName()*. Unfortunately, these two methods don't provide the control needed to make more subtle kinds of selections. For example, if you want to select every <a> tag with a class of *navButton*, you first need to select every tag, and then go through each and find only the ones that have the proper class name.

Fortunately, jQuery offers a very powerful technique for selecting and working on a collection of elements—CSS selectors. That's right, if you're used to using Cascading Style Sheets to style your web pages, you're ready to use jQuery. A CSS selector is simply the instruction that tells a web browser which tag the style applies to. For example, *h1* is a basic element selector, which applies a style to every <h1> tag, while *.copyright*, is a class selector, which styles any tag that has a class attribute of copyright like this:

```
<p class="copyright">Copyright, 2011</p>
```

With jQuery, you select one or more elements using a special command called the *jQuery object*. The basic syntax is like this:

```
$('selector')
```

You can use nearly all CSS 2.1 and many CSS 3 selectors when you create a jQuery object (even if the browser itself doesn't understand the particular selector—like IE with certain CSS 3 selectors). For example, if you want to select a tag with a specific ID of *banner* in jQuery, you can write this:

```
$('#banner')
```

The *#banner* is the CSS selector used to style a tag with the ID name *banner*—the # part indicates that you're identifying an ID. Of course, once you select one or more elements, you'll want to do something with them—jQuery provides many tools for working with elements. For example, say you want to change the HTML inside an element; you can write this:

```
$('#banner').html('<h1>JavaScript was here</h1>');
```

You'll learn more about how to work with page elements using jQuery starting on page 138, and throughout the rest of this book. But first, you need learn more about using jQuery to select page elements.

Note: The latest versions of most browsers now include the ability to select elements by class name and by using CSS selectors. However, since support for this isn't the same across the browsers used worldwide, jQuery helps out by making sure that your selections work even in that old antique, IE6.

Basic Selectors

Basic CSS *selectors* like IDs, classes, and element selectors make up the heart of CSS. They're a great way to select a wide range of elements using jQuery.

Because reading about selectors isn't the best way to gain an understanding of them, this book includes an interactive web page so you can test selectors. In the *testbed* folder of the book's tutorial files, you'll find a file named *selectors.html*. Open the file in a web browser. You can test various jQuery selectors by typing them into the selector box and clicking Apply (see Figure 4-4).

Note: See page 29 for information on where to find the tutorial files for this book.

ID selectors

You can select any page element that has an ID applied to it using jQuery and a CSS ID selector. For example, say you have the following HTML in a web page:

```
<p id="message">Special message</p>
```

To select that element using the old DOM way, you'd write this:

```
var messagePara = document.getElementById('message');
```

The jQuery method looks like this:

```
var messagePara = $('#message');
```

Unlike with the DOM method, you don't just use the ID name (*'message'*); you have to use the CSS-syntax for defining an ID selector (*'#message'*). In other words, you include the pound sign before the ID name, just as if creating a CSS style for that ID.

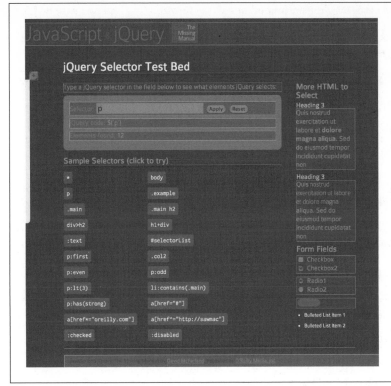

Figure 4-4:
The file selectors.html, provided with this book's tutorial files, lets you try out jQuery selectors. Type a selector in the Selector form field (circled), and then click Apply. The page converts your selector into a jQuery object, and any elements that match the selector you typed turn red. Below the field is the jQuery code used to select the item, as well as the total number or elements selected. In this case, p is the selector, and all <p> tags on the page (there are 12 on this page) are highlighted in red.

Element selectors

jQuery also has its own replacement for the *getElementsByTagName()* method. Just pass the tag's name to jQuery. For example, using the old DOM method to select every <a> tag on the page, you'd write this:

```
var linksList = document.getElementsByTagName('a');
```

With jQuery, you'd write this:

```
var linksList = $('a');
```

Tip: jQuery supports an even wider range of selectors than are listed here. Although this book lists many useful ones, you can find a complete list of jQuery selectors at *http://api.jquery.com/category/selectors/*.

Class selectors

Another useful way of selecting elements is by class name. For example, suppose you want to create a navigation bar that includes drop-down menus; when a visitor mouses over one of the main navigation buttons, you want a drop-down menu to appear. You need to use JavaScript to control those menus, and you need a way to program each of the main navigation buttons to open a drop-down menu when someone mouses over the button.

Note: Because finding all elements with a particular class name is such a common task, the latest version of most browsers support a method to do that. But since not all browsers have a built-in way to find elements of a specific class (like IE8 and earlier), a library like jQuery, which takes the different browsers into account, is invaluable.

One technique is to add a class—like *navButton*—to each of the main navigation bar links, and then use JavaScript to search for links with *just* that class name and apply all of the magical menu-opening power to those links (you'll learn how to do that, by the way, on page 249). This scheme may sound confusing, but the important point for now is that to make this navigation bar work, you need a way to select only the links with a specific class name.

Fortunately, jQuery provides an easy method to select all elements with the same class name. Just use a CSS class selector like this:

```
$('.submenu')
```

Again, notice that you write the CSS class selector just like, well, a CSS class selector, with the period before the class name. Once you select those tags, you can manipulate them using jQuery. For example, to hide all tags with the class name of *.submenu*, you'd write this:

```
$('.submenu').hide();
```

You'll learn more about the jQuery *hide()* function on page 187, but for now, this example gives you a bit of an idea of how jQuery works.

UP TO SPEED

Understanding CSS

Cascading Style Sheets are a big topic in any discussion of JavaScript. To get the most out of this book, you need to have at least some background in web design and know a bit about CSS and how to use it. CSS is the most important tool a web designer has for creating beautiful websites, so if you don't know much about it, now's the time to learn. Not only will CSS help you use jQuery, but you'll find that you can use JavaScript in combination with CSS to easily add interactive visual effects to a web page.

If you need some help getting up to speed with CSS, there are plenty of resources at your disposal:

For a basic overview on CSS, try the HTML Dog CSS Tutorials *www.htmldog.com/guides/*. You'll find basic, intermediate, and advanced tutorials at the site.

You can also pick up a copy of *CSS: The Missing Manual,* which provides thorough coverage of CSS (including many hands-on tutorials just like the ones in this book).

Most of all, when working with jQuery, it's very important to understand *CSS selectors*—the instructions that tell a web browser which tag a CSS rule applies to. To get a handle on selectors, the resources in this box are very good. There are also a few places to go if you just want a refresher on the different selectors that are available:

- *http://css.maxdesign.com.au/selectutorial/*
- *http://www.456bereastreet.com/archive/200601/ css_3_selectors_explained/*

Advanced Selectors

jQuery also lets you use more complicated CSS selectors to accurately pinpoint the tags you wish to select. Don't worry too much about mastering these right now: Once you've read a few more chapters and gained a better understanding of how jQuery works and how to use it to manipulate a web page, you'll probably want to turn back to this section and take another look.

- **Descendent selectors** provide a way to target a tag inside another tag. For example, say you've created an unordered list of links and added an ID name of *navBar* to the list's <ul> tag like this: *<ul id="navBar">*. The jQuery expression *$('a')* selects all <a> tags on the page. However, if you want to select only the links inside the unordered list, you use a descendent selector like this:

  `$('#navBar a')`

  Again, this syntax is just basic CSS: a selector, followed by a space, followed by another selector. The selector listed last is the target (in this case, *a*), while each selector to the left represents a tag that wraps around the target.

- **Child selectors** target a tag that's the child of another tag. A child tag is the direct descendent of another tag. For example, in the HTML diagrammed in Figure 4-3, the <h1> and <p> tags are children of the <body> tag, but the <strong> tag is not (since it's wrapped by the <p> tag). You create a child selector by first listing the parent element, followed by a >, and then the child element. For example, to select <p> tags that are the children of the <body> tag, you'd write this:

  `$('body > p')`

- **Adjacent sibling** selectors let you select a tag that appears directly after another tag. For example, say you have an invisible panel that appears when you click a tab. In your HTML, the tab might be represented by a heading tag (say <h2>), while the hidden panel is a <div> tag that follows the header. To make the <div> tag (the panel) visible, you'll need a way to select it. You can easily do so with jQuery and an adjacent sibling selector:

  `$('h2 + div')`

  To create an adjacent sibling selector, just add a plus sign between two selectors (which can be any type of selector: IDs, classes, or elements). The selector on the right is the one to select, but only if it comes directly after the selector on the left.

- **Attribute selectors** let you select elements based on whether the element has a particular attribute, and even check to make sure the attribute matches a specific value. With an attribute selector, you can find <img> tags that have the alt attribute set, or even match an <img> tag that has a particular alt text value. Or you could find every link tag that points outside your site, and add code to just those links, so they'll open in new windows.

  You add the attribute selector after the name of the element whose attribute you're checking. For example, to find <img> tags that have the alt attribute set, you write this:

```
$('img[alt]')
```

There are a handful of different attribute selectors:

- *[attribute]* selects elements that have the specified attribute assigned in the HTML. For example, *$(a[href])* locates all <a> tags that have an *href* attribute set. Selecting by attribute lets you exclude named anchors—<a name="placeOnPage"></a>—that are simply used as in-page links.

- *[attribute="value"]* selects elements that have a particular attribute with a specific value. For example, to find all text boxes in a form, you can use this:
  ```
  $('input[type="text"]')
  ```
  Since most form elements share the same tag—<input>—the only way to tell the type of form element is to check its type attribute (selecting form elements is so common that jQuery includes specific selectors just for that purpose, as described on page 259).

- *[attribute^="value"]* matches elements with an attribute that *begins* with a specific value. For example, if you want to find links that point outside your site, you can use this code:
  ```
  $('a[href^="http://"]')
  ```
  Notice that the entire attribute value doesn't have to match just the beginning. So *href^=http://* matches links that point to *http://www.yahoo.com*, *http://www.google.com*, and so on. Or you could use this selector to identify mailto: links like this:
  ```
  $('a[href^="mailto:"]')
  ```

- *[attribute$="value"]* matches elements whose attribute ends with a specific value, which is great for matching file extensions. For example, with this selector, you can locate links that point to PDF files (maybe to use JavaScript to add a special PDF icon, or dynamically generate a link to Adobe.com so your visitor can download the Acrobat Reader program). The code to select links that point to PDF files looks like this:
  ```
  $('a[href$=".pdf"]')
  ```

- *[attribute*="value"]* matches elements whose attribute contains a specific value anywhere in the attribute. For example, you can find any type of link that points to a particular domain. For example, here's how to find a link that points to missingmanuals.com (*http://missingmanuals.com*):
  ```
  $('a[href*="missingmanuals.com"]')
  ```
  This selector provides the flexibility to find not only links that point to *http://www.missingmanuals.com*, but also *http://missingmanuals.com* and *http://www.missingmanuals.com/library.html*.

Note: jQuery has a set of selectors that are useful when working with forms. They let you select elements such as text fields, password fields, and selected radio buttons. You'll learn about these selectors on page 259.

---

jQuery Filters

jQuery also provides a way to filter your selections based on certain characteristics. For example, the *:even* filter lets you select every even element in a collection of elements. In addition, you can find elements that contain particular tags, specific text, elements that are hidden from view, and even elements that do *not* match a particular selector. To use a filter, you add a colon followed by the filter's name after the main selector. For example, to find every even row of a table, write your jQuery selector like this:

```
$('tr:even')
```

This code selects every even <tr> tag. To narrow down the selection, you may want to just find every even table row in a table with class name of *striped*. You can do that like this:

```
$('.striped tr:even')
```

Here's how *:even* and other filters work:

- *:even* and *:odd* select every *other* element in a group. These filters work a little counter-intuitively; just remember that a jQuery selection is a list of all elements that match a specified selector. In that respect, they're kind of like arrays (see page 59). Each element in a jQuery selection has an index number—remember that index values for arrays always start at 0 (see page 62). So, since *:even* filters on even index values (like 0, 2, and 4), this filter actually returns the first, third, and fifth items (and so on) in the selection—in other words, it's really selecting every other odd element! The *:odd* filter works the same except it selects every odd index number (1, 3, 5, and so on).

- *:first* and *:last* select the first or the last element in a group. For example, if you wanted to select the first paragraph on a page, you'd type this:
  ```
  $('p:first');
  ```
  And to select the last paragraph on a page, you'd type this:
  ```
  $('p:last');
  ```

- You can use *:not()* to find elements that *don't* match a particular selector type. For example, say you want to select every <a> tag except ones with a class of *navButton*. Here's how to do that:
  ```
  $('a:not(.navButton)');
  ```
  You give the *:not()* function the name of the selector you wish to ignore. In this case, *.navButton* is a class selector, so this code translates to "does not have the class of *.navButton*." You can use *:not()* with any of the jQuery filters and with most jQuery selectors; so, for example, to find every link that doesn't begin with http://, you can write this:
  ```
  $('a:not([href^="http://"])')
  ```

- *:has()* finds elements that contain another selector. For example, say you want to find all <li> tags, but only if they have an <a> tag inside them. You'd do that like this:
  ```
  $('li:has(a)')
  ```

This setup is different from a descendent selector, since it doesn't select the <a>; it selects <li> tags, but only those <li> tags with a link inside them.

- *:contains()* finds elements that contain specific text. For example, to find every link that says "Click Me!" you can create a jQuery object like this:
  ```
  $('a:contains(Click Me!)')
  ```
- *:hidden* locates elements that are hidden, which includes elements that either have the CSS *display* property set to *none* (which means you won't see them on the page), elements you hide using jQuery's *hide()* function (discussed on page 187), elements with width and height values set to 0, and hidden form fields. (This selector doesn't apply to elements whose CSS *visibility* property is set to *invisible*.) For example, say you've hidden several <div> tags; you can find them and then make them visible using jQuery, like this:
  ```
  $('div:hidden').show();
  ```
  This line of code has no effect on <div> tags that are currently visible on the page. (You'll learn about jQuery's *show()* function on page 187.)
- *:visible* is the opposite of *:hidden*. It locates elements that are visible on the page.

Understanding jQuery Selections

When you select one or more elements using the jQuery object—for example, *$('#navBar a')*—you don't end up with a traditional list of DOM nodes, like the ones you get if you use *getElementById()* or *getElementsByTagName()*. Instead, you get a special jQuery-only selection of elements. These elements don't understand the traditional DOM methods; so, if you learned about the DOM in another book, you'll find that none of the methods you learned there work with the jQuery object as-is. That may seem like a major drawback, but nearly all of the properties and methods of a normal DOM node have jQuery equivalents, so you can do anything the traditional DOM can do—only usually much faster and with fewer lines of code.

There are, however, two big conceptual differences between how the DOM works and how jQuery selections work. jQuery was built to make it a lot easier and faster to program JavaScript. One of the goals of the library is to let you do a lot of stuff with as few lines of code as possible. To achieve that, jQuery uses two unusual principles.

Automatic loops

Normally, when you're using the DOM and you select a bunch of page elements, you then need to create a loop (page 93) to go through each node selected and do something to that node. For example, if you want to select all the images in a page and then hide them—something you might do if you want to create a JavaScript-driven slideshow—you must first select the images and then create a loop to go through the list of images.

Because looping through a collection of elements is so common, jQuery functions have that feature built right in. In other words, when you apply a jQuery function to a selection of elements, you don't need to create a loop yourself, since the function does it automatically.

For example, to select all images inside a <div> tag with an ID of *slideshow* and then hide those images, you write this in jQuery:

```
$('#slideshow img').hide();
```

The list of elements created with *$('#slideshow img')* might include 50 images. The *hide()* function automatically loops through the list, hiding each image individually. This setup is so convenient (imagine the number of *for* loops you won't have to write) that it's surprising that this great feature isn't just part of the JavaScript.

Chaining functions

Sometimes you'll want to perform several operations on a selection of elements. For example, say you want to set the width and height of a <div> tag (with an ID of *popUp*) using JavaScript. Normally, you'd have to write at least two lines of code. But jQuery lets you do so with a single line:

```
$('#popUp').width(300).height(300);
```

jQuery uses a unique principle called *chaining*, which lets you add functions one after the other. Each function is connected to the next by a period, and operates on the same jQuery collection of elements as the previous function. So the code above changes the width of the element with the ID *popUp, and* changes the height of the element. Chaining jQuery functions lets you concisely carry out a large number of actions. For example, say you not only want to set the width and height of the <div> tag, but also want to add text inside the <div> and make it fade into view (assuming it's not currently visible on the page). You can do that very succinctly like this:

```
$('#popUp').width(300).height(300).text('Hi!').fadeIn(1000);
```

This code applies four jQuery functions—*width(), height(), text(),* and *fadeIn()*—to the tag with an ID name of *popUp*.

Tip: A long line of chained jQuery functions can be hard to read, so some programmers break it up over multiple lines like this:

```
$('#popUp').width(300)
    .height(300)
    .text('Message')
    .fadeIn(1000);
```

As long as you only add a semicolon on the *last line* of the chain, the JavaScript interpreter treats the lines as a single statement.

The ability to chain functions is pretty unusual and is a specific feature of jQuery—in other words, you can't add non-jQuery functions (either ones you create or built-in JavaScript functions) in the chain.

Adding Content to a Page

jQuery provides many functions for manipulating elements and content on a page, from simply replacing HTML, to precisely positioning new HTML in relation to a selected element, to completely removing tags and content from the page.

Note: An example file, *content_functions.html*, located in the *testbed* tutorial folder, lets you take each of these jQuery functions for a test drive. Just open the file in a web browser, type some text in the text box, and click any of the boxes to see how each function works.

To study the following examples of these functions, assume you have a page with the following HTML:

```
<div id="container">
  <div id="errors">
    <h2>Errors:</h2>
  </div>
</div>
```

- *.html()* can both read the current HTML inside an element and replace the current contents with some other HTML. You use the *html()* function in conjunction with a jQuery selection.

  To retrieve the HTML currently inside the selection, just add *.html()* after the jQuery selection. For example, you can run the following command using the HTML snippet at the beginning of this section:

  ```
  alert($('#errors').html());
  ```

  This code creates an alert box with the text *"<h2>Errors:</h2>"* in it. When you use the *html()* function in this way, you can make a copy of the HTML inside a specific element and paste it into another element on a page.

  If you supply a string as an argument to *.html()*, you replace the current contents inside the selection:

  ```
  $('#errors').html('<p>There are four errors in this form</p>');
  ```

  This line of code replaces all of the HTML inside an element with an ID of *errors*. It would change the example HTML snippet to:

  ```
  <div id="container">
    <div id="errors">
      <p>There are four errors in this form</p>
    </div>
  </div>
  ```

  Notice that it replaces the <h2> tag that was already there. You can avoid replacing that HTML using other functions listed below.

- *.text()* works like *.html()* but it doesn't accept HTML tags. It's useful when you want to replace the text within a tag. For example, in the code at the beginning of this section, you'll see an <h2> tag with the text "Errors:" in it. Say, after running a program to check to see if there were any errors in the form, you wanted to replace the text "Errors:" with "No errors found", you could use this code:

```
$('#errors h2').text('No errors found');
```

The <h2> tag stays in place; only the text inside changes. jQuery encodes any HTML tags that you pass to the text() function, so that <p> is translated to *<p>*. This can come in handy if you want you to actually display the brackets and tag names *on* the page. For example, you can use it to display example HTML code for other people to view.

- *.append()* adds HTML as the last child element of the selected element. For example, say you select a <div> tag, but instead of replacing the contents of the <div>, you just want to add some HTML before the closing </div> tag. The *.append()* function is a great way to add an item to the end of a bulleted (<ul>) or numbered (<ol>) list. As an example, say you run the following code on a page with the HTML listed at the beginning of this section:

```
$('#errors').append('<p>There are four errors in this form</p>');
```

After this function runs, you end up with HTML like this:

```
<div id="container">
  <div id="errors">
    <h2>Errors:</h2>
    <p>There are four errors in this form</p>
  </div>
</div>
```

Notice that the original HTML inside the <div> remains the same, and the new chunk of HTML is added after it.

- *.prepend()* is just like *.append()*, but adds HTML directly after the opening tag for the selection. For example, say you run the following code on the same HTML listed previously:

```
$('#errors').prepend('<p>There are four errors in this form</p>');
```

After this *prepend()* function, you end up with the following HTML:

```
<div id="container">
  <div id="errors">
    <p>There are four errors in this form</p>
    <h2>Errors:</h2>
  </div>
</div>
```

Now the newly added content appears directly after the <div>'s opening tag.

- If you want to add HTML just *outside* of a selection, either before the selected element's opening tag or directly after the element's closing tag, use the *.before()* or *.after()* functions. For example, it's common practice to check a text field in a form to make sure that the field isn't empty when your visitor submits the form. Assume that the HTML for the field looks like the following before the form is submitted:

```
<input type="text" name="userName" id="userName">
```

Now suppose that when the visitor submits the form, this field is empty. You can write a program that checks the field and then adds an error message after the field. To add the message after this field (don't worry right now about how you actually check that the contents of form fields are correct—you'll find out on page 278), you can use the *.after()* function like this:

```
$('#userName').after('<span class="error">User name required</span>');
```

That line of code makes the web page show the error message, and the HTML component would look like this:

```
<input type="text" name="userName" id="userName">
<span class="error">User name required</span>
```

The *.before()* function simply puts the new content before the selected element.

Note: The functions listed in this section—html(), text(), and so on—are the most popular ways of adding and altering content on a page but they're not the only ones. You can find more functions at http://api .jquery.com/category/manipulation/.

Replacing and Removing Selections

At times you may want to completely replace or remove a selected element. For example, say you've created a pop-up dialog box using JavaScript (not the old-fashioned *alert()* method, but a more professional-looking dialog box that's actually just an absolutely-positioned <div> floating on top of the page). When the visitor clicks the "Close" button on the dialog box, you naturally want to remove the dialog box from the page. To do so, you can use the jQuery *remove()* function. Say the pop-up dialog box had an ID of *popup*; you can use the following code to delete it:

```
$('#popup').remove();
```

The *.remove()* function isn't limited to just a single element. Say you want to remove all <span> tags that have a class of *error* applied to them; you can do this:

```
$('span.error').remove();
```

You can also completely replace a selection with new content. For example, suppose you have a page with photos of the products your company sells. When a visitor clicks on an image of a product, it's added to a shopping cart. You might want to replace the <img> tag with some text when the image is clicked ("Added to cart," for example). You'll learn how to make particular elements react to events (like an image being clicked) in the next chapter, but for now just assume there's an <img> tag with an ID of *product101* that you wish to replace with text. Here's how you do that with jQuery:

```
$('#product101').replaceWith('<p>Added to cart</p>');
```

This code removes the <img> tag from the page and replaces it with a <p> tag.

Note: jQuery also includes a function named *clone()* that lets you make a copy of a selected element. You'll see this function in action in the tutorial on page 150.

Skip View Source

One problem with using JavaScript to manipulate the DOM by adding, changing, deleting, and rearranging HTML code is that it's hard to figure out what the HTML of a page looks like when JavaScript is finished. For example, the View Source command available in every browser only shows the web page file as it was downloaded from the web server. In other words, you see the HTML *before* it was changed by JavaScript, which can make it very hard to figure out if the JavaScript you're writing is really producing the HTML you're after. For example, if you could see what the HTML of your page looks like after your JavaScript adds 10 error messages to a form page, or after your JavaScript program creates an elaborate pop-up dialog box complete with text and form fields, it would be a lot easier to see if you're ending up with the HTML you want.

Fortunately, most major browsers offer a set of developer tools that let you view the *rendered HTML*—the HTML that the browser displays after JavaScript has done its magic. Usually the tools appear as a pane at the bottom of the browser window, below the web page. Different tabs let you access JavaScript code, HTML, CSS, and other useful resources. The exact name of the tab and method for turning on the tools panel varies from browser to browser:

- In Firefox, install the Firebug plug-in (discussed on page 477). Open a page with the JavaScript code you wish to see and open Firebug (Tools→Firebug→Open Firebug). Click the HTML tab in the Firebug panel, and you'll see the complete DOM (including any

HTML generated by JavaScript). Alternatively, you can use the Web Developer toolbar (*https://addons .mozilla.org/en-US/firefox/addon/web-developer/*) in Firefox to view both the regular HTML source, and the generated HTML.

- In IE 9, press the F12 key to open the Developer Tools panel, then click the HTML tab to see the page's HTML. In the case of IE9, the HTML tab starts by showing the downloaded HTML (the same as the View Source command). But if you click the refresh icon (or press F5), the HTML tab shows the rendered HTML complete with any JavaScript-created changes.

- In Chrome, select View→Developer→Developer Tools and click the Elements tab in the panel at the bottom of the browser window.

- In Safari, make sure the Developer menu is on (choose Safari→Preferences, click the Advanced button, and make sure the "Show Develop menu in menu bar" is checked. Then open the page you're interested in looking at, and choose Develop→Show Web Inspector. Click the Elements tab in the panel that appears at the bottom of the browser window.

- In Opera, choose Tools→Advanced→Opera Dragonfly. (Dragonfly is the name of Opera's built-in set of developer tools.) In the panel that appears at the bottom of the browser window, click the Documents tab.

Setting and Reading Tag Attributes

Adding, removing, and changing elements isn't the only thing jQuery is good at, and it's not the only thing you'll want to do with a selection of elements. You'll often want to change the value of an element's attribute—add a class to a tag, for example, or change a CSS property of an element. You can also get the value of an attribute—for instance, what URL does a particular link point to?

Classes

Cascading Style Sheets are a very powerful technology, letting you add all sorts of sophisticated visual formatting to your HTML. One CSS rule can add a colorful background to a page, while another rule might completely hide an element from view. You can create some really advanced visual effects simply by using JavaScript to remove, add, or change a class applied to an element. Because web browsers process and implement CSS instructions very quickly and efficiently, simply adding a class to a tag can completely change that tag's appearance—even make it disappear from the page.

jQuery provides several functions for manipulating a tag's class attribute:

- *addClass()* adds a specified class to an element. You add the *addClass()* after a jQuery selection and pass the function a string, which represents the class name you wish to add. For example, to add the class *externalLink* to all links pointing outside your site, you can use this code:

  ```
  $('a[href^="http://"]').addClass('externalLink');
  ```

  This code would take HTML like this:

  ```
  <a href="http://www.oreilly.com/">
  ```

  And change it to the following:

  ```
  <a href="http://www.oreilly.com/" class="externalLink">
  ```

  For this function to be of any use, you'll need to create a CSS class style beforehand and add it to the page's style sheet. Then, when the JavaScript adds the class name, the web browser can apply the style properties from the previously defined CSS rule.

Note: When using the *addClass()* and *removeClass()* functions, you only supply the class name—leave out the period you normally use when creating a class selector. For example, *addClass('externalLink')* is correct, but *addClass('.externalLink')* is wrong.

  This jQuery function also takes care of issues that arise when a tag already has a class applied to it—the *addClass()* function doesn't eliminate the old classes already applied to the tag; the function just adds the new class as well.

Note: Adding multiple class names to a single tag is perfectly valid and frequently very helpful. Check out *www.cvwdesign.com/txp/article/177/use-more-than-one-css-class* for more information on this technique.

- *removeClass()* is the opposite of *addClass()*. It removes the specified class from the selected elements. For example, if you wanted to remove a class named *highlight* from a <div> with an ID of alertBox, you'd do this:

  ```
  $('#alertBox').removeClass('highlight');
  ```

- Finally, you may want to *toggle* a particular class—meaning add the class if it doesn't already exist, or remove the class if it does. Toggling is a popular way to show an element in either an on or off state. For example, when you click a radio button, it's checked (on); click it again, and the checkmark disappears (off).

Say you have a button on a web page that, when clicked, changes the <body> tag's class. By so doing, you can add a complete stylistic change to a web page by crafting a second set of styles using descendent selectors. When the button is clicked again, you want the class removed from the <body> tag, so that the page reverts back to its previous appearance. For this example, assume the button the visitor clicks to change the page's style has an ID of *changeStyle* and you want to toggle the class name *altStyle* off and on with each click of the button. Here's the code to do that:

```
$('#changeStyle').click(function() {
  $('body').toggleClass('altStyle');
});
```

At this point, don't worry about the first and third lines of code above; those have to do with events that let scripts react to actions—like clicking the button—that happen on a page. You'll learn about events in the next chapter. The bolded line of code demonstrates the *toggleClass()* function; it either adds or removes the class *altStyle* with each click of the button.

Reading and Changing CSS Properties

jQuery's *css()* function also lets you directly change CSS properties of an element, so instead of simply applying a class style to an element, you can immediately add a border or background color, or set a width or positioning property. You can use the *css()* function in three ways: to find the current value for an element's CSS property, to set a single CSS property on an element, or to set multiple CSS properties at once.

To determine the current value of a CSS property, pass the name of the property to the *css()* function. For example, say you want to find the background color of a <div> tag with an ID of *main*:

```
var bgColor = $('#main').css('background-color');
```

After this code runs, the variable *bgColor* will contain a string with the element's background color value.

Note: jQuery may not always return CSS values the way you expect. In the case of colors (like the CSS background color, or color properties), jQuery always returns either an rgb value like rgb(255, 0, 10) or, if there is any transparency in the color, an rgba color value like rgba(255,10,10,.5). jQuery returns RGB values regardless of whether the color in the stylesheet was defined using hexadecimal notation (#F4477A), RGB using percentages (rgb(100%,10%,0%)), or HSL (hsl(72,100%,50%)). In addition, jQuery doesn't understand shorthand CSS properties like *font, margin, padding,* or *border.* Instead, you have to use the specific CSS properties like *font-face, margin-top, padding-bottom,* or *border-bottom-width* to access styles that can be combined in CSS shorthand. Finally, jQuery translates all unit values to pixels, so even if you use CSS to set the <body> tag's font-size to 150%, jQuery returns a pixel value when checking the *font-size* property.

The *css()* function also lets you set a CSS property for an element. To use the function this way, you supply two arguments to the function: the CSS property name and a value. For example, to change the font size for the <body> tag to 200% size, you can do this:

```
$('body').css('font-size', '200%');
```

The second argument you supply can be a string value, like *'200%'*, or a numeric value, which jQuery translates to pixels. For example, to change the padding inside all of the tags with a class of *.pullquote* to 100px, you can write this code:

```
$('.pullquote').css('padding',100);
```

In this example, jQuery sets the padding property to 100 pixels.

Note: When you set a CSS property using jQuery's *.css()* function, you can use the CSS shorthand method. For example, here's how you could add a black, one-pixel border around all paragraphs with a class of *highlight:*

```
$('p.highlight').css('border', '1px solid black');
```

It's often useful to change a CSS property based on its current value. For example, say you want to add a "Make text bigger" button on a web page, so when a visitor clicks the button, the page's font-size doubles. To make that happen, you read the value, and then set a new value. In this case, you first determine the current font-size and then set the font-size to twice that value. It's a little trickier than you might think. Here's the code, and a full explanation follows:

```
var baseFont = $('body').css('font-size');
baseFont = parseInt(baseFont,10);
$('body').css('font-size',baseFont * 2);
```

The first line retrieves the <body> tag's font-size value—the returned value is in pixels and is a string like this: '16px'. Since you want to double that size—multiplying it by 2—you must convert that string to a number by removing the "px" part of the string. The second line accomplishes that using the JavaScript *parseInt()* method discussed on page 446. That function essentially strips off anything following the number, so after line 2, *baseFont* contains a number, like 16. Finally, the third line resets the *font-size* property by multiplying the *baseFont* value by 2.

Note: This code affects the page's type size only if the other tags on the page—paragraphs, headlines, and so on—have their font-size set using a relative value like ems or percentages. If the other tags use absolute values like pixels, changing the <body> tag's font size won't affect them.

Changing Multiple CSS Properties at Once

If you want to change more than one CSS property on an element, you don't need to resort to multiple uses of the *.css()* function. For example, if you want to dynamically highlight a <div> tag (perhaps in reaction to an action taken by a visitor), you can change the <div> tag's background color *and* add a border around it, like this:

```
$('#highlightedDiv').css('background-color','#FF0000');
$('#highlightedDiv').css('border','2px solid #FE0037');
```

Another way is to pass what's called an *object literal* to the *.css()* function. Think of an object literal as a list of property name/value pairs. After each property name, you insert a colon (:) followed by a value; each name/value pair is separated by a comma, and the whole shebang is surrounded by braces—{}. Thus, an object literal for the two CSS property values above looks like this:

```
{ 'background-color' : '#FF0000', 'border' : '2px solid #FE0037' }
```

Because an object literal can be difficult to read if it's crammed onto a single line, many programmers break it up over multiple lines. The following is functionally the same as the previous one-liner:

```
{
  'background-color' : '#FF0000',
  'border' : '2px solid #FE0037'
}
```

The basic structure of an object literal is diagrammed in Figure 4-5.

Warning: When creating an object literal, make sure to separate each name/value pair by adding a comma after the value (for instance, in this example, the comma goes after the value '#FF0000'. However, the last property/value pair should *not* have a comma after it, since no property/value pair follows it. If you do add a comma after the last value, some web browsers (including Internet Explorer) will generate an error.

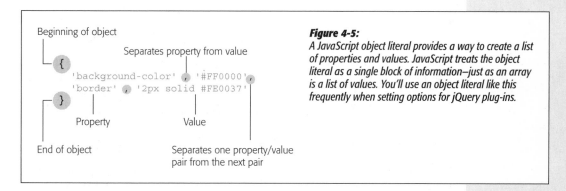

Figure 4-5:
A JavaScript object literal provides a way to create a list of properties and values. JavaScript treats the object literal as a single block of information—just as an array is a list of values. You'll use an object literal like this frequently when setting options for jQuery plug-ins.

To use an object literal with the *css()* function, just pass the object to the function like this:

```
$('#highlightedDiv').css({
  'background-color' : '#FF0000',
  'border' : '2px solid #FE0037'
});
```

Study this example closely, because it looks a little different from what you've seen so far, and because you'll be encountering lots of code that looks like it in future chapters. The first thing to notice is that this code is merely a single JavaScript statement (essentially just one line of code)—you can tell because the semicolon that ends the statement doesn't appear until the last line. The statement is broken over four lines to make the code easier to read.

Next, notice that the object literal is an argument (like one piece of data) that's passed to the *css()* function. So in the code *css({*, the opening parenthesis is part of the function, while the opening { marks the beginning of the object. The three characters in the last line break down like this: } is the end of the object and the end of the argument passed to the function;) marks the end of the function, the last parenthesis in *css()*; and ; marks the end of the JavaScript statement.

And if all this object literal stuff is hurting your head, you're free to change CSS properties one line at a time, like this:

```
$('#highlightedDiv').css('background-color','#FF0000');
$('#highlightedDiv').css('border','2px solid #FE0037');
```

Or, a better method is to use jQuery's built-in chaining ability (page 137). Chaining is applying several jQuery functions to a single collection of elements by adding that function to the end of another function, like this:

```
$('#highlightedDiv').css('background-color','#FF0000')
                    .css('border','2px solid #FE0037');
```

This code can be translated as: find an element with an ID of *highlightedDiv* and change its background color, then change its border color. Chaining provides better performance than making the selection—*$('#highlightedDiv')*—twice as in the code above, because each time you make a selection you make the web browser run all of the jQuery code for selecting the element. Thus, this code is not optimal.

```
$('#highlightedDiv').css('background-color','#FF0000');
$('#highlightedDiv').css('border','2px solid #FE0037');
```

This code forces the browser to select the element, change its CSS, select the element a second time (wasting processor time), and apply CSS again. Using the chaining method, the browser only needs to select the element a single time and then run the CSS function twice; selecting the element once is faster and more efficient.

Reading, Setting, and Removing HTML Attributes

Since changing classes and CSS properties using JavaScript are such common tasks, jQuery has built-in functions for them. But the *addClass()* and *css()* functions are really just shortcuts for changing the HTML *class* and *style* attributes. jQuery includes general-purpose functions for handling HTML attributes—the *attr()* and *removeAttr()* functions.

The *attr()* function lets you read a specified HTML attribute from a tag. For example, to determine the current graphic file a particular <img> points to, you pass the string '*src*' (for the <img> tag's *src* property) to the function:

```
var imageFile = $('#banner img').attr('src');
```

The *attr()* function returns the attributes value as it's set in the HTML. This code returns the *src* property for the first <img> tag inside another tag with an ID of *banner*, so the variable *imageFile* would contain the path set in the page's HTML: for instance, 'images/banner.png' or '*http://www.thesite.com/images/banner.png*'.

Note: When passing an attribute name to the *.attr()* function, you don't need to worry about the case of the attribute name—href, HREF, or even HrEf will work.

If you pass a second argument to the *attr()* function, you can set the tag's attribute. For example, to swap in a different image, you can change an <img> tag's *src* property like this:

```
$('#banner img').attr('src','images/newImage.png');
```

If you want to completely remove an attribute from a tag, use the *removeAttr()* function. For example, this code removes the *bgColor* property from the <body> tag:

```
$('body').removeAttr('bgColor');
```

Acting on Each Element in a Selection

As discussed on page 136, one of the unique qualities of jQuery is that most of its functions automatically loop through each item in a jQuery selection. For example, to make every <img> on a page fade out, you only need one line of JavaScript code:

```
$('img').fadeOut();
```

The *.fadeOut()* function causes an element to disappear slowly, and when attached to a jQuery selection containing multiple elements, the function loops through the selection and fades out each element. There are plenty of times when you'll want to loop through a selection of elements and perform a series of actions on each element. jQuery provides the *.each()* function for just this purpose.

For example, say you want to list of all of the external links on your page in a bibliography box at the bottom of the page, perhaps titled "Other Sites Mentioned in This Article." (OK, you may not ever want to do that, but just play along.) Anyway, you can create that box by:

1. **Retrieving all links that point outside your site.**

2. **Getting the HREF attribute of each link (the URL).**

3. **Adding that URL to the other list of links in the bibliography box.**

jQuery doesn't have a built-in function that performs these exact steps, but you can use the *each()* function to do it yourself. It's just a jQuery function, so you slap it on at the end of a selection of jQuery elements like this:

```
$('selector').each();
```

Anonymous Functions

To use the *each()* function, you pass a special kind of argument to it—an *anonymous function*. The anonymous function is simply a function containing the steps that you wish to perform on each selected element. It's called *anonymous* because, unlike the functions you learned to create on page 100, you don't give it a name. Here's an anonymous function's basic structure:

```
function() {
  //code goes here
}
```

Because there's no name, you don't have a way to call the function. For example, with a regular named function, you use its name with a set of parentheses like this: *calculateSalesTax( );*. Instead, you use the anonymous function as an argument that you pass to another function (strange and confusing, but true!). Here's how you incorporate an anonymous function as part of the *each()* function:

```
$('selector').each(function() {
// code goes in here
});
```

Figure 4-6 diagrams the different parts of this construction. The last line is particularly confusing, since it includes three different symbols that close up three parts of the overall structure. The } marks the end of the function (that's also the end of the argument passed to the *each()* function); the) is the last part of the *each()* function; and ; indicates the end of a JavaScript statement. In other words, the JavaScript interpreter treats all of this code as a single instruction.

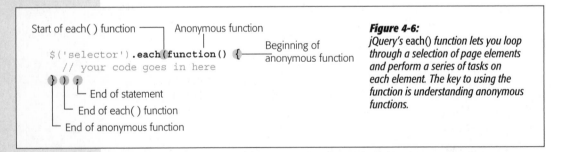

Figure 4-6:
jQuery's each() function lets you loop through a selection of page elements and perform a series of tasks on each element. The key to using the function is understanding anonymous functions.

Now that the outer structure's in place, it's time to put something inside the anonymous function: all of the stuff you want to happen to each element in a selection. The *each()* function works like a loop—meaning the instructions inside the anonymous function will run once for each element you've retrieved. For example, say you have 50 images on a page and add the following JavaScript code to one of the page's scripts:

```
$('img').each(function() {
  alert('I found an image');
});
```

Fifty alert dialog boxes with the message "I found an image" would appear. (That'd be really annoying, so don't try this at home.)

Note: This may look somewhat familiar. As you saw on page 123, when you add jQuery to a page, you should use the *document.ready()* function to make sure a page's HTML has loaded before the browser executes any of the JavaScript programming. That function also accepts an anonymous function as an argument:

```
$(document).ready(function() {
  // programming goes inside this
  // anonymous function
});
```

---

this and *$(this)*

When using the *each()* function, you'll naturally want to access or set attributes of each element—for example, to find the URL for each external link. To access the current element through each loop, you use a special keyword called *this*. The *this* keyword refers to whatever element is calling the anonymous function. So the first time through the loop, *this* refers to the first element in the jQuery selection, while the second time through the loop, *this* refers to the second element.

The way jQuery works, *this* refers to a traditional DOM element, so you can access traditional DOM properties. But, as you've read in this chapter, the special jQuery selection lets you tap into all of the wonderful jQuery functions. So to convert *this* to its jQuery equivalent, you write *$(this)*.

At this point, you're probably thinking that all of *this* stuff is some kind of cruel joke intended to make your head swell. It's not a joke, but it sure is confusing. To help make clear how to use *$(this)*, take another look at the task described at the beginning of this section—creating a list of external links in a bibliography box at the bottom of a page.

Assume that the page's HTML already has a <div> tag ready for the external links. For example:

```
<div id="bibliography">
<h3>web pages referenced in this article</h3>
<ul id="bibList">
</ul>
</div>
```

The first step is to get a list of all links pointing outside your site. You can do so using an attribute selector (page 133):

```
$('a[href^="http://"]')
```

Now to loop through each link, we add the *each()* function:

```
$('a[href^="http://"]').each()
```

Then add an anonymous function:

```
$('a[href^="http://"]').each(function() {

});
```

The first step in the anonymous function is to retrieve the URL for the link. Since each link has a different URL, you must access the current element each time through the loop. The *$(this)* keyword lets you do just that:

```
$('a[href^=http://]').each(function() {
  var extLink = $(this).attr('href');
});
```

The code in the middle, bolded line does several things: First, it creates a new variable (*extLink*) and stores the value of the current element's *href* property. Each time through the loop, *$(this)* refers to a different link on the page, so each time through the loop, the *extLink* variable changes.

After that, it's just a matter of appending a new list item to the <ul> tag (see the HTML on page 149), like this:

```
$('a[href^=http://]').each(function() {
  var extLink = $(this).attr('href');
  $('#bibList').append('<li>' + extLink + '</li>');
});
```

You'll use the *$(this)* keyword almost every time you use the *each()* function, so in a matter of time, *$(this)* will become second nature to you. To help you practice this concept, you'll try it out in a tutorial.

Note: The example script used in this section is a good way to illustrate the use of the *$(this)* keyword, but it probably isn't the best way to accomplish the task of writing a list of external links to a page. First, if there are no links, the <div> tag (which was hardcoded into the page's HTML) will still appear, but it'll be empty. In addition, if someone visits the page without JavaScript turned on, he won't see the links, but will see the empty box. A better approach is to use JavaScript to create the enclosing <div> tag as well. You can find an example of that in the file *bibliography.html* accompanying the tutorials for this chapter.

Automatic Pull Quotes

In the final tutorial for this chapter, you'll create a script that makes it very easy to add pull quotes to a page (like the one pictured in Figure 4-7). A *pull quote* is a box containing an interesting quote from the main text of a page. Newspapers, magazines, and websites all use these boxes to grab readers' attention and emphasize an important or interesting point. But adding pull quotes manually requires duplicating text from the page and placing it inside a <div> tag, <span> tag, or some other container.

Creating all that HTML takes time and adds extra HTML and duplicate text to the finished page. Fortunately, with JavaScript, you can quickly add any number of pull quotes to a page, adding just a small amount of HTML.

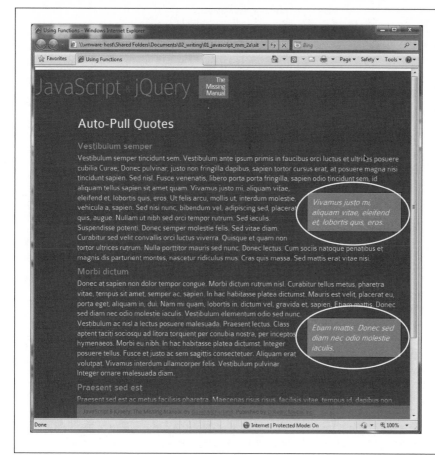

Figure 4-7:
Adding pull quotes manually to the HTML of a page is a pain, especially when you can just use JavaScript to automate the process.

Overview

The script you're about to create will do several things:

1. **Locate every <span> tag containing a special class named *pq* (for pull quote).**

   The only work you have to do to the HTML of your page is to add <span> tags around any text you wish to turn into a pull quote. For example, suppose there's a paragraph of text on a page and you want to highlight a few words from that paragraph in pull quote box. Just wrap that text in the <span> tag like this:

   ```
   <span class="pq">...and that's how I discovered the Loch Ness monster.</span>
   ```

2. **Duplicate each <span> tag.**

Each pull quote box is essentially another span tag with the same text inside it, so you can use JavaScript to just duplicate the current <span> tag.

3. **Remove the *pq* class from the duplicate <span> and add a new class *pullquote*.**

The formatting magic—the box, larger text, border, and background color—that makes up each pull quote box isn't JavaScript's doing. The page's style sheet contains a CSS class selector, *.pullquote*, that does all of that. So by simply using JavaScript to change the duplicate tags' class name, you completely change the look of the new <span> tags.

4. **Add the duplicate <span> tag to the page.**

Finally, you add the duplicate <span> tag to the page. (Step 2 just makes a copy of the tag in the web browser's memory, but doesn't actually add that tag to the page yet. This gives you the opportunity to further manipulate the duplicated tag before displaying it for the person viewing the page.)

Programming

Now that you have an idea of what you're trying to accomplish with this script, it's time to open a text editor and make it happen.

Note: See the note on page 29 for information on how to download the tutorial files.

---

1. **In a text editor, open the file *pull-quote.html* in the *chapter04* folder.**

You'll start at the beginning by adding a link to the jQuery file.

2. **Click in the empty line just above the closing </head> tag and type:**

```
<script src="../_js/jquery-1.6.3.min.js"><script>
```

This loads the jQuery file from the site. Note that the name of the folder containing the jQuery file is *_js* (don't forget the underscore character at the beginning). Next, you'll add a set of <script> tags for your programming.

3. **Press Enter (or Return) to create a new line below the jQuery code and add the code listed in bold below:**

```
1   <script src="../_js/jquery-1.6.3.min.js"><script>
2   <script>
3
4   </script>
```

Note: The line numbers to the left of each line of code are just for your reference. Don't actually type them as part of the script on the web page.

Now add the *document.ready()* function.

4. **Click on the empty line between the <script> tags and add the code in bold:**

```
1  <script src="../_js/jquery-1.6.3.min.js"><script>
2  <script>
3  $(document).ready(function() {
4
5  }); // end ready
6  </script>
```

The JavaScript comment *// end ready* is particularly helpful as your programs get longer and more complicated. On a long program, you'll end up with lots of *});* scattered throughout, each marking the end of an anonymous function and a function call. Putting a comment that identifies what the *});* matches makes it much easier to later return to your code and understand what is going on.

Steps 1–4 cover the basic setup for any program you'll write using jQuery, so make sure you understand what it does. Next, you'll get into the heart of your program by selecting the <span> tags containing the text that should appear in the *pullquote* boxes.

5. **Add the bolded code on line 4:**

```
1  <script src="../_js/jquery-1.6.3.min.js"><script>
2  <script>
3  $(document).ready(function() {
4    $('span.pq')
5  }); // end ready
6  </script>
```

The *$('span.pq')* is a jQuery selector that locates every <span> tag with a class of *pq* applied to it. Next you'll add the code needed to loop through each of these <span> tags and do something to them.

6. **Add the bolded code on lines 4 and 6:**

```
1  <script src="../_js/jquery-1.6.3.min.js"><script>
2  <script>
3  $(document).ready(function() {
4    $('span.pq').each(function() {
5
6    }); // end each
7  }); // end ready
8  </script>
```

As discussed on page 147, *.each()* is a jQuery function that lets you loop through a selection of elements. The function takes one argument, which is an anonymous function.

Next you'll start to build the function that will apply to each matching <span> tag on this page: Get started by creating a copy of the <span>.

7. **Add the code listed in bold on line 5 below to the script:**

```
1  <script  src="../_js/jquery-1.6.2.min.js"></script>
2  <script >
3  $(document).ready(function() {
4    $('span.pq').each(function() {
5    var quote=$(this).clone();
```

```
6     }); // end each
7   }); // end ready
8   </script>
```

This function starts by creating a new variable named *quote*, which contains a "clone" (just a copy) of the current <span> (see page 149 if you forgot what *$(this)* means). The jQuery *.clone()* function duplicates the current element, including all of the HTML within the element. In this case, it makes a copy of the <span> tag, including the text inside the <span> that will appear in the pull quote box.

Cloning an element copies everything, including any attributes applied to it. In this instance, the original <span> had a class named *pq*. You'll remove that class from the copy.

8. **Add the two lines of code listed in bold on lines 6 and 7 below to the script:**

```
1    <script src="../_js/jquery-1.6.3.min.js"></script>
2    <script>
3    $(document).ready(function() {
4      $('span.pq').each(function() {
5        var quote=$(this).clone();
6        quote.removeClass('pq');
7        quote.addClass('pullquote');
8      }); // end each
9    }); // end ready
10   </script>
```

As discussed on page 142, the *removeClass()* function removes a class name from a tag, while the *.addClass()* function adds a class name to a tag. In this case, we're replacing the class name on the copy, so you can use a CSS class named *.pullquote* to format the <span> as a pull quote box.

Finally, you'll add the <span> to the page.

9. **Add the bolded line of code (line 8) to the script:**

```
1    <script src="../_js/jquery-1.6.3.min.js"></script>
2    <script>
3    $(document).ready(function() {
4      $('span.pq').each(function() {
5        var quote=$(this).clone();
6        quote.removeClass('pq');
7        quote.addClass('pullquote');
8        $(this).before(quote);
9      }); // end each
10   }); // end ready
11   </script>
```

This line is the final piece of the function—up until this line, you've just been manipulating a copy of the <span> in the web browser's memory. No one viewing the page would see it until the copy is actually added to the DOM.

In this case, you're inserting the copy of the <span> tag, just before the one in your HTML. In essence, the page will end up with HTML sort of like this:

```
<span class="pullquote">...and that's how I discovered the Loch Ness monster.
</span> <span class="pq">...and that's how I discovered the Loch Ness
monster.</span>
```

Although the text looks like it will appear duplicated side by side, the CSS formatting makes the pull quote box float to the right edge of the page.

Note: To achieve the visual effect of a pull quote box, the page has a CSS style that uses the CSS *float* property. The box is moved to the right edge of the paragraph in which the text appears, and the other text in the paragraph wraps around it. If you're unfamiliar with this technique, you can learn about the CSS *float* property at *http://css.maxdesign.com.au/floatutorial/*. If you wish to examine the .pullquote style, just look in the head of the tutorial file. That style and all its properties are listed there.

At this point, all of the JavaScript is complete. However, you won't see any pull quote boxes until you massage the HTML a bit.

10. **Find the first <p> tag in the page's HTML. Locate a sentence and wrap *<span class="pq"> </span>* around it. For example:**

    ```
    <span class="pq">Nullam ut nibh sed orci tempor rutrum.</span>
    ```

    You can repeat this process to add pull quotes to other paragraphs as well.

11. **Save the file and preview it in a web browser.**

    The final result should look something like Figure 4-7. If you don't see a pull quote box, make sure you added the <span> tag in step 10 correctly. Also, check out the tips on page 34 for fixing a malfunctioning program. You can find a completed version of this tutorial in the file *complete_pull-quote.html*.

Action/Reaction: Making Pages Come Alive with Events

W hen you hear people talk about JavaScript, you usually hear the word "interactive" somewhere in the conversation: "JavaScript lets you make interactive web pages." What they're really saying is that JavaScript lets your web pages react to something a visitor does: moving a mouse over a navigation button produces a menu of links; selecting a radio button reveals a new set of form options; clicking a small photo makes the page darken and a larger version of the photo pop onto the screen.

All the different visitor actions that a web page can respond to are called *events*. JavaScript is an *event-driven* language: Without events, your web pages wouldn't be able to respond to visitors or do anything really interesting. It's like your desktop computer. Once you start it up in the morning, it doesn't do you much good until you start opening programs, clicking files, making menu selections, and moving your mouse around the screen.

What Are Events?

Web browsers are programmed to recognize basic actions like the page loading, someone moving a mouse, typing a key, or resizing the browser window. Each of the things that happens to a web page is an *event*. To make your web page interactive, you write programs that respond to events. In this way, you can make a <div> tag appear or disappear when a visitor clicks the mouse, a new image appear when she mouses over a link, or check the contents of a text field when she clicks a form's Submit button.

An event represents the precise moment when something happens. For example, when you click a mouse, the precise moment you release the mouse button, the web browser signals that a *click event* has just occurred. The moment that the web browser indicates that an event has happened is when the event *fires*, as programmers put it.

Web browsers actually fire several events whenever you click the mouse button. First, as soon as you press the mouse button, the mousedown event fires; then, when you let go of the button, the mouseup event fires; and finally, the click event fires (see Figure 5-1).

Note: Understanding when and how these events fire can be tricky. To let you test out different event types, this chapter includes a demo web page with the tutorial files. Open *events.html* (in the *testbed* folder) in a web browser. Then move the mouse, click, and type to see some of the many different events that constantly occur on a web page (see Figure 5-1).

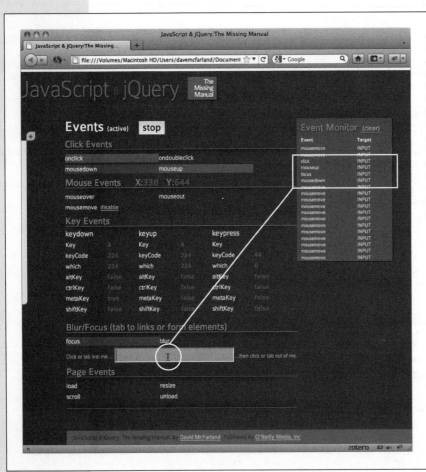

Figure 5-1:
While you may not be aware of it, web browsers are constantly firing off events whenever you type, mouse around, or click. The events .html file (included with the tutorial files in the testbed folder) shows you many of these events in action. For example, clicking into a text field (circled) starts the mousedown, focus, mouseup, *and* click *events.*

Mouse Events

Ever since Steve Jobs introduced the Macintosh in 1984, the mouse has been a critical device for all personal computers. Folks use it to open applications, drag files into folders, select items from menus, and even to draw. Naturally, web browsers provide lots of ways of tracking how a visitor uses a mouse to interact with a web page:

- **click**. The *click* event fires after you click and release the mouse button. You'll commonly assign a click event to a link: For example, a link on a thumbnail image can display a larger version of that image when clicked. However, you're not limited to just links. You can also make any tag on a page respond to an event—even just clicking anywhere on the page.

Note: The click event can also be triggered on links via the keyboard. If you tab to a link, then press the Enter (Return) key, the click event fires.

- **dblclick**. When you press and release the mouse button twice, a double-click (*dblclick*) event fires. It's the same action you use to open a folder or file on your desktop. Double-clicking a web page isn't a usual web-surfer action, so if you use this event, you should make clear to visitors where they can double-click and what will happen after they do. Also note that a double-click event is the same thing as two click events, so don't assign click and double-click events to the same tag. Otherwise, the function for the click will run twice before the double-click function runs.

- **mousedown**. The *mousedown* event is the first half of a click—the moment when you click the button before releasing it. This event is handy for dragging elements around a page. You can let visitors drag items around your web page just like they drag icons around their desktop—by clicking on them (without releasing the button) and moving them, and then releasing the button to drop them.

- **mouseup**. The *mouseup* event is the second half of a click—the moment when you release the button. This event is handy for responding to the moment when you drop an item that has been dragged.

- **mouseover**. When you move your mouse over an element on a page, a *mouseover* event fires. You can assign an event handler to a navigation button using this event and have a submenu pop up when a visitor mouses over the button. (If you're used to the CSS *:hover* pseudo-class, then you know how this event works.)

- **mouseout**. Moving a mouse off an element triggers the *mouseout* event. You can use this event to signal when a visitor has moved her mouse off the page, or to hide a pop-up menu when the mouse travels outside the menu.

- **mousemove**. Logically enough, the *mousemove* event fires when the mouse moves—which means this event fires all of the time. You use this event to track the current position of the cursor on the screen. In addition, you can assign this event to a particular tag on the page—a <div>, for example—and respond only to movements within that tag.

Note: Some web browsers, like Internet Explorer, support many events (*http://msdn2.microsoft.com/en-us/library/ms533051(VS.85).aspx*), but most browsers share just a handful of events.

Document/Window Events

The browser window itself understands a handful of events that fire from when the page loads to when the visitor leaves the page:

- **load.** The *load* event fires when the web browser finishes downloading all of a web page's files: the HTML file itself, plus any linked images, Flash movies, and external CSS and JavaScript files. Web designers have traditionally used this event to start any JavaScript program that manipulated the web page. However, loading a web page and all its files can take a long time if there are a lot of graphics or other large linked files. In some cases, this meant the JavaScript didn't run for quite some time after the page was displayed in the browser. Fortunately, jQuery offers a much more responsive replacement for the load event, as described on page 169.

- **resize.** When you resize your browser window by clicking the maximize button, or dragging the browser's resize handle, the browser triggers a *resize* event. Some designers use this event to change the layout of the page when a visitor changes the size of his browser. For example, after a visitor resizes his browser window, you can check the window's width—if the window is really wide, you could change the design to add more columns of content to fit the space.

Note: Internet Explorer, Opera, and Safari fire multiple resize events as you resize the window, whereas Firefox only fires the resize event a single time after you've let go of the resize handle.

- **scroll.** The *scroll* event is triggered whenever you drag the scroll bar, or use the keyboard (for example, the up, down, home, end, and similar keys) or mouse scroll wheel to scroll a web page. If the page doesn't have scrollbars, no scroll event is ever triggered. Some programmers use this event to help figure out where elements (after a page has scrolled) appear on the screen.

- **unload.** When you click a link to go to another page, close a browser tab, or close a browser window, a web browser fires an *unload* event. It's like the last gasp for your JavaScript program and gives you an opportunity to complete one last action before the visitor moves on from your page. Nefarious programmers have used this event to make it very difficult to ever leave a page. Each time a visitor tries to close the page, a new window appears and the page returns. But you can also use this event for good: For example, a program can warn a visitor about a form he's started to fill out but hasn't submitted, or the program could send form data to the web server to save the data before the visitor exits the page.

Form Events

In the pre-JavaScript days, people interacted with websites mainly via forms created with HTML. Entering information into a form field was really the only way for visitors to provide input to a website. Because forms are still such an important part of the web, you'll find plenty of form events to play with.

- **submit**. Whenever a visitor submits a form, the *submit* event fires. A form might be submitted by clicking the Submit button, or simply by hitting the Enter (Return) key while the cursor is in a text field. You'll most frequently use the submit event with form validation—to make sure all required fields are correctly filled out *before* the data is sent to the web server. You'll learn how to validate forms on page 278.

- **reset**. Although not as common as they used to be, a Reset button lets you undo any changes you've made to a form. It returns a form to the state it was when the page was loaded. You can run a script when the visitor tries to reset the form by using the *reset* event. For example, if the visitor has made some changes to the form, you might want to pop up a dialog box that asks "Are you sure you want to delete your changes?" The dialog box could give the visitor a chance to click a "No" button and prevent the process of resetting (erasing) the form.

- **change**. Many form fields fire a *change* event when their status changes: for instance, when someone clicks a radio button, or makes a selection from a drop-down menu. You can use this event to immediately check the selection made in a menu, or which radio button was selected.

- **focus**. When you tab or click into a text field, it gives the field *focus*. In other words, the browser's attention is now focused on that page element. Likewise, selecting a radio button, or clicking a checkbox, gives those elements focus. You can respond to the focus event using JavaScript. For example, you could add a helpful instruction inside a text field—"Type your full name." When a visitor clicks in the field (giving it focus), you can erase these instructions, so he has an empty field he can fill out.

- **blur**. The *blur* event is the opposite of focus. It's triggered when you exit a currently focused field, by either tabbing or clicking outside the field. The blur event is another useful time for form validation. For example, when someone types her email address in a text field, then tabs to the next field, you could immediately check what she's entered to make sure it's a valid email address.

Note: Focus and blur events also apply to links on a page. When you tab to a link, a focus event fires; when you tab (or click) off the link, the blur event fires.

Keyboard Events

Web browsers also track when visitors use their keyboards, so you can assign commands to keys or let your visitors control a script by pressing various keys. For example, pressing the space bar could start and stop a JavaScript animation.

Unfortunately, the different browsers handle keyboard events differently, even making it hard to tell which letter was entered! (You'll find one technique for identifying which letter was typed on a keyboard in the Tip on page 175.)

- **keypress**. The moment you press a key, the *keypress* event fires. You don't have to let go of the key, either. In fact, the keypress event continues to fire, over and over again, as long as you hold the key down.

- **keydown**. The *keydown* event is like the keypress event—it's fired when you press a key. Actually, it's fired right *before* the keypress event. In Firefox and Opera, the keydown event only fires once. In Internet Explorer and Safari, the keydown event behaves just like the keypress event—it fires over and over as long as the key is pressed.

- **keyup**. Finally, the *keyup* event is triggered when you release a key.

Using Events the jQuery Way

Traditionally, programming with events has been tricky. For a long time, Internet Explorer had a completely different way of handling events than other browsers, requiring two sets of code (one for IE and one for all other browsers) to get your code to work. Fortunately, IE9 now uses the same method for handling events as other browsers, so programming is a lot easier. However, there are still a lot of people using IE8 and earlier, so a good solution that makes programming with events easy and cross-browser compatible is needed. Fortunately, you have jQuery.

As you learned in the last chapter, JavaScript libraries like jQuery solve a lot of the problems with JavaScript programming—including pesky browser incompatibilities. In addition, libraries often simplify basic JavaScript-related tasks. jQuery makes assigning events and *event helpers* (the functions that deal with events) a breeze.

As you saw on page 126, jQuery programming involves (a) selecting a page element and then (b) doing something with that element. In fact, since events are so integral to JavaScript programming, it's better to think of jQuery programming as a three-step process:

1. **Select one or more elements.**

   The last chapter explained how jQuery lets you use CSS selectors to choose the parts of the page you want to manipulate. When assigning events, you want to select the elements that the visitor will interact with. For example, what will a visitor click—a link, a table cell, an image? If you're assigning a mouseover event, what page element does a visitor mouse over to make the action happen?

2. **Assign an event.**

In jQuery, most DOM events have an equivalent jQuery function. So to assign an event to an element, you just add a period, the event name, and a set of parentheses. So, for example, if you want to add a mouseover event to every link on a page, you can do this:

```
$('a').mouseover();
```

To add a click event to an element with an ID of *menu*, you'd write this:

```
$('#menu').click();
```

You can use any of the event names listed on pages 159–162 (and a couple of jQuery-only events discussed on page 171).

After adding the event, you still have some work to do. In order for something to happen when the event fires, you must provide a function for the event.

3. **Pass a function to the event.**

Finally, you need to define what happens when the event fires. To do so, you pass a function to the event. The function contains the commands that will run when the event fires: for example, making a hidden <div> tag visible or highlighting a moused-over element.

You can pass a previously defined function's name like this:

```
$('#start').click(startSlideShow);
```

When you assign a function to an event, you omit the () that you normally add to the end of a function's name to call it. In other words, the following won't work:

```
$('#start').click(startSlideShow())
```

However, the most common way to add a function to an event is to pass an *anonymous function* to the event. You read about anonymous functions on page 148—they're basically a function without a name. The basic structure of an anonymous function looks like this:

```
function() {
// your code here
}
```

The basic structure for using an anonymous function with an event is pictured in Figure 5-2.

Note: To learn more about how to work with jQuery and events, visit *http://api.jquery.com/category/events/*.

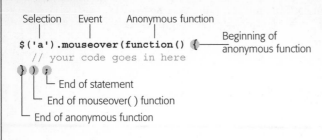

Figure 5-2:
In jQuery, an event works like a function, so you can pass an argument to the event. You can think of an anonymous function, then, as an argument—like a single piece of data that's passed to a function. If you think of it that way, it's easier to see how all of the little bits of punctuation fit together. For example, in the last line, the } marks the end of the function (and the end of the argument passed to the mouseover function); the) is the end of the mouseover() *function; and the semicolon is the end of the entire statement that began with the selector* $('a').

Here's a simple example. Assume you have a web page with a link that has an ID of *menu* applied to it. When a visitor moves his mouse over that link, you want a hidden list of additional links to appear—assume that the list of links has an ID of *submenu*. So what you want to do is add a mouseover event to the menu, and then call a function that shows the submenu. The process breaks down into four steps:

1. **Select the menu:**

   ```
   $('#menu')
   ```

2. **Attach the event:**

   ```
   $('#menu').mouseover();
   ```

3. **Add an anonymous function:**

   ```
   $('#menu').mouseover(function() {

   }); // end mouseover
   ```

   You'll encounter lots of collections of closing brace, closing parenthesis, and semicolons—});—which frequently mark the end of an anonymous function inside a function call. Since you see them everywhere, it's always a good idea to add a JavaScript comment—in this example, // end mouseover—to specify what that trio of punctuation means.

4. **Add the necessary actions (in this case, it's showing the submenu):**

   ```
   $('#menu').mouseover(function() {
    $('#submenu').show();
   }); // end mouseover
   ```

   A lot of people find the crazy nest of punctuation involved with anonymous functions very confusing (that last }); is always a doozy). And it *is* confusing, but the best way to get used to the strange world of JavaScript is through lots of practice, so the following hands-on tutorial should help reinforce the ideas just presented.

Note: The *show()* function is discussed in the next chapter on page 187.

Tutorial: Introducing Events

This tutorial gives you a quick introduction to using events. You'll make the page react to several different types of events so you can get a handle on how jQuery events work and how to use them.

Note: See the note on page 29 for information on how to download the tutorial files.

---

1. **In a text editor, open the file *events_intro.html* in the *chapter05* folder.**

   You'll start at the beginning by adding a link to the jQuery file.

2. **Click in the empty line just above the closing </head> tag and type:**

   ```
   <script src="../_js/jquery-1.6.3.min.js"></script>
   ```

   This line loads the jQuery file from the site. Note that the name of the folder containing the jQuery file is _js (don't forget the underscore character at the beginning). Next, you'll add a set of <script> tags for your programming.

3. **Press Enter (or Return) to create a new line below the jQuery code and add the code listed in bold below:**

   ```
   <script src="../_js/jquery-1.6.3.min.js"></script>
   <script>

   </script>
   ```

   Now add the *document.ready()* function.

4. **Click in the empty line between the <script> tags and add the code in bold:**

   ```
   <script src="../_js/jquery-1.6.3.min.js"></script>
   <script>
   $(document).ready(function() {

   }); // end ready
   </script>
   ```

   Don't forget the JavaScript comment after the });. Even though adding comments requires a little extra typing, they'll be very helpful in identifying the different parts of a program. At this point, you've completed the steps you'll follow whenever you use jQuery on a page.

   Next, it's time to add an event. Your first goal will be simple: have an alert box appear when a visitor clicks anywhere on the page twice. To begin, you need to select the element (the page in this case) that you wish to add the event to.

5. **Click in the empty line inside the *.ready()* function and add the bolded code below:**

   ```
   <script src="../_js/jquery-1.6.3.min.js"></script>
   <script>
   $(document).ready(function() {
     $('html')
   }); // end ready
   </script>
   ```

The *$('html')* selects the HTML element; basically, the entire browser window. Next, you'll add an event.

6. **Type .dblclick(); after the jQuery selector so your code looks like this:**

```
<script src="../_js/jquery-1.6.3.min.js"></script>
<script>
$(document).ready(function() {
  $('html').dblclick(); // end double click
}); // end ready
</script>
```

.dblclick() is a jQuery function that gets the browser ready to make something happen when a visitor double-clicks on the page. The only thing missing is the "make something happen" part, which requires passing an anonymous function as an argument to the *dblclick()* function (if you need a recap on how functions work and what "passing an argument" means, turn to page 102).

7. **Add an anonymous function by typing the code in bold below:**

```
<script src="../_js/jquery-1.6.3.min.js"></script>
<script>
$(document).ready(function() {
  $('html').dblclick(function() {

  }); // end double click
}); // end ready
</script>
```

Don't worry, the rest of this book won't crawl through every tutorial at this glacial pace; but, it's important for you to understand what each piece of the code is doing. The *function( ) { }* is just the outer shell; it doesn't do anything until you add programming inside the { and }: That's the next step.

8. **Finally, add an alert statement:**

```
<script src="../_js/jquery-1.6.3.min.js"></script>
<script>
$(document).ready(function() {
  $('html').dblclick(function() {
    alert('ouch');
  }); // end double click
}); // end ready
</script>
```

If you preview the page in a web browser and double-click anywhere on the page, a JavaScript alert box with the word "ouch" should appear. If it doesn't, double-check your typing to make sure you didn't miss anything.

Note: After that long build-up, having "ouch" appear on the screen probably feels like a let-down. But keep in mind that the *alert()* part of this script is unimportant—it's all the other code you typed that demonstrates the fundamentals of how to use events with jQuery. As you learn more about programming and jQuery, you can easily replace the alert box with a series of actions that (when a visitor double-clicks the page) moves an element across the screen, displays an interactive photo slideshow, or starts a car-racing game.

Now that you've got the basics, you'll try out a few other events.

9. **Add the code in bold below so your script looks like this:**

```
<script src="../_js/jquery-1.6.3.min.js"></script>
<script>
$(document).ready(function() {
  $('html').dblclick(function() {
    alert('ouch');
  }); // end double click
  $('a').mouseover(function() {

  }); // end mouseover
}); // end ready
</script>
```

This code selects all links on a page (that's the *$('a')* part), then adds an anonymous function to the mouseover event. In other words, when someone mouses over any link on the page, something is going to happen.

10. **Add two JavaScript statements to the anonymous function you added in the last step:**

```
<script src="../_js/jquery-1.6.3.min.js"></script>
<script>
$(document).ready(function() {
  $('html').dblclick(function() {
    alert('ouch');
  }); // end double click
  $('a').mouseover(function() {
    var message = "<p>You moused over a link</p>";
    $('.main').append(message);
  }); // end mouseover
}); // end ready
</script>
```

The first line here—*var message = "<p>You moused over a link</p>";*—creates a new variable named message and stores a string in it. The string is an HTML paragraph tag with some text. The next line selects an element on the page with a class name of main (that's the *$('.main')*) and then appends (or adds to the end of that element) the contents of the message variable. The page contains a <div> tag with the class of main, so this code simply adds "You moused over a link" to the end of that div each time a visitor mouses over a link on the page. (See page 139 for a recap of jQuery's *append()* function.)

11. **Save the page, preview it in a browser, and mouse over any link on the page.**

Each time you mouse over a link, a paragraph is added to the page (see Figure 5-3). Now you'll add one last bit of programming: when a visitor clicks on the form button on the page, the browser will change the text that appears on that button.

12. **Lastly, add the code in bold below so that your finished script looks like this:**

```
<script src="../_js/jquery-1.6.3.min.js"></script>
<script>
$(document).ready(function() {
  $('html').dblclick(function() {
```

```
    alert('ouch');
  }); // end double click
  $('a').mouseover(function() {
    var message = "<p>You moused over a link</p>";
    $('.main').append(message);
  }); // end mouseover
  $('#button').click(function() {
    $(this).val("Stop that!");
  }); // end click
}); // end ready
</script>
```

You should understand the basics here: *$('#button')* selects an element with the ID button (the form button in this case), and adds a *click* event to it, so when someone clicks the button, something happens. In this example, the words "Stop that!" appear on the button. Here's how the code inside the anonymous function makes that happen:

On page 149, you saw how to use *$(this)* inside of a loop in jQuery. It's the same idea inside of an event: *$(this)* refers to the element that is responding to the event—the element you select and attach the event to. In this case, this is the form button. (You'll learn more about the jQuery *val()* function on page 261, but basically you use it to read the value from or change the value of a form element. In this example, passing the string "Stop that!" to the *val()* function sets the button's value to "Stop that!")

13. **Save the page, preview it in a browser, and click the form button.**

    The button's text should instantly change (see Figure 5-3). For an added exercise, add the programming to make the text field's background color change to red when a visitor clicks or tabs into it. Here's a hint: You need to (a) select the text field; (b) use the *focus( )* event (page 264); (c) use *$(this)* (as in step 12) to address the text field inside the anonymous function; and (d) use the *.css( )* function (page 143) to change the background color of the text field. You can find the answer (and a complete version of the page) in the *complete_events_intro .html* file in the *chapter05* folder.

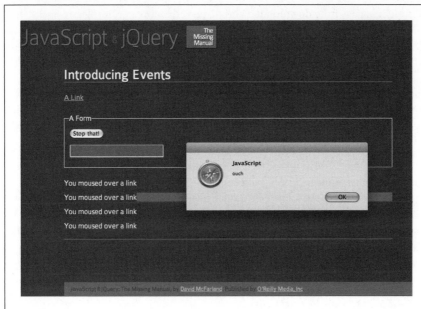

Figure 5-3:
jQuery makes it easy for your web pages to respond to user interaction, such as opening an alert box when the page is clicked twice, adding text to the page in response to mousing over a link, or clicking a form button.

More jQuery Event Concepts

Because events are a critical ingredient for adding interactivity to a web page, jQuery includes some special jQuery-only functions that can make your programming easier and your pages more responsive.

Waiting for the HTML to Load

When a page loads, a web browser tries immediately to run any scripts it encounters. So scripts in the head of a page might run before the page fully loads—you saw this in the Moon Quiz tutorial on page 108, where the page was blank until the script asking the questions finished. Unfortunately, this phenomenon often causes problems. Since a lot of JavaScript programming involves manipulating the contents of a web page—displaying a pop-up message when a particular link is clicked, hiding specific page elements, adding stripes to the rows of a table, and so on—you'll end up with JavaScript errors if your program tries to manipulate elements of a page that haven't yet been loaded and displayed by the browser.

The most common way to deal with that problem has been to use the load event to wait until a page is fully downloaded and displayed before executing any JavaScript. Unfortunately, waiting until a page fully loads before running JavaScript code can create some pretty strange results. The load event only fires *after* all of a web page's files have downloaded—meaning all images, movies, external style sheets, and so on. As a result, on a page with lots of graphics, the visitor might actually be staring at a page for several seconds while the graphics load *before* any JavaScript runs. If the JavaScript makes a lot of changes to the page—for example, styles table rows, hides currently visible menus, or even controls the layout of the page—visitors will suddenly see the page change before their very eyes.

Fortunately, jQuery comes to the rescue. Instead of relying on the load event to trigger a JavaScript program, jQuery has a special function named *ready()* that waits just until the HTML has been loaded into the browser and then runs the page's scripts. That way, the JavaScript can immediately manipulate a web page without having to wait for slow-loading images or movies. (That's actually a complicated and useful feat—another reason to use a JavaScript library.)

You've already used the *ready()* function in a few of the tutorials in this book. The basic structure of the function goes like this:

```
$(document).ready(function() {
  //your code goes here
});
```

Basically, all of your programming code goes inside this function. In fact, the *ready()* function is so fundamental, you'll probably include it on every page on which you use jQuery. You only need to include it once, and it's usually the first and last line of a script. You must place it within a pair of opening and closing <script> tags (it is JavaScript, after all) and after the <script> tag that adds jQuery to the page.

So, in the context of a complete web page, the function looks like this:

```
<!DOCTYPE HTML PUBLIC "-//W3C//DTD HTML 4.01//EN" "http://www.w3.org/TR/
html4/strict.dtd">
<html>
<head>
<meta http-equiv="Content-Type" content="text/html; charset=UTF-8">
<title>Page Title</title>
<script type="text/javascript" src="js/jquery.js"></script>
<script type="text/javascript">
$(document).ready(function() {

    // all of your JavaScript goes in here.

}); // end of ready() function
</script>
</head>
<body>
The web page content...
</body>
</html>
```

Tip: Because the *ready()* function is used nearly anytime you add jQuery to a page, there's a shorthand way of writing it. You can remove the *$(document).ready* part, and just type this:

```
$(function() {
    // do something on document ready
});
```

jQuery Events

jQuery also provides special events for dealing with two very common interactivity issues—moving the mouse over and then off of something, and switching between two actions when clicking.

The hover() *event*

The mouseover and mouseout events are frequently used together. For example, when you mouse over a button, a menu might appear; move your mouse off the button, and the menu disappears. Because coupling these two events is so common, jQuery provides a shortcut way of referring to both. jQuery's *hover()* function works just like any other event, except that instead of taking one function as an argument, it accepts two functions. The first function runs when the mouse travels over the element, and the second function runs when the mouse moves off the element. The basic structure looks like this:

```
$('#selector').hover(function1, function2);
```

You'll frequently see the *hover()* function used with two anonymous functions. That kind of code can look a little weird; the following example will make it clearer. Suppose when someone mouses over a link with an ID of *menu*, you want a (currently invisible) DIV with an ID of *submenu* to appear. Moving the mouse off of the link hides the submenu again. You can use *hover()* to do that:

```
$('#menu').hover(function() {
    $('#submenu').show();
}, function() {
    $('#submenu').hide();
}); // end hover
```

To make a statement containing multiple anonymous functions easier to read, move each function to its own line. So a slightly more readable version of the code above would look like this:

```
$('#menu').hover(
  function() {
    $('#submenu').show();
  }, // end mouseover
  function() {
    $('#submenu').hide();
  } // end mouseout
); // end hover
```

Figure 5-4 diagrams how this code works for the mouseover and mouseout events.

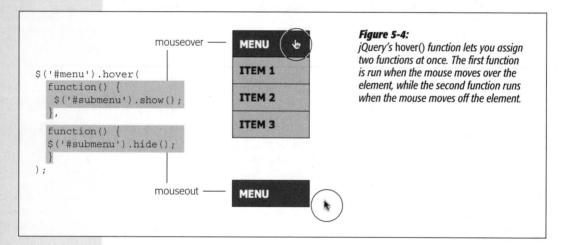

Figure 5-4:
jQuery's hover() *function lets you assign two functions at once. The first function is run when the mouse moves over the element, while the second function runs when the mouse moves off the element.*

If the anonymous function method is just too confusing, you can still use plain old named functions (page 100) to get the job done. First, create a named function to run when the mouseover event triggers; create another named function for the mouseout event; and finally, pass the names of the two functions to the *hover()* function. In other words, you could rewrite the code above like this:

```
function showSubmenu() {
  $('#submenu').show();
}
function hideSubmenu() {
  $('#submenu').hide();
}
$('#menu').hover(showSubmenu, hideSubmenu);
```

If you find this technique easier, then use it. There's no real difference between the two, though some programmers like the fact that by using anonymous functions you can keep all of the code together in one statement, instead of spread out amongst several different statements.

The toggle() *Event*

jQuery's *toggle()* event works identically to the *hover()* event, except that instead of responding to mouseover and mouseout events, it responds to clicks. One click triggers the first function; the next click triggers the second function. Use this event when you want to alternate between two states using clicks. For example, you could make an animation begin when a button is first clicked, and then pause that animation when the button is clicked a second time. Click yet again, and the animation begins again.

For example, say you want to make the *submenu* <div> (from the *hover()* examples above) appear when you first click the link, then disappear when the link is next clicked. Just swap "toggle" for "hover" like this:

```
$('#menu').toggle(
  function() {
    $('#submenu').show();
  }, // end first click
  function() {
    $('#submenu').hide();
  } // end second click
); // end toggle
```

Or, using named functions, like this:

```
function showSubmenu() {
  $('#submenu').show();
}
function hideSubmenu() {
  $('#submenu').hide();
}
$('#menu').toggle(showSubmenu, hideSubmenu);
```

The *toggle( )* function can accept more than two functions as arguments: for example, if you want one thing to happen on the first click, another thing happen on the second click, and yet another thing to happen on the third click. Each function passed to *toggle( )* will respond to its corresponding click. For example, the first function runs on the first click, the second function runs on the second click, the third function runs on the third click, and so on. Once jQuery has executed all of the functions, it returns to the first function on the following click (for example, if you passed three functions to *toggle( )* then, on the fourth click, the first function would run a second time).

The Event Object

Whenever a web browser fires an event, it records information about the event and stores it in an *event object*. The event object contains information that was collected when the event occurred, like the vertical and horizontal coordinates of the mouse, the element on which the event occurred, or whether the Shift key was pressed when the event was triggered.

In jQuery, the event object is available to the function assigned to handling the event. In fact, the object is passed as an argument to the function, so to access it, you just include a parameter name with the function. For example, say you want to find the X and Y position of the cursor when the mouse is clicked anywhere on a page.

```
$(document).click(function(evt) {
  var xPos = evt.pageX;
  var yPos = evt.pageY;
  alert('X:' + xPos + ' Y:' + yPos);
}); // end click
```

The important part here is the *evt* variable. When the function is called (by clicking anywhere in the browser window), the event object is stored in the *evt* variable. Within the body of the function, you can access the different properties of the event object using dot syntax—for example, *evt.pageX* returns the horizontal location of the cursor (in other words, the number of pixels from the left edge of the window).

Note: In this example, *evt* is just a variable name supplied by the programmer. It's not a special JavaScript keyword, just a variable used to store the event object. You could use any name you want such as *event* or simply *e*.

The event object has many different properties, and (unfortunately) the list of properties varies from browser to browser. Table 5-1 lists some common properties.

Table 5-1. *Every event produces an event object with various properties that you can access within the function handling the event*

Event property	Description
pageX	The distance (in pixels) of the mouse pointer from the left edge of the browser window.
pageY	The distance (in pixels) of the mouse pointer from the top edge of the browser window.
screenX	The distance (in pixels) of the mouse pointer from the left edge of the monitor.
screenY	The distance (in pixels) of the mouse pointer from the top edge of the monitor.
shiftKey	Is *true* if the shift key is down when the event occurs.
which	Use with the keypress event to determine the numeric code for the key that was pressed (see tip, next).
target	The object that was the "target" of the event—for example, for a *click()* event, the element that was clicked.
data	A jQuery object used with the *bind()* function to pass data to an event handling function (see page 177).

Tip: If you access the event object's *which* property with the *keypress()* event, you'll get a numeric code for the key pressed. If you want the specific key that was pressed (a, K, 9, and so on), you need to run the *which* property through a JavaScript method that converts the key number to the actual letter, number, or symbol on the keyboard:

```
String.fromCharCode(evt.which)
```

Stopping an Event's Normal Behavior

Some HTML elements have preprogrammed responses to events. A link, for example, usually loads a new web page when clicked; a form's Submit button sends the form data to a web server for processing when clicked. Sometimes you don't want the web browser to go ahead with its normal behavior. For example, when a form is submitted (the *submit()* event), you might want to stop the form data from being sent if the person filling out the form left out important data.

You can prevent the web browser's normal response to an event with the *prevent-Default()* function. This function is actually a part of the event object (see the previous section), so you'll access it within the function handling the event. For example, say a page has a link with an ID of *menu*. The link actually points to another menu page (so that visitors with JavaScript turned off will be able to get to the menu page). However, you've added some clever JavaScript, so when a visitor clicks the link, the menu appears right on the same page. Normally, a web browser would follow the link to the menu page, so you need to prevent its default behavior, like this:

```
$('#menu').click(function(evt){
  // clever javascript goes here
 evt.preventDefault(); // don't follow the link
});
```

Another technique is simply to return the value false at the end of the event function. For example, the following is functionally the same as the code above:

```
$('#menu').click(function(evt){
  // clever javascript goes here
 return false; // don't follow the link
});
```

Removing Events

At times, you might want to remove an event that you had previously assigned to a tag. jQuery's *unbind()* function lets you do just that. To use it, first create a jQuery object with the element you wish to remove the event from. Then add the *unbind()* function, passing it a string with the event name. For example, if you want to prevent all tags with the class *tabButton* from responding to any click events, you can write this:

```
$('.tabButton').unbind('click');
```

Take a look at a short script to see how the *unbind()* function works.

```
1  $('a').mouseover(function() {
2    alert('You moved the mouse over me!');
3  });
4  $('#disable').click(function() {
5    $('a').unbind('mouseover');
6  });
```

Lines 1–3 add a function to the mouseover event for all links (<a> tags) on the page. Moving the mouse over the link opens an alert box with the message "You moved your mouse over me!" However, because the constant appearance of alert messages would be annoying, lines 4–6 let the visitor turn off the alert. When the visitor clicks a tag with an ID of *disable* (a form button, for example), the mouseover events are unbound from all links, and the alert no longer appears.

Note: For more information on jQuery's *unbind()* function, visit *http://api.jquery.com/unbind/*.

POWER USERS' CLINIC

Stopping an Event in Its Tracks

Both Internet Explorer and the W3C event model supported by Firefox, Safari, and Opera let an event pass beyond the element that first receives the event. For example, say you've assigned an event helper for click events on a particular link; when you click the link, the click event fires and a function runs. The event, however, doesn't stop there. Each ancestor element (a tag that wraps around the element that's clicked) can also respond to that same click. So if you've assigned a click event helper for a <div> tag that the link is inside, the function for that <div> tag's event will run as well.

This concept, known as *event bubbling*, means that more than one element can respond to the same action. Here's another example: Say you add a click event to an image so when the image is clicked, a new graphic replaces it. The image is inside a <div> tag to which you've also assigned a click event. In this case, an alert box appears when the <div> is clicked. Now when you click the image, both functions will run. In other words, even though you clicked the image, the <div> also receives the click event.

You probably won't encounter this situation too frequently, but when you do, the results can be disconcerting. Suppose in the example in the previous paragraph, you don't want the <div> to do anything when the image is clicked. In this case, you have to stop the click event from passing on to the <div> tag without stopping the event in the function that handles the click event on the image. In other words, when the image is clicked, the function assigned to the image's click event should swap in a new graphic, but then stop the click event.

jQuery provides a function called *stopPropagation()* that prevents an event from passing onto any ancestor tags. The function is a method of the event object (see page 173), so you access it within an event-handling function:

```
$('#theLink').click(function(evt) {
  // do something
  evt.stopPropagation(); // stop event from
continuing
});
```

Advanced Event Management

You can live a long, happy programming life using just the jQuery event methods and concepts discussed on the previous pages. But if you really want to get the most out of jQuery's event-handling techniques, then you'll want to learn about the *bind()* function.

Note: If your head is still aching from the previous section, you can skip ahead to the tutorial on page 180 until you've gained a bit more experience with event handling.

The *bind()* method is a more flexible way of dealing with events than jQuery's event-specific functions like *click()* or *mouseover()*. It not only lets you specify an event and a function to respond to the event, but also lets you pass additional data for the event-handling function to use. This lets different elements and events (for example, a click on one link, or a mouseover on an image) pass different information to the same event-handling function—in other words, one function can act differently based on which event is triggered.

The basic format of the *bind()* function is the following:

```
$('#selector').bind('click', myData, functionName);
```

The first argument is a string containing the name of the event (like click, mouseover, or any of the other events listed on page 159). The second argument is the data you wish to pass to the function—either an object literal or a variable containing an object literal. An object literal (discussed on page 145) is basically a list of property names and values:

```
{
    firstName : 'Bob',
    lastName : 'Smith'
}
```

You can store an object literal in a variable like so:

```
var linkVar = {message:'Hello from a link'};
```

The third argument passed to the *bind()* function is another function—the one that does something when the event is triggered. The function can either be an anonymous function or named function—in other words, this part is the same as when using a regular jQuery event, as described on page 163.

Note: Passing data using the *bind()* function is optional. If you want to use *bind()* merely to attach an event and function, then leave the data variable out:

```
$('selector').bind('click', functionName);
```

This code is functionally the same as:

```
$('selector').click(functionName);
```

Suppose you wanted to pop up an alert box in response to an event, but you wanted the message in the alert box to be different based on which element triggered the event. One way to do that would be to create variables with different object literals inside, and then send the variables to the *bind()* function for different elements. Here's an example:

```
var linkVar = { message:'Hello from a link'};
var pVar = { message:'Hello from a paragraph'};
function showMessage(evt) {
    alert(evt.data.message);
}
$('a').bind('click',linkVar,showMessage);
$('p').bind('mouseover',pVar,showMessage);
```

Figure 5-5 breaks down how this code works. It creates two variables, *linkVar* on the first line and *pVar* on the second line. Each variable contains an object literal, with the same property name, *message*, but different message text. A function, *showMessage()*, takes the event object (see page 173) and stores it in a variable named *evt*. That function runs the *alert()* command, displaying the *message* property (which is itself a property of the event object's *data* property). Keep in mind that *message* is the name of the property defined in the object literal.

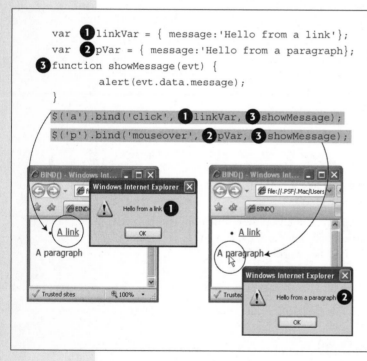

Figure 5-5:
jQuery's bind() *function lets you pass data to the function responding to the event. That way, you can use a single named function for several different elements (even with different types of events), while letting the function use data specific to each event helper.*

Other Ways to Use the *bind()* Function

jQuery's *bind()* function gives you a lot of programming flexibility. In addition to the techniques listed in the previous section, it also lets you tie two or more events to the same function. For example, say you write a program that makes a large image appear on the screen when a visitor clicked a thumbnail image (the common "light-box" effect found on thousands of websites; you'll learn how it works on page 222). You want the larger image to disappear when the visitor either clicks anywhere on the page or hits any key on the keyboard (providing both options makes your program respond to people who prefer the keyboard over the mouse and vice-versa). Here's some code that does that:

```
$(document).bind('click keypress', function() {
  $('#lightbox').hide( );
}); // end bind
```

The important part is *'click keypress'*. By providing multiple event names, each sepa-rated by a space, you're telling jQuery to run the anonymous function when any of the events in the list happen. In this case, when either the *click* or *keypress* event fires on the document.

In addition, if you want to attach several events that each trigger different actions, you don't need to use the *bind()* function multiple times. In other words, if you want to make one thing happen when a visitor clicks an element, and another when a visitor mouses over that same element, you might be tempted to write this:

```
$('#theElement').bind('click', function() {
  // do something interesting
}); // end bind
$('#theElement').bind('mouseover', function() {
  // do something else interesting
}); // end bind
```

You can do the same thing by passing an object literal (see page 145) to the *bind()* function that is composed of an event name, followed by a colon, followed by an anonymous function. Here's the code above rewritten, calling the *bind()* function only once and passing it an object literal (in bold):

```
$('#theElement').bind({
    'click' : function() {
        // do something interesting
      }, // end click function
    'mouseover' : function() {
        // do something interesting
      }; // end  mouseover function
}); // end bind
```

Note: As if that's not enough to digest, jQuery provides still other ways to attach events to elements. In particular, the *delegate( )* function comes in very handy whenever you wish to attach an event to an ele-ment that's added to a page after the page loads (that is, an element that's either added to the page with JavaScript programming, or that's downloaded to the page using the Ajax techniques described in Part 4 of this book). You can read about the *delegate()* function starting on page 421.

Tutorial: A One-Page FAQ

"Frequently Asked Questions" pages are a common sight on the web. They can help improve customer service by providing immediate answers 24/7. Unfortunately, most FAQ pages are either one very long page full of questions and complete answers, or a single page of questions that link to separate answer pages. Both solutions slow down the visitors' quest for answers: in the first case, forcing a visitor to scroll down a long page for the question and answer she's after, and in the second case, making the visitor wait for a new page to load.

In this tutorial, you'll solve this problem by creating a JavaScript-driven FAQ page. All of the questions will be visible when the page loads, so it's easy to locate a given question. The answers, however, are hidden until the question is clicked—then the desired answer fades smoothly into view (see Figure 5-6).

Overview of the Task

The JavaScript for this task will need to accomplish several things:

- When a question is clicked, the corresponding answer will appear.
- When a question whose answer is visible is clicked, then the answer should disappear.

In addition, you'll want to use JavaScript to hide all of the answers when the page loads. Why not just use CSS to hide the answers to begin with? For example, setting the CSS *display* property to *none* for the answers is another way to hide the answers. The problem with this technique is what happens to visitors who don't have JavaScript turned on: They won't see the answers when the page loads, nor will they be able to make them visible by clicking the questions. To make your pages viewable to both those with JavaScript enabled and those with JavaScript turned off, it's best to use JavaScript to hide any page content.

Note: See the note on page 29 for information on how to download the tutorial files.

The Programming

1. **In a text editor, open the file *faq.html* in the *chapter05* folder.**

    This file already contains a link to the jQuery file, and the *$(document).ready()* function (page 169) is in place. First, you'll hide all of the answers when the page loads.

2. **Click in the empty line after the *$(document).ready()* function, and then type *$('.answer').hide();*.**

    The text of each answer is contained within a <div> tag with the class of *answer* applied to it. This one line of code selects each <div> and hides it (the *hide()*

function is discussed on page 187). Save the page and open it in a web browser. The answers should all be hidden.

The next step is determining which elements you need to add an event listener to. Since the answer appears when a visitor clicks the question, you must select every question in the FAQ. On this page, each question is a <h2> tag in the page's main body.

3. **Press Return to create a new line and add the code in bold below to the script:**

```
<script src="../_js/jquery-1.6.3.min.js"></script>
<script>
$(document).ready(function() {
  $('.answer').hide();
  $('.main h2')
}); // end of ready()
</script>
```

That's a basic descendent selector used to target every <h2> tag inside an element with a class of *main* (so it doesn't affect any <h2> tags elsewhere on the page). Now it's time to add an event. The click event is a good candidate; however, you can better meet your requirements—that clicking the question either shows or hides the answer—using the jQuery *toggle()* function (see page 173). This function lets you switch between two different functions with each mouse click.

4. **Immediately following the code you typed in step 2 (on the same line), type** *.toggle(.*

This code marks the beginning of the *toggle()* function, which takes two anonymous functions (page 148) as arguments. The first anonymous function runs on the first click, the second function runs on the next click. You'll get the basic structure of these functions in place first.

5. **Press Return to create a new line, and then type:**

```
function() {

}
```

This code is the basic shell of the function and represents the first argument passed to the *toggle()* function. You'll add the basic structure for the second function next.

6. **Add the code in bold, so that your script looks like this:**

```
1    <script src="../_js/jquery-1.6.3.min.js"></script>
2    <script>
3    $(document).ready(function() {
4      $('.answer').hide();
5      $('#main h2').toggle(
6        function() {
7
8        },
9        function() {
10
11       }
```

```
12    ); // end of toggle()
13    }); // end of ready()
14    </script>
```

Be sure you don't leave out the comma at the end of line 8 above. Remember that the two functions here act like arguments passed to a function (page 102). When you call a function, you separate each argument with a comma, like this: *prompt('Question', 'type here')*. In other words, the comma on line 8 separates the two functions. (You can leave out the comment on line 12—// *end of toggle*— if you want. It's just there to make clear that this line marks the end of the *toggle()* function.)

Now it's time to add the effect you're after: The first time the <h2> tag is clicked, the associated answer needs to appear. While each question is contained in a <h2> tag, the associated answer is in a <div> tag immediately following the <h2> tag. In addition, the <div> has a class of *answer* applied to it. So what you need is a way to find the <div> tag following the clicked <h2>.

7. **Within the first function (marked as line 6 in step 5 above), add $(this) .next ('.answer').fadeIn(); to the script.**

As discussed on page 149, *$(this)* refers to the element currently responding to the event—in this case, a particular <h2> tag. jQuery provides several functions to make moving around a page's structure easier. The *.next()* function finds the tag immediately following the current tag. In other words, it finds the tag following the <h2> tag. You can further refine this search by passing an additional selector to the *.next()* function—the code *.next('answer')* finds the first tag following the <h2> that also has the class *answer* applied to it. Finally, *.fadeIn()* gradually fades the answer into view (the *fadeIn()* function is discussed on page 187).

Note: The *.next()* function is just one of the many jQuery functions that help you navigate through a page's DOM. To learn about other helpful functions, visit *http://docs.jquery.com/Traversing*.

Now's a good time to save the page and check it out in a web browser. Click one of the questions on the page—the answer below it should open (if it doesn't, double-check your typing and refer to the troubleshooting tips on page 34).

In the next step, you'll complete the second half of the toggling effect—hiding the answer when the question is clicked a second time.

8. **Add the code bolded on line 10 below:**

```
1    <script src="../_js/jquery-1.6.3.min.js"></script>
2    <script>

3    $(document).ready(function() {
4      $('.answer').hide();
5      $('#main h2').toggle(
6        function() {
7          $(this).next('.answer').fadeIn();
8        },
```

```
9      function() {
10        $(this).next('.answer').fadeOut();
11      }
12    ); // end of toggle()
13  }); // end of ready()
14  </script>
```

Now the answer fades out on a second click. Save the page and give it a try. While the page functions fine, there's one nice design touch you can add. Currently, each question has a small plus sign to the left of it. The plus sign is a common icon used to mean, "Hey, there's more here." To indicate that a visitor can click to hide the answer, replace the plus sign with a minus sign. You can do it easily by just adding and removing classes from the <h2> tags.

9. **Add two final lines of code (lines 8 and 12 below). The finished code should look like this:**

```
1   <script src="../_js/jquery-1.6.3.min.js"></script>
2   <script>
3   $(document).ready(function() {
4     $('.answer').hide();
5     $('#main h2').toggle(
6       function() {
7         $(this).next('.answer').fadeIn();
8         $(this).addClass('close');
9       },
10      function() {
11        $(this).next('.answer').fadeOut();
12        $(this).removeClass('close');
13      }
15    ); //end toggle
15  });
16  </script>
```

This code simply adds a class named *close* to the <h2> tag when it's clicked the first time, then removes that class when it's clicked a second time. The minus sign icon is defined within the style sheet as a background image. (Once again, CSS makes JavaScript programming easier.)

Save the page and try it out. Now when you click a question, not only does the answer appear, but the question icon changes (see Figure 5-6).

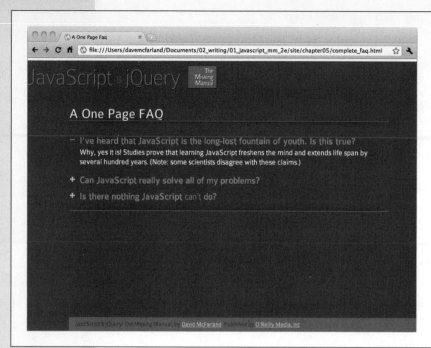

Figure 5-6:
With just a few lines of JavaScript, you can make page elements appear or disappear with a click of the mouse.

Animations and Effects

I n the last two chapters, you learned the basics of using jQuery: how to load the jQuery library, select page elements, and respond to events like a visitor clicking on a button or mousing over a link. Most jQuery programs involve three steps: selecting an element on the page, attaching an event to that element, and then responding to that event by doing something. In this chapter, you'll start learning about the "doing something" part with jQuery's built-in effect and animation functions. You'll also get a little CSS-refresher covering a few important CSS properties related to creating visual effects.

jQuery Effects

Making elements on a web page appear and disappear is a common JavaScript task. Drop-down navigation menus, pop-up tooltips, and automated slideshows all rely on the ability to show and hide elements when you want to. jQuery supplies a handful of functions that achieve the goal of hiding and showing elements.

To use each of these effects, you apply them to a jQuery selection, like any other jQuery function. For example, to hide all tags with a class of *submenu*, you can write this:

```
$('.submenu').hide();
```

Each effect function also can take an optional speed setting and a *callback* function. The speed represents the amount of time the effect takes to complete, while a callback is a function that runs when the effect is finished. (See "Performing an Action After an Effect is Completed" on page 196 for details on callbacks.)

To assign a speed to an effect, you supply one of three string values—*'fast'*, *'normal'*, or *'slow'*—or a number representing the number of milliseconds the effect takes

(1,000 is 1 second, 500 is half of a second, and so on). For example, the code to make an element fade out of view slowly would look like this:

```
$('element').fadeOut('slow');
```

Or if you want the element to fade out *really* slowly, over the course of 10 seconds:

```
$('element').fadeOut(10000);
```

When you use an effect to make an element disappear, the element isn't actually removed from the web browser's understanding of the page. The element still exists in the DOM, or Document Object Model (page 127). The element's code is still in the browser's memory, but its *display* setting (same as the CSS display setting) is set to *none*. Because of that setting, the element no longer takes up any visual space, so other content on the page may move into the position previously filled by the hidden element. You can see all of the jQuery effects in action on the *effects.html* file included in the *testbed* tutorial folder (see Figure 6-1).

Note: The keywords used for setting the speed of an effect—'fast,' 'normal,' and 'slow'—are the same as 200 milliseconds, 400 milliseconds, and 600 milliseconds. So

```
$('element').fadeOut('slow');
```

is the same as

```
$('element').fadeOut(600);
```

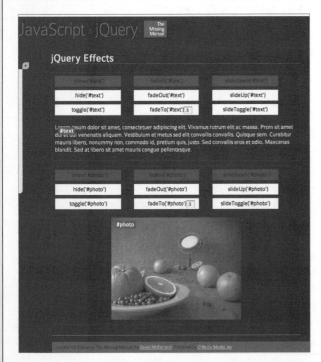

Figure 6-1:
You can test out jQuery's visual effects on the effects.html file located in the testbed folder. Click the function text—fadeOut('#photo'), for example—to see how text and images look when they fade out, slide up, or appear. Some effects will appear in grey to indicate that they don't apply to the element. For example, it doesn't make much sense for the code to make a photo appear if it's already visible on the page.

Basic Showing and Hiding

jQuery provides three functions for basic hiding and showing of elements:

- *show()* makes a hidden element visible. It doesn't have any effect if the element is already visible on the page. If you don't supply a speed value, the element appears immediately. However, if you supply a speed value—*show(1000)*, for example—the element animates from the top-left corner down to the bottom-left corner.

- *hide()* hides a visible element. It doesn't have any effect if the element is already hidden, and as with the *show()* function, if you don't supply a speed value, the element immediately disappears. However, with a speed value the element animates out of view in a kind of shrinking motion.

- *toggle()* switches an element's current display value. If the element is currently visible, *toggle()* hides the element; if the element is hidden, then *toggle()* makes the element appear. This function is ideal when you want to have a single control (like a button) alternately show and hide an element.

In the tutorial on page 180 of the previous chapter, you saw both the *hide()* and *toggle()* functions in action. That script uses *hide()* to make all of the answers on an FAQ page disappear when the page's HTML loads, then uses *toggle()* to alternately show and hide those answers when you click the question.

Fading Elements In and Out

For a more dramatic effect, you can fade an element out or fade it in—in either case, you're just changing the opacity of the element over time. jQuery provides three fade-related functions:

- *fadeIn()* makes a hidden element fade into view. First, the space for the element appears on the page (this may mean other elements on the page move out of the way); then the element gradually becomes visible. This function doesn't have any effect if the element is already visible on the page. If you don't supply a speed value, the element fades in using the *'normal'* setting (400 milliseconds).

- *fadeOut()* hides a visible element by making it fade out of view like a ghost. It doesn't have any effect if the element is already hidden, and like the *fadeIn()* function, if you don't supply a speed value, the element fades out over the course of 400 milliseconds.

- *fadeToggle()* combines both fade in and fade out effects. If the element is currently hidden, it fades into view; if it's currently visible, the element fades out of view. You could use this function to make an instruction box appear or disappear from a page. For example, say you have a button with the word "instructions" on it. When a visitor clicks the button, a div with instructions fades into view; clicking the button a second time fades the instructions out of view. To make the box fade in or out over the course of half a second (500 milliseconds), you could write this code:

```
$('#button').click(function() {
    $('#instructions').fadeToggle(500);
}); // end click
```

- *fadeTo()* works slightly differently than other effect functions. It fades an image to a specific opacity. For example, you can make an image fade so that it's semi-transparent. Unlike other effects, you must supply a speed value. In addition, you supply a second value from 0 to 1 that indicates the opacity of the element. For example, to fade all paragraphs to 75% opacity, you'd write this:

```
$('p').fadeTo('normal',.75);
```

This function changes an element's opacity regardless of whether the element is visible or invisible. For example, say you fade a currently hidden element to 50% opacity, the element fades into view at 50% opacity. If you hide a semitransparent element and then make it reappear, its opacity setting is recalled.

If you fade an element to 0 opacity, the element is no longer visible, but the space it occupied on the page remains. In other words, unlike the other disappearing effects, fading to 0 will leave an empty spot on the page where the element is.

Sliding Elements

For a little more visual action, you can also slide an element in and out of view. The functions are similar to the fading elements in that they make page elements appear and disappear from view, and may have a speed value:

- *slideDown()* makes a hidden element slide into view. First, the top of the element appears and anything below the element is pushed down as the rest of the element appears. It doesn't have any effect if the element is already visible on the page. If you don't supply a speed value, the element slides in using the *'normal'* setting (400 milliseconds).

- *slideUp()* removes the element from view by hiding the bottom of the element and moving anything below the element up until the element disappears. It doesn't have any effect if the element is already hidden, and as with the *slideDown()* function, if you don't supply a speed value, the element slides out over the course of 400 milliseconds.

- *slideToggle()* applies the *slideDown()* function if the element is currently hidden, and the *slideUp()* function if the element is visible. This function lets you have a single control (like a button) both show and hide an element.

Absolute Positioning with CSS

Normally, when you hide an element on a web page, other elements move to fill the space. For example, if you hide an image on a page, the image disappears, and content below that image moves up the page. Likewise, making an element appear forces other content to move to make room for the newly displayed element. You may not want content on your page to jump around like that. In that case, you can turn to CSS and *absolute positioning* to place an element outside the flow of normal page content. In other words, you can have a div, image, or paragraph appear on top of the page, as if sitting on its own separate layer, using the CSS position property.

To make an element appear above the page, give it a position value of absolute. You can then specify the placement for that element on the page using the left, right, top and/or bottom properties. For example, say you have a <div> tag containing a login form. The login form won't normally be visible, but when a visitor clicks a link, that form slides into place, sitting above other content on the page. You could position that div like this:

```
#login {
    position: absolute;
    left: 536px;
    top: 0;
    width: 400px;
}
```

This style places the div at the top of the browser window and 536px from the left edge. You can also place an element from the right edge of the browser window using the right property, or in relationship to the bottom edge of the browser window using the bottom property.

Of course, you may want to place an element in relation to something other than the browser window. For example, pop-up tooltips are usually positioned in relation to some other element: A word on the page might have a ? next to it, that when clicked, opens a small box with a definition for that word. In this case, the tooltip needs to be positioned not in relationship to the top, left, right, or bottom of the browser window, but next to the word. To achieve this, you need to supply a position of relative to an element that surrounds the absolutely positioned item. For example, look at this HTML:

```
<span class="word">Heffalump

<span class="definition">An imaginary, el-
ephant-like creative from Winnie the Pooh</
span>

</span>
```

To make the definition span appear below the word, you first need to position the word span relatively, and then position the definition absolutely like this:

```
.word { position: relative; }
.definition {
    position: absolute;
    bottom: -30px;
    left: 0;
    width: 200px;
}
```

For more information on absolute positioning, visit *www .elated.com/articles/css-positioning/* or pick up a copy of CSS: The Missing Manual.

Tutorial: Login Slider

In this tutorial, you'll get a little practice with using jQuery effects by creating a common user interface element: a panel that slides into and out of view with a click of the mouse (see Figure 6-2).

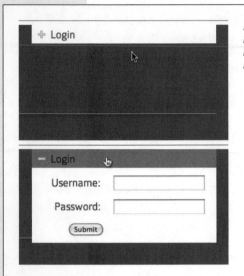

Figure 6-2:
Now you don't see it, now you do. The login form is normally hidden from view (top), but a simple mouse click reveals the form, ready for the visitor to fill out and log on.

The basic task is rather simple:

1. **Select the paragraph with the "Login" message on it.**

   Remember that a lot of jQuery programming first begins with selecting an element on the page. In this case, the "Login" paragraph will receive clicks from a visitor.

2. **Attach a *click* event to that paragraph.**

   JavaScript isn't interactive without events: The visitor needs to interact with the selection (the Login paragraph) to make something happen.

3. **Toggle the display of the form on and off.**

   The previous two steps are just review (but necessary for so much of jQuery programming). This last step is where you'll use the effects you've learned about. You can make the form instantly appear (the *show()* function), slide into view (the *slideDown()* function), or fade into view (the *fadeIn()* function.)

Note: See the note on page 29 for information on how to download the tutorial files.

The Programming

1. **In a text editor, open the file *signup.html* in the *chapter06* folder.**

   This file already contains a link to the jQuery file, and the *$(document).ready()* function (page 169) is in place. First, you'll select the paragraph with the "Login" text.

2. **Click in the empty line after the *$(document).ready()* function, and then type *$('#open')*.**

   The "Login" text is inside a paragraph tag with the ID of open: <p id="open" >Login</p>, so the code you just typed will select that element. Now, it's time to add an event handler.

3. **Add the bolded code below, so that the script looks like this:**

   ```
   $(document).ready(function() {
       $('#open').click(function() {

       }); // end click
   }); // end ready
   ```

   This code adds a click handler, so each time a visitor clicks on the paragraph, something happens. In this case, the form should appear when clicked once and then disappear when clicked again, appear on the next click, and so on. In other words, the form toggles between visible and invisible. jQuery offers three functions that will serve this purpose: *toggle()*, *fadeToggle()*, and *slideToggle()*. The difference is merely in how the effect looks.

4. **Click in the empty line inside the click function and type:**

   ```
   $('#login form').slideToggle(300);
   ```

   This code selects the login form, then slides it into view if it currently isn't visible, and then slides it back out of view if it is visible. Finally, you'll change the class of the paragraph, so that the "Login" can change appearance using a CSS class style.

5. **Add the code in bold below, so the finished script looks like this:**

   ```
   1  $(document).ready(function() {
   2      $('#open').click(function() {
   3          $('#login form').slideToggle(300);
   4          $(this).toggleClass('close');
   5      }); // end click
   6  }); // end ready
   ```

   As you'll recall from page 149, when you're inside of an event handler, you can use *$(this)* to refer to the element that responds to the event. In this case, *$(this)* refers to the paragraph the visitor clicks on—the *$('#open')* in line 2 above. The *toggleClass()* function simply adds or removes a class from the element. Like the other toggle functions, *toggleClass()* adds the specified class if it's missing or removes the class if it's present. In this example, there's a class style—.close—in a style sheet on the page. (Look in the <head> of the file and you can see the style and what it does.)

6. **Save the page and preview it in a web browser.**

Make sure you click the "Login" paragraph several times to see how it works. You'll find a finished version of the tutorial—*complete_signup.html*—in the *chapter06* folder. Try out the other toggle effects as well, by replacing *slideToggle()* with *toggle()* or *fadeToggle()*.

But what if you want two different effects? One for making the form appear—slide the form down into view, for example—and a different effect to make it disappear—fade out of view, for example. The code in step 5 won't exactly work, since the *click()* function doesn't really let you choose between two different actions. However, as you read on page 173, jQuery offers a special event—the *toggle()* event—for dealing with this kind of situation. Not to be confused with the *toggle() effect*—which makes an element appear and disappear—the *toggle()* event lets you run different code alternating between odd and even clicks. So on the first click, the form appears, and on the second click, it disappears.

To make the form slide into view, then fade out of view on alternating clicks, you use this code:

```
$(document).ready(function() {
    $('#open').toggle(
        function() {
            $('#login form').slideDown(300);
            $(this).addClass('close');
        },
        function() {
            $('#login form').fadeOut(600);
            $(this).removeClass('close');
        }
    ); // end toggle
}); // end ready
```

Animations

You aren't limited to just the built-in effects jQuery supplies. Using the *animate()* function, you can animate any CSS property that accepts numeric values such as pixel, em, or percentage values. For example, you can animate the size of text, the position of an element on a page, the opacity of an object, or the width of a border.

Note: jQuery, by itself, can't animate color—for example, the color of text, background color, or border color. However, the jQuery *Color* plug-in can do this. We've included a copy of the plug-in with the tutorials, and you'll see an example of animated colors in action on page 198. You can get the latest version of the color plug-in at *https://github.com/jquery/jquery-color*. (In a nutshell, a plug-in is a separate file containing additional JavaScript programming that adds features to jQuery.)

To use this function, you must pass an object literal (see page 145) containing a list of CSS properties you wish to change and the values you wish to animate to. For example, say you want to animate an element by moving it 650 pixels from the left edge of the page, changing its opacity to 50%, and enlarging its font size to 24 pixels. The following code creates an object with those properties and values:

```
{
    left: '650px',
    opacity: .5,
    fontSize: '24px'
}
```

Note that you only have to put the value in quotes if it includes a measurement like px, em, or %. In this example, you need quotes around '*650px*' since it contains '*px*', but not around the opacity value, since .5 is simply a number and doesn't contain any letters or other characters. Likewise, putting quotes around the property (left, opacity, and fontSize) is optional.

Note: JavaScript doesn't accept hyphens for CSS properties. For example, *font-size* is a valid CSS property, but JavaScript doesn't understand it because the hyphen has special meaning (it's JavaScript's minus operator). When using CSS properties in JavaScript, remove the hyphen and capitalize the first letter of the word following the hyphen. For example, *font-size* becomes *fontSize*, and *border-left-width* becomes *borderLeftWidth*. However, jQuery lets you use the hyphen, but only if you put the property name in quotes like this:

```
{
    'font-size': '24px',
    'border-left-width': '2%'
}
```

Suppose you want to animate an element with an ID of *message* using these settings. You can use the *animate()* function like this:

```
$('#message').animate(
{
    left: '650px',
    opacity: .5,
    fontSize: '24px'
},
1500
);
```

The *animate()* function can take several arguments. The first is an object literal containing the CSS properties you wish to animate. The second is the duration (in milliseconds) of the animation. In the above example, the animation lasts 1,500 milliseconds, or 1.5 seconds.

Note: In order to animate a position of an element using the CSS *left, right, top,* or *bottom* properties, you must set that element's CSS *position* property to either *absolute* or *relative*. Those are the only two positioning properties that let you assign positioning values to them (see the box on page 189).

You can also set a property relative to its current value using += or -= as part of the animation options. For example, say you want to animate an element by moving it 50 pixels to the right each time you click on it. Here's how:

```
$('#moveIt').click(function() {
  $(this).animate(
    {
      left:'+=50px'
    },
  1000);
});
```

Note: You can't animate the border-width property. It's a shorthand property that sets the width of all four borders at once:

```
border-width: 2px 5px 2px 6px;
```

If you want to animate the width of a border, you need to use the full name for each border you wish to animate. For example, if you want to animate all four borders so that they end up 20 pixels wide each, you need to add each border width property (*border-width-left, border-width-top,* and so on) to the object literal passed to the animate function:

```
$('#element').animate(

  {

    borderTop: 20px,

    borderRight: 20px,

    borderBottom: 20px,

    borderLeft: 20px

  }, 1000 );
```

Easing

The jQuery effects functions (*slideUp(), fadeIn(),* an so on) and the *animation()* function accept another argument that controls the speed during the animation: *easing,* which refers to the speed during different points of the animation. For example, while moving an element across the page, you could have the element's movement start slowly, then get really fast, and finally slow down as the animation completes. Adding easing to an animation can make it more visually interesting and dynamic.

jQuery includes only two easing methods: swing and linear. The linear method provides a steady animation so each step of the animation is the same (for example, if you're animating an element across the screen, each step will be the same distance as the previous one). Swing is a bit more dynamic, as the animation starts off a bit more quickly, then slows down. Swing is the normal setting, so if you don't specify any easing, jQuery uses the swing method.

The easing method is the second argument for any jQuery effect, so to make an element slide up using the linear method, you'd write code like this:

```
$('#element').slideUp(1000,'linear');
```

When using the *animate()* function, the easing method is the third argument after the object literal containing the CSS properties you wish to animate, and the overall speed of the animation. For example, to use the linear easing method with the animation code from page 193, you'd write:

```
$('#message').animate(
{
  left: '650px',
  opacity: .5,
  fontSize: '24px'
},
1500,
'linear'
);
```

You're not limited to the two easing methods jQuery supplies, however. Thanks to the industrious work of other programmers, you can add a whole bunch of other easing methods—some quite dramatic and fun to watch. Using the jQuery easing plug-in (available at *http://gsgd.co.uk/sandbox/jquery/easing/* and in the tutorials download), you can effect an animation in some pretty dramatic ways. For example, the easeInBounce method makes an animation rapidly change in speed and direction as if the element where bouncing.

Tip: There are many different easing methods available with the easing plug-in, and most of the names don't really help you understand what the easing method will look like. To get a better visual understanding of the different easing options, visit *www.robertpenner.com/easing/easing_demo.html,* where you can try each method yourself.

To use the easing plug-in (which is an external JavaScript file), you attach the file to your page following the code that links to the jQuery library. Once you've linked to the easing plug-in, you can use any of the easing methods available (see *http://gsgd.co.uk/sandbox/jquery/easing/* for a complete list). For example, say you want to make a div tag grow in size when a visitor clicks on it, and you want to make the animation more interesting by using the easeInBounce method. Assuming the div has an ID of *animate* applied to it, your code may look like this:

```
1  <script src="js/jquery-1.6.3.min.js"></script>
2  <script src="js/jquery.easing.1.3.js"></script>
3  <script>
4  $(document).ready(function() {
5    $('#animate').click(function() {
6      $(this).animate(
7        {
8          width: '400px',
9          height: '400px'
10       },
11       1000,
12       'easeInBounce'); // end animate
13   }); // end click
14 }); // end ready
15 </script>
```

Lines 1 and 2 load jQuery and the easing plug-in. Line 4 is the every-present *ready()* function (page 169), and line 5 adds a click handler to the div. The heart of the action are lines 6–12. As you'll recall from page 149, when you're inside of an event, *$(this)* refers to the element that's responding to the event—in this case, the <div> tag. In other words, by clicking the div, you also animate that div by changing its width and height (lines 8 and 9). Line 11 makes the animation occur over 1 second (1000 milliseconds), and line 12 sets the easing method to easeInBounce (you can substitute any easing method, like *easeInOutSine, easeInCubic,* and so on).

Note: You can find an example of this code in action in the *chapter06* folder of the tutorial files. Open the file *easing_example1.html* in a web browser. The file *easing_example2.html* shows how to use the *toggle()* event (page 173) to apply two different easing methods to the div.

Performing an Action After an Effect Is Completed

Sometimes you want to do something once an effect is complete. For example, suppose when a particular photo fades into view, you want a caption to appear. In other words, the caption must pop onto the page after the photo finishes fading into view. Normally, effects aren't performed one after the other; they all happen at the same time they're called. So if your script has one line of code to fade the photo into view, and another line of code to make the caption appear, the caption will appear while the photo is still fading in.

To get around this dilemma, you can pass a *callback function* to any effect. That's a function that runs only after the effect is completed. The callback function is passed as the second argument to most effects (the third argument for the *fadeTo()* function).

For example, say you have an image on a page with an ID of *photo*, and a paragraph below it with an ID of *caption*. To fade the photo into view and then make the caption fade into view, you can use a callback function like this:

```
$('#photo').fadeIn(1000, function() {
  $('#caption').fadeIn(1000);
});
```

Of course, if you want to run the function when the page loads, you'd want to hide the photo and caption first, and then do the *fadeIn* effect:

```
$('#photo, #caption').hide();
$('#photo').fadeIn(1000, function() {
    $('#caption').fadeIn(1000);
});
```

If you use the *animate()* function, then the callback function appears after any other arguments—the object literal containing the CSS properties to animate, the animation duration, and the easing setting. The easing setting is optional, however, so you can also just pass the *animate()* function, property list, duration, and callback function. For instance, say you want to not only fade the photo into view but also increase its width and height from zero to full size (a kind of zooming effect). You can use the *animate()* function to do that, and then display the caption like this:

```
1  $('#photo').width(0).height(0).css('opacity',0);
2  $('#caption').hide();
3  $('#photo').animate(
4    {
5       width: '200px',
6       height: '100px',
7       opacity: 1
8    },
9    1000,
10   function() {
11      $('#caption').fadeIn(1000);
12   }
13 ); // end animate
```

Line 1 of the code above sets the width, height, and opacity of the photo to 0. (This hides the photo and gets it ready to be animated.) Line 2 hides the caption. Lines 3–13 are the animation function in action and the callback occurs on lines 10–12. This probably looks a little scary, but, unfortunately, the callback function is the only way to run an action (including an effect on a different page element) at the completion of an effect.

Note: The file *callback.html* in the *chapter06* folder shows the above code in action.

Callback functions can get tricky when you want to animate several elements in a row: for example, to make an image move into the center of the screen, followed by a caption fading into view, and then having both the image and caption fade out. To make that happen, you need to pass a callback function to a callback function like this:

```
$('#photo').animate(
  {
     left: '+=400px',
  },
  1000,
  function() { // first callback function
     $('#caption').fadeIn(1000,
      function() { // second callback function
         $('#photo, #caption').fadeOut(1000);
      } // end second callback
    ); // end fadeIn
  } // end first callback function
); // end animate
```

Note: The file *multiple-callbacks.html* in the *chapter06* folder shows this code in action.

However, you don't need to use a callback function if you want to add additional animations to the same page element. For example, say you want to move a photo onto the screen, then make it fade out of view. In this case, you simply use the *animate()* function to move the photo and then fade the image out of view. You can do that like this:

```
$('#photo').animate(
    {
        left: '+=400px',
    },
    1000
); // end animate
$('#photo').fadeOut(3000);
```

In this case, although the browser executes the code immediately, jQuery places each effect into a queue, so that first the animation runs and then the *fadeOut()* function runs. Using jQuery chaining (page 137), you could rewrite the code above like this:

```
$('#photo').animate(
    {
        left: '+=400px',
    },
    1000).fadeOut(3000);
```

If you want a photo to fade in, fade out, and then fade in again, you can use chaining like this:

```
$('#photo').fadeIn(1000).fadeOut(2000).fadeIn(250);
```

Note: For more information on how the effects queue works visit the jQuery website: *http://api.jquery.com/jQuery.queue/*.

One additional jQuery function that can come in handy when queueing up effects on an element is the *delay()*. This function simply waits the specified number of milliseconds before beginning the next effect in the queue. For example, say you want to fade an image into view, wait 10 seconds, and then fade it out of view. You can use the *delay()* function like this:

```
$('#photo').fadeIn(1000).delay(10000).fadeOut(250);
```

Tutorial: Animated Dashboard

In this tutorial, you'll use the *animate()* function to move a <div> tag right from off the left edge of the page into view. The div is absolutely positioned (see the box on page 189 for more on absolute positioning) so that most of the box hangs off the left edge of the page outside the boundaries of the browser window (Figure 6-3, left). When a visitor mouses over the visible edge of the div, that div moves completely into view (Figure 6-3, right). To make this effect more fun, you'll also use two plug-ins to animate the background color of the div and to use a couple of different easing methods.

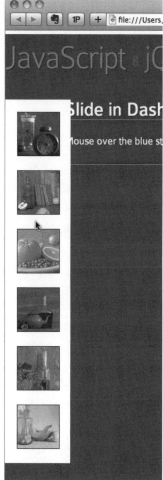

Figure 6-3:
*You can have a lot
of fun by hiding
page elements off
one of the edges of
the browser window
(like the div in the
left image, which is
mostly out of view).
Using the* animate()
*function, you can
then bring that page
element fully into
view (right).*

Note: See the note on page 29 for information on how to download the tutorial files.

The basic task is rather simple:

1. **Select the <div> tag.**

   Remember that a lot of jQuery programming begins with selecting an element on the page—in this case, the div tag which a visitor mouses over.

2. **Attach a *hover* event.**

The *hover* event (described on page 171) is a special jQuery function, not a real JavaScript event, that lets you perform one set of actions when a visitor mouses over an element, then a second set of actions when the visitor mouses off the element (the *hover* event is really just a combination of the mouseOver and mouseOut events described on page 159).

3. **Add the animate function for the mouseover event.**

   When a visitor mouses over the div, you'll animate the left position of the div, moving it from out of view on the left edge of the browser window. In addition, you'll animate the background color of the div.

4. **Add another animate function for the mouseout event.**

   When a visitor moves the mouse off the div, you'll animate the div back to its original position and with its original background color.

The Programming

1. **In a text editor, open the file *animate.html* in the *chapter06* folder.**

   This file already contains a link to the jQuery file, and the *$(document).ready()* function (page 169) is in place. However, since you'll be animating the background color of the div and using a couple of interesting easing methods, you need to attach two jQuery plug-ins—the color plug-in and the easing plug-in.

2. **Click in the empty line after the first <script> tag and add the code in bold below:**

   ```
   <script src="../_js/jquery-1.6.3.min.js"></script>
   <script src="../_js/jquery.easing.1.3.js"></script>
   <script src="../_js/jquery.color.js"></script>
   ```

   jQuery plug-ins (which you'll learn more about in the next chapter) are simply external JavaScript files that add functionality to jQuery, and often let you add complex effects or functionality to your site, without a lot of programming (on your part). Next you'll select the div and then add the *hover()* function to it.

3. **Click in the empty line inside the *$(document).ready()* function and type *$('#dashboard').hover(); // end hover* so your code looks like this:**

   ```
   $(document).ready(function() {
     $('#dashboard').hover(); // end hover
   }); // end ready
   ```

   $('#dashboard') selects the <div> tag (which has the id dashboard applied to it). The *hover()* function takes two arguments—two anonymous functions (page 148)—that describe what to do when a visitor moves his mouse over the div, and then moves his mouse off the div. Instead of typing all of the code at once, you'll build it up piece by piece, first adding the *hover()* function, then adding the "shell" for two anonymous functions. This approach is helpful since the nest of parentheses, braces, commas, and semicolons can overwhelm you if you're not careful.

4. **Click between the parentheses of the *hover()* function and add two empty, anonymous functions:**

```
$(document).ready(function() {
  $('#dashboard').hover(
    function() {

    },
    function() {

    }
  ); // end hover
}); // end ready
```

jQuery plug-ins (which you'll learn more about in the next chapter) are simply external JavaScript files that add functionality to jQuery, and often let you add complex effects or functionality to your site, without a lot of programming on your part. Next you'll add the *hover()* function.

Tip: It's a good idea to test your code frequently to make sure you haven't made any typos. In step 4, you can type *alert('mouseOver')* inside the first anonymous function and *alert('mouseOut')* inside the second anonymous function, and then preview the page in a web browser. You should see an alert box appear when you mouse over the div, and then when you mouse out (for example, to close the first alert dialog box), you'll see a second alert box. If no alert box appears, you've made a typo. Double-check your code against these steps, or use the steps on page 34 to find errors using the browser's error console.

---

5. **Inside the first anonymous function, type $(this).animate(); // end animate.**

   As discussed on page 149, inside an event, *$(this)* refers to the page element to which you've attached the event. In this case, *$(this)* refers to the <div> tag with the ID dashboard. In other words, mousing over this div will also animate this div.

6. **Add an object literal with the CSS properties you wish to animate:**

```
$(document).ready(function() {
  $('#dashboard').hover(
    function() {
      $(this).animate(
        {
          left: '0',
          backgroundColor: 'rgb(255,255,255)'
        }
      ); // end animate
    },
    function() {

    }
  ); // end hover
}); // end ready
```

The first argument to the *animate()* function is an object literal (page 145) containing CSS properties. In this case, the div currently has a left value of -92px, so that most of the div is hidden, hanging off the left edge of the browser window. By animating its left value to 0, you're essentially moving it completely into view on the left edge. Likewise, thanks to the color plug-in, you're changing its background color from blue to white. Next, you'll set a duration for the animation.

7. **Type a comma after the closing } of the object literal, press Returns and then type *500*.**

The comma marks the end of the first argument passed to the *animate()* function, while the 500 sets the length of the animation to half a second or 500 milliseconds. Lastly, you'll set an easing method.

8. **Type a comma after the 500, hit Return, and type *'easeInSine'* so your code looks like this:**

```
$(document).ready(function() {
  $('#dashboard').hover(
    function() {
      $(this).animate(
        {
          left: '0',
          backgroundColor: 'rgb(255,255,255)'
        }
        500,
        'easeInSine'
      ); // end animate
    },
    function() {

    }
  ); // end hover
}); // end ready
```

The last argument to the *animate()* function here—*'easeInSine'*—tells the function to use an easing method that starts off somewhat slowly and then speeds up.

9. **Save the file. Preview it in a browser and mouse over the div.**

The div should scoot into view. If it doesn't, troubleshoot using the techniques described on page 34. Of course, when you mouse off the div, nothing happens. You have to add the animate function to the second anonymous function.

10. **Add the code below to the second anonymous function:**

```
$(this).animate(
    {
      left: '-92px',
      backgroundColor: 'rgb(110,138,195)'
    },
    1500,
    'easeOutBounce'
); // end animate
```

This code reverses the process of the first animation, moving the div back off the left edge of the window and reverting the background color to blue. The timing is a bit different—1.5 seconds instead of half a second—and the easing method is different.

11. **Save the file. Preview it in a browser and move your mouse over and off of the div.**

You'll see the div move into view and then out of view. However, if you move the mouse over and off the div repeatedly and quickly, you'll notice some strange behavior: The div will keep sliding in and out of view long after you've finished moving the mouse. This problem is caused by how jQuery queues up animations on an element. As described on page 198, any animation you add to an element gets put into a sort of queue for that element. For example, if you have an element fade into view, fade out of view, and then fade back into view, jQuery performs each effect in order, one after the other.

What's happening in the code for this tutorial is that each time you mouse onto and off of the div, an animation is added to the queue; so, rapidly mousing over the div creates a long list of effects for jQuery to perform: Animate the div into view, animate the div out of view, animate the div into view, animate the div out of view, and so on. The solution to this problem is to stop all animations on the div before performing a new animation. In other words, when you mouse over the div, and that div is in the process of being animated, then jQuery should stop the current animation, and proceed with the animation required by the mouseover. Fortunately, jQuery supplies a function—the *stop()* function—for just such a problem.

12. Add *.stop()* between *$(this)* and *.animate* in the two anonymous functions. The finished code should look like this (additions are in bold):

```
$(document).ready(function() {
  $('#dashboard').hover(
    function() {
      $(this).stop().animate(
        {
          left: '0',
          backgroundColor: 'rgb(255,255,255)'
        }
        500,
        'easeInSine'
      ); // end animate
    },
    function() {
      $(this).stop().animate(
        {
          left: '-92px',
          backgroundColor: 'rgb(110,138,195)'
        },
        1500,
        'easeOutBounce'
      ); // end animate
    }
  ); // end hover
}); // end ready
```

The *.stop()* function here simply ends any animations on the div before starting a new one, and prevents multiple animations from building up in the queue.

Save the page and try it out in a web browser. You can find a finished version of this tutorial—*complete_animate.html*—in the *chapter06* folder.

Part Three: Building Web Page Features

3

Chapter 7: Improving Your Images

Chapter 8: Improving Navigation

Chapter 9: Enhancing Web Forms

Chapter 10: Expanding Your Interface

Improving Your Images

Web designers use images to improve a page's design, decorate navigation bars, highlight elements on a page—and to show the world what fun they had on their last vacation. Adding an image to a web page immediately injects interest and visual appeal. When you add JavaScript to the mix, however, you can really add excitement by dynamically changing images on a page, presenting an animated photo gallery, or showing off a series of photos in a self-running slideshow. In this chapter, you'll learn a slew of tricks for manipulating and presenting images on your website.

Swapping Images

One of the most common uses of JavaScript is the simple *image rollover*: When you move your mouse over an image, it changes to another image. This basic technique has been used since the dawn of JavaScript to create interactive navigation bars whose buttons change appearance when the mouse hovers over them.

But in the past couple of years, more and more designers have turned to CSS to achieve this same effect (for example, see *www.monkeyflash.com/css/image-rollover-navbar/*). However, even if you're using CSS to create interactive navigation bars, you still need to understand how to use JavaScript to swap one image for another if you want to create slide shows, image galleries, and adding other types of interactive graphic effects to a web page.

Changing an Image's src Attribute

Every image displayed on a web page has a *src* (short for *source*) attribute that indicates a path to a graphic file; in other words, it points to an image on a web server. If you change this property to point to a different graphic file, the browser displays the new image instead. Say you have an image on a page and you assign it an ID of *photo*. Using jQuery, you can dynamically change the src attribute for an image.

For example, suppose you have an image on a page and that you've assigned it an ID of photo. The HTML might look something like this:

```
<img src="images/image.jpg" width="100" height="100" id="photo">
```

To swap in another image file, you just use the attr() function (page 146) to set the tag's src property to a new file, like this:

```
$('#photo').attr('src','images/newImage.jpg');
```

> **Note:** When you change the *src* property of an image using JavaScript, the path to the image file is based on the page location, *not* the location of the JavaScript code. This point can be confusing when you use an external JavaScript file (page 27) located in a different folder. In the example above, the web browser would try to download the file *newImage.jpg* from a folder named *images*, which is located in the same folder as the web page. That method works even if the JavaScript code is included in an external file located in another folder elsewhere on the site. Accordingly, it's often easier to use root-relative links inside external JavaScript files (see the box on page 28 for more information on the different link types).

Changing an image's *src* attribute doesn't change any of the <img> tag's other attributes, however. For example, if the *alt* attribute is set in the HTML, the swapped-in image has the same *alt* text as the original. In addition, if the *width* and *height* attributes are set in the HTML, changing an image's *src* property makes the new image fit inside the same space as the original. If the two graphics have different dimensions, then the swapped-in image will be distorted.

In a situation like rollover images in a navigation bar, the two images will most likely be the same size and share the same *alt* attribute, so you don't get that problem. But you can avoid the image distortion problem entirely by simply leaving off the *width* and *height* property of the original image in your HTML. Then when the new image is swapped in, the web browser displays the image at the dimensions set in the file.

Another solution is to first download the new image, get its dimensions, and then change the *src, width, height,* and *alt* attributes of the <img> tag:

```
1   var newPhoto = new Image();
2   newPhoto.src = 'images/newImage.jpg';
3   var photo = $('#photo');
4   photo.attr('src',newPhoto.src);
5   photo.attr('width',newPhoto.width);
6   photo.attr('height',newPhoto.height);
```

> **Note:** The line numbers on the left aren't part of the code, so don't type them. They're just to make the code easier to read.

The key to this technique is line 1, which creates a new image object. To a web browser, the code *new Image()*says, "Browser, I'm going to be adding a new image to the page, so get ready." The next line tells the web browser to actually download the new image. Line 3 gets a reference to the current image on the page, and lines 4–6 swap in the new image and change the width and height to match the new image.

Tip: The jQuery *attr()* function can set multiple HTML attributes at once. Just pass an object literal (see page 145) that contains each attribute name and new value. You could write the jQuery code from above more succinctly, like this:

```
var newPhoto = new Image();
newPhoto.src = 'images/newImage.jpg';
$('#photo').attr({
    src: newPhoto.src,
    width: newPhoto.width,
    height: newPhoto.height
});
```

Normally, you'd use this image swap technique in conjunction with an event handler. For example, you can make an image change to another image when a visitor mouses over the image. This rollover effect is commonly used for navigation bars, and you'll learn how to create it on page 210. However, you can change an image in response to any event: For example, you can make a new photo appear each time an arrow on a page is clicked, like a slideshow.

Preloading Images

There's one problem with swapping in a new image using the techniques listed above: When you swap the new file path into the *src* attribute, the browser has to download the image. If you wait until someone mouses over an image before downloading the new graphic, there'll be an unpleasant delay before the new image appears. In the case of a navigation bar, the rollover effect will feel sluggish and unresponsive.

To avoid that delay, preload any images that you want to immediately appear in response to an action. For example, when a visitor mouses over a button on a navigation bar, the rollover image should appear instantly. *Preloading* an image simply means forcing the browser to download the image before you plan on displaying it. When the image is downloaded, it's stored in the web browser's cache so that any subsequent requests for that file are served from the visitor's hard drive instead of downloaded a second time from the web server.

Preloading an image is as easy as creating a new image object and setting the object's *src* property. In fact, you already know how to do that:

```
var newPhoto = new Image();
newPhoto.src = 'images/newImage.jpg';
```

What makes this preloading is that you do it before you need to replace an image currently on the web page. One way to preload is to create an array (page 59) at the beginning of a script containing the paths to all graphics you wish to preload, then loop through that list, creating a new image object for each one:

```
1   var preloadImages = ['images/roll.png',
2                        'images/flower.png',
3                        'images/cat.jpg'];
4   var imgs = [];
5   for (var i=0; i<preloadImages.length;i++) {
6     imgs[i] = new Image();
7     imgs[i].src = preloadImages[i];
8   }
```

Lines 1–3 are a single JavaScript statement that creates an array named *preloadImages*, containing three values—the path to each graphic file to preload. (As mentioned on page 61, it's often easier to read an array if you place each array item on its own line.) Line 4 creates a new empty array, *imgs*, which will store each of the preloaded images. Lines 5–8 show a basic JavaScript *for* loop (see page 97), which runs once for each item in the array *preloadImages*. Line 6 creates a new image object, while line 7 retrieves the file path from the *preloadImages* array—that's the magic that causes the image to download.

Rollover Images

A *rollover image* is just an image swap (as discussed on page 207) triggered by the mouse moving over an image. In other words, you simply assign the image swap to the mouseover event. For example, say you have an image on the page with an ID of *photo*. When the mouse rolls over that image, you want the new image to appear. You can accomplish that with jQuery like this:

```
1   <script src="js/jquery-1.6.3.min.js"></script>
2   <script >
3   $(document).ready(function() {
4     var newPhoto = new Image();
5     newPhoto.src = 'images/newImage.jpg';
6     $('#photo').mouseover(function() {
7         $(this).attr('src', newPhoto.src);
8     }); // end mouseover
9   }); // end ready
10  </script>
```

Line 3 waits until the HTML has loaded, so the JavaScript can access the HTML for the current photo. Lines 4 and 5 preload the image that you want to swap in. The rest of the code assigns a mouseover event to the image, with a function that changes the image's *src* attribute to match the new photo.

Since rollover images usually revert back to the old image once you move the mouse off the image, you need to also add a mouseout event to swap back the image. As discussed on page 171, jQuery provides its own event, called *hover()*, which takes care of both the mouseover and mouseout events:

```
1  <script src="js/jquery-1.6.3.min.js"></script>
2  <script>
3  $(document).ready(function() {
4    var newPhoto = new Image();
5    newPhoto.src = 'images/newImage.jpg';
6    var oldSrc=$('#photo').attr('src');
7  $('#photo').hover(
8    function() {
9      $(this).attr('src', newPhoto.src);
10    },
11    function() {
12      $(this).attr('src', oldSrc);
13  }); // end hover
14 }); // end ready
15 </script>
```

The *hover()* function takes two arguments: The first argument is an anonymous function telling the browser what to do when the mouse moves over the image; the second argument is a function telling the browser what to do when the mouse moves off the image. This code also adds a variable, *oldSrc*, for tracking the original *src* attribute—the path to the file that appears when the page loads.

You aren't limited to rolling over just an image, either. You can add a *hover()* function to any tag—a link, a form element, even a paragraph. In this way, any tag on a page can trigger an image elsewhere on the page to change. For example, say you want to make a photo swap out when you mouseover a page's <h1> tag. Assume that the target image is the same as the previous example. You just change your code as shown here in bold:

```
1  <script src="js/jquery-1.6.3.min.js"></script>
2  <script>
3  $(document).ready(function() {
4    var newPhoto = new Image();
5    newPhoto.src = 'images/newImage.jpg';
6  var oldSrc=$('#photo').attr('src');
6    var oldSrc = $('#photo').attr('src');
7    $('h1').hover(
8      function() {
9        $('#photo').attr('src', newPhoto.src);
10      },
11      function() {
12        $('#photo').attr('src', oldSrc);
13  }); //  end hover
14 }); // end ready
15 </script>
```

Tutorial: Adding Rollover Images

In this tutorial, you'll add a rollover effect to a series of images (see Figure 7-1). You'll also add programming to preload the rollover images in order to eliminate any delay between mousing over an image and seeing the rollover image. In addition, you'll learn a new technique to make the process of preloading and adding the rollover effect more efficient.

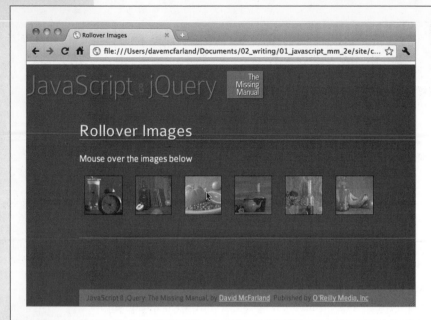

Figure 7-1:
Make a navigation bar, link, or simply a photo more visually interactive with rollovers.

Overview of the Task

The tutorial file *rollover.html* (located in the *chapter07* tutorial folder) contains a series of six images (see Figure 7-2). Each image is wrapped by a link that points to a larger version of the photo, and all of the images are wrapped in a <div> tag with an ID of *gallery*. Basically, you're trying to achieve two things:

- Preload the rollover image associated with each of the images inside the <div>.
- Attach a *hover()* function to each image inside the <div>. The *hover()*function swaps the rollover image when the mouse moves over the image, then swaps back to the original image when the mouse moves off.

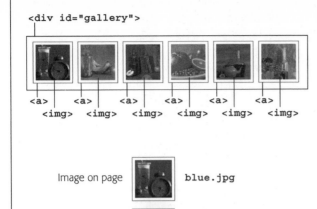

Figure 7-2:
The basic structure of the HTML for this tutorial includes a <div> tag that surrounds a series of links with images in them. To make swapping in the new image easy, its file name is simply a version of the original image's file name.

From this description, you can see that both steps are tied to the images inside the <div>, so one way to approach this problem is to first select the images inside the <div>, then loop through the selection, preloading each images' rollover and attaching a *hover()* function.

Note: See the note on page 29 for information on how to download the tutorial files.

The Programming

1. **In a text editor, open the file *rollover.html* in the *chapter07* folder.**

   This file already contains a link to the jQuery file, and the *$(document).ready()* function (page 123). The first step is to select all of the images within the <div> tag and set up a loop with the jQuery *each()* function discussed on page 147.

2. **Click in the empty line after the *$(document).ready()* function and type *$('#gallery img').each(function() {*.**

   The selector *#gallery img* selects all <img> tags within a tag that has the ID *gallery*. jQuery's *each()* function provides a quick way to loop through a bunch of page elements, performing a series of actions on each element. The *each()* function takes an anonymous function (page 148) as its argument. It's a good idea to close (end) the anonymous and each functions before actually writing the code that runs inside the function, so you'll do that next.

3. **Press Return twice, and then type** *});* // *end each* **to close the anonymous function, end the call to the** *each()* **function, and terminate the JavaScript statement. Your code should now look like this:**

```
1   <script src="../_js/jquery-1.6.3.min.js"></script>
2   <script>
3   $(document).ready(function() {
4     $('#gallery img').each(function() {
5
6     }); // end each
7   }); // end ready
```

At this point, the script loops through each of the images in the gallery, but doesn't actually do anything yet. The first order of business is to capture the image's *src* property and store it in a variable that you'll use later on in the script.

Note: The JavaScript comments—// *end each* and // *end ready*—aren't required for this script to work. However, they do make it easier to identify what part of the script the line goes with.

---

4. **Click inside the empty line (line 5 in step 3) and type:**

   `var imgFile = $(this).attr('src');`.

   As described on page 149, you can use *$(this)* to refer to the current element in the loop; in other words, *$(this)* will refer to each of the image tags in turn. The jQuery *attr()* function (see page 146) retrieves the specified HTML attribute. In this case, it retrieves the *src* property of the image and stores it in a variable named *imgFile*. For example, for the first image, the *src* property is *_images/small/blue.jpg*, which is the path to the image that appears on the page.

   You can use that very *src* value to preload the image.

5. **Hit Return to create a blank line, and then add the following two lines of code:**

   ```
   var preloadImage = new Image();
   var imgExt = /(\.\w{3,4}$)/;
   preloadImage.src = imgFile.replace(imgExt,'_h$1');
   ```

   As described on page 209, to preload an image you must first create an image object. In this case, the variable *preloadImage* is created to store the image object. Next, we preload the image by setting the Image object's *src* property.

   One way to preload images (as discussed on page 210) is to create an array of images you wish to preload, then loop through each item in the array, creating an image object and adding the image's source to the object. However, that approach can require a lot of work, since you need to know the path to each of the rollover images and type those paths into the array.

   In this example, you'll use a more creative (and less labor-intensive method) to preload images. You just have to make sure you store the rollover image in the same location as the original image and name it similarly. For this web page, each image on the page has a corresponding rollover image with an *_h* added to the end of the image name. For example, for the image *blue.jpg*, there's a rollover image named *blue_h.jpg*. Both files are stored in the same folder, so the path to both files is the same.

Here's the creative part: Instead of manually typing the *src* of the rollover to preload it like this, *preloadImage.src='_images/small/blue_h.jpg'*, you can let JavaScript figure out the *src* by simply changing the name of the original image's source so it reflects the name of the rollover. In other words, if you know the path to the image on the page, then its rollover image simply has an h added directly before the .jpg in that path. So *_images/small/blue.jpg* becomes *_images/small/blue_h.jpg*, and *_images/small/orange.jpg* becomes *_images/small/orange_h.jpg*.

That's what the other two lines of code do. The first line—*var imgExt = /(\.\w{3,4}$)/;*—creates a *regular expression*. A regular expression (which you'll learn about on page 430) is a pattern of characters that you can search for in a string: for example, three numbers in a row. Regular expressions can be tricky, but essentially this one matches a period followed by three or four characters at the end of a string. For example, it will match both *.jpeg* in */images/small/blue.jpeg* and *.png* in */images/orange.png*.

The next line—*preloadImage.src = imgFile.replace(imgExt, '_h$1');*—uses the *replace()* method (see page 443) to replace the matched text with something else. Here a *.jpg* in the path name will be replaced with *_h.jpg*, so *images/small/blue.jpg* is changed to *images/small/blue_h.jpg*. This technique is a little tricky since it uses a regular expression subpattern (see the box on page 444 for full details), so don't worry if you don't exactly understand how it works.

Now that the rollover image is preloaded, you can assign the *hover()* event to the image.

6. **Hit Return and then add the code listed on lines 9–11 below:**

```
1   <script src="../_js/jquery-1.6.3.min.js"></script>
2   <script>
3   $(document).ready(function() {
4     $('#gallery img').each(function() {
5       var imgFile = $(this).attr('src');
6       var preloadImage = new Image();
7       var imgExt = /(\.\w{3,4}$)/;
8       preloadImage.src = imgFile.replace(imgExt,'_h$1');
9       $(this).hover(
10
11      ); // end hover
12    }); // end each
13  }); // end ready
```

jQuery's *hover()* function is just a shortcut method of applying a mouseover and mouseout event to an element (see page 157). To make it work, you pass two functions as arguments. The first function runs when the mouse moves over the element—in this case, the image changes to the rollover. The second function runs when the mouse moves off the element—here, the rollover image swaps back to the original image.

7. **In the empty line (line 9 in step 6), add the following three lines of code:**

```
function() {
  $(this).attr('src', preloadImage.src);
},
```

This first function simply changes the *src* property of the current image to the *src* of the rollover image. The comma at the end of the last line is required because the function you just added is acting as the first argument in a call to the *hover()* function—a comma separates each argument passed to a function.

8. **Finally, add the second function (lines 13–15 below). The finished script should look like this:**

```
1   <script src="../_js/jquery-1.6.3.min.js"></script>
2   <script>
3   $(document).ready(function() {
4   $('#gallery img').each(function() {
5     var imgFile = $(this).attr('src');
6     var preloadImage = new Image();
7     var imgExt = /(\.\w{3,4}$)/;
8     preloadImage.src = imgFile.replace(imgExt,'_h$1');
9     $(this).hover(
10      function() {
11        $(this).attr('src', preloadImage.src);
12      },
13      function() {
14      $(this).attr('src', imgFile);
15      }
16    ); // end hover
17  }); // end each
18  }); // end ready
```

This second function simply changes the *src* attribute back to the original image. In line 5, the path to the image originally on the page is stored in the variable *imgFile*. In this function (line 14), you access that value again to set the *src* back to its original value. Save the page, view it in a web browser, and mouse over each of the black and white images to see them pop into full color.

Tutorial: Photo Gallery with Effects

Now you'll expand on the last tutorial to create a single-page photo gallery. You'll be able to load a larger image onto the page when a visitor clicks a thumbnail image (see Figure 7-3). In addition, you'll use a couple of jQuery's effect functions to make the transition between larger images more visually interesting.

Figure 7-3:
The finished photo gallery page. Clicking a thumbnail makes a larger image fade into view and the current image fade out. The completed version of this tutorial file, complete_gallery.html, *is in the* chapter07 *folder.*

Overview of Task

The way the gallery works is pretty straightforward—click a thumbnail to see a larger image. However, this tutorial shows you how to add a few features that make the presentation more interesting by using fade effects to swap larger images in and out of the page.

Another important technique you'll use here is *unobtrusive JavaScript*. That simply means that users who have JavaScript turned off will still be able to access the larger versions of the photos. To achieve that, each thumbnail image is wrapped in a link that points to the larger image file (see Figure 7-4). For those without JavaScript, clicking the link exits the current web page and follows the link to load the larger image file. It won't look fantastic, since the visitor has to exit the gallery page and will see just the single larger image, but the photos will at least be accessible. For folks who have JavaScript turned on, clicking a link will make the larger image fade into view on the page.

Figure 7-4:
The basic structure of the photo gallery. All of the thumbnail images are wrapped in links that point to the larger version of the photo. Clicking each link will load the larger image inside a <div> tag with the ID of photo.

All of the action occurs when the link is clicked, so this script uses the link's click event to achieve the following steps:

- **Stop the default behavior of the link**. Normally, clicking a link takes you to another page. On this page, clicking the link around a thumbnail exits the web page and displays a larger image. Since you'll use JavaScript to display the image, you can add some JavaScript code to prevent the browser from following that link.

- **Get the href value of the link**. The link actually points to the larger image, so by retrieving the link's *href*, you also get the path to the larger image file.

- **Create a new image tag to insert into the page**. This image tag will include the path from the *href* value.

- **Fade the old image out while fading the new image in**. The current image fades out of view as the large version of the clicked thumbnail fades into view.

The tutorial includes a few additional nuances, but these four steps cover the basic process.

The Programming

This tutorial expands on the previous one, but the starting web page has been reorganized a little: There's a new set of thumbnails and they are now in a left column, and a <div> tag with an ID of *photo* has been added to the page (see Figure 7-4).

Note: See the note on page 29 for information on how to download the tutorial files.

---

1. **In a text editor, open the file *gallery.html* in the *chapter07* folder.**

   This file contains the programming from the previous tutorial, plus a new <div> tag to display the large version of each thumbnail image. Since the process of displaying a gallery image is triggered by clicking one of the links wrapped around the thumbnail images, the first step is to create a selection of those links and add the click event to each.

2. **Locate the JavaScript comment that reads "insert new programming below this line" and add the following code:**

   ```
   $('#gallery a').click(function(evt) {

   }); // end click
   ```

   The selector *#gallery a* selects all link tags inside another tag with the ID *gallery*. The *.click* is a jQuery function for adding an event handler (see page 162 if you need a refresher on events). Also, the code passes an anonymous function to the click event (as mentioned on page 173, functions that are executed in response to an event automatically have the event object passed to them). In this case, the variable *evt* stores that event object. You'll use it in the next step to stop the browser from following the clicked link.

3. **Between the two lines of code you added in step 2, type *evt.preventDefault();*.**

   Normally, clicking a link makes the web browser load whatever the link points to (a web page, graphic file, PDF document, and so on). In this case, the link is just there so that people who don't have JavaScript turned on will be able to go to a larger version of the thumbnail image. To prevent the web browser from following the link for those who have JavaScript enabled, you run the event object's *preventDefault()* function (see page 175).

   Next, we'll get the *href* attribute for the link.

4. **Hit Return to create a new, blank line, and then add the bold line of code below:**

   ```
   $('#gallery a').click(function(evt) {
     evt.preventDefault();
     var imgPath = $(this).attr('href');
   }); // end click
   ```

   Here, *$(this)* refers to the element that's clicked—in other words, a link. A link's href attribute points to the page or resource the link goes to. In this case, each link contains a path to the larger image. That's important information, since you can use it to add an image tag that points to the image file. But before you do that, you need to get a reference to the large image that's currently displayed on the page. After all, you need to know what it is so you can fade it out of view.

Tip: You'll see that each line of code inside the *click()* event in step 4 is indented. That's optional, but it helps make the code more readable, as described in the box on page 49. Many programmers use two spaces (or a tab) for each level of indentation.

---

5. **Hit Return and type** *var oldImage = $('#photo img');*.

The variable *oldImage* holds a jQuery selection containing the <img> tag inside the photo <div> (see Figure 7-4). Now it's time to create a tag for the new image.

6. **Hit Return again and add** *var newImage = $('<img src="' + imgPath +'">');* **to the script.**

There are quite a few things going on here. jQuery lets you select an element that's in the page's HTML. For example, *$('img')* selects all images on the page. In addition, the jQuery object can add a *new* element to the page. For example, *$('<p>Hello</p>')* creates a new paragraph tag containing the word Hello. This line creates a new <img> tag and stores it in a variable named *newImage*.

Since the jQuery object expects a string as an argument (*'<p>Hello</p>'*, for example), this line of code *concatenates* or *combines* several strings to make one. The first string (surrounded by single quotes) is *<img src="*; the second string is stored in the variable *imgPath* (which you created in step 4) and is the path to the image file (for example, *../_images/large/slide1.jpg*); the third string (also surrounded by single quotes) is *">*. Taken altogether, they add up to an HTML tag: *<img src="../_images/large/slide1.jpg">*. When the script passes it to the jQuery object like this, *$('<img src="../_images/large/slide2.jpg">')*, the browser creates a page element. It isn't displayed on the page yet, but the browser is ready to add it to the page at anytime.

7. **Add the code listed below on lines 6–8 so the code you've added so far looks like this:**

```
1   $('#gallery a').click(function(evt) {
2       evt.preventDefault();
3       var imgPath = $(this).attr('href');
4       var oldImage = $('#photo img');
5       var newImage = $('<img src="' + imgPath +'">');
6       newImage.hide();
7       $('#photo').prepend(newImage);
8       newImage.fadeIn(1000);
9   }); // end click
```

In line 6, the newly created image (which is stored in the variable *newImage*) is hidden using the *hide()* function described on page 187. This step is necessary because if you just added the image tag created in line 5, the image would be immediately visible on the page—no cool fade-in effect. So you first hide the image, and then add it to the page inside the photo <div> (line 7). The *prepend()* function (described on page 139) adds HTML inside a tag. Specifically, it adds the HTML at the very beginning of the tag. At this point, there are two images on the page inside the photo <div>—Figure 7-5 shows how one image can sit on top of the other. The image on top is invisible, but in line 8, the *fadeIn()* function makes the image slowly fade in over the course of 1,000 milliseconds (1 second).

Now it's time to make the original image fade out.

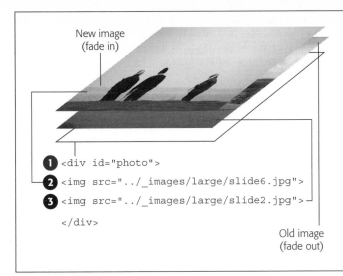

New image
(fade in)

Figure 7-5:
*To achieve the effect where two photos ap-
pear in the same spot on the page, but one
photo fades in and another fades out, you
need to use some creative CSS. Absolute positioning lets an element sit above the page,
and even on top of another element. In this
case, both images are absolutely positioned
within the <div> tag, making them float one
on top of the other. The style sheet embedded in the <head> of gallery.html file
included in the chapter07 folder has all the
CSS required—make sure to check out the
#photo img style. In addition, the tag contain-
ing the photos needs a position of relative, in
order to allow the photos to be positioned in
relation to that spot on the page.*

❶ `<div id="photo">`
❷ `<img src="../_images/large/slide6.jpg">`
❸ `<img src="../_images/large/slide2.jpg">`
`</div>`

Old image
(fade out)

8. **Press Return and then add these three lines of code:**

```
oldImage.fadeOut(1000,function(){
  $(this).remove();
}); // end fadeout
```

In step 5, you created a variable named *oldImage* and stored a reference to the
original image on the page into it. That's the image we want to fade out, so you
apply the *fadeOut()* function. You pass two arguments to the function: The first
is the duration of the effect—1,000 milliseconds (1 second); the second is a callback function (as described on page 196 in Chapter 6). The callback function
runs *after* the fade out effect finishes, and removes the <img> tag for that image.

Note: The *remove()* function is discussed on page 419. It actually removes the tag from the DOM, which
erases the HTML from the browser's memory, freeing up computer resources. If you didn't take this step,
each time your visitor clicks a thumbnail, a new <img> tag would be added (see step 7), but the old one
would simply be hidden, not deleted. You'd end up with lots and lots of hidden <img> tags still embedded in the web page, slowing down the responsiveness of the web browser.

There's one final step—loading the first image. Currently the <div> tag where
the photo goes is empty. You could type an <img> tag in that spot, so when
the page loads there'd be a larger image for, say, the first thumbnail. But why
bother—you've got JavaScript!

9. Add one last line after the end of the *click()* function (line 13 below), so your completed code looks like this:

```
1   $('#gallery a').click(function(evt) {
2       evt.preventDefault();
3       var imgPath = $(this).attr('href');
4       var oldImage = $('#photo img');
5       var newImage = $('<img src="' + imgPath +'">');
6       newImage.hide();
7       $('#photo').prepend(newImage);
8       newImage.fadeIn(1000);
9       oldImage.fadeOut(1000,function(){
10          $(this).remove();
11      }); // end fadeout
12  }); // end click
13  $('#gallery a:first').click();
```

This last statement has two parts. First the selector—*#gallery a:first*—selects just the first link only in the gallery <div>. Next is the *click()* function. So far, you've used jQuery's *click()* function to assign a function that runs when the event occurs. However, if you don't pass any arguments to an event function, jQuery simply triggers that event, causing any previously defined event handlers to run. So, this line triggers a *click* on the first link that makes the web browser run the function that you created earlier in lines 1–11. That is, it makes the larger image for the first thumbnail fade into view when the page loads.

Save the page and preview it in a web browser. Not only do the thumbnails change color when you mouse over them, clicking a thumbnail makes its associated large image fade into view. (If you're having trouble with your code, the file *complete_gallery.html* contains a working copy of the script.)

Advanced Gallery with jQuery FancyBox

Displaying a gallery of photos is such a common task that you'll find dozens of different ways to show off your imagery. One very popular technique dims the web page and displays the larger version of the thumbnail as if it were floating on top of the browser window (see Figure 7-6). The most well-known version of this method is a JavaScript program called Lightbox (*www.huddletogether.com/projects/lightbox2/*). There have been many imitations of the original, as well as several written as jQuery plug-ins. This section uses the powerful FancyBox jQuery plug-in (*http://fancybox .net/),* which is easy to use and customize. With just a single line of code, FancyBox creates a spectacular way to present images as part of a portfolio, gallery, or slideshow.

Note: Before continuing, you might want to open the file *complete_fancybox.html* in the *chapter07* folder included with this book's tutorial files. It has a working demo of FancyBox. Watching it in action first will probably make the rest of this section easier to understand.

Figure 7-6:
The FancyBox jQuery plug-in, created by Janis Skarnelis, gives you an easy way to create an attractive, single-page photo gallery. You can even set up FancyBox so that visitors can navigate through a series of photos by clicking a Next or Previous button that appears when you mouse over the image. In addition, you're not limited to just photos. You can pop open YouTube video players, or embed regular HTML content (even content from other websites) using FancyBox.

The Basics

FancyBox is very easy to use—you just need to set up your web page with links to the images you wish to display, attach .css and .js files to the page, and add one line of code to call the light box into action.

1. **Set up your gallery page.**

   There's not really much you need to do—just add links to the larger images you wish to display on the page. These could be links added to thumbnail images, so when the thumbnail is clicked, the larger image appears (that's how the gallery you programmed in the previous tutorial worked). The important thing to remember is that the link points to a graphic file—a .png, .jpeg, or .gif file—not to a web page. (On page 245, though, you'll learn how to use FancyBox to display non-image content like other web pages and videos of Flash movies).

   In addition, you need a way to identify just the gallery links (as opposed to other links on the page). One way is to wrap the links in a <div> tag with a specific ID—*gallery*, for example. Then you can target just those links with a selector like '*#gallery a*'. Another approach is to add specific class names to each gallery link: for example, *<a href="images/potato.jpg" class="gallery">*. Then you can target those links with a selector like '*a.gallery*'. This last method is handy if the links are scattered around the page and aren't contained in a single <div>.

> **Tip:** To add a caption to a photo, just supply a *title* attribute to the <a> tag that links to the large image. For example:
>
> ```
> <a href="images/potato.jpg" title="A handsome potato">
> ```

2. **Download the FancyBox files and put them into your site.**

   You can find the files at *http://fancybox.net*. They're also provided with the tutorial files for this book in a folder named *fancybox* in the *chapter07* folder. A good approach is to simply copy the fancybox folder from the tutorial folder to your own website (the root folder's a good place for it). There are a handful of files you'll need: a JavaScript file, a CSS file, and several graphics files:

   - The JavaScript file is named something like *jquery.fancybox-1.3.4.js*, where 1.3.4 represents a version number. You'll also find a minified (or compressed) version of the file named *jquery.fancybox-1.3.4.min.js* in the fancybox folder in the chapter07 tutorials folder. You can place this file anywhere in your site, but it's easiest to keep it in the fancybox folder with the other files.

   - The CSS file, *jquery.fancybox-1.3.4.css*, contains the CSS that formats different aspects of the lightbox effect, such as drop shadows, the Next, Previous, and Close buttons, and the appearance of captions. Since this file references many different image files (*fancybox.png, fancy_title_main.png*, and so on), it's best to keep this CSS file in the same folder as those images (that's one reason it's good to keep all the FancyBox-related files together in one folder).

   - FancyBox also requires a bunch of graphic files: Some of these files are specifically used to overcome IE6 bugs, while others are used to add visual elements like a drop shadow, a graphic box for captions, and images for navigation buttons. You'll read more about the different files on page 226.

3. **Attach the external style sheet to your page.**

   jQuery FancyBox uses some fancy CSS to achieve the dark, transparent overlay effect and display the pop-up image. Attach this file as you would any CSS file. For example:

   ```
   <link href="fancybox/jquery.fancybox-1.3.4.css".css" rel="stylesheet">
   ```

   Most JavaScript programmers place any style sheet information before their JavaScript programming—some JavaScript programs depend on having the style sheet information available first, in order for the program to work correctly. That's especially true of many jQuery plug-ins, so get in the habit of placing all style sheets before JavaScript files and programs.

4. **Attach the JavaScript files.**

   jQuery FancyBox gets most of its power from the jQuery library (no surprise), so you must first attach the jQuery file to the page (see page 122 for a recap of this procedure). Also, the FancyBox JavaScript file (like any JavaScript that uses jQuery) must be attached after the jQuery file. For example:

```
<script src="js/jquery-1.6.3.min.js"></script>
<script src="fancybox/jquery.fancybox-1.3.4.js"></script>
```

In addition, FancyBox can use the easing methods described on page 194 to control how the larger images zoom into or out of the page. If you wish to use any easing method besides jQuery's standard swing and linear, then you must attach the easing plug-in as well. For example:

```
<script src="js/jquery-1.6.3.min.js"></script>
<script src="js/jquery.easing.1.3.js"></script>
<script src="fancybox/jquery.fancybox-1.3.4.js"></script>
```

5. **Add a <script> tag, the jQuery *ready()* function, and call FancyBox.**

   Believe it or not, steps 1–4 above are the hardest part of the whole process. Getting FancyBox to work requires just a single line of JavaScript. Of course, as you read on page 169, you should put that code inside a jQuery *ready()* function, so the browser has processed the HTML and is ready to manipulate the DOM. For example:

```
<script>
$(document).ready(function() {
  $('#gallery a').fancybox();
});
</script>
```

   The *fancybox()* function must be applied to just the links that point to the image files you wish to display. You use a jQuery selector (*$('#gallery a')*, for example) to tell FancyBox which links to use: In this example, any <a> tag inside another tag with an ID of *gallery* becomes part of the FancyBox effect. As mentioned in step 1, you need to set up your HTML so you can use jQuery to identify the specific links that make up your light box.

   And that's it. Now, when you click each of the gallery links, a transparent background appears over the page, and a large version of the image appears in the middle of the window.

Creating a Gallery of Images

Normally, when you apply FancyBox to a collection of links, each thumbnail is treated like a separate, unrelated image. In other words, if you apply FancyBox to a collection of links, to see the larger version of each image, your visitor first has to click a link to open a larger image, close that larger image by clicking a close button or (anywhere on the page), and then click a different thumbnail to see a larger image, and so on and so on. This constant opening and closing of images can be annoying and time consuming.

A better approach is to treat a collection of thumbnails and links as a unified gallery. The visitor clicks a thumbnail to open a larger version of the image, and then clicks Next or Previous buttons on the larger image to jump back and forth among all the larger images in the gallery. The FancyBox example pictured in Figure 7-6 works this way; notice the Next button (circled).

To create a gallery of related images, simply add the rel attribute to the <a> tag and assign the same value for each image in the gallery. For example:

```
<a href="large_slide1.jpg"  rel="gallery">
  <img src="slide1.jpg" width="70" height="70">
</a>
<a href="large_slide2.jpg"  rel="gallery">
  <img src="slide2.jpg" width="70" height="70">
</a>
<a href="large_slide3.jpg"  rel="gallery">
  <img src="slide3.jpg" width="70" height="70">
</a>
```

With the above code, if you apply the FancyBox function to these three links, then the larger images will be considered part of the same gallery so you can jump back and forth between the images without needing to first close a larger image and then click a thumbnail. (You'll see an example of this in the tutorial on page 231.)

Customizing FancyBox

While the general look of the FancyBox effect is really nice, you may want to tinker a bit with its appearance. You can customize a variety of different parts of the Fancy-Box look, including the buttons that let you close the FancyBox window or navigate to the previous and next images; you can also change the color and opacity of the transparent background that overlays the page or change the background color of the caption box and picture frame. Some of the changes involve providing different options to the FancyBox function, while other changes require you to make changes directly to the CSS file.

FancyBox options

The FancyBox plug-in lets you supply custom options that affect the appearance of the light box effect. Basically, you pass a JavaScript object literal (see page 145) to the FancyBox function containing the names of the options you wish to set and the values you wish to set them to. For example, to change the background color and opacity of the background placed over the page, you can pass an object literal with your new settings to FancyBox like this:

```
$('#gallery a').fancybox({
    overlayOpacity: .5,
    overlayColor: '#F64',
    transitionIn: 'elastic',
    transitionOut: 'elastic',
});
```

In this example, the color of the overlay is set to a bright red (#F65), and its opacity is set to 50% (.5). Also, the in and out transitions are set to *elastic*, which affects how the larger image appears on the screen: In this case, the elastic setting makes the larger image zoom into view when the thumbnail is clicked, and zoom out of view when the Close button (or any other place on the page) is clicked (normally the larger image just appears and disappears without any animation effect).

jQuery FancyBox accepts a lot of different options (visit *http://fancybox.net/api/* for the complete list), but here are the most useful:

- **overlayColor**. The background color that covers the page while FancyBox displays an image. This option accepts a hex color value like #FF0033. If you don't set this option, the plug-in uses a gray color, #666 to be specific. Set this option like this:

  `overlayColor : '#ff6346'`

- **overlayOpacity**. The opacity of the overlay. This option sets how much of the page below the overlay should show through. You specify a number from 0 to 1: .5, for example, is 50% opacity. If you don't want to be able to see through the overlay—for example, you want to completely cover the rest of the web page while the image appears—set this option to 1. If you don't set this option, FancyBox sets the opacity to 30% (.3). Set this value to 0 to hide the overlay.

  `overlayOpacity : .5`

- **padding.** The space around the image; it creates a visual border around the image. Normally, FancyBox sets the padding to 10 pixels, but you can change this to any value you wish. A value of 0 completely removes the border around a pop-up photo (see page 231 for instructions on how to change the color of the border around the image). Simply supply a number (FancyBox assumes it's a pixel value so you don't need to include the px you'd normally add in CSS):

  `padding: 5`

- **changeSpeed**. When you move from image to image in a FancyBox-powered page, the box containing the image is animated as it changes size from the dimensions of the current image to match the dimensions of the next image. You can control the speed of this transition by setting this option. The default is 300, meaning 300 milliseconds, or slightly less than half of a second. For example:

  `changeSpeed : 500`

- **transitionIn and transitionOut.** These two options control how the larger, pop-up image appears on the screen. The *fade* setting makes the larger image fade into view on the screen. That's also how FancyBox normally makes a pop-up image appear. The *none* setting makes the image pop abruptly onto the screen. Finally, the *elastic* option is the most visually fun: It makes the image zoom onto the page. In conjunction with an easing method (see the next option), you can create some very dynamic (and potentially annoying) visuals. The transitionIn option controls how the larger image appears on the screen, while the transitionOut option controls how the image disappears. You can have different settings for each:

  `transitionIn : 'elastic',`
  `transitionOut : 'none'`

- **easingIn and easingOut.** These two options work when the transitionIn and transitionOut options are set to *elastic* (see the previous bullet point). They take an easing method such as jQuery's swing or linear options, or, if you've attached the easing plug-in (page 194), you can use any of the easing methods supported by that plug-in:

```
easingIn : 'easeInBounce',
easingOut : 'easeOutSine'
```

- **titlePosition.** Normally, when you add a caption to an image (see the Note on page 231), FancyBox places the caption inside a graphic box (a lozenge-shaped image). You can change this graphic (see page 229), or simply not use it by setting the titlePosition option to either *outside* (the caption appears below the box containing the image), *inside* (the caption appears inside the white box surrounding the image), or over (the caption appears over the bottom edge of the photo). You set this option like this:

```
titlePosition: 'outside'
```

- **cyclic.** Normally, when you reach the last image in a gallery of images, only the Previous button appears; and when you're at the first image, only a Next button appears. When you set the cyclic property to true—cyclic: true—visitors will be able to jump to the first image when they reach the last image in the gallery by pressing the Next button, and will be able to jump to the last image when viewing the first image by pressing the Previous button. In other words, this option lets you cycle through the images continually without end.

```
cyclic : true
```

Here's an example of how you might set these options. Say you are applying Fancy-Box to a collection of links to create a navigable gallery of pop-up images. You want to make the gallery endless, so when a visitor reaches the last photo, she can click the Next button to jump back to the beginning of the gallery. Also, you want to remove any border around the pop-up photos, make them zoom in and out of view, and position the captions below the bottom of each photo. You can do that with this code:

```
$('#gallery a').fancybox({
  cyclic : true,
  padding : 0,
  transitionIn : 'elastic',
  transitionOut : 'elastic'
  titlePosition : 'outside'
});
```

Styling FancyBox

FancyBox uses a combination of graphics and CSS to style its appearance. It uses images for the Close button, navigation buttons, and drop shadow that appear beneath the pop-up image, as well as CSS styles to format the placement and size of those controls. An animated loading graphic also displays as the larger image is retrieved. You can adjust these graphics, but you first need to understand how FancyBox organizes its graphic files.

First, for all browsers except Internet Explorer 6, the main graphics are stored in a single file: *fancybox.png* (see Figure 7-7). FancyBox uses a method known as *CSS sprites,* which stores multiple images in a single file, but using CSS and the background-image property displays only a portion of that image in each instance. For example, to display the Close button, FancyBox loads *fancybox.png* as a background image into a link on the page, but sets the width and height of that link to 30 pixels, and shifts the image using the background-position property so that only the top-right corner of the *fancybox.png* file appears. The reasoning behind this approach is that by only loading a single file—*fancybox.png*—instead of separate files for each control, your website will download more quickly and feel more responsive to visitors. (You can find read more about the CSS sprites technique at *http://css-tricks .com/158-css-sprites/*.

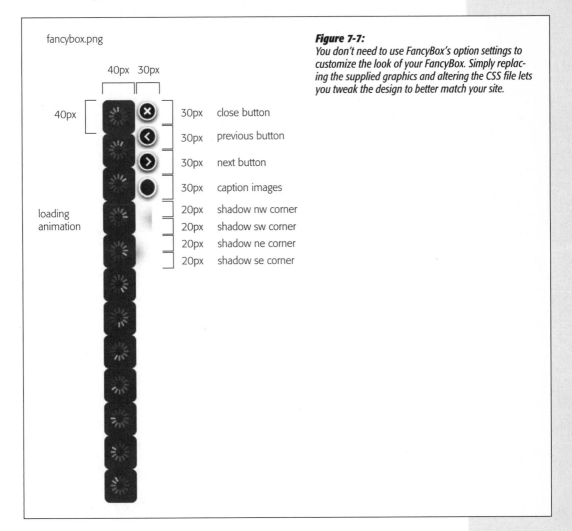

fancybox.png

40px   30px

40px   30px   close button

30px   previous button

30px   next button

30px   caption images

loading
animation   20px   shadow nw corner

20px   shadow sw corner

20px   shadow ne corner

20px   shadow se corner

Figure 7-7:
You don't need to use FancyBox's option settings to customize the look of your FancyBox. Simply replacing the supplied graphics and altering the CSS file lets you tweak the design to better match your site.

In addition to graphics, FancyBox also includes styles in its external style sheet to format different elements of its presentation. Here's a run-down of the most common elements and how to format them:

- **The Close button.** FancyBox uses a graphic Close button that appears at the top-right corner of a pop-up image. The image is 30 pixels by 30 pixels and appears in the upper-right corner of the *fancybox.png* file. There are a couple of ways to modify this. If you're not happy with the 30-pixel by 30-pixel size, you can simply edit the *fancybox.png* file: Delete the 30×30 image in the top-right of that file and replace it with a design of your own.

In the FancyBox stylesheet (the *jquery.fancybox-1.3.4.css* file included in the tutorial files), you can edit the #fancybox-close style for even greater control. In this style, you can control the placement of the Close button (change the top and right settings), the height and width of the button (change the height and width properties), and even point to a different graphic file by editing the background property.

IE6 Note: FancyBox uses special CSS styles to overcome bugs in Internet Explorer 6. The styles don't reference the *fancybox.png* file, but instead use different images for each of the controls. IE6 is a nearly dead web browser, so you're most likely safe to ignore it, but if you're still worried and want to change the appearance of the control graphics, then you need to edit the following image files: *fancy_close.png* (the close button), *fancy_nav_left.png* (the previous button), *fancy_nav_right.png* (the next button), *fancy_loading.png* (the animated loading image), *fancy_title_main.png* (for the center part of the caption graphic), *fancy_title_right.png* (for the right edge of the caption graphic), and *fancy_title_left.png* (for the left edge of the caption graphic). Or you can save yourself all this trouble and ignore IE6 altogether.

- **The Previous and Next buttons.** As with the Close button, the Previous and Next buttons are images within the *fancybox.png* file (see Figure 7-7). You can edit that file (make sure to stay within the 30×30 pixel boundary). You can also use different graphic files and at different sizes by editing the styles for these two controls: a group selector (#fancybox-left-ico, #fancybox-right-ico), which provides properties (like width and height) that are common to both controls, and the individual styles (#fancybox-left-ico for the Previous button and #fancybox-right-ico for the Next button), which set the image for the controls.

- **The "loading" graphic.** When a visitor clicks on a thumbnail to make a larger image pop onto the page, the browser has to download that file. While it waits, an animated image appears on the screen to indicate that image is being retrieved. This image is actually a series of "frames" in the *fancybox.png* file (see Figure 7-7). Its 12 frames are 40 pixels tall by 40 pixels wide. To change this image, you need to edit the *fancybox.png* file and create your own 12-frame animation. The CSS style controlling which image is loaded and its width is the #fancybox-loading div style. But if you want to control the placement, width, and height of the image, you need to also edit the #fancybox-loading style. It's a lot of work, and since the normal "loading" graphic looks great, you may want to avoid changing it.

- **Drop shadows.** The drop shadows that appear around the pop-up image are generated by a bunch of individual image files, including a couple of parts of the *fancybox.png* file. Editing these is complex and is best avoided. If you do make separate graphic files for the various controls discussed in this list and edit the CSS to point to those files, don't delete the *fancybox.png* file—it supplies the corners for the drop shadows.

- **Border color around pop-up images.** Normally, FancyBox displays a white border around a pop-up image. As mentioned in the previous section, you can control the size of that border by sending a *padding* value to the FancyBox function. However, to control its color, you need to edit the FancyBox style sheet. Locate the style #fancybox-content and change its border color from #FFF to whatever color you prefer.

- **Color behind photos.** When you create a gallery effect where a visitor can click the previous and next buttons to jump from large image to large image, Fancy-Box displays a background color as one image fades out and the next fades in. This color is defined by the background property in the #fancybox-outer style. It's a good idea to have this value match whatever color you define for the border color (previous bullet point).

- **Captions.** You can control the color, font, and size of captions by editing various CSS Styles. The #fancybox-title style defines the font and font size of the caption, while the .fancybox-title-inside, .fancybox-title-outside, and .fancybox-title-over styles affect the look of the caption based on its titlePosition setting (discussed on page 228). For example, if you set the "titlePosition" option to *inside,* the caption appears inside the border for the image. If you change the border color (see above bullet point), then you should change the background property on the .fancybox-title-inside style to match that border color. If you don't set the titlePosition option, FancyBox uses images inside the *fancybox.png* file to generate a graphical caption box. It takes three slices of that image (one for the left edge of the box, another for the middle section of the box, and a third for the right edge of the box). To alter the images used, you can edit the following styles: *#fancybox-title-float-left, #fancybox-title-float-main,* and *#fancybox-title-float-right.*

Tip: FancyBox lets you customize the HTML used to display the captions in many different ways by creating a custom function. You can find out how and see more tips and tricks for using FancyBox at *http://fancybox.net/blog.*

Tutorial: FancyBox Photo Gallery

Although FancyBox is really easy to use, it's always helpful to have a step-by-step tutorial showing you how it's done. In this tutorial, you'll take a page with a basic set of thumbnail images and turn it into a fancy pop-up gallery.

Note: See the note on page 29 for information on how to download the tutorial files.

---

1. **In a text editor, open the file *fancybox.html* in the *chapter07* folder.**

   This file contains a simple group of thumbnail images. Each image is linked to a larger version of the photo, and all of the thumbnails are contained within a <div> tag with an ID of *gallery*.

   The first step is to attach the CSS file used by FancyBox.

2. **In the <head> of the document, locate the empty line below the <link> tag, which attaches the *site.css* style sheet file (it's the blank line that appears directly above the first <script> tag). On that line, type:**

   ```
   <link href="fancybox/jquery.fancybox-1.3.4.css" rel="stylesheet">
   ```

   The *jquery.fancybox-1.3.4.css* file contains all of the styles used to format various elements of the FancyBox interface, including the placement of the close button, and the look of the photo caption text. Next, you need to attach the plug-in's JavaScript file. Notice that the page already has the jQuery and jQuery easing (page 194) files attached.

3. **On the blank line immediately after the <script> tag that attaches the *jquery .easing.1.3.js* file to this page, type:**

   ```
   <script src="fancybox/jquery.fancybox-1.3.4.min.js"></script>
   ```

   This JavaScript file is stored in the *fancybox* folder inside the *chapter07* folder. Since FancyBox requires a collection of files—JavaScript, CSS, and images—it's easiest to just keep them all in one place. That way you need only to copy the *fancybox* folder from this tutorial to your own site to use FancyBox.

   This page already has another <script> tag, complete with the jQuery *ready()* function and the preloading/rollover magic you created in the first tutorial in this chapter. You just need to add the fancybox() function and you're good to go.

4. **Click in blank line directly below *$(document).ready(function() {*, and type:**

   ```
   $('#gallery a').fancybox();
   ```

   All of the links that point to larger images are contained inside a <div> tag with the ID *gallery*, so *$('#gallery a')* selects those, and the *.fancybox()* function applies the FancyBox effect to the page.

   Believe it or not, you're done! Save the page and preview it in a web browser. Click one of the thumbnail images to see the magic happen. Now you can see why plug-ins are so useful—you don't really have to do any programming to get some fantastic effects!

   Click the Close button or anywhere else on the page to make the large image disappear. Click another thumbnail to see another larger image. One problem with this setup is that each thumbnail is independent of the others. In other words, in order to see another pop-up image, you need to first close the current pop-up, then click a thumbnail. It would be nicer if, once one pop-up image appears, you could just navigate from one large photo to another. A simple change to the HTML will do that.

5. **Locate the first link inside the gallery <div>—<a href=".._images/large/slide1 .jpg">—and add rel="gallery" so that the HTML looks like this:**

```
<a href="../_images/large/slide1.jpg" rel="gallery">
```

The actual value you supply the rel attribute—*gallery* in this case—doesn't matter. What's important is that the value be the same for every image you wish to include in the group.

6. **Add *rel="gallery"* to each of the 5 remaining links inside the gallery div. Save and preview the page.**

Now, after you click one thumbnail, you can mouse over the right side of the pop-up image to see a Next button. Click that button and you'll jump to the next photo in the group. Mouse over the left side to see the Previous button.

One thing that's missing are captions for each photo. To add a caption, you don't need any JavaScript, just an HTML *title* attribute added to each <a> tag.

7. **Locate the first link again—*<a href="../_images/large/slide1.jpg" rel="gallery">*—and add *title="Lotsa golf balls"* to the tag, so it looks like this:**

```
<a href="../_images/large/slide1.jpg" rel="gallery" title="Lotsa golf balls">
```

Save the file and preview it in a web browser. Click the first thumbnail on the left—voila, the caption appears. Add title attributes to the other <a> tags in this <div>. Now, you'll tweak some of FancyBox's default settings to customize its look.

8. **Change the code you added in step 4 by adding an object literal between the *fancybox()* function's parentheses. The new code is bolded below:**

```
$('#gallery a').fancybox({
  overlayColor : '#060',
  overlayOpacity : .3
});
```

This code passes an object literal (page 145) to the *fancybox()* function. An object literal is made up of a property name, followed by a colon and then a value. So overlayColor is the name of an option for FancyBox (see page 227), and you're setting its value to *'#060'*. This particular option changes the background color that appears between the page and the pop-up image. The overlayOpacity setting controls how transparent the overlay is; in this case, .3 means 30% opacity.

Note: Object literals look kind of weird and have some strange rules. Make sure to add a comma after each property/value pair for each pair except the last one. For example, the last line *above overlayOpacity : .3* must not have a comma at the end. However, if you add more options (as you will in step 10), you must add a comma. You'll find more information about object literals on page 145.

---

9. **Save the page and preview it in a web browser.**

Now when you click on a thumbnail, a greenish tint appears covering the page. Next, you'll adjust how the pop-up images pop onto the screen.

10. **Change the code once again, by adding a few additional options. The new code is bolded below:**

```
$('#gallery a').fancybox({
  overlayColor : '#060',
```

```
overlayOpacity : .3,
transitionIn: 'elastic',
transitionOut: 'elastic',
easingIn: 'easeInSine',
easingOut: 'easeOutSine',
titlePosition: 'outside' ,
cyclic: true
});
```

Don't forget to add a comma at the end of *overlayOpacity : .3.* When you set transitionIn and transitionOut properties to *elastic,* the pop-up image zooms onto the page when you click a thumbnail and zoom off the page when you close the pop-up image. The easingIn and easingOut options use the jQuery easing plug-in (page 194) to control how the elastic in and out transitions animate. Finally, the cyclic option makes it so that visitors, once they get to the last pop-up image in a group, can click the Next button to cycle back to the first image in the group.

11. **Save the page and preview it in a web browser.**

    Who says JavaScript is hard? The file *complete_fancybox.html* is a completed, working version of the tutorial.

FancyBox is a fun and useful plug-in. As you'll see in the next chapter, it's not limited to just displaying images, either. You can also use it to display HTML, videos, or complete web pages in a pop-up window on the page.

Improving Navigation

Links make the web go around. Without the instant access to information provided by linking from page to page and site to site, the web wouldn't have gotten very far. In fact, it wouldn't be a *web* at all. Since links are one of the most common and powerful pieces of HTML, it's only natural that there are lots of JavaScript techniques for enhancing how links work. In this chapter, you'll learn the basics of using JavaScript to control links, and how to open links in new windows and in windows within a page.

Some Link Basics

You undoubtedly know a lot about links already. After all, they're the heart of the web, and the humble <a> tag is one of the first pieces of HTML a web designer learns. Adding JavaScript to a page can turn a basic link into a supercharged gateway of interactivity...but only if you know how to use JavaScript to control your links. Once you've got the basics, later sections of this chapter will give you real-world techniques for controlling links with JavaScript.

Selecting Links with JavaScript

To do anything with a link on a web page, you must first select it. You can select all of the links on a page, just one, or a particular group of related links—for example, links that are grouped together in the same part of a page, or that share a certain characteristic such as external links that point to other websites.

jQuery gives you great flexibility in selecting document elements. For example, the code *$('a')* creates a jQuery selection of all links on a page. Furthermore, jQuery lets you refine your selections, so you can quickly select all the links within a particular area of a page. For example, you can select all of the links contained inside a bulleted list with an ID of *mainNav* like this: *$('#mainNav a')*. Likewise, you can use attribute selectors (page 133) to select links whose HREF values (the paths to the files they point to) match a certain pattern such as links that point to other sites, or that point to PDF files (see "Opening External Links in a New Window" on page 238 for an example).

And once you've used jQuery to select those links, you can use the jQuery functions to work with those links. For example, you can loop through each link using the *each()* function (page 147), apply a class to those links with the addClass() function (page 142), or add event functions to them (page 162). You'll see many examples of what you can do to links later in this chapter.

Determining a Link's Destination

After you've selected one or more links, you may be interested in where they lead. For example, in the slideshow you built on page 222, each link pointed to a larger image; by retrieving the path, you used JavaScript to display that larger image. In other words, you extracted the link's *href* value and used that path to create a new <img> tag on the page. Likewise, you can retrieve the *href* value that leads to another web page and, instead of going to that page when you click the link, you can actually display the new web page on top of the current page. (See page 245 to learn how to do that.)

In each case, you need to access the *href* attribute, which is an easy process using jQuery's *attr()* function (page 146). For example, say you've applied an ID to the link that leads back to a site's home page. You can retrieve that link's path like this:

```
var homePath = $('#homeLink').attr('href');
```

You'll find this information handy in many instances. For example, say you want to add the full URL of a link pointing outside of your site next to the link text itself. In other words, suppose you have a link with the text "Learn more about bark beetles" that points to *http://www.barkbeetles.org/*. Now suppose you'd like to change the text on the page to read "Learn more about bark beetles (*www.barkbeetles.org*)" (so when people print the page they'll know where that link leads to).

You can do that easily with the following JavaScript:

```
1   $('a[href^="http://"]').each(function() {
2     var href = $(this).attr('href');
3     href = href.replace('http://','');
4     $(this).after(' (' + href + ')');
5   });
```

Note: The line numbers at left aren't part of the code, so don't type them. They're just for examining the code line by line.

Line 1 selects all external links (page 146) then runs the *each()* function (page 147), which simply applies a function to each link (in other words, it "loops" through the list of links). In this case, lines 2–4 make up the function body. Line 2 retrieves the link's *href* of the link (for example, *http://www.barkbeetles.org*). Line 3 is optional—it just simplifies the URL for display purposes by removing the *http://*, so the *href* variable now holds something like *www.barkbeetles.org* (you can learn about JavaScript's *replace()* method on page 443). Finally, line 4 adds the contents of the variable *href* (wrapped in parentheses) after the link: (*www.barkbeetles.org*), and line 5 closes the function.

You can take this basic premise even further by creating a bibliography at the bottom of the page listing all the links mentioned in the article. Instead of adding each web address after each link, you list each web address at the bottom of the page in a separate div.

Don't Follow That Link

When you add a click event to a link, you may not want the web browser to follow its normal behavior of exiting the current page and loading the link's destination. For example, in the image gallery on page 216, when you click a link on a thumbnail image, the page loads a larger image. Normally, clicking that link would exit the page and show the larger image by itself on a blank page. However, in this case, instead of following the link to the image, you stay on the same page, where the larger image is loaded.

There are a couple of ways you can stop a link in its tracks—you can return a *false* value or use jQuery's *preventDefault()* function (page 175). For example, say you have a link that takes a visitor to a login page. To make your site feel more responsive, you want to use JavaScript to show a login form when the visitor clicks that link. In other words, if the visitor's browser has JavaScript turned on, when he clicks that link, a form will appear on the page; if the browser has JavaScript turned off, clicking the link will take the visitor to the login page.

There are several steps to achieve this goal:

1. **Select the login link.**

   See the first part of this section on the previous page, if you need ideas for how to do this.

2. **Attach a click event.**

   You can use jQuery's *click()* function to do so. The *click()* function takes another function as an argument. That function contains the steps that happen when a user clicks the link. In this example, only two steps are required.

3. **Show the login form.**

   The login form might be hidden from view when the page loads—perhaps an absolutely positioned <div> tag directly under the link. You can show the form using the *show()* function or one of jQuery's other show effects (see page 189).

4. **Stop the link!**

This step is the most important. If you don't stop the link, the web browser will simply leave the current page and go to the login web page.

Here's how to stop the link using the "return false" method. Assume that the link has an ID of *showForm* and the hidden <div> tag with the login form has an ID of *loginForm:*

```
1   $('#showForm').click(function() {
2     $('#loginForm').fadeIn('slow');
3     return false;
4   });
```

Line 1 accomplishes both steps 1 and 2 above; line 3 displays the hidden form. Line 2 is the part that tells the web browser "Stop! Don't follow that link." You must put the *return false;* statement as the last line of the function, because once the JavaScript interpreter encounters a return statement, it exits the function.

You can also use jQuery's *preventDefault()* function, like this:

```
1   $('#showForm').click(function(evt) {
2     $('#loginForm').fadeIn('slow');
3     evt.preventDefault();
4   });
```

The basic details of this script are the same as the one before it. The main difference is that the function assigned to the click event now accepts an argument—*evt*—which represents the event itself (the event object is described on page 173). The event has its own set of functions and properties—the *preventDefault()* function simply stops any default behavior associated with the event: For a click on a link, that's loading a new web page.

Opening External Links in a New Window

Losing visitors is one of the great fears for any site that depends on readership. Online magazines that make money from ad revenue don't want to send people away from their site if they can help it; an e-commerce site doesn't want to lose a potential customer by letting a shopper click a link that leaves the site behind; and while displaying a portfolio of completed websites, a web designer might not want to let a potential client leave her site while viewing one of the designer's finished projects.

Many sites deal with these fears by opening a new window whenever a link to another site is clicked. That way, when the visitor finishes viewing the other site and closes its window, the original site is still there. HTML has long provided a method of doing that using a link's *target* attribute—if you set that attribute to *_blank*, a web browser knows to open that link in a new window (or, with browsers that use tabs, open the link a new tab).

Note: There's a quite a bit of debate amongst web usability experts about whether the strategy of opening new windows is a good or bad idea. For example, see *www.useit.com/alertbox/990530.html*.

Manually adding *target="_blank"* to each link that points outside your site takes a long time and is easy to forget. Fortunately, using JavaScript and jQuery, there's a quick, easy method to force web browsers to open external links (or any links you want) in a new window or browser tab. The basic process is simple:

1. **Identify the links you wish to open in a new window.**

   In this chapter, you'll use a jQuery selector (page 129) to identify those links.

2. **Add the *target* attribute with a value of *_blank* to the link.**

   You might be thinking, "Hey, that's invalid HTML. I can't do that." Well, first, it's only invalid for the strict versions of HTML 4.01 and XHTML 1.0, so it's fine for any other document type, including the new HTML5 doctype. Second, your page will still validate, since an HTML validator (for example, *http://validator .w3.org/*) only analyzes the actual HTML code in the web page file and not any HTML that JavaScript adds. And, lastly, every browser understands the *target* attribute, so you know that the link will open in a new window, regardless of the standards for strict document types.

In jQuery, you can complete the previous two steps in one line of code:

```
$('a[href^="http://"]').attr('target','_blank');
```

The jQuery selector—*$('a[href^="http://"]')*—uses an attribute selector (page 133) to identify <a> tags that begin with *http://* (for example, *http://www.yahoo.com*). The selector identifies all of these types of links and then uses the jQuery *attr()* function (page 146) to set the *target* attribute to *_blank* for each link. And that's it!

If you use absolute paths to specify links to files on your own site, you need one more step. For example, if your site's address is *www.your_site.com*, and you link to other pages or files on your site like this: *http://www.your_site.com/a_page.html*, then the previous code also forces those links to open in a new window. If you don't want to open up a new window for every page of your site (your poor visitors), you need code like the following:

```
var myURL = location.protocol + '//' + location.hostname;
$('a[href^="http://"]').not('[href^="'+myURL+'"]').attr('target','_blank');
```

This code first specifies the URL for your site and assigns it to a variable—*myURL*. The URL of your site is accomplished with a little bit of help from the browser's window object. A browser knows the protocol used for accessing a URL—*http:*, or for secured sites, *https:*. It's stored in the location object's *protocol* property. Likewise, the name of the site—*www.sawmac.com*, for example—is stored in the *hostname* property. So the JavaScript *location.protocol + '//' + location.hostname* generates a string that looks like *http://www.sawmac.com*. Of course, the hostname in this case changes depending upon where the page with this JavaScript code comes from. For example, if you put this code on a page that comes from *http://www.your_site.com*, then when someone views the page from that site, *location.hostname* would be *www .your_site.com*.

The second line of code starts with a jQuery selector, which retrieves all links that start with *http://*. Then, the *not()* function removes any links start with your URL—in this example, links that point to *http://www.sawmac.com*. (The *not()* function is a useful way of excluding some elements from a jQuery selection—to learn about it, visit *http://api.jquery.com/not*.)

So to actually use this code on a page, you just link to the jQuery file, add the *$(document).ready() function* (page 169), and then insert the previous code inside like this:

```
<script src="js/jquery-1.6.3.min.js"></script>
<script>
$(document).ready(function() {
  var myURL = location.protocol + '//' + location.hostname;
  $('a[href^="http://"]').not('[href^="'+myURL+'"]').attr('target','_blank');
});
</script>
```

Another approach would be to create an external JavaScript file (see page 27); in that file, create a function that runs the code to make external links open in a new window; attach that file to the page; and then call the function on that page.

For example, you could create a file named *open_external.js* with the following code:

```
function openExt() {
  var myURL = location.protocol + '//' + location.hostname;
  $('a[href^="http://"]').not('[href^="'+myURL+'"]').attr('target','_blank');
}
```

Then add the following code to each page on your site that you'd like to apply this function to:

```
<script src="js/jquery-1.6.3.min.js"></script>
<script src="js/open_external.js"></script>
<script>
$(document).ready(function() {
  openExt();
  // add any other JavaScript code to the page
});
</script>
```

The benefit of using an external file is that if you've used this function throughout your site on hundreds of pages, you can easily update the script so it's fancier—for example, you can later change the *openExt()* function to open external pages in a frame within the current page (see page 245 for how to do that). In other words, an external *.js* file makes it easier for you to keep your scripts consistent across your entire site.

Creating New Windows

Web browsers let you open new windows and customize many of their properties, like width and height, onscreen placement, and even whether they display scrollbars, menus, or the location (address) bar. The basic technique uses the *open()* method, which follows this basic structure:

```
open(URL, name, properties)
```

The *open()* method takes three arguments. The first is the URL of the page you wish to appear in the new open window—the same value you'd use for the *href* attribute for a link (*http://www.google.com*, */pages/map.html*, or *../../portfolio.html*, for example). The second argument is a name for the window, which can be any name you'd like to use; follow the same naming rules used for variables as described on page 46. Finally, you can pass a string containing the settings for the new window (its height and width, for example).

In addition, when opening a new window, you usually create a variable to store a reference to that window. For example, if you want to open Google's home page in a new window that's 200 pixels square, you can write this code:

```
var newWin= open('http://www.google.com/', ↵
'theWin','height=200,width=200');
```

Note: The ↵ symbol at the end of a line of code indicates that the next line should really be typed as part of the first line. But since a *really* long line of JavaScript code won't fit on this book's page, it's broken up over two lines.

This code opens a new window and stores a reference to that window in the variable *newWin*. The section "Use the Window reference" on the next page describes how to use this reference to control the newly opened window.

Note: The name you provide for the new window (*'theWin'* in this example) doesn't do much. However, once you've provided a name, if you try to open another window using the same name, you won't get a new window. Instead, the web page you request with the *open()* method just loads in the previously created window with the same name.

Window Properties

Browser windows have many different components: scroll bars, resize handles, toolbars, and so on (see Figure 8-1). In addition, windows have a width and height and a position on the screen. You can set most of these properties when creating a new window by creating a string containing a comma-separated list of each property and its setting as the third argument for the *open()* method. For example, to set the width and height of a new window and to make sure the location bar appears, you can write this:

```
var winProps = 'width=400,height=300,location=yes';
var newWin = open('about.html','aWin',winProps);
```

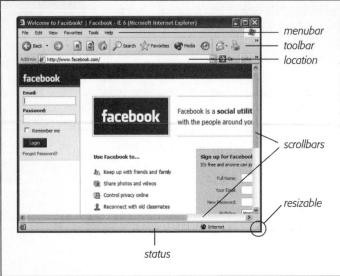

Figure 8-1:
The different properties of a browser window like scroll bars, toolbars, and resize handles are collectively called a browser's chrome. Each browser has its own take on these properties, and web developers have little control over how they work or look. Don't despair—when you create a new window using JavaScript, you can turn off some of these features.

menubar

toolbar

location

scrollbars

resizable

status

You set the properties that control the size or position of the window using pixel values, while the other properties take either the value *yes* (to turn on that property) or *no* (to turn off that property). In the case of any of the yes/no properties (like toolbar or location), if you don't specify a property value, the web browser turns that property off (for example, if you don't set the location property, the web browser hides the location field that normally appears at the top of the window). Only *height, width, left, top,* and *toolbar* work consistently across browsers. As noted in the following list, some browsers ignore some of these properties entirely, so if you create pop-up windows with JavaScript, make sure to test on every browser you can.

- *height* dictates the height of the window, in pixels. You can't specify percentage values or any other measurement besides pixels. If you don't specify a height, the web browser matches the height of the current window.

- *width* specifies the width of the window. As with height, you can only use pixels, and if you leave this property out, the web browser matches the width of the current window.

- *left* is the position, in pixels, from the left edge of the monitor.

- *top* is the position, in pixels, from the top edge of the monitor.

- *scrollbars* appear at the right and bottom edges of a browser window whenever a page is larger than the window itself. To completely hide the scrollbar, set this property to *no*. You can't control which scrollbar is hidden (it's either both or neither), and some browsers, like Chrome and Safari, won't let you hide scrollbars.

- *status* controls the appearance of the status bar at the bottom of the window. Firefox and Internet Explorer normally don't let you hide the status bar, so it's always visible in those browsers.

- *toolbar* sets the visibility of the toolbar containing the navigation buttons, book-mark button, and other controls available to the particular browser. On Safari, the toolbar and location settings are the same: Turning on either one displays both the toolbar buttons and the location field.

- *location* specifies whether the location field is visible. Also known as the address bar, this field displays the page's URL and lets visitors go to another page by typing a new URL. Opera, Internet Explorer, and Firefox don't let you hide a page's location entirely. This feature is supposed to stop nefarious uses of JavaScript like opening a new window and sending you off to another site that looks like the site you just left. Also, Safari displays the toolbars as well as the location field with this property turned on.

- *menubar* applies to browsers that have a menu at the top of their windows (for example, the common File and Edit menus that appear on most programs). This setting applies only to Windows browsers—Macs have the menu at the top of the screen, not the individual window. And it doesn't apply to IE 7 and later, which doesn't normally display a menu bar.

Note: For amazing examples of JavaScript programming that use the *window.open()* method, check out *http://experiments.instrum3nt.com/markmahoney/ball/* and *http://thewildernessdowntown.com/*.

Use the window reference

Once you open a new window, you can use the reference to that window to control it. For example, say you open a new window with the following code:

```
var newWin = open('products.html','theWin','width=300,height=300');
```

The variable *newWin*, in this case, holds a reference to the new window. You can then apply any of the browser's window methods to that variable to control the window. For example, if you want to close that window, you could use the *close()* method like this:

```
newWin.close();
```

Browsers support many different methods for the window object, but here are some of the most commonly used to control the window itself:

- *close()* closes the specified window. For example, the command *close()* closes the current window. But you can also apply this to a window reference: *newWin* *.close(),* for example. You can use any event to trigger this close, like a mouse click on a button that says, "Close this window."

Note: If you use any one of these commands by itself, it applies to the window running the script. For example, adding the statement *close();* to a script closes the window the script is in. However, if you've opened a window and have a reference to that window (for example, a variable that you created when the window was opened, like *newWin*), then you can close that window from the page that originally created the window using the reference like this: *newWin.close()*.

- *blur()* forces the window to "lose focus." That is, the window moves behind any already opened windows. It's a way to hide an opened window, and web advertisers use it to create "pop under" ads—windows that open underneath any current windows, so when the visitor closes all of his windows, there's an annoying ad waiting for him.

- *focus()* is the opposite of *blur()* and forces the window to come to the top of the stack of other windows.

- *moveBy()* lets you move the window a set number of pixels to the right and down. You provide two arguments to the method—the first specifies the number of pixels to move to the right, and the second specifies how many pixels to move the window down. For example, *newWin.moveBy(200,300);* moves the window that's referenced by the *newWin* variable 200 pixels to the right and 300 pixels down on the screen.

- *moveTo()* moves the window to a specific spot on the monitor specified by a left and top values. This command is the same as setting the *left* and *top* properties (page 242) when opening a new window. For example, to move a window to the top-left corner of the monitor, you can run this code: *moveTo(0,0);*.

Note: To see many of these methods in action, visit the All Is Not Lost website: *http://www.allisnotlo.st/*.

- *resizeBy()* changes the width and height of the window. It takes two arguments: The first specifies how many pixels wider to make the window; the second specifies how many pixels taller the window should be. For example, *resizeBy(100,200);* makes the current window 100 pixels taller and 200 pixels wider. You use negative numbers to make the window smaller.

- *resizeTo()* changes the windows dimensions to a set width and height. For example, *resizeTo(200,400);* changes the current window so it's 200 pixels wide and 400 pixels tall.

- *scrollBy()* scrolls the document inside the window by the specified number of pixels to the right and down. For example, *scrollBy(100,200);* scrolls the current document down 200 pixels and 100 pixels to the right. If the document can't scroll (in other words, the document fits within the window without scrollbars or the document has been scrolled to the end), then this function has no effect.

- *scrollTo()* scrolls the document inside the window to a specific pixel location to the right and from the top of the page. For example, *scrollTo(100,200);* scrolls the current document down 200 pixels from its top and 100 pixels from its left edge. If the document can't scroll (in other words, the document fits within the window without scrollbars or the document has been scrolled to the end), then this function has no effect.

Tip: The jQuery ScrollTo plug-in provides a simple way to control document scrolling using JavaScript. Find out more about this plug-in at *http://plug-ins.jquery.com/project/ScrollTo*.

Events that can open a new window

In the short history of the web, pop-up windows have gotten a bad name. Unfortunately, many websites have abused the *open()* method to force unwanted pop-up ads on unsuspecting visitors. These days, most browsers have a pop-up blocking feature that prevents unwanted pop-up windows, so even though you can add the JavaScript code to make a new window open as soon as a page loads, or when the visitor closes a window, most browsers won't let it happen. The visitor will either see a message letting her know that the browser prevented a new window from opening, or maybe get no indication at all that a pop-up window was blocked.

In fact, many browsers won't let you open a browser window using most events like mouseover, mouseout, or keypress. The only reliable way to use JavaScript to open windows is to trigger the action when the user clicks a link or submits a form. To do so, you add a click event to any HTML element (it doesn't have to be a link) and open a new window. For example, say you want some links on a page to open in a new window that's 300 pixels square, has scrollbars, and is resizable, but doesn't have any of the other browser chrome like toolbars. You can add a class name—*popup*, for example—to each of those special links, and then add this jQuery code to your page:

```
$('.popup').click(function() {
  var winProps='height=300,width=300,resizable=yes,scrollbars=yes';
  var newWin=open($(this).attr('href'),'aWin',winProps);
}
```

Opening Pages in a Window on the Page

Opening new windows can be problematic. Not only do many browsers try to block pop-up windows, but like many designers, you may not like the fact that you can't really control how the browser window looks. What if you just want a clean, simple way to display a new web page without exiting the current page? Use JavaScript, of course! You can create a window-within-a-page effect by using JavaScript to dynamically add an *iframe* to a page and display another web page within that iframe. The final effect looks as if the linked page is simply floating above the current page (see Figure 8-2).

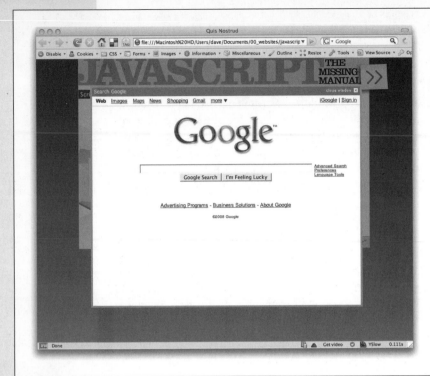

Figure 8-2:
You can quickly create a page-within-a-page effect using the FancyBox jQuery plug-in.

The <iframe> (short for inline frame) is similar to old-school HTML frames, but you can insert an iframe anywhere in a page's HTML. By setting the dimensions of the iframe and specifying a src attribute (a web page address), you can load another web page so it looks like it's part of the current page. To make the process easy, you can use a jQuery plug-in to handle all of the heavy lifting, so you can concentrate on the design.

In fact, you already have used a plug-in that can do this in the last chapter—FancyBox. In the last chapter you used FancyBox to create a gallery of images, and you can also use its pop-up window goodness to display entire web pages from your site or any other site on the web.

Note: You can learn more about iframes at *http://www.w3schools.com/tags/tag_iframe.asp*. The <iframe> tag is not valid HTML for HTML 4.01 Strict or XHTML 1.0 Strict. However, the Greybox plug-in uses JavaScript to add the <iframe> tag, so your actual HTML will pass validation. In addition, since HTML 5 supports the <iframe> tag, all major browsers will continue to support it into the future.

Using FancyBox to display links within a page is nearly the identical to using the plug-in for an image gallery as described on page 222. In a nutshell, the steps are:

1. **Download the FancyBox files from** *http://fancybox.net.*

   See step 2 on page 224 for more information on which files you'll need.

2. **Attach the FancyBox CSS file to your web page.**

   FancyBox uses some, ahem, fancy CSS to achieve its page-within-a-page look, and it won't look or work correctly without it.

3. **Attach the JavaScript files.**

   Of course FancyBox requires jQuery as well as its own external JavaScript file, so you'll add those to your page; for example:

   ```
   <script src="js/jquery-1.6.3.min.js"></script>
   <script src="fancybox/jquery.fancybox-1.3.4.js"></script>
   ```

   As mentioned on page 227, you may also want to use the jQuery easing plug-in if you want to add more interesting effects when opening and closing the web pages on screen.

4. **Add** *class="iframe"* **to any links that you wish to open in a pop-up window on the page.**

   Because FancyBox needs to open external web pages inside of <iframe> tags (something that's not required for a simple image gallery), you need to identify the links that require iframes. The easiest way to do this is to simply add *class="iframe"* to each link, like this:

   ```
   <a href="http://www.google.com" class="iframe">Google</a>
   ```

5. **Add a <script> tag, the jQuery** *ready()* **function, and call FancyBox.**

   ```
   <script>
   $(document).ready(function() {
     $('.iframe').fancybox();
   }); // end ready
   </script>
   ```

   As you read in the last chapter, FancyBox is pretty simple to get working: Just one line of code is needed. In this case, you can use the jQuery selector *$('.iframe')* since the class *iframe* was applied to each of the links.

6. **Insert an object literal, with the width and height you want for the pop-up window.**

   FancyBox accepts mean different settings. As you read on page 227, you can control the speed at which the effect runs, the opacity of the page overlay, and more by passing an object literal to the *fancybox()* function. Normally for images, the height and width of the pop-up is determined by the size of the image. In the case of linked pages, there is no set dimension, so you need to supply both a width and a height value. For example, say you want to make the pop-up window 760 pixels wide and 400 pixels tall. You can add the code in bold below to the code from step 5:

   ```
   <script>
   $(document).ready(function() {
     $('.iframe').fancybox({
         width : 760,
         height : 400
   ```

```
    }); // end fancybox
  }); // end ready
</script>
```

You can also use percentage values so the box is a percentage of the total width and height of the browser window—this is a good way to make sure the box takes advantage of very large screens for some visitors, but still fits within a smaller screen. Instead of using a number, you need to use a string value for the width and height so that you can include the % sign, like this:

```
<script>
$(document).ready(function() {
  $('.iframe').fancybox({
      width : '85%',
      height : '75%'
  }); // end fancybox
}); // end ready
</script>
```

Tutorial: Opening a Page Within a Page

In this tutorial, you'll take the FancyBox plug-in for a spin by applying it to a page and customizing its appearance.

Note: See the note on page 29 for information on how to download the tutorial files.

---

1. **In a text editor, open the file *in-page-links.html* in the *chapter08* folder.**

   Your fingers are probably pretty tired by this point in the book, so this file provides a link to the FancyBox style sheet, script tags to load jQuery and the FancyBox plug-in, and a <script> tag with the *$(document).ready()* function.

   The first step is to mark the links you wish to open in a window on the page.

2. **Locate the first link—*<a href="http://www.google.com/">Search Google </a>*—and add *class="iframe"* so the code looks like this:**

   ```
   <a href="http://www.google.com/" class="iframe">Search Google</a>
   ```

   As with the FancyBox image gallery discussed on page 224, you can add captions to the pop up window by adding a title attribute to the <a> tag.

3. **Add *title="Google"* to the link you edited in the last step so it looks like this:**

   ```
   <a href="http://www.google.com/" class="iframe" title="Google">Search Google
   </a>
   ```

   Now you just need to set up the other links similarly.

4. **Repeat steps 2 and 3 for the next 4 links.**

   Use the text inside the link for the title attribute (or make up your own). Now you can apply FancyBox to those links.

5. **Near the top of the file, click in the empty line after the *$(document).ready()* function and add the code listed on lines 3–7:**

```
1  <script>
2  $(document).ready(function() {
3      $('.iframe').fancybox({
4          width : '90%',
5          height : '90%',
6          titlePosition: 'outside',
7      }); // end fancybox
8  }); end ready()
9  </script>
```

Here, the width and height are set to 90% so the pop-up window will adjust to the visitor's browser window. The *titlePosition* option (page 228) positions the title outside of the pop-up window.

6. **Save the page and preview it in a web browser. Click the links.**

The links open in a pop-up window. Very cool. You can use any of the other FancyBox options discussed on page 226 to modify the appearance of the page: changing the overlay color, adding a zoom-in and zoom-out effect when opening and closing links, and altering the Close button. The file *complete_in-page-links.html* includes the finished version of this tutorial.

Note: The previous edition of this book included a section on creating "bigger links"—that is, a link that contains block level elements like divs, headings, and paragraphs. This technique let you create a large, clickable target, complete with rollover effects. You don't need JavaScript to do that anymore. HTML5 (and all current browsers) let you wrap the <a> tag around any block level element including divs.

Basic, Animated Navigation Bar

As websites grow in size, it gets harder and harder to provide access to every section of a site without overwhelming the page (and its visitors) with links. To make navigating a site more manageable, many web designers use drop-down menu systems to keep links hidden until they're asked for (see Figure 8-3). While there are CSS-only solutions to this problem, these aren't always ideal. First, CSS-only pop-up menus are temperamental: If you roll off the menu for just a split second, the menu disappears. In addition, CSS doesn't let you add any visual effects, like fading the menu into view or animating it into position.

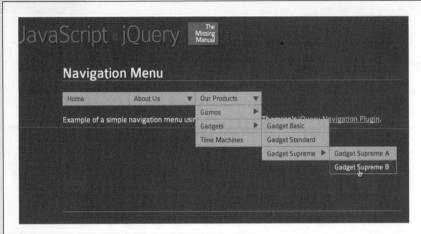

Figure 8-3:
Navigating a website filled with many pages and sections can be confusing. A navigation bar with drop-down menus is an elegant way to simplify the presentation of your site's links. It lets you include many navigation options and reduce clutter on your page.

Fortunately, with just a little JavaScript, you can create an animated menu system that works smoothly for your visitors in all browsers. This navigation menu relies a lot more on HTML and CSS than other JavaScript techniques you've learned in this book so far. You'll use HTML to create a nested set of links, and CSS to format those links to look like a navigation bar and position and hide any submenus. You'll then add some JavaScript to animate the display of menus as the mouse moves over the navigation bar's buttons.

The HTML

The HTML for your navigation menu is a straightforward bulleted list created with the <ul> tag. Each of the top-level <li> tags represent the main buttons on the navigation bar. To create a submenu, you add a nested <ul> tag within the <li> tag the menu belongs to. For example, the HTML for the menu pictured in Figure 8-3 looks like this:

```
<ul id="navigation" >
  <li><a href="#">Home</a></li>
  <li><a href="#">About Us </a>
    <ul>
      <li><a href="#">Our History</a></li>
      <li><a href="#">Driving Directions</a></li>
      <li><a href="#">Hours</a></li>
    </ul>
  </li>
  <li><a href="#">Our Products </a>
    <ul>
      <li><a href="#">Gizmos </a>
        <ul>
          <li><a href="#">Gizmo Basic</a></li>
          <li><a href="#">Gizmo Standard</a></li>
          <li><a href="#">Gizmo Supreme</a></li>
```

```
        </ul>
      </li>
      <li><a href="#">Gadgets </a>
        <ul>
          <li><a href="#">Gadget Basic</a></li>
          <li><a href="#">Gadget Standard</a></li>
          <li><a href="#">Gadget Supreme</a>
            <ul>
              <li><a href="#">Gadget Supreme A</a></li>
              <li><a href="#">Gadget Supreme B</a></li>
            </ul>
          </li>
        </ul>
      </li>
      <li><a href="#">Time Machines</a></li>
    </ul>
  </li>
</ul>
```

Note: To keep this example looking simple, the HTML uses a # symbol in place of an actual URL for the href property on each <a> tag—*<a href="#">*, for example. In an actual navigation bar, each <a> tag would point to a real web page, like this: *<a href="products/gadgets/basic.html">*.

The three main navigation buttons are Home, About Us, and Our Products. Under About Us is a menu, represented by a nested list that includes the options Our History, Driving Directions, and Hours. The Our Products button contains another menu with the options Gizmo, Gadget, and Time Machines. Both Gizmo and Gadgets have their own menus (two other nested lists); and under the Gadget Supreme option found under the Gadget menu), there are two more options (yet another nested list). A nested list is just another list that's indented one more level. Visually, the HTML above translates to a list like the following:

- Home
- About Us
  - Our History
  - Driving Directions
  - Hours
- Our Products
  - Gizmos
    - Gizmo Basic
    - Gizmo Standard
    - Gizmo Supreme
  - Gadgets
    - Gadget Basic

- Gadget Standard
- Gadget Supreme
  - Gadget Supreme A
  - Gadget Supreme B
- Time Machines

Keep in mind that a nested list goes within the <li> tag of its parent item. For example, the <ul> tag containing the list items Gizmos, Gadgets, and Time Machines is contained within the <li> tag for the Products list item (if you need a refresher on creating HTML lists, check out *www.htmldog.com/guides/htmlbeginner/lists/*).

Note: Make sure that the top-level links (Home, About Us, and Our Products in this example) always point to a page that links to the subpages in its section (for example, the Our History, Driving Directions, and Hours links under About Us). That way, if the browser doesn't have JavaScript turned on, it can still access the links in the submenus.

The CSS

The jQuery Navigation Plugin by Daniel Thomson (*www.pollenizer.com/jquery-navigation-plugin/*) does most of the work of placing the list items so you don't need to worry about creating the CSS necessary to create the side-by-side button or the drop-down and flyout menus. However, you will want to customize the appearance of the buttons; for example, add a backgound color, remove underlines for the links, and so on. Here are a few helpful styles you can create to control different elements of the menu. (For an example, open the *complete_menu.html* file in the *chapter08* tutorial folder and look at the CSS in the <head> of the page.)

Note: The styles listed below assume that the main <ul> tag containing all of the menus and buttons has an ID of *navigation* like this: *<ul id="navigation">*. You're free to use another ID name if you like—*mainNav, menu*, for example—just adjust the style names listed below accordingly. For example, if you use the ID of *mainNav*, change the style #*navigation a* listed below to #*mainNav a*.

- #*navigation ul* controls the overall appearance of each menu. It's a good idea to set the padding and margin of this style to 0.
- #*navigation li* controls the styling for each button (however, as you'll see in this example, it's best to put most of the styling on the <a> tag inside each <li> tag). However, you should at least set the padding and margin to 0 and the *list-style-type* property to none in order to eliminate the bullets next to each button. Here's a good default style for both the ul and li tags:

```
#navigation ul, #navigation li {
```

```
    margin: 0;
    padding: 0;
    list-style-type: none;
}
```

- *#navigation a* controls the appearance of each link. You can have fun with this style: Apply background colors, fonts, font color, border lines to make your buttons standout. However, avoid setting margin and padding values to anything but 0; otherwise, your buttons will overlap each other.

- *#navigation a:hover* controls the hover or mouseover appearance of the links. You can change the background color so that when a visitor mouses over a button, the button is highlighted, which provides excellent visual feedback.

- *#navigation .stack > a* and *#navigation .stack > a:hover* control the appearance of links that have menus. You may want to add a background image (like a down-pointing arrow) to indicate that these buttons open a menu, or somehow visually distinguish these buttons from other buttons without menus.

- *#navigation ul .stack > a* and *#navigation ul .stack > a:hover* provide styling for a sub-submenu; that is, a menu that opens off of button that is itself part of a menu. For example, in Figure 8-4, the Gizmos and Gadgets buttons have sub-submenus. You don't need to style these buttons differently, but the plug-in displays those menus somewhat differently. In Figure 8-4, you see a menu that opens from the top-level (when mousing over Our Products, for instance) produces a drop-down menu below the button, but the sub-submenus open off to the *right side* of the button (Gizmos and Gadgets). If you want to use an arrow graphic to indicate a menu, you may want a down-pointing arrow for the top-level menu and a right-pointing arrow for the other menus. Look at the CSS in the *complete_menu.html* file for examples.

- Clear the float after the menu. The plug-in uses the CSS *float* CSS property to position the menu buttons side-by-side in the main menu. Because of this, text or other content that follows after the menu may slide up to the right next to the menu. In order to prevent this wrapping, you should add *clear:left* to a style formatting the content immediately following the menu. An easy way to do this is to create a class style like this:

```
.clearLeft { clear : left; }
```

And then apply that class to the tag following the <ul> of the menu. For example, say there's a paragraph tag following the nav menu. You could just write this to create the opening <p> tag:

```
<p class="clearLeft">
```

The JavaScript

The basic concept behind using JavaScript to control the display of menus is simple. Mouse over a list item, and if it has a nested list (a pop-up menu), then show that nested list; mouse off the list, and hide any nested lists.

There are a few subtleties that make this basic idea a bit more complicated. For example, pop-up menus that disappear the very instant the mouse moves off of its parent list item require precise mouse technique. It's easy to mouse off a list item when trying to navigate to a pop-up menu. If the menu suddenly disappears, your visitor is forced to move the mouse back over the original list item to open the menu again. And when there are a couple of levels of pop-up menus, it's frustratingly easy to miss the target and lose the menus.

To deal with this problem, most navigation menu scripts add a timer feature that delays the disappearance of pop-up menus. This timer accommodates not-so-precise mouse technique and makes the pop-up menus feel less fragile.

The jQuery Navigation plug-in is a very easy-to-use method of creating a basic drop-down menu, and provides the option of either a fade in or slide in effect.

The Tutorial

Now that you understand the basics of creating a navigation menu, here's how to make it happen. In this tutorial, you'll add CSS and JavaScript to transform the basic HTML menu list shown on page 250 into a navigation bar.

Note: See the note on page 29 for information on how to download the tutorial files.

---

1. **In a text editor, open the file *menu.html* in the *chapter08* folder.**

   This file contains the bulleted list of links that you'll turn into a navigation bar. To see what it looks like without any JavaScript, the first step is to attach the plug-in file.

2. **Click in the empty line after *<script src="../_js/jquery-1.6.3.min.js"></script>* and type:**

   ```
   <script src="../_js/nav1.1.min.js"></script>
   ```

   This links the jQuery Navigation plug-in to the page. Now you'll add the programming—we've already provide a set of <script> tags with the *$(document) .ready()* function in place.

3. **Click in the empty line inside the *$(document).ready()* function and add the following code in bold below:**

   ```
   $(document).ready(function() {
    $("#navigation").navPlugin({
      'itemWidth': 150,
      'itemHeight': 30
    });
   });
   ```

To activate the menu, you first use jQuery to select the <ul> tag used for the main navigation bar—in this example, that tag has the ID *navigation* applied to it, so the code *$('#navigation')* selects that tag, and the *.navPlugin()* applies the jQuery Navigation plug-in programming to the menu.

To control the plug-in, you pass an object literal as an argument. There aren't many options for this plug-in, but the two most important are itemWidth and itemHeight, which control the width and height of the buttons. You can't set different width and heights for each button on the menu, so make sure you provide a width and height that will fit all the content in the button that has the *most* text. You can also add effects to how the menus appear.

4. **Edit the code you just added so it looks like the code below (additions are in bold):**

```
1  $(document).ready(function() {
2    $('#navigation').navPlugin({
3      'itemWidth': 150,
4      'itemHeight': 30,
5      'navEffect': 'slide'
6    });
7  });
```

Don't forget the comma after 30 in line 4. The navEffect option controls how the menus appear on the page. Normally they just pop into view, but you can make a menu slide down into view with a value of *'slide'* or fade into view with a value of *'fade'*. You can also control the speed at which the menus appear and disappear.

5. **Edit the code so it looks like the code below (additions are in bold):**

```
1  $(document).ready(function() {
2    $("#navigation").navPlugin({
3      'itemWidth': 150,
4      'itemHeight': 30,
5      'navEffect': 'slide',
6      'speed': 250
7    });
8  });
```

Don't forget the comma after *'slide'* in line 5. The speed option controls is set in milliseconds, so 250 means 250 milliseconds or ¼ of a second, which is a pretty good setting. Larger numbers will make the menu feel sluggish and non-responsive.

6. **Save the page and preview it in a browser.**

You should now have a fully functional navigation bar. That was easy. Check out the CSS in the file to see how the buttons are formatted and try different CSS properties to customize the appearance of the menu. A completed version of the tutorial *complete_menu.html* is in the *chapter08* folder.

Other jQuery Plug-ins for Enhancing Page Navigation

The jQuery Navigation plug-in is simple and effective, but there are a ton of other jQuery plug-ins for creating more advanced navigation.

- The DD Mega Menu plug-in (*http://dynamicdrive .com/dynamicindex1/ddmegamenu.htm*) lets you create not just drop-down menus, but entire <divs> that can drop into view. Imagine a navigation bar that slides a big box of content into view when you mouse over a button. In this way, you can hide content but show it when someone mouses over a menu button.

The plug-in supports regular drop-down menus as well.

- The jqDock plug-in (*www.wizzud.com/jqDock/*) lets you simulate the Mac's Dock: a band of images across the screen that enlarge as you rollover them. A fun visual effect.

If neither of these plug-ins tickle your fancy, check out the large list of 45 jQuery navigation plug-ins and tutorials at *www.noupe.com/jquery/45-jquery-navigation-plugins-and-tutorials.html*.

Enhancing Web Forms

S ince the earliest days of the web, forms have made it possible for websites to collect information from their visitors. Forms can gather email addresses for a newsletter, collect shipping information to complete an online sale, or simply receive visitor feedback. Forms also require your site's visitors to *think*: read labels, type information, make selections, and so on. Since some sites depend entirely on receiving form data—Amazon wouldn't be in business long if people couldn't use forms to order books—web designers need to know how to make their forms as easy to use as possible. Fortunately, JavaScript's ability to inject interactivity into forms can help you build forms that are easier to use and ensure more accurate visitor responses.

Understanding Forms

HTML provides a variety of tags to build a web form like the one pictured in Figure 9-1. The most important tag is the <form> tag, which defines the beginning (the opening <form> tag) and the end (the closing </form> tag) of the form. It also indicates what type of method the form uses to send data (*post* or *get*), and specifies where on the web the form data should be sent.

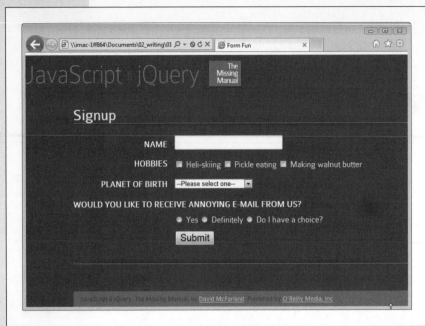

Figure 9-1:
A basic form can include many different types of controls, including text fields, radio buttons, checkboxes, menu lists, submit buttons, and so on. For a complete rundown on HTML form fields and how to use them, visit www.w3schools.com/html/html_forms.asp.

You create the actual form controls—the buttons, text fields, and menus—using either the <input>, <textarea>, or <select> tags. Most of the form elements use the <input> tag. For example, text fields, password fields, radio buttons, checkboxes, and submit buttons all share the <input> tag, and you specify which one with the *type* attribute. For example, you create a text field by using the <input> tag and setting the *type* attribute to *text* like this:

```
<input name="user" type="text">
```

Here's the HTML that creates the form pictured in Figure 9-1; the <form> tag and *form* elements are shown in bold:

```
<form action="process.php" method="post" name="signup" id="signup">
  <div>
    <label for="username" class="label">Name</label>
    <input name="username" type="text" id="username" size="36">
  </div>
  <div><span class="label">Hobbies</span>
    <input type="checkbox" name="hobby" id="heliskiing" value="heliisking">
      <label for="heliskiing">Heli-skiing</label>
    <input type="checkbox" name="hobby" id="pickle" value="pickle">
      <label for="pickle">Pickle eating</label>
    <input type="checkbox" name="hobby" id="walnut" value="walnut">
      <label for="walnut">Making walnut butter</label>
  </div>
  <div>
      <label for="planet" class="label">Planet of Birth</label>
    <select name="planet" id="planet">
      <option>Earth</option>
```

```
       <option>Mars</option>
       <option>Alpha Centauri</option>
       <option>You've never heard of it</option>
      </select>
    </div>
    <div class="labelBlock">Would you like to receive annoying e-mail from
us?</div>
    <div class="indent">
    <input type="radio" name="spam" id="yes" value="yes" checked="checked">
      <label for="yes">Yes</label>
    <input type="radio" name="spam" id="definitely" value="definitely">
      <label for="definitely">Definitely</label>
    <input type="radio" name="spam" id="choice" value="choice">
      <label for="choice">Do I have a choice?</label>
    </div>
    <div>
    <input type="submit" name="submit" id="submit" value="Submit">
    </div>
  </form>
```

Note: The <label> tag in this sample is another tag commonly used in forms. It doesn't create a form control like a button, though. It lets you add a text label, visible on the page, that explains the purpose of the form control.

Selecting Form Elements

As you've seen repeatedly in this book, working with elements on the page first requires selecting those elements. To determine the value stored in a form field, for example, you must select that field. Likewise, if you want to hide or show *form* elements, you must use JavaScript to identify those elements.

As you've read, jQuery can use almost any CSS selector to select page elements. The easiest way to select a single *form* element is to assign an ID to it, like this:

```
<input name="user" type="text" id="user">
```

You can then use jQuery's selection function:

```
var userField = $('#user');
```

Once you select a field, you can do something with it. For example, say you want to determine the value in a field—to check what a visitor has typed into the field, for instance. If the form field has an ID of *user*, you can use jQuery to access the field's value like this:

```
var fieldValue = $('#user').val();
```

Note: The jQuery *val()* function is discussed on page 261.

But what if you wanted to select all *form* elements of a particular type? For example, you might want to add a click event to every radio button on a page.

Since the <input> tag is used for radio buttons, text fields, password fields, checkboxes, submit buttons, reset buttons, and hidden fields, you can't just select the <input> tag. Instead, you need to be able to find a particular type of input tag.

Fortunately, jQuery has taken the burden out of selecting specific types of form fields (see Table 9-1). Using one of the jQuery form selectors, you can easily identify and work with all fields of a particular type. For example, suppose when the visitor submits the form, you want to check to make sure all text fields hold some value. You need to select those text fields and then check each to see if each field holds a value. jQuery lets you complete the first step like this:

```
$(':text')
```

Then, you simply loop through the results using the *.each()* function (see page 147) to make sure there's a value in each field. (You'll learn a lot more about validating form fields on page 278).

Table 9-1. jQuery includes lots of selectors to make it easy to work with specific types of form fields

Selector	Example	What it does
:input	$(':input')	Selects all input, textarea, select, and button elements. In other words, it selects all form elements.
:text	$(':text')	Selects all text fields.
:password	$(':password')	Selects all password fields.
:radio	$(':radio')	Selects all radio buttons.
:checkbox	$(':checkbox')	Selects all checkboxes.
:submit	$(':submit')	Selects all submit buttons.
:image	$(':image')	Selects all image buttons.
:reset	$(':reset')	Selects all reset buttons.
:button	$(':button')	Selects all fields with type *button*.
:file	$(':file')	Selects all file fields (used for uploading a file).
:hidden	$(':hidden')	Selects all hidden fields.

You can combine the form selectors with other selectors as well. For example, say you have two forms on a page, and you want to select the text fields in just one of the forms. Assuming that the form with the fields you're after has an ID of *signup*, you can select text fields in that form only like this:

```
$('#signup :text')
```

In addition, jQuery provides a few very useful filters that find form fields matching a particular state:

- *:checked* selects all fields that are checkmarked or turned on—that is, checkboxes and radio buttons. For example, if you want to find all checkboxes and radio buttons that are turned on, you can use this code:

```
$(':checked')
```

Even better, you can use this filter to find which radio button within a group has been selected. For example, say you have a group of radio buttons ("Pick a delivery method") with different values (UPS, USPS, and FedEx, for instance) and you want to find the value of the radio button that your visitor has selected. A group of related radio buttons all share the same HTML *name* attribute; assume that you have a group of radio buttons that share the name *shipping*. You can use jQuery's attribute selector (page 133) in conjunction with the *:checked* filter to find the value of the checked radio button like this:

```
var checkedValue = $('input[name="shipping"]:checked').val();
```

The selector—*$('input[name="shipping"]')*—selects all input elements with the name *shipping*, but adding the *:checked*—*$('input[name="shipping"]:checked')*—selects only the one that's checked. The *val()* function returns the value stored in that checkbox—USPS, for example.

- *:selected* selects all selected *option* elements within a list or menu, which lets you find which selection a visitor makes from a menu or list (<select> tag). For example, say you have a <select> tag with an ID of *state*, listing all 50 U.S. states. To find which state the visitor has selected, you can write this:

```
var selectedState=$('#state:selected').val();
```

Notice that unlike in the example for the *:checked* filter, there's a space between the ID name and the filter (*'#state :selected'*). That's because this filter selects the <option> tags, not the <select> tag. To put it in English, this jQuery selection means "find all selected options that are inside the <select> tag with an ID of *state*." The space makes it work like a CSS descendent selector: First it finds the element with the proper ID, and then searches inside that for any elements that have been selected.

Note: You can enable multiple selections for a <select> menu. This means that the *:selected* filter can potentially return more than one element.

Getting and Setting the Value of a Form Element

At times you'll want to check the value of a *form* element. For example, you may want to check a text field to make sure an email address was typed into it. Or you may want to determine a field's value to calculate the total cost of an order. On the other hand, you may want to *set* the value of a *form* element. Say, for example, you have an order form that asks for both billing and shipping information. It would helpful to give your visitors a "Same as billing" checkbox and have the shipping information fields automatically filled out using the information from the billing fields.

jQuery provides a simple function to accomplish both tasks. The *val()* function can both set and read the value of a form field. If you call the function without passing any arguments, it reads the field's value; if you pass a value to the function, it sets the form field's value. For example, say you have a field for collecting a user's email address with an ID of *email*. You can find the contents of that field like this:

```
var fieldValue = $('#email').val();
```

You can set the value of a field simply by passing a value to the *val()* function. For example, say you have a form for ordering products and you wanted to automatically calculate the total cost of a sale based on the quantity a visitor specifies (Figure 9-2). You can *get* the quantity the visitor supplies, multiply it by the cost of the products, and then *set* the value in the total field.

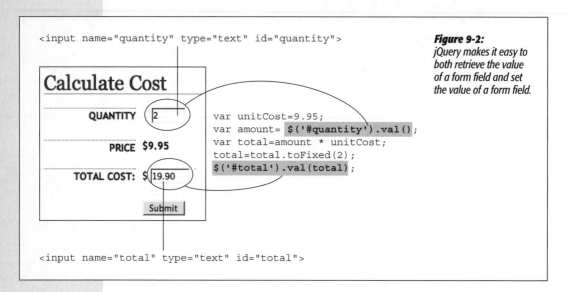

```
<input name="quantity" type="text" id="quantity">
```

Calculate Cost

QUANTITY `2`

PRICE **$9.95**

TOTAL COST: $ `19.90`

Submit

```
var unitCost=9.95;
var amount= $('#quantity').val();
var total=amount * unitCost;
total=total.toFixed(2);
$('#total').val(total);
```

```
<input name="total" type="text" id="total">
```

Figure 9-2:
jQuery makes it easy to both retrieve the value of a form field and set the value of a form field.

The code to retrieve the quantity and set the total cost for the form in Figure 9-2 looks like this:

```
1   var unitCost=9.95;
2   var amount=$('#quantity').val(); // get value
3   var total=amount * unitCost;
4   total=total.toFixed(2);
5   $('#total').val(total); // set value
```

The first line of code creates a variable that stores the cost for the product. The second line creates another variable and retrieves the amount the visitor entered into the field with an ID of *quantity*. Line 3 determines the total cost by multiplying the order amount by the unit cost, and line 4 formats the result to include two decimal places (see page 448 for a discussion of the *toFixed()* method). Finally, line 5 sets the value in the field with ID *total* to the total cost. (You'll learn how to trigger this code using an event on the next page.)

Determining Whether Buttons and Boxes Are Checked

While the *val()* function is helpful for getting the value of any *form* element, for some fields, the value is important only if the visitor has selected the field. For example, radio buttons and checkboxes require visitors to make a choice by selecting a particular value. You saw on page 260 how you can use the *:checked* filter to find checked radio buttons and checkboxes, but once you find it, you need a way to determine the status of a particular button or box.

In HTML, the *checked* attribute determines whether a particular element is checked. For example, to turn on a box when the web page is loaded, you add the *checked* attribute like this for XHTML:

```
<input type="checkbox" name="news" id="news" checked="checked" />
```

And this for HTML5:

```
<input type="checkbox" name="news" id="news" checked>
```

Since *checked* is an HTML attribute, you can easily use jQuery to check the status of the box like this:

```
if ($('#news').attr('checked')) {
  // the box is checked
} else {
  // the box is not checked
}
```

The code *$('#news').attr('checked')* returns the value *true* if the box is checked. If it's not, it returns the value *undefined*, which the JavaScript interpreter considers the same as *false*. So this basic conditional statement lets you perform one set of tasks if the box is turned on or a different set of tasks if the box is turned off. (If you need a refresher on conditional statements, turn to page 79.)

The *checked* attribute applies to radio buttons as well. You can use the *attr()* function in the same way to check whether the radio button's *checked* attribute is set.

Form Events

As you read in Chapter 5, events let you add interactivity to your page by responding to different visitor actions. Forms and *form* elements can react to many different events, so you can tap into a wide range of events to make your forms respond intelligently to your visitors' actions.

Submit

Whenever a visitor submits a form by clicking a submit button or pressing Enter or Return when typing into a text field, the *submit* event is triggered. You can tap into this event to run a script when the form is submitted. That way, JavaScript can validate form fields to make sure they're correctly filled out. When the form is submitted, a JavaScript program checks the fields, and if there's a problem, JavaScript can stop the form submission and let the visitor know what's wrong; if there are no problems, then the form is submitted as usual.

To run a function when the form's submit event is triggered, first select the form, then use jQuery's *submit()* function to add your script. For example, say you want to make sure that the name field on the form pictured in Figure 9-1 has something in it when the form is submitted—in other words, a visitor can't leave the field blank. You can do so by adding a submit event to the form, and checking the value of the field before the form is submitted. If the field is empty, you want to let the visitor know and stop the submission process; otherwise, the form will be allowed to go through.

If you look at the HTML for the form on page 258, you can see that the form has an ID of *signup* and the name field has an ID of *username*. So you can validate this form using jQuery like this:

```
1   $(document).ready(function() {
2       $('#signup').submit(function() {
3           if ($('#username').val() == '') {
4               alert('Please supply a name in the Name field.');
5               return false;
6           }
7       }); // end submit()
8   }); // end ready()
```

Line 1 sets up the required *$(document).ready()* function so the code runs only after the page's HTML has loaded (see page 169). Line 2 attaches a function to the form's *submit* event (see page 157 if you need a reminder of how to use events). Lines 3–6 are the validation routine. Line 3 checks to see if the value of the field is an empty string (''), meaning the field is empty. If the field has nothing in it, then an alert box appears letting the visitor know what he did wrong.

Line 5 is very important: It stops the form from being submitted. If you omit this step, then the form will be submitted anyway, without the visitor's name. Line 6 completes the conditional statement, and line 7 is the end of the *submit()* function.

Note: You can also stop the form from submitting by using the event object's *preventDefault()* function, described on page 175.

The *submit* event only applies to forms, so you must select a form and attach the *submit* event function to it. You can select the form either by using an ID name that's supplied in the <form> tag of the HTML, or, if there's just a single form on the page, you can use a simple element selector like this:

```
$('form').submit(function() {
    // code to run when form is submitted
});
```

Focus

Whenever someone either clicks into a text field on a form or tabs into a text field, that field receives what's called *focus*. Focus is an event that the browser triggers to indicate that a visitor's cursor is on or in a particular field; you can be sure that that's where your visitor's attention is focused. You probably won't use this event very often, but some designers use it to erase any text that's already present in a field. For example, say you have the following HTML inside a form:

```
<input name="username" type="text" id="username"↵
value="Please type your user name">
```

This code creates a text field on the form with the text "Please type your user name" inside it. This technique lets you provide instructions as to how the visitor is supposed to fill out the field. Then instead of forcing the visitor filling out the form to erase all that text herself, you can erase it when she focuses on the field, like this:

```
1   $('#username').focus(function() {
2     var field = $(this);
3     if (field.val()==field.attr('defaultValue')) {
4       field.val('');
5     }
6   });
```

Line 1 selects the field (which has an ID of *username*) and assigns a function to the focus event. Line 2 creates a variable, *field*, that stores a reference to the jQuery selection; as discussed on page 149, *$(this)* refers to the currently selected element within a jQuery function—in this case, the form field.

Line 4 is what actually erases the field. It sets the value of the field to an empty string—represented by the two single quote marks—thus removing any value from the field. But you don't want to erase this field every time the field gets the focus. For example, say someone comes to the form and clicks in the form field; the first time, that erases the "Please type your user name" text. However, if the visitor then types his name in the field, clicks outside the field, and then clicks back into the field, you don't want his name to suddenly disappear. That's where the conditional statement in line 3 comes into play.

Text fields have an attribute called *defaultValue*, which represents the text inside the field when the page first loads. Even if you erase that text, the web browser still remembers what was in the field when the page was loaded. The conditional statement checks to see if what is currently inside the field (*field.val()*) is the same as what was originally inside the field (*field.attr('defaultValue')*). If they are the same, then the JavaScript interpreter erases the text in the field.

Here's an example that explains the entire process. When the HTML on the previous page first loads, the text field has the value "Please type your user name." That's the field's *defaultValue*. So when a visitor first clicks into that field, the conditional statement asks the question "Is what's currently in the field the same as what was first in the field when the page loaded?" In other words, is "Please type your user name" equal to "Please type your user name"? The answer is yes, that field is erased.

However, say you typed *helloKitty* as your username, then tabbed into another field, and then realized that you mistyped your username. When you click back into the field to fix the mistake, the focus event is triggered again, and the function assigned to that event runs again. This time the question is "Is 'helloKitty' equal to 'Please type your username.'" The answer is no, so the field isn't erased and you can fix your typo.

Blur

When you tab out of a field or click outside of the currently focused field, the browser triggers a *blur* event. This event is commonly used with text and textarea fields to run a validation script when someone clicks or tabs out of a field. For example, say you have a long form with a lot of questions, many of which require particular types of values (for example, email address, numbers, Zip codes, and so on). Say a visitor doesn't fill out any of those fields correctly, but hits the Submit button—and is faced with a long list of errors pointing out how she failed to fill out the form correctly. Rather than dumping all of those errors on her at once, you can also check fields as she fills out the form. That way, if she makes a mistake along the way, she'll be notified immediately and can fix the mistake right then.

Say, for instance, that you have a field for collecting the number of products the visitor wants. The HTML for that might look like this:

```
<input name="quantity" type="text" id="quantity">
```

You want to make sure that the field contains numbers only (for example, 1, 2, or 9, but not One, Two, or Nine). You can check for that after the visitor clicks out of the field like this:

```
1  $('#quantity').blur(function() {
2    var fieldValue=$(this).val();
3    if (isNaN(fieldValue)) {
4      alert('Please supply a number');
5    }
6  });
```

Line 1 assigns a function to the blur event. Line 2 retrieves the value in the field and stores it in a variable named *fieldValue*. Line 3 checks to make sure that the value is numeric using the *isNaN()* method (see page 447). If it's not a number, then line 4 runs and an alert appears.

Click

The *click* event is triggered when any form element is clicked. This event is particularly useful for radio buttons and checkboxes, since you can add functions that alter the form based on the buttons a visitor selects. For example, say you have an order form that provides separate fields for both billing and shipping information. To save visitors whose shipping and billing information are the same from having to type their information twice, you can provide a checkbox—"Same as billing information", for example—that, when checked, hides the shipping information fields and makes the form simpler and more readable. (You'll see this example in action on page 276.)

Like other events, you can use jQuery's *click()* function to assign a function to a form field's click event:

```
$(':radio').click(function() {
  //function will apply to every radio button when clicked
});
```

Note: The click event also applies to text fields, but it's not the same as the focus event. Focus is triggered whenever you click *or* tab into a text field, while the click event is only triggered when the field is clicked into.

Change

The *change* event applies to form menus (like the "Planet of Birth" menu pictured in Figure 9-1). Whenever you make a selection from the menu, the change event is triggered. You can use this event to run a validation function: For example, many designers commonly add an instruction as the first option in a menu, like "Please choose a country." To make sure a visitor doesn't pick a country, then accidentally change the menu back to the first option ("Please choose a country"), you can check the menu's selected value each time someone makes a new selection from the menu.

Or, you could program the form to change based on a menu selection. For example, you can run a function so that whenever an option is selected from a menu, the options available from a second menu change. For example, Figure 9-3 shows a form with two menus; selecting an option from the top menu changes the list of available colors from the bottom menu.

To apply a change event to a menu, use jQuery's *change()* function. For example, say you have a menu listing the names of countries; the menu has an ID of *country*, and each time a new selection is made, you want to make sure the new selection isn't the instruction text "Please choose a country." You could do so like this:

```
$('#country').change(function() {
  if ($(this).val()=='Please choose a country') {
    alert('Please select a country from this menu.');
  }
}
```

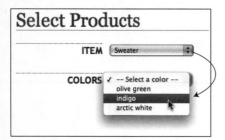

Figure 9-3:
A form menu's change event lets you do interesting things when a visitor selects an option from a menu. In this case, selecting an option from the top menu dynamically changes the options presented in the second menu. Choose a product from the top menu, and the second menu displays the colors that product is available in.

Adding Smarts to Your Forms

Web forms demand a lot from your site's visitors: Text fields need to be filled out, selections made, checkboxes turned on, and so on. If you want people to fill out your forms, it's in your interest to make the forms as simple as possible. Fortunately, JavaScript can do a lot to make your web forms easier to use. For example, you can hide form fields until they're needed, disable form fields that don't apply, and calculate totals based on form selections. JavaScript gives you countless ways to improve the usability of forms.

Focusing the First Field in a Form

Normally, to begin filling out a form, you have to click into the first text field and start typing. On a page with a login form, why make your visitors go to the extra trouble of moving their mouse into position and clicking into the login field before they can type? Why not just place the cursor in the field, ready to accept their login information immediately? With JavaScript, that's a piece of cake.

The secret lies in focus, which isn't just an event JavaScript can respond to but a command that you can issue to place the cursor inside a text field. You simply select the text field, and then run the jQuery *focus()* function. Let's say, for example, that you'd like the cursor to be inside the name field pictured in Figure 9-1 when the page loads. If you look at the HTML for this form on page 258, you'll see that field's ID is *username*. So the JavaScript to place the focus on—that is, place the cursor in—that field looks like this:

```
$(document).ready(function() {
  $('#username').focus();
});
```

In this example, the text field has the ID *username*. However, you can also create a generic script that always focuses the first text field of a form, without having to assign an ID to the field:

```
$(document).ready(function() {
  $(':text:first').focus();
});
```

As you read on page 260, jQuery provides a convenient method of selecting all text fields—*$(':text')*. In addition, by adding *:first* to any selector, you can select the first instance of that element, so the jQuery selector *$(':text:first')* selects the first text field on the page. Adding *.focus()* then places the cursor in that text field, which waits patiently for the visitor to fill out the field.

If you have more than one form on a page (for example, a "search this site" form, and a "sign up for our newsletter" form), you need to refine the selector to identify the form whose text field should get focus. For example, say you want the first text field in a sign up form to have the cursor blinking in it, ready for visitor input, but the first text field is in a search form. To focus the sign up form's text field, just add an ID (*signup*, for example) to the form, and then use this code:

```
$(document).ready(function() {
  $('#signup :text:first').focus();
});
```

Now, the selector—*$('#signup :text:first')*—only selects the first text field inside the sign up form.

Disabling and Enabling Fields

Form fields are generally meant to be filled out—after all, what good is a text field if you can't type into it? However, there are times when you might *not* want a visitor to be able to fill out a text field, check a checkbox, or select an option from a menu. Say you have a field that should only be filled out if a previous box was turned on. For example, on the 1040 form used for determining U.S. income tax, there's a field for collecting your spouse's Social Security number. You'd fill out that field only if you're married.

To "turn off" a form field that shouldn't be filled out, you can *disable* it using Java-Script. Disabling a field means it can't be checked (radio buttons and checkboxes), typed into (text fields), selected (menus), or clicked (submit buttons).

To disable a form field, simply set the field's *disabled* attribute to *true*. For example, to disable all input fields on a form, you can use this code:

```
$(':input').attr('disabled', true);
```

You'll usually disable a field in response to an event. Using the 1040 form example, for instance, you can disable the field for collecting a spouse's Social Security number when the "single" button is clicked. Assuming that the radio button for declaring yourself as single has an ID of *single*, and the field for a spouse's SSN has an ID of *spouseSSN*, the JavaScript code will look like this:

```
$('#single').click(function() {
  $('#spouseSSN').attr('disabled', true);
});
```

Of course, if you disable a field, you'll probably want a way to enable it again. To do so, simply set the disabled attribute to *false*. For example, to enable all fields on a form:

```
$(':input').attr('disabled', false);
```

Note: When disabling a form field, make sure to use the Boolean values (page 44) *true* or *false* and not the strings *'true'* or *'false'*. For example, this is wrong:

```
$(':input').attr('disabled', 'false');
```

And this is correct:

```
$(':input').attr('disabled', false);
```

Back to the tax form example: If the visitor selects the "married" option, then you need to make sure that the field for collecting the spouse's Social Security number is active. Assuming the radio button for the married option has an ID of married, you can add the following code:

```
$('#married').click(function() {
  $('#spouseSSN').attr('disabled', false);
});
```

You'll run through an example of this technique in the tutorial on page 273.

Stopping Multiple Submissions

Sometimes I get the same form information submitted more than once. How can I prevent that from happening?

Web servers aren't always the fastest creatures…and neither is the Internet. Often, there's a delay between the time a visitor presses a form's submit button, and when a new "We got your info" page appears. Sometimes this delay can be pretty long, and impatient web surfers hit the submit button a second (or third, or fourth) time, thinking that the first time they submitted the form, it simply didn't work.

This phenomenon can lead to the same information being submitted multiple times. In the case of an online sale, it can also mean a credit card is charged more than once! Fortunately, with JavaScript, there's an easy way to disable a submit button once the form submission process has begun. Using the submit button's *disabled* attribute, you can "turn it off" so it can't be clicked again.

Assume the form has an ID of *formID*, and the submit button has an ID of *submit*. First, add a *submit()* function to the form, and then, within the function, disable the submit button, like this:

```
$('#formID').submit(function() {
```

```
  $('#submit').attr('disabled',true);
});
```

If the page has only a single form, you don't even need to use IDs for the tags:

```
$('form').submit(function() {
  $('input[type=submit]').
attr('disabled',true);
});
```

In addition, you can change the message on the submit button by changing the button's value. For example, the button says "Submit" at first, but when the form is submitted, the button changes to say "…sending information" You could do that like this:

```
$('#formID').submit(function() {
  var subButton = $(this).find(':submit');
  subButton.attr('disabled',true);
  subButton.val('...sending information');
});
```

Make sure to put this code inside a *$(document).ready()* function, as described on page 169.

Hiding and Showing Form Options

In addition to disabling a field, there's another way to make sure visitors don't waste time filling out fields unnecessarily—just hide the unneeded fields. For instance, using the tax form example from the last section, you may want to hide the field for a spouse's Social Security number when the "single" option is selected and show the field when the "married" option is turned on. You can do so like this:

```
$('#single').click(function() {
  $('#spouseSSN').hide();
});
$('#married').click(function() {
  $('#spouseSSN').show();
});
```

> **Note:** jQuery's *hide()* and *show()* functions (as well as other functions for revealing and concealing elements) are discussed on page 187.

One usability benefit of hiding a field (as opposed to just disabling it) is that it makes the layout of the form simpler. After all, a disabled field is still visible and can still attract (or more accurately, distract) a person's attention.

In many cases, you'll want to hide or show more than just the form field: You'll probably want to hide that field's label and any other text associated with it. One strategy is to wrap the code you wish to hide (field, labels, and whatever other HTML) in a <div> tag, add an ID to that <div>, and then hide the <div>. You'll see an example of this technique in the following tutorial.

Tutorial: Basic Form Enhancements

In this tutorial, you'll add three usability improvements to a basic ordering form composed of fields for collecting billing and shipping information. First, you'll place the text cursor in the first field of the form when the page loads. Second, you'll disable or re-enable form fields based on selections a visitor makes. Finally, you'll hide an entire section of the form when it's not needed (see Figure 9-4).

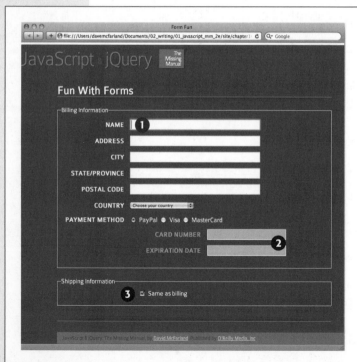

Figure 9-4:
Using JavaScript, you can increase the usability of your web forms and add interactive features, like hiding fields that aren't needed and disabling fields that shouldn't be filled out.

Note: See the note on page 29 for information on how to download the tutorial files.

Focusing a Field

The first field on this tutorial's order form page collects the name of the person placing the order (see Figure 9-4). To make using the form easier to fill out, you'll place the cursor in this field when the page loads.

1. **In a text editor, open the file *form.html* in the *chapter09* folder.**

   This file already contains a link to the jQuery file and the *$(document).ready()* function (page 169). There's a form that includes two sections—one for collecting billing information and another for collecting shipping information. (Check the page out in a web browser before continuing.)

   The first step (actually, the only step for this part of the tutorial) is to focus the field.

2. **Click in the empty line after the *$(document).ready()* function and type *$(':text:first').focus();* so the code looks like this:**

   ```
   $(document).ready(function() {
    $(':text:first').focus();
   }); // end ready()
   ```

   This selects the first text field and applies the *focus()* function to it to make a browser place the insertion point in that field.

   Save the file and preview it in a web browser.

   When the page loads, the first field should have a blinking insertion bar—meaning that field has focus, and you can immediately start filling it out.

Disabling Form Fields

That last section was just a warm-up. In this part of the tutorial, you'll disable or enable two form fields in response to selections on the form. If you preview the form in a web browser (or just look at Figure 9-4), you'll see that at the end of the billing information section of the form, there are three radio buttons for selecting a payment method: PayPal, Visa, and MasterCard. In addition, there are two fields below for collecting a card number and expiration date. Those two options only apply for credit cards, not for PayPal payments, so you'll disable those fields when the PayPal button is clicked.

The HTML for that section of the page looks like this (the form fields are in bold):

```
1    <div><span class="label">Payment Method</span>
2    <input type="radio" name="payment" id="paypal" value="paypal">
3      <label for="paypal">PayPal</label>
4    <input type="radio" name="payment" id="visa" value="visa">
5      <label for="visa">Visa</label>
6    <input type="radio" name="payment" id="mastercard" value="mastercard">
```

```
7      <label for="mastercard">MasterCard</label>
8    </div>
9    <div id="creditCard" class="indent">
10     <div>
11       <label for="cardNumber" class="label">Card Number</label>
12     <input type="text" name="cardNumber" id="cardNumber">
13     </div>
14     <div>
15       <label for="expiration" class="label">Expiration Date</label>
16     <input type="text" name="expiration" id="expiration">
17     </div>
18   </div>
```

3. **Return to your text editor and the file *form.html*.**

   You'll add to the code you created in the previous section. First, assign a function to the click event for the PayPal radio button.

4. **To the script at the top of the page, add the code in bold below:**

```
$(document).ready(function() {
  $('#name').focus();
  $('#paypal').click(function() {

  }); // end click
}); // end ready()
```

   The radio button for the PayPal option has an ID of *paypal* (see line 2 in the HTML code above), so selecting that field is just a matter of typing *$('#paypal')*. The rest of the code assigns an anonymous function to the click event (if this isn't clear, check out the discussion on assigning functions to events on page 162). In other words, not only does clicking the PayPal radio button select it (that's normal web browser behavior), but it also triggers the function you're about to create.

   Next, you'll disable the credit card number and expiration date fields, since they don't apply when the PayPal option is selected.

5. **Inside the anonymous function you added in the previous step, add a new line of code (line 4):**

```
1    $(document).ready(function() {
2      $('#name').focus();
3      $('#paypal').click(function() {
4        $('#creditCard input').attr('disabled', true);
5      }); // end click
6    }); // end ready()
```

   Although you want to disable two form fields, there's a simple way to do that with just one line of code. Both of the form fields are inside a <div> tag with an ID of *creditCard* (see line 9 of the HTML code above). So, the jQuery selector *$('#creditCard input')* translates to "select all <input> tags inside of an element with the ID *creditCard*." This flexible approach makes sure you select all of the input fields, so if you add another field, such as a CVV field, it gets selected as well (CVVs are those three numbers on the back of your credit card that web forms often request to enhance the security of online orders).

To disable the fields, all you have to do is set the *disabled* attribute to *true* (see page 269). However, this doesn't do anything to the text labels ("Card Number" and "Expiration Date"). Even though the fields themselves are disabled, those text labels remain bright and bold, sending the potentially confusing signal that the visitor can fill out the fields. To make the disabled status clearer, you'll change the labels to a light shade of gray. While you're at it, you'll also add a gray color to the background of the fields to make them look disabled.

6. **Add the bolded code below to your script:**

```
1    $(document).ready(function() {
2      $('#name').focus();
3      $('#paypal').click(function() {
4        $('#creditCard input').attr('disabled', true) ↵
5        .css('backgroundColor','#CCC');
6        $('#creditCard label').css('color','#BBB');
7      }); // end click
8    }); // end ready()
```

Note: The ↵ symbol at the end of a line of code indicates that you should type the next line as part of the previous line. Since a *really* long line of JavaScript code won't fit on this book's page, it's broken up over two lines. However, as described on page 49, JavaScript is rather flexible when it comes to line breaks and spacing, so it's actually perfectly acceptable (and sometimes easier to read) if you break a single JavaScript statement over multiple lines like this:

```
$('#creditCard input').attr('disabled',true)
                      .css('backgroundColor','#CCC');
```

Note that some programmers indent code formatted over multiple lines—in this case, indenting the .css( ) function so that it lines up with the .attr( ) function.

First, you use the jQuery's *css()* function to alter the background color of the text fields (note that the code is part of line 4, so you should type it onto the same line as the *attr()* function). Next, you use the *css()* function to adjust the font color of any <label> tags inside the <div> tag (the *css()* function is described on page 143).

If you preview the page in a web browser at this point, you'll see that clicking the PayPal button does indeed disable the credit card number and expiration date fields and dims the label text. However, if you click either the Visa or MasterCard buttons, the fields stay disabled! You need to re-enable the fields when either of the other radio buttons is selected.

7. **After the *click()* function, add a new blank line (you're adding new code between lines 7 and 8 in step 6) and then add the following:**

```
$('#visa, #mastercard').click(function() {
    $('#creditCard input').attr('disabled', false) ↵
    .css('backgroundColor','');
    $('#creditCard label').css('color','');
}); // end click
```

The selector *$('#visa, #mastercard')* selects both of the other radio buttons (see lines 4 and 6 of the HTML on page 273). Notice that to remove the background color and text colors added by clicking the PayPal button, you simply pass an empty string as the color value: *$('#creditCard label').css('color','');*. That removes the color for that element, but leaves in place the color originally defined in the style sheet.

You're nearly done with this tutorial. In the final section, you'll completely hide a part of the page based on a form selection.

JQUERY PLUG-IN ALERT

Making It Easier to Select a Date

Whether you're joining a social network site, reserving seats on a plane, or searching a calendar of events, you'll frequently encounter forms that ask you to enter a date. In most cases, you'll see a basic text field into which you're supposed to type a date. Unfortunately, you don't always know what the date is going to be two Fridays from now. In addition, an empty text field means a visitor is free to type a date in any format he'd like: 10-20-2009, 10.20.2009, 10/20/2009, or even 20/10/2009.

The best way to make selecting a date easy and ensure you'll receive dates in the same format is to use a calendar *widget*—a pop-up calendar that lets visitors select a date by clicking a day on the calendar. HTML5 defines a way to add a date picker to forms, and some web browsers have implemented basic date pickers—unfortunately, we're a ways away from relying solely on HTML, and for the time being, we'll need to stick with JavaScript. Fortunately, you can download a jQuery plug-in that makes adding calendar widgets to your forms a piece of cake.

The jQuery UI Datepicker plug-in is a sophisticated date-picking pop-up calendar that you can customize in many ways. To use it, you need to get the plug-in from the jQuery UI website at *http://jqueryui.com/*. You can use the custom download page (*http://jqueryui.com/download*) to get just the date picker, or, if you like other elements of the jQuery

UI plug-in, you can select them as well. You can also create a custom style sheet using the jQuery UI Themeroller (*http://jqueryui.com/themeroller/*).

Once you've downloaded those files, you attach the jQuery UI CSS file to the page; attach the jQuery library (see page 122); and then link to the *jQuery UI* file (follow the instructions for linking to an external JavaScript file on page 27). You'll read more about jQuery UI on page 312.

After you set up all of those basic steps, you just need to apply the *datepicker()* function to a text field. For example, say you have a form and a text field with an ID of *dateOfBirth*. To make it so that when someone clicks inside that field a pop-up calendar appears, add a <script> tag with the basic *$(document).ready()* function (see page 169 for instructions on this) and invoke the Datepicker like this:

```
$('#dateOfBirth').datepicker();
```

Of course, *$('#dateOfBirth')* is the old jQuery way of selecting the text field; the *datepicker()* function then handles the rest. The Datepicker plug-in supports options that include selecting a range of dates, opening the pop-up calendar by clicking a calendar icon, and more. To learn more about this useful plug-in, visit *http://jqueryui.com/demos/datepicker/*.

Hiding Form Fields

As is common on many product order forms, this tutorial's form includes separate fields for collecting billing and shipping information. In many cases, this information is exactly the same, so there's no need to make someone fill out both sets of fields if they don't have to. You'll frequently see a "Same as billing" checkbox on forms like these to indicate that the information is identical for both sets of fields. However, wouldn't it be even more useful (not to mention cooler) if you could completely hide the shipping fields when they aren't needed? With JavaScript, you can.

1. **Open the file *form.html* in a text editor.**

   You'll expand on the code you've been writing in the last two sections of this tutorial. First, add a function to the click event for the checkbox that has the label "Same as billing." The HTML for that checkbox looks like this:

   ```
   <input type="checkbox" name="hideShip" id="hideShip">
   ```

2. **Add the following code after the code you added in step 4 on page 274, but before the end of the script (the last line of code, which reads *}); // end ready())*:**

   ```
   $('#hideShip').click(function() {

   }); // end click
   ```

   Since the checkbox has the ID *hideShip*, the code above selects it and adds a function to the click event. In this case, instead of hiding just a single field, you want the entire group of fields to disappear when the box is checked. To make that easier, the HTML that makes up the shipping information fields is wrapped in a <div> tag with the ID of *shipping*: To hide the fields, you just need to hide the <div> tag.

   However, you'll only want to hide those fields when the box is checked. If someone clicks the box a second time to uncheck it, the <div> tag and its form fields should return. So the first step is to find out whether the box is checked.

3. **Add the code in bold below:**

   ```
   $('#hideShip').click(function() {
     if ($(this).attr('checked')) {
     }
   }); // end click
   ```

   A simple conditional statement (page 79) makes it easy to test the state of the checkbox and either hide or show the form fields. The *$(this)* refers to the object being clicked—the checkbox in this case. The element's *checked* attribute lets you know if the box is checked or not. If it's checked, then this attribute returns *true*; otherwise, it returns *false*. To finish this code, you just need to add the steps for hiding and showing the form fields.

4. **Add the bolded code below (lines 16–18) to your script. The completed script should look like this:**

   ```
   1   <script>
   2   $(document).ready(function() {
   3     $('#name').focus();
   4     $('#paypal').click(function() {
   5       $('#creditCard input').attr('disabled', true) ↵
   6       .css('backgroundColor','#CCC');
   7       $('#creditCard label').css('color','#BBB');
   8     }); // end click
   9     $('#visa, #mastercard').click(function() {
   10      $('#creditCard input').attr('disabled', false) ↵
   ```

```
11          .css('backgroundColor','');
12        $('#creditCard label').css('color','');
13      }); // end click
14    $('#hideShip').click(function() {
15      if ($(this).attr('checked')) {
16        $('#shipping').slideUp('fast');
17      } else {
18        $('#shipping').slideDown('fast');
19      }
20    }); // end click
21  }); // end ready()
22  </script>
```

The *$('#shipping')* refers to the <div> tag with the form fields, while the *slideUp()* and *slideDown()* functions (described on page 188) hide and show the <div> tag by sliding the <div> up and out of view or down and into view. You can try out some of the other jQuery effects like *fadeIn()* and *fadeOut(),* or even create your own custom animation using the *animate()* function (page 192).

A finished version of this tutorial—*complete_form.html*—is in the *chapter09* folder. If your version isn't working, compare your code with the finished tutorial and refer to the troubleshooting steps on page 34.

Form Validation

It can be frustrating to look over feedback that's been submitted via a form on your website, only to notice that your visitor failed to provide a name, email address, or some other piece of critical information. That's why, depending on the type of form you create, you might want to make certain information mandatory.

For instance, a form used for subscribing to an email newsletter isn't much use if the would-be reader doesn't type in an email address for receiving the newsletter. Likewise, if you need a shipping address to deliver a brochure or product, you'll want to be sure that the visitor includes his address on the form.

In addition, when receiving data from a web form, you want to make sure the data you receive is in the correct format—a number, for example, for an order quantity, or a correctly formatted URL for a web address. Making sure a visitor inputs information correctly is known as *form validation*, and with JavaScript, you can identify any errors before the visitor submits incorrect information.

Basically, form validation requires checking the form fields before the form is submitted to make sure required information is supplied and that information is properly formatted. The form's submit event—triggered when the visitor clicks a submit button or presses Return when the cursor's in a text field—is usually where the validation occurs. If everything is fine, the form information travels, as it normally would, to the web server. However, if there's a problem, the script stops the submission process and displays errors on the page—usually next to the problem form fields (Figure 9-5).

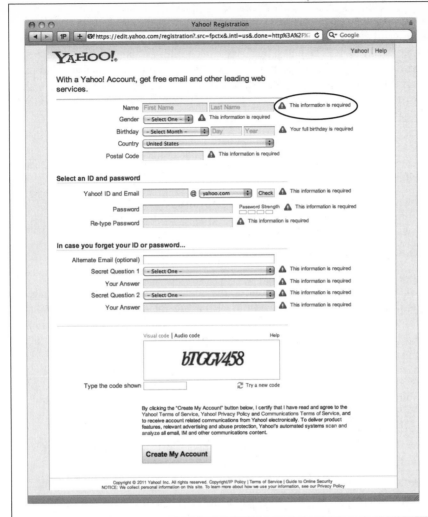

Checking to make sure a text field has been filled out is easy. As you read on page 261, you can simply access the form's *value* property (using the jQuery *val()* function, for example) and if the value is an empty string, then the field is empty. But it gets trickier when you're checking other types of fields, like checkboxes, radio buttons, and menus. In addition, you need to write some complicated JavaScript when you want to check to make sure the visitor submits particular *types* of information, like email addresses, Zip codes, numbers, dates, and so on. Fortunately, you don't need to write the code yourself; there's a wealth of form validation scripts on the web, and one of the best is a plug-in for the jQuery library.

jQuery Validation Plug-in

The Validation plug-in (*http://bassistance.de/jquery-plugins/jquery-plugin-validation/*) is a powerful but easy-to-use jQuery plug-in created by Jörn Zaefferer. It can check a form to make sure all required fields have been filled out, and check to make sure that visitor input meets particular requirements. For example, a quantity field must contain a number, and an email field must contain an email address. If a visitor doesn't fill out a form correctly, the plug-in will display error messages describing the problems.

Here's the basic process of using the Validation plug-in:

1. **Download and attach the *jquery.js* file to the web page containing the form you wish to validate.**

    Read "Getting jQuery" (on page 119) for more info on downloading the jQuery library. The Validation plug-in uses the jQuery library, so you need to attach the *jQuery* file to the page first.

2. **Download and attach the Validation plug-in.**

    You can find the plug-in at *http://bassistance.de/jquery-plugins/jquery-plugin-validation/*. The download includes lots of extra stuff, including a demo, tests, and more. You really only need the *jquery.validate.min.js* file. (You'll also find this plug-in in the tutorial files in the *_js* folder, named *jquery.validate.min.js*— see the tutorial on page 291). This file is just an external JavaScript file, so follow the instructions on page 27 for linking the file to your page.

3. **Add validation rules.**

    Validation rules are just the instructions that say "make this field required, make sure that field gets an email address," and so on. In other words, this step is where you assign which fields get validated and how. There are a couple of methods for adding validation rules: a simple way using just HTML (page 281), and a more flexible but slightly more complicated way (page 284).

4. **Add error messages.**

    This step is optional. The Validation plug-in comes with a predefined set of error messages, like "This field is required," "Please enter a valid date," "Please enter a valid number," and so on. These basic messages are fine and to the point, but you may want to customize them for your form, so that the errors provide more definite instruction for each form field—for example, "Please type your name," or "Please tell us your date of birth."

    There are two methods for adding error messages—the simple way is discussed on page 283, and the more flexible method on page 288.

Note: You can also control the style and placement of error messages as described on page 290.

---

5. **Apply the *validate()* function to the form.**

   The plug-in includes a function that makes all of the magic happen: *validate()*. To apply it, you first use jQuery to select the form, and then attach the function to that selection. For example, say you have a form with an ID of *signup* applied to it. The HTML might look like this:

   ```
   <form action="process.php" method="post" name="signup" id="signup">
   ```

   The simplest way to apply validation would be like this:

   ```
   $('#signup').validate();
   ```

   The *validate()* function can accept many different pieces of information that affect how the plug-in works. For example, while you can specify validation rules and error messages in the HTML of the form (see below), you can also specify rules and errors when you call the *validate()* function. (You'll learn about this method on page 284.)

   The entire JavaScript code for a very basic form validation (including the two steps already described in this section) could be as simple as this:

   ```
   <script src="js/jquery-1.6.3.min.js"></script>
   <script src="js/jquery.validate.min.js"></script>
   <script>
   $(document).ready(function() {
     $('#signup').validate();
   }); // end ready
   </script>
   ```

Note: Remember to always wrap your script in jQuery's *document.ready()* function to make sure the script runs after the page's HTML is loaded (see page 169).

Basic Validation

Using the Validation plug-in can be as simple as attaching the plug-in's JavaScript file, adding a few class and title attributes to the form elements you want to validate, and applying the *validate()* function to the form. The *validate()* method is the easiest way to validate a form, and may be all you need for most forms. (However, if you need to control where error messages are placed on a page, or apply more than one rule to a form field, or set a minimum or maximum number of characters for a text field, you'll need to use the advanced method described on page 278).

To add validation, follow the basic steps outlined in the previous sections (attaching the jQuery and Validation plug-in files, and so on), but in addition, you can embed rules and error messages in your form fields' HTML.

Adding validation rules

The simplest way to validate a field using the Validation plug-in is to assign one or more of the class names listed in Table 9-2 to the *form* element. The plug-in is cleverly programmed to scan the class names for each *form* element to determine if one of the validation terms is present, and if so, to apply the particular validation rule to that field.

For example, say you have a text field to collect a person's name. The basic HTML might look like this:

```
<input name="name" type="text">
```

To tell the plug-in that the field is mandatory—in other words, the form can't be submitted unless the visitor types something into this field—add a *required* class to the tag. For example, to make this text field required, add a class attribute to the tag like this:

```
<input name="name" type="text" class="required">
```

Adding a class in this way actually has nothing to do with CSS, even though usually you assign a class to a tag to provide a way of formatting that tag by creating a CSS class style. In this case, you're using a class name to provide the plug-in the information it needs to determine what kind of validation you're applying to that field.

Note: JavaScript validation is a great way to provide friendly feedback to visitors who accidentally skip a field or provide the wrong type of information, but it's not a good way to prevent malicious input. JavaScript validation is easy to circumvent, so if you want to make absolutely sure that you don't receive bad data from visitors, you'll need to implement a server-side validation solution as well.

Requiring visitors to fill out a field is probably the most common validation task, but often you also want to make sure the data supplied matches a particular format. For example, if you're asking how many widgets someone wants, you're expecting a number. To make a field both mandatory *and* contain a specific type of value, you add both the *required* class plus one of the other classes listed in Table 9-2.

Table 9-2. *The Validation plug-in includes methods that cover the most common validation needs*

Validation rule	Explanation
required	The field won't be submitted unless this field is filled out, checked, or selected.
date	Information must be in the format MM/DD/YYYY. For example, 10/30/2009 is considered valid, but 10-30-2009 is not.
url	Must be a full, valid web address like *http://www.chia-vet.com*. Partial URLs like *www.chia-vet.com* or *chia-vet.com* are considered invalid.
email	Must be formatted like an email address: *bob@chia-vet.com*. This class doesn't actually check to make sure the email address is real, so someone could still enter *nobody@noplace.com* and the field would pass validation.
number	Must be a number like 32 or 102.50 or even –145.5555. However, the input can't include any symbols, so $45.00 and 100,000 are invalid.
digits	Can only include positive integers. So 1, 20, 12333 are valid, but 10.33 and –12 are not valid.
creditcard	Must be a validly formatted credit card number.

For example, say you have a field asking for someone's date of birth. This information is not only required, but should also be in a date format. The HTML for that field could look like this:

```
<input name="dob" type="text" class="required date">
```

Notice that the class names—*required* and *date*—are separated by a space.

If you exclude the *required* class and just use one of the other validation types—for example, *class="date"*—then that field is optional, but if someone does type something into the field, it must be in the proper format (a date).

Tip: When you require a specific format for field information, make sure to include specific instructions in the form so your visitors know how they should add their information. For example, if you require a field to be a date, add a message near the field that says something like "Please enter a date in the format 01/25/2009."

Adding error messages

The Validation plug-in supplies generic error messages to match the validation problems it checks for. For example, if a required field is left blank, the plug-in displays the message "This field is required." If the field requires a date, then the message "Please enter a valid date" appears. You can, however, override these basic messages and supply your own.

The easiest way is to add a *title* attribute to the form field and supply the error message as the title's value. For example, say you're using the *required* class to make a field mandatory, like this:

```
<input name="name" type="text" class="required">
```

To supply your own message, just add a *title* attribute:

```
<input name="name" type="text" class="required" ↵
title="Please give us your name.">
```

Normally, web designers use the *title* attribute to increase a form field's accessibility by providing specific instructions that appear when someone mouses over the field, or for screen-reading software to read aloud. But with the Validation plug-in, you use the *title* attribute to supply the error message you wish to appear. The plug-in scans all validated fields and sees if there's a *title* attribute. If there is, then the plug-in uses the attribute's value as the error-message text.

If you use more than one validation method, you should supply a title that makes sense for either situation. For example, if you have a field that's required and that also must be a date, a message like "This field is required" doesn't make much sense if the visitor enters a date in the wrong format. Here's an example of an error message that makes sense whether the visitor leaves the field blank or enters the date the wrong way:

```
<input name="dob" type="text" class="required date" ↵
title="Please enter a date in the format 01/28/2009.">
```

Adding validation rules and error messages by adding class names and titles to fields is easy, and it works great. But sometimes you may have more complicated validation needs; the Validation plug-in offers a second, more advanced method of adding validation to a form. For example, you may want to have different error messages based on the type of error—like one message when a field is left blank and another when the visitor enters the wrong type of information. You can't do that using the basic validation method described in this section. Fortunately, the Validation plug-in offers a second, more advanced method that lets you implement a wider range of validation rules.

For example, you must use the advanced method if you want to make sure a minimum number of characters is entered into a field. When setting a password, for instance, you might want to make sure the password is at least six characters long.

Advanced Validation

The Validation plug-in provides another way of adding validation to a form that doesn't require changing the fields' HTML. In addition, the plug-in supports a wide variety of additional options for controlling how the plug-in works. You set these options by passing an object literal (page 145) to the *validate()* function, containing separate objects for each option. For example, to specify a validation rule, you pass one object containing the code for the rule. First, you include an opening brace directly after the first parentheses for the validation function and a closing brace directly before the closing parentheses:

```
$('idOfForm').validate({
    // options go in here
}); // end validate();
```

These braces represent an object literal, which will contain the option settings. Using the Validation plug-in in this way gets a little confusing, and the best way to understand how the plug-in's author intended it to work is to look at a simple example, like the one in Figure 9-6.

Figure 9-6:
Even with a simple form like this one, you can use the Validation plug-in's advanced options for greater control.

Tip: You can combine the basic validation method described on page 281 and the advanced method described here on the same form. For fields that have just one validation rule and error message, you can use the simple method since it's fast, and just use the advanced method for more complicated validation. The tutorial on page 291, for instance, uses both methods for validating a single form.

The HTML for the form in Figure 9-6 is as follows:

```
<form action="process.php" method="post" id="signup">
  <div>
    <label for="name">Name</label>
    <input name="name" type="text">
  </div>

  <div>
    <label for="email">E-mail Address</label>
    <input name="email" type="text">
  </div>
  <div>
    <input type="submit" name="submit" value="Submit">
  </div>
</form>
```

This form contains two text fields, shown in bold: one for a person's name and one for an email address. This section walks through the process of validating both of these fields using advanced rules to make sure the name field is filled and the email field is both filled in and correctly formatted.

Note: You can find a complete list of options for the Validation plug-in at *http://docs.jquery.com/Plugins/Validation/validate#toptions*.

Advanced rules

The advanced way to specify validation rules involves passing an object (see page 145) containing the names of the form fields and the validation rule or rules you want to apply to the field. The basic structure of that object looks like this:

```
rules: {
  fieldname : 'validationType'
}
```

The object is named *rules*, and inside it you specify the fields and validation types you want to apply to the field. The entire object is then passed to the *validate()* function. For example, in the form pictured in Figure 9-6, to make the name field mandatory, you apply the *validate()* function to the form as described on the previous page, and then pass the *rules* object to the function like this:

```
$('#signup').validate({
  rules: {
    name: 'required'
  }
}); // end validate()
```

In this case, the field is named *name*, and the rule specifies that the field is required. To apply more than one validation rule to a form field, you must create another object for that field. For example, to expand the validation rules for the form in Figure 9-6, you can add a rule that would not only make the email field required, but also specify that the email address must be validly formatted:

```
1   $('#signup').validate({
2     rules: {
3       name: 'required',
4       email: {
5         required:true,
6         email:true
7       }
8     }
9   }); // end validate()
```

Note: According to the rules of JavaScript object literals, you must end each name/value pair except the last one with a comma. For example, in line 3 above, *name: 'required'* must have a comma after it, because another rule (for the email field) follows it. Turn to page 145 for a refresher on how object literals work.

Lines 4–7, shown in bold, specify the rules for the email field. The field's name is *email*, as specified in the HTML (see the HTML code on page 285); *required:true* make the field required; and *email:true* makes sure the field contains an email address.

You can use any of the validation types listed in Table 9-2. For example, say you add a field named *birthday* to the form used in this example. To ensure that a date is entered into the field, you can expand the list of rules like this:

```
$('#signup').validate({
  rules: {
    name: 'required',
    email: {
      required:true,
      email:true
    },
      birthday: 'date'
  }
}); // end validate()
```

If you also want the birthday field to be *required*, adjust the code as follows:

```
$('#signup').validate({
  rules: {
    name: 'required',
    email: {
      required:true,
      email:true
    },
      birthday: {
      date:true,
      required:true
      }
  }
}); // end validate()
```

As mentioned earlier, one of the most powerful and useful things you can do with advanced validation rules is require visitors' entries to be a certain minimum or maximum length. For example, on a complaint report form, you may want to limit comments to, say, 200 characters in length, so your customers will get to the point instead of writing *War and Peace*. There are also rules to make sure that numbers entered are within a certain range; for example, unless you're accepting information from mummies or vampires, you won't accept birth years earlier than 1900.

- *minlength.* The field must contain *at least* the specified number of characters. For example, the rule to make sure that at least six characters are entered into a field is this:

  `minlength:6`

- *maxlength.* The field must contain *no more* than the specified number of characters. For example, the rule to ensure that no more than 100 characters are entered into the field looks like this:

  `maxlength:100`

- *rangelength.* A combination of both *minlength* and *maxlength*. Specifies both the minimum and maximum number of characters allowed in a field. For example, the rule to make sure a field contains at least six characters but no more than 100 is as follows:

  `rangelength:[6,100]`

- *min.* Requires that the field contain a number that's equal to or greater than the specified number. For example, the following rule requires that the field both contains a number and that the number is greater than or equal to 10.

  `min:10`

  In this example, if the visitor enters *8*, the field won't validate because 8 is less than 10. Likewise, if your visitor types a word—*eight*, for example—the field won't validate and she'll get an error message.

- *max.* Like *min*, but specifies the largest number the field can contain. To make sure a field contains a number less than 1,000, for example, use the following:

  `max:1000`

- *range.* Combines *min* and *max* to specify both the smallest and largest numbers that the field must contain. For example, to make sure a field contains at least 10 but no more than 1,000, use this:

  ```
  range:[10,1000]
  ```

- *equalTo.* Requires that a field's contents match another field. For example, on a sign-up form, it's common to ask a visitor to enter a password and then verify that password by typing it a second time. This way, the visitor can make sure he didn't mistype the password the first time. To use this method, you must specify a string containing a valid jQuery selector. For example, say the first password field has an ID of *password* applied to it. If you want to make sure the "verify password" field matches the first password field, you use this code:

  ```
  equalTo: '#password'
  ```

You can use these advanced validation rules in combination. Just take it one field at a time. Here's an example of how they work together: Assume you have a form that includes two fields, one for creating a password, and another for confirming that password. The HTML for those two fields might look like this:

```
<input name="password" type="password" id="password">
<input name="confirm_password" type="password" id="confirm_password">
```

Both fields are required, and the password must be at least 8 characters but no more than 16. And finally, you want to make sure the "confirm password" field matches the other password field. Assuming the form has an ID of *signup*, you can validate those two fields with the following code:

```
$('#signup').validate({
  rules: {
    password: {
      required:true,
      rangelength:[8,16]
    },
    confirm_password: {
      equalTo:'#password'
    }
  }
}); // end validate()
```

Advanced error messages

As you read on page 283, you can easily add an error message for a field by adding a *title* with the error message text. However, this approach doesn't let you create separate error messages for each type of validation error. For example, say a field is required and must have a number in it. You might want two different messages for each error: "This field is required", and "Please enter a number." You can't do that using the *title* attribute. Instead, you must pass a JavaScript object to the *validate()* function containing the different error messages you wish to display.

Validating with the Server

While JavaScript validation is great for quickly checking user input, sometimes you need to check in with the server to see if a field is valid. For example, say you have a sign-up form that lets visitors create their own username for use on the forums of your site. No two people can share the same username, so it would be helpful if you could inform the person filling out the form if the username he wants is already taken before submitting the form. In this case, you have to consult with the server to find out whether the username is available.

The Validation plug-in provides an advanced validation method, named *remote*, that lets you check in with the server. This method lets you pass both the field name and the value the visitor has typed into that field to a server-side page (like a PHP, JSP, ASP, or Cold Fusion page). The server-side page can then take that information and do something with it, such as check to see if a username is available, and then respond to the form with either a value of *true* (passed validation) or *false* (failed validation).

Assume you have a field named "username" that's both required and must not be a name currently in use on your site. To create a rule for the field (using the advanced rules method described on the previous page), you can add the following to the *rules* object:

```
username : {
    required: true,
    remote: 'check_username.php'
}
```

The remote method takes a string containing the path from the current page to a page on the web server. In this example, the page is named *check_username.php*. When the validation plug-in tries to validate this field, it sends the field's name (username) and the visitor's input to the *check_username.php*, which then determines if the username is available. If the name is available, the PHP page returns the word 'true'; if the username is already taken, the page returns the word 'false', and the field won't validate.

All of this magic takes place via the power of Ajax, which you'll learn about in Part 4. To see a working example of this validation method, visit *http://jquery.bassistance.de/ validate/demo/captcha/*.

The process is similar to creating advanced rules, as described in the previous section. The basic structure of the *messages* object is as follows:

```
messages: {
  fieldname: {
    methodType: 'Error message'
  }
}
```

In the above example, replace *fieldname* with the field you're validating, and *methodType* with one of the assigned validation methods. For example, to combine the validation methods for the password fields and messages for each of those errors, add the following code shown in bold:

```
$('#signup').validate({
  rules: {
    password: {
      required:true,
      rangelength:[8,16]
    },
    confirm_password: {
      equalTo:'#password'
    }
  }, // end of rules
  messages: {
    password: {
      required: "Please type the password you'd like to use.",
      rangelength: "Your password must be between 8 and 16 characters long."
    },
    confirm_password: {
      equalTo: "The two passwords don't match."
    }
  } // end of messages
}); // end validate()
```

Tip: As you can see, using the advanced method can require a lot of object literals, and the number of { and } characters required can often make the code confusing to understand. A good approach when using the Validation plug-in's advanced method is to go slow and test often. Instead of trying all your rules and messages in one furious typing session, add one rule, then test the page. If the validation doesn't work, you've probably made a typo somewhere, so fix it before continuing on and adding a second rule. Once the rules are finished and they work, add the object literal for any error messages. Again, go slow, add the messages one at a time, and test often.

Styling Error Messages

When the Validation plug-in checks a form and finds an invalid form field, it does two things: First, it adds a class to the form field; then it adds a <label> tag containing an error message. For example, say your page has the following HTML for an email field:

```
<input name="email" type="text" class="required">
```

If you add the Validation plug-in to the page with this form and your visitor tries to submit the form without filling out the email field, the plug-in would stop the submission process and change the field's HTML, adding an additional tag. The new HTML would look like this:

```
<input name="email" type="text" class="required error">
<label for="email" generated="true" class="error">
This field is required.</label>
```

In other words, the plug-in adds the class name *error* to the form field. It also inserts a <label> tag with a class named *error* containing the error-message text.

To change the appearance of the error messages, you simply need to add a style to your style sheet defining the look for that error. For example, to make the error text bold and red, you can add this style to your style sheet:

```
label.error {
  color: #F00;
  font-weight: bold;
}
```

Since the Validation plug-in also adds an error class to the invalid form field, you can create CSS styles to format those as well. For example, to place a red border around invalid fields, you can create a style like this:

```
input.error, select.error, textarea.error {
  border: 1px red solid;
}
```

Validation Tutorial

In this tutorial, you'll take a form and add both basic and advanced validation options to it (see Figure 9-7).

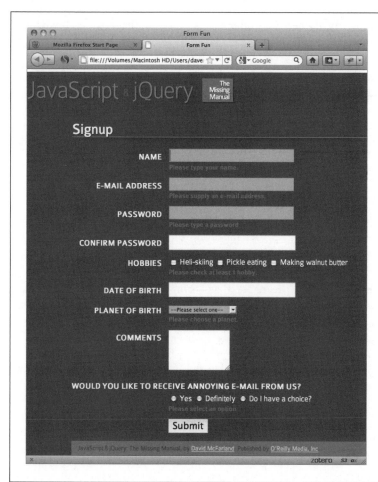

Figure 9-7:
Don't let visitors submit your forms incorrectly! With a little help from the jQuery Validation plug-in, you can make sure that you get the information you're after.

Note: See the note on page 29 for information on how to download the tutorial files.

Basic Validation

In this tutorial, you'll get started with the Validation plug-in by applying the basic validation methods described on page 281. Then you'll learn more complex validation procedures using the advanced method discussed on page 284. As you'll see, it's perfectly OK to mix and match the two approaches on the same form.

1. **In a text editor, open the file *validation.html* in the *chapter09* folder.**

    This file contains a form with a variety of form fields, including text fields, checkboxes, radio buttons, and menus. You'll add validation to this form, but first you need to attach the validation plug-in to the page.

2. **On the blank line immediately after the <script> tag that attaches the jQuery file to this page, type:**

    ```
    <script src="../_js/jquery.validate.min.js"></script>
    ```

    The validation plug-in is contained in the *_js* folder in the main tutorials folder—along with the jQuery file.

    This page already has another <script> tag, complete with the jQuery *ready()* function. You just need to add the *validate()* function to this page's form.

3. **In the blank line directly below *$(document).ready(function()*, type:**

    ```
    $('#signup').validate();
    ```

    The form has an ID of *signup*:

    ```
    <form action="process.php" method="post" name="signup" id="signup">
    ```

    So *$('#signup')* uses jQuery to select that form, and *validate()* applies the validation plug-in to the form. However, the form won't get validated until you specify some validation rules. So first, you'll make the name field required and supply a custom error message.

4. **Locate the HTML for the name field—<*input name="name" type="text" id="name"*>—and add class and title attributes, so the tag looks like this (changes are in bold):**

    ```
    <input name="name" type="text" id="name"
    class="required" title="Please type your name.">
    ```

    The *class="required"* part of the code lets the Validation plug-in know that this field is mandatory, while the *title* attribute specifies the error message that the visitor will see if she doesn't fill out this field.

5. **Save the page, open it in a web browser, and click Submit.**

    Since the name field isn't filled out, an error message appears to the right of the field (circled in Figure 9-8).

Congratulations—you've just added validation to your form using the basic method discussed on page 281. Next, you'll add another validation rule for the "date of birth" field.

Note: If you don't see an error message and instead get a page with the headline "Form Processed," the validation didn't work and the form was submitted anyway. Go over steps 1–4 again to make sure you didn't make any typos.

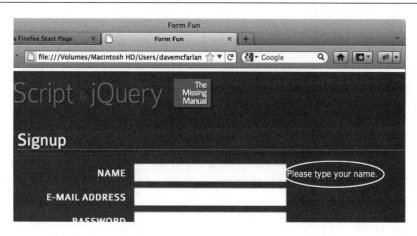

Figure 9-8:
Don't worry about the appearance of the error message just yet. You'll learn how to format errors on page 299.

6. **Locate the HTML for the date of birth field**—*<input name="dob" type="text" id="dob">*—**and add class and title attributes so the tag looks like this (changes are in bold):**

   ```
   <input name="dob" type="text" id="dob" class="date" ↵
   title="Please type your date of birth using this format: 01/19/2000">
   ```

   Because you didn't add the *required* class, filling out this field is optional. However, if the visitor does type anything into the field, the *class="date"* tells the plug-in that the input must be formatted like a date. You use the *title* attribute again to hold the error message if this field isn't valid. Save the page and try it out in a web browser—type something like *kjsdf* in the date of birth field and try to submit the form.

Note: If you did want to require that the visitor fill out the date of birth field *and* that enter a valid date, just add *required* to the class attribute. Just make sure *date* and *required* are separated by a space:

   ```
   class="date required"
   ```

You can use the same technique for validating a menu (<select> tag).

7. **Locate the HTML for the opening select tag—<select name="planet" id="planet">—and add class and title attributes so that the tag looks like this (changes are in bold):**

```
<select name="planet" id="planet" class="required" ↵
title="Please choose a planet.">
```

You can validate menus just like text fields by adding a validation *class* and *title* attribute.

Now it's time to try the advanced validation method.

Advanced Validation

As mentioned on page 284, there are some things you can't do with the basic validation methods, like assign different error messages for different validation problems, or require a specific number of characters for input. In these cases, you need to use the Validation plug-in's advanced approach for creating validation rules and error messages.

To start, you'll add two validation rules and two different error messages for the form's email field.

1. **In the JavaScript code near the top of the file, locate the line *$('#signup')* .validate(); and edit it to look like this:**

```
$('#signup').validate({

}); // end validate()
```

In other words, add opening and closing braces between the parentheses in *validate()*, add an empty line between the braces, and add a JavaScript comment at the end. The comment is a note to identify the end of the *validate()* function. You'll soon be filling the script with braces and parentheses, so it can get tricky to remember which brace goes with what. This comment can help keep you from getting confused, but like all comments in code, it's optional.

Next, you'll create the basic skeleton for adding validation rules.

2. **In the empty line (between the braces) you added in the last step, type:**

```
rules: {

} //end rules
```

To make the code easier to read, you might also want to put two spaces before the *rules* and }. Indenting those lines makes it more visually obvious that these lines of code are part of the *validate()* function.

This code creates an empty object, which you'll fill with specific field names and validation methods. In addition, a JavaScript comment identifies the end of the rules object. Next, you'll add rules for the email field.

3. **Edit the *validate()* function so that it looks like this (changes are in bold):**

```
$('#signup').validate({
  rules: {
    email: {
```

```
    required: true,
    email: true
  }
 } // end rules
}); // end validate()
```

Here, you've added another object literal. The first part, *email*, is the name of the field you wish to validate and matches the field's name in the HTML. Next, two validation methods are specified—the field is required (meaning visitors must fill it in if they want to submit the form), and the input must match the form of an email address. "Test early and often" is a good motto for any programmer. Before moving on, you'll test to make sure the script is working.

4. **Save the file; preview it in a web browser and try to submit the form.**

   You'll see the plug-in's default error message for missing information: "This field is required." Click in that field and type a couple letters. The error message changes to "Please enter a valid email address" (that's the standard message the plug-in prints when a visitor types something other than an email address into an email field). If you don't see any error messages, then go over your code and compare it to step 3 above.

   Now you'll add custom error messages for this field.

5. **Return to your text editor. Type a comma after the closing brace for the *rules* object (but before the // end rules comment), and then type:**
   ```
   messages: {
   ```

   ```
   } // end messages
   ```
   This code represents yet another object literal, named *messages*. This object will contain any error messages you wish to add to your form fields. Again, the comment at the end—*// end messages*—is optional. Now you'll add the actual error messages for the email field.

6. **Edit the *validate()* function so it looks like this (the additions are in bold):**
   ```
   1   $('#signup').validate({
   2     rules: {
   3       email: {
   4         required: true,
   5         email: true
   6       }
   7     }, //end rules
   8     messages: {
   9       email: {
   10        required: "Please supply your e-mail address.",
   11        email: "This is not a valid e-mail address."
   12      }
   13    } // end messages
   14  }); // end validate(),
   ```
   Save the page and preview it in a web browser again. Try to submit the form without filling out the email address field. You should now see your custom error message: "Please supply your email address." Now, type something like

"hello" into the email field. This time you should get the "This is not a valid email address" error.

If you don't get any error messages and, instead, end up on the "Form Processed!" page, there's a JavaScript error somewhere in your code. The most likely culprit is a missing comma after the *rules* object (see line 7), or in the *email* message object (see line 10).

Now it's time to add validation rules for the two password fields.

7. **Edit the rules object so that it looks like this (changes are in bold):**

```
1   rules: {
2       email: {
3           required: true,
4           email: true
5       },
6       password: {
7           required: true,
8           rangelength:[8,16]
9       },
10      confirm_password: {
11          equalTo:'#password'
12      }
13  }, //end rules
```

Don't miss the comma on line 5—it's necessary to separate the email rules from the password rules.

The first set of rules applies to the first password field. It makes the field mandatory and requires the password to be at least 8 but not more than 16 characters long. The second rule applies to the email confirmation field and requires that its contents match the value in the first password field (details on how these rules work can be found on page 287).

Tip: It's a good idea to save the file and test it after each step in this tutorial. That way, if the validation stops working, you know which step you made the error in.

These rules also need accompanying error messages.

8. **Edit the *messages* object so it looks like this (changes in bold):**

```
1   messages: {
2       email: {
3           required: "Please supply an e-mail address.",
4           email: "This is not a valid email address."
5       },
6       password: {
7           required: 'Please type a password',
8           rangelength: 'Password must be between 8 and 16 characters long.'
9       },
10      confirm_password: {
11          equalTo: 'The two passwords do not match.'
12      }
13  } // end messages
```

Don't forget the comma on line 5.

At this point, you should be feeling comfortable adding rules and error messages. Next you'll add validation for the checkboxes and radio buttons.

Validating Checkboxes and Radio Buttons

Checkboxes and radio buttons usually come in groups, and typically, adding validation to several checkboxes or radio buttons in a single group is a tricky process of finding all boxes or buttons in a group. Fortunately, the Validation plug-in takes care of the hard parts, and makes it easy for you to quickly validate this form fields.

1. **Locate the HTML for the first checkbox—*<input name="hobby" type= "checkbox" id="heliskiing" value="heliskiing">*—and add *class* and *title* attributes so that the tag looks like this (changes are in bold):**

   ```
   <input name="hobby" type="checkbox" id="heliskiing"
   value="heliskiing" class="required"
   title="Please check at least 1 hobby.">
   ```

   Here, you're using the basic validation technique described on page 281. You could also use the advanced technique and include the rules and error messages as part of the *validate()* function, but if you only require one validation rule and error message, the basic technique is more straightforward and less error-prone.

   In this case, all three checkboxes share the same name, so the Validation plug-in treats them as a group. In other words, this validation rule applies to *all three boxes*, even though you've only added the *class* and *title* attributes to one box. In essence, you've required that visitors checkmark at least one box before they can submit the form.

   You'll do the same thing for the radio buttons at the bottom of the form.

2. **Locate the HTML for the first radio button—*<input type="radio" name= "spam" id="yes" value="yes">*—and add *class* and *title* attributes so the tag looks like this (changes are in bold):**

   ```
   <input type="radio" name="spam" id="yes" value="yes"
   class="required" title="Please select an option">
   ```

   A related group of radio buttons always shares the same name (*spam*, in this case), so even though you've added a rule and error message to just one button, it will apply to all three. Because the field is required, visitors must select one of the three radio buttons to submit the form.

3. **Save the file, preview it in a web browser, and click Submit.**

   You may notice something looks a bit odd: When the error messages for the checkbox and radio buttons appear, they come directly after the first checkbox and radio button (circled in Figure 9-9). Even worse, the messages appear between the form field and its label (for example, between the checkbox and the label "Heli-skiing").

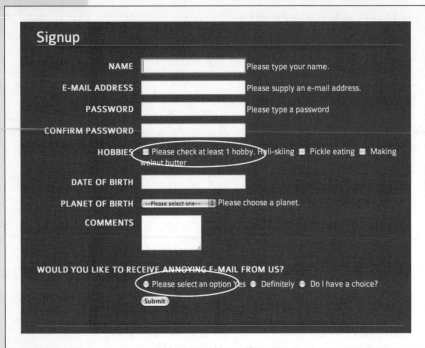

Figure 9-9:
The Validation plug-in places error messages after the invalid form field. In the case of checkboxes and radio buttons, that looks awful. In order to place the error message elsewhere, you need to provide some instruction to the plug-in's validate() function.

The Validation plug-in places the error message directly after the form field that you apply the validation rule to. Normally, that's OK: When the message appears directly after a text field or menu, it looks fine (as in the earlier examples in this tutorial). But in this case, the message should go somewhere else, preferably after all of the checkboxes or radio buttons.

Fortunately, the Validation plug-in has a way to control the placement of error messages. You can create your own rules for error-message placement by passing another object literal to the *validate()* function.

4. **Locate the validation script you added earlier, and type a comma after the closing brace for the *messages* object (but before the // *end messages* comment). Insert a blank line after the *messages* object, and then type:**

```
errorPlacement: function(error, element) {
   if ( element.is(":radio") || element.is(":checkbox")) {
      error.appendTo( element.parent());
   } else {
      error.insertAfter(element);
   }
} // end errorPlacement
```

The Validation plug-in is programmed to accept an optional *errorPlacement* object, which is just an anonymous function (page 148) that determines where an error message is placed. Every error is sent through this function, so if you only want to change the placement of some error messages, you'll need to use a conditional statement to identify the form elements whose errors you wish to place. The function receives both the error message and the *form* element the error applies to, so you can use a conditional statement (page 79) to check whether the form field is either a radio button of a checkbox. If it is, the error message is added to the end of the element containing the button or checkbox. In this page's HTML, a <div> tag wraps around the group of checkboxes, and another <div> tag wraps the radio buttons. So the error message is placed just before the closing </div> tag using jQuery's *appendTo()* function (see page 139).

You're done with all of the JavaScript programming for this form. Here's the complete script, including the *$(document).ready()* function:

```
1    $(document).ready(function() {
2      $('#signup').validate({
3        rules: {
4          email: {
5             required: true,
6             email: true
7          },
8          password: {
9             required: true,
10            rangelength:[8,16]
11         },
12         confirm_password: {equalTo:'#password'},
13         spam: "required"
14       }, //end rules
15       messages: {
16         email: {
17            required: "Please supply an e-mail address.",
18            email: "This is not a valid email address."
19          },
20         password: {
21           required: 'Please type a password',
22           rangelength: 'Password must be between 8 and 16 characters long.'
23         },
24         confirm_password: {
25           equalTo: 'The two passwords do not match.'
26         }
27       }, // end messages
28       errorPlacement: function(error, element) {
29          if ( element.is(":radio") || element.is(":checkbox")) {
30             error.appendTo( element.parent());
31          } else {
32             error.insertAfter(element);
33          }
34       } // end errorPlacement
35     }); // end validate
36   }); // end ready()
```

Formatting the Error Messages

Now the page has working form validation, but the error messages don't look very good. Not only are they spread around the page, but they don't stand out the way they should. They'd look a lot better if they were bold, red, and appeared underneath the form field they apply to. You can make all of those formatting changes with a little simple CSS.

1. **Near the top of the validation.html file, click on the blank line between the opening <style> and closing </style> tags.**

   This page has an empty style sheet into which you'll add the styles. In a real-world situation, you'd probably use an external style sheet—either the main style sheet used by the other pages of the site, or a specific style sheet intended just for forms (*forms.css*, for example). But to keep things simpler for this tutorial, you'll just add the new styles to this page.

2. **Add the following CSS rule inside the <style> tags:**

   ```
   #signup label.error {
     font-size: 0.8em;
     color: #F00;
     font-weight: bold;
     display: block;
     margin-left: 215px;
   }
   ```

   The CSS selector *#signup label.error* targets any <label> tag with a class of *error* that appears inside another element with the ID *signup*. In this case, the <form> tag has an ID *signup*, and the Validation plug-in puts error messages inside a <label> tag and adds the class *error* (see page 290). In other words, this CSS rule only applies to the error message inside this form.

   The CSS properties themselves are pretty basic: First, the font size is reduced to .8 em; next, the color is changed to red, and the text is bolded. The *display: block* instruction informs the browser to treat the <label> tag as a block-level element. That is, instead of putting the error message *next* to the form field, the browser treats the error like a paragraph of its own, with line breaks above and below. Finally, to make the error message line up with the form fields (which are indented 215 pixels from the left edge of the main content area), you need to add a left margin.

   To make it even clearer which fields have validation problems, you can add CSS rules to change the look of invalid form fields.

3. **Add one final rule to the *form.css* file:**

   ```
   #signup input.error, #signup select.error {
     background: #FFA9B8;
     border: 1px solid red;
   }
   ```

   This rule highlights an invalid form field by adding a red border around its edges and a background color to the field.

That's all there is to it. Save the CSS file and preview the *validation.html* page in a web browser to see how the CSS affects the error messages (you may need to hit the browser's reload button to see the changes you made to the CSS file).

The final form should look like Figure 9-7. You can find a completed version of the tutorial (*complete_validation.html*) in the *chapter09* folder.

Expanding Your Interface

A web page can feel like a long one-page brochure. Visitors are overwhelmed if there seem to be acres of text and pictures to scroll through, and they are unable to quickly get the information they need. It's up to you to provide your visitors tools to find what they're after. Using JavaScript and jQuery, you can streamline your web page and make it simpler for visitors to deal with—hiding content until it's required and providing easier access to information.

In this chapter, you'll learn common techniques to make your pages easier to read and use. Tabs fit lots of information in a small space and let visitors click a tab to access content in smaller chunks. Tooltips—pop-up windows with additional information about moused-over links, form fields, and other HTML elements—provide supplemental information. An increasingly popular tactic for controlling page content is a slider—sort of a window on the page where content slides in and out of view. Sliders let you showcase content and are commonly used on home pages.

You'll also learn a few useful techniques for building your own interface widgets: how to determine the dimensions of the browser window, a page element, and the position of elements on a page.

Organizing Information in Tabbed Panels

Putting too much information on a page can overwhelm your visitors and make a web page look crowded. JavaScript gives you many ways to present a lot of information in a small space. One technique is the *tabbed panel* effect. A tabbed panel consists of tabs along the top, and panels that are visible one at a time. When your visitor clicks a tab, the currently visible panel disappears and the hidden panel appears, as Figure 10-1 illustrates.

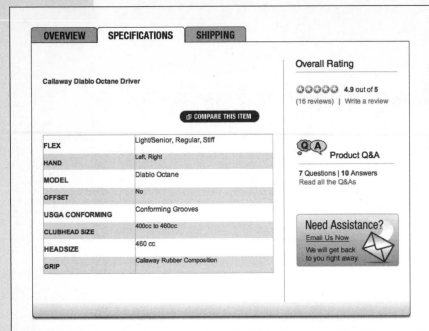

Figure 10-1:
Tabbed panels are common on e-commerce sites, where information is often displayed in separate panels. This example (just a fragment of a complete web page) presents a product overview, product specifications, and shipping information in separate panels, so visitors can click a tab to see the information that interests them.

Tabbed panels, like all user interface widgets, are composed of HTML, CSS, and JavaScript programming. You have numerous ways to tackle each of these components, but read on for a straightforward approach.

The HTML

There are two main components to tabbed panels: the tabs, which are buttons presented side-by-side at either the top or bottom of the panels, and the panels, which are <divs> containing the content you want to display. In addition, a few other tags are useful to keep everything organized and to make programming easier:

- **Wrapper element.** This isn't strictly necessary, but having a <div> tag that wraps around the tabs and panels can help mark the beginning and end of the tabbed panels and can make programming easier if you include more than one tabbed panel on a page. The HTML for this is simple:

```
<div class="tabbedPanels">

</div>
```

Adding a class to the div helps identify the div, as well as providing "hooks" for styling the elements inside the tabbed panels and for using jQuery to identify and select the tabs and panels. If you only have a single tabbed panel on a page, an ID works just as well.

- **Tabs** are commonly structured as unordered list items, with links inside them:

```
<ul class="tabs">
  <li><a href="#panel1">Overview</a></li>
  <li><a href="#panel2">Specifications</a></li>
  <li><a href="#panel3">Shipping</a></li>
</ul>
```

The links inside the list items are in-page links pointing to IDs assigned to the panels (described next). Linking to the panels makes it possible for a visitor who doesn't have JavaScript enabled to jump directly to corresponding content—just as a regular in-page link that simply scrolls the page up to the associated point on the page.

Note: If you're not familiar with in-page links, you can find a short explanation at *www.yourhtmlsource .com/text/internallinks.html*.

- **Panel wrapper.** A <div> tag that surrounds all the panels is helpful for styling and to provide a way to zero in on the tabs using jQuery:

  ```
  <div class="panelContainer">

  </div>
  ```

- **Panels** are where the content goes. Each panel is represented by a <div> tag and can hold any content you'd like: headlines, paragraphs, images, and other divs. Each <div> should have a unique ID that matches the ID used in the HREF for the tab links (see above):

  ```
  <div class="panel" id="panel1">
    <!-- put content here -->
  </div>
  <div class="panel" id="panel2">
    <!-- put content here -->
  </div>
  <div class="panel" id="panel3">
    <!-- put content here -->
  </div>
  ```

  Adding a class to each panel div is a good idea—class="panel", for example—since it provides another way to style these elements and select them with jQuery.

All of the panel divs go inside the panel wrapper div and the main wrapper element. Altogether the HTML for the basic structure of set of three tabbed panels would look like this:

```
<div class="tabbedPanels">
  <ul class="tabs">
    <li><a href="#panel1">Overview</a></li>
    <li><a href="#panel2">Specifications</a></li>
    <li><a href="#panel3">Shipping</a></li>
  </ul>
   <div class="panelContainer">
      <div class="panel" id="panel1">
         <!-- put content here -->
      </div>
```

```
            <div class="panel" id="panel2">
                <!-- put content here -->
            </div>
            <div class="panel" id="panel3">
                <!-- put content here -->
            </div>
        </div>
    </div>
```

The CSS

The CSS for tabbed panels lets you create the tab effect (side-by-side buttons) as well as style the panels to make them appear to be a cohesive whole, integrated with the tabs.

- The **container.** You don't need to set a style for the <div> tag that surrounds all the other tabbed panels code (in fact, you don't actually need that div at all). However, it is handy to create a style if you'd like to constrain the width of the tabbed panels to a certain size, perhaps to place a tabbed panel next to another page element or to place two sets of tabbed panels side-by-side. In this case, you can create a style and set its *width* property like this:

```
.tabbedPanels {
    width: 50%;
}
```

- The **bulleted list and list items.** Because bulleted lists are normally indented, you need to remove any left and right padding from them, if you want the tabs to butt up to the left edge. In addition, to get the tabs to appear side-by-side, instead of on top of each other, you must float the list items. Finally, since list items normally have bullets next to them, you should remove them. These basic styles do the trick:

```
.tabs {
    margin: 0;
    padding: 0;
}
.tabs li {
    float: left;
    list-style: none;
}
```

Note: The CSS code listed here applies to the HTML listed above. In other words, *.tabs* refers to the bulleted list—the *<ul class="tabs">* HTML—while *.tabs li* refers to list items inside of that <ul> tag.

- The **tabs** themselves are represented by the <a> tags inside the list items. There are a few properties you definitely want to set for these. First, you'll want to remove the underline that normally appears under links; next you'll want to set the display property of the links to *block* so padding and margin properties applies to them. Here's a basic style:

```
.tabs a {
    display: block;
    text-decoration: none;
    padding: 3px 5px;
}
```

Of course, you'll probably want to add more properties to really make the tabs look great: *background-color* to give the tabs life, fonts, font colors and sizes to make the tab text stand out, and so on.

- The **active tab.** It's a good idea to highlight the tab associated with the currently displayed panel. This is a kind of "you are here" signal that identifies for the visitor the information in the panel. A common technique is to create a class style that jQuery applies dynamically after a visitor clicks the tab. There's no mandatory properties for this style, but giving the active tab the same background color as a panel (and making the regular tabs style a color different than the panels) creates a visual unity between the selected tab and its panel:

```
.tabs a.active {
    background-color: white;
}
```

Tip: A common technique is to add a border around the panels and around the tabs. When you click a tab, the bottom border of the tab disappears and the tab appears to blend in with the panel (see Figure 10-1). To make this happen, first add to the *.tabs a* style a border and set the bottom margin to -1px. The negative value moves the tabs down one pixel, actually overlapping the panels. Then, give the *tabs a.active* style a bottom border color that matches the background color of the panels—the border will still be there, but because it matches the background color of the panel and overlaps the top border of the panel, it will appear as if the tab and panel are one unit (you also need to add *position: relative* to the style for this to work in IE8 and earlier). Finally, add a border to the panel container—make it the same style, width, and color as the border for the *.tabs a* style. The tutorial on page 307 shows this effect in action.

- The **panel container.** The style for the div tag that surrounds all of the panels requires is important: Because all of the tabs are floated to the left (so they appear side-by-side), you must "clear" the panel container. Otherwise, it will try to wrap around the right side of the tabs, rather than appear below them:

```
.panelContainer {
    clear: left;
}
```

You can also use this style to format the appearance of the panels. Because the panel container is a box around the panels, you could add a background color, border, padding, and so on for this style.

- The **panels.** As mentioned in the previous bullet point, you can use the panel container style to create the basic format for panels—border, background color, and so on. However, you can, if you want, apply that formatting to the individual panel divs by creating a *.panel* style.

- **Panel content.** To style the content inside of a panel, you can use descendent selectors to target the tags inside each panel div. For example, if you want to make a <h2> tag inside an orange panel displaying the Arial font face, you could create this style:

```
.panel h2 {
    color: orange;
    font-family: Arial, Helvetica, sans-serif;
}
```

To format a paragraph inside a panel, create a style named *.panel p*.

The JavaScript

With the HTML and CSS in place, you see tabs along the top, and three divs (the panels) below them stacked one on the next as diagrammed in Figure 10-2. The basic look is in place. You just need to add the programming to make the panels open and close, and to change the class on the tabs to make one the "active" tab and the others regular tabs. The basic program involves:

1. **Add a click event to the links inside the tabs.**

   Tabbed panels are all about a visitor interacting with the tabs: Click a tab to reveal a panel; click another tab to reveal another panel.

2. **Add an anonymous function to the click event to:**

   - (a) Hide the currently visible panel.
   - (b) Remove the *active* class from the previously selected tab.
   - (c) Add the *active* class to the just-clicked tab to make it active.
   - (d) Display the panel associated with that tab.

3. **Trigger the click event on the first tab.**

   This step is necessary because when the page first loads, all the panels are visible and no tab is selected. You could just write the code to highlight the first tab and hide all the panels except the first one, but you don't need to—the anonymous function for the click event (step 2) does that for you, so you need only programmatically "click" that tab, and trigger the function.

So, in a nutshell, that's how its done. Now you'll go through the programming step-by-step in the following tutorial.

Figure 10-2:
*The HTML structure for tabbed pan-els is really pretty simple: a div tag,
an unordered list, some links, and
more div tags.*

Tabbed Panels Tutorial

Now that you understand the basics of creating a navigation menu, here's how to
make it happen. In this tutorial, you'll add CSS and JavaScript to transform the basic
HTML menu list shown on page 303 into a navigation bar.

Note: See the note on page 29 for information on how to download the tutorial files.

---

1. **In a text editor, open the file *tabs.html* in the *chapter10* folder.**

   This file contains the HTML described on page 302: a container div, an unordered list of links for the tabs, a div to contain the panels, and one div for each
   panel. The basic CSS formatting is in place as well. If you view the page in a web
   browser, you'll see three tabs and the content for three panels (each panel is
   stacked on top of the other).

Note: To make the CSS for the tabbed panels as clear as possible, we've put it directly in this page's HTML in an internal stylesheet. If you want to reuse this CSS for your own tabbed panels, it's best to put it into the main external stylesheet used by your site.

The jQuery file is already linked and the *$(document).ready()* function is in place, so the first step is to hide the panels.

2. **Click in the empty line inside the *$(document).ready()* function and add the following code in bold below:**

```
$(document).ready(function() {
  $('.tabs a').click(function() {

  }); // end click
}); // end ready
```

$('.tabs a') selects all the <a> tags inside the unordered list (it has a class of *tabs*). (The *click()* function is described on page 162.) At this point you have an empty anonymous function, so you'll begin filling it with programming. First, you'll add a statement to make your code just a tad more efficient.

3. **Inside the anonymous function, add the bolded code below:**

```
$('.tabs a').click(function() {
    $this = $(this);
}); // end click
```

As mentioned on page 149, when inside an event handler's anonymous function, *$(this)* refers to the element the event is added to: In this case, *$(this)* refers to the tab the visitor clicks. Each time you use *$()* to select an element, you're actually calling the jQuery function, forcing the web browser to execute many lines of JavaScript programming. If you need to use the same selector more than once inside a function, it's a good idea to save it into a variable. In this example, *$this* is simply a variable created by the programmer (that's you).

Storing the value of *$(this)* into that variable means that anytime you need to access the link, you only need to use the variable *$this*—you don't need to make jQuery select the link all over again. In other words, if you have *$(this)* twice in a function, then the browser has to run the jQuery function two times to select the exact same element. If you first store *$(this)* into a variable—*$this*—you can use that variable multiple times in your code without forcing the browser to do extra work (page 404 describes the benefits of storing jQuery selectors in variables in greater depth).

Now, you'll hide the panels, and activate the clicked tab.

4. **Add the code listed in lines 3 and 4 below.**

```
1  $('.tabs a').click(function() {
2      $this = $(this);
3      $('.panel').hide();
4      $('.tabs a.active').removeClass('active');
5  }); // end click
```

Line 3 hides the panels. Because each panel is a <div> tag with the class of *panel*, *$('.panel')* selects them all and jQuery's *.hide()* function (page 187) hides them. You need to do this because otherwise, when you open one panel, the previous panel will still be visible.

Line 4 removes the *active* class from any of the links inside the tabs. On page 305, we discussed how creating an *active* class style will let you provide a different look for the tab the user clicks (a sort of "you are here" look). Of course, when a visitor clicks a tab to make it active, you also need to remove that class from the previously selected tab—that's what line 4 does using jQuery's *removeClass()* function (page 142). Next, you'll highlight the tab the visitor just clicked.

5. **Add the code listed in line 5 below.**

```
1  $('.tabs a').click(function() {
2      $this = $(this);
3      $('.panel').hide();
4      $('.tabs a.active').removeClass('active');
5      $this.addClass('active').blur();
6  }); // end click
```

Remember that *$this* is a variable you created in line 2, and it holds a reference to the link the visitor clicks. So *$this.addClass('active')* adds the active class to the link: The web browser will use the CSS to style that tab. The *.blur()* at the end uses jQuery's chaining feature discussed on 137. It's just another function that's run after the *.addClass()*. The *.blur()* function removes the focus of a link (or form field): In this case, it also removes the fuzzy line that web browsers display around links that a visitor has clicked or tabbed to. Without it, an active tab wouldn't look very good.

This function is almost done: You just need to make the panel appear.

6. **Add the code listed in lines 6 and 7 below.**

```
1  $('.tabs a').click(function() {
2      $this = $(this);
3      $('.panel').hide();
4      $('.tabs a.active').removeClass('active');
5      $this.addClass('active').blur();
6      var panel = $this.attr('href');
7      $(panel).fadeIn(250);
8  }); // end click
```

Every tab is really a link pointing to its associated panel. Remember, a panel's HTML looks something like this: *<div id="panel1" class="panel">*; and every tab's HTML looks like something like this: *<a href="#panel1">*. Notice that the href value looks just like a CSS ID selector; since jQuery uses CSS selector to select a page element, you can retrieve the link's HREF and use it to locate the panel you wish to display. Line 6 creates a new variable—*panel*—to hold the HREF property of the link (using jQuery's *.attr()* function discussed on page 146).

Line 7 uses the HREF to select the panel, and then fade it into view using jQuery's *fadeIn()* function (page 187). You could replace *fadeIn()* with one of jQuery's other effect functions like *show()*, *slideDown()*, or *animate()*.

Now that the programming is in place, if you trigger a click when the page loads, then you can run this function, hide the panels, select a tab and display its associated panel. Fortunately, jQuery makes it easy to simulate any event and trigger an event handler.

7. **After the *click()* function, add one more line of code to trigger a "click" on the first tab.**

```
1  $('.tabs a').click(function() {
2      $this = $(this);
3      $('.panel').hide();
4      $('.tabs a.active').removeClass('active');
5      $this.addClass('active').blur();
6      var panel = $this.attr('href');
7      $(panel).fadeIn(250);
8  }); // end click
9  $('.tabs li:first a').click();
```

This code uses a pretty complex selector—.*tabs li:first a*—to select the first tab. Basically, you can read the selector (like all descendent selectors) from right to left. On the right side, *a* indicates that our goal is to select an <a> tag. In the middle, *li:first* is a *first child pseudo-element*, it matches an <li> tag that is the first child of another tag. Since the tabs are constructed by a bulleted list, the *li:first* means the first list item, or in this case, the first tab. Finally, .tabs makes sure we're selecting a link inside a list item that's part of our tabbed panels. This prevents us from accidentally selecting a link inside another bulleted list (like a navigation bar) elsewhere on the page.

Finally, you can use the .*click()* function not just to set a function to respond to the click event, but to actually trigger the event. So line 9 is basically saying "web browser, click the first tab," which triggers a whole cascade of actions: hiding the panels, highlighting the tab, and fading the proper panel into view. Whew! You're almost there. If you preview the page in a web browser, you may notice one small problem. Because the tabs are actually in-page links, if you view the page in a small monitor, you might see the browser jump down to the panel, in addition to displaying it. You need to tell the browser not to follow the link.

8. **Add *return false;* to the end of the click handler (see line 9 below). The completed code should look like this:**

```
1   $(document.ready(function() {
2       $($('.tabs a').click(function() {
3           $this = $(this);
4           $('.panel').hide();
5           $('.tabs a.active').removeClass('active');
6           $this.addClass('active').blur();
7           var panel = $this.attr('href');
8           $(panel).fadeIn(250);
9           return false;
10      }); // end click
11      $('.tabs li:first a').click();
12  }); // end ready
```

9. **Save the page and try it out in a web browser.**

    The completed tutorial should look like Figure 10-3. You can add more tabs
    and more panels simply by inserting additional list items to the unordered
    list containing links that point to new div tags for the new panels.

Note: You'll find a completed version of this tutorial–*complete_tabs.html*–in the chapter10 tutorial
folder. In addition, a more advanced version of the tabbed panels code, which allows for multiple tabbed
panels on a single page can be found in the *complete_complex_tabs.html* file–it uses some of jQuery's
advanced DOM Traversal functions discussed on page 413.

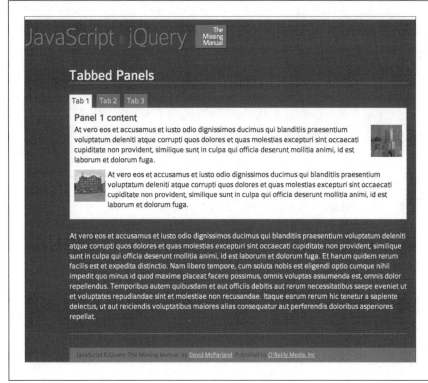

Figure 10-3:
*Tabbed panels
provide an elegant
way to provide access
to lots of information
while preserving web
page real estate.*

The jQuery UI Project

You'll find a more advanced version of tabbed panels as part of jQuery UI. An official project of the jQuery team, jQuery UI aims to provide plug-ins that solve basic user interface problems: accordions, tabs, dialog boxes, calendar widgets, and draggable page elements. The goal is to provide a single plug-in that solves the majority of user interface problems for web applications. The project has its own website (*http://jqueryui.com/*), where you can find the latest code, along with demonstrations and a link to documentation on the main jQuery website.

jQuery UI provides a lot of tools for web designers, and even supports CSS themes, which let you create a uniform look and feel across all of the jQuery UI elements. jQuery UI is pretty complex and contains a lot of different elements. You can customize the jQuery UI files to fit your needs—leaving out components you don't need to save on file size and download speed—and even create your own custom CSS themes to match the colors, fonts, and textures of your website. An online download tool—*http://jqueryui .com/download*—helps you with this process.

The previous edition of this book used jQuery UI in several chapters, but since that time, the jQuery UI team decided to rewrite all of the code for the project and add a host of new and exciting user interface widgets and utilities. Unfortunately, the new version of jQuery UI (version 1.9) wasn't out at the time of this writing, and so you won't waste time learning a bunch of user interface widgets that are destined to be replaced in the near future, this book doesn't cover jQuery UI as it stands today.

However, jQuery UI has great promise and is worth keeping your eye on. Visit the jQuery UI site to see whether version 1.9 is out. If so, go check it out.

Adding a Content Slider to Your Site

Another tool web designers use to battle information overload is a *content slider*— a simple slideshow-like interface for showing one picture or chunk of content at a time. Many information-heavy sites like Microsoft.com use sliders to show images, text, and links in bite-sized chunks that slide across the screen (Figure 10-4). A slider is like a tabbed panel, except that the panels are usually the same size, are animated across the screen in a sliding motion, and often run on a timer, with the panels sliding across the screen every couple of seconds. Sliders are commonly used on home pages to keep the page simple and attractive while still highlighting lots of content. Frequently, they act like teasers, advertising content or products on other pages in the site. Clicking a panel in a slider usually leads to another web page.

Content sliders require mastering a few elements of JavaScript and jQuery programming including animations, timers, and manipulating CSS and HTML. While it's possible to program your own slider, there are many jQuery plug-ins that offer a wide range of useful features. One of the most versatile jQuery slider plug-ins is called AnythingSlider (available at *https://github.com/ProLoser/AnythingSlider/*).

Figure 10-4:
To minimize on-screen clutter, sites like Microsoft.com use content sliders (outlined in black) to display a single image or chunk of content at a time. In this example, the image outlined can slide out of sight to the left, revealing another image with more information.

Using AnythingSlider

AnythingSlider requires several files to work: jQuery (of course), an external JavaScript file with the slider programming, a CSS file for styling the basic slider effect, and an image file for the sliders controls (next and previous buttons). You can download Anything Slider from *https://github.com/ProLoser/AnythingSlider/*. (We've also included a copy of the necessary files with the tutorial files for this chapter.) The basic process for using the plug-in is straightforward:

1. **Attach the *anythingslider.css* file to your web page.**

   This external CSS provides formatting instructions for the slider's navigation buttons, as well as behind-the-scenes styles for placing the individual slides. You'll be able to modify basic elements of the slider by altering styles in this file (see below).

2. **Link to the jQuery file.**

   jQuery provides the basic toolset AnythingSlider needs. As when using any jQuery plug-in, you must load the jQuery JavaScript file first. If you load jQuery after the plug-in file loads, it won't work.

3. **Link to the AnythingSlider file.**

   This file contains the basic programming to transform your HTML into a slider.

4. **Add HTML.**

   AnythingSlider doesn't require any complex HTML. You only need add a container div with the ID of slider—*<div id="slider">*—and, inside that div, insert one div for each panel, or "slide." This is very similar to how panels are set up with tabbed panels (page 302).

5. **Add <script> tags and the *$(document).ready()* function, and then call the AnythingSlider function:**

   One of the pleasures of working with jQuery plug-ins is that they often require very little code to work. In this case, adding simple code to the page after the link to the AnythingSlider file (step 3) is all you need:

   ```
   <script>
   $(document).ready(function) {
       $('#slider').anythingSlider();
   }); // end ready
   </script>
   ```

   There are many ways to customize the AnythingSlider effect, as you'll see later in this chapter. But, first you'll take the plug-in for a spin.

AnythingSlider Tutorial

Creating a basic slider is really quite easy. This tutorial will take you through the process. You can use any HTML editor you'd like for this.

Note: See the note on page 29 for information on how to download the tutorial files.

---

1. **In a text editor, open the file *slider.html* in the *chapter10* folder.**

   The first step is to add AnythingSlider's CSS file.

2. **Click in the empty line following *<link href="../_css/site.css" rel="stylesheet">*, and type:**

   ```
   <link rel="stylesheet" href="anythingSlider/anythingslider.css">
   ```

   This line loads the *anythingslider.css* file, which contains specific styles for formatting the slider. You'll revisit this file later when we look at how to update the look of the slider. Next, you'll link to the necessary JavaScript files.

3. **Below the line of code you just added, type:**

   ```
   <script src="../_js/jquery-1.6.3.min.js"></script>
   <script src="anythingSlider/jquery.anythingslider.min.js"></script>
   ```

   The first line loads the jQuery file, while the second loads the plug-in file. Now it's time to add the HTML.

Tip: For this tutorial, the JavaScript, CSS, and image files for the AnythingSlider plug-in are all stored inside a folder named *anythingSlider* in the *chapter10* tutorial folder. Keeping all of the files required for the plug-in together in a specific folder is a good way to make sure you don't misplace one of the files; it also makes it easy to reuse the plug-in on another site. If you like this effect, you can just copy the *anythingslider* folder to your site (put it inside the main root folder or inside a folder dedicated to JavaScript files).

---

4. **Locate the heading 1 tag—*<h1>Anything Slider</h1>*—in the code, and on the blank line below it, type:**

```
<div id="slider">

</div>
```

This is a <div> tag (an HTML tag meant to mark a region or *division* in a web page). This particular div represents the slider itself. Inside it, you'll add more <div> tags, one for each slide you wish to display.

5. **Inside the slider div (that is, between the opening <div> and closing </div> tags), type:**

```
<div>
<a href="page1.html"><img src="images/pumpkin.jpg" width="700" height="390"
alt="Pumpkin"></a>
</div>
```

This is a second div, containing a link and image. Clicking the image takes you to another page: This is a common approach with content sliders, which often act as a kind of animated banner ad for your site. Each slider acts as a teaser for other content, so visitors click a slide to jump to an article or other section of the site.

With AnythingSlider, you can add any HTML you'd like. You're not limited to one large image. You could have text, images, other div tags—anything you'd like to place inside the slide.

6. **Add two more <div> tags inside the slider div:**

```
<div>
<a href="page2.html"><img src="images/grapes.jpg" width="700" height="390"
alt="Grapes"></a>
</div>
<div>
<a href="page3.html"><img src="images/various.jpg" width="700" height="390"
alt="Various"></a>
</div>
```

These two divs represent two more slides. You can add as many slides as you'd like. Now it's time to add some programming.

7. **Near the top of the file, add an empty line after the second <script> tag, but before the closing </head> tag, and type:**

```
<script>
$(document).ready(function() {
    $('#slider').anythingSlider();
});
</script>
```

Believe it or not, all you need to do is select the div containing the slides— *$('#slider')*—and apply the *anythingSlider()* function. The plug-in takes care of the rest.

8. **Save the file, and open it in a web browser.**

The page should look like Figure 10-5. (If it doesn't, double-check your code. You can also compare your work to the file *complete_slider.html*, which is a completed version of this tutorial.) Try out the different controls: Click the right arrow button to move to the next slider to the right, the left arrow button to move back one slider, the numbered buttons to jump to a specific slider, and the start button to begin an automated slideshow.

Figure 10-5:
Using the AnythingSlider jQuery plug-in, you can quickly create an interactive slideshow to highlight pages and products throughout your site.

Customizing the Slider Appearance

As you can see, it's pretty easy to use AnythingSlider. Of course, the slider's "out-of-the-box" appearance may not match your site's design, and you may not want or need all of its features (like the automated slideshow or the forward and backward buttons). AnythingSlider's appearance can be changed in a few ways: editing a graphics file, editing the style sheet, and setting options for the plug-in (discussed in the next section).

Using a technique called CSS Sprites, a single graphic file does quintuple-duty as both the regular and "hover" states of the back and forward arrows, as well as shadow background of the numbered buttons and the "Start" button (for an introduction to CSS Sprites, visit *http://css-tricks.com/158-css-sprites/*). You can edit this graphics file (each arrow is 45×140 pixels, the drop shadow) and add your own arrow images.

You can also edit the stylesheet to customize the appearance of the slideshow. Here's a list of some of the most common formatting changes and styles you may need to edit:

- **Height and width of the slider.** The first style in the *anythingslider.css* file— *#slider*—controls the overall width and height of the slideshow. You can adjust the width value to allow for either a wider or thinner slideshow, and the height value if your slides are shorter or taller than the default 390 pixels.

- **Color of the navigation buttons.** The numbered buttons at the bottom of the slider are normally green. If you don't like that color, edit this long-winded style: *div .anythingSlider.activeSlider .anythingControls ul a.cur, div.anythingSlider.active Slider .anythingControls ul a.* Change the background-color from #7C9127 to a color that matches your site. If you want to change the font color, you can also add the color property with the color you want. For example:
  ```
  color: #F44439;
  ```

- **Rollover color for navigation buttons.** You can give the navigation buttons a new background-color, change the font or whatever you'd like by editing the *div .anythingSlider .anythingControls ul a:hover* style. Currently, it simply removes the background-image (the drop shadow) from the button.

- **Currently selected navigation button.** You can highlight the button associated with the currently displayed slide by adding a style named *div.anythingSlider .activeSlider .anythingControls ul a.cur* to the style sheet and setting a different background color, font, and so on. Make sure you either place this style after the style listed above for the "Color of the navigation buttons" or edit that style by removing *div.anythingSlider.activeSlider .anythingControls ul a.cur* from it. Since the style listed above already has a background color associated with it, it will override your new style, unless you place the new style later in the style sheet.

- **Colors of the start and stop buttons.** The button used to for starting and stopping an automated slideshow is controlled by two styles. To change the green background color of the start button as well as the font color, edit the *div.anythingSlider .start-stop.* To change the red color of the stop button, edit the *div .anythingSlider .start-stop.playing* style.

- **Remove drop shadows and make other changes to navigation buttons.** If you don't like the drop shadows that appear on the navigation buttons and the start/stop button, then edit the *div.anythingSlider .anythingControls ul a* and *div .anythingSlider .start-stop* styles: Remove the background-image property. You can also edit the *border-radius, -moz-border-radius,* and *–webkit-border-radius* properties on these styles to remove or increase the rounded corners on this button. These styles control the basic look of the buttons, so they're worth playing around with to see what new looks you can create.

- **Green borders above and below the slideshow.** The slider has a green, 3-pixel border above and below it. Edit the *div.anythingSlider .anythingWindow* style to change this. Simply remove the border-top and border-bottom properties to remove the borders completely, or just alter their settings to change the color and width of the borders.

- **Placement of the arrows.** You can control where the back and forward arrows are placed by editing the *div.anythingSlider .back* (for the left arrow) and *div .anythingSlider .forward* (for the right arrow) styles. In addition, the *div.any thingSlider .arrow* style sets some basic properties for both arrows, including their position in the middle of the slide. If, for example, you want the arrows closer to the top of the slider, simply edit the *div.anythingSlider .arrow* style and change *top: 50%* to something like *top: 20%,* or even use a pixel value like *top: 45px;.*

Customizing the Slider Behavior

You can make a lot of changes to the slider simply by editing the CSS file. But to make fundamental changes to how the slider works, you need to set a few options for the plug-in. To do this, you pass an object literal (page 145) to the plug-in:

```
{
    buildArrows : false,
    startText : "Start slideshow",
    stopText : "Stop slideshow"
}
```

In this example, *buildArrows* is an AnythingSlider option, and *false* is the setting. This setting prevents AnythingSlider from adding the left and right arrows. You add a comma at the end of each option/value pair except for the last one (notice that there's no comma after *stopText :* "Stop Slideshow".

You then place this object literal inside the function call to the plug-in. For example:

```
$('#slider').anythingslider({
    buildArrows : false,
    startText : "Start slideshow",
    stopText : "Stop slideshow"
});
```

Here are some of the most useful options.

- **Hide navigation arrows.** To hide the left and right arrows, set the *buildArrows* option to false like this:
  ```
  buildArrows : false
  ```

- **Change slideshow labels.** To change the text that appears on the start and stop buttons, set the startText and stopText options like this:
  ```
  startText : "Start slideshow",
  stopText : "Stop slideshow"
  ```

- **Turn off the autoplay option.** You might not want the start and stop buttons to appear, preferring that visitors manually select the slide they wish to view. In this case, set the *buildStartStop* setting to *false*:
  ```
  buildStartStop : false
  ```

- **Vertical slideshow.** To have slides move vertically up and down instead of left to right, set the vertical option to true:
  ```
  vertical : true
  ```

- **Autoplay.** To have the slideshow feature automatically begin when the page loads, set the *autoPlay* option to true:
  ```
  autoPlay : true
  ```

  Automatically beginning a slideshow when the page loads is a particularly common feature on websites that include sliders, since it exposes visitors to more content without requiring them to hit a "play slideshow" button.

- **Variable size slides.** If each slide holds different amounts of content, you can make the slider window change size to grow or shrink the content of each slide. For example, say the first slide is a div with a single paragraph in it, while the second slide was a div with a headline, two large images, and three paragraphs. If you set the *resizeContents* property to *true*, then AnythingSlider will change the size of the slider for each slide—in the above example, the slider would start off shorter, displaying the single paragraph. Hitting the next button moves to the next slide with a lot more content, so the slider grows in height. You set the option like this:

  ```
  resizeContents: true
  ```

To see some of these options in action, open the *complete_slider2.html* file in the tutorial files.

As you can see, AnythingSlider is easy to add to a site, and just as easy to customize. We've just scratched the surface of what this plug-in can do. You can embed video, add special effects, and add custom programming to make it work exactly like you want it to. Check out the AnythingSlider Wiki for more information at *https://github .com/ProLoser/AnythingSlider/wiki*.

Determining the Size and Position of Page Elements

When you dynamically add to and alter a web page with JavaScript and jQuery, it's often handy to know the size and position of elements on a page. For example, you might want to place an oh-so-common *overlay* on top of a page (the effect where the page seems to dim, as shown in the FancyBox tutorial on page 231). To do that, you place an absolutely positioned <div> tag so that it covers the browser window. To fully cover the window, you need to make sure the div is the same size as the window, so you must first determine the width and height of the browser window.

Likewise, if you want to create a tooltip effect—where a small box with information pops up when a visitor mouses over something on the page—you need to determine the position of the cursor on the screen, so you can place the tooltip.

Determining the Height and Width of Elements

jQuery provides *.height()* and *.width()* functions to find the height and width of page elements. By providing the proper selector, you can determine the height and width of any tag on the page and even determine the size of the browser window, and the size of the document itself.

- **Height and width of browser window.** If you want to retrieve the height and width of the browser window (often referred to as the *viewport*), use the *$(window)* selector and the *height()* and *width()* functions like this:

  ```
  var winH = $(window).height();
  var winW = $(window).width();
  ```

  The code above retrieves the width and height, and stores them into two variables. Getting the width and height of the browser window is useful when you want to make sure you don't position an element outside the visible area of the browser window.

- **Height and width of the document.** The document isn't the same thing as the browser window and most often has a different height and width. The document represents your web page: If the page has just a little bit of content—a single paragraph, for example—the document is the height of that paragraph (plus top and bottom margins). On a large monitor, the document's height would be less than the height of browser window.

   Conversely, if a web page has a lot of content, so a visitor has to scroll down the page to read it all, then the document is taller than the browser window. Likewise, if you've set a style for the body tag or for a <div> tag containing the content of the page and set the width of that style to, say, 1500 pixels, the document might be wider than the browser window. To find the width and height for the document, use the *$(document)* selector and the *height()* and *width()* functions:

   ```
   var docH = $(document).height();
   var docW = $(document).width();
   ```

You can also use the *height()* and *width()* functions on regular HTML elements like paragraphs, divs, and images, however, it may not always give you the information you're after. The *height()* and *width()* functions return the values of the CSS height and width properties—these are not necessarily the same as the height and width of the element on the page. In CSS, the width and height properties define the space given to the content inside a tag—the text inside a paragraph tag, for example. However, if you add padding, borders, or margins to the element, then the amount of space the element takes up on the page is greater than the element's CSS height and width.

To understand how this works, let's look at some simple CSS for a <div> tag:

```
div {
    width : 300px;
    height : 300px;
    padding : 20px;
    border : 10px solid black;
}
```

Figure 10-6 shows a diagram of that div. The actual on-screen width and height of that div is 360 pixels, since its space on the page is a total of the height (or width), padding, and border. So the actual width is the left border + left padding + CSS width + right padding + right border, and the actual height is the total of the top border + top padding + CSS height + bottom padding + bottom border.

Because of these different dimensions, jQuery provides three sets of functions for determining various widths and heights for page elements:

- *width() and height()* functions return the CSS width and height of the element. For example, say your page has the CSS style listed above, and a <div> tag on it:

   ```
   var divW = $('div').width(); // 300
   var divH = $('div').height(); // 300
   ```

   In the code above, the variables divW and divH hold the value 300—the height and width set in the CSS.

- *innerWidth()* returns the width + the left and right padding; *innerHeight()* returns the CSS height + top and bottom padding:

```
var divW = $('div').innerWidth(); // 340
var divH = $('div').innerHeight(); // 340
```

In the code above, the variables divW and divH hold the value 340—the height and width set in the CSS + the padding values on either side.

- *outerWidth()* returns the width + the left and right padding + left and right borders; *outerHeight()* returns the CSS height + top and bottom padding + top and bottom borders:

```
var divW = $('div').outerWidth(); // 360
var divH = $('div').outerHeight(); // 360
```

In the code above, the variables *divW* and *divH* hold the value *360*—the height and width set in the CSS + the padding and border values on either side.

The *outerWidth()* and *outerHeight()* properties also take an optional argument—*true*—which also takes the margins around the element into account. For example, say the CSS for the div tag looks like this:

```
div {
    width : 300px;
    height : 300px;
    padding : 20px;
    border : 10px solid black;
    margin: 20px;
}
```

Notice the 20px margin setting. If you wanted to also include the margins into the overall width and height calculation, you can write this jQuery code:

```
var divW = $('div').outerWidth(true); // 400
var divH = $('div').outerHeight(true); // 400
```

Which function you use depends on what you're trying to accomplish. For example, perhaps you want to cover some text on the page—the answer to a quiz, for instance—with a black box, then, later reveal the text; one way would be to cover the text with a div filled with black background color. In this case, you'd use the *width()* and *height()* functions to determine the width and height of just the text (not the padding or borders) to properly size the div before placing it over the text.

Or, say you want to create a Pong-like game—a little ball bouncing around the screen—and want the ball to remain contained inside the borders of playing area (a div perhaps with a border line around it). Then you need to know the area available inside the borders so you could make sure the animated ball doesn't cross outside the box or over the borders. In this case, you'd use *innerHeight()* and *innerWidth()* since the ball can move anywhere inside the box, even over any padding applied to it.

Note: Don't use *innerHeight()*, *innerWidth()*, *outerHeight()*, or *outerWidth()* with the window (*$('window')*) or document (*$(document)*) objects. Only *height()* and *width()* work with those.

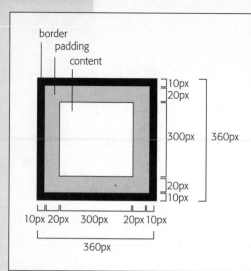

Figure 10-6:
Width and height aren't always straightforward when it comes to CSS. The CSS width and height properties only dictate the space dedicated to the content inside a tag. The overall height and width of an element on a page is calculated by combining width or height with any padding and borders on the element.

Determining the Position of Elements on a Page

It's often useful to locate the position of an element on the page: Perhaps you wish to display a tooltip above an image when a visitor mouses over the image. The tooltip is placed in relationship to that image on the page, so you need to determine where on the page the image is, then place the tooltip in that spot. jQuery provides several functions to help with this:

- *offset()*. The *offset()* function returns an object containing the left and top positions of an element from the top-left corner of the document. For example, say you wanted to place a caption across the top of an image when a visitor moused over the image. You'll want to know the position of that image. Say the image has an ID of *captionImage*. You could gather its top, left position like this:

  ```
  var imagePosition = $('#captionImage').offset();
  ```

  In this example, the variable *imagePosition* holds the coordinates of the image. Those coordinates are stored in a JavaScript object and can be accessed using the dot-syntax discussed on page 70. The left position is stored in a property named *left* and the top position in a property name *top*:

  ```
  imagePosition.top // number of pixels from the top of the document
  imagePosition.left // number of pixels from the left edge of the document
  ```

  Let's say you wanted to use this information to place a div with the id of *caption*— you could use jQuery's *.css()* function (page 143) to set the *top*, *left*, and *position* properties of the caption:

```
$('#caption').css({
    'position' : 'absolute',
    'left' : imagePosition.left,
    'top' : imagePosition.top
});
```

Note: The *offset()* and *position()* functions always return numbers representing the number of pixels from the left and top positions. That is, even if you use ems or percentages to place an element on a page, these two functions only retrieve the pixel position of the element.

* **position().** The *position()* function returns an object containing the left and top position of an element from the top-left corner of its nearest positioned ancestor. That's a bit of a mindful to take in, so let's look at how it works using Figure 10-7, which displays two divs. Both are absolutely positioned—the *outerBox* is positioned in relation to the document, but the *innerBox,* whose HTML code is inside the *outerBox* div, is positioned in relation to the outer box. The outer box is positioned in relation to the document (since it's not nested inside of any elements with either absolute, relative, or fixed positioning). For the outer box, *position()* works just like offset, so the following code:

  ```
  $('#outerBox').position() // { left : 100, top : 300 }
  ```

  returns an object with a left property of 100 and a top property of 300, since those are the values set in the CSS.

  However, in the case of the inner box, which is positioned in relation to the outer box, you'll get two different results for *offset()* and *position()*:

  ```
  $('#innerBox').offset() // { left : 300, top : 550 }
  $('#innerBox').position() // { left : 200, top : 250 }
  ```

  In this case, *offset()* returns the position in relationship to the document; that is, the inner box is 300 pixels from the left edge of the document and 550 pixels from its top. The *position()* function, on the other hand, returns the CSS left and CSS top properties for the div.

The *offset()* function is usually the more useful of the two, since it lets you know where an element is in relationship to the overall web page, and provides the information you need to place other elements on the page in relationship to the element.

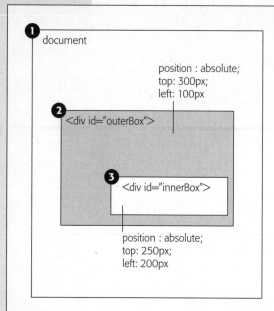

Figure 10-7:
jQuery provides two functions that let you determine the top and left position of an element on the page. In the case where you have an absolutely positioned element (#innerBox) inside another positioned element (#outerBox), the two functions will return different results.

Tip: You can also use the *offset()* function to set the position of an element on a page; just pass the function an object with left and top values like this:

```
$('#element').offset({
    left : 100,
    top : 200
});
```

You can only use pixel values for left and top; em values–(20em)–or percentages–(20%)–won't work.

Determining a Page's Scrolling Position

A web page is often larger than the browser window that displays that page: Web documents with lots of content are frequently taller and sometimes wider than the browser, forcing visitors to scroll to see all of the page (see Figure 10-8). When a visitor scrolls a page, some of the document disappears from view. For example, In Figure 10-8, the web page doesn't fit in the browser window, the document is scrolled in left and up, so the top of the page and left side of the page are out of view. This means the top-left corner of the browser window isn't the same as the top-left corner of the document. If you tried to place a new element like an animated banner at the top of the screen, you'd run into trouble if you merely set the left and top position of the element to 0—you'd actually be placing it at the top of the document, but outside of the browser window.

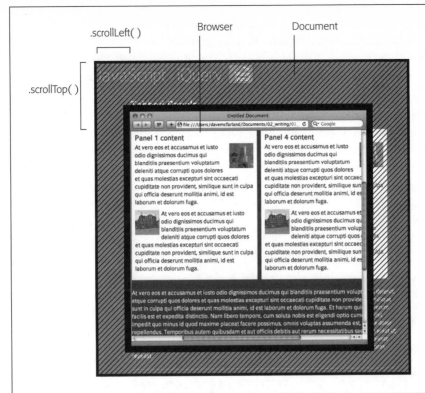

.scrollLeft( )

Browser

Document

.scrollTop( )

Figure 10-8:
Often, a web page won't completely fit inside a visitor's browser window. The visitor then has to scroll to see other parts of the page. But even though you only see part of the document, it's still always there in its entirety.

Fortunately, jQuery supplies two functions that let you determine how much the page has scrolled from the top and from the left (in other words, how many pixels of document exist above and to the left of the browser window). To determine how much of the document is above the browser window, use this code:

```
$(document).scrollTop()
```

To determine how much of the document is off the screen to the left, use this code:

```
$(document).scrollLeft()
```

Both functions return a pixel value that you can use to position another element on the page. For example, if you want to position a pop-up window in the center of the page, even after someone has scrolled down, you need to determine how far down the visitor has scrolled and move the pop-up window that many additional pixels down the page. In the case of pop-up tooltips, you need to be careful when positioning a tooltip on a page that the visitor has scrolled down: It's easy to accidentally position the tooltip in a space on the page, but outside the visible area in the browser's viewport. In fact, in step 12 of the next tutorial on page 334, you'll see how to use the *scrollTop()* to avoid positioning a tooltip above the viewable area of the top of the browser window.

Adding Tooltips

Tooltips are a common way to provide supplemental information. They are small pop-up windows triggered when a visitor mouses over a link, word, photo or any page element. They're often used to show a definition for a word, a caption for a photo, or even more detailed information like the time, cost, and location for an event.

The basic idea behind a tooltip is pretty straightforward: mouse over an element, display another element (usually a <div> tag) near the mousedover element; mouse off the element and the tooltip disappears. You have learned all the programming needed to do this, so we'll take you through the process in a step-by-step tutorial.

You'll use a combination of CSS, HTML, and JavaScript to produce the effect shown in Figure 10-9. You use HTML to both identify a tooltip trigger (the thing you mouse over) and to construct the tooltip. You use CSS to provide the basic look for the tooltip box and finally JavaScript to hide the tooltips when the page loads. You also add a hover event handler to all the tooltip triggers on the page.

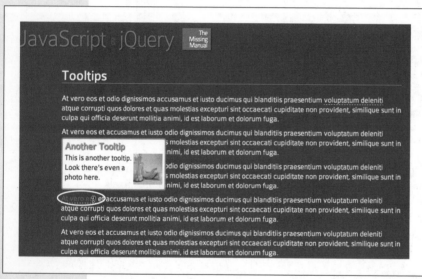

Figure 10-9:
Tooltips are boxes with supplemental information. They pop onto the page when a visitor mouses over another element—a trigger—on the page (circled) and then disappear when the visitor mouses off the element.

The HTML

There are two components to a tooltip: the tooltip itself, which is the element that appears when the visitor mouses over the trigger. The second component, the trigger, is any element like an image, link, heading, paragraph, or <span> tag.

The tooltip is a <div> tag with the class of *tooltip* and a unique ID. You can put additional HTML inside the div tag like headings, paragraphs, and images. However, don't insert links, since they won't work properly: Mousing over the tooltip to click the link also mouses off the trigger, causing the tooltip to disappear.

Here's the HTML for a basic tooltip:

```
<div class="tooltip" id="aardvarkTooltip">
    <h2>The Aardvark</h2>
    <p>A medium-sized, burrowing, nocturnal mammal native to Africa</p>
</div>
```

While you can put the tooltip divs just about anywhere in a page's HTML (they're hidden from view most of the time anyway), a good spot to place them is directly before the closing </body> tag. This location is good because it avoids any weird display problems that might arise if you put them inside another tag that has absolute or relative positioning.

The trigger can be any element—a <h1> tag, a <div> tag, an <img> tag. If you want just a single word or a several words to be a trigger, you need to wrap those words in a <span> tag. The trigger requires two pieces of information to work:

- **A class name.** All of the triggers need to share the same class name—trigger, for example. The class name is required so that our JavaScript code can identify the triggers on the page, and apply the proper event handlers to open and close the associated tooltip.

- **Data identifying the tooltip.** Each trigger has an associated tooltip. The tooltip is a <div> tag that's normally invisible, but is displayed when a visitor mouses over the trigger. Each tooltip needs a unique ID, and we need a way to associate the trigger with the proper tooltip div, so that when a visitor mouses over a trigger, we know which div to show. A simple approach is to embed the ID for the tooltip in an attribute on the trigger (add a # before the name and it'll be really easy to use jQuery to select the proper tooltip). HTML5 lets you embed data into HTML tags using the *data-* prefix.

For example, let's say the trigger for a tooltip was the word *aardvark*. Mousing over it would open the tooltip (actually a <div> tag on the page with the ID of *aardvarkTooltip*). You could wrap that word in a <span> like this:

```
<span class="trigger" data-tooltip="#aardvarkTooltip">aardvark</span>
```

HTML5's custom data attributes feature is really quite nifty. It lets web designers embed all sorts of information into their tags that they can later retrieve with JavaScript. For a detailed description of the HTML5 data attributes, read *http://html5doctor.com/html5-custom-data-attributes/*.

If you're using XHTML 1 or HTML 4.01 doctypes and are worried about validation, you can't use the data attribute. Instead you can piggy-back on a valid HTML 4 attribute for the tag such as the title:

```
<span class="trigger" title="#aardvarkTooltip">aardvark</span>
```

Using a title attribute in this way isn't how that attribute is meant to be used, and some designers might not approve of this method. You're probably better off going the HTML5 route, and using the custom data attributes.

You can put as many triggers and tooltips as you'd like in a page.

The CSS

Each div has a class of tooltip, so adding a .tooltip style to the page's stylesheet will format the overall look of the tooltip (such as background color, border, width, and so on). Here's a basic style that's already in the tutorial file:

```
.tooltip {
    width: 25%;
    padding: 5px;
    background-color: white;
    border: 3px solid rgb(195,151,51);
    border-radius : 5px;
}
```

In addition, without some styling, visitors won't know that a trigger does anything special. This is especially true if you add a tooltip to a word inside a paragraph. You can use CSS to make triggers stand out—adding a border, a background color, and so on. For example, here's a basic style that adds a bottom border to any element with the trigger class:

```
.trigger {

    border-bottom: 1px dashed white;
    cursor : help;

}
```

The CSS cursor property is particularly handy—it controls what the cursor looks like when the element is moused over. On regular text, a cursor looks like a selection bar, but you can change the cursor's appearance: The help value turns the cursor into a question mark (good for tooltips that offer definitions of terms), while the pointer value makes the cursor behave as it does when mousing over a link. For more cursor options, check out *www.w3schools.com/cssref/pr_class_cursor.asp*.

You can also add a *:hover* state to the trigger so that it changes appearance when moused over:

```
.trigger:hover {
    color: rgb(255,0,0);
}
```

The JavaScript

At its most basic, a tooltip simply appears, then disappears as a visitor mouses over a trigger. You've already learned how to make elements appear and disappear in Chapter 6. However, there's more going on that just that. A crucial part of any tooltip is placing it near the trigger; this involves using the jQuery's functions for determining the height, width, and position of an element. That's the tricky part. To make things clearer, this tutorial breaks down the tooltip programming into three parts:

1. **Hide the tooltips.**

   When the page loads, all of the tooltips (the div tags at the bottom of the page) should be hidden. You could, of course, do this in the CSS before the page loads, but anyone browsing without JavaScript enabled wouldn't be able to access the tooltip content. If the tooltip content isn't necessary information, and it's OK if some visitors (including search engines) don't see the tooltips, then go ahead and hide the tooltips in your CSS:

```css
.tooltip {
    display: none;
}
```

2. **Add a mouseover event handler to the trigger.**

   This part is the heart of the tooltip functionality. When a visitor mouses over the trigger, a couple of things need to happen:

   - The associated tooltip div needs to be shown.

   - The tooltip needs to be placed near the trigger. To do this, you need to determine the current location of the trigger element. In addition, you want to make sure the tooltip doesn't cover up the trigger, and that the tooltip doesn't extend off the screen.

3. **Add a mouseout event handler to the trigger.**

   This part is simple—just hide the div when the visitor mouses off the trigger.

To get a handle on how the programming works, it's time to jump into the tutorial and create our own tooltips.

Tooltips Tutorial

Creating a basic tooltip is really quite easy. This tutorial will take you through the process. You can use any HTML editor you'd like for this.

Note: See the note on page 29 for information on how to download the tutorial files.

---

1. **In a text editor, open the file *tooltip.html* in the *chapter10* folder.**

   This page already has an internal stylesheet with a few styles for formatting the tooltips and triggers—they're the same styles as described above on page 328. However, the page doesn't yet have any tooltips, so you'll add the code for those next.

2. **Locate the closing </body> tag near the bottom of the file and add the following HTML for a tooltip:**

```html
<div class="tooltip" id="tip1">
    <h2>A Tooltip</h2>
    <p>This is the tooltip text. It's inside a div tag
    so you can put anything inside one of these.</p>
</div>
```

   The most important part is the outer <div> tag. It contains the class tooltip, which is necessary for both the CSS and for the programming you'll add in a little bit. In addition, a unique ID identifies this particular tooltip and will let you connect the trigger you'll add next to this tooltip. The content inside the div can be any HTML; in this case, a headline and a paragraph.

3. **Locate the <p> tag below just below the <h1>Tooltips</h1> header about halfway up the file. Wrap a few words in that paragraph in a <span> tag like this:**

```
<span class="trigger" data-tooltip="#tip1">accusamus et iusto</span>
```

The class identifies this particular span as a trigger for a tooltip—some CSS in the page formats any tag with a trigger class in a special way. In addition, the *data-tooltip* attribute identifies the tooltip HTML that this trigger belongs to.

Now you'll add another tooltip.

4. **After the <div> you added in step 2 (but before the closing </body>) tag, add:**

```
<div class="tooltip" id="tip2">
    <h2>Another Tooltip</h2>
    <p><img src="../_images/small/yellow_h.jpg"
    alt="yellow" width="70" height="70" class="imgRight">
    This is another tooltip. Look there's even a photo here.</p>
</div>
```

You've just added another tooltip. Notice that it shares the same class as the previous tooltip, but has its own unique ID: *tip2*. This tooltip also includes an image. Now, you'll add the trigger for this tooltip.

5. **Locate another few words inside a paragraph somewhere in the file and wrap it in a span tag, like so:**

```
<span class="trigger" data-tooltip="#tip2">At vero eos</span>
```

Make sure to use the ID for the new tooltip—*#tip2*. You could go on adding more tooltips and triggers—just make sure to use a unique ID for each tooltip, and use that same ID when setting the *data-tooltip* attribute for the trigger.

Now, time for some programming. This page already has the jQuery file added to it, and the *$(document).ready()* function in place. The first step is to hide all the tooltips when the page loads.

6. **Click in the empty line inside the *$(document).ready()* function and type:**

```
$('.tooltip').hide();
```

This line is pretty straightforward. jQuery's *hide()* function (page 187) simply hides all the tooltips so visitors won't see them when the page loads. You will, of course, want individual tooltips to appear when a visitor mouses over a trigger, so the next step is to select all the triggers and add a mouseover event handler.

7. **After the code you added in line 6, type:**

```
$('.trigger').mouseover(function() {

}); // end mouseover
```

This is a basic event handler, like those discussed on page 162. In this case, all of the elements with a class of trigger are selected and a mouseover event is assigned to them. This function is the heart of the tooltip programming, because it controls showing and placing the tooltips on the screen. Identifying exactly where on the screen to place the tooltip is a little tricky, and you'll need a lot of different pieces of information to figure it out. So the first part of this function creates a bunch of variables.

8. **Inside the anonymous function you just added, type the bolded code below:**

```
1  $('.trigger').mouseover(function() {
2      var ttLeft,
3          ttRight,
4  }); // end mouseover
```

You start by creating two variables; *ttLeft* holds the left position of the tooltip, and *ttTop* the top position. The variables are empty at this point, since you don't know exactly what the values should be yet.

This way of creating variables might look a little weird; you may be used to creating two variables using two *var* keywords like this:

```
var ttLeft;
var ttRight;
```

That's perfectly acceptable, but when you're creating a whole bunch of variables at once, it's common practice to use a single var keyword, followed by a bunch of variables, separated by commas. It saves your fingers from typing *var* over and over again. The comma at the end of line 3 isn't a typo—there are a lot more variables you need to create.

9. **Add another variable to your code (line 4 below):**

```
1  $('.trigger').mouseover(function() {
2      var ttLeft,
3          ttRight,
4          $this=$(this),
5  }); // end mouseover
```

$(this) refers to the trigger element, and *$this=$(this)* is used to store a reference to the trigger element into a variable. You did the same thing in step 3 of the tabbed panels tutorial on page 308. You'll be referencing the trigger element a lot in this function, and if you used *$(this)* over and over again, you'd force the browser's JavaScript interpreter to run the jQuery function each time, wasting computer power and time. Instead, by storing *$(this)* into a variable, the jQuery function needs to only run once to retrieve the trigger element, making your program more efficient (see page 404 for more information on the benefits of storing jQuery selections into variables).

Next, you'll select the tooltip that's associated with this trigger.

Tip: When storing a jQuery selection in a variable, it's common practice to add a $ before the variable name like this:

```
var $banner = $('#banner');
```

It's not necessary to include the dollar sign—*var banner = $('#banner')*—would work just as well. However, the dollar sign reminds you that the variable holds a jQuery selection and not just any old value like a number or a string.

---

10. **Add another variable (line 5):**

```
1  $('.trigger').mouseover(function() {
2      var ttLeft,
3          ttRight,
4          $this=$(this),
5          $tip = $($this.attr('data-tooltip')),
6  }); // end mouseover
```

The variable $tip holds a jQuery selection of the tooltip. The code *$($this .attr('data-tooltip'))* does a lot, so here's how it breaks down. The part inside the *$()*—*$this.attr('data-tooltip')*—uses jQuery's *.attr()* function to retrieve the *'data-tooltip'* attribute for the trigger (remember, *$this* refers to the trigger). In other words, this code takes the current trigger element, looks for a data-tooltip attribute, and retrieves its value. For example, for the trigger you added in step 3, this code would return '*#tip1*'; for the trigger in step 5, this code would return '*#tip2*'.

Once the *data-tooltip* value is retrieved, it's passed to the jQuery function— that's the outer *$( )* in line 5 above. In other words, the code ends up being something like *$('#tip1')* or *$('#tip2')*. Hey, that looks familiar: It's a jQuery selection! Once line 5 above runs, you end up with a variable named tip containing the jQuery selection for the proper tooltip. You can then use that to show, animate, and position the tooltip on the screen.

Next, you need to collect a lot of information in order to place the tooltip on the screen.

11. **Add lines 6–12 below to the mouseover function.**

```
1  $('.trigger').mouseover(function() {
2      var ttLeft,
3          ttRight,
4          $this=$(this),
5          $tip = $($this.attr('data-tooltip')),
6          triggerPos = $this.offset(),
7          triggerH = $this.outerHeight(),
8          triggerW = $this.outerWidth(),
9          tipW = $tip.outerWidth(),
10         tipH = $tip.outerHeight(),
11         screenW = $(window).width(),
12         scrollTop = $(document).scrollTop();
13 }); // end mouseover
```

Here, you're collecting a lot of information about the position and dimensions of different elements. Figure 10-10 can help you picture these values: It shows a web page (gray box) that's larger than the browser window (outlined box). The page is scrolled up, so part of it is out of view above the browser window, and, because the page is longer and wider than the browser window, part of the page extends off the right and bottom edges.

Line 6 above retrieves the top and left position of the trigger (#1 in Figure 10-10)—since you'll be positioning the tooltip in relation to the trigger, you need to know this.

Lines 7 and 8 use the *outerHeight()* function (page 321) and *outerWidth()* function (page 321) to retrieve the height (#2) and width (#3) (including padding and borders) of the trigger; while lines 9 and 10 get the width (#4) and height (#5) of the tooltip. Because you don't want a tooltip to appear outside window, you need to also know the width of the screen (line 11 in the code above, and #6 in Figure 10-10) and whether the visitor has scrolled the page down and if so, how far (line 12, #7). Don't forget the ; at the end of line 12, since this is the end of the var statement that you started way back at line 2.

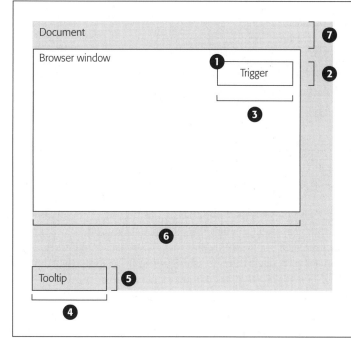

Figure 10-10:
This diagram displays a web page (gray box) that's taller and wider than the browser window (black outline). The visitor viewing the page has scrolled down, so the top part of the page isn't visible, nor are the right edge and bottom of the page. The tooltip is pictured at the bottom of the document, because this is where it is positioned when the page loads. It's not until the code in step 15 runs that the program determines where the tooltip needs to go, and then positions it there.

You may be wondering why you need all this information. Wouldn't it be easier to determine where the trigger is on the page, then position the tooltip right above it? In most cases you could do that, but there are a few situations where it wouldn't work out. For example, in Figure 10-11, the trigger is at the top right of the browser window; part of the document extends above and to the left of the window. If the tooltip is simply placed above the trigger, then most of it won't be visible to the visitor. In other words, the code needs to be smart: It has to figure out whether placing the tooltip above the trigger will make it appear outside of the browser window. If that's the case, then the program must reposition the tooltip.

You'll start by seeing whether a tooltip placed directly above the trigger will fit inside the top part of the browser window.

12. **Add lines 13-17 below to the mouseover function:**

```
1  $('.trigger').mouseover(function() {
2      var ttLeft,
3          ttRight,
4          $this=$(this),
5          $tip = $($this.attr('data-tooltip')),
6          triggerPos = $this.offset(),
7          triggerH = $this.outerHeight(),
8          triggerW = $this.outerWidth(),
9          tipW = $tip.outerWidth(),
10         tipH = $tip.outerHeight(),
11         screenW = $(window).width(),
12         scrollTop = $(document).scrollTop();
13     if (triggerPos.top - tipH - scrollTop > 0 ) {
14         ttTop = triggerPos.top - tipH - 10;
15     } else {
16         ttTop = triggerPos.top + triggerH +10 ;
17     }
18 }); // end mouseover
```

There's a lot going on here, but it helps to start by taking a look at where you want to position the top of the tooltip in relation to the trigger. Normally, you'd place a tooltip about 10 pixels above the trigger, so it doesn't cover the trigger. To determine the top position, you start by getting the top position of the trigger, then subtracting the height of the tooltip, and then subtracting another 10 pixels. For example, say the trigger is 150 pixels from the top of the document and the tooltip is 100 pixels tall. To place the tooltip so that it doesn't cover the trigger, take the trigger's 150 top position, subtract 100 to get 50 pixels, and then subtract another 10 (just to give a little breathing room from above the trigger). As a result, the tooltip is placed 40 pixels from the top of the document.

What happens if the trigger is 10 pixels from the top of the document and the tooltip is 100 pixels tall? If you simply followed the above equation, you'd end up with 10-100, or a top position of -90 pixels: in other words, off the top of the document and out of view!

Here's where the condition in line 13 comes in: You take the trigger's top position, subtract the height of the tooltip, and also subtract the amount the visitor has scrolled down the page. You then test to make sure that value is greater than 0 (if it's less than zero, the tooltip is placed outside the top of the browser window). You need to account for the scrolling as well, since it's possible that a tooltip will fit above a trigger without being placed outside the top of the document, but, if the page is scrolled, it could still be placed above the viewport of the browser window (that's the situation pictured in Figure 10-11).

If the condition is true, then the tooltip's top position—*ttTop*—is set above the trigger (line 14). However, if the condition is false, line 16 runs, which sets the top position to 10 pixels below the bottom of the trigger (you calculate the bottom of the trigger by finding its top positon—*triggerPos.right*—and add its height—*triggerH*).

We next need to calculate the left position of the tooltip.

Note: The example in this section places the tooltip above the trigger, but you don't have to do it that way. Feel free to play around with the programming to see if you can make the tooltip appear below or to the left or right of the trigger.

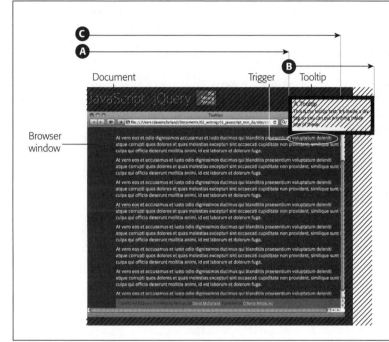

Figure 10-11:
You need to be careful when dynamically positioning an element on a page. You never know what size a visitor's browser window might be, nor whether he has scrolled the page. If you don't take these things into consideration, it's easy to accidentally place an element partly or completely off the screen (the hatched areas of the diagram).

13. **Add line 18 below to the mouseover function:**

```
1  $('.trigger').mouseover(function() {
2      var ttLeft,
3          ttRight,
4          $this=$(this),
5          $tip = $($this.attr('data-tooltip')),
6          triggerPos = $this.offset(),
7          triggerH = $this.outerHeight(),
8          triggerW = $this.outerWidth(),
9          tipW = $tip.outerWidth(),
10         tipH = $tip.outerHeight(),
11         screenW = $(window).width(),
12         scrollTop = $(document).scrollTop();
13     if (triggerPos.top - tipH - scrollTop > 0 ) {
14         ttTop = triggerPos.top - tipH - 10;
15     } else {
16         ttTop = triggerPos.top + triggerH +10 ;
17     }
18     var overFlowRight = (triggerPos.left + tipW) - screenW;
19 }); // end mouseover
```

Calculating the left position is a bit trickier than the right position. You need to know not only whether part of a tooltip is positioned off the right edge of the browser window, but by how much. For example, say a trigger's left position is 850 pixels (marked as A in Figure 10-11), the tooltip is 250 pixels wide (B), and the browser window is 1,000 pixels wide (C). If you position the left edge of the tooltip at 850 pixels, it will span from the 850 pixel mark to the 1,100 mark (A+B). That means the right 100 pixels of the tooltip won't be visible! To fix that, you need to know how much of the tooltip extends outside of the right edge of the browser, and adjust the tip's left position by moving it that same amount to the left.

Line 18 above calculates the total amount (if any) that the tooltip extends of the right edge of the browser window. To do that, first calculate the far-left edge of the tooltip if it were positioned at the left edge of the trigger—*triggerPos.left + tipW* (A+B in Figure 10-11). Then subtract the screen width (C). If the result is a positive value, some part of the tooltip will be outside the browser window. If the result is negative, there's plenty of screen space, and the tooltip will fit just fine.

14. **Add the following code below the line you added in the last step (line 18 above).**

```
if (overFlowRight > 0) {
    ttLeft = triggerPos.left - overFlowRight - 10;
} else {
    ttLeft = triggerPos.left;
}
```

Basically this code says that if the *overFlowRight* variable holds a number greater than zero (that means the tooltip won't fit), then set the left edge of the tooltip—*ttLeft*—to the trigger's left position, minus the amount the tooltip would extend off the window. Subtracting an additional 10 pixels keeps the tooltip from touching the edge of the window. If the value of *overFlowRight* is less then zero, the tooltip will fit so just set its left position to match the trigger's left position—*ttLeft = triggerPos.left;*.

Wow, that's a lot of math! Fortunately, you're done. The top and left position for the tooltip is calculated so now you can make it appear onscreen. Finally!

15. **Add lines 24-28 below to finish up the mouseover function:**

```
1  $('.trigger').mouseover(function() {
2      var ttLeft,
3          ttRight,
4          $this=$(this),
5          $tip = $($this.attr('data-tooltip')),
6          triggerPos = $this.offset(),
7          triggerH = $this.outerHeight(),
8          triggerW = $this.outerWidth(),
9          tipW = $tip.outerWidth(),
10         tipH = $tip.outerHeight(),
11         screenW = $(window).width(),
12         scrollTop = $(document).scrollTop();
```

```
13    if (triggerPos.top - tipH - scrollTop > 0 ) {
14        ttTop = triggerPos.top - tipH - 10;
15    } else {
16        ttTop = triggerPos.top + triggerH +10 ;
17    }
18    var overFlowRight = (triggerPos.left + tipW) - screenW;
19    if (overFlowRight > 0) {
20        ttLeft = triggerPos.left - overFlowRight - 10;
21    } else {
22        ttLeft = triggerPos.left;
23    }
24    $tip.css({
25        left : ttLeft ,
26        top : ttTop,
27        position: 'absolute'
28        }).fadeIn(200);
29 }); // end mouseover
```

Now the moment of truth. Using jQuery's chaining feature (page 137), first the *.css()* function (page 143) is applied to the tooltip, with its left position and right position set. Because you're positioning the tooltip, its *position* property is also set to *absolute*; then, the *fadeIn()* function (page 187) quickly fades the tooltip into view. Fortunately, making the tooltip disappear when you mouse off the trigger is a lot simpler.

16. **Finish the programming by adding lines 30-32 below, so that the finished code looks like this:**

```
1 $('.trigger').mouseover(function() {
2    var ttLeft,
3        ttRight,
4        $this=$(this),
5        $tip = $($this.attr('data-tooltip')),
6        triggerPos = $this.offset(),
7        triggerH = $this.outerHeight(),
8        triggerW = $this.outerWidth(),
9        tipW = $tip.outerWidth(),
10        tipH = $tip.outerHeight(),
11        screenW = $(window).width(),
12        scrollTop = $(document).scrollTop();
13    if (triggerPos.top - tipH - scrollTop > 0 ) {
14        ttTop = triggerPos.top - tipH - 10;
15    } else {
16        ttTop = triggerPos.top + triggerH +10 ;
17    }
18    var overFlowRight = (triggerPos.left + tipW) - screenW;
19    if (overFlowRight > 0) {
20        ttLeft = triggerPos.left - overFlowRight - 10;
21    } else {
22        ttLeft = triggerPos.left;
23    }
24    $tip.css({
25        left : ttLeft ,
26        top : ttTop,
27        position: 'absolute'
```

```
28          }).fadeIn(200);
29      }); // end mouseover
30      $('.trigger').mouseout(function () {
31          $('.tooltip').fadeOut(200);
32      }); // end mouseout
```

The mouseout stuff is easy: Just fade out any visible tooltips when you mouse off the trigger. And that's it. Save the file and test it out in a web browser. A completed version of the file—*complete_tooltip.html*—is in the *chapter10* tutorial folder.

PLUG-IN ALERT

Tooltips, the Easier Way

Learning to program your own tooltips is a great way to master jQuery's functions for working with the dimensions and positions of elements. But if you're looking for additional features like cooler-looking tooltip boxes, speech-bubble effects, the ability to download tooltip content using Ajax, or precise positioning of the tooltip, there are plenty of jQuery plug-ins that offer more features than the simple script we created in this chapter:

- qTip2 (*http://craigsworks.com/projects/qtip2/*) is a powerhouse tooltip plug-in. Not only can it create simple tooltips like in our tutorial, but it can also create speech bubbles, follow a mouse as it moves around the screen, download content from the server to display in the tooltip, and a lot more. You can even use it to create dialog boxes, drop-down menus, and more. It's like the Swiss army knife of tooltips.

- jQuery Tools Tooltip (*http://flowplayer.org/tools/tooltip/index.html*) is another great tooltip plug-in. The tooltips it creates are very slick looking and highly customizable. While you're looking at this plug-in, check out the entire jQuery Tools collection (*http://flowplayer.org/tools/*). It bills itself as "The Missing UI Library for the Web," and despite this grandiose claim, it comes pretty close to answering the needs of many web designers. jQuery tools includes plug-ins for tabs, overlays, forms, a slider (like the Anything-Slider discussed on page 312), and more.

- The jQuery UI Tooltip (*http://wiki.jqueryui.com/w/page/12138112/Tooltip*). You read about jQuery UI in the box on page 312: It's a large collection of user interface widgets and tools for web designers. Although (at the time of this writing) the jQuery UI team hasn't officially released a tooltip plug-in, a substantial amount of work on it is already completed and it's scheduled to come out with version 1.9 of the jQuery UI library. All of the plug-ins that come with jQuery UI are top-notch.

Part Four: Ajax: Communication with the Web Server

4

Chapter 11: Introducing Ajax

Chapter 12: Flickr and Google Maps

Introducing Ajax

J avaScript is great, but it can't do everything. If you want to display information
from a database, dash off an email with results from a form, or just download
additional HTML, you need to communicate with a web server. For these tasks,
you usually need to load a new web page. For example, when you search a database
for information, you usually leave the search page and go to another page of results.

Of course, waiting for new pages to load takes time. And, if you think about it, the
concept of a page disappearing and then reappearing is pretty strange in general.
Imagine if you were using Microsoft Word and every time you opened a new file the
program's menus, panels, and windows suddenly disappeared and then reappeared
when the new file opened. Sites like Facebook, Twitter, Google Maps, and Gmail are
blurring the line between websites and desktop computer programs. If anything,
people want websites to feel faster and more responsive, like their desktop programs.
The technology that makes this new generation of web applications possible is a
programming technology called Ajax.

Ajax lets a web page ask for and receive a response from a web server and then update itself without ever having to load a new web page. The result is a website that
feels more responsive. When you visit Google Maps, for example (see Figure 11-1),
you can zoom into the map; move north, south, east, or west, and even grab the map
and drag it around. All of these actions happen without ever loading a new web page.

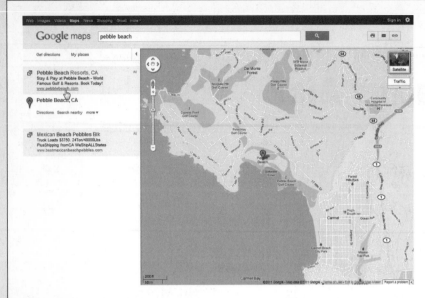

Figure 11-1:
*Google Maps (http://
maps.google.com)
was one of the first
large sites to use Ajax
to refresh page con-
tent without loading
new web pages. The
site's responsiveness
is due to the fact that
only the map data
changes—the other
parts of the page,
like the logo, search
box, search results
sidebar, and map
controls, remain the
same even as you
request new map
information.*

What Is Ajax?

The term Ajax was originally coined in 2005 to capture the essence of new web-sites coming from Google—Google Maps (*http://maps.google.com*), Gmail (*www .gmail.com*), and Google Suggest (*www.google.com/webhp?complete=1&hl=en*). Ajax stands for *Asynchronous JavaScript and XML*, but it isn't an "official" technology like HTML, JavaScript, or CSS. It's a term that refers to the interaction of a mix of tech-nologies—JavaScript, the web browser, and the web server—to retrieve and display new content without loading a new web page.

Note: If you want to read the original blog post where the term Ajax was first used, visit *www.adaptivepath .com/ideas/ajax-new-approach-web-applications*.

In a nutshell, current web browsers let you use JavaScript to send a request to a web server, which, in turn, sends some data back to the web browser. The JavaScript program takes that data, and does something with it. For example, if you're on a Google Maps page and click the "north" arrow button, the page's JavaScript requests new map data from the Google server. That new information is then used to display a new chunk of the map.

While you may not create the next Google Maps, there are many simple things that you can do with Ajax technologies:

- **Display new HTML content without reloading the page**. For example, on a page that lists news headlines and displays the article when a visitor clicks a headline, you can save him the tiresome wait for a new page to load. Instead, the news story could appear right on the same web page, without the banner, sidebar, footer, or other page content needing to reload. You'll learn how on page 352.

- **Submit a form and instantly display results**. For example, imagine a "sign up for our newsletter" form; when someone fills out and submits the form, the form disappears and a "you're signed up for our newsletter" message immediately appears. You'll learn how to make such forms using Ajax on page 356.

- **Log in without leaving the page**. Here's another form-related use of JavaScript—a page with a small "login" form. Fill out the form, hit the "login" button, and you're not only logged in, the page transforms to show your login status, user name, and perhaps other information specific to you.

- **Star-rating widget**. On sites that list books, movies, and other products, you often see a star rating—usually 1 to 5 stars—to indicate how visitors have rated the item's quality. These rating systems usually let you voice your opinion by clicking a number of stars. Using Ajax, you can let your visitors cast votes without actually leaving the web page—all they have to do is click the stars. There's a cool jQuery plug-in that does just that: *www.wbotelhos.com/raty/*.

- **Browsing through database information**. Amazon is a typical example of an online database you can browse. When you search Amazon for books on, say, JavaScript, you get a list of the JavaScript books Amazon sells. Usually, there are more books than can fit on a single web page, so you need to jump from page to page to see "the next 10 items." Using Ajax, you can move through database records without having to jump to another page. Here's how Twitter uses Ajax: When you view your Twitter page, you see a bunch of tweets from the people you follow. If you scroll to the bottom of the page, Twitter loads more tweets. Scroll again and more tweets appear. It's like a never-ending web page!

There's nothing revolutionary about any of the tasks listed above—except for the "without loading a new page" part, you can achieve the same basic results using regular HTML and some server-side programming (to collect form data, or access database information, for example). However, Ajax makes web pages feel more responsive, and improves the user experience of a site. In fact, Ajax lets you create websites that feel more like desktop programs and less like web pages.

Ajax: The Basics

Taken together, the technologies behind Ajax are pretty complicated. They include JavaScript, server-side programming, and the web browser all working together. However, the basic concept is easy to grasp, as long as you understand all of the steps involved. Figure 11-2 shows the difference between how traditional HTML web pages and web pages with Ajax communicate with the web server.

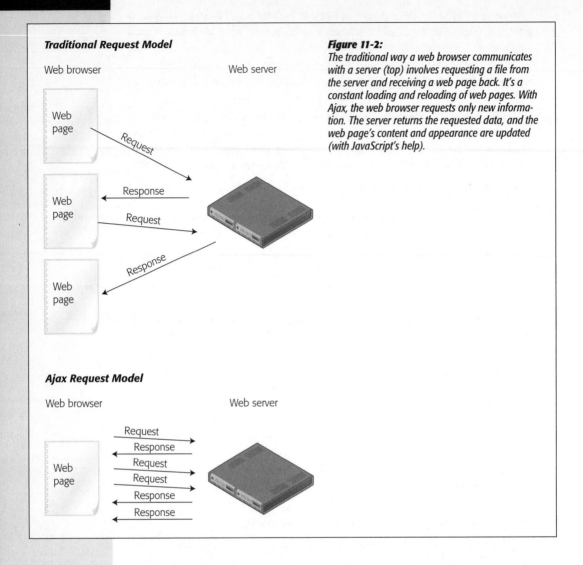

Traditional Request Model

Web browser

Web server

Web page

Request

Response

Web page

Request

Response

Web page

Figure 11-2:
The traditional way a web browser communicates with a server (top) involves requesting a file from the server and receiving a web page back. It's a constant loading and reloading of web pages. With Ajax, the web browser requests only new information. The server returns the requested data, and the web page's content and appearance are updated (with JavaScript's help).

Ajax Request Model

Web browser

Web server

Web page

Request
Response
Request
Request
Response
Response

Pieces of the Puzzle

Ajax isn't a single technology—it's a mixture of several different technologies that work together to make a more effective user experience. In essence, Ajax brings together three different components:

- **The web browser**. Obviously, you need a web browser to view web pages and run JavaScript, but there's a secret ingredient built into most web browsers that makes Ajax possible: the *XMLHttpRequest object*. This odd-sounding term is what lets JavaScript talk to a web server and receive information in response.

The *XMLHttpRequest* object was actually introduced in Internet Explorer 5 many years ago, but has gradually made its way into all the major web browsers. You'll learn more about it on page 346.

- **JavaScript** does most of the heavy lifting in Ajax. It sends a request to the web server, waits for a response, processes the response, and (usually) updates the page by adding new content or changing the display of the page in some way. Depending upon what you want your program to do, you might have JavaScript send information from a form, request additional database records, or simply send a single piece of data (like the rating a visitor just gave to a book). After the data is sent to the server, the JavaScript program will be ready for a response back from the server—for example, additional database records or just a simple text message like "Your vote has been counted."

  With that information, JavaScript will update the web page—display new database records, for example, or inform the visitor that he's successfully logged in. Updating a web page involves manipulating a page's DOM (Document Object Model, discussed on page 127) to add, change, and remove HTML tags and content. In fact, that's what you've been doing for most of this book: changing a page's content and appearance using JavaScript.

- **The web server** receives requests from and sends information back to the web browser. The server might simply return some HTML or plain text, or it might return an XML document (see the box on page 365) or JSON data (page 370). For example, if the web server receives information from a form, it might add that information into a database and send back a confirmation message like "record added." Or, the JavaScript program might send a request for the next 10 records of a database search, and the web server will send back the information for those next 10 records.

  The web server part of the equation can get a bit tricky. It usually involves several different types of technologies, including a web server, application server, and database server. A web server is really kind of a glorified filing cabinet: It stores documents and when a web browser asks for a document, the web server delivers it. To do more complicated tasks such as putting data from a form into a database, you also need an *application server* and a *database server*. An application server understands a server-side programming language like PHP, Java, C#, Ruby, or Cold Fusion Markup language and lets you perform tasks that aren't possible with only an HTML page, like sending email, checking Amazon for book prices, or storing information in a database. The database server lets you store information like the names and addresses of customers, details of products you sell, or an archive of your favorite recipes. Common database servers include MySQL, PostgreSQL, and SQL Server.

Note: The term *server* can refer either to a piece of hardware or software. In this book, the terms *application, web,* and *database* server refer to different pieces of software that can (and often do) run on the same machine.

There are many different combinations of web servers, application servers, and database servers. For example, you might use Microsoft's IIS web server, with ASP.NET (application server) and SQL server (a database server). Or you can use Apache (a web server), PHP (an application server), and MySQL (a database).

Note: The combination of Apache, PHP, and MySQL (often referred to simply as AMP) is free and very common. You'll find that most web hosting companies provide these servers. This book's examples also use AMP (see the box below).

UP TO SPEED

Setting Up a Web Server

Ajax works with a web server—after all, its main purpose is to let JavaScript send and retrieve information from a server. While all but one of the tutorials in this and the following chapter will run on your local computer without a web server, you'll probably want to have access to a web server if you want to further explore the world of Ajax. If you've already got a website on the Internet, one choice is to test your Ajax programs by moving your files to the web server. Unfortunately, this technique is cumbersome—you have to create the pages on your computer and then move them to your web server using a FTP program just to see if they work.

A better approach is to set up a *development server*, which involves installing a web server on your desktop computer so you can program and test your Ajax pages directly on your own computer. This task may sound daunting, but there are plenty of free programs that make installing all of the necessary components as easy as double-clicking a file.

On the Windows side, you can install Apache, PHP, and MySQL using WAMP (*www.wampserver.com/en/*). WAMP

is a free installer that sets up all of the required elements needed to simulate a real website hosted on the Internet. You can find a video demonstrating how to install WAMP at *http://uptospeedguides.com/wamp/*.

For Mac fans, MAMP (*www.mamp.info/en*) provides an easy-to-use program that includes Apache, PHP, and MySQL. It's also free. You can find a video demonstrating how to install WAMP at *http://uptospeedguides.com/mamp/*.

The tutorial on page 365 requires AMP. So if you want to follow along with that tutorial, you'll need to install AMP on your computer using one of the two programs above. If you already have a website that uses a different web server (for example, Microsoft's IIS), you'll probably want to install it on your computer if you plan to create Ajax applications that you'd like to use on your real website. There are many resources for installing IIS. If you want to install IIS on Vista, visit *http://learn.iis.net/page.aspx/85/installing-iis7/*. XP Pro users can visit *www.webwiz.co.uk/kb/asp-tutorials/installing-iis-winxp-pro.htm*.

Talking to the Web Server

The core of any Ajax program is the *XMLHttpRequest* object. Sometimes just referred to as *XHR*, the XMLHttpRequest object is a feature built into current web browsers that allows JavaScript to send information to a web server and receive information in return. There are basically five steps, all of which can be accomplished with JavaScript.

1. **Create an instance of the *XMLHttpRequest* object.**

   This first step simply tells the web browser "Hey, I want to send some information to the web server, so get ready." In its most basic form, creating an *XML-
   HttpRequest* object in JavaScript looks like this:

   ```
   var newXHR = new XMLHttpRequest();
   ```

   Unfortunately, there are enough cross-browser problems with Ajax that is better to use a JavaScript library—like jQuery—to make your Ajax requests. You'll
   learn the jQuery way on page 349.

2. **Use the XHR's *open()* method to specify what kind of data you'll send and
   where the data will go.**

   You can send data in two ways, using either the GET or POST method—these
   are the same options as used with HTML forms. The GET method sends any
   information to the web server as part of the URL—*shop.php?productID=34*,
   for example. In this example, the data is the information that follows the *?*:
   productID=34, which indicates a name/value pair, where *productID* is the name
   and *34* is the value. Think of the name like the name of a field on a form and
   value as what a visitor would type into that field.

Note: The URL you specify for the *open()* method must be on the same website as the page making the
request. For security, web browsers won't let you make Ajax requests to other domains.

   The POST method sends data separately from the URL. Usually, you use the
   GET method to get data back from the server, and the POST method to update
   information on the server (for example, to add, update, or delete a database
   record). You'll learn how to use both methods on page 356.

   You also use the *open()* method to specify the page on the server the data is
   sent to. That's usually a page on your web server that uses a server-side scripting language like PHP to retrieve data from a database or perform some other
   programming task, and you point to it by its URL. For example, the following
   code tells the XHR object what method to use (GET) and which page on the
   server to request:

   ```
   newXHR.open('GET', 'shop.php?productID=34');
   ```

3. **Create a function to handle the results.**

   When the web server returns a result like new database information, a confirmation that a form was processed, or just a simple text message, you usually
   want to do something with that result. That could be as simple as writing the
   message "form submitted successfully," or replacing an entire table of database
   records with a new table of records. In any case, you need to write a JavaScript
   function to deal with the results—this function (called a *callback function*) is
   often the meat of your program.

Usually, this function will manipulate the page's content (that is, change the page's DOM) by removing elements (for example, removing a form that was just submitted using Ajax), adding elements (a "form submitted successfully" message, or a new HTML table of database records), or changing elements (for example, highlighting the number of stars a visitor just clicked to rate a product).

There are a few other steps involved here, but you'll be using jQuery to handle the details, so the only thing you really need to understand about the callback function is that it's the JavaScript that deals with the server's response.

4. **Send the request.**

To actually send information to the web server, you use the XHR object's *send()* method. Everything up to this point is just setup—*this* step is what tells the web browser, "We're good to go…send the request!" If you're using the GET method, this step is as simple as:

```
newXHR.send(null);
```

The *null* part indicates that you're not sending any additional data. (Remember, with the GET method, the data is sent in the URL like this: *search .php?q=javascript*, where the *q=javascript* is the data.) With the POST method, on the other hand, you must provide the data along with the *send()* method like this:

```
newXHR.send('q=javascript');
```

Again, don't sweat the details here—you'll see how jQuery greatly simplifies this process starting in the next section.

Once the request is sent, your JavaScript program doesn't necessarily stop. The "A" in Ajax stands for *asynchronous*, which means that once the request is sent, the JavaScript program can continue doing other things. The web browser doesn't just sit around and wait for the server to respond.

5. **Receive the response.**

After the server has processed the request, it sends back a response to the web browser. Actually, the callback function you created in step 3 handles the response, but meanwhile, the XHR object receives several pieces of information when the web server responds, including the *status* of the request, a *text* response, and possibly an *XML* response.

The status response is a number indicating how the server responded to the request: You're probably familiar with the status number *404*—it means the file wasn't found. If everything went according to plan, you'll get a status of 200 or possibly 304. If there was an error processing the page, you'll get a 500 "Internal Server Error" status report, and if the file you requested is password protected, you'll get a 403 "Access Forbidden" error.

In addition, most of the time, you'll receive a text response, which is stored in the XHR object's *responseText* property. This response could be a chunk of HTML, a simple text message, or a complex set of JSON data (see page 370). Finally, if the server responds with an XML file, it's stored in the XHR object's *responseXML* property. Although XML is still used, it's more common for program server pages to return text, HTML, or JSON data, so you may never have a need to process an XML response.

Whatever data the server returns, it's available to the callback function to use to update the web page. Once the callback function finishes up, the entire Ajax cycle is over. (However, you may have multiple Ajax requests shooting off at the same time.)

Ajax the jQuery Way

There are enough differences between browsers that you have to write extra code for your Ajax programs to work in Internet Explorer, Firefox, Safari, and Opera. And although the basic *XMLHttpRequest* process isn't too complicated, since you must take so many steps each time you make an XHR request, your Ajax programming will go faster if you turn to a JavaScript library.

The jQuery library provides several functions that greatly simplify the entire process. After all, if you look at the five steps in an Ajax request (page 347), you'll see that the interesting stuff—the programming that actually does something with the server's response—happens in just a single step (step 3). jQuery simplifies all of the other steps so you can concentrate on the really fun programming.

Using the *load()* Function

The simplest Ajax function offered by jQuery is *load()*. This function loads an HTML file into a specified element on the page. For example, say you have an area of a web page dedicated to a short list of news headlines. When the page loads, the five most recent news stories appear. You may want to add a few links that let visitors choose what type of news stories are displayed in this area of the page: for example, yesterday's news, local news, sports news, and so on. You can do this by linking to separate web pages, each of which contain the proper news items—but that would force your visitors to move onto another web page (and wouldn't use Ajax at all!).

Another approach would be to simply load the selected news stories into the news headlines box on the page. In other words, each time a visitor clicks a different news category, the web browser requests a new HTML file from the server, and then places that HTML into the headlines box—without leaving the current page (see Figure 11-3).

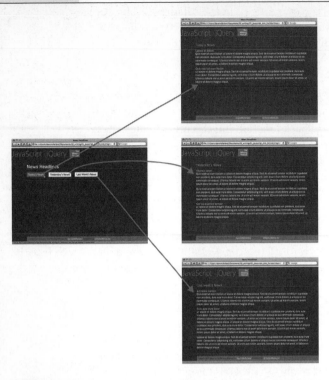

Figure 11-3:
The top set of images shows how links work—the typical method of accessing additional HTML. Click a link on a page (top left) and it loads a brand new page (top right). However, using Ajax and jQuery's load() function, you can access the same HTML without leaving the current web page (bottom). Clicking a link loads the HTML content into a <div> tag (outlined).

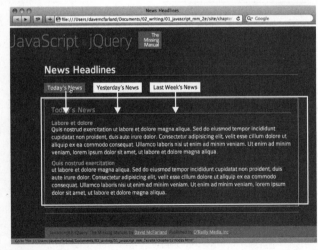

Learning the Ways of the Server Side

Unless you're using jQuery's basic *load()* function (discussed previously) to insert HTML from a page on the server into the page in the web browser, you'll need to have server-side programming to use Ajax. The main point of Ajax is to let JavaScript talk to and get information from the server. Most of the time, that means there's another script running on the web server that completes tasks JavaScript can't do, like reading information from a database, sending off an email, or logging a user in.

This book doesn't cover the server side, so you'll need to learn how to program using a server-side technology like PHP, .NET, JSP, ASP, or Cold Fusion (or you'll need someone who can program the server-side bit for you). If you haven't picked a server-side language yet, PHP is a good place to start: It's one of the most popular web server programming languages, it's free, and nearly every web

hosting company offers PHP on its servers. It's a powerful language that's built for the web, and it's *relatively* easy to learn. If you want to get started learning server-side programming with PHP, you should check out *Learning PHP, MySQL, and JavaScript* (O'Reilly), *Head First PHP & MySQL* (O'Reilly), or *PHP Solutions: Dynamic Web Design Made Easy* (Friends of Ed). Any of these books is a good place to start.

There are also plenty of free online resources for learning PHP. PHP 101 (*http://devzone.zend.com/node/view/id/627*) from Zend (one of the main companies that supports the development of PHP) has plenty of basic (and advanced) information. The W3Schools website also has a lot of information for the beginning PHP programmer at *www.w3schools.com/PHP*.

To use the *load()* function, you first use a jQuery selector to identify the element on the page where the requested HTML should go; you then call the *load()* function and pass the URL of the page you wish to retrieve. For example, say you have a <div> tag with the ID *headlines* and you want to load the HTML from the file *todays_news .html* into that div. You can do that like this:

```
$('#headlines').load('todays_news.html');
```

When this code runs, the web browser requests the file *todays_news.html* from the web server. When that file is downloaded, the browser replaces whatever is currently inside the <div> with the ID *headlines* with the contents of the new file. The HTML file can be a complete web page (including the <html>, <head>, and <body> tags), or just a snippet of HTML—for example, the requested file might just have a single <h1> tag and a paragraph of text. It's OK if the file isn't a complete web page, since the *load()* function inserts only that HTML snippet into the current (complete) page.

Note: You can only load HTML files from the same site. For example, you can't load Google's home page into a <div> on a page from your site using the *load()* function. (You can display a page from another website using an iframe—this is the technique used by the FancyBox plug-in presented on page 245.)

When using the *load()* function, you must be very careful with file paths. First, the URL you pass to the *load()* function is in relation to the current page. In other words, you use the same path as if you were linking from the current page to the HTML file you wish to load. In addition, any file paths in the HTML don't get rewritten when the HTML is loaded into the document, so if you have a link or include images in the HTML file that's loaded, those URLs need to work in relation to the page using the *load()* function. In other words, if you're using document-relative paths (see the box on page 28) and the loaded HTML file is located in another folder on your website, images and links might not work when the HTML is loaded into the current page. Here's a simple workaround: Just use root-relative links, or make sure the file you load is located in the same directory as the page that's using the *load()* function.

The *load()* function even lets you specify which part of the downloaded HTML file you wish to add to the page. For example, say the page you request is a regular web page from the site; it includes all of the normal web page elements such as a banner, navigation bar, and footer. You may just be interested in the content from a single area of that page—for example, just a particular <div> and its contents. To specify which part of the page you wish to load, insert a space after the URL, followed by a jQuery selector. For example, say in the above example you want to insert the content only inside a <div> with the ID *news* in the *todays_news.html* file. You could do that with this code:

```
$('#headlines').load('todays_news.html #news');
```

In this case, the web browser downloads the page *todays_news.html*, but instead of inserting the entire contents of the file into the *headlines* <div>, it extracts just the <div> tag (and everything inside it) with an ID of *news*. You'll see this technique in the following tutorial.

Tutorial: The *load()* Function

In this tutorial, you'll use jQuery to replace the traditional click-and-load method of accessing HTML (Figure 11-3, top) with a more responsive method that simply replaces content on the current page with new HTML (Figure 11-3, bottom).

Overview

To get a handle on what you'll be doing in this tutorial, you first need to understand the HTML of the page you're about to "Ajaxify." Take a look at Figure 11-4: The page has a bulleted list of links, each of which points to a different page containing different news headlines. The <ul> tag used to create the list has the ID *newslinks*. In addition, there's an empty <div> tag in the right sidebar (below the "News Headlines" header). That div has an ID of *headlines* and is, at this point, an empty placeholder. Eventually, once you use jQuery's *load()* function, clicking one of the links will load news stories into the <div>.

Currently, clicking a link just opens a web page with a series of news items. In other words, this page works the regular HTML way—it has links that point to other pages. In fact, without the nifty JavaScript you're about to add, the page works perfectly fine—it'll get any visitors to the news they're after. That's a good thing, because not everyone has JavaScript enabled in their browsers. In addition, if the only way to get to those news items is through JavaScript, search engines would skip over that valuable content.

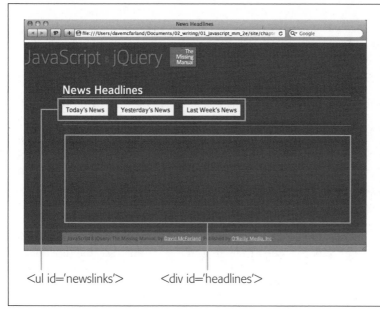

Figure 11-4:
When you want to use JavaScript to add content to a page, it's common to insert an empty <div> tag with an ID. You can then select that <div> and insert content when you want. For example, this page has an empty div (<div id="headlines">) in the right sidebar. With a little Ajax power, it's a simple matter to fill that div with the contents of any of the three linked pages listed in the middle of the page.

Note: You can use the *load()* function directly from your hard drive without a web server, so you don't need to set up a server on your computer (see the box on page 346) to follow along.

This tutorial provides an example of *progressive enhancement*—it functions just fine without JavaScript, but works even better with JavaScript. In other words, everyone can access the content, and no one's left out. To implement progressive enhancement, you'll add JavaScript to "hijack" the normal link function, then get the URL of the link, and then download the link to the page and put its contents into the empty <div>. It's as simple as that.

Note: See the note on page 29 for information on how to download the tutorial files.

The programming

1. **In a text editor, open the file *load.html* in the *chapter11* folder.**

   You'll start by assigning a *click* event function to each of the links in the bulleted list in the main part of the page. The bulleted list (the <ul> tag) has an ID of *newslinks*, so you can easily use jQuery to select each of those links and assign a *click()* function to them.

2.   **Click in the empty line inside the *$(document).ready()* function, and type:**

```
$('#newslinks a').click(function() {

});
```

The *$('#newslinks a')* is the jQuery way to select each of those links, and the *.click()* function lets you assign a function (an event handler) to the *click* event (see page 162) if you need a refresher on events).

The next step is to extract the URL from each link.

3.   **Inside the *click()* function (the blank line in step 2 above), type *var url=$(this). attr('href');* and press Return to create an empty line.**

This line of code creates a new variable (*url*) and assigns it the value of the link's *href* attribute. As you'll recall from page 136, when you attach a function (like the *click()* function) to a jQuery selection (*$('#newslinks a')* in this case), jQuery loops through each element in the selection (each link) and applies the function to each one. The *$(this)* is just a way to get hold of the current element being worked on. In other words, *$(this)* will refer to a different link as jQuery loops through the collection of elements. The *attr()* function (discussed on page 146) can retrieve or set a particular element for a tag; in this case, the function extracts the *href* property to get the URL of the page the link points to. In the next step, you'll use that URL along with the *load()* function to retrieve the page's content and display it inside a <div> on the page.

4.   **Type *$('#headlines').load(url);* so the script looks like this:**

```
$('#newslinks a').click(function() {
  var url=$(this).attr('href');
  $('#headlines').load(url);
});
```

Remember that the empty <div> tag on the page—where the downloaded HTML will go—has an ID of *headlines*, so *$('#headlines')* selects that <div>. The *load()* function then downloads the HTML at the URL that the previous line of code retrieved, and then puts that HTML in the <div> tag. Yes, there's actually *lots* of other stuff going on under the hood to make all that happen, but thanks to jQuery, you don't have to worry about it.

The page isn't quite done yet. If you save the file and preview it in a web browser— go ahead, try it—you'll notice that clicking one of the links doesn't load new content onto the page—it actually leaves the current page and loads the linked page instead! What happened to the Ajax? It's still there, it's just that the web browser is following its normal behavior of loading a new web page when a link is clicked. To stop that, you have to prevent the browser from following the link.

5.   **Add a new empty line after the code you typed in the previous step and type *return false;* so the script now looks like this:**

```
$('#newslinks a').click(function() {
  var url=$(this).attr('href');
  $('#headlines').load(url);
  return false;
});
```

This simple step tells the web browser, "Hey, web browser, don't follow that link." It's one way of preventing a browser from following its normal behavior in response to an event. You can also use jQuery's *preventDefault()* function as described on page 175 to achieve the same effect.

6. **Save the file and preview it in a web browser. Click one of the links.**

   Now there's another problem, as you can see in Figure 11-5. The *load()* function is working, it's just that the downloaded file has a lot of HTML you don't want—in particular, the banner "JavaScript & jQuery" appears a second time. What you really want is only a portion of that web page—the area containing the news items. Fortunately, the *load()* function can help here as well.

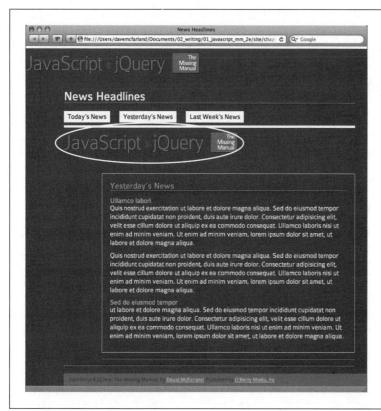

Figure 11-5:
jQuery's load() *function will download all of the HTML for a specified file and place it into an element on the current page. If the downloaded file includes unneeded HTML, like a duplicate banner, and footer, the result can look like a page within a page.*

7. **Locate the line with the *load()* function and add + ' #newsItem' after *url*. The finished code should look like this:**

```
$('#newslinks a').click(function() {
  var url=$(this).attr('href');
  $('#headlines').load(url + ' #newsItem');
  return false;
});
```

As described on page 352, you can specify which part of a downloaded file you want the *load()* function to add to the page. To do that, you add a space after the URL, followed by a selector that identifies the part of the downloaded page you wish to display.

Here's how the code breaks down into bit-sized chunks: First, on each of the linked pages, there's a <div> tag with the ID *newsItem*. That div contains the HTML you want—the news items. So you can tell the *load()* function to only insert that part of the downloaded HTML by adding a space followed by *#newsItem* to the URL passed to *load()*. For example, if you want to load the file *today .html* and place just the HTML inside the *newsItem* div inside the *headlines* div, you can use this code:

```
$('#headlines').load('today.html #newsItem');
```

In this case, you need to combine two strings—the contents of the *url* variable and '*#newsItems*' to get the proper code—so you use JavaScript's string concatenation operator (the + symbol) like this: *load(url + '#newsItems')*. (See page 51 if you need a refresher on how to combine two strings.)

8. **Save the file and preview it in a web browser. Click the links to test it out.**

   Now the news items—and only the news items—from each linked page should appear in the box in the middle of the page. Ajax in just a few lines of code! (You'll find a completed version of the tutorial—*complete_load.html*—in the *chapter12* file for reference.)

The *get()* and *post()* Functions

The *load()* function described on page 349 is a quick way to get HTML from a web server and inject it into a page. But the server may not always return straight HTML—it may return a message, a code number, or data that you then need to process further using JavaScript. For example, if you want to use Ajax to get some database records, the server may return an XML file containing those records (see the box on page 365) or a JSON object (page 370). You wouldn't just insert that data into the page—you first have to get the data and process it in some way to generate the HTML you want.

jQuery's *get()* and *post()* functions provide simple tools to send data to and retrieve data from a web server. As mentioned in step 2 on page 347, you need to treat the *XMLHttpRequest* object slightly differently when using either the GET or POST method. However, jQuery takes care of any differences between the two methods so the *get()* and *post()* functions work identically. (So which should you use? Read the box on page 358.)

The basic structure of these functions is:

```
$.get(url, data, callback);
```

Or:

```
$.post(url, data, callback);
```

Unlike most other jQuery functions, you don't add *get()* or *post()* to a jQuery selector—in other words, you'd never do something like this: *$('#mainContent') .get('products.php')*. The two functions stand by themselves and aren't connected with any element on the page, so you just use the *$* symbol, followed by a period, followed by either *get* or *post*: *$.get()*.

The *get()* and *post()* functions accept three arguments: *url* is a string that contains the path to the server-side script that processes the data (for example, 'processForm. php'). The *data* argument is either a string or a JavaScript object literal containing the data you want to send to the server (you'll learn how to create this in the next section). Finally, *callback* is the function that processes the information returned from the server (see the box on page 196 for details on writing a callback function).

When either the *get()* or *post()* function runs, the web browser sends off the data to the specified URL. When the server sends data back to the browser, the browser hands that data to the callback function, which then processes that information and usually updates the web page in some way. You'll see an example of this in action on page 365.

Formatting Data to Send to the Server

Most of the time when writing a JavaScript program that uses Ajax, you'll be sending some information to the server. For example, if you want to get information about a particular product stored in a database, you could send a single number representing a product. When the web server gets the number from the XHR request, it looks for a product in the database that matches that number, retrieves the product information, and sends it back to the web browser. Or, you might use Ajax to submit an entire form's worth of information as part of an online order or a "sign up for our email newsletter" form.

In either case, you need to format the data for your request in a way that the *get()* and *post()* functions understand. The second argument sent to either function contains the data you wish to send the server—you can format this data either as a query string or as a JavaScript object literal, as described in the next two sections.

Query string

You've probably seen query strings before: They frequently appear at the end of a URL following a *?* symbol. For example, in this URL *http://www.chia-vet.com/products.php?prodID=18&sessID=1234,* the query string is *prodID=18&sessID=1234*. This query string contains two name/value pairs, *prodID=18* and *sessID=1234*. This string does basically the same as creating two variables, *prodID* and *sessID*, and storing two values into them. A query string is a common method for passing information in a URL.

GET or POST?

The two methods for submitting data to a web server, GET and POST, seem pretty much the same. Which should I use?

The answer really depends. In some cases, you don't have a choice. For example, suppose you're sending information to a server-side script that's already up and running on your server. In other words, the server-side programming is already done, and you just need to use JavaScript to talk to it. In that case, you use the method that the script is expecting. Most likely, the programmer set up the script to accept either GET or POST data. So you can either talk to the programmer or look at the script to see which method it uses, then use the jQuery function that matches—either *get()* or *post()*.

If you (or another programmer) hasn't yet written the server-side script that your JavaScript program will talk to, then you get to choose the method. The GET method is suited to requests that don't affect the state of a database or files

on the server. In other words, use it when you want to *get* information, like requesting the price of a particular product or obtaining a list of most popular products. The POST method is for sending data that will change information on the server, like a request to delete a file, update a database, or insert new information into a database.

In reality, you can use either method, and often programmers will use a GET method to delete database information, and the POST method just to retrieve information from the server. However, there is one situation where POST is required. If you're submitting a lot of form data to a server—for example, a blog post that might include hundreds of words—use POST. The GET method has a built-in limit on the amount of data it can send (this limit varies from browser to browser but it's usually around several thousand characters). Most of the time, web designers use POST for forms that include more than just a few fields.

You can also format data sent to the server using Ajax in this format. For example, say you've created a web page that lets visitors rate movies by clicking a number of stars. Clicking five stars, for instance, submits a rating of five to the server. In this case, the data sent to the server might look like this: *rating=5*. Assuming the name of the page processing these ratings is called *rateMovie.php*, the code to send the rating to the server using Ajax would look like this:

```
$.get('rateMovie.php','rating=5');
```

Or, if you're using the POST method:

```
$.post('rateMovie.php','rating=5');
```

Note: jQuery's *get()* and *post()* functions don't require you to define data or a callback function. You only need to supply the URL of the server-side page. However, you'll almost always provide data as well. For example, in this code *$.get('rankMovie.php','rating=5');* only the URL and the data are supplied—no callback function is specified. In this case, the visitor is merely submitting a ranking, and there's no need for the server to respond or for a callback function to do anything.

If you need to send more than one name/value pair to the server, insert an *&* between each pair:

```
$.post('rateMovie.php','rating=5&user=Bob');
```

You need to be careful using this method, however, since some characters have special meaning when you insert into a query string. For instance, you use the & symbol to include additional name/value pairs to the string; the = symbol assigns a value to a name. For example, the following query string isn't valid:

```
'favFood=Mac & Cheese' // incorrect
```

The & symbol here is supposed to be part of "Mac & Cheese," but when used as part of a query string, the & will be interpreted to mean a second name/value pair. If you want to use special characters as part of the name or value in a name/value pair, you need to *escape* or *encode* them so that they won't be mistaken for a character with special meaning. For example, the space character is represented by *%20*, the & symbol by *%26*, and the = sign by *%3D*. So you need to write out the "Mac & Cheese" example like this:

```
'favFood=Mac%20%26%20Cheese' // properly escaped
```

JavaScript provides a method for properly escaping strings—the *encodeURICompo-nent()* method. You supply the *endcodeURIComponent()* method with a string, and it returns a properly escaped string. For example:

```
var queryString = 'favFood=' + encodeURIComponent('Mac & Cheese');
$.post('foodChoice.php', queryString);
```

Object literal

For short and simple pieces of data (that don't include any punctuation symbols), the query string method works well. But a more foolproof method supported by jQuery's *get()* and *post()* functions is to use an object literal to store data. As you'll recall from page 145, an object literal is a JavaScript method for storing name/value pairs. The basic structure of an object literal is this:

```
{
  name1: 'value1',
  name2: 'value2'
}
```

You can pass the object literal directly to the *get()* or *post()* function. For example, this code uses the query string method:

```
$.post('rankMovie.php','rating=5');
```

To use an object literal, rewrite the code like this:

```
$.post('rankMovie.php', { rating: 5 });
```

You can either pass the object literal directly to the *get()* or *post()* functions, or first store it in a variable and pass that variable to *get()* or *post()*:

```
var data = { rating: 5 };
$.post('rankMovie.php', data);
```

Of course, you can include any number of name/value pairs in the object that you pass to the *get()* or *post()* function:

```
var data = {
  rating: 5,
  user: 'Bob'
}
$.post('rankMovie.php', data);
```

Or, if you directly pass an object literal to .post():

```
var data = $.post('rankMovie.php',
  {
    rating: 5,
    user: 'Bob'
  }
); // end post
```

jQuery's serialize() *function*

Creating a query string or object literal for an entire form's worth of name/value pairs can be quite a chore. You have to retrieve the name and value for each form element, and then combine them all to create one long query string or one large JavaScript object literal. Fortunately, jQuery provides a function that makes it easy to convert form information into data that the *get()* and *post()* functions can use.

You can apply the *serialize()* function to any form (or even just a selection of form fields) to create a query string. To use it, first create a jQuery selection that includes a form, then attach the *serialize()* function to it. For example, say you have a form with an ID of *login*. If you wanted to create a query string for that form, you can do so like this:

```
var formData = $('#login').serialize();
```

The *var formData* part just creates a new variable; *$('#login')* creates a jQuery selection containing the form; finally, *.serialize()* collects all of the field names and the values currently in each field and creates a single query string.

To use this with either the *get()* or *post()* functions, just pass the serialized results to the function as the second argument after the URL. For example, say you want to send the contents of the login form to a page named *login.php*. You can do so like this:

```
var formData = $('#login').serialize();
$.get('login.php',formData,loginResults);
```

This code sends whatever the visitor enters into the form to the *login.php* file using the GET method. The final argument for *get()* here—*loginResults*—is the callback function: the function that takes the data sent back from the server and does something with it. You'll learn how to create a callback function next.

Processing Data from the Server

Ajax is usually a two-way street—a JavaScript program sends some data to the server and the server returns data to the JavaScript program, which can then use that data to update the page. In the previous pages, you saw how to format data and send it to a server using the *get()* and *post()* functions. Now you'll learn how to receive and process the server's response.

When the web browser sends off a request to the server using the XMLHttpRequest object, it keeps listening for a response from the server. When the server responds, a callback function handles the server's response. That function is passed several arguments that can be used by the function. First, and most important, the data returned by the server is sent as the first argument.

You can format the data the server returns in any number of ways. The server-side script can return a number, a word, a paragraph of text, or a complete web page. In cases where the server is sending a lot of information (like a bunch of records from a database), the server often uses XML or JSON. (See the box on page 365 for more about XML; see page 370 for a discussion of JSON.)

The second argument to the callback function is a string indicating the status of the response. Most of the time, the status is "success," meaning that the server has successfully processed the request and returned data. However, sometimes a request doesn't succeed—for example, the request was made to a file that doesn't exist, or there was an error in the server-side programming. If a request fails, the callback function receives an "error" status message.

The callback function processes the information in some way, and, most of the time, updates the web page in some way—replacing a submitted form with results from the server, or simply printing a "request successful" message on the page, for example. Updating the content of a web page is easy using jQuery's *html()* and *text()* functions described on page 138. Other methods of manipulating a page's DOM are discussed in Chapter 4.

To get a handle on a complete request/response cycle, take a look at a basic movie-rating example (see Figure 11-6). A visitor can rate a movie by clicking one of five links. Each link indicates a different rating. When the visitor clicks a link, the rating and ID of the movie being rated are sent to a server-side program, which adds the rating to the database, and then returns the average rating for that movie. The average rating is then displayed on the web page.

In order for this page to work without JavaScript, each of the links on the page points to a dynamic server-side page that can process the visitor's rating. For example, the five-star rating link (see Figure 11-6) might be *rate.php?rate=5&movie=123*. The name of the server-side file that processes the ratings is called *rate.php*, while the query string (*?rate=5&movie=123*) includes two pieces of information for the server: a rating (*rate=5*) and a number that identifies the movie being rated (*movie=123*). You can use JavaScript to intercept clicks on these links and translate them into Ajax calls to the server:

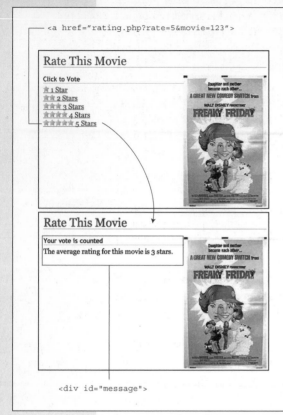

```
<a href="rating.php?rate=5&movie=123">
```

Rate This Movie

Click to Vote
- ★ 1 Star
- ★★ 2 Stars
- ★★★ 3 Stars
- ★★★★ 4 Stars
- ★★★★★ 5 Stars

Rate This Movie

Your vote is counted

The average rating for this movie is 3 stars.

```
<div id="message">
```

Figure 11-6:
On this page, a visitor clicks a link to rate the movie (top). By adding Ajax to the mix, you can submit the rating to the server without leaving the page. In fact, using the response from the server, you can update the page's contents (bottom).

```
1   $('#message a').click(function() {
2     var href=$(this).attr('href');
3     var querystring=href.slice(href.indexOf('?')+1);
4     $.get('rate.php', querystring, processResponse);
5     return false; // stop the link
6   });
```

Line 1 selects every link (<a> tag) inside of another tag with an ID of *message* (in this example, each link used to rate the movie is contained within a <div> with the ID *message*). A function is then applied to the click event for each of those links.

Line 2 extracts the HREF attribute of the link—so, for example, the *href* variable might hold a URL like *rate.php?rate=5&movie=123*. Line 3 extracts just the part after the *?* in the URL using the *slice()* method (discussed on page 428) to extract part of the string, and the *indexOf()* method (see page 427) to determine where the *?* is located (this information is used by the *slice()* method to determine where to start slicing).

Line 4 is the Ajax request. Using the GET method, a request containing the query string for the link is sent to the server file *rate.php* (see Figure 11-7). The results will then go to the callback function *processResponse*. Line 5 just stops the normal link behavior and prevents the web browser from unloading the current page and loading the linked-to page.

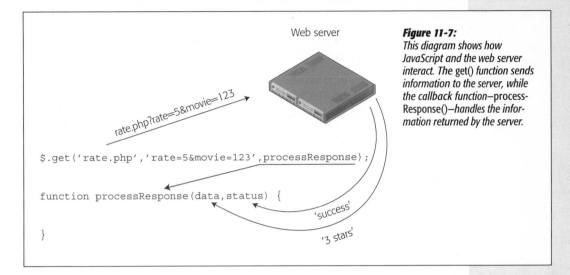

Web server

Figure 11-7:
This diagram shows how JavaScript and the web server interact. The get() *function sends information to the server, while the callback function—process-Response()—handles the information returned by the server.*

```
rate.php?rate=5&movie=123

$.get('rate.php','rate=5&movie=123',processResponse);

function processResponse(data,status) {



}
```
'success'

'3 stars'

Note: If you need a refresher on how functions work and how to create them, see page 100.

Finally, it's time to create the callback function. The callback function receives data and a string with the status of the response (*'success'* if the server sent information back). Remember the callback function's name is used in the request (see line 4 of the code on the previous page). So in this example, the function's name is *process-Response*. The code to deal with the server's response might look like this:

```
1    function processResponse(data) {
2      var newHTML;
3      newHTML = '<h2>Your vote is counted</h2>';
4      newHTML += '<p>The average rating for this movie is ';
5      newHTML += data + '.</p>';
6      $('#message').html(newHTML);
7    }
```

The function accepts data arguments, which is the information returned by the web server. This data could be plain text, HTML, XML, or JSON. Line 2 creates a new variable that holds the HTML that will be displayed on the page (for example, "Your vote is counted"). In lines 3 and 4, the *newHTML* variable is filled with some HTML, including a <h2> tag and a <p> tag. The server's response doesn't come into play until line 5—there the response from the server (stored in the *data* variable) is added to the *newHTML* variable. In this case, the server returns a string with the average rating for the movie: for example, '3 stars'.

Note: If you want to add a star rating system to your site, there's a great jQuery plug-in that handles most of the details available at *http://www.wbotelhos.com/raty/*.

Finally, line 6 modifies the HTML on the web page using jQuery's *html()* function (see page 138) by replacing the contents of the <div> with the ID of *message* with the new HTML. The result is something like the bottom image in Figure 11-6.

In this example, the callback function was defined outside of the *get()* function; however, you can use an anonymous function (see page 148) if you want to keep all of the Ajax code together:

```
$.get('file.php', data, function(data,status) {
    // callback function programming goes here
});
```

For example, you could rewrite line 4 on page 362 to use an anonymous function like this:

```
$.get('rate.php', querystring, function(data) {
    var newHTML;
    newHTML = '<h2>Your vote is counted</h2>';
    newHTML += '<p>The average rating for this movie is ';
    newHTML += data + '.</p>';
    $('#message').html(newHTML);
}); // end get
```

Handling Errors

Unfortunately, things don't always go as planned. When using Ajax to talk to a web server, things can go wrong. Maybe the web server is down for a moment, or a visitor's Internet connection drops momentarily. If that happens, the *.get()* and *.post()* functions will fail without letting the visitor know. While this type of problem is rare, it's best to be prepared and letting your visitors know that something has temporarily gone wrong can help them figure out what to do (like reload the page, try again, or come back later).

To respond to an error, you simply add a *.error()* function to the end of the *.get()* or *.post()* functions. The basic structure looks like this:

```
$.get(url, data, successFunction).error(errorFunction);
```

For example, you could rewrite line 4 on page 362 to look like this:

```
$.get('rate.php', querystring, processResponse).error(errorResponse);
```

Then create a new function named *errorResponse* that notifies the visitor that there was a problem. For example:

```
function errorResponse() {
    var errorMsg = "Your vote could not be processed right now.";
    errorMsg += "Please try again later.";
    $('#message').html(errorMsg);
}
```

In this case, the function *errorResponse* runs only if there's some kind of error with the server or the server's connection.

Tutorial: Using the *get()* Function

In this tutorial, you'll use Ajax to submit information from a login form. When a visitor supplies the correct user name and password, a message will appear letting her know she's successfully logged in. If the login information isn't correct, an error message will appear on the same page—without loading a new web page.

Note: In order to successfully complete this tutorial, you'll need to have a running web server to test the pages on. See the box on page 346 for information on how to set up a testing server on your computer.

POWER USERS' CLINIC

Receiving XML from the Server

XML is a common format for exchanging data between computers. Like HTML, XML lets you use tags to identify information. Unlike HTML, you're free to come up with tags that accurately reflect the content of your data. For example, a simple XML file might look like this:

```
<?xml version="1.0" ?>
<message id="234">
  <from>Bob</from>
  <to>Janette</to>
  <subject>Hi Janette</subject>
  <content>Janette, let's grab lunch to-
day.</content>
</message>
```

As you can see, there's a main tag (called the *root element*) named <message>–the equivalent of HTML's <html> tag– and several other tags that define the meaning of each piece of data.

When using Ajax, you might have a server program that returns an XML file. jQuery has no problem reading and extracting data from an XML file. When you use the *get()* or *post()* functions, if the server returns an XML file, the data argument that's sent to the callback function (see page 196) will contain the DOM of the XML file. In other words, jQuery will read the XML file and treat it like another document. You can then use jQuery's selector tools to access the data inside the XML.

For example, say a server-side file named *xml.php* returned the XML listed above, and you want to retrieve the text within the <content> tag. The XML file becomes the returned data, so the callback function can process it. You can use the jQuery *find()* function to search the XML to find a particular CSS element using any of the regular selectors you'd use with jQuery. For example, you can find an element, class, ID, descendent selector (page 133), or jQuery's filters (page 135).

For example:

```
$.get('xml.php','id=234',processXML);
function processXML(data) {
  var messageContent=$(data).
find('content').text();
}
```

The key here is *$(data).find('content')*, which tells jQuery to select every <content> tag within the *data* variable. Since, in this case, the *data* variable contains the returned XML file, this code tells jQuery to look for the <content> tag within the XML.

For learn more about XML, visit *www.w3schools.com/XML*. If you want a little information on how to produce XML from a server, check out *www.w3schools.com/XML/xml_server.asp*. And if you want to read about jQuery's *find()* function you'll find more information at *http://api.jquery.com/find*.

Overview

You'll start with the form pictured in Figure 11-8. It includes fields for supplying a username and password to the server. When the form is submitted, the server attempts to verify that the user exists and the password matches. If the information supplied matches valid login credentials, then the server logs the visitor in.

Figure 11-8:
A basic login page is a simple affair: just a couple of fields and a Submit button. However, there's really no reason to leave the page when the user logs in. By adding Ajax, you can submit the visitor's credentials, then notify whether he logged in successfully or not.

You'll add Ajax to the form by sending the login information via an *XMLHttpRequest*. The server will send a message to the callback function, which removes the form and displays a "logged in" message if the login information is valid, or an error message if it's not.

The programming

See the note on page 29 for information on how to download the tutorial files. The starting file contains the HTML form, ready for you to add some jQuery and Ajax programming.

1. **In a text editor, open the file *login.html* in the *chapter11* folder.**

    The link to the jQuery library file and the *$(document).ready()* function are already in place. You'll start by using jQuery to select the form and adding a *submit* event to it.

2. **Click in the empty line inside the *$(document).ready()* function and type:**

    ```
    $('#login').submit(function() {

    }); // end submit
    ```

The <form> tag has the ID login applied to it, so the jQuery selector—
$('#login')—selects that form, while the *submit()* function adds an event handler
to the *submit* event. In other words, when a visitor tries to submit the form, the
function you're about to create will run.

The next step is to collect the information from the form and format it as a
query string to submit to the server. You could do this by finding each form
field, extracting the value that the visitor had typed in, then constructing a query string by concatenating those different pieces of information. Fortunately,
jQuery's *serialize()* function takes care of all these details in one shot.

3. **Hit return to create an empty line and type:**

   ```
   var formData = $(this).serialize();
   ```

   This line starts by creating a new variable to hold the form data, and then applies the *serialize()* function to the form. Recall that *$(this)* refers to the current
   element, so in this case it refers to the login form, and is the same as *$('#login')*
   (see page 149 for more on how *$(this)* works). The *serialize()* function (see page
   360), takes a form and extracts the field names and values and puts them in the
   proper format for submitting to the server.

   Now you'll use the *get()* function to set up the *XMLHttpRequest*.

4. **Hit Return to create another empty line and type:**

   ```
   $.get('login.php',formData,processData);
   ```

   This code passes three arguments to the *get()* function. The first—*'login.php'*—
   is a string identifying where the data should be sent—in this case, a file on the
   server named *login.php*. The second argument is the query string containing
   the data that's being sent to the server—the login information. Finally, *process-
   Data* refers to the callback function that will process the server's response. You'll
   create that function now.

5. **Add another blank line below the last one and type:**

   ```
   1    function processData(data) {
   2
   3    } // end processData
   ```

   These lines form the shell of the callback function; there's no programming inside it yet. Notice that the function is set up to accept one argument (*data*),
   which will be the response coming from the server. The server-side page is programmed to return a single word—*pass* if the login succeeded, or *fail* if the login
   failed.

   In other words, based on the response from the server, the script will either
   print a message letting the visitor know he's successfully logged on, or that he
   hasn't—this is the perfect place for a conditional statement.

Note: The server-side page used in this tutorial isn't a full-fledged login script. It does respond if the proper credentials are supplied, but it's not something you could use to actually password-protect a site. There are many ways to effectively password protect a site, but most require setting up a database or setting up various configuration settings for the web server—these steps are beyond this basic tutorial. For a real, PHP-based login script, visit *http://www.html-form-guide.com/php-form/php-login-form .html*. This YouTube video also explains how to write the necessary PHP: http://www.youtube.com/watch?v=4oSCuEtxRK8.

6. **Inside the *processData()* function (line 2 in step 5), type:**

```
1    if (data=='pass') {
2       $('#content').html('<p>You have successfully logged on!</p>');
3    }
```

Line 1 here checks to see if the information returned from the server is the string *'pass'*. If it is, the login was successful and a success message is printed (line 2). The form is inside a <div> tag with the ID content, so *$('#content'). html('<p>You have successfully logged on!</p>')* will replace whatever's inside that <div> with a new paragraph. In other words, the form disappears and the success message appears in its place.

To finish up, you'll add an *else* clause to let the visitor know if he didn't supply the correct login information.

7. **Add an *else* clause to the *processData()* function so that it looks like this (additions are in bold):**

```
1    function processData(data) {
2       if (data=='pass') {
3          $('#content').html('<p>You have successfully logged on!</p>');
4       } else {
5          $('#formwrapper).prepend('<p id="fail">Incorrect 🔲
6          login information. Please try again</p>');
7    }}
8    } // end processData
```

Line 5 prints the message that the login failed. Notice that the *prepend()* function is used. As discussed on page 139, *prepend()* lets you add content to the beginning of an element. It doesn't remove what's already there; it just adds more content. In this case, you want to leave the form in place, so the visitor can try again to log in a second time.

8. **Save the file, and preview it in a web browser.**

You must view this page through a web browser using a URL, like *http://localhost/ chapter11/login.html*, for this tutorial to work. See the box on page 346 for more information on how to set up a web server.

9. **Try to log into the site.**

"But wait—you haven't given me the username and password yet!" you're probably thinking. That's the point—to see what happens when you don't log in correctly. Try to log in a second time: You'll see the "Incorrect login information" message appear a second time (see Figure 11-9). Since the *prepend()* function doesn't remove the first error message, it just adds the message a second time. That doesn't look right at all.

You have several ways to deal with this problem. You could, for example, insert an empty div—*<div id="failMessage">*—below the form. Then simply replace its HTML when the login fails. However, in this case, there's no empty div tag on the page. Instead, use a basic conditional statement to check whether the error message already exists—if it does, there's no need to add it a second time.

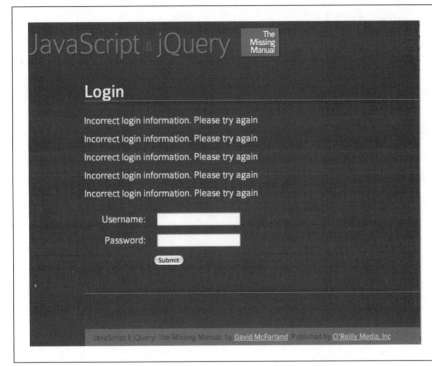

Figure 11-9:
jQuery's prepend() function adds HTML to an already existing element. It doesn't delete anything, so if you're not careful, you may end up adding the same message over and over again.

10. **Add another conditional statement (lines 5 and 7 below):**

```
1    function processData(data) {
2        if (data=='pass') {
3            $('#content').html('<p>You have successfully logged on!</p>');
4        } else {
5            if ($('#fail').length==0) {
6                $('#formwrapper').prepend('<p id="fail">Incorrect ↵
7                login information. Please try again</p>');
8            }
9        }
10    } // end processData
```

Notice that the error message paragraph has an ID—*fail*—so you can use jQuery to check to see if that ID exists on the page. If it doesn't, then the program writes the error message on the page. One way to check if an element already exists on the page is to try to use jQuery to select it. You can then check the *length* attribute of the results. If jQuery couldn't find any matching elements, the *length* attribute is *0*. In other words, *$('#fail')* tries to find an element with the ID *fail*. If jQuery can't find it—in other words, the error message hasn't yet been written to the page—then the length attribute is *0*, the conditional statement will be true, and the program writes the error message. Once the error message is on the page, the conditional statement always evaluates to false, and the error message doesn't appear again.

Finally, you need to tell the web browser that it shouldn't submit the form data itself—you already did that using Ajax.

11. **Add *return false;* at the end of the submit event (line 15 below). The finished script should look like this:**

```
1    $(document).ready(function() {
2    $('#login').submit(function() {
3      var formData = $(this).serialize();
4      $.post('login.php',formData,processData);
5      function processData(data) {
6        if (data=='pass') {
7          $('#formwrapper').html('<p>You have successfully logged on!</p>');
8        } else {
9          if (! $('#fail').length) {
10           $('#formwrapper').prepend('<p id="fail">Incorrect ↵
11           login information. Please try again</p>');
12         }
13       }
14     } // end processData
15     return false;
16   }); // end submit
17   }); // end ready
```

12. **Save the file and preview the page once again.**

Try to log in again: the user name is *007* and the password is *secret*. A completed version of this tutorial *complete_login.html* is in the *chapter12* folder.

Note: As mentioned on page 356, jQuery's *post()* and *get()* functions work identically even though, behind the scenes, jQuery has to do two different set of steps to make the Ajax request work correctly. You can check this out yourself by just changing *get* to *post* in the script (see line 4 in step 11). The server-side script for this tutorial is programmed to accept either GET or POST requests.

JSON

Another popular format for sending data from the server is called JSON, which stands for *JavaScript Object Notation*. JSON is a data format that's written in JavaScript, and it's kind of like XML (see the box on page 365), in that it's a method for exchanging data. JSON is usually better than XML; however, since JSON is JavaScript, it works quickly and easily in JavaScript program. XML needs to be taken apart—also called *parsed*—by JavaScript, which is generally slower and requires more programming.

Note: Another type of JSON, known as JSONP, lets you request data from other domains, so you can, for example, request images from Flickr (*www.flickr.com*) and display them on a page on your own site. (As mentioned in the note on page 351, usually you can only make an Ajax request to your own domain.) You'll see JSONP in action in the next chapter.

You already learned how to create JSON back on page 370. In essence, JSON is simply a JavaScript object literal, or a collection of name/value pairs. Here's a simple example of JSON:

```
{
    firstName: 'Frank',
    lastName: 'Smith',
    phone: '503-555-1212'
}
```

The *{* marks the beginning of the JSON object, while the *}* marks its end. In between are sets of name/value pairs; for example, *firstName: 'Frank'*. Every name/value pair is separated by a comma, but don't put a comma at the end of the last pair (otherwise, Internet Explorer will cough up an error).

Note: Alternatively, you can put the name in the name/value pair in quotes as well, like this:

```
{
    'firstName': 'Frank',
    'lastName': 'Smith',
    'phone': '503-555-1212'
}
```

You *must* use quotes if the name has a space in it, or other non-alphanumeric characters.

Think of a name value/pair just like a variable—the name is like the name of the variable, and the value is what's stored inside that variable. In the above example, *lastName* acts like a variable, with the string *'Smith'* stored in it.

When the web server responds to an Ajax request, it can return a string formatted like a JSON. The server doesn't actually send JavaScript: It just sends text that's formatted like a JSON object. It isn't actually real, usable JavaScript until the string is converted into an actual JSON object. Fortunately, jQuery provides a special function, *getJSON()*, that handles all of the details. The *getJSON()* function looks and works much like the *get()* and *post()* functions. The basic structure looks like this:

```
$.getJSON(url, data, callback);
```

The three arguments passed to the function are the same as for *post()* or *get()*—the URL of the server-side page, data to send to the server-side page, and the name of a callback function. The difference is that *getJSON()* will process the response from the server (which is just a string) and convert it (through some JavaScript wizardry) into a usable JSON object.

Note: PHP 5.2 has a built-in function—*json_encode*—to make it easy to create a JSON object out of a traditional PHP array. So for AJAX applications, you can take a PHP array and quickly convert to a JSON object to send back to the awaiting JavaScript code in the web browser. Visit *www.php.net/manual/en/ function.json-encode.php* to learn more.

In other words, *getJSON()* works just like *post()* or *get(),* but the data passed to the callback is a JSON object. To use the *getJSON()* function, then, you only need to learn how to process a JSON object with the callback function. For a basic example, say you want to use Ajax to request information on a single contact from a server-side file named *contacts.php*; that file returns contact data in JSON format (like the JSON example on the previous page). A basic request would look like this:

```
$.getJSON('contacts.php','contact=123',processContacts);
```

This code sends a query string—*contact=123*—to *contacts.php*. Say the *contacts.php* file uses that information to locate a single contact in a database and retrieve that contact's information. The result is sent back to the web browser and handed to the callback function *processContacts*. The basic structure of the callback, then, would look like this:

```
function processContacts(data) {

}
```

The *processContacts()* function has one argument—*data*—that contains the JSON object from the server. Let's look at how the callback can access information from the JSON object.

Accessing JSON Data

There are two ways to access data in a JSON object: *dot syntax* or *array notation.* Dot-syntax (see page 70) is a way of indicating an object's property—specifically, by adding a period between the name of the object and the property you wish to access. You've seen this in use with properties of different JavaScript objects like strings and arrays. For example, *'abc'.length* accesses the string's length property, and, in this example, returns the number of letters in the string *'abc'*, which is *3*.

For example, suppose you create a variable and store an object literal inside it like this:

```
var bday = {
  person: 'Raoul',
  date: '10/27/1980'
};
```

In this case, the variable *bday* contains the object literal, so if you want to get the value of person in the object, use dot syntax like this:

```
bday.person // 'Raoul'
```

To get the birth date:

```
bday.date // '10/27/1980'
```

The same is true with a JSON object that's returned by the web server. For example, take the following *getJSON()* example and callback function:

```
$.getJSON('contacts.php','contact=123',processContacts);
function processContacts(data) {

}
```

Assuming that the server returned the JSON example on page 371, that JSON object is assigned to the variable *data* (the argument for the callback function *processContacts()*), just as if this code had been executed:

```
var data = {
   firstName: 'Frank',
   lastName: 'Smith',
   phone: '503-555-1212'
};
```

Now within the callback function, you can access the value of *firstName* like this:

```
data.firstName // 'Frank'
```

And retrieve the last name of the contact like this:

```
data.lastName // 'Smith'
```

So, let's say the whole point of this little Ajax program is to retrieve contact information and display it inside of a <div> with the ID *info*. All of the programming for that might look like this:

```
$.get JSON('contacts.php','contact=123',processContacts);
function processContacts(data) {
   var infoHTML='<p>Contact: ' + data.firstName;
   infoHTML+=' ' + data.lastName + '<br>';
   infoHTML+='Phone: ' + data.phone + '</p>';
   $('#info').html(infoHTML);
}
```

The final outcome would be a paragraph added to the page that looks something like this:

```
Contact: Frank Smith
Phone: 503-555-1212
```

Complex JSON Objects

You can create even more complex collections of information by using object literals as the values inside a JSON object—in other words, object literals nested within object literals. (Sorry, but don't put down this book yet.)

Here's an example: Say you want the server to send back contact information for more than one individual using JSON. You'll send a request to a file named *contacts .php* with a query string that dictates how many contacts you wish returned. That code may look something like this:

```
$.getJSON('contacts.php','limit=2',processContacts);
```

The *limit=2* is the information sent to the server, and indicates how many contacts should be returned. The web server would then return two contacts. Say the contact info for the first person matched the example above (Frank Smith), and a second set of contact information was another JSON object like this:

```
{
   firstName: 'Peggy',
   lastName: 'Jones',
   phone: '415-555-5235'
}
```

The web server may return a string that represents a single JSON object, which combines both of these objects like this:

```
{
  contact1: {
    firstName: 'Frank',
    lastName: 'Smith',
    phone: '503-555-1212'
  },
  contact2: {
    firstName: 'Peggy',
    lastName: 'Jones',
    phone: '415-555-5235'
  }
}
```

Assume that the callback function accepts a single argument named *data* (for example, *function processContacts(data)*). The variable *data* would then be assigned that JSON object, just as if this code had been executed:

```
var data = {
  contact1: {
    firstName: 'Frank',
    lastName: 'Smith',
    phone: '503-555-1212'
  },
  contact2: {
    firstName: 'Peggy',
    lastName: 'Jones',
    phone: '415-555-5235'
  }
};
```

Now, you could access the first contact object within the callback function like this:

```
data.contact1
```

And retrieve the first name of the first contact like this:

```
data.contact1.firstName
```

But, in this case, since you want to process multiple contacts, jQuery provides a function that lets you loop through each item in a JSON object—the *each()* function. The basic structure of the function is this:

```
$.each(JSON,function(name,value) {

});
```

You pass the JSON object, and an anonymous function (page 148) to the *each()* function. That anonymous function receives the name and value of each item in the JSON object. Here's how the JSON object would look in use in the current example:

```
1    $.getJSON('contacts.php','limit=2',processContacts);
2    function processContacts(data) {
3      // create variable with empty string
4      var infoHTML='';
5
6      //loop through each object in the JSON data
7      $.each(data,function(contact, contactInfo) {
8        infoHTML+='<p>Contact: ' + contactInfo.firstName;
9        infoHTML+=' ' + contactInfo.lastName + '<br>';
10       infoHTML+='Phone: ' + contactInfo.phone + '</p>';
11     }); // end of each()
12
13     // add finished HTML to page
14     $('#info').html(infoHTML);
15   }
```

Here's how the code breaks down:

1. **Line 1 creates the Ajax request with data (limit=2) and assigns the callback function (processContacts).**

2. **Line 2 creates the callback function, which accepts the JSON object sent back from the server and stores it in the variable** *data.*

3. **Line 4 creates an empty string. The HTML that eventually gets added to the page will fill it.**

4. **Line 7 is the** *each()* **function, which will look through the objects in the JSON data.**

   The *each()* function takes the JSON object as its first argument (*data*) and an anonymous function as the second argument. The process is diagrammed in Figure 11-10. Essentially, for each of the main objects (in this example, *contact1* and *contact2*), the anonymous function receives the name of the object as a string (that's the *contact* argument listed in line 7) and the value for that object (that's the *contactInfo* argument). In this case, the *contactInfo* variable will hold the object literal containing the contact information.

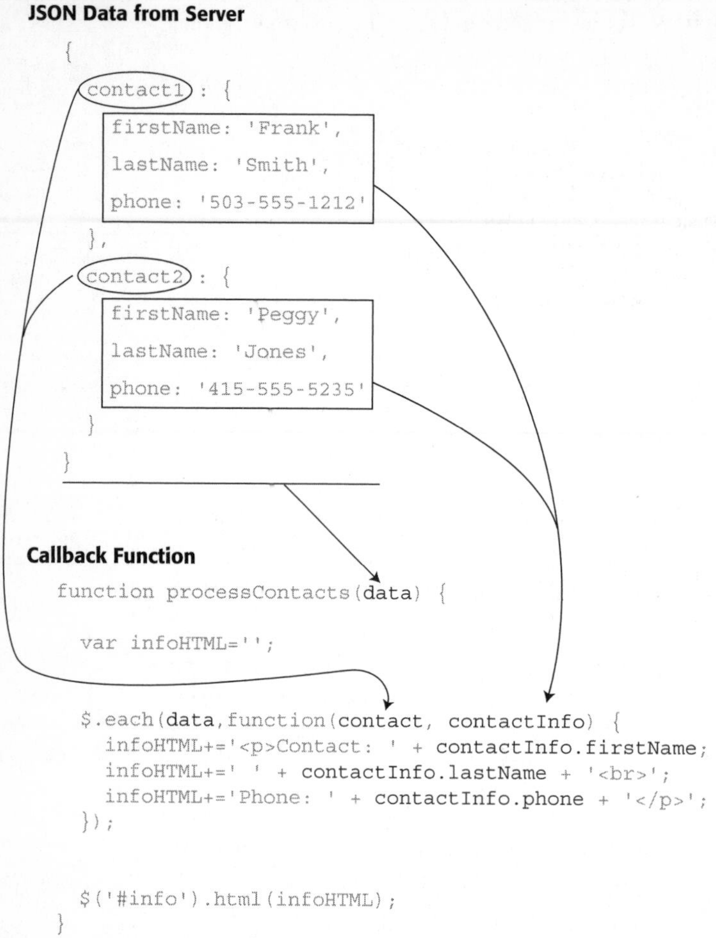

JSON Data from Server

```
{
    contact1 : {
        firstName: 'Frank',
        lastName: 'Smith',
        phone: '503-555-1212'
    },
    contact2 : {
        firstName: 'Peggy',
        lastName: 'Jones',
        phone: '415-555-5235'
    }
}
```

Figure 11-10:
*You can use jQuery's each()
function to loop through a
JSON object to perform tasks
on nested objects. You can
also use the* each() *function
to loop through arrays. To
learn more about this useful
function, visit* http://docs
.jquery.com/Utilities/jQuery
.each#objectcallback.

Callback Function

```
function processContacts(data) {

    var infoHTML='';

    $.each(data,function(contact, contactInfo) {
        infoHTML+='<p>Contact: ' + contactInfo.firstName;
        infoHTML+=' ' + contactInfo.lastName + '<br>';
        infoHTML+='Phone: ' + contactInfo.phone + '</p>';
    });


    $('#info').html(infoHTML);
}
```

5. **Lines 8–10 extract the information from one contact.**

   Remember that the *each()* function is a loop, so lines 8–10 will run twice—once for each of the contacts.

6. **Line 14 updates the web page by adding the HTML to the page.**

   The final result will be the following HTML:

   ```
   <p>Contact: Frank Smith<br>
   Phone: 503-555-1212</p>
   <p>Contact: Peggy Jones<br>
   Phone: 415-555-5235</p>
   ```

Flickr and Google Maps

I n the previous chapter, you learned the basics of Ajax: what it is, how it works, and how jQuery can simplify the process of Ajax programming. Since Ajax is all about the two-way communication between web browser and web server, understanding server-side programming is necessary if you really want to harness Ajax's power. However, you don't need to be a server-side programming guru to use Ajax successfully. In fact, you can take advantage of the services offered by popular websites like Flickr, Twitter, and Google Maps to retrieve photos, tweets, and maps, and place them directly inside your web pages.

Introducing JSONP

In the last chapter you learned that, for security reasons, Ajax requests are limited to the same domain. That is, the page making an Ajax request must be on the same server as the page responding to the request. This is a policy enforced by the web browser to keep one site from maliciously attempting to contact another site (like your bank). There's one way around that however. While a web browser can't send an XMLHTTP request to a different website, it can download resources from other sites, including pictures, style sheets, and external JavaScript files.

JSONP (which stands for *JSON with padding*) provides one way to retrieve information from another site. Basically, instead of making an Ajax request of the foreign site, you load a script that contains the JSON code in it. In other words, it's like linking to an external JavaScript file on Google.

You can't request just any bit of information that you'd like from another site, however. For JSONP to work, the foreign site must be set up to respond with JSONP. Most sites aren't set up to send information this way, but many of the big sites like Google Maps, Twitter, Flickr, Facebook, Netflix, and YouTube offer an API (Application Programming Interface) that lets you request data like a map, a photo, movie review text, and so on, using jQuery's *$.getJSON()* function (see Figure 12-1).

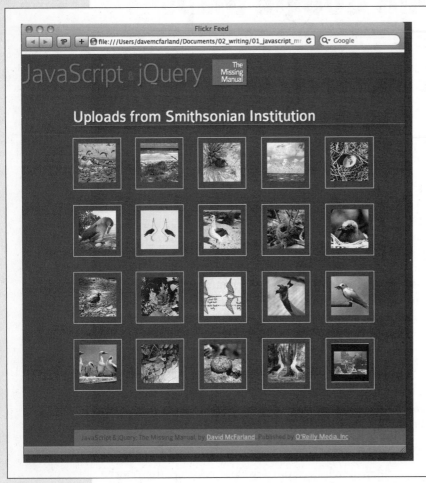

Figure 12-1:
While AJAX is restricted to the requesting information from the same domain, a workaround called JSONP lets you retrieve JSON data from another site by requesting a JavaScript file from that site. This technique lets you access tweets from Twitter, maps from Google, and photos from Flickr (pictured here) and embed them directly in your own web pages.

Adding a Flickr Feed to Your Site

Flickr is a popular photo-sharing site. It's been around for years and has millions of photographs. A lot of websites like to include photos either taken by the site owner or within a Flickr group (a group is a collection of photos submitted by multiple people around a common subject like Web Design, landscape photography, and so on).

Flickr gives you a couple of ways to retrieve photos and related information. The most powerful, but also most complex, method is to use Flickr's API to search for photos. This method requires that you sign up at Flickr and get a special API *key* (a string of numbers and letters that identifies you). It also requires some fancy programming to work. The simplest way is to use the Flickr Feed Service. Feeds are a way to keep people up-to-date with a site's information. For example, you may have seen sites with RSS feeds that let you view the latest news and information from that website. Flickr offers a similar service for its photos—you can get a listing of the 20 most recent photos from a particular person or a particular group.

In this section, you'll use the feed method to get a collection of photos from Flickr and display them on a web page, and in the process, learn how to use jQuery's *$.getJSON()* function to retrieve JSONP data from another website.

Note: If you want more control in selecting and displaying Flickr photos, there are plenty of jQuery plug-ins to help. The jQuery Flickr Photo Gallery plug-in (*http://johnpatrickgiven.com/jquery/flickr-gallery/*) is particularly nice.

Constructing the URL

Flickr offers several different URLs for accessing feeds for different types of photos (see *www.flickr.com/services/feeds/* for a full list). For example, you use *http://api.flickr.com/services/feeds/photos_public.gne* to access photos from specific Flickr accounts (such as your own account if you have one), and *http://api.flickr.com/services/feeds/groups_pool.gne* to retrieve photos from a particular group (like the Web Design group, which features photos and images to inspire great web design).

Once you know which type of photo feed you'd like and the basic URL that accompanies it, you need to add some additional information to retrieve the photos you're interested in. To do so, you add a query string with several pieces of information tagged on. (As you'll recall from page 357, a query string is a ? mark at the end of a URL, followed by one or more name/value pairs: *http://api.flickr.com/services/feeds/groups_pool.gne?id= 25053835@N03&&format=json*, for example.)

- **Add one or more IDs**. To select photos from a particular group or one or more individual accounts, you add *id*, plus an = sign followed by a individual or group account number. For example, to access a group photo feed for the Web Design group, you'd use this group photo feed and add the ID for the group, like this:
  ```
  http://api.flickr.com/services/feeds/ ↵
  groups_pool.gne?id=37996591093@N01
  ```
  For individual Flickr feeds, you'd use the public photos feed and use one or more IDs. For example, to retrieve photos from both the Smithsonian (which has its own Flickr account) and the Library of Congress, you can use the *ids* names and the public photo feed like this:
  ```
  http://api.flickr.com/services/feeds/ ↵
  photos_public.gne?ids=8623220@N02,25053835@N03
  ```

To use multiple IDs, separate each with a comma. Note that you can only use multiple IDs for retrieving individual accounts: You can't use the group feed and retrieve photos from multiple groups.

Tip: If you know someone's Flickr user name, you can get his Flickr ID using this website: http://idgettr.com/.

- **Add the JSON format.** The Flickr photo feed service is very flexible and can return photo information in many different formats from RSS, to Atom, CSV, and JSON. To let Flickr know that you want data in JSON format, you need to add *&format=json* to the query string. For example, to get the a Flickr feed of the Smithsonian Museum's Flickr photos in JSON format, you'd use this URL:

  ```
  http://api.flickr.com/services/feeds/ ↵
  photos_public.gne?ids=25053835@N03&format=json
  ```

  Go ahead and type the URL above into a web browser (if you're feeling lazy, you can copy and paste the URL from the *flickr_json.txt* file in the *chapter12* folder of the tutorial files). You'll see a bunch of data; actually, an object literal containing a bunch of information. That's what you receive from Flickr when you use the *$.getJSON()* function (discussed on page 371). You need to use JavaScript to dissect that object and then use it to build a neat little gallery of images. (The structure of Flickr's JSON feed is discussed on page 382, and taking apart the feed so you can use it is shown in the tutorial on page 383.)

- **Add a JSONP callback to the URL.** Finally, for a page on your site to successfully request JSON data from another website, you need to add one last bit to the URL: *&jsoncallback=?*. Remember that for security reasons you can't just send an XMLHTTP request to a different domain. To get around that problem, the *&jsoncallback=?* piece notifies Flickr that you want to receive JSONP data and lets jQuery's *$.getJSON()* function treat this request as if the web browser were simply requesting an external JavaScript file. In other words, to receive a feed of the Smithsonian Museum's latest Flickr photos, you'd need to pass the *$.getJSON()* function a URL like this:

  ```
  http://api.flickr.com/services/feeds/ ↵ photos_public.gne?ids=25053835@
  N03&format=json&jsoncallback=?
  ```

A few other options for the public photos feed

For Flickr's public photos feed, you can add a couple of other options to refine the information the feed returns. For example, say you and a couple of friends like to take pictures of chipmunks and post them up on Flickr, and you want to get a feed of the 20 latest chipmunk photos you and your friends have taken. You can do this by filtering the feed by specifying one or more tags.

On Flickr, you can *tag* any photo with one or more words; a tag is a word or short phrase that describes an element of the photo. For example, you might tag a particularly bright photo of a sunset with the word "sunset." Any photo can have multiple tags, so you might tag that sunset photo with the words "sunset, orange, beach."

Note: You can only search for tags on Flickr's public photo feed (*www.flickr.com/services/feeds/docs/ photos_public/*). You can't, for example, search for photos with a particular tag or tags from a group (like the Flickr Web Design group).

Flickr's feed service provides options that let you search a feed for specific tags:

- **tags**. Add the tag keyword with one or more comma, separated keywords to the URL to specify a tag; for example: &tags=fireworks,night. Say your Flickr ID is 8623220@N02, and your friend's is 25053835@N03. You could get both of your feeds, plus search only for photos with the tag of "chipmunk" with a long-winded URL like this:

  ```
  http://api.flickr.com/services/feeds/ ↵
  photos_public.gne?ids=25053835@N03,8623220@N02 ↵
  &tags=chipmunk&format=json&jsoncallback=?
  ```

- **tagmode**. Normally when you search for a set of tags, Flickr only retrieves photos that match all of the tags. For example, say you added ?tags=chipmunks,baseball,winter to a feed. This code finds only photos of chipmunks playing baseball in the winter. If you wanted pictures of chipmunks, or baseball or the winter (in other words, at least one of the tags), add &tagmode=any to the URL. For example:

  ```
  http://api.flickr.com/services/feeds/ ↵
  photos_public.gne?ids=25053835@N03,8623220@N02 ↵
  &tags=chipmunk&tagmode=any&format=json&jsoncallback=?
  ```

Using the *$.getJSON()* Function

Using the *$.getJSON()* function to retrieve a photo feed from Flickr works the same as retrieving JSON data from your own site. The basic structure for the function is the same. For example, here's the setup for retrieving the Smithsonian's Flickr feed:

```
1  var flickrURL = "http://api.flickr.com/services/feeds/ ↵
   photos_public.gne?ids=25053835@N03&format=json&jsoncallback=?"
2  $.getJSON(flickrURL, function(data) {
3  // do something with the JSON data returned
4  }); // end get
```

In this example, line 1 creates a variable named FlickrURL and stores the URL (using the rules discussed in the last section). Line 2 sends the AJAX request to the URL and sets up an anonymous function for processing that data. After sending an Ajax request, the code retrieves data back from the server—in this example, that data is sent to the anonymous function and is stored in the variable called *data*. You'll learn how to process the data in a few pages, but first, you need to understand what Flickr's JSON data looks like.

Understanding the Flickr JSON Feed

As discussed on page 370, JSON is simply a JavaScript object literal. It can be as simple as this:

```
{
    firstName : 'Bob',
    lastName : 'Smith'
}
```

In this code, *firstName* acts like a key with a value of Bob—a simple string value. However, the value can also be another object (see Figure 11-10 on page 376), so you can often end up with a complex nested structure—like dolls within dolls. That's what Flickr's JSON feed is like. Here's a small snippet of one of those feeds. It shows the information retrieved for two photos:

```
1  {
2      "title": "Uploads from Smithsonian Institution",
3      "link": "http://www.flickr.com/photos/smithsonian/",
4      "description": "",
5      "modified": "2011-08-11T13:16:37Z",
6      "generator": "http://www.flickr.com/",
7      "items": [
8          {
9              "title": "East Island, June 12, 1966.",
10             "link": "http://www.flickr.com/photos/smithsonian/5988083516/",
11             "media": {"m":"http://farm7.static.flickr.com/6029/5988083516_
   bfc9f41286_m.jpg"},
12             "date_taken": "2011-07-29T11:45:50-08:00",
13             "description": "Short description here",
14             "published": "2011-08-11T13:16:37Z",
15             "author": "nobody@flickr.com (Smithsonian Institution)",
16             "author_id": "25053835@N03",
17             "tags": "ocean birds redfootedbooby"
18         },
19         {
20             "title": "Phoenix Island, April 15, 1966.",
21             "link": "http://www.flickr.com/photos/smithsonian/5988083472/",
22             "media": {"m":"http://farm7.static.flickr.com/6015/5988083472_
   c646ef2778_m.jpg"},
23             "date_taken": "2011-07-29T11:45:48-08:00",
24             "description": "Another short description",
25             "published": "2011-08-11T13:16:37Z",
26             "author": "nobody@flickr.com (Smithsonian Institution)",
27             "author_id": "25053835@N03",
28             "tags": ""
29         }
30  }
```

Flickr's JSON object has a bit of information about the feed in general: That's the stuff at the beginning—*"title"*, *"link"*, and so on. The *"title"* element (line 2) is the name of that feed. In this case, *"Uploads from Smithsonian Institution"*—the *"link"* element (line 3)—points to the main Flickr page for the Smithsonian institution. You can use this information, for example, as a headline presented before displaying the photos.

To access that information, you use the dot-syntax described on page 70. For example, say you used the code from the previous section (page 381): The anonymous function used to process the data stores the JSON response in a variable named *data* (see line 2 on page 381). Then, to access the title of the feed, you'd access the *"title"* property of the *"data"* object like this:

```
data.title
```

The most important part of the feed is the *"items"* property (line 7), which contains additional objects, each containing information about one photo. For example, lines 8–18 provide information for one photo, while lines 19-29 are about another photo. Within each item object, you'll find other properties like the title of the photo (line 9), a link to that photo's Flickr page (line 10), the date the photo was taken (line 12), a description (the "*Short description here*" on line 13 [the curators at the Smithsonian must have been feeling a little lazy that day]), and so on.

Another important element for each photo is *"media"*—it's another object. For example:

```
{
    "m":"http://farm7.static.flickr.com/6029/5988083516_bfc9f41286_m.jpg"
}
```

The *"m"* means "medium," and its value is a URL to the photo. Flickr photos are often available in different sizes, like medium, thumbnail, and small (which is a small square image). If you want to display the image on a page, then this URL is what you're after. You can use it to insert a <img> tag in the page and point to that photo on the Flickr server. You'll see how in the tutorial.

Tutorial: Adding Flickr Images to Your Site

In this tutorial, you'll put together all the pieces to retrieve the photo feed from the Smithsonian Institution, display thumbnail images of the photos, and add links to each image, so a visitor can click the thumbnail to go to Flickr and see the photos page.

Note: See the note on page 29 for information on how to download the tutorial files.

---

1. **In a text editor, open the file *flickr.html* in the *chapter12* folder.**

   You'll start by creating a few variables to store the components of the URL required to talk to Flickr.

2. **Click in the empty line inside the *$(document).ready()* function, and type:**

```
var URL = "http://api.flickr.com/services/feeds/photos_public.gne";
var ID = "25053835@N03";
var jsonFormat = "&format=json&jsoncallback=?";
```

   Each variable here is just part of that much longer URL discussed on page 379. Breaking each piece into a separate variable makes it easy to adjust this code. For example, if you want to get a photo feed from another Flickr user, just change the ID variable (if you have a Flickr account, go ahead and plug in your ID number in here [if you don't know your Flickr ID, visit *http://idgettr.com/*]).

Tip: If you want to retrieve the photos from a Flickr group, like the Web Design Group, then change the URL in step 2 to: *http://api.flickr.com/services/feeds/groups_pool.gne?id=37996591093@N01* and the ID to the ID of the Flickr group.

Next you'll put these variables together to construct a complete URL.

3. **Add another line of code after the three you just typed:**

    ```
    var ajaxURL = URL + "?id=" + ID + jsonFormat;
    ```

    This combines all the variables plus the opening part of the query string—*?id=*—to form a complete URL like the ones you learned about on page 379: *http://api.flickr.com/services/feeds/photos_public.gne?id=25053835@N03&format =json&jsoncallback=?*. Now it's time to get into the Ajax part of this and use jQuery *$.getJSON()* function.

4. **After the line you just added, type this:**

    ```
    $.getJSON(ajaxURL,function(data) {

    }); // end get JSON;
    ```

    Here's the basic shell of the *$.getJSON()* function: It will contact the URL you constructed in steps 2 and 3, and receive data back from Flickr. That data is passed to an anonymous function and stored in a variable named *data*. You can then take that data and begin to use it on the page. First, you'll get the title of the feed and replace the <h1> tag that's currently on the page with it.

5. **Add the bolded line of code below to the code from the last step:**

    ```
    $.getJSON(ajaxURL,function(data) {
      $('h1').text(data.title);
    }); // end get JSON;
    ```

    This is a basic jQuery selector—*$('h1')*—and function—*.text()*—that selects the <h1> tag currently on the page and replaces the text inside it. The actual JSON feed is stored in the data variable. To access its components you can use dot-syntax (page 70), so *data.title* retrieves the title of the feed. If you save the page now and preview it in a web browser, you should see a bold headline reading "Uploads from Smithsonian Institution."

    To add the photos, you'll need to loop through the *items* object (see page 383) returned by the Flickr feed.

6. **Add the bolded lines of code below to the code from the last step:**

    ```
    $.getJSON(ajaxURL,function(data) {
      $('h1').text(data.title);
      $.each(data.items,function(i,photo) {
      }); // end each
    }); // end get JSON;
    ```

    You read about the *.each()* function on page 147—that function is used to loop through a jQuery selection. The *$.each()* function is different, but similar. It's a generic loop utility that you can use to loop through either an array (page 59) or a series of objects. You pass the *$.each()* function an array or an object literal and an anonymous function. The *$.each()* function then loops through the array or the object literal and runs the anonymous function once for each item. That anonymous function receives two arguments (*i* and *photo* in the code in this step), which are variables that contain the index of the item and the item itself. The index is the number of the item through the loop: This works just like an index for an array (page 62). For example, the first item in the loop has an index of 0. The second argument (*photo* in this example), is the actual photo object containing the photo's name, description, URL, and so on as described on page 383.

In the case of the Flickr feed, *data.items* represents the photo objects in the JSON feed (page 383), so the *$.each()* function passes the object for each photo to the anonymous function in the *photo* variable. In other words, this code loops through each of the photos in the feed and then does something. In this case, you'll simply create a series of thumbnail images that links to each photo's Flickr page. The goal will be to create some basic HTML to display each image and include a link. For example:

```
<span class="image">
<a href="http://www.flickr.com/photos/smithsonian/5988083516/">
<img src="http://farm7.static.flickr.com/6029/5988083516_bfc9f41286_s.jpg">
</a>
</span>
```

Only two pieces of information—the URL of the photo's Flickr page, and the path to the photo file—are required to build this. You'll just build up a long string that looks just like the HTML above, only replacing the URL and image path for each of the images.

7. **Inside the *$.each()* function add the code below in bold:**

```
$.each(data.items,function(i,photo) {
    var photoHTML = '<span class="image">';
    photoHTML += '<a href="' + photo.link + '">';
    photoHTML += '<img src="' + photo.media.m + '"></a>';
}); // end each
```

This code starts by creating a variable—*photoHTML*—which stores an opening <span> tag; each subsequent line adds more to the variable (for a refresher on what += means and how it works, see page 54). The key elements here are photo.link and photo.media.m. If you look at the JSON code on page 382, you can see that each photo has various properties like title (the name of the photo) and description (a short description of the photo). The link property points to the photo's page on Flickr.com, while the media object has a property named "m," which contains the path to the medium size version of the graphic file. Altogether this code builds up HTML like that pictured in step 6. Now you just need to add that code to the page.

8. **Add the code in bold below:**

```
$.each(data.items,function(i,photo) {
    var photoHTML = '<span class="image">';
    photoHTML += '<a href="' + photo.link + '">';
    photoHTML += '<img src="' + photo.media.m + '"></a>';
```

```
    $('#photos').append(photoHTML);
}); // end each
```

The *$('#photos')* part selects an already existing <div> tag on the page, while the *append()* function (discussed on page 139) adds the HTML to the end of that div. In other words, each time through the loop, another chunk of HTML is added to that div.

9. **Save the page and preview it in a web browser.**

You should see 20 photos load on the page. (If you don't see anything, double-check your code and use your web browser's error console [page 34] to look for any syntax errors.) The problem is the photos all vary in size and don't form a nice grid on the page. That's because the Flickr feed only provides the path to medium-sized Flickr images.

Flickr does have nice square thumbnails of all their photos as well. Displaying those identically-sized photos together on a page makes a nice, orderly presentation. Fortunately, it's easy to request those thumbnail images. Flickr uses a consistent naming convention for their photos: The path to a medium-sized image is something like *http://farm7.static.flickr.com/6029/5988083516_bfc9f41286_m.jpg*, while the thumbnail path for that same image is *http://farm7.static.flickr.com/6029/5988083516_bfc9f41286_s.jpg*. The only difference is at the end of the file name: *_m* indicates a medium image, *_s* is a small square thumbnail image (75 pixels by 75 pixels), *_t* is a small image that's at most 100 pixels on the longest side, *_o* indicates the original image (the original size the file that the was uploaded to Flickr), and *_b* is a large image (at most, 1,024 pixels tall or wide). Simply by adjusting the file name (replacing the *_m* with *_s*, for example), you can display a different size file. Fortunately, JavaScript provides a handy method of quickly swapping characters in a string.

10. **In the code change *photo.media.m* to *photo.media.m.replace('_m','_s')*. The final code on the page should look like this:**

```
$(document).ready(function() {
var URL = "http://api.flickr.com/services/feeds/photos_public.gne";
var ID = "25053835@N03";
var jsonFormat = "&format=json&jsoncallback=?";
var ajaxURL = URL + "?id=" + ID + jsonFormat;
$.getJSON(ajaxURL,function(data) {
    $('h1').text(data.title);
    $.each(data.items,function(i,photo) {
        var photoHTML = '<span class="image">';
        photoHTML += '<a href="' + photo.link + '">';
        photoHTML += '<img src="' + photo.media.m.replace('_m','_s') + '"></
a>';
        $('#photos').append(photoHTML);
    }); // end each
}); // end get JSON

}); // end ready
```

JavaScript's *replace()* method (discussed on page 443) works with strings, and takes two arguments—the string to find ('*_m*' in this case) and the string to replace it with ('*_s*').

11. **Save the page and preview it in a web browser.**

Now you should see 20 neatly aligned, square thumbnails (see Figure 12-1). Click a thumbnail to see a larger image on Flickr's site. A working version of this tutorial—*complete_flickr.html*—is available in the *chapter12* folder.

Note: The Flickr feed only provides 20 images maximum. You can retrieve more than 20 from any one feed. What if you only want to display 10 images from the feed? See the file *complete_flickr_limit_photos* *.html* in the *chapter12* folder for the solution.

Adding Google Maps to Your Site

Google Maps (*http://maps.google.com*) is an original poster-child for the JavaScript revolution. The ability to zoom in and out of a map, move around city streets, and get driving directions in a flash makes Google Maps an incredibly useful site. And thanks to the clever use of Ajax, the site's responsiveness makes it feel nearly like a desktop program.

But Google Maps offers even more power to web designers: The Google Maps service lets you embed a map in your own site. If you run a brick-and-mortar business (or build sites for businesses), being able to provide an easy-to-understand map and directions can bring more customers through your door. Fortunately, thanks to Go-Map, a jQuery plug-in, it's easy to add interactive maps directly to your own web pages (see Figure 12-2).

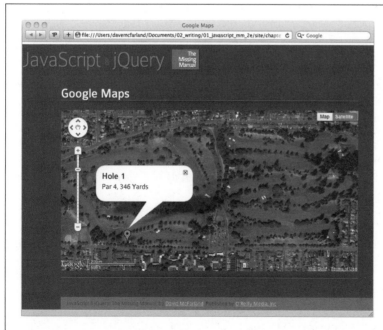

Figure 12-2:
While a simple picture of a map is a fine way to indicate the location of your (or your client's) business, an interactive map like those available at http://maps.google.com *is better. Visitors can zoom into, zoom out of, and pan across a Google Map with ease. Thanks to the GoMap jQuery plug-in, it's easy to add a Google Map to your website.*

Going Further with jQuery and Ajax

There are loads of other jQuery plug-ins that can make Ajax development go faster. In some cases, you need to provide the server-side programming—the plug-in just takes care of the JavaScript part. A few other programs supply the basic server-side programming as well. Here are a few good ones:

- **Form plug-in**. The jQuery Form plug-in is a simple way to add Ajax to your form submissions. The plug-in goes far beyond the basics discussed in the previous chapter and includes file uploading ability. It works with form validation as well. For more information, visit *http://jquery.malsup.com/form/*.

- **Autocomplete**. The jQuery UI project offers an autocomplete plug-in (*http://jqueryui.com/demos/autocomplete/*) that lets you add the nifty functionality you'll find in search fields on Google and Amazon. Begin typing a word into a text field, and a drop-down menu suggesting possible matches appears. This saves your visitors from having to type so much and also provides a helpful list of suggestions. Working with your web server and Ajax, you can add mind-reading like abilities to search forms.

- **Ajax File Upload**. If you want to add file uploads to your site, make the process seamless for your users by using Ajax to send the files. The Uploadify plug-in (*www.uploadify.com/*) makes the process easy.

- **Taconite**. Using Ajax, you can receive information from a server and update a web page. However, you may want to update multiple areas of a page—for example, if a visitor logs in using an Ajax form, you might want to show his login status in one part of the page, a list of the pages he visited last time he was at the site in another part of the page, and display a shopping cart in yet another area of the page. The Taconite plug-in lets you receive a basic XML file from the web server with simple instructions on what areas of a web page to update and what information to use. You can find out more about this plug-in at *http://jquery.malsup.com/taconite/*.

- **Twitter**. If you want an easy way to add a Twitter stream to your web pages, check out the Tweet! plug-in (*http://tweet.seaofclouds.com/*). Tweet! lets you add your own Twitter stream, search for tweets from other Twitter users, or even just search Twitter for key words.

The GoMap plug-in (*www.pittss.lv/jquery/gomap/*), created by Jevgenijs Shtrauss, lets you add a Google map to any web page, request driving directions between two points on a map, add markers to highlight locations on a map, and much more. The basic steps to using the plug-in are:

1. **Attach an external JavaScript file from Google Maps.**

   In order to access the maps service, you need to load a script from Google. The <script> tag you use looks like this:

   ```
   <script src="http://maps.google.com/maps/api/js?sensor=false"></script>
   ```

   This code loads the necessary JavaScript that Google relies on for accessing its map services. The gmap3 plug-in builds off of the code in this file to provide a more friendly way to add maps to your pages.

Note: GoMap uses version 3 of the Google Maps API (Application Programming Interface). The older Google Maps API required you to sign up at Google and get a unique key to use Google Maps on your site. Fortunately, you no longer have to sign up with Google to add maps to your site.

2. **Attach two jQuery files.**

   Of course, you need the jQuery library, as well as the GoMap file. The GoMap file is available from *www.pittss.lv/jquery/gomap*. This file provides all the programming that makes adding a map to your site so easy. So in addition to the <script> tag from step 2, you'll add code that's something like this:

   ```
   <script src="js/jquery-1.6.3.min.js"></script>
   <script src="js/jquery.gomap-1.3.2.min.js"></script>
   ```

Note: We've included a copy of the GoMap plug-in file in the _js folder in the tutorial files (see the Note on page 29 for information on accessing the tutorial files).

3. **Add an empty <div> tag with an ID to the page.**

   GoMap will add a map in this empty tag, so place the <div> where you want the map to appear on the page. Also, you need to provide a way of identifying that tag, so add an ID. The HTML for this might look like this:

   ```
   <div id="map"></div>
   ```

   In addition, you must add a CSS rule to the page's stylesheet to define the height and width of the map on the page. For example:

   ```
   #map {
     width: 760px;
     height: 400px;
   }
   ```

4. **Call the *goMap()* function.**

   Finally, add a new <script> tag, the *document.ready()* function, and call the *goMap()* function. To use the *goMap()* function, you select the map <div> using a jQuery selector—*$('#map')*—then add *gmap3()*:

   ```
   <script>
   $(document).ready(function() {
    $('#map').goMap();
   });
   </script>
   ```

   Just calling the *jmapgoMap()* function, though, will give you a map that's centered somewhere in Latvia. Most likely (unless you're from Latvia) you'll want to have the map point to a specific location (such as your or your client's business location) and zoom in to a level that shows more detail like the names of streets. You'll learn how to do that next.

Setting a Location for the Map

A Google Map has a center point as defined by numbers that represent the location's longitude and latitude. If you want to center your map on a place—such as your business's address or the location of your next birthday party—you need to get that location's longitude and latitude. That's easy:

1. **Go to** *http://itouchmap.com/latlong.html,* **type an address in the Address box, and then click Go.**

   This helpful website provides the latitude and longitude of any location of the address you specify. Write down or copy this information; you'll use it in the next step.

Tip: You can also get latitude and longitude information directly from Google Maps. Go to *http://maps .google.com* and search for a location you'd like to use in your map. Then in your browser's address bar, type *javascript:void(prompt('',gApplication.getMap().getCenter()));*. A JavaScript alert box appears with the latitude and longitude of the center point of the current map.

---

2. **Update the** *goMap()* **function by adding the following code:**

```
1 <script>
2 $(document).ready(function() {
3   $('#map').goMap({
4     latitude : 45.53940,
5     longitude : -122.59025
6   }); // end goMap
7 }); // end ready
8 </script>
```

In this case, you pass an object literal—that's the opening { at the end of line 3 and the closing } at the beginning of line 6—that contains options for the plug-in. The first item—*latitude*—specifies the latitude of the center of the map, while the second item—*longitude*—is the longitude of the center of the map. You should replace the two numbers listed on lines 5 and 6 with the latitude and longitude you'd like for your map.

Fortunately, the GoMap plug-in is versatile enough to simply use an address as the location for the map. You can simply replace the *latitude* and *longitude* items with an *address* item that contains a string with the desired address. For example:

```
$('#map').goMap({
    address : '2200 NE 71st Ave Portland, OR, USA'
}); // end goMap
```

If you only need a rough area, such as a map centered on a particular city, you can do that too:

```
$('#map').goMap({
    address : 'Portland, OR, USA'
}); // end goMap
```

In fact, you can use anything that works in the Google Maps search box (*http://
maps.google.com*) as the address element, even the names of well-known land-
marks like "Kennedy Space Center" or "Eiffel Tower." However, Google may not
always be able to locate an address, and addresses aren't very good when you
want to highlight a particular spot in a very large area—like a spot in a favorite
park. In that case, you'll need to use latitude and longitude values as described
above.

Note: Another Google Maps plug-in worth checking out is GMAP3 (*http://gmap3.net/*). It offers many
more features than the GoMap plug-in, but it's also more complex to use and is a larger file. One nice
feature of GMAP3 is the ability to generate driving directions on the map.

Other GoMap Options

In addition to *address, latitude,* and *longitude,* you can set many other options when
creating a new map. You should incorporate each option into the object literal that's
passed to the *goMap()* function. For example, to center the map at a longitude and
latitude of 45/–122, and set the map so that's zoomed in to show details you'd call the
goMap function like this:

```
$('#map').goMap(
{
    latitude : 45,
    longitude : -122,
    zoom : 15
}); // end goMap
```

In other words, the options you're reading about in this section are just passed in as
part of the object literal.

Here are a few options you can set.

- **Control the scale of the map**. Sometimes you want your map focused on the
  finest details, such as a street-level map. Other times, you might want to have
  a broader picture and see an entire city or state on the screen. You can control
  how zoomed-in the map is by providing a number for the *zoom* option. A setting of 0 is completely zoomed out (that is, a map of the entire globe), while
  each number above 0 represents greater zoom. As a general rule, 15 is a good
  setting if you want to see the names of each street, while 13 is good for more of
  a bird's-eye view. The upper limit (greatest amount of zoom) depends on how
  detailed a map Google has for the area, and varies anywhere from 17 to 23. Set
  the option like this:
  ```
  zoom:15
  ```

- **Specify the type of map you'd like**. Normally, GoMap displays what's called a
  hybrid map—a satellite photo with street and landmark names superimposed
  on top. However, you may want your map to be a plain road map, only a satellite image, or a terrain map that shows vegetation, elevation changes, and so on.

Set the maptype option to one of the following values: 'HYBRID', 'ROADMAP', 'SATELLITE', or 'TERRAIN'. For example:

```
maptype: 'TERRAIN'
```

- **Add a scale marker.** It's common on printed maps to have some kind of scale listed on the map: 1" equals 1 mile, for example. A Google Map can also have a scale marker (see Figure 12-3). To add a small visual scale marker to the lower left of the map, set *scaleControl* to *true*:

```
scaleControl : true
```

If you don't want to see the scale marker, you don't need to do anything—goMap normally doesn't display a scale.

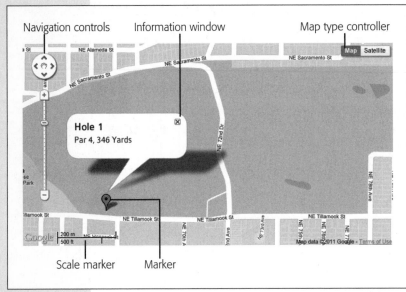

Navigation controls   Information window   Map type controller

Hole 1
Par 4, 346 Yards

Scale marker   Marker

Figure 12-3:
Beyond the map itself, a Google Map offers various controls and information markers that make it possible to zoom into a map, move the map within the window, determine the scale of the map, and pinpoint exact locations.

- **Remove navigation controls.** If you want to show a map without the zoom in/ zoom out or pan controls, you can set the navigationControl item to false like this:

```
navigationControl : false
```

That line hides those controls from visitors, but they can still use the scroll wheel or double-click to zoom in. If you really want to keep a visitor from navigating the map, then add this to the object literal passed to the *goMap()* function:

```
navigationControl: false,
scrollwheel: false,
disableDoubleClickZoom: true,
```

GoMap doesn't let you turn off dragging, however, so visitors could still drag around the map even if you prevent them from zooming in or out.

- **Map Type Controls.** You can present a Google Map as a road map, a satellite image, a hybrid of the two, or a map with terrain details like elevation. Normally a map includes controls to switch between the different types of maps. You can hide that control by setting the *mapTypeControl* item to *false* like this:

```
mapTypeControl : false
```

If you do like the map type buttons, you can control the style of those buttons and their position. You give the *mapTypeControlOptions* item an object literal composed of a position setting and a style. The possible values for placing the map type controls on the page are *TOP, TOP_LEFT, TOP_RIGHT, BOTTOM, BOTTOM_LEFT, BOTTOM_RIGHT, LEFT, RIGHT*; the values for the style of control are *DEFAULT, DROPDOWN_MENU, HORIZONTAL_BAR*. For example, say you want to use the drop-down menu style and place it in the bottom right of the map. You'd pass this into the object literal for the *goMap()* function:

```
mapTypeControlOptions: {
  position: 'BOTTOM_RIGHT',
  style: 'DROPDOWN_MENU'
}
```

Adding Markers

To highlight a point on a map, you can add a red pushpin marker like the one in Figure 12-3. These markers are a great way to mark the location of your business or a point of interest on the map. To provide even more information for the marker, you can also add a pop-up bubble with HTML (Figure 12-3). The GoMap plug-in makes adding these details easy.

GoMap gives you a couple of ways to add a marker: You can create a marker and a map at the same time. Or, you can add a map to a page and then add one or more markers to the map. This second approach gives you the ability to control a marker dynamically—for example, add a marker when a visitor clicks a button on the page.

The first approach involves calling the *goMap()* function and passing an object literal with a *markers* item. Here's an example:

```
$('#map').goMap({
  markers : [
    {
      latitude : 45.53940,
      longitude : -122.59025,
      title : 'Marker 1'
    }
  ]
}); // end goMap
```

The *markers* property creates one or more markers on the map. It's an array, which is like a grocery list containing one or more items (page 59). To create an array named *arrayItems* containing three strings, you'd write this:

```
var  arrayItems = [ 'item1', 'item2', 'item3' ];
```

The markers item is an array like this as well, but instead of containing strings, it contains object literals (page 145). In other words, one marker is an object literal:

```
{
  latitude : 45.53940,
  longitude : -122.59025,
  title : 'Marker 1'
}
```

This code represents one marker and, at its most basic, is composed of a latitude, longitude, and title for the marker (the title is the text that appears when a visitor mouses over the marker).

By adding additional object literals to the array, you can add more markers to the map. For example, here's the code for adding three markers:

```
$('#map').goMap({
  markers : [
    {
      latitude : 45.53940,
      longitude : -122.59025,
      title : 'Marker 1'
    },
    {
      latitude : 45.53821,
      longitude : -122.59796,
      title : 'Marker 2'
    },
    {
      latitude : 45.53936,
      longitude :-122.58159,
      title : 'Marker 3'
    }
  ]
}); // end goMap
```

When you create a map this way, you can still pass the same options described above to the *goMap()* function. For example, to create a road map with one marker, zoomed into level 15, with a scale marker on it, you could write code like this (note that the options go outside the *markers* array):

```
$('#map').goMap({
  markers : [
    {
      latitude : 45.53940,
      longitude : -122.59025,
      title : 'Marker 1'
    }
  ],
  zoom : 15,
  maptype : 'ROADMAP',
  scaleControl : true
}); // end goMap
```

You can also use an address to set a marker, instead of latitude and longitude, like this:

```
$('#map').goMap({
  markers : [
    {
      address : '2200 NE 71st Ave Portland, OR, USA',
      title : 'Marker 1'
    }
  ],
  zoom : 15,
}); // end goMap
```

You can also add a marker after the map is created. This technique is handy if you don't want a marker in the center of the map: For example, you might want to have a map of a park, and highlight various points of interest in the park with markers. You'll want the park centered in the map, but don't want a marker in the center (which is what happens when you create markers and maps at the same time as described on page 395).

You also might want to add markers dynamically—maybe in response to something a user clicks. For instance, using the park map example, you might have a button that says "Show me all the slides in the park." Clicking that button makes markers appear highlighting all the slides in the park.

Following this approach, you start by first adding a map, and then calling a special function of the GoMap plug-in—*createMarker()*. For example, to create a map and then add a marker, you can write code like this:

```
$('#map').goMap(
{
    latitude : 45,
    longitude : -122,
    zoom : 15
}); // end goMap
$.goMap.createMarker({
  latitude : 45.53940,
  longitude : -122.59025,
  title : 'Marker 1'
});
```

Notice that the GoMap plug-in isn't attached to a jQuery selection to add a marker in this way. In other words, it's *$.goMap.createMarker()*, instead of *$('#map').goMap .createMarker()*. You can add only one marker at a time like this, so you need to call this function multiple times to add more than one marker. A good approach is to define all of your markers as an array and then use jQuery's *$.each()* function to loop through the array and apply the *createMarker()* function. Here's an example:

```
var markers = [
   {
       latitude : 45.53940,
       longitude : -122.59025,
       title : 'Marker 1'
   },
   {
       latitude : 45.53821,
       longitude : -122.59796,
       title : 'Marker 2'
   },
   {
       latitude : 45.53936,
       longitude :-122.58159,
       title : 'Marker 3'
   }
]
$('#map').goMap(
{
```

```
        latitude : 45,
        longitude : -122,
        zoom : 15
    }); // end goMap
    $.each(markers,function(i,marker) {
     $.goMap.createMarker(marker);
    }); // end each
```

In addition, you might want to remove markers (for example, a button that says Hide Markers). GoMap includes a *clearMarkers()* function. You use it like the *createMarker()* function; that is, you attach it to the jQuery object instead of a selection, like this:

```
    $.goMap.clearMarkers();
```

So say you have a button on the page with the ID of *removeMarkers*. You can attach a click handler to it that will remove the markers from the page:

```
    $('#removeMarkers').click(function() {
        $.goMap.clearMarkers();
    }); // end click
```

If you wish to remove just a particular marker, you need to first add an ID to a marker, then call GoMap's *removeMarker* function. For example, the code below creates a new map (lines 1–13), and then adds a click event to a page element with the ID of *remove*.

```
1  $('#map').goMap({
2    markers : [
3      {
4        latitude : 45.53940,
5        longitude : -122.59025,
6        title : 'Marker 1',
7        id : 'marker1'
8      }
9    ],
10   zoom : 15,
11   maptype : 'ROADMAP',
12   scaleControl : true
13 }); // end goMap
14 $('#remove').click(function() {
15     $.goMap.removeMarker('marker1');
16 });
```

The important part in creating the marker is line 7—*id : 'marker1'*—which assigns an name to that marker. Once a marker has an ID, you can identify it and remove it using the *removeMarker* function (line 15). GoMap also provides a *showHideMarker()* function, which toggles a marker from visible to invisible and vice versa. For example, you could rewrite lines 14–16 so each time the page element is clicked, the particular marker is either hidden or shown, like this:

```
    $('#remove').click(function() {
        $.goMap.showHideMarker('marker1');
    });
```

Adding Information Windows to Markers

You can also add a pop-up bubble (called an information window) to each marker. To do that, add another item to the object literal for each marker named *html* containing yet another object literal with the property's content and popup. For example:

```
$('#map').goMap({
  markers : [
    {
      address : '2200 NE 71st Ave Portland, OR, USA',
      title : 'Marker 1',
      html : {
          content : '<p>A fun place to play</p>',
          popup : true
      }
    }
  ],
  zoom : 15,
}); // end goMap
```

The *content* property sets the text you'd like to appear in the pop-up bubble, which you can do using regular HTML tags and text. The *popup* property specifies whether the pop-up bubble is visible when the map appears (set the property to true as in the above example) or whether a visitor needs to click the marker before seeing the information bubble (set *popup* to false like this—popup : false).

You can add any HTML you wish, such as tables, images, and bulleted lists. You can add quite a bit of content to these information bubbles—they automatically resize.

Tip: To style the HTML inside the HTML bubble, you can use a descendent selector. For example, if you used the name *map* for the ID of the <div> containing the map (see step 3 on page 389), you could create a descendent selector #*map p* to format the look of <p> tags inside the bubble.

GoMap Tutorial

In this tutorial, you'll go through the steps necessary to add the GoMap plug-in to a web page. You'll also add programming so that visitors can request driving directions.

Note: See the note on page 29 for information on how to download the tutorial files.

---

1. **In a text editor, open the file *map.html* in the *chapter12* folder.**

   Before you start adding any JavaScript to this page, you'll modify the HTML by adding an empty <div> to hold the map.

2. **Locate the <h1> tag in the body of the page *(<h1 class="shadowLine">Google Maps</h1>)*. Click inside the empty line directly below this tag and add:**

   ```
   <div id="map"></div>
   ```

You've just created a placeholder, where the GoMap plug-in will eventually add a Google Map.

Next, you'll add a CSS style to set the height and width of the map.

3. **At the top of the file is an internal style sheet; add a CSS rule, just after the opening <style> tag, type:**

```
#map {
  height:400px;
  width:760px;
}
```

At this point, the map area is 500 pixels square. Now it's time to add some JavaScript.

4. **Click in the empty line just *above* the closing </head> tag and type:**

```
<script src="http://maps.google.com/maps/api/js?sensor=false"></script>
<script src="../_js/jquery-1.6.3.min.js"></script>
<script src="../_js/jquery.gomap-1.3.2.min.js"></script>
```

The first <script> tag loads a JavaScript file from Google.com containing the code needed to talk to the Google Maps service. The second <script> tag loads jQuery, while the third one loads the GoMap plug-in file. Now, you're ready to create the map.

5. **Add one additional <script> tag below the ones you added in step 4, and include jQuery's *$(document).ready()* function:**

```
<script>
$(document).ready(function() {

}); // end ready
</script>
```

Now, you just need to apply the *goMap()* function to the empty <div> you created in step 2.

6. **Inside the *$(document).ready()* function, add the following code:**

```
$('#map').goMap({
    latitude : 45.53940,
    longitude : -122.59025
}); // end goMap
```

This code places a map inside the div you added in step 2, displaying a specific longitude and latitude as the center point on the map. (Feel free to change these values if you want to display a map with a different location.)

7. **Save the file and preview it in a web browser.**

Provided you're connected to the Internet (so the browser can contact Google .com), you'll see a 760×400 pixel map.

Let's zoom in a bit more on the map.

8. **Edit the script by adding a comma after the *longitude* option and inserting a *zoom* setting (changes are in bold):**

```
$('#map').goMap({
    latitude : 45.53940,
    longitude : -122.59025,
    zoom : 16
}); // end goMap
```

You can zoom completely out (0), or in to street level (17). Feel free to save the page and preview the changes in a web browser. Next you'll add a scale marker so visitors can get some sense of the distances on the map.

9. **Edit the script again. This time add a comma after the *zoom* option and insert another line of code:**

```
$('#map').goMap({
    latitude : 45.53940,
    longitude : -122.59025,
    zoom : 16,
    scaleControl : true
}); // end goMap
```

This line adds a small scale marker in the bottom left of the map, Finally, you'll change the type of map (normally GoMap displays a hybrid—satellite imagery with streets and street names) to just a Satellite photo.

10. **Edit the *goMaps()* function one last time by adding one last option:**

```
$('#map').goMap({
    latitude : 45.53940,
    longitude : -122.59025,
    zoom : 16,
    scaleControl : true,
    maptype : 'SATELLITE'
}); // end goMap
```

The basic map is now in place. To highlight a location on the map, you'll add a red pushpin marker.

11. **After the *goMap()* function you added earlier, type:**

```
$.goMap.createMarker({
        latitude : 45.53743,
        longitude :  -122.59473,
        title : 'hole1'
}); // end createMarker
```

This sets up a marker at the same location as the center of the map. You can provide different longitude and latitude values, of course, to add a marker elsewhere on the map.

Lastly, you'll add an information window for this marker.

12. **Edit the code you typed in the last step to add an information window (changes in bold):**

```
$.goMap.createMarker({
      latitude : 45.53743,
      longitude :  -122.59473,
      title : 'hole1' ,
      html : {
        content : '<h2>Hole 1</h2><p>Par 4, 346 yards</p>',
        popup : true
      }
}); // end createMarker
```

This code adds a pop-up window with some HTML in it. Save the page and give it one final check in a web browser. You'll find a completed version of the tutorial file—*complete_map.html*—in the *chapter12* folder.

Part Five: Tips, Tricks, and Troubleshooting

5

Chapter 13: Getting the Most from jQuery

Chapter 14: Going Further with JavaScript

Chapter 15: Troubleshooting and Debugging

Getting the Most from jQuery

jQuery greatly simplifies JavaScript programming, and provides web designers with a tool that lets them add sophisticated interactivity quickly and easily. But jQuery isn't always simple, and you need a certain amount of knowledge to use it to its full extent. In this chapter, you'll learn how to take jQuery further: how to use the jQuery documentation and how to take advantage of prepackaged interactivity with plug-ins, plus some useful tips and tricks for working with jQuery.

Useful jQuery Tips and Information

jQuery makes programming easier, but on top of that, there are ways you can make programming jQuery easier. Here are a few bits of information that give you insight into jQuery so you can get the most from it.

$() Is the Same as *jQuery()*

In the many articles and blog posts on jQuery out there on the Web, you may encounter code like this:

```
jQuery('p').css('color','#F03');
```

While you're familiar with *$('p')*, which selects all the <p> tags on a page, you may be wondering about this *jQuery()* function. Actually, they are one and the same. The code above could also be written like this:

```
$('p').css('color','#F03');
```

$() is an alias for *jQuery()*, and the two are interchangeable. John Resig, the creator of jQuery, realized that programmers would be using the main jQuery function a LOT, so rather than force people to type *jQuery()* over and over, he decided the shorter *$()* would be a good substitute.

In practice, you can use either *jQuery()* or *$()*; it's your choice. However, since *$()* is faster to type, you'll probably want to stick with it (as most programmers do).

Note: Another JavaScript library named Prototype (*www.prototypejs.org*) also uses *$()*. If you happen to also use Prototype on your site, you might want to use the *jQuery()* method. In addition, jQuery provides a special function to deal with this situation, named *.noConflict()*. You can read about it at *http:// api.jquery.com/jQuery.noConflict/*.

Saving Selections Into Variables

Every time you make a selection of page elements using *$()—$('#tooltip')*, for example—you're calling the jQuery function. And each time you do that, a visitor's browser has to run a bunch of code. This can often slow your programs down unnecessarily. For example, say you wanted to apply several jQuery functions to a selection like this:

```
$('#tooltip').html('<p>An aardvark</p>');
$('#tooltip').fadeIn(250);
$('#tooltip').animate({left : 100px},250);
```

This code selects an element with an ID of *tooltip* and inserts a <p> tag into it. It then selects the element again and fades it into view. Finally, it selects the element a third time and then animates its left property to 100px. Each of those selections—each *$('#tooltip')*—runs the jQuery function. Since these three lines of code affect the same element, you really only need to select it once.

One approach (discussed earlier in the book on page 137) is to use jQuery's chaining abilities. You select the elements then add one function after another to it like this:

```
$('#tooltip').html('<p>An aardvark</p>').fadeIn(250).animate({left :
100px},250);
```

But sometimes chaining gets unwieldy and hard to read. Another option is to only run the jQuery function a single time, and store its result in a variable that you reuse. Here's how you could do that with the above code:

```
1 var tooltip = $('#tooltip')
2 tooltip.html('<p>An aardvark</p>');
3 tooltip.fadeIn(250);
4 tooltip.animate({left : 100px},250);
```

Line 1 runs the jQuery function, creating a selection of an element with the ID of *tooltip* and stores it into a variable named *tooltip*. Once the selection is made and stored, you don't need to do it again. You can simply use that variable (which now contains a jQuery selection) and run jQuery functions on it.

When using this approach, many programmers like to add a *$* before the variable name, which helps remind them that the variable is storing a jQuery selection as opposed to other data types like strings, variables, arrays, or object literals. For example:

```
var $tooltip = $('#tooltip');
```

Storing a selection into a variable is also very common when using events. As you'll recall from page 149, when you are inside an event function, the variable *$(this)* refers to the element the event is applied to. However, each time you use *$(this)* you are calling the jQuery function, so repeated use of *$(this)* inside an event function just wastes computer power. Instead, you can store *$(this)* into a variable at the beginning of the event function and use it repeatedly without needing to continually call the jQuery function:

```
$('a').click(function() {
  var $this = $(this); // store a reference to the <a> tag
  $this.css('outline','2px solid red');
  var href = $this.attr('href');
  window.open(href);
  return false;
}); // end click
```

Adding Content as Few Times as Possible

In Chapter 4, you learned about some jQuery functions that let you add content to page elements: The *.text()* function (page 138) for example, lets you replace the text inside an element, and the *.html()* function (page 138) lets you replace the HTML inside of an element. For example, if you wished to insert an error message inside a span tag with the ID of *passwordError,* you could write this code:

```
$('#passwordError').text('Passwords must by at least 7 characters long.');
```

Other functions let you add content after an element (*append()*; discussed on page 139) or before an element (*prepend()*; discussed on page 139).

Adding and changing content lets you add error messages, pop-up tooltips (page 326), insert pull quotes (page 150), but it does require a lot from a browser. Each time you add content, the browser needs to do a lot of work—you're basically changing the DOM (page 127) and when that happens, browsers do a lot of behind-the-scenes work. Changing the content a lot of times can significantly affect the performance of a web page.

It's not the amount of content that matters—it's the number of times you change the page that affects performance. For example, say you wanted to create a tooltip effect: When someone mouses over a box, for example, a div appears with some additional content. To do this, you need to add the box and the additional content to the page. This is one approach to add that div:

```
1  // add div to end of element
2  $('#elemForTooltip').append('<div id="tooltip"></div>');
3  // add headline to tooltip
4  $('#tooltip').append('<h2>The tooltip title</h2>');
5  // add contents
6  $('#tooltip').append('<p>The tooltip contents here</p>');
```

The code above will work just fine: Line 2 adds a div to the element the visitor will mouse over; line 3 adds a headline to the tooltip box; and line 4 adds a paragraph to the tooltip. However, the DOM is modified three times in the process with three different append operations. All of this processing is actually quite taxing on a web browser, and reducing the number of times you have to modify the DOM can significantly improve the performance of a page.

In this example, you can reduce the number of append operations to just one by building the entire tooltip HTML, storing it in a variable, and then appending that variable's contents to the page, like this:

```
1 var tooltip = '<div id="tooltip"><h2>The tooltip title</h2> ↵
  <p>The tooltip contents here</p></div>';
2 $('#elemForTooltip').append(tooltip);
```

Note: The ↵ symbol at the end of a line of code indicates that the next line should really be typed as part of the first line. But since a *really* long line of JavaScript code won't fit on this book's page, it's broken up over two lines.

In this code, line 1 creates a variable containing all of the HTML for the tooltip, and line 2 appends that HTML to a page element. There's only one append operation, and depending upon which browser the visitor views the page in, this code can be up to 20 times faster than using the three *.append()* functions.

The bottom line is that if you want to inject a chunk of HTML into a spot on the page, do it in one single operation rather than add the HTML in parts using multiple inserts.

Optimizing Your Selectors

jQuery's flexibility means you have many ways to achieve the same goal. For example, you can select a page element in a number of ways; for example, you can use any CSS selector, or refine a jQuery selection using the DOM Traversal functions discussed on page 413. However, the following techniques will make your selections faster and your JavaScript programs more efficient.

- **Use ID selectors if at all possible.** The fastest way to select a page element is to use an ID selector. Browsers from the dawn of JavaScript have provided a method for selecting elements with IDs, and it's still the fastest way. If you're worried about performance, then you might want to slap an ID on each element that you plan on selecting rather than depending upon other methods like a descendent selector.

- **Use IDs first, as part of a descendent selector.** The problem with using just an ID selector is that you only ever retrieve a single element. What if you need to retrieve multiple elements like all the <a> tags inside a div, or the paragraphs on a page? If your page is structured in such a way that all the elements you wish to select are within an element with an ID, then use a descendent selector that includes the ID first. For example, say you want to select all the <a> tags on a page. It just so happens that all of those tags are also inside a div tag with an ID of *main*. It's faster to use this selector:

```
$('#main a')
```

than this selector:

```
$('a')
```

- **Use the** *.find()* **function.** jQuery includes a function for finding elements within a selection. It works kind of like a descendent selector in that it locates tags inside of other tags. You'll read more about this function on page 414, but in a nutshell, you start with a jQuery selection, slap on *.find()*, and pass a selector to it. In other words, you could write *$('#main a')* like this:

```
$('#main').find('a');
```

In fact, in some situations using *.find()* instead of a descendent selector is over two times as fast!

Note: You can try a speed test for the *.find()* function at *http://jsperf.com/sawmac-selector-test.*

- **Avoid too much specificity.** You may be used to using CSS's specificity rules to create CSS styles that target particular elements on a page. A rule like *#main .sidebar .note ul.nav li a* is very specific, but when you run it through the jQuery function, it can also perform slowly. If possible, either use a descendent selector that's shorter and more refined—*$('.sidebar .nav a')*, for example—or use the *.find()* function mentioned in the previous point: *$('#main').find('.sidebar). find('.nav a').*

Note: If you're interested in learning about other ways to improve jQuery's performance, check out this presentation: *http://addyosmani.com/jqprovenperformance/* and *http://jqfundamentals.com/#chapter-9.* For many good tips and tricks for working with jQuery, visit this blog post *http://tutorialzine.com/2011/06/15-powerful-jquery-tips-and-tricks-for-developers/.*

Using the jQuery Docs

The jQuery website provides very detailed documentation for jQuery at *http://docs .jquery.com/* (see Figure 13-1). You'll find useful links for how to get started with jQuery, where to seek help, tutorials, and more, but the most important section of the site deals with the jQuery API. API stands for Application Programming Interface, and simply means the set of functions that jQuery lets you use, like the event handler functions you read about in Chapter 5 (*.click()*, *.hover()*, and so on), the CSS functions you learned about in Chapter 4 (*.css()*, *.addClass()*, and *.removeClass()*), and most importantly, the basic jQuery function itself—*$()*—which lets you select elements on a page.

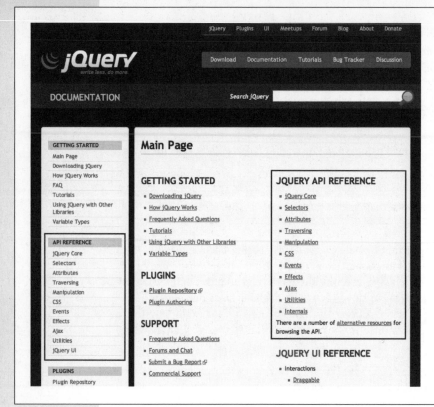

Figure 13-1:
*The main jQuery
docs page contains
links to lots of useful
information, but the
ones that will help
you figure out all of
the functions jQuery
offers are listed under
the API heading in
the main area of the
page (outlined on
right) or on the left
sidebar (outlined on
left). You'll find the
left sidebar is avail-
able when you visit
other pages.*

Figure 13-1 highlights the main categories of the API. Click one of the categories
to jump to a page listing functions related to that aspect of jQuery. The main categories are:

- **jQuery Core** (*http://api.jquery.com/category/core/*). Here, you'll find information on just a handful of functions, most of which are advanced functions that
  you might never need to access. You will find the main *jQuery()* function, which
  is the heart of jQuery. Visiting its page (*http://api.jquery.com/jQuery/*) will give
  you in-depth information on the *jQuery()* function.

Note: You've learned about the *$()* function and how to use it to select a page element—*$('p')*, for
example. That same function also goes by the name *jQuery()*. That is, *$()* is an alias for a function name
jQuery(). The two are interchangeable, so you may see code in a tutorial or in a book that looks like this:

```
jQuery('p').css('color','#F03');
```

That is functionally equivalent to:

```
$('p').css('color','#F03');
```

- **Selectors** (*http://api.jquery.com/category/selectors/*) provides access to some of the most helpful jQuery functions. This page is worth visiting often since it lists the many different ways to use jQuery to select page elements. You learned about many of these in Chapter 4, but you'll find even more ways when you visit this section of the jQuery documentation.

- **Attributes** (*http://api.jquery.com/category/attributes/*). Visit this page to find the various jQuery functions that get and set attributes of HTML elements such as adding a class to a tag, finding or setting the value of an attribute (like the href attribute on a <a> tag), or getting the value of a form element.

Note: You'll often find the same function listed in more than one section of the jQuery documentation site. For example, the *.val()* function used to read and set the value of a form field is listed both under the Attributes and the Forms categories of the site.

- **Traversing** (*http://api.jquery.com/category/traversing/*) refers to functions used to manipulate a set of page elements. For example, the *.find()* function lets you find an element inside a jQuery selection: This is handy when you want to select a page element (a <ul> tag for example), perform an operation on it (like add a class, or fade it into view), and then find another element inside that page element to do something else (for example, find an <li> tag inside the original <ul> tag). jQuery provides lots of functions for traversing HTML elements and you'll read about some of them later in this chapter.

- **Manipulation** (*http://api.jquery.com/category/manipulation/*). Whenever you want to add or remove something from a page, you need to manipulate the page's DOM (Document Object Model [see page 127]). This page lists the many functions available for changing a page, including the ones you read about in Chapter 4 (page 138) like *.html()* to add HTML to a page, *.text()* to add text to a page and so on. This category of functions is very important, since a lot of JavaScript programming is about dynamically changing the content and appearance of a web page.

- The **CSS** page (*http://api.jquery.com/category/css/*) lists jQuery functions used for reading or setting CSS-related properties on elements including adding or removing classes, directly setting CSS properties, and controlling or reading the height, width, and position of an element. You'll learn about some of these functions on page 143.

- **Events** (*http://api.jquery.com/category/events/*). In Chapter 5, you learned how to use jQuery to respond to user interaction like the mouse moving over a link, or the visitor clicking a button on the page. You'll find a list of jQuery's many event-related functions on this page. On page 427, you'll learn about some advanced event functions.

- The **Effects** page (*http://api.jquery.com/category/effects/*) provides access to information on jQuery's effects-related functions like the *.slideDown()*, *.fadeIn()*, and *.animate()* functions you learned about in Chapter 6.

- The **Ajax** category (*http://api.jquery.com/category/ajax/*) lists functions related to dynamically updating a page based on information sent to or received from a web server. You'll learn about Ajax in Part 4 of this book.

- **Utilities** (*http://api.jquery.com/category/utilities/*). jQuery also provides a handful of functions dedicated to simplifying common programming tasks like finding an element inside an array (page 59), acting on each item inside an array or object (the *$.each()* function discussed on page 147), and a bunch of other geeky niceties. You may not need any of these functions at this point in your programming career (they don't really tap into any cool effects, or help you update the content or appearance of a page), but as you get more advanced, it's worth visiting this page on the jQuery documentation site.

Strangely, when you visit one of the category pages (like Ajax or Selectors), the left sidebar adds more categories of functions for the jQuery API that aren't listed on the home page:

- The **Data** category (*http://api.jquery.com/category/data/*) lists functions related to adding data to page elements. jQuery provides a *.data()* function to add data to an element—think of it as a way to add name/value pairs to any page element, kind of like a mini-database. This and the other data-related functions can come in handy when working on a web application where you need to store and track data. For an understandable introduction to using these data functions, check out *http://tutorialzine.com/2010/11/jquery-data-method/*.

- **Deferred Object** (*http://api.jquery.com/category/deferred-object/*). You don't need to look much further than the introduction to this category (which explains that a deferred object "is a chainable utility object that can register multiple callbacks into callback queues, invoke callback queues, and relay the success or failure state of any synchronous or asynchronous function") to understand that jQuery's Deferred Object is a complex beast. Basically, it helps with queuing up functions to control the order in which they run. If you want to learn more, visit the category page of the jQuery docs site.

- **Dimensions** (*http://api.jquery.com/category/dimensions/*) refers to functions used to determine the width and height of objects. These functions are also listed under the CSS category mentioned above.

- The **Forms** category (*http://api.jquery.com/category/forms/*) lists functions related to—drum-roll please—forms. It mainly lists events used with form elements, but also includes the *.val()* function for reading or setting the value of a form field, and a couple of functions to make it easy to submit a form using Ajax (see section 4).

- **Internals** (*http://api.jquery.com/category/internals/*) are a handful of functions of various usefulness. The *.jquery* property, for example, returns the version of jQuery in use on the page:

```
// open alert box with version number
alert($().jquery); // 1.6.2, for example
```

  You can lead a long, happy life without using any of the functions here.

- The **Offset** category page (*http://api.jquery.com/category/offset/*) lists functions related to determining the position of an object relative to the screen or to its parent element. You'll use these functions when setting or getting the position of an element on the page.

Reading a Page on the jQuery Docs Site

Each jQuery function has its own page, documenting what it does and how it works. Figure 13-2 shows part of the page explaining jQuery's *.css()* function. The page lists the functions name (*.css()* in this case), as well as listing the category and subcategories the function falls under. You can click on the category and subcategory links to jump up to a page listing all functions that fit that category.

In some cases, a function serves double- or even triple-duty and acts differently based on the type and number of arguments you provide it. In that case, you'll see the function listed in several different ways under the function title. For example, in Figure 13-2, you'll see that the *.css()* function can be used in two different ways (numbers 1 and 2 in the figure).

The first way, #1, is listed as *css(propertyName)*. Here, *propertyName* indicates that you pass one argument to the function, which should be a CSS property name. jQuery then returns the value of that property for the specified element (notice *Returns: String* on the right side of the dark bar in the middle of the figure). The information listed on the page then lets you know that you pass one argument and receive a string in return. For example, say you want to determine the width of a <div> tag with the ID of tooltip; you can use this code:

```
var tipWidth = $('#tooltip').css('width'); // get the width value
```

In the code above, '*width*' is passed to the function, and a string value is returned. (However, in this case since it's a width, the string will actually be the number of pixels wide; the element is—'*300*', for example.)

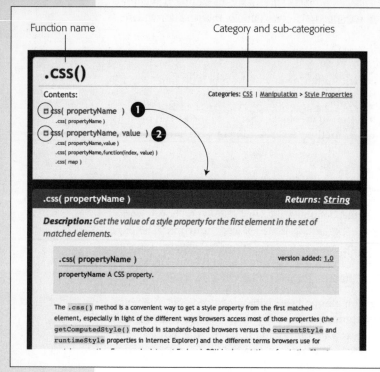

Function name   Category and sub-categories

Figure 13-2:
The docs page for each jQuery function lists all the different ways you can use a function. In this case, listed under Contents: you'll see that you can pass the .css() function either a single argument (#1) or two arguments (#2). The function behaves differently depending on which of those two routes you go. By clicking the small blue down-pointing arrow (circled), you can jump directly to the spot on the page that describes that use of the function.

A second way to use the *.css()* function is listed (#2) as *css(propertyName, value)*, indicating that you pass the function two arguments—the name of a CSS property and a value. Used this way, the *.css()* function sets the CSS property for the element. For example, if you wanted to set the width of a <div> tag with the ID of tooltip, you would pass *width* as the first argument, and the value you wish for the width as the second like this:

```
$('#tooltip').css('width',300); // set div to 300px wide
```

The documentation also lists two other ways to use the *.css()* function to set CSS properties:

- *.css(propertyName, function(index,value))* indicates that you can set a CSS property using a function to dynamically generate a value. This is handy when you have a collection of page elements and you want to set slightly different values for each; for example, a series of divs that you wish to set the *left* property on to position, but you want each div to be positioned next to each other at a different *left* position.

- *.css(map)* is described on page 143, and means that you can pass an object literal in order to set several CSS properties and values in one step.

The important thing to understand is that the same jQuery function can and often does take different arguments and does different things. The *.css()* function, for example, can both retrieve a CSS value and set a CSS value. You'll frequently find jQuery functions working in this way as both "getters" (that is, they retrieve information about an element) and "setters" (that is, they set the value of a particular property for an element).

The docs page will describe each use of the function and usually provides working examples of how the function works. The jQuery docs are well-maintained, and as far as technical documentation goes, pretty easy to read and understand. You should spend some time visiting these pages and especially reading up on the functions you use most often.

Traversing the DOM

You've learned how to select page elements using jQuery and basic CSS syntax: $('p'), for example, selects all of the paragraphs on a page. Once you select elements, you can do stuff to them, such as add or remove a class, change a CSS property, or make the elements disappear. But sometimes you want to find *other* page elements in relationship to your original selection. In JavaScript-speak, this is called *Traversing the DOM* (Document Object Model).

Traversing the DOM happens frequently when you attach an event to an element but then want to do something to another element. For example, say you have a <div> tag with an ID of gallery; the div contains a series of thumbnail images. When a visitor clicks the div, you want the thumbnails to do something: shrink, grow, shake, or something like that. The event is attached to the <div> tag like this:

```
$('#gallery').click(function() {

}); // end click
```

Inside the function, you need to add the programming code to animate the images. So, although the user clicks the *div*, you want do something to the *images*. In the code above, you've merely selected the <div> tag, and inside the function *$(this)* will refer to that div (if that's news to you, turn to page 149 for a refresher on what *$(this)* means). So, although the <div> tag is the selected element inside the click function, you need to find the images inside that div. Fortunately, jQuery provides just such a solution: the *.find()* function. Its purpose is to generate a new selection of page elements by searching *inside* the current selection for other tags that match a given selector. So you can select the images inside the div by adding the bolded code below:

```
$('#gallery').click(function() {
  $(this).find('img');
}); // end click
```

The *$(this).find('img')* creates a new selection of elements; *$(this)* refers to the div, then *.find('img')* looks for every image inside that div. Of course, this code doesn't do anything to the new selection, but you could add any of the effects you learned about in the last chapter. For example, say you want the images to fade out temporarily and then fade back in. You could use this code:

```
$('#gallery').click(function() {
  $(this).find('img').fadeTo(500,.3).fadeTo(250,1);
}); // end click
```

As you read on page 187, the *fadeTo()* function takes a duration and an opacity value as arguments. So this code first fades all of the images to 30% opacity in 500 milliseconds, and then fades it back to 100% opacity in 250 milliseconds (see the file *find .html* in the *chapter07* tutorial folder to see this effect in action).

In fact, traversing the DOM is such a common task that jQuery provides many functions that help you take a selection of elements and then locate other elements in relationship to the first. To better understand how they work, we'll use a simple chunk of HTML represented in Figure 13-3: *http://api.jquery.com/category/manipulation/*. It's a <div> tag with an ID of *gallery* containing four links, each of which is wrapped around an image.

As discussed on page 127, you can use the relationships of a family to describe the relationships between tags on a page. For example, in Figure 13-3, the <div> tag is the parent of the <a> tags, and each <a> tag is the parent of the <img> tag inside it. Conversely, the <a> tags are children of the <div> tag, and each <a> tag is the sibling of the other <a> tags. Each <img> tag is the child of the <a> tag that wraps around them, and since there are no other tags inside each <a>, the <img> tags don't have siblings.

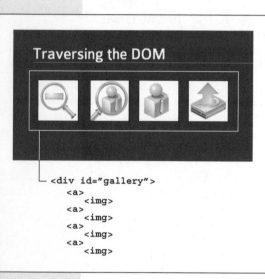

Figure 13-3:
When you make a jQuery selection—for example to add an event handler to an element, such as the <a> tags pictured here—you'll often want to act on another tag in relation to that selection (for example add an outline to the div tag or alter the img tag). jQuery's DOM traversing functions can help.

Here are a few jQuery's most useful DOM traversing functions:

- *.find()*. Finds particular elements inside the current selection. You start with a jQuery selection, add *.find()* and pass it a CSS selector like this:

  ```
  $('#gallery').find('img')
  ```

  This code finds all of the images inside the gallery div. Of course, you could achieve the same goals with a descendent selector like this *$('#gallery img')*. As mentioned above, you're more likely to use *.find()* in a situation where you already have a selection that you've done something too—like attach a click event—to create a new selection to act on.

You use *.find()* to select a descendent (a tag inside another tag) of the current selection. So in the example pictured in Figure 13-3, you could use *.find()* on a selection including the div to select either the <a> tags or the <img> tags.

Note: See the previous page to read about the huge performance benefits *.find()* offers. It's generally a faster way to select elements than using a descendent selector.

- *.children()* is similar to *.find()*. It also accepts a selector as an argument, but it limits its selection to immediate children of the current selection. For example, say you had a div tag that contains a series of other divs. When you click on the main div, it reveals previously hidden divs, and adds a red outline around them. Let's say you used the *.find()* function to achieve this goal like this:

```
$('#mainDiv').click(function() {
    $(this).find('div').show().css('outline','red 2px solid');
});
```

  A problem arises if one of the divs inside the main div also has a div tags inside it. *.find('div')* locates all div tags, even divs inside other divs. You may end up with a page that has outlines around all the divs, when what you want is simply an outline around the immediate child divs of the main div. To solve that dilemma, you can rewrite the code above using *.children()* like this:

```
$('#mainDiv').click(function() {
    $(this).children('div').show().css('outline','red 2px solid');
});
```

  Now this code finds only the divs that are immediate children of the main div and avoids any divs that might exist inside the child divs.

- *.parent().* Whereas *.find()* locates elements inside the current element, *.parent()* travels up the DOM locating the parent of the current tag. This could come in handy, for example, if you attach a hover event to the <a> tags pictured in Figure 13-3, but you want to perform an action on the <div> tag (for example, add a border or background color to the div. In this case, you'd use *.parent()* to locate the div and apply an action to it, like this:

```
$('#gallery a').hover(
    function() {
      // add outline to link
      $(this).css('outline','2px solid red');
      // add background color to div
      $(this).parent().css('backgroundColor','white');
    },
    function() {
      // remove outline from link
      $(this).css('outline','');
      // remove background color from div
      $(this).parent().css('backgroundColor','');

    }
); // end hover
```

In this example, hovering over a link adds an outline around that link, then selects the link's parent (the div) and applies a background color. Mousing off the link removes both the outline and background color (see page 171 for more information on the *.hover()* event). (See the file *parent.html* in the *chapter13* tutorial folder for an example of this function in action.)

- *.closest()* finds the nearest ancestor that matches a particular selector. Unlike *.parent()*, which finds the immediate parent of the current tag, *.closest()* accepts a selector as an argument and finds the nearest ancestor that matches. For example, in Figure 13-3, each image is inside a <a> tag; in other words, the <a> tag is the parent of the image. However, what if you wanted to select the <div> tag that surrounds the <a> tags (an ancestor further up the HTML chain)? You could then use *.closest()* like this:

```
1  $('#gallery img').click(function() {
2      $(this).css('outline','2px red solid');
3      $(this).closest('div').css('backgroundColor','white');
4  }); // end click
```

In line 4, *$(this)* refers to the <img> tag; *.closest('div')* means find the nearest ancestor that's a <div> tag. The closest ancestor is the <a> tag, but since it isn't a div, jQuery skips it and finds the next ancestor, and so on and so on until it locates a <div>.

- *.siblings()* comes in handy when you wish to select an element that's at the same level as the current selection. Say you had the setup pictured in Figure 13-3; when a visitor clicks a link, you want all the other links to gently fade out and into view. In this case the event—*click*—applies to a link tag, but the effect you wish to perform is to all the other links inside that div. In other words, you start with a link, but you want to select all that link's siblings. You could do that like this:

```
1  $('#gallery a').click(function() {
2      $(this).siblings().fadeTo(500,.3).fadeTo(250,1);
3  }); // end click
```

In the above code, *$(this)* refers to the clicked link, so *.siblings()* selects all of the other links in that div.

The *.siblings()* function also can take an argument—the name of a selector—to limit the selected siblings to a certain type of tag. For example, say inside the <div> tag pictured in Figure 13-3, there's a headline and introductory paragraph prior to the links. Since the headline and paragraph are both inside the <div> tag along with all of the <a> tags, they're also siblings of the <a> tag. In other words, give the code above, clicking a link would also cause that headline and paragraph to fade out and back into view. To limit the effect to just other links, you could rewrite line 2 above to look like the following:

```
$(this).siblings('a').fadeTo(500,.3).fadeTo(250,1);
```

The *'a'* inside *siblings('a')* limits the selection to just siblings that are also <a> tags. See the *siblings.html* file in the *chapter13* tutorial folder to see how this function works.

- *.next()* finds the next sibling of the current selection. You already saw this function in action in the One Page FAQ tutorial on page 180. In that tutorial, clicking a question opens and then closes a <div> tag containing the answer to that question. Each question is represented by a <h2> tag, and each answer by a div tag immediately following that <h2> tag. The headline and div are siblings, but they are also the siblings of all the other questions and answers on that page. So when the headline is clicked, you must select the immediate sibling (in other words, the next sibling). Like *.siblings()*, *.next* accepts an optional selector so that you can limit selection to the next sibling of a particular type. (See the *complete_faq.html* file in the *chapter05* tutorial folder for an example of *.next()* in action.)

- *.prev()* works just like *.next()*, except that it selects the immediately preceding sibling.

Note: For more jQuery functions that let you traverse the DOM, visit *http://api.jquery.com/category/traversing/*.

Putting an *.end()* to DOM Traversal

In order to get the most done while writing the least amount of code, jQuery lets you chain functions together. Chaining is discussed on page 137, but in a nutshell it lets you select some pages elements, do one thing to them, then do another and another thing to them, simply by adding one function after another. For example, if you wanted to select all the paragraphs on a page and have them fade out of view then fade back into view, you could write this code:

```
$('p').fadeOut(500).fadeIn(500);
```

You can chain as many functions together as you'd like including the DOM Traversal methods discussed above. For example, you could select a <div> tag, add an outline around it, and then select all of the <a> tags inside that <div> and change the color of their text like this:

```
$('div').css('outline','2px red solid').
find('a').css('color','purple');
```

Broken into pieces, this means:

1. *$('div')* selects all <div> tags.

2. *.css('outline','2px red solid')* adds a 2-pixel red outline to the div.

3. *.find('a')* then changes the selection from the div to all of the <a> tags inside the div.

4. *.css('color','purple')* makes the text of all of the links (not the div tag) purple.

When adding one of the DOM Traversal functions to the chain, you alter the selection. For example, in the above code, jQuery first selects the div, then halfway through the chain, changes the selection to links inside the div. But sometimes when you want to return the selection to its original state. In other words, you want to select one thing, then select another thing in relation to the first selection, then return to the first selection. For example, say when a visitor clicks a div that has an opacity of 50%, you want to make the div fade to 100% opacity, change the color of the headline inside the div, add a background color to each p

inside the div. One action—a click—needs to trigger several actions on different elements of the page. One way to do this would be like this:

```
$('div').click(function() {
    $(this).fadeTo(250,1); // fade div in
    $(this).find('h2').css('color','#F30');
                    $(this).find('p').
('backgroundColor','#F343FF');
}); // end click
```

Here's a case where chaining would be really helpful—instead of calling *$(this)* three times, you could call it once and chain together the functions. However, you'd run into trouble if you tried to chain the functions like this:

```
$('div').click(function() {
  $(this).fadeTo(250,1)
    .find('h2').css('color','#F30')
  .find('p').('backgroundColor','#F343FF');
}); // end click
```

This might look right, but the problem occurs after the *.find('h2')*—which changes the selection from the div to the h2 tag inside the div. When the next *.find()* function runs—*.find('p')*—jQuery tries to find p tags inside the h2 tag, not inside the div. Fortunately, you can use jQuery's *.end()* function to "rewind" a changed selection back to its original state. In the example above, you can use *.end()* to return the selection back to the div, and then find the <p> tags inside the div like this.

```
$('div').click(function() {
  $(this).fadeTo(250,1)
    .find('h2').css('color','#F30').end()
  .find('p').('backgroundColor','#F343FF');
}); // end click
```

Notice the *.end()* after the *.css('color', '#F30)*; this code returns the jQuery selection back to the div so that the following *.find('p')* will find all <p> tags inside the div.

More Functions For Manipulating HTML

You'll often want to add, remove, and change the HTML of a page dynamically. For example, when a visitor clicks a submit button on a form, you might want the text "Send form information. Please wait." to appear on the screen. Or when a visitor mouses over a photo, you want a box to appear on top of the photo with a caption and photo credits. In both cases, you need to add HTML to a page. You learned about the most common functions in Chapter 4 on page 138. Here's a quick recap:

- *.text()* replaces the text inside a selection with selection you pass to the function. For example:

  ```
  $('#error').text('You must supply an e-mail address');
  ```

- *.html()* works like *.text()* but lets you insert HTML instead of just text:

  ```
  $('#tooltip').html('<h2>Esquif Avalon</h2><p>Designed for canoe camping.</p>');
  ```

- *.append()* lets you add HTML to the end of an element (for example, at the end of a div just before the closing </div> tag. This function is perfect for adding items to the bottom of a list.

- *.prepend()* lets you add HTML to the beginning of an element (for instance, at the beginning of a div just after the opening <div> tag).

- *.before()* adds content before the selection.

- *.after()* works just like *.before()*, except that the content is added after the selection (after its closing tag).

Which of these you use really depends on what your final goal is. Page 124 discussed how JavaScript is really just about automating the tasks web designers normally perform manually: adding HTML and CSS to create a web page. If you're writing a program to add content to a page dynamically—like a tooltip, an error message, a pull quote, and so on—just imagine what your finished product should look like and the HTML and CSS required to achieve it.

For example, if you want to create a special message on the page when a visitor mouses over a button, try building a web page that demonstrates that message without using JavaScript—just build it with CSS and HTML. Once you have the HTML/CSS mockup working, take a look at the HTML you used to achieve the effect: Is it placed before some other element? If so, use the *.before()* function.) Is the HTML inside a specific tag? (Then use the *.append()* or *.prepend()* functions.)

jQuery also supplies some functions for removing content from a page:

- *.replaceWith()* completely replaces the selection (include the tag and everything inside it) with whatever you pass the function. For example, to replace a submit button on the page with the text "processing…" you could use this code:

  ```
  $(':submit').replaceWith('<p>processing…</p>');
  ```

- *.remove()* removes the selection from the DOM; essentially erasing it from the page. For example, to remove a div with the ID of error from the page, you'd write this code:

  ```
  $('#error').remove();
  ```

While you may only need the functions listed above and discussed in Chapter 4, jQuery provides other functions that provide additional ways of manipulating the HTML of a page:

- *.wrap()* wraps each element in a selection in a pair of HTML tags. For example, what if you want to create a fancy caption effect for images on a page? You can start by selecting images from the page and wrapping them in a <div> with a class like *figure* and adding a <p> tag inside that div with a class of caption. Then, using CSS, you can format the div and caption in whatever way you'd like. Here's one way to accomplish that:

```
1  // loop through the list of images
2  $('img').each(function() {
3    // save reference to current image
4    var $this = $(this);
5    // get the alt property for the caption
6    var caption = $this.attr('alt');
7    // add the HTML
8    $this.wrap('<div class="figure"></div>').after('<p>' + caption + '</p>');
9  }); // end each
```

The code above first selects all the images on the page and then loops through the list of images using the *.each()* function (page 147); on line 4, the current image in the loop is saved into a variable (a good practice, as described on page 404 in this chapter). In line 6, the alt attribute is retrieved from the image and stored in a variable named caption. Finally, line 8 wraps the image in a <div> tag, and adds a captions after the image using the *.after()* function described above.

Note: You can see the *.wrap()* code listed on line 8 in action in the file *wrap.html* in the *chapter13* tutorial folder.

You pass a complete set of tags to the *.wrap()* function—*$('p').wrap('<div></div>')*—or even a nested set of tags like this:

```
$('#example').wrap('<div id="outer"><div id="inner"></div></div>');
```

In the above code, jQuery will wrap the selection with the two divs, leaving the HTML something like this:

```
<div id="outer">
  <div id="inner">
    <div id="example">This is the original code on the page</div>
  </div>
</div>
```

- *.wrapInner()* wraps the contents of each element in a selection in HTML tags. For example, say you had the following code in your HTML:

```
<div id="outer">
<p>This is the contents of outer</p>
</div>
```

If the browser encounters the code *$('#outer').wrapInner('<div id="inner"></div>');* it transforms the HTML on the page into this:

```
<div id="outer">
<div id="inner">
<p>This is the contents of outer</p>
</div>
</div>
```

- *.unwrap()* simply removes the parent tag surrounding the selection. For example, say a page has the following HTML:

```
<div>
<p>a paragraph</p>
<div>
```

Running the code *$('p').unwrap()* changes the HTML to:

```
<p>a paragraph</p>
```

The outer <div> is simply removed. Note that unlike the other functions discussed here, *.unwrap()* takes no arguments—in other words, don't put anything inside the parentheses in *.unwrap()* or it won't work.

- *.empty()* removes all of the contents of a selection, but leaves the selection in place. For example, say you had a div on a web page with the ID of *messageBox*. Using JavaScript, you can dynamically add content to this div to display messages to a visitor as she interacts with the page. You might fill that div with lots of content headlines, images, and paragraphs to provide status messages to the visitor. You may want to empty that box at some point in the program (when there are no current messages to display, for example), but leave the box in place so you can later add status messages to it. To remove all the tags inside that box, you can use this code.

```
$('#messageBox').empty();
```

As with *.unwrap()*, *.empty()* takes no arguments.

Note: jQuery provides even more functions for manipulating HTML. You can read about all of them at *http://api.jquery.com/category/manipulation/*.

Advanced Event Handling

In Chapter 5 you learned about jQuery's handy functions for assigning events to elements. For example, if you want to make an alert box pop up each time someone clicked on a heading 1, you could use the *.click()* event like this:

```
$('h1').click(function() {
  alert('ouch!');
}); // end click
```

jQuery provides functions for responding to different events, like *.submit()* for when a visitor submits a form, or the .mouseout() function to do something when a visitor mouses off of an element. All of those functions are simply shorthand methods of using the jQuery *.bind()* function described on page 177.

The *.bind()* function receives a few arguments: the event type (*'click'*, *'mouseover'*, and so on) and a function to run when that event occurs. For example, you can rewrite the code above like this:

```
$('h1').bind('click', function() {
  alert('ouch!');
}); // end bind
```

There's one big problem with both *.bind()* and the shorthand event functions like *.click()* and *.hover()*: They're only applied to the HTML currently on the page. For the examples in this book, that's OK; the HTML is loaded, the browser applies event listeners to the HTML, and a user interacts with the page. However, as you get more advanced in your programming, you'll begin to do a lot dynamic updates to web page content using jQuery's manipulation functions (like *.append()*, *.before()*, and so on discussed earlier in this chapter). Unfortunately, event handlers already on the page aren't applied to HTML you add later, and that can cause problems.

For example, say you create a web game: The object of the game is to remove all the weeds in a garden. The player has to click a weed to remove it from the screen. But, of course, as weeds do, they continue to fill up the screen. Basically, the program keeps adding weeds, and the player needs to click on weeds until they're all gone. In this example, each "weed" can be represented by a <div> tag with a picture of a weed in it. The program continually adds divs to the page, while the player tries to eliminate all the divs by clicking on them. In other words, each div must have a *click* handler applied to it, so it responds to a visitor clicking it. You might add some code in your program to do that like this:

```
$('.weed').click(function() {
  $(this).remove();
}); // end click
```

The problem with this code is that it only applies to elements that already exist. If you programmatically add new divs—*<div class="weed">*—the click handler isn't applied to them.

Code that applies only to existing elements is also a problem when you use Ajax as described in Part 4 of this book. Ajax lets you update content on a page using information retrieved from a web server. Gmail, for example, can display new mail as you receive it by continually retrieving it from a web server and updating the content in the web browser. In this case, your list of received emails changes after you first started using Gmail. Any events that were applied to the page content when the page loads won't apply to the new content added from the server.

You can reapply event handlers whenever the page is updated, but this method is slow and inefficient. Fortunately, jQuery provides another function to handle this situation: *.delegate()*. The *.delegate()* function remains active even when new elements are added to the page; that is, you only need to use it once in your program, and it will be able to respond to events on elements added to the page later. Here's the basic syntax of *.delegate()*:

```
$('#container').delegate('selector','event',function() {
    //code to respond to event
}); // end delegate
```

The syntax is a little strange, so let's break it down:

- First, you start by selecting a container element. This is confusing, since with .*bind()* you select the elements that you want to add events to, but here you select an element that *contains* the elements you wish to attach events to. For example, if you wanted to attach a click event handler to all of the list items inside a div with the ID of sidebar, you'd start by selecting the div like this:

  ```
  $('#sidebar')
  ```

  If you want to apply a mouseover event handler to all the <a> tags on a page, on the other hand, you select the body itself:

  ```
  $('body')
  ```

- Next, you call the *delegate()* function and pass it three arguments: the selector you wish to attach the event to, the name of the event, and the function that responds to that event. For example, using delegate to apply a click event handler to list items inside a div with the ID of sidebar, you'd write this code:

  ```
  $('#sidebar').delegate('li','click',function() {
      //do something here
  }); // end delegate
  ```

  Likewise, to apply a mouseover event handler to all <a> tags on a page, you write this:

  ```
  $('body').delegate('a','mouseover',function() {
      //do something here
  }); // end delegate
  ```

To see .*delegate()* in action, open the *delegate.html* file in the *chapter13* tutorial folder.

Note: jQuery also provides a function named .*live()*, which functions similarly to .*delegate()* in that it applies event handlers to page elements that are added after the function runs. However, it is significantly slower than .*delegate()* and is best avoided.

Going Further with JavaScript

This chapter covers various concepts that can help make you a better JavaScript programmer. You don't need most of the ideas here to write functioning JavaScript programs, so don't worry if you don't understand them all. The first few sections provide helpful tips and methods for working with strings, numbers, and dates, and once you've mastered the basics, these sections can really help you process visitor input in forms, work with HTML and HTML attributes, and generate dates for calendars. The section "Putting It All Together" on page 457 contains some good advice for beginners, but you can program happily for a long time without needing the information in the other sections in this chapter. But if you want to expand your skills, this chapter can point you in the right direction.

Working with Strings

Strings are the most common type of data you'll work with: input from form fields, the path to an image, a URL, and HTML that you wish to replace on a page are all examples of the letters, symbols, and numbers that make up strings. You learned the basics of strings in Chapter 2, but JavaScript provides a lot of useful methods for working with and manipulating strings.

Determining the Length of a String

There are times when you want to know how many characters are in a string. For example, say you want to make sure that when someone creates an account on your top secret website, they create a new password that's more than 6 letters but no more than 15. Strings have a *length* property that gives you just this kind of information.

Add a period after the name of the variable, followed by *length* to get the number of characters in the string: *name.length.*

For example, assume you have a form with a text field. The field has the ID of password. To make sure the password has the proper number of characters, you could use a conditional statement (page 79) to test the password's length like this:

```
var password = $('#password').val();
if (password.length <= 6) {
  alert('That password is too short.');
} else if (password.length > 15) {
  alert('That password is too long.');
}
```

Note: In the above example, this little snippet of code would also go inside of a *submit()* event handler (page 263), so that you'd test whether the visitor entered a long enough password when the form was submitted.

Changing the Case of a String

JavaScript provides two methods to convert strings to all uppercase or all lowercase, so you can change "hello" to "HELLO" or "NOT" to "not". Why, you might ask? Converting letters in a string to the same case makes comparing two strings easier. For example, say you created a quiz program like the one from Chapter 3 (see page 108) and one of the questions is, "Who was the first American to win the Tour De France?" You might have some code like this to check the quiz-taker's answer:

```
var correctAnswer = 'Greg LeMond';
var response = prompt('Who was the first American to win the Tour De⏎
France?', '');
if (response == correctAnswer) {
  // correct
} else {
  // incorrect
}
```

The answer is Greg LeMond, but what if the person taking the quiz typed *Greg Le-mond*? The condition would look like this: *'Greg Lemond' == 'Greg LeMond'*. Since JavaScript treats uppercase letters as different than lowercase letters, the lowercase 'm' in Lemond wouldn't match the 'M' in LeMond, so the quiz-taker would have gotten this question wrong. The same would happen if her caps lock key was down and she typed GREG LEMOND.

To get around this difficulty, you can convert both strings to the same case and then compare them:

```
if (response.toUpperCase() == correctAnswer.toUpperCase()) {
  // correct
} else {
  // incorrect
}
```

In this case, the conditional statement converts both the quiz-taker's answer and the correct answer to uppercase, so *'Greg Lemond'* becomes *'GREG LEMOND' and 'Greg LeMond'* becomes *'GREG LEMOND'*.

To get the string all lowercase, use the *toLowerCase()* method like this:

```
var answer = 'Greg LeMond';
alert(answer.toLowerCase()); // 'greg lemond'
```

Note that neither of these methods actually alters the original string stored in the variable—they just return that string in either all uppercase or all lowercase. So in the above example, *answer* still contains *'Greg LeMond'* even after the alert appears. (In other words, these methods work just like a function that returns some other value as described on page 104.)

Searching a String: *indexOf()* Technique

JavaScript provides several techniques for searching for a word, number, or other series of characters inside a string. Searching can come in handy, for example, if you want to know which web browser a visitor is using to view your website. Every web browser identifies information about itself in a string containing a lot of different statistics. You can see that string for yourself by adding this bit of JavaScript to a page and previewing it in a web browser:

```
<script>
alert(navigator.userAgent);
</script>
```

Navigator is one of a web browser's objects, and *userAgent* is a property of the navigator object. The *userAgent* property contains a long string of information; for example, on Internet Explorer 7 running on Windows XP, the *userAgent* property is: Mozilla/4.0 (compatible; MSIE 7.0; Windows NT 5.1). So, if you want to see if the Web browser was IE 7, you can just search the *userAgent* string for "MSIE 7".

One method of searching a string is the *indexOf()* method. Basically, after the string you add a period, *indexOf()*, and supply the string you're looking for. The basic structure looks like this:

```
string.indexOf('string to look for')
```

The *indexOf()* method returns a number: If the search string isn't found, the method returns –1. So if you want to check for Internet Explorer, you can do this:

```
var browser = navigator.userAgent; // this is a string
if (browser.indexOf('MSIE') != -1) {
  // this is Internet Explorer
}
```

In this case, if *indexOf()* doesn't locate the string *'MSIE'* in the *userAgent* string, it will return –1, so the condition tests to see if the result is not (*!=*) –1.

When the *indexOf()* method *does* find the searched-for string, it returns a number that's equal to the starting position of the searched-for string. The following example makes things a lot clearer:

```
var quote = 'To be, or not to be.'
var searchPosition = quote.indexOf('To be'); // returns 0
```

Here, *indexOf()* searches for the position of *'To be'* inside the string *'To be, or not to be.'* The larger string begins with *'To be'*, so *indexOf()* finds *'To be'* at the first position. But in the wacky way of programming, the first position is considered 0, the second letter (o) is at position 1, and the third letter (a space in this case) is 2 (as explained on page 62, arrays are counted in the same way).

The *indexOf()* method searches from the beginning of the string. You can also search from the end of the string by using the *lastIndexOf()* method. For example, in the Shakespeare quote, the word 'be' appears in two places, so you can locate the first *'be'* using *indexOf()* and the last 'be' with *lastIndexOf()*:

```
var quote = "To be, or not to be."
var firstPosition = quote.indexOf('be'); // returns 3
var lastPosition = quote.lastIndexOf('be'); // returns 17
```

The results of those two methods are pictured in Figure 14-1. In both cases, if *'be'* didn't exist anywhere in the string, the result would be –1, and if there's only one instance of the searched-for word, *indexOf()* and *lastIndexOf()* will return the same value—the starting position of the searched-for string within the larger string.

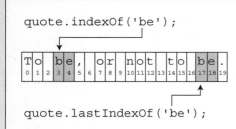

Figure 14-1:
The indexOf() *and* lastIndexOf() *methods search for a particular string inside a larger string. If the search string is found, its position in the larger string is returned.*

Extracting Part of a String with *slice()*

To extract part of a string, use the *slice()* method. This method returns a portion of a string. For example, say you had a string like *http://www.sawmac.com* and you wanted to eliminate the http:// part. One way to do this is to extract every character in the string that follows the http:// like this:

```
var url = 'http://www.sawmac.com';
var domain = url.slice(7); // www.sawmac.com
```

The *slice()* method requires a *number* that indicates the starting *index* position for the extracted string (see Figure 14-2). In this example—*url.slice(7)*—the 7 indicates the eighth letter in the string (remember, the first letter is at position 0). The method returns all of the characters starting at the specified index position to the end of the string.

Figure 14-2:
If you don't supply a second argument to the slice() method, it just extracts a string from the specified position (7 in this example) all the way to the end of the string.

You can also extract a specific number of characters within a string by supplying a second argument to the *slice()* method. Here's the basic structure of the *slice()* method:

```
string.slice(start, end);
```

The *start* value is a number that indicates the first character of the extracted string. The end *value* is a little confusing—it's not the position of the last letter of the extracted string; it's actually the position of the last letter + 1. For example, if you wanted to extract the first five letters of the string 'To be, or not to be', you would specify 0 as the first argument, and 5 as the second argument. As you can see in Figure 14-3, 0 is the first letter in the string, and 5 is the sixth letter, but the last letter specified is not extracted from the string. In other words, the character specified by the second argument is *never* part of the extracted string.

Tip: If you want to extract a specific number of characters from a string, just add that number to the starting value. For example, if you want to retrieve the first 10 letters of a string, the first argument would be 0 (the first letter) and the last would be 0 + 10 or just 10: *slice(0,10)*.

You can also specify negative numbers; for example, *quote.slice(-6,-1)*. A negative number counts backwards from the end of the string, as pictured in Figure 14-3.

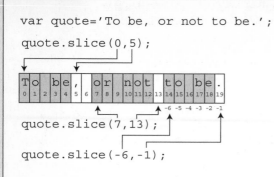

```
var quote='To be, or not to be.';

quote.slice(0,5);
```

Figure 14-3:
*The slice() method extracts a portion of a string. The
actual string is not changed in any way. For instance,
the string contained in the quote variable in this
example isn't changed by quote.slice(0,5). The method
simply returns the extracted string, which you can store
inside a variable, display in an alert box, or even pass
as an argument to a function.*

```
quote.slice(7,13);

quote.slice(-6,-1);
```

Tip: If you want, say, to extract a string that includes all of the letters from the 6th letter from the end of
the string all the way to the end, you leave off the second argument:

```
quote.slice(-6);
```

Finding Patterns in Strings

Sometimes you wish to search a string, not for an exact value, but for a specific pattern of characters. For example, say you want to make sure when a visitor fills out an order form, he supplies a phone number in the correct format. You're not actually looking for a specific phone number like 503-555-0212. Instead, you're looking for a general pattern: three numbers, a hyphen, three numbers, another hyphen, and four numbers. You'd like to check the value the visitor entered, and if it matches the pattern (for example, it's 415-555-3843, 408-555-3782, or 212-555-4828, and so on), then everything's OK. But if it doesn't match that pattern (for example, the visitor typed *823lkjxdfglkj*), then you'd like to post a message like "Hey buddy, don't try to fool us!"

JavaScript lets you use *regular expressions* to find patterns within a string. A regular expression is a series of characters that define a pattern that you wish to search for. As with many programming terms, the name "regular expression" is a bit misleading. For example, here's what a common regular expression looks like:

```
/^[-\w.]+@([a-zA-Z0-9][-a-zA-Z0-9]+\.)+[a-zA-Z]{2,4}$/
```

Unless you're a super-alien from Omicron 9, there's nothing very *regular*-looking about a regular expression. To create a pattern, you use characters like *, +, ?, and \w, which are translated by the JavaScript interpreter to match real characters in a string like letters, numbers, and so on.

Note: Pros often shorten the name regular expression to *regex*.

Creating and Using a Basic Regular Expression

To create a regular expression in JavaScript, you must create a regular expression object, which is a series of characters between two forward slashes. For example, to create a regular expression that matches the word "hello", you'd type this:

```
var myMatch = /hello/;
```

Just as an opening and closing quote mark creates a string, the opening / and closing / create a regular expression.

There are several string methods that take advantage of regular expressions (you'll learn about them starting on page 441), but the most basic method is the *search()* method. It works very much like the *indexOf()* method, but instead of trying to find one string inside another, larger string, it searches for a pattern (a regular expression) inside a string. For example, say you want to find '*To be*' inside the string '*To be or not to be.*' You saw how to do that with the *indexOf()* method on page 427, but here's how you can do the same thing with a regular expression:

```
var myRegEx = /To be/; // no quotes around regular expression
var quote = 'To be or not to be.';
var foundPosition = quote.search(myRegEx);  // returns 0
```

If the *search()* method finds a match, it returns the position of the first letter matched, and if it doesn't find a match, it returns –1. So in the above example, the variable *foundPosition* is 0, since 'To be' begins at the very beginning (the first letter) of the string.

As you'll recall from page 427, the *indexOf()* method works in the same way. You might be thinking that if the two methods are the same, why bother with regular expressions? The benefit of regular expressions is that they can find patterns in a string, so they can make much more complicated and subtle comparisons than the *indexOf()* method, which always looks for a match to an exact string. For example, you could use the *indexOf()* method to find out if a string contains the Web address *http://www. missingmanuals.com/*, but you'd have to use a regular expression to find any text that matches the format of a URL—exactly the kind of thing you want to do when verifying if someone supplied a Web address when posting a comment to your blog.

However, to master regular expressions, you need to learn the often confusing symbols required to construct a regular expression.

Building a Regular Expression

While a regular expression can be made up of a word or words, more often you'll use a combination of letters and special symbols to define a pattern that you hope to match. Regular expressions provide different symbols to indicate different types of characters. For example, a single period (.) represents a single character, any character, while \w matches any letter or number (but not spaces, or symbols like $ or %). Table 14-1 provides a list of the most common pattern-matching characters.

Note: If this entire discussion of "regular" expressions is making your head hurt, you'll be glad to know this book provides some useful regular expressions (see page 436) that you can copy and use in your own scripts (without really knowing how they work).

Table 14-1. Common pattern-matching symbols for regular expressions

Character	Matches
.	Any one character—will match a letter, number, space, or other symbol.
\w	Any word character including a–z, A–Z, the numbers 0–9, and the underscore character: _.
\W	Any character that's not a word character. It's the exact opposite of \w.
\d	Any digit 0–9.
\D	Any character except a digit. The opposite of \d.
\s	A space, tab, carriage return, or new line.
\S	Anything but a space, tab, carriage return, or new line.
^	The beginning of a string. This is useful for making sure no other characters come before whatever you're trying to match.
$	The end of a string. Use $ to make sure the characters you wish to match are at the end of a string. For example, /com$/ matches the string "com", but only when it's the last three letters of the string. In other words, /com$/ would match "com" in the string "Infocom", but not 'com' in 'communication'.
\b	A space, beginning of the string, end of string, or any nonletter or number character such as +, =, or '. Use \b to match the beginning or ending of a word, even if that word is at the beginning or ending of a string.
[]	Any one character between the brackets. For example, [aeiou] matches any one of those letters in a string. For a range of characters, use a hyphen: [a-z] matches any one lower case letter; [0-9] matches any one number (the same as \d).
[^]	Any character except one in brackets. For example, [^aeiouAEIOU] will match any character that isn't a vowel. [^0-9] matches any character that's not a number (the same as \D).

Character	Matches
|	Either the characters before or after the | character. For example, a|b will match either *a* or *b*, but not both. (See page 440 for an example of this symbol in action.)
\	Used to escape any special regex symbol (*,.,\/, for instance) to search for a literal example of the symbol in a string. For example, . in regex-speak means "any character," but if you want to really match a period in a string you need to escape it, like this: \..

Learning regular expressions is a topic better presented by example, so the rest of this section walks you through a few examples of regular expressions to help you wrap your mind around this topic. Assume you want to match five numbers in a row—perhaps to check if there's a U. S. Zip code in a string:

1. **Match one number.**

   The first step is simply to figure out how to match one number. If you refer to Table 15-1, you'll see that there's a special regex symbol for this, \d, which matches any single number.

2. **Match five numbers in a row.**

   Since \d matches a single number, a simple way to match five numbers is with this regular expression: \d\d\d\d\d. (Page 435, however, covers a more compact way to write this.)

3. **Match only five numbers.**

   A regular expression is like a precision-guided missile: It sets its target on the first part of a string that it matches. So, you sometimes end up with a match that's part of a complete word or set of characters. This regular expression matches the first five numbers in a row that it encounters. For example, it will match 12345 in the number 12345678998. Obviously, 12345678998 isn't a Zip code, so you need a regex that targets just five numbers.

   The \b character (called the *word boundary* character) matches any nonletter or non-number character, so you could rewrite your regular expression like this: \b\d\d\d\d\d\b. You can also use the ^ character to match the beginning of a string and the $ character to match the end of a string. This trick comes in handy if you want the entire string to match your regular expression. For example, if someone typed "kjasdflkjsdf 88888 lksadflkjsdkfjl" in a Zip code field on an order form, you might want to ask the visitor to clarify (and fix) her Zip code before ordering. After all, you're really looking for something like 97213 (with no other characters in the string). In this case, the regex would be ^\d\d\d\d\d$.

Note: Zip codes can have more than five numbers. The ZIP + 4 format includes a dash and four additional numbers after the first five, like this: 97213-1234. For a regular expression to handle this possibility, see page 436.

---

4. **Put your regex into action in JavaScript.**

Assume you've already captured a user's input into a variable named *zip*, and you want to test to see if the input is in the form of a valid five-number Zip code:

```
var zipTest = /^\d\d\d\d\d$/; //create regex
if (zip.search(zipTest) == -1) {
  alert('This is not a valid zip code');
} else {
  // is valid format
}
```

The regex example in these steps works, but it seems like a lot of work to type \d five times. What if you want to match 100 numbers in a row? Fortunately, JavaScript includes several symbols that can match multiple occurrences of the same character. Table 15-2 includes a list of these symbols. You place the symbol directly *after* the character you wish to match.

For example, to match five numbers, you can write *\d{5}*. The *\d* matches one number, then the *{5}* tells the JavaScript interpreter to match five numbers. So *\d{100}* would match 100 digits in a row.

Let's go through another example. Say you wanted to find the name of any GIF file in a string. In addition, you want to extract the file name and perhaps use it somehow in your script (for example, you can use the *match()* method described on page 441). In other words, you want to find any string that matches the basic pattern of a GIF file name, such as *logo.gif, banner.gif,* or *ad.gif*.

1. **Identify the common pattern between these names.**

To build a regular expression, you first need to know what pattern of characters you're searching for. Here, since you're after GIFs, you know all the file names will end in *.gif*. In other words, there can be any number of letters or numbers or other characters before *.gif*.

2. **Find .gif.**

Since you're after the literal string '*.gif*', you might think that part of the regular expression would just be *.gif*. However, if you check out Table 4-3, you'll see that a period has special meaning as a "match any character" character. So *.gif* would match ".gif," but it would also match "tgif." A period matches any single character so in addition to matching a period, it will also match the "t" in tgif. To create a regex with a literal period, add a slash before it; so \. translates to "find me the period symbol." So the regex to find *.gif* would be \.*gif*.

3. **Find any number of characters before .gif.**

To find any number of characters, you can use .*, which translates to "find one character (.) zero or more times (*)." That regular expression matches all of the letters in any string. However, if you used that to create a regular expression like .*\.*gif*, you could end up matching more than just a file name. For example, if you have the string 'the file is logo.gif', the regex .*\.*gif* will match the entire

string, when what you really want is just *logo.gif*. To do that, use the \S character, which matches any nonspace character: \S*\.gif matches just *logo.gif* in the
string.

4. **Make the search case-insensitive.**

   There's one more wrinkle in this regular expression: It only finds files that end
   in *.gif*, but *.GIF* is also a valid file extension, so this regex wouldn't pick up on a
   name like *logo.GIF*. To make a regular expression ignore the difference between
   upper and lowercase letters, you use the *i* argument when you create the regular
   expression:

   ```
   /\S*\.gif/i
   ```

   Notice that the *i* goes outside of the pattern and to the right of the / that defines
   the end of the regular expression pattern.

5. **Put it into action:**

   ```
   var testString = 'The file is logo.gif'; // the string to test
   var gifRegex = /\S*\.gif/i; // the regular expression
   var results = testString.match(gifRegex);
   var file = results[0]; // logo.gif
   ```

   This code pulls out the file name from the string. (You'll learn how the *match()*
   method works on page 441.)

Grouping Parts of a Pattern

You can use parentheses to create a subgroup within a pattern. Subgroups come in
very handy when using any of the characters in Table 14-2 to match multiple instances of the same pattern.

Table 14-2. *Characters used for matching multiple occurrences of the same character or pattern*

Character	Matches
?	Zero or one occurrences of the previous item, meaning the previous item is optional, but if it does appear, it can only appear once. For example, the regex *colou?r* will match both "color" and "colour", but not "colouur".
+	One or more occurrences of the previous item. The previous item must ap-pear at least once.
*	Zero or more occurrences of the previous item. The previous item is optional and may appear any number of times. For example, .* matches any number of characters.
{n}	An exact number of occurrences of the previous item. For example, \d{3} only matches three numbers in a row.
{n, }	The previous item *n* or more times. For example, a{2,} will match the letter "a" two or more times, which would match "aa" in the word "aardvark" and "aaaa" in the word "aaaahhhh".
{n,m}	The previous item at least *n* times but no more than *m* times. So \d{3,4} will match three or four numbers in a row (but not two numbers in a row, nor five numbers in a row).

For example, say you want to see if a string contains either "Apr" or "April"—both of those begin with "Apr", so you know that you want to match that, but you can't just match "Apr", since you'd also match the "Apr" in "Apricot" or "Aprimecorp." So, you must match "Apr" followed by a space or other word ending (that's the \b regular expression character described in Table 15-1) or April followed by a word ending. In other words, the "il" is optional. Here's how you could do that using parentheses:

```
var sentence = 'April is the cruelest month.';
var aprMatch = /Apr(il)?\b/;
if (sentence.search(aprMatch) != -1) {
  // found Apr or April
} else {
  //not found
}
```

The regular expression used here—/Apr(il)?\b/—makes the "Apr" required, but the subpattern—(il)—optional (that ? character means zero or one time). Finally, the \b matches the end of a word, so you won't match "Apricot" or "Aprilshowers." (See the box on page 444 for another use of subpatterns.)

Tip: You can find a complete library of regular expressions at *www.regexlib.com*. At this website, you'll find a regular expression for any situation.

Useful Regular Expressions

Creating a regular expression has its challenges. Not only do you need to understand how the different regular expression characters work, but you then must figure out the proper pattern for different possible searches. For example, if you want to find a match for a Zip code, you need to take into account the fact that a Zip code may be just five numbers (97213) or 5+4 (97213-3333). To get you started on the path to using regular expressions, here are a few common ones.

Note: If you don't feel like typing these regular expressions (and who could blame you), you'll find them already set up for you in a file named *example_regex.txt* in the *chapter14* folder that's part of the tutorial download. (See page 29 for information on downloading the tutorial files.)

U.S. Zip code

Postal codes vary from country to country, but in the United States they appear as either five numbers, or five numbers followed by a hyphen and four numbers. Here's the regex that matches both those options:

```
\d{5}(-\d{4})?
```

Note: For regular expressions that match the postal codes of other countries, visit *http://regexlib.com/Search.aspx?k=postal+code*.

That regular expression breaks down into the following smaller pieces:

- *\d{5}* matches five digits, as in 97213.

- *()* creates a subpattern. Everything between the parentheses is considered a single pattern to be matched. You'll see why that's important in a moment.

- *-\d{4}* matches the hyphen followed by four digits, like this: -1234.

- *?* matches zero or one instance of the preceding pattern. Here's where the parentheses come in: *(-\d{4})* is treated as a single unit, so the *?* means match zero or one instance of a hyphen followed by four digits. Because you don't have to include the hyphen + four, that pattern might appear zero times. In other words, if you're testing a value like 97213, you'll still get a match because the hyphen followed by four digits is optional.

Note: To make sure an entire string matches a regular expression, begin the regex with ^ and end it with $. For example, if you want to make sure that someone only typed a validly formatted Zip code into a Zip code form field, use the regex ^\d{5}(-\d{4})?$. to prevent a response like "blah 97213 blah blah."

U.S. phone number

U.S. phone numbers have a three-digit area code followed by seven more digits. However, people write phone numbers in many different ways, like 503-555-1212, (503) 555-1212, 503.555.1212, or just 503 555 1212. A regex for this pattern is:

```
\(?(\d{3})\)?[ -.](\d{3})[ -.](\d{4})
```

Note: For regular expressions that match the phone number format of other countries, visit *http://regexlib.com/Search.aspx?k=phone+number*.

This regex looks pretty complicated, but if you break it down (and have a good translation like the following), it comes out making sense:

- *\(* matches a literal opening parenthesis character. Because parentheses are used to group patterns (see the previous Zip code example), the opening parentheses has special meaning in regular expressions. To tell the JavaScript interpreter to match an actual opening parenthesis, you need to escape the character (just like escaping the quotes discussed on page 44) with the forward slash character.

- *?* indicates that the (character is optional, so a phone number without parentheses like 503-555-1212 will still match.

- *(\d{3})* is a subpattern that matches any three digits.

- \)? matches an optional closing parenthesis.

- [-.] will match either a space, hyphen, or period. (Note that normally you have to escape a period like this \. in order to tell the JavaScript interpreter that you want to match the period character and not treat it as the special regular expression symbol that matches *any* character; however, when inside brackets, a period is always treated literally.)

- (\d{3}) is another subpattern that matches any three digits.

- [-.] will match either a space, hyphen, or period.

- (\d{4}) is the last subpattern, and it matches any four digits.

Note: Subpatterns are patterns that appear inside parentheses, as in *(\d{3})* in the phone number regular expression above. They come in very handy when you use the *replace()*, method as described in the box on page 444.

Email address

Checking for a valid email address is a common chore when accepting user input from a form. A lot of people try to get away without trying to provide a valid email using a response like "none of your business," or people just mistype their email address (*missing@sawmac.commmm*, for example). The following regex can check to see if a string contains a properly formatted email address:

```
[-\w.]+@([A-z0-9][-A-z0-9]+\.)+[A-z]{2,4}
```

Note: This regex doesn't check to see if an address is somebody's real, working email address; it just checks that it's *formatted* like a real email address.

This regex breaks down like this:

- *[-\w.]+* matches a hyphen, any word character, or a period one or more times. So it will match "bob," "bob.smith," or "bob-smith."

- *@* is the @ sign you find in an email address: *missing@sawmac.com*.

- *[A-z0-9]* matches one letter or number.

- *[-A-z0-9]+* matches one or more instances of a letter, number, or hyphen.

- *\.* is a period character, so it would match the period in sawmac.com (*http://www.sawmac.com*).

- *+* matches one or more instances of the pattern that includes the above three matches. This character allows for subdomain names like *bob@mail.sawmac.com*.

- *[A-z]{2,4}* is any letter 2, 3, or 4 times. This matches the com in .com, or uk in .uk.

Note: The email regex listed above doesn't match *all* technically valid email addresses. For example, *!#$%&'*+-/=?^_`.{|}~@example.com* is technically a valid email address, but the regex described here won't match it. It's designed to find email addresses that people would actually use. If you really want to be accurate, you can use the following regex. Type this expression on a single line:

```
/^[\w!#$%&\'*+\/=?^`{|}~.-]+@(?:[a-z\d][a-z\d-]*(?:\.[a-z\d][a-z\d-]*)?)+\.(?:[a-z]
[a-z\d-]+)$/i
```

Date

A date can be written in many different ways; for example, 09/28/2008, 9-28-2007, 09 28 2007, or even 09.28.2007. (And those are just formats for the United States. In other parts of the world, the day appears before the month, like 28.09.2007.) Because your visitors may enter a date in any one of these formats, you need a way to check to see if they supplied a validly formatted date. (In the box on page 453, you'll learn how to convert any of these formats into a single, standard format, so that you can make sure all the dates you receive on a form are formatted correctly.)

Here's the regex that checks for a correctly entered date:

```
([01]?\d)[-\/ .]([0123]?\d)[-\/ .](\d{4})
```

- () surrounds the next two regex patterns to group them. Together they form the number for the month.

- *[01]?* matches either 0 or 1 and the ? makes this optional. This is for the first number in a month. Obviously it can't be bigger than 1—there's no 22 month. In addition, if the month is January through September, you might just get 5 instead of 05. That's why it's optional.

- \d matches any number.

- *[-\/ .]* will match a hyphen, a forward slash, a period, or a space character. These are the acceptable separators between the month and day, like 10/21, 10 21, 10.21, or 10-21.

- () is the next subpattern, which is meant to capture the day of the month.

- *[0123]?* matches either 0, 1, 2, or 3 zero or more times. Since there's no 40th day of the month, you limit the first number of the month to one of these four digits. This pattern is optional (as determined by the ? character), because someone might just type 9 instead of 09 for the ninth day of the month.

- \d matches any digit.

- [-\/ .] is the same as above.

- () captures the year.

- \d{4} matches any four digits, like 1908 or 2880.

Web address

Matching a web address is useful if you're asking a visitor for his website address and you want to make sure he's supplied one, or if you want to scan some text and identify every URL listed. A basic regular expression for URLs is:

```
((\bhttps?:\/\/)|(\bwww\.))\S*
```

This expression is a little tricky because it uses lots of parentheses to group different parts of the expression. Figure 14-4 can help guide you through this regular expression. One set of parentheses (labeled 1) wraps around two other parenthetical groups (2 and 3). The | character between the two groups represents "or". In other words, the regular expression needs to match either 2 or 3.

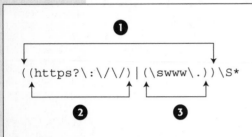

Figure 14-4:
You can group expressions using parentheses and look for either one of two expressions by using the | (pipe) character. For example, the outer expression (1) will match any text that matches either 2 or 3.

- (is the start of the outer group (1 in Figure 14-4).

- (is the start of inner group (2 in Figure 14-4).

- *b* matches the beginning of a word.

- *http* matches the beginning of a complete web address that begins with *http*.

- *s?* is an optional *s*. Since a web page may be sent via a secure connection, a valid web address may also begin with *https*.

- :\\/\\/ matches ://. Since the forward slash has meaning in regular expressions, you need to precede it by a backslash to match the forward slash character.

-) is the end of the inner group (2 in Figure 14-4). Taken together, this group will match either *http://* or *https://*.

- | matches either one or the other group (2 or 3 in Figure 14-4).

- (is the start of second inner group (3 in Figure 14-4).

- *b* matches the beginning of a word.

- *www\\.* matches *www..*

-) is the end of the second inner group (3 in Figure 14-4). This group will capture a URL that is missing the *http://* but begins with *www*.

-) is the end of the outer group (1 in Figure 14-4). At this point, the regular expression will match text that begins with *http://*, *https://*, or *www*.

- *\\S** matches zero or more nonspace characters.

This expression isn't foolproof (for example, it would match a nonsensical URL like *http://#$*%&*@**), but it's relatively simple, and will successfully match real URLs like *http://www.sawmac.com/missing/js/index.html*.

Tip: To see if a string only contains a URL (nothing comes before or after the URL), use the ^ and $ characters at the beginning and end of the regular expression and remove the |b characters: *^((https?:\/\/)|(www\.))\S*$*.

Matching a Pattern

The *search()* method described on page 431 is one way to see if a string contains a particular regular expression pattern. The *match()* method is another. You can use it with a string to not only see if a pattern exists within the string, but to also capture that pattern so that you can use it later in your script. For example, say you have a text area field on a form for a visitor to add a comment to your site. Perhaps you want to check if the comments include a URL, and if so, get the URL for further processing.

The following code finds and captures a URL using *match()*:

```
// get the contents of the text area
var text='my website is www.missingmanuals.com';
// create a regular expression
var urlRegex = /((\bhttps?:\/\/)|(\bwww\.))\S*/
// find a match for the regular expression in the string
var url = text.match(urlRegex);
alert(url[0]); // www.missingmanuals.com
```

First, the code creates a variable containing a string that includes the URL *www.missingmanuals.com*. This variable is just for test purposes here (so you can see what the *match()* method does. If you actually wanted to test the contents of a text area on a form, you could use code like this:

```
var text = $('#comments').val() ;
```

Next, the code creates a regular expression to match a URL (see page 440 for the details on this regex). Finally, it runs the *match()* method on the string. The *match()* function is a string method, so you start with the name of a variable containing a string, add a period, followed by *match()*. You pass the *match()* method a regular expression to match.

In the above example, the variable *url* holds the results of the match. If the regular expression pattern isn't found in the string, then the result is a special JavaScript value called *null*. If there is a match, the script returns an array—the first value of the array is the matched text. For instance, in this example, the variable *url* contains an array, with the first array element being the matched text. In this case, *url[0]* contains *www.missingmanuals.com* (see page 59 for more on arrays).

Note: In JavaScript, a *null* value is treated the same as false, so you could test to see if the *match()* method actually matched something like this:

```
var url = text.match(urlRegex);
if (! url) {
  //no match
} else {
  //match
}
```

Matching every instance of a pattern

The *match()* method works in two different ways, depending on how you've set up your regular expression. In the above example, the method returns an array with the first matched text. So, if you had a long string containing multiple URLs, only the first URL is found. However, you can also turn on a regular expression's *global* search property to search for more than one match in a string.

You make a search global by adding a *g* at the end of a regular expression when you create it (just like the *i* used for a case-insensitive search, as discussed on page 435):

```
var urlRegex = /((\bhttps?:\/\/)|(\bwww\.))\S*/g
```

Notice that the *g* goes outside of the ending / (which is used to enclose the actual pattern). This regular expression performs a global search; when used with the *match()* method, it searches for every match within the string and will return an array of all matched text—a great way to find every URL in a blog entry, for example, or every instance of a word in a long block of text.

You could rewrite the code from page 441 using a global search, like this:

```
// create a variable containing a string with a URL
var text='there are a lot of great websites like ⏎
        www.missingmanuals.com and http://www.oreilly.com';
// create a regular expression with global search
var urlRegex = /((\bhttps?:\/\/)|(\bwww\.))\S*/g
// find a match for the regular expression in the string
var url = text.match(urlRegex);
alert(url[0]); // www.missingmanuals.com
alert(url[1]); // http://www.oreilly.com
```

You can determine the number of matches by accessing the *length* property of the resulting array: *url.length*. This example will return the number 2, since two URLs were found in the tested string. In addition, you access each matched string by using the array's index number (as described on page 62); so in this example, *url[0]* is the first match and *url[1]* is the second.

Replacing Text

You can also use regular expressions to replace text within a string. For example, say you have a string that contains a date formatted like this: 10.28.2008. However, you want the date to be formatted like this: 10/28/2008. The *replace()* method can do that. It takes this form:

```
string.replace(regex,'replace');
```

The *replace()* method takes two arguments: The first is a regular expression that you wish to find in the string; the second is a string that replaces any matches to the regular expression. So, to change the format of 10.28.2008 to 10/28/2008, you could do this:

```
1   var date='10.28.2008'; // a string
2   var replaceRegex = /\./g // a regular expression
3   var date = date.replace(replaceRegex, '/'); // replace . with /
4   alert(date); // 10/28/2008
```

Line 1 creates a variable and stores the string '*10.28.2008*' in it. In a real program, this string could be input from a form. Line 2 creates the regular expression: The / and / mark the beginning and end of the regular expression pattern; the \. indicates a literal period; and the *g* means a global replace—every instance of the period will be replaced. If you left out the *g*, only the first matched period would be replaced, and you'd end up with '*10 /28.2008*'. Line 3 performs the actual replacement—changing each . to a /, and stores the result back into the date variable. Finally the newly formed date—10/28/2008—is displayed in an alert box.

Using Subpatterns to Replace Text

The *replace()* method not only can replace matched text (like the . in 10.28.2008) with another string (like /), but it can also remember *subpatterns* within a regular expression and use those subpatterns when replacing text. As explained in the Note on page 438, a subpattern is any part of a regular expression enclosed in parentheses. For example, the *(il)* in the regular expression */Apr(il)?\b/* is a subpattern.

The use of the *replace()* method demonstrated on page 443 changes 10.28.2008 to 10/27/2008. But what if you also want to put other formatted dates like 10 28 2008 or 10-28-2008 into the same 10/27/2008 format? Instead of writing multiple lines of JavaScript code to replace periods, spaces, and hyphens, you can create a general pattern to match any of these formats:

```
var date='10-28-2008';
```

```
var regex = /([01]?\d)[-\/ .]([0123]?\d)
[-\/ .](\d{4})/;

date = date.replace(regex, '$1/$2/$3');
```

This example uses the regular expression described on page 439 to match a date. Notice the groups of patterns within parentheses—for example, *([01]?\d)*. Each subpattern matches one part of the date. The *replace()* method remembers matches to those subpatterns, and can use them as part of the replacement string. In this case, the replacement string is *'$1/$2/$3'*. A dollar sign followed by a number represents one of the matched subpatterns. $1, for example, matches the first subpattern—the month. So this replacement string translates to "put the first subpattern here, followed by a /, followed by the second subpattern match, followed by another /, and finally followed by the last subpattern."

Trying Out Regular Expressions

You'll find sample regular expressions in the *example_regex.txt* file that accompanies the tutorial files. In addition, you'll find a file named *regex_tester.html* in the testbed folder. You can open this web page in a browser and try your hand at creating your own regular expressions (see Figure 14-5). Just type the string you'd like to search in the "String to Search" box, and then type a regular expression in the box (leave out the beginning and ending / marks used when creating a regex in JavaScript and just type the search pattern). You can then select the method you'd like to use—Search, Match, or Replace—and any options, like case-insensitivity or global search. Click the Run button and see how your regex works.

JavaScript & jQuery: The Missing Manual, by David McFarland. Published by O'Reilly Media, Inc.

Figure 14-5:
This sample page, included with the tutorial files, lets you test out regular expressions using different methods–like Search or Match–and try different options such as case-insensitive or global searches.

Working with Numbers

Numbers are an important part of programming. They let you perform tasks like calculating a total sales cost, determining the distance between two points, or simulating the roll of a die by generating a random number from 1 to 6. JavaScript gives you many different ways of working with numbers.

Changing a String to a Number

When you create a variable, you can store a number in it like this:

```
var a = 3.25;
```

However, there are times when a number is actually a string. For example, if you use the *prompt()* method (page 57) to get visitor input, even if someone types 3.25, you'll end up with a string that contains a number. In other words, the result will be '*3.25*' (a string) and not 3.25 (a number). Frequently, this method doesn't cause a problem, since the JavaScript interpreter usually converts a string to a number when it seems like a number is called for. For example:

```
var a = '3';
var b = '4';
alert(a*b); // 12
```

In this example, even though the variables *a* and *b* are both strings, the JavaScript interpreter converts them to numbers to perform the multiplication (3 x 4) and return the result: 12.

However, when you use the + operator, the JavaScript interpreter won't make that conversion, and you can end up with some strange results:

```
var a = '3';
var b = '4';
alert(a+b); // 34
```

In this case, both *a* and *b* are strings; the + operator not only does mathematical addition, it also combines (concatenates) two strings together (see page 51). So instead of adding 3 and 4 to get 7, in this example, you end up with two strings fused together: 34.

When you need to convert a string to a number, JavaScript provides several ways:

- *Number()* converts whatever string is passed to it into a number, like this:

```
var a = '3';
a = Number(a); // a is now the number 3
```

So the problem of adding two strings that contain numbers could be fixed like this:

```
var a = '3';
var b = '4';
var total = Number(a) + Number(b); // 7
```

A faster technique is the + operator, which does the same thing as *Number()*. Just add a + in front of a variable containing a string, and the JavaScript interpreter converts the string to a number.

```
var a = '3';
var b = '4';
var total = +a + +b // 7
```

The downside of either of these two techniques is that if the string contains anything except numbers, a single period, or a + or – sign at the beginning of the string, you'll end up with a non-number, or the JavaScript value *NaN*, which means "not a number" (see the next page).

- *parseInt()* tries to convert a string to a number as well. However, unlike *Number()*, *parseInt()* will try to change even a string with letters to a number, as long as the string begins with numbers. This command can come in handy when you get a string like '20 years' as the response to a question about someone's age:

```
var age = '20 years';
age = parseInt(age,10); //20
```

The *parseInt()* method looks for either a number or a + or – sign at the beginning of the string and continues to look for numbers until it encounters a non-number. So in the above example, it returns the number 20 and ignores the other part of the string, ' *years*'.

Note: You're probably wondering what the 10 is doing in *parseInt(age,10);*. JavaScript can handle Octal numbers (which are based on 8 different digits 0-7, unlike decimal numbers which are based on 10 different digits 0-9); when you add the, *10* to *parseInt()*, you're telling the JavaScript interpreter to treat whatever the input is as a decimal number. That way, JavaScript correctly interprets a string like '08' in a prompt window or form field—decimally. For example, in this code *age* would be equal to 0:

```
var age = '08 years';
age = parseInt(age);
```

However, in the following code the variable *age* would hold the value 8:

```
var age = '08 years';
age = parseInt(age,10);
```

In other words, always add the *,10* when using the *parseInt()* method.

- *parseFloat()* is like *parseInt()*, but you use it when a string might contain a decimal point. For example, if you have a string like '*4.5 acres*', you can use *parseFloat()* to retrieve the entire value including decimal places:

```
var space = '4.5 acres';
space = parseFloat(space); // 4.5
```

If you used *parseInt()* for the above example, you'd end up with just the number 4, since *parseInt()* only tries to retrieve whole numbers (integers).

Which of the above methods you use depends on the situation: If your goal is to add two numbers, but they're strings, then use *Number()* or + operator. However, if you want to extract a number from a string that might include letters, like '*200px*' or '*1.5em*', then use *parseInt()* to capture whole numbers (200, for example) or *parseFloat()* to capture numbers with decimals (1.5, for example).

Testing for Numbers

When using JavaScript to manipulate user input, you often need to verify that the information supplied by the visitor is of the correct type. For example, if you ask for people's years of birth, you want to make sure they supply a number. Likewise, when you're performing a mathematical calculation, if the data you use for the calculation isn't a number, then your script might break.

To verify that a string is a number, use the *isNaN()* method. This method takes a string as an argument and tests whether the string is "not a number." If the string contains anything except a plus or minus (for positive and negative numbers) followed by numbers and an optional decimal value, it's considered "not a number," so the string '*-23.25*' is a number, but the string '*24 pixels*' is not. This method returns either *true* (if the string is not a number) or *false* (if it is a number). You can use *isNaN()* as part of a conditional statement like this:

```
var x = '10'; // is a number
if (isNaN(x)) {
  // won't run because x IS a number
} else {
  // will run because x is a number
}
```

Rounding Numbers

JavaScript provides a way to round a fractional number to an integer—for example, rounding 4.5 up to 5. Rounding comes in handy when you're performing a calculation that must result in a whole number. For example, say you're using JavaScript to dynamically set a pixel height of a <div> tag on the page based on the height of the browser window. In other words, the height of the <div> is calculated using the window's height. Any calculation you make might result in a decimal value (like 300.25), but since there's no such thing as .25 pixels, you need to round the final calculation to the nearest integer (300, for example).

You can round a number using the *round()* method of the Math object. The syntax for this looks a little unusual:

```
Math.round(number)
```

You pass a number (or variable containing a number) to the *round()* method, and it returns an integer. If the original number has a decimal place with a value below .5, the number is rounded down; if the decimal place is .5 or above, it is rounded up. For example, 4.4 would round down to 4, while 4.5 rounds up to 5.

```
var decimalNum = 10.25;
var roundedNum = Math.round(decimalNum); // 10
```

Note: JavaScript provides two other methods for rounding numbers: *Math.ceil()* and *Math.floor()*. You use them just like *Math.round()*, but *Math.ceil()* always rounds the number up (for example, *Math.ceil(4.0001)* returns 5), while *Math.floor()* always rounds the number down: *Math.floor(4.99999)* returns 4. To keep these two methods clear in your mind, think a *ceiling* is up, and a *floor* is down.

Formatting Currency Values

When calculating product costs or shopping cart totals, you'll usually include the cost, plus two decimals out, like this: 9.99. But even if the monetary value is a whole number, it's common to add two zeros, like this: 10.00. And a currency value like 8.9 is written as 8.90. Unfortunately, JavaScript doesn't see numbers that way: It leaves the trailing zeros off (10 instead of 10.00, and 8.9 instead of 8.90, for example).

Fortunately, there's a method for numbers called *toFixed()*, which lets you convert a number to a string that matches the number of decimal places you want. To use it, add a period after a number (or after the name of a variable containing a number), followed by *toFixed(2)*:

```
var cost = 10;
var printCost = '$' + cost.toFixed(2); // $10.00
```

The number you pass the *toFixed()* method determines how many decimal places to go out to. For currency, use 2 to end up with numbers like 10.00 or 9.90; if you use 3, you end up with 3 decimal places, like 10.000 or 9.900.

If the number starts off with more decimal places than you specify, the number is rounded to the number of decimal places specified. For example:

```
var cost = 10.289;
var printCost = '$' + cost.toFixed(2); // $10.29
```

In this case, the 10.289 is rounded up to 10.29.

Note: The *toFixed()* method only works with numbers. So if you use a string, you end up with an error:

```
var cost='10';//a string
```

```
var printCost='$' + cost.toFixed(2);//error
```

To get around this problem, you need to convert the string to a number as described on page 445, like this:

```
var cost='10';//a string
```

```
cost = +cost; // or cost = Number(cost);
```

```
var printCost='$' + cost.toFixed(2);//$10.00
```

Creating a Random Number

Random numbers can help add variety to a program. For example, say you have an array of questions for a quiz program (like the quiz tutorial on page 108). Instead of asking the same questions in the same order each time, you can randomly select one question in the array. Or, you could use JavaScript to randomly select the name of a graphic file from an array and display a different image each time the page loads. Both of these tasks require a random number.

JavaScript provides the *Math.random()* method for creating random numbers. This method returns a randomly generated number between 0 and 1 (for example, .9716907176080688 or .10345038010895868). While you might not have much need for numbers like those, you can use some simple math operations to generate a whole number from 0 to another number. For example, to generate a number from 0 to 9, you'd use this code:

```
Math.floor(Math.random()*10);
```

This code breaks down into two parts. The part inside the *Math.floor()* method— *Math.random()*10*—generates a random number between 0 and 10. That will generate numbers like 4.190788392268892; and since the random number is *between* 0 and 10, it never *is* 10. To get a whole number, the random result is passed to the *Math.floor()* method, which rounds any decimal number down to the nearest whole number, so 3.4448588848 becomes 3 and .1111939498984 becomes 0.

If you want to get a random number between 1 and another number, just multiply the *random()* method by the uppermost number, and use the Math.ceil() method (which rounds a number up to the neareast integer). For example, if you want to simulate a die roll to get a number from 1 to 6:

```
var roll = Math.ceil(Math.random()*6); // 1,2,3,4,5 or 6
```

Randomly selecting an array element

You can use the *Math.random()* method to randomly select an item from an array. As discussed on page 62, each item in an array is accessed using an index number. The first item in an array uses an index value of 0, and the last item in the array is accessed with an index number that's 1 minus the total number of items in the array. Using the *Math.random()* method makes it really easy to randomly select an array item:

```
var people = ['Ron','Sally','Tricia','Bob']; //create an array
var random = Math.floor(Math.random() * people.length);
var rndPerson = people[random]; //
```

The first line of this code creates an array with four names. The second line does two things: First, it generates a random number between 0 and the number of items in the array (*people.length*)—in this example, a number *between* 0 and 4. Then it uses the *Math.floor()* method to round down to the nearest integer, so it will produce the number 0, 1, 2, or 3. Finally, it uses that number to access one element from the array and store it in a variable named *rndPerson*.

A function for selecting a random number

Functions are a great way to create useful, reusable snippets of code (page 100). If you use random numbers frequently, you might want a simple function to help you select a random number between any two numbers—for example, a number between 1 and 6, or 100 and 1,000. The following function is called using two arguments: The first is the lowest possible value (1 for example), and the second is the largest possible value (6 for example):

```
function rndNum(from, to) {
  return Math.floor((Math.random()*(to - from + 1)) + from);
}
```

To use this function, add it to your web page (as described on page 100), and then call it like this:

```
var dieRoll = rndNum(1,6); // get a number between 1 and 6
```

Dates and Times

If you want to keep track of the current date or time, turn to JavaScript's *Date* object. This special JavaScript object lets you determine the year, month, day of the week, hour, and more. To use it, you create a variable and store a new *Date* object inside it like this:

```
var now = new Date();
```

The *new Date()* command creates a *Date* object containing the current date and time. Once created, you can access different pieces of time and date information using various date-related methods as listed in Table 14-3. For example, to get the current year, use the *getFullYear()* method like this:

```
var now = new Date();
var year = now.getFullYear();
```

Note: *new Date()* retrieves the current time and date as determined by each visitor's computer. In other words, if someone hasn't correctly set his computer's clock, then the date and time won't be accurate.

Table 14-3. Methods for accessing parts of the Date object

Method	What it returns
getFullYear()	The year: 2008, for example.
getMonth()	The month as an integer between 0 and 11: 0 is January and 11 is December.
getDate()	The day of the month—a number between 1 and 31.
getDay()	The day of the week as a number between 0 and 6. 0 is Sunday, and 6 is Saturday.
getHours()	Number of hours on a 24-hour clock (a number between 0 and 23). For example, 11p.m. is 23.
getMinutes()	Number of minutes between 0 and 59.
getSeconds()	Number of seconds between 0 and 59.
getTime()	Total number of milliseconds since January 1, 1970 at midnight (see box on page 453).

Getting the Month

To retrieve the month for a *Date* object, use the *getMonth()* method, which returns the month's number:

```
var now = new Date();
var month = now.getMonth();
```

However, instead of returning a number that makes sense to us humans (as in 1 meaning January), this method returns a number that's one less. For example, January is 0, February is 1, and so on. If you want to retrieve a number that matches how we think of months, just add 1 like this:

```
var now = new Date();
var month = now.getMonth()+1;//matches the real month
```

There's no built-in JavaScript command that tells you the name of a month. Fortunately, JavaScript's strange way of numbering months comes in handy when you want to determine the actual name of the month. You can accomplish that by first creating an array of month names, then accessing a name using the index number for that month:

```
var months = ['January','February','March','April','May',
              'June','July','August','September',
              'October','November','December'];
var now = new Date();
var month = months[now.getMonth()];
```

The first line creates an array with all twelve month names, in the order they occur (January–December). Remember that to access an array item you use an index number, and that arrays are numbered starting with 0 (see page 62). So to access the first item of the array *months*, you use *months[0]*. So, by using the *getMonth()* method, you can retrieve a number to use as an index for the *months* array and thus retrieve the name for that month.

Getting the Day of the Week

The *getDay()* method retrieves the day of the week. And as with the *getMonth()* method, the JavaScript interpreter returns a number that's one less than what you'd expect: 0 is considered Sunday, the first day of the week, while Saturday is 6. Since the name of the day of the week is usually more useful for your visitors, you can use an array to store the day names and use the *getDay()* method to access the particular day in the array, like this:

```
var days = ['Sunday','Monday','Tuesday','Wednesday',
            'Thursday','Friday','Saturday'];
var now = new Date();
var dayOfWeek = days[now.getDay()];
```

Getting the Time

The *Date* object also contains the current time, so you can display the current time on a web page or use the time to determine if the visitor is viewing the page in the a.m. or p.m. You can then do something with that information, like display a background image of the sun during the day, or the moon at night.

The Date Object Behind the Scenes

JavaScript lets you access particular elements of the *Date* object, such as the year or the day of the month. However, the JavaScript interpreter actually thinks of a date as the number of *milliseconds* that have passed since midnight on January 1, 1970. For example, Wednesday, February 1, 2012 is actually 131328083200000 to the JavaScript interpreter.

That isn't a joke: As far as JavaScript is concerned, the beginning of time was January 1, 1970. That date (called the "Unix epoch") was arbitrarily chosen in the 70s by programmers creating the Unix operating system, so they could all agree on a way of keeping track of time. Since then, this way of tracking a date has become common in many programming languages and platforms.

Whenever you use a *Date* method like *getFullYear()*, the JavaScript interpreter does the math to figure out (based on how many seconds have elapsed since January 1, 1970) what year it is. If you want to see the number of milliseconds for a particular date, you use the *getTime()* method:

```
var sometime = new Date();
var msElapsed = sometime.getTime();
```

Tracking dates and times as milliseconds makes it easier to calculate differences between dates. For example, you can determine the amount of time until next New Year's Day by first getting the number of milliseconds that will have elapsed from 1/1/1970 to when next year rolls around and then subtracting the number of milliseconds that have elapsed from 1/1/1970 to today:

```
// milliseconds from 1/1/1970 to today
var today = new Date();
// milliseconds from 1/1/1970 to next new year
var nextYear = new Date(2013,0,1);
// calculate milliseconds from today to next year
var timeDiff = nextYear - today;
```

The result of subtracting two dates is the number of milliseconds difference between the two. If you want to convert that into something useful, just divide it by the number of milliseconds in a day (to determine how many days) or the number of milliseconds in an hour (to determine how many hours), and so on.

```
var second = 1000; // 1000 milliseconds in a second
var minute = 60*second; // 60 seconds in a minute
var hour = 60*minute; // 60 minutes in an hour
var day = 24*hour; // 24 hours in a day
var totalDays = timeDiff/day; // total number of days
```

(In this example, you may have noticed a different way to create a date: *new Date(2009,0,1)*. You can read more about this method on page 450.)

You can use the *getHours()*, *getMinutes()*, and *getSeconds()* methods to get the hours, minutes, and seconds. So to display the time on a web page, add the following in the HTML where you wish the time to appear:

```
var now = new Date();
var hours = now.getHours();
var minutes = now.getMinutes();
var seconds = now.getSeconds();
document.write(hours + ":" + minutes + ":" + seconds);
```

This code produces output like 6:35:56 to indicate 6 a.m., 35 minutes, and 56 seconds. However, it will also produce output that you might not like, like 18:4:9 to indicate 4 minutes and 9 seconds after 6 p.m. One problem is that most people reading this book, unless they're in the military, don't use the 24-hour clock. They don't recognize 18 as meaning 6 p.m. An even bigger problem is that times should be formatted with two digits for minutes and seconds (even if they're a number less than 10), like this: 6:04:09. Fortunately, it's not difficult to adjust the above script to match those requirements.

Changing hours to a.m. and p.m.

To change hours from a 24-hour clock to a 12-hour clock, you need to do a couple of things. First, you need to determine if the time is in the morning (so you can add '*am*' after the time) or in the afternoon (to append '*pm*'). Second, you need to convert any hours greater than 12 to their 12-hour clock equivalent (for example, change 14 to 2 p.m.).

Here's the code to do that:

```
1    var now = new Date();
2    var hour = now.getHours();
3    if (hour < 12) {
4       meridiem = 'am';
5    } else {
6       meridiem = 'pm';
7    }
8    hour = hour % 12;
9    if (hour==0) {
10      hour = 12;
11   }
12   hour = hour + ' ' + meridiem;
```

Note: The column of numbers at the far left is just line numbering to make it easier for you to follow the discussion below. Don't type these numbers into your own code!

Lines 1 and 2 grab the current date and time and store the current hour into a variable named *hour*. Lines 3–7 determine if the hour is in the afternoon or morning; if the hour is less than 12 (the hour after midnight is 0), then it's the morning (a.m.); otherwise, it's the afternoon (p.m.).

Line 8 introduces a mathematical operator called *modulus* and represented by a percent (%) sign. It returns the remainder of a division operation. For example, 2 divides into 5 two times (2 x 2 is 4), with 1 left over. In other words, 5 % 2 is 1. So in this case, if the hour is 18, 18 % 12 results in 6 (12 goes into 18 once with a remainder of 6). 18 is 6 p.m., which is what you want. If the first number is smaller than the number divided into it (for example, 8 divided by 12), then the result is the original number. For example, 8 % 12 just returns 8; in other words, the modulus operator doesn't change the hours before noon.

Lines 9–11 take care of two possible outcomes with the modulus operator. If the hour is 12 (noon) or 0 (after midnight), then the modulus operator returns 0. In this case, *hour* is just set to 12 for either 12 p.m. or 12 a.m.

Finally, line 12 combines the reformatted hour with a space and either "am" or "pm", so the result is displayed as, for example, "6 am" or "6 pm".

Padding single digits

As discussed on the previous page, when the minutes or seconds values are less than 10, you can end up with weird output like 7:3:2 p.m. To change this output to the more common 7:03:02 p.m., you need to add a 0 in front of the single digit. It's easy with a basic conditional statement:

```
1    var minutes = now.getMinutes();
2    if (minutes<10) {
3       minutes = '0' + minutes;
4    }
```

Line 1 grabs the minutes in the current time, which in this example could be 33 or 3. Line 2 simply checks if the number is less than 10, meaning the minute is a single digit and needs a 0 in front of it. Line 3 is a bit tricky, since you can't normally add a 0 in front of a number: 0 + 2 equals 2, not 02. However, you can combine strings in this way so '0' + *minutes* means combine the string '0' with the value in the *minutes* variable. As discussed on page 446, when you add a string to a number, the JavaScript interpreter converts the number to a string as well, so you end up with a string like '08'.

You can put all of these parts together to create a simple function to output times in formats like 7:32:04 p.m., or 4:02:34 a.m., or even leave off seconds altogether for a time like 7:23 p.m.:

```
function printTime(secs) {
    var sep = ':'; //seperator character
    var hours,minutes,seconds,time;
    var now = new Date();
    hours = now.getHours();
    if (hours < 12) {
        meridiem = 'am';
    } else {
        meridiem = 'pm';
    }
    hours = hours % 12;
    if (hours==0) {
        hours = 12;
```

```
    }
    time = hours;
    minutes = now.getMinutes();
    if (minutes<10) {
        minutes = '0' + minutes;
    }
    time += sep + minutes;
    if (secs) {
        seconds = now.getSeconds();
        if (seconds<10) {
            seconds = '0' + seconds;
        }
        time += sep + seconds;
    }
    return time + ' ' + meridiem;
}
```

You'll find this function in the file *printTime.js* in the *chapter14* folder in the Tutorials. You can see it in action by opening the file *time.html* (in that same folder) in a web browser. To use the function, either attach the *printTime.js* file to a web page, or copy the function into a web page or another external JavaScript file. To get the time, just call the function like this: *printTime()*, or, if you want the seconds displayed as well, *printTime(true)*. The function will return a string containing the current time in the proper format.

Creating a Date Other Than Today

So far, you've seen how to use *new Date()* to capture the current date and time on a visitor's computer. But what if you want to create a *Date* object for next Thanksgiving or New Year's? JavaScript lets you create a date other than today in a few different ways. You might want to do this if you'd like to do a calculation between two dates: for example, "How many days until the new year?" (Also see the box on page 453.)

When using the *Date()* method, you can also specify a date and time in the future or past. The basic format is this:

```
new Date(year,month,day,hour,minutes,seconds,milliseconds);
```

For example, to create a *Date* for noon on New Year's Day 2012, you could do this:

```
var ny2012 = new Date(2012,0,1,12,0,0,0);
```

This code translates to "create a new Date object for January 1, 2012 at 12 o'clock, 0 minutes, 0 seconds, and 0 milliseconds." You must supply at least a year and month, but if you don't need to specify an exact time, you can leave off milliseconds, seconds, minutes, and so on. For example, to just create a date object for January 1, 2012, you could do this:

```
var ny2012 = new Date(2012,0,1);
```

Note: Remember that JavaScript uses 0 for January, 1 for February, and so on, as described on page 451.

Creating a date that's one week from today

As discussed in the box on page 453, the JavaScript interpreter actually treats a date as the number of milliseconds that have elapsed since Jan 1, 1970. Another way to create a date is to pass a value representing the number of milliseconds for that date:

```
new Date(milliseconds);
```

So another way to create a date for January 1, 2012 would be like this:

```
var ny2012 = new Date(1325404800000);
```

Of course, since most of us aren't human calculators, you probably wouldn't think of a date like this. However, milliseconds come in very handy when you're creating a new date that's a certain amount of time from another date. For example, when setting a cookie using JavaScript, you need to specify a date at which point that cookie is deleted from a visitor's browser. To make sure a cookie disappears after one week, you need to specify a date that's one week from today.

To create a date that's one week from now, you could do the following:

```
var now = new Date(); // today
var nowMS = now.getTime(); // get # milliseconds for today
var week = 1000*60*60*24*7; // milliseconds in one week
var oneWeekFromNow = new Date(nowMS + week);
```

The first line stores the current date and time in a variable named *now*. Next, the *getTime()* method extracts the number of milliseconds that have elapsed from January 1, 1970 to today. The third line calculates the total number of milliseconds in a single week (1000 milliseconds * 60 seconds * 60 minutes * 24 hours * 7 days). Finally, the code creates a new date by adding the number of milliseconds in a week to today.

Putting It All Together

So far in this book, you've seen lots of tasks that JavaScript can accomplish: form validation, image rollovers, photo galleries, user interface improvements like tabbed and accordion panels, and more. But you might be wondering, how do you put them together to work with your site? After all, once you start using JavaScript, you'll probably want to use it to improve every page of your site. Here are some tips for how to use multiple scripts on your site.

Using External JavaScript Files

As mentioned on page 27, external JavaScript files are an efficient way to share the same JavaScript code among web pages. An external file makes updating your Java-Script easier—there's just one file to edit if you need to enhance (or fix) your Java-Script code. In addition, when an external JavaScript file is downloaded, it's stored in the browser's cache, so it doesn't need to be downloaded a second time, making web pages feel more responsive and load more quickly.

In the case of a JavaScript library like jQuery, external JavaScript files are a necessity—after all, your web pages would be unnecessarily large and difficult to maintain if you put the actual jQuery JavaScript code into each page. Furthermore, jQuery plug-ins are supplied as external files, so you need to link them to a web page if you want to use them. Linking to an external JavaScript file is as easy as this:

```
<script src="js/ui.tabs.js"></script>
```

Putting your own JavaScript code into external JavaScript files can also help make your code more reusable and your site feel faster—but only if you actually share that code among web pages. For example, with the form validation script you created on page 278, it doesn't make sense to put the code used to create the validation rules and error messages into an external file, since all of those rules and error messages are specific to the form elements on that page, and wouldn't work on a form that has different form fields. In that case, it's best to just use the JavaScript to validate the form within the web page itself.

However, the validation plug-in file you learned about on page 278 can be used for any form, so it makes sense to have that in a separate file. The same is true for any code that you'll use in multiple pages. For example, on page 273 you learned how to focus the first field of a form using JavaScript—that's something you might want to do for every form. Likewise, the box on page 271 presents the JavaScript necessary to prevent a visitor from hitting the submit button multiple times (and thus submitting the form data more than once), which is also useful for any form page. So, you might want to combine these two scripts into a single external file named something like *forms.js*. The JavaScript code would look something like this:

```
1   $(document).ready(function() {
2     // focus first text field
3     $(":text")[0].focus();
4
5     // disable submit button on submit
6     $('form').submit(function() {
7       var subButton = $(this).find(':submit');
8       subButton.attr('disabled',true);
9       subButton.val('...sending information...');
10    });
11  }); //end ready
```

Note that since this code relies on jQuery, you must wrap it inside the *$(document). ready()* function (lines 1 and 11). In fact, every external file that relies on jQuery must start with the code on line 1 above and end with the code on line 10.

Note: jQuery can handle multiple *$(document).ready()* functions without any problems. For example, you can have several external JavaScript files that do various things to the page, and each file can have a *$(document).ready()* function, and you can include a *$(document).ready()* function within <script> that appears only on that page. That's perfectly fine with jQuery.

Using the same script across multiple pages requires a little planning on your part. For example, line 3 places the cursor into the first text field on a web page. In most cases, that makes sense—you want the focus to be on the first field so that a visitor can start filling out the form. However, if the page has more than one form, this code might not work as you want it to.

For example, if you have a search box at the top of the page and a separate form for submitting a product order, the code in line 3 will put the focus on the search box and not the first text field in the order form. In this case, you need to think through the problem a bit and come up with a way of making sure the proper text field has the focus when the page loads. Here are two possible solutions:

- Add a class name to the field you want the focus on when the page loads. For example, say you add the class name *focus* to the text field like this:

```
<input type="text" class="focus" name="firstName">
```

You could then you use this JavaScript to make sure that field is focused:

```
$('.focus').focus();
```

To use this code, you just need to make sure that you add the *focus* class to a text field on each form page, and make sure you link the external JavaScript file containing this code to each of those form pages.

- You can get the same effect by adding a class name to the <form> tag itself, using this JavaScript:

```
$('.focus :text')[0].focus();
```

This code automatically focuses the first text field of a form with the class *focus*. The benefit of this approach is that the first text field always gets the focus, so if you reorganize your form (add a few more text fields to the beginning, for example), you know that the first text field will get focus and not some other field (with the focus class) further down the page.

Once you start using JavaScript, you might end up using several scripts on all (or nearly all) of your web pages. For example, you might have some rollover images (page 207), and use JavaScript to make sure links outside your site open in a new window (page 238). In this situation, it's useful to create an external JavaScript file with all of the scripts you share among your site—you could call the file something like *site_scripts.js* or simply *site.js*.

Note: jQuery has a built-in mechanism to protect you from producing unwanted JavaScript errors. JavaScript usually spits out an error if you try to perform an action on something that doesn't exist—for example, trying to select a text field on a page that doesn't have a text field. Fortunately, jQuery ignores these kinds of errors.

Writing More Efficient JavaScript

Programming is a lot of work. Programmers are always looking for ways to do things faster and with fewer lines of code. While there are lots of tips and tricks, the following techniques are especially useful for working with JavaScript and jQuery.

Putting Preferences in Variables

One important lesson that programmers learn is how to extract details from scripts so that they are more flexible and easier to update. For example, say you want to change the color of a paragraph of text to orange when a visitor clicks on it. You could do that with jQuery using the *css()* function (page 143) like this:

```
$('p').click(function() {
  $(this).css('color','#F60');
});
```

In this case, the color orange (#F60) is hard-coded into this step. Say you apply this same color in other steps (maybe to add a background color when the visitor mouses over a table cell). You might be tempted to write *#F60* into those steps as well. A better approach is to place the color into a variable at the beginning of your script and then use that variable throughout your script:

```
1   $(document).ready(function() {
2   var hColor='#F60';
3   $('p').click(function() {
4     $(this).css('color',hColor);
5   });
6   $('td').hover(
7     function() {
8       $(this).css('backgroundColor',hColor);
9     },
10    function() {
11      $(this).css('backgroundColor','transparent');
12    }
13  );
14  }); //end ready()
```

In this example, the variable *hColor* now holds a hexadecimal color value—that variable is used both in the *click* event for the <p> tags, and in a *hover* event for the <td> tags. If you later decide orange isn't your thing, you can change the value stored in the variable—*var hColor='#F33';*—and now the script will use that color.

You could make the above code even more flexible by uncoupling the connection between the color used for the <p> tags and <td> tags. Currently, they're both set to the same color, but if you want to make it so that you could eventually assign different colors to each, you could add an additional variable to your code:

```
1   $(document).ready(function() {
2   var pColor='#F60';
3   var tdColor=pColor;
4   $('p').click(function() {
5     $(this).css('color',pColor);
6   });
7   $('td').hover(
8     function() {
9       $(this).css('backgroundColor',tdColor);
10    },
11    function() {
12      $(this).css('backgroundColor','transparent');
13    }
```

```
14    );
15    }); //end ready()
```

Now, the *click* and *hover* events use the same color—#F60 (since the *tdColor* variable is set to the value of *pColor* in line 3 of the code). However, if you later decide that you want the table cells to have a different color, just change line 3 like this:

```
var tdColor='#FF3';
```

When writing a JavaScript program, identify values that you explicitly name in your code and turn them into variables. Likely candidates are colors, fonts, widths, heights, times (such as 1,000 milliseconds), file names (such as image files), message text (such as alert and confirmation messages), and paths to files (such as the path for a link or an image). For example:

```
var highlightColor = '#33A';
var upArrow = 'ua.png';
var downArrow='da.png';
var imagePath='/images/';
var delay=1000;
```

Put these variable definitions at the beginning of your script (or if you're using jQuery, right inside the *.ready()* function).

Tip: It's particularly useful to put text that you plan on printing to a page into variables. For example, error messages like "Please supply a valid email address," or confirmation messages like "Thank you for supplying your mailing information" can be variables. When these messages are grouped together as variables at the beginning of a script, it's easier to edit them later (and to translate the text if you ever need to reach an international audience).

Ternary Operator

It's a common programming task to set the value of a variable based on some kind of condition. For example, say you want to set up a variable that contains text with the login status of a user. In your script there's a variable named *login*, which contains a Boolean value—*true* if the user is logged in, or *false* if she isn't. Here's one way to create a new variable for this situation:

```
var status;
if (login) {
  status='Logged in';
} else {
  status='Not logged in';
}
```

In this case, a basic conditional statement (page 79) sets the value of a variable named *status* based on whether the user is logged in or not. JavaScript offers a shortcut for this common procedure, called a *ternary operator*. A ternary operator provides a one-line approach to creating a simple conditional statement. The basic format of the ternary operator is:

```
(condition) ? A : B
```

Depending upon the result of the condition, either A (if the condition is *true*) or B (if the condition is *false*) is returned. The ? precedes the *true* result, while the : precedes the *false* result. So, for example, the above code could be rewritten like this:

```
var status=(login)?'Logged in':'Not logged in';
```

What was once six lines of code is now a single line of code. Figure 14-6 diagrams how this code works.

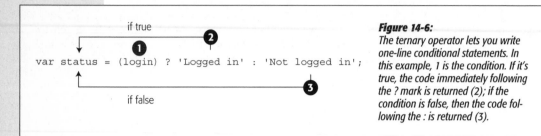

Figure 14-6:
The ternary operator lets you write one-line conditional statements. In this example, 1 is the condition. If it's true, the code immediately following the ? mark is returned (2); if the condition is false, then the code following the : is returned (3).

The ternary operator is simply a shortcut—you don't have to use it, and some programmers find it too dense to easily understand and prefer the easier-to-read if/else statement. In addition, the best use of the ternary operator is for setting the value of a variable based on a condition. It doesn't work for every type of conditional statement; for example, you can't use it for multiple-line statements where many lines of code are executed based on a particular condition. But even if you don't use ternary operators, recognizing how they work will help you understand other peoples' programs, since you'll probably encounter them frequently.

The Switch Statement

There's more than one way to skin a conditional statement. While the ternary operator is great for assigning a value to a variable based on the results of a condition, the *switch* statement is a more compact way of writing a series of if/else statements that depend on the value of a single variable.

For example, say you ask visitors to your site to type their favorite color into a form field, then print a different message based on the color they submit. Here's how you might write part of this code using the typical conditional statement.

```
if (favoriteColor == 'blue') {
  message = 'Blue is a cool color.';
} else if (favoriteColor == 'red') {
  message = 'Red is a warm color.';
} else if (favoriteColor == 'green') {
  message = 'Green is the color of the leaves.';
} else {
  message = 'What kind of favorite color is that?';
}
```

Notice that there's an awful lot of *favoriteColor == 'some value'* in that code. In fact, *'favoriteColor =='* appears three times in just nine lines of code. If all you're doing is testing the value of a variable repeatedly, then the switch statement provides a more elegant (and easy to read) solution. The basic structure of a switch statement is diagrammed in Figure 14-7.

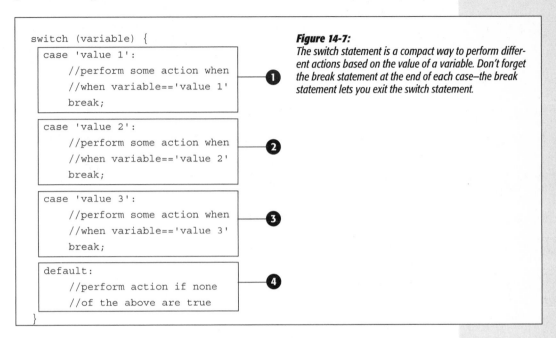

```
switch (variable) {
    case 'value 1':
        //perform some action when
        //when variable=='value 1'
        break;

    case 'value 2':
        //perform some action when
        //when variable=='value 2'
        break;

    case 'value 3':
        //perform some action when
        //when variable=='value 3'
        break;

    default:
        //perform action if none
        //of the above are true
}
```

Figure 14-7:
The switch statement is a compact way to perform different actions based on the value of a variable. Don't forget the break statement at the end of each case—the break statement lets you exit the switch statement.

The first line of a switch statement begins with the keyword *switch*, followed by a variable name inside parentheses, followed by an opening brace symbol. Essentially, this code says, "Let's get the value of this variable and see if it matches one of several other values." Each test is called a *case*, and a switch statement has one or more cases. In Figure 14-7, there are three cases, numbered 1–3. The basic structure of a case looks like this:

```
case value1:
    // do something
    break;
```

The *case* keyword indicates the beginning of a case; it's followed by some value and then a colon. This line is shorthand for the longer *if (variable=='value1')*. The value can be a number, string, or Boolean (or a variable containing a number, string, or Boolean), so if you want to test whether the variable is equal to 37, for example, then the case would look like this:

```
case 37:
//do something
break;
```

To test whether the variable is true or not, you'd write this:

```
case true:
//do something
break;
```

After the first line, you add the statements you want to execute if the variable match-es the test case value. Finally, you add a *break;* statement. This step is important—the *break;* statement exits the switch statement. If you leave it out, the JavaScript inter-preter will skip to the next test case and see if it matches.

Leaving out the break; statement can cause problems, especially if you use the final *default* keyword with a switch statement (number 4 in Figure 14-7). The default statement applies if none of the test cases is true—it's the equivalent of the final *else* clause in a conditional statement. If you leave out the break; statement in one of the earlier test cases, then if one of the cases is true, the JavaScript interpreter will also run whatever code is listed in the default statement.

Here's how the switch statement can help with the *if/else* if code on page 463:

```
switch (favoriteColor) {
  case 'blue':
    message = 'Blue is a cool color.';
    break;
  case 'red':
    message = 'Red is a warm color.';
    break;
  case 'green':
    message = 'Green is the color of the leaves.';
    break;
  default:
    message = 'What kind of favorite color is that?';
}
```

This code is the equivalent to the *if/else* if code, but is more compact and easier to read.

In fact, you can also put more than one *case* statement right after one another (and intentionally exclude the *default* keyword) if you want to run the same code for sev-eral values. For example:

```
switch (favoriteColor) {
  case 'navy':
  case 'blue':
  case 'indigo':
    message = 'Blue is a cool color.';
    break;

  case 'red':
    message = 'Red is a warm color.';
    break;
  case 'green':
    message = 'Green is the color of the leaves.';
```

```
      break;
    default:
      message = 'What kind of favorite color is that?';
  }
```

This is similar to using *if (favoriteColor == 'navy' || favoriteColor == 'blue' || favor-iteColor == 'indigo')* in an *if/else* statement.

Creating Fast-Loading JavaScript

Once you starting using external JavaScript files for your scripts, your visitors should start to feel like your site is faster. Thanks to a browser's cache, once your external JavaScript files download for one page of your site, they don't have to be downloaded a second time for a different page. However, there's still another way to make your site download more quickly: compressing your external JavaScript files.

Note: Files sent securely via SSL (secure socket layer) are *never* cached. So if people access the pages of your site using *https://* as the protocol (for example, *https://www.oreilly.com*), then any files they download, including external JavaScript files, must be downloaded every time they're needed.

To make a script more understandable, programmers usually insert empty spaces, carriage returns, and comments to explain what the script does. These are all important additions for the programmer, but not necessary for the web browser, which can happily understand JavaScript without carriage returns, tabs, extraneous spaces, or comments. Using a compression program, you can minimize the space your JavaScript takes up. The version of jQuery recommended in this book, for example, is *minified*, and is nearly half the file size of the uncompressed version.

There are several programs aimed at making JavaScript more petite. Douglas Crockford's JSMin (*http://crockford.com/javascript/jsmin.html*) is one example, and Dean Edward's Packer (*http://dean.edwards.name/packer*) is another. However, we'd recommend the same compressor Yahoo uses (and jQuery), because it achieves great file size savings without changing your code (some compressors actually rewrite your code and in some cases can break your scripts!).

Yahoo's JavaScript compressor, *YUI Compressor*, lives at *http://developer.yahoo.com/yui/compressor*. In the last edition of this book, we gave instructions that only a computer hacker would love: They involved downloading a JAR file (Java) as well as using the dreaded command line. Fortunately, some friendly and enterprising fellow has made an online version you can use by either pasting in the JavaScript code you wish to minimize or even selecting a JavaScript file on your computer and uploading it to the website.

1. **Launch a web browser and visit** *http://www.refresh-sf.com/yui/.*

   This is the site for the Online YUI Compressor.

2. **Click the File(s) link.**

   Alternatively, you can just copy the JavaScript code from your text editor and paste it into the large text box at the site's homepage; you can then skip to step 4.

3. **Click the Choose File button and locate the external JavaScript file on your computer.**

   The file must contain only JavaScript. For example, you can't select a HTML file that also has JavaScript programming in it.

4. **Select the "Redirect to gzipped output" box (just above the Compress button).**

   This option lets you download the minimized code in a new, zipped file. This will be your new, compressed, external JavaScript file, which you can save to your site.

5. **Click the Compress button.**

   The website processes your code and downloads the compressed file to your computer. You can then rename this file (since it's always saved as min.js), and put it into your site for use. The Online YUI Compressor site provides a nice report after you compress a file, listing the original file size, the new, compressed file size, and a percentage that represents how much smaller the new file is.

Warning: Make sure you keep the original JavaScript file on hand after using the Online YUI Compressor, since the new, compressed version is unreadable and you'll never be able to edit it if you wish to make changes to your original code.

Troubleshooting and Debugging

Everybody makes mistakes, but in JavaScript, mistakes can keep your programs from running correctly—or at all. When you first start out with JavaScript, you'll probably make a lot of mistakes. Trying to figure out why a script isn't behaving the way it should can be frustrating, but it's all a part of programming. Fortunately, with experience and practice, you'll be able to figure out why an error has occurred and how to fix it.

This chapter describes some of the most common programming mistakes, and, more importantly teaches you how to diagnose problems in your scripts—*debug* them, as programmers say. In addition, the tutorial will take you step-by-step through debugging a problematic script.

Top JavaScript Programming Mistakes

There are countless ways a program can go wrong, from simple typos to more subtle errors that only pop up every now and again. However, there are a handful of mistakes that routinely plague beginning (and even advanced) JavaScript programmers. Go over the list in this section, and keep it in the back of your mind when programming. You'll probably find that knowing these common mistakes makes it a lot easier to identify and fix problems in your own programs.

Non-Closed Pairs

As you've noticed, JavaScript is filled with endless parentheses, braces, semicolons, quotation marks, and other punctuation. Due to the finicky nature of computers, leaving out a single punctuation mark can stop a program dead in its tracks. One of the most common mistakes is simply forgetting to include a closing punctuation mark. For example, *alert('hello';* will produce an error because the closing parenthesis is missing: *alert('hello');*.

Leaving off a closing parenthesis will cause a syntax error (see the box on page 471). This kind of "grammatical" error prevents scripts from running at all. When you give your script a test run, the browser lets you know if you've made a syntax error, but, confusingly, they all describe the problem differently. In the Firefox error console (page 35), you get an error message like "missing) after argument list"; Internet Explorer 9's console (page 37) reports this error as "Expected ')'"; Chrome's error consoles reads "Uncaught SyntaxError: Unexpected token ;"; and Safari's error console (page 38) gives you the less-helpful message "SyntaxError: ParseError." As mentioned on page 39, Firefox tends to provide the most understandable error messages, so it's a good browser to start with when trying to figure out why a script isn't working (see Figure 15-1).

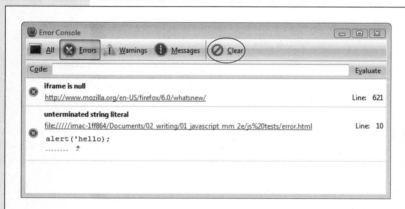

Figure 15-1:
Firefox's Error Console lists all JavaScript errors that the browser encounters. You can display the console by choosing Web Developer→Error Console (Ctrl+Shift+J) on Windows, or Tools→Web Developer→Error Console (⌘-Shift-J) on Macs. Since the console lists the errors it has encountered on all pages, you'll want to frequently erase the list by clicking the Clear button (circled).

The syntax error in *alert('hello';* is pretty easy to spot. When you've got a nest of parentheses, though, it's very easy to leave off a closing parenthesis and difficult to spot that error at a glance. For example:

```
if ((x>0) && (y<10) {
    // do something
}
```

In this example, the final closing parentheses for the conditional statement is missing—the one that goes directly after *(y<10)*. The first line should really be: *if ((x>0) and (y<10)) {*. Again, Firefox provides the clearest description of the problem: "missing) after condition." Table 14-1 provides a list of Firefox's error console syntax error messages.

You'll encounter a syntax error when you forget to include the second quote mark as well. For example, *alert('hello);* produces an error because the final single quote is missing: *alert('hello');*. In Firefox, if you forget to include both quote marks, you'll get an "unterminated string literal" error, while Internet Explorer reports an "unterminated string constant"; Safari again provides the less-than-useful "SyntaxError: Parse Error" message.

Braces also come in pairs, and you'll use them in conditional statements (page 79), in loops (page 93), when creating JavaScript object literals (page 145), and with JSON (page 370):

```
if (score==0) {
   alert('game over');
```

In this example, the closing *}* is missing, and the script will produce a syntax error.

One approach to overcome the problem of missing closing punctuation marks is to always add them before adding other programming. For example, say you want to end up with the following code:

```
if ((name=='bob') && (score==0)) {
    alert('You lose (but at least you have a great name');
}
```

Start by typing the outside elements first, creating a basic skeleton for the condition like this:

```
if () {

}
```

At this point, there's not much code, so it's easy to see if you've mistakenly left out any punctuation. Next, add more code, bit by bit, until the program is in place. The same is true when creating a complex JavaScript object literal like the one used to set the options for the Validation plug-in described on page 278, or like a JSON object described on page 370. Start with the basic structure:

```
var options = {

};
```

Then add more structure:

```
var options = {
   rules : {

   },
   messages : {

   }
};
```

Then finish the object:

```
var options = {
  rules : {
    name : 'required',
    email: 'email'
  },
  messages : {
    name : 'Please type your name',
    email: 'Please type your e-mail address.'
  }
};
```

This approach lets you check your work through various steps and makes it a lot easier to identify any mistakes in punctuation.

Table 15-1. *Firefox's Error Console (discussed on page 35) provides the clearest description of syntax error messages. When a script isn't working, preview it in Firefox and review the Error Console. Here are a few of the most common error messages and what they mean.*

Firefox error message	Explanation

Unterminated string literal	Missing opening or closing quote mark:
	`var name = Jane' ;`
	Error also appears with mismatched quote marks:
	`var name = 'Jane";`

Missing) after argument list	Missing closing parenthesis when calling a function or method: `alert('hello' ;`
Missing) after condition	Missing closing parenthesis within a conditional statement: `if (x==0`
Missing (before condition	Missing opening parenthesis within a conditional statement: `if x==0)`

Missing } in compound statement	Missing closing brace as part of conditional loop:
	`if (score == 0) { alert('game over'); // missing }`
	`on this line`

Missing } after property list	Missing closing brace for JavaScript object:
	`var x = { fName: 'bob', lName: 'smith' // missing`
	`} on this line`

Syntax Error	General problem that prevents JavaScript interpreter from reading the script.
Missing ; before statement	Lets you know when you've run two statements together on a single line, without separating them with a semicolon. You'll also see this when you incorrectly nest quotation marks: `var message='There's an error here.';`
Missing variable name	Appears if you attempt to use a JavaScript reserved word (see page 47) for a variable name: `var if="Syntax error.";`

Types of Errors

There are three basic categories of errors that you'll encounter as you program JavaScript. Some of these errors are immediately obvious, while others don't always rear their ugly heads until the script is up and running.

Syntax Errors. A syntax error is essentially a grammatical mistake that makes a web browser's JavaScript interpreter throw up its hands and say, "I give up." Any of the errors involving a missing closing parenthesis, brace, or quote mark generates a syntax error. The web browser encounters syntax errors immediately, as it reads the script, so the script never has a chance to run. An error message for a syntax error always appears in a web browser's error console.

Runtime errors. After a browser reads a script's code successfully and the JavaScript interpreter interprets it, it can still encounter errors. Even if the program's syntax is fine, other problems might pop up as the program runs—called *runtime* errors. For example, say you define a variable named *message* at the beginning of a script; later in the script, you add a click function to an image so an alert box appears when the image is clicked. Say the alert code for this example looks like this: *alert(MESSAGE);*. There's nothing wrong with this statement's syntax, but it calls the variable *MESSAGE* instead of lowercase *message*. As mentioned on page 473, JavaScript is case-sensitive, so *MESSAGE* and *message* refer to two different variables. When a visitor clicks the image, the JavaScript interpreter looks for the variable *MESSAGE* (which doesn't exist) and generates a runtime error.

Another common runtime error occurs when you try to access an element on a page that either doesn't exist or the browser hasn't yet read into its memory. See the discussion of jQuery's *$(document).ready()* function on page 169 for more detail on this problem.

Logic errors. Sometimes even though a script seems to run, it doesn't produce the results you're after. For example, you may have an if/else statement (page 79) that performs step A if a condition is true or step B if it's false. Unfortunately, the program never seems to get to step B, even if you're sure the condition is false. This kind of error happens when you use the equality operator incorrectly (see page 50). From the JavaScript interpreter's perspective, everything is technically correct, but you've made a mistake in the logic of your programming that prevents the script from working as planned.

Another example of a logic error is an infinite loop, which is a chunk of code that runs *forever*, usually causing your programming to hang up and sometimes even crashing the web browser. Here's an example of an infinite loop:

```
for (var i=1; i>0; i++) {
    // this will run forever
}
```

In a nutshell, this loop will run as long as the test condition *(i>0)* is true. Since *i* starts out with a value of 1 *(var i=1)*, and each time it goes through the loop *i* is increased by 1 *(i++)*, the value of *i* will always be greater than 0. In other words, the loop never stops. (Turn to page 97 if you need a refresher on *for* loops.)

Logic errors are amongst the most difficult to uncover. However, with the debugging techniques described on page 477, you should be able to uncover just about any problem you encounter.

Quotation Marks

Quote marks often trip up beginning programmers. Quote marks are used to create strings of letters and other characters (see page 43) to use as messages on the page, or as variables in a program. JavaScript, like other programming languages, lets you use either *double* or *single* quote marks to create a string. So,

```
var name="Jane";
```

is the same as:

```
var name='Jane';
```

As you read in the previous section, you must include both the opening and closing quote marks, or you'll end up with an "Unterminated string literal" error in Firefox (and all other browsers will give up on your script as well). In addition, as you read on page 44, you must use the same type of quote mark for each pair—in other words, both single quotes or both double quotes. So *var name='Jane"* will also generate an error.

Another common problem can arise with the use of quotations within a string. For example, it's very easy to make the following mistake:

```
var message='There's an error in here.';
```

Notice the single quote in *There's*. The JavaScript interpreter treats that quote mark as a closing quote, so it actually sees this: *var message='There'*, and the rest of the line is seen as an error. In the Firefox error console, you'll get the message "Missing ; before statement," because Firefox thinks that second quote is the end of a simple JavaScript statement and what follows is a second statement.

You can get around this error in two ways. First, you can mix and match double and single quotes. In other words, you can put double quotes around a string with single quotes, or you can put single quotes around a string containing double quotes. For example, you can fix the above error this way:

```
var message="There's no error in here.";
```

Or, if the string contains double quotes:

```
var message='He said, "There is no problem here."';
```

Another approach is to *escape* quote marks within a string. Escaping quote marks is discussed in greater detail in the box on page 44, but here's a recap: To escape a character, precede it with a forward slash, like this:

```
var message='There\'s no error here.';
```

The JavaScript interpreter treats \' as a single quote character and not as the symbol used to begin and end strings.

Using Reserved Words

As listed on page 47, the JavaScript language has many words that are reserved for its private use. These words include words used in the language's syntax like *if, do, for*, and *while*, as well as words used as part of the browser object, like *alert, location, window*, and *document*. These words are not available to use as variable names.

For example, the following code generates a syntax error:

```
var if = "This won't work.";
```

Since *if* is used to create conditional statements—as in *if (x==0)*—you can't use it as a variable name. Some browsers, however, won't generate an error if you use words that are part of the Browser Object Model for your variable names. For example, *document* refers to the HTML document. For example, look at the following code:

```
var document='Something strange is happening here.';
alert(document);
```

Firefox, Safari, and Opera don't generate an error, but instead pop up an alert with the text "[object HTMLDocument]," which refers not to the HTML document itself. In other words, those browsers won't let you overwrite the document object with a string. Chrome and Internet Explorer 9 generate error messages and won't display a pop up alert.

Single Equals in Conditional Statements

Conditional statements (page 79) provide a way for a program to react in different ways depending upon a value of a variable, the status of an element on a page, or some other condition in the script. For example, a conditional statement can display a picture *if* it's hidden or *else* hide it if it's visible. Conditional statements only make sense, however, if a particular condition can be *true* or *false*. Unfortunately, it's easy to create a conditional statement that's always true:

```
if (score=0) {
    alert('game over');
}
```

This code is supposed to check the value stored in the variable *score*—if the value is 0, then an alert box with the message "game over" should appear. However, in this case, the alert message will *always* display, no matter what value is stored in *score* prior to the conditional statement. That's because a single equal sign is an *assignment* operator, so *score=0* stores the value *0* in *score*. The JavaScript interpreter treats an assignment operation as *true*, so not only does the code above always pop up the alert box, it also rewrites the value of *score* to *0*.

To avoid this error, make sure to use *double* equal signs when testing whether two values are the same:

```
if (score==0) {
  alert('game over');
}
```

Case-Sensitivity

Remember that JavaScript is case-sensitive, meaning that the JavaScript interpreter tracks not only the letters in the names of variables, functions, methods, and keywords, but also whether the letters are uppercase or lowercase. So *alert('hi')* is not the same as *ALERT('hi')* to the JavaScript interpreter. The first, *alert('hi')*, calls the browser's built-in *alert()* command, while the second *ALERT('hi')* attempts to call a user-defined function named *ALERT()*.

You can run into this problem if you use the long-winded DOM selection methods *getElementsByTagName()* or *getElementById()*, since they use both upper and lower-case letters (another good reason to stick with jQuery). Likewise, if you include both upper and lowercase letters in variable and function names, you may run into this problem from time to time.

If you see an "*x* is not defined" error message (where *x* is the name of your variable, function, or method), mismatched case may be the problem.

Incorrect Path to External JavaScript File

Another common mistake is incorrectly linking to an external JavaScript file. Page 27 discusses how to attach an external JavaScript file to a web page. Basically, you use the <script> tag's *src* property to point to the file. So in the HTML page, you'd add the <script> tag to the <head> of the document like this:

```
<script src="site_js.js"></script>
```

The *src* property works like a link's *href* property—it defines the path to the JavaScript file. As mentioned in the box on page 28, there are three ways you can point to a file: absolute links (*http://www.site.com/site_js.js*), root-relative links (*/site_js.js*), and document-relative links (*site_js.js*).

A document-relative path describes how a web browser gets from the current page (the web page) to a particular file. Document-relative links are commonly used because they let you test your web page and JavaScript file right on your own computer. If you use root-relative links, you'll need to set up a web server on your own computer to test your pages (or move them up to your web server to test them).

You can read more about how link paths work on page 28. But, in a nutshell, if you find that a script doesn't work and you're using external JavaScript files, double-check to make sure you've specified the correct path to the JavaScript file.

Tip: If you're using the jQuery library and you get the error "$ is not defined" in the Firefox error console, you probably haven't correctly linked to the *jquery.js* file (see page 122 for more).

Incorrect Paths Within External JavaScript Files

Another problem related to file paths occurs when using document-relative paths in an external JavaScript file. For example, you might create a script that displays images on a page (like a slideshow or just a "random image of the day" script). If the script uses document-relative links to point to the images, you can run into trouble if you put that script into an external JavaScript file. Here's why: When an external JavaScript file is loaded into a web page, its frame of reference for document-relative paths is the location of the web page itself. So, any document-relative paths you include in the JavaScript file must be relative to the *web page* and not the JavaScript file.

Here's a simple example to illustrate this problem. Figure 15-2 represents the structure of a very simple website. There are two web pages (*page.html* and *about.html*), four folders (*libs, images, pages,* and *about*), an external JavaScript file (*site_js.js* inside the *libs* folder) and an image (*photo.jpg* in the *images* folder.) Say the *site_js.js* file references the *photo.jpg* file—perhaps to preload the image (page 209), or display it dynamically on a web page.

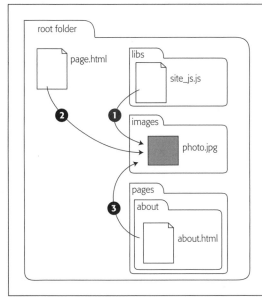

Figure 15-2:
Document-relative paths depend on both the location of the file that the path starts at as well as the location of the destination file. For example, the document-relative path from the site_js.js *file to the* photo.jpg *file (#1) is* ../images/photo.jpg; *the path to the same file from the* page.html *file (#2) is* images/photo.jpg; *and the path from the* about.html *file (#3) is* ../../images/photo.jpg.

From the *site_js.js* file's perspective, a document-relative path to the *photo.jpg* file is *../images/photo.jpg* (#1 in Figure 14-2). The path tells the browser to exit the *libs* folder (*../*), enter the *images* folder (*images/*), and select the *photo.jpg* file. However, from the perspective of the *page.html* file, the path to the *photo.jpg* file (#2 in Figure 14-2) is just *images/photo.jpg*. In other words, the path to the same photo differs between the two files.

If you want to use the *site_js.js* script within the *page.html* file, then, you have to use path #2 in the *site_js.js* file to reference the location of *photo.jpg* (that is, specify a path relative to *page.html*). By the same token, you can't use the *site_js.js* file in a web page located in another directory in your site, since the relative path would be different for that file (#3 in Figure 15-2).

There are a few ways around this problem. First, well, you may never encounter it—you may not find yourself listing paths to other files in your JavaScript files. But if you do, you can use root-relative paths (see page 28), which are the same from any page in the site. Alternatively, you can define the path to the files within each web page. For example, you can link to the external JavaScript file (see page 27), and then, in each web page, define variables to hold document-relative paths from the current web page to the correct file.

Finally, you could use an approach like the one used in the slideshow on page 222. The paths come from the web page and are embedded within links on the page—the JavaScript simply pulls the paths out of the HTML. As long as those paths work in the HTML, they'll work in a script as well.

Disappearing Variables and Functions

You may occasionally encounter an "*x* is not defined" error, where *x* is either the name of a variable or a function you're trying to call. The problem may just be that you mistyped the name of the variable or function, or used the wrong case. However, if you look through your code and can clearly see that the variable or function is defined in your script, then you may be running into a "scope" problem.

Variable and function scope is discussed in greater detail on page 105, but in a nutshell, if a variable is defined inside of a function, it's only available to that function (or to other functions defined inside that function). Here's a simple example:

```
1   function sayName(name) {
2     var message = 'Your name is ' + name;
3   }
4   sayName();
5   alert(message); // error: message is not defined
```

The variable *message* is defined within the function *sayName()*, so it only exists for that function. Outside the function, *message* doesn't exist, so an error is generated when the script tries to access the variable outside the function (line 5).

You may also encounter this error when using jQuery. On page 169, you read about the importance of the *$(document).ready()* function for jQuery. Anything inside that function only runs once the page's HTML is loaded. You'll run into problems if you define variables or functions within the *$(document).ready()* function and try to access them outside of it, like this:

```
$(document).ready(function() {
  var msg = 'hello';
});
alert(msg); // error: msg is not defined
```

So, when using jQuery, be sure to put all of your programming inside the *$(document).ready()* function:

```
$(document).ready(function() {
  var msg = 'hello';
  alert(msg); // msg is available
});
```

Programming Tips to Reduce Errors

The best way to deal with errors and bugs in your programs is to try to stop them as early as possible. It can be really difficult to track down the cause of errors in a program if you wait until you've written a 300-line script before testing it in a web browser. The two most important tips to avoiding errors are:

Build a script in small chunks. As you've probably figured out by now, JavaScript programs can be difficult to read, what with all of the },), ', ifs, elses, functions, and so on. Don't try to write an entire script in one go (unless you're really good, the script is short, or you're feeling lucky). There are so many ways to make a mistake while programming, and you're better off writing a script in bits.

For example, say you want to display the number of letters typed into a "Comments" box, right next to the box. In other words, as a visitor types into the field, a running total of the number of letters typed appears next to the box. (Some sites do this when they limit the amount a visitor can type into a field—say, 300 letters.) This task is pretty easy JavaScript, but it involves several steps: responding to the keydown event (when a visitor types a letter in the

field), reading the value of that field, counting the numbers of characters in the field, and then displaying that number on the page. You can try to write this script in one go, but you can also write the code for step 1 (responding to a keydown event) and then test it immediately in a web browser (using the *alert()* command or Firebug's *console.log()* function, described on the next page, can help you see the results of a keydown event). If it works, you can then move on to step 2, test it, and so on.

As you gain more experience, you won't need to test such small steps. You can write a few steps at once, and then test that chunk.

Test frequently. You should also test your script in a web browser frequently. At a minimum, test after you complete each chunk of the program, as suggested in the previous point. In addition, you should test the script in different browsers—preferably Internet Explorer 7, 8, and 9; Firefox 5 and 6; the latest versions of Chrome and Safari; and whatever other browsers you think your site's visitors might be using.

Debugging with Firebug

If you haven't been using Firebug, you've been missing out on one of the best tools a web designer could have. It's free, easy to install and use, and can help you improve your HTML, CSS, and JavaScript. Firebug is an extension for Firefox that adds a bunch of helpful diagnostic tools to let you pick apart your HTML, CSS, and (most importantly for this book) JavaScript programs.

Installing and Turning On Firebug

You can find the extension at *www.getfirebug.com*, or from the Mozilla Add-Ons site. Here's how to install it:

1. Visit *http://addons.mozilla.org/firefox/addon/firebug* using Firefox, and click the "Add to Firefox" button.

   To protect you from accidentally installing a malicious extension, Firefox stops your first attempt at installing the extension. A Software Installation window appears, warning you that malicious software is bad (oh, really?). Don't worry; Firebug is perfectly safe.

2. Click the Install Now button.

   Firefox installs the extension, but it won't work until you restart Firefox. A small window appears explaining that very thing.

3. Click the Restart button.

   Voila, Firebug is installed and ready to use, but first you need to open it.

4. On Windows, choose Firefox→Web Developer→Firebug→Open Firebug or Press F12; on Macs, choose Tools→ Web Developer→Firebug→Enable Firebug.

   Now you can begin using Firebug to help you debug your scripts.

Viewing Errors with Firebug

Firebug provides an easier and more useful way to view errors than Firefox's built-in error console. With Firebug, when you load a web page with JavaScript errors, you'll see a counter in the upper right listing the number of errors encountered (see Figure 15-3). Click the Firebug icon to open the Firebug console, which lists any JavaScript errors.

The errors listed in the console are the same as Firefox's error console (Figure 15-1), but Firebug only lists errors for the page you're currently viewing (unlike the error console, which lists all errors on all pages Firefox has visited). Because Firebug provides such easy access to error information, you'll probably find yourself skipping the Firefox error console entirely once you've experienced Firebug.

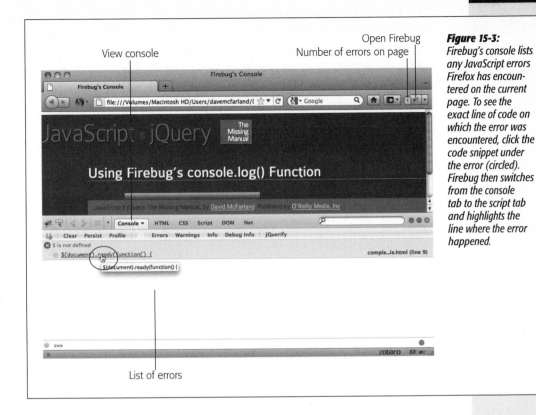

View console

Open Firebug

Number of errors on page

List of errors

Figure 15-3:
Firebug's console lists any JavaScript errors Firefox has encountered on the current page. To see the exact line of code on which the error was encountered, click the code snippet under the error (circled). Firebug then switches from the console tab to the script tab and highlights the line where the error happened.

Using *console.log()* to Track Script Progress

Once a script begins to run, it's kind of like a black box. You don't really know what's going on inside the script and only see the end result, like a message on the page, a pop-up window, and so on. You can't always tell exactly whether a loop is working correctly or see the value of a particular variable at any point in time.

JavaScript programmers have long used the *alert()* method (page 29) to pop up a window with the current value of a variable. For example, if you want to know what value is being stored in the variable *elementName* as a loop is running, you can insert an alert command inside the loop: *alert(elementName);*. That's one way to look into the "black box" of the script. However, the alert box is pretty intrusive: You have to click it to close it, and in a loop that might run 20 times, that's a lot of pop-up alerts to close.

Firebug provides a better way to look into your program. The Firebug console not only lists errors (see previous section), but can also be used to output messages from the program. The *console.log()* function works similar to the *document.write()* function (page 31), but instead of printing a message to the web page, *console.log()* prints a message to the console.

Tip: All current browsers support the *console.log()* method. So you can use it in Chrome, Safari, Internet Explorer, and Opera's consoles as discussed in Chapter 1.

For example, you could print the current value of the variable *elementName* to the console using this code:

```
console.log(elementName);
```

Unlike the *alert()* method, this method won't interrupt your program's flow—you'll just see the message in the console.

To make the log message more understandable, you can include a string with additional text. For example, if you have a variable named *name* and you want to determine what value is stored in *name* at some point in your program, you can use the *console.log()* function like this:

```
console.log(name);
```

But if you wanted to precede the name with a message, you can write this:

```
console.log('User name: %s', name);
```

In other words, you first pass a string to the *log()* function, followed by a comma and the name of the variable whose value should be displayed. The special *%s* is way of saying "substitute the variable value with me." In other words, *%s* gets replaced with the value of *name*, so you'll end up with a message in the console like "User name: Bob."

You can add more than one variable to the message; just include one *%s* for each variable. For example, if you have two variables, *name* and *score*, and want to print both along with a custom log message, you can do the following:

```
console.log('%s has a score of %s', name, score);
```

You can use *%s* for numeric values, but Firebug provides two other tokens—*%d* and *%f*—to represent integers (like 1, 2, and 10) and floating point numbers (like 1.22 and 2.4444). Using one of the two numeric tokens means the numbers are printed in a different color—just an easy way to tell them apart from the rest of the text.

For example, you can rewrite the line of code above to display the number stored in the variable *score*:

```
console.log('%s has a score of %d', name, score);
```

The *log()* function is merely a way to give you some information about the functioning of your script as you *develop* it. Once your program is finished and working, you should remove all of the *console.log()* code from your script. Web browsers that don't understand the *console.log()* method (like older versions of Internet Explorer) generate errors when they encounter the *log()* function.

Tutorial: Using the Firebug Console

In this tutorial, you'll learn how to use the *console.log()* function to see what's going on inside your program. You'll create a script that displays the number of characters typed into a text box on a form.

Note: See the note on page 29 for information on how to download the tutorial files.

To get started, first install Firebug in Firefox using the instructions on page 477 (remember, Firebug only works with the Firefox web browser).

1. **Open the file *console.html* in a text editor.**

   This script uses the jQuery library. The external *jQuery* file is already attached to the page, and the opening and closing <script> tags are in place. You'll start by adding jQuery's *$(document).ready()* function.

2. **Between the <script> tags near the top of the page, add the code in bold below:**

   ```
   <script>
   $(document).ready(function() {

   }); // end ready
   </script>
   ```

   You learned about the basic *$(document).ready()* function on page 147, which makes the browser load all of the page's code before starting to run any JavaScript. You'll first use the Firebug *log()* function to simply print out a message that the script has executed the *.ready()* function.

3. **Add the bolded code below to the script:**

   ```
   <script>
   $(document).ready(function() {
     console.log('READY');
   }); // end ready
   </script>
   ```

   The *console.log()* function runs wherever you place it in the script. In other words, after this page's HTML is loaded (that's what the *ready()* function waits for), Firebug writes "READY" to the Firebug console. Adding the *ready()* function is a pretty common and basic move, so you may not always add a *console.log()* function here, but for this tutorial, you'll add one to see how the *log()* function works. In fact, you'll be adding a lot of log messages to this page to get the hang of the *console.log()* function.

4. **Save the file, and open it in Firefox. If Firebug isn't already open, click the Firebug icon in the upper-right corner of Firefox's tool bar.**

   You can also choose FirefoxTools→Web Developer→Firebug→Open Firebug to see the Firebug console.

The word READY should appear in the console (circled in Figure 15-4). The
script you're creating will display the number of characters typed into a form's
text field each time your visitor types a character. To accomplish this, you'll add
a keyup event (page 162) to that text box. During each step of this script, you'll
also add a *console.log()* function, to clue you in to what's happening.

Figure 15-4:
*If a number appears to
the left of the Firebug
icon in the upper-right
corner of Firefox's tool
bar there's a JavaScript
error (probably just a
typo). Open Firebug
(click the Firebug icon)
to view the error in the
console.*

5. **After the line of code you added in step 3, add the following:**

```
$('#comments').keyup(function() {
  console.log('Event: keyup');
}); // end keyup
```

The <textarea> tag on this page has an ID of comments, so we can select that
element using jQuery (*$('#comments')*) and add a function to the *keyup* event
(see page 162 if you need a refresher on adding events). In this case, the *console.
log()* function is just printing a status message to the Firebug console telling
you each time the keyup event is triggered. This function is an easy way to see
whether an event function is actually running or something's preventing the
event from happening.

Save the page; reload it in Firefox and type a few characters into the text box. Make sure Firebug's console is open, and you should see several lines (one for each character you typed) of *'Event: keyup'*, Now that the *keyup* event is working, you might want to retrieve the contents of the text box and store it in a variable. To be sure you're getting the information you're after, you'll print the contents of the variable to the console.

6. **Add lines 3 and 4 below to the code you typed in step 5:**

```
1    $('#comments').keyup(function() {
2      console.log('Event: keyup');
3      var text = $(this).val();
4      console.log('Contents of comments: %s',text);
5    }); // end keyup
```

Line 3 retrieves the value from the text box and stores it inside a variable named *text* (see page 261 for more information on extracting the value from a form field). Line 4 writes a message to the console. In this case, it combines a string 'Contents of comments: ' and the value currently stored in the text box. When a program isn't working correctly, a very common diagnostic step is to print out the values of variables in the script to make sure the variable contains the information you're expecting it to have.

7. **Save the file, reload it in Firefox, and type some text into the comments box.**

The console should now display the contents in the comments box each time you type a letter into the field. By now you should be getting the hang of the console, so you'll add one more message, and then finish this script.

8. **Edit the keyup event function by adding two more lines (5 and 6 below):**

```
1    $('#comments').keyup(function() {
2      console.log('Event: keyup');
3      var text = $(this).val();
4      console.log('Contents of comments %s',text);
5      var chars = text.length;
6      console.log('Number of characters: %d',chars);
7    }); // end keyup
```

Line 5 counts the number of characters stored inside the *text* variable (see page 425 for more on the *length* property) and stores it inside the variable *chars*. Just to make sure the script is correctly calculating the number of characters, use the *log()* function (line 6) to print a message to the console. Since the variable *chars* holds a number, you use the *%d* token to display an integer value.

There's just one last thing to do: Finish the script so it prints the number of characters typed so your visitor can see it.

9. **Add one last line to the end of the keyup event function (line 10), so the completed script for the page looks like this:**

```
1    <script>
2    $(document).ready(function() {
3      console.log('READY');
4      $('#comments').keyup(function() {
```

```
5       console.log('Event: keyup');
6       var text = $(this).val();
7       console.log('Contents of comments: %s',text);
8       var chars = text.length;
9       console.log('Number of characters: %d',chars);
10   $('#count').text(chars + " characters");
11     }); // end keyup
12   }); // end ready
13   </script>
```

10. **Save the file, and preview it in Firefox.**

Make sure Firebug is open, and the page and console should now look something like Figure 15-5. You'll find a finished version of this tutorial—*complete_console.html*—in the *chapter15* folder in the tutorials folder.

Note: Once you have a functioning program, you should remove all *console.log()* code from your script. The *log()* function will generate errors in some browsers.

Figure 15-5:
The Firebug console is a great way to print out diagnostic information as a program is running. You can also group together a series of log entries (for example, to group all the log messages printed during a loop) by adding console. group() *before the first* console. log() *message in the group, and* console.groupEnd() *after the last message. These same functions work in Safari and Chrome's consoles (but not in Opera or Internet Explorer 9).*

More Powerful Debugging

The Firebug console is a great way to print out messages so you can see what's going on when a program runs. But sometimes a program zips by so quickly it's hard to see what's going on during each step. You need a way to slow things down. Fortunately, Firebug includes a powerful JavaScript debugger. It lets you step through a script line by line so you can see what's happening at each step of the program.

Note: You'll also find JavaScript debuggers with similar functionality in Chrome, Opera, Safari, and Internet Explorer 9.

Debugging is the process of fixing an incorrectly functioning program—getting the bugs out. To really understand how a program is functioning (or malfunctioning), you need to see how the program works, step-by-step.

To use the debugger, you mark certain lines of code as *breakpoints*. A breakpoint is a spot where the JavaScript interpreter stops running and waits. You can then use controls inside Firebug that let you run a program one line at a time. In this way, you can see exactly what's happening at any particular line. Here's the basic process.

1. **Open a web page in Firefox.**

   You need Firebug installed and enabled as described on page 477.

2. **Open Firebug.**

   Click the Firebug icon (in the upper-right corner of the Firefox toolbar). Alternatively, press F12 (Windows only) or choose Firefox→Web Developer→Firebug→Open Firebug (Windows) or Tools→ Web Developer→Firebug→Enable Firebug (Mac).

Note: If you don't like the cramped appearance of the web page stacked directly on top of Firebug, choose Firefox→Web Developer→Firebug→"Open Firebug in New Window" (Windows) or Tools→ Web Developer→Firebug→"Open Firebug in New Window" (Mac).

3. **Click the Script tab (see Figure 15-6).**

   The Script tab lists the source code for the file you wish to debug. In the case of a script that's written into a web page, you see the source code for the entire web page (including HTML). For an external JavaScript file, you see just the JavaScript in that file.

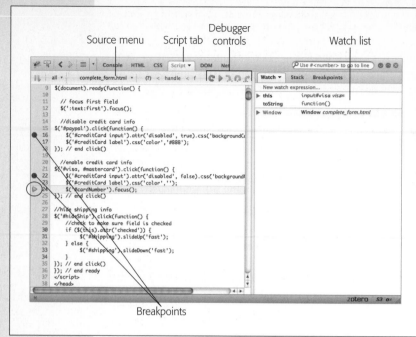

Source menu   Script tab   Debugger
controls   Watch list

Figure 15-6:
*The Firebug debugger
lets you set breakpoints
(lines where the script
stops and waits), control
the execution of the
script, and watch vari-
ables in the Watch list. As
the debugger executes
the script, the current line
(the one that's about to
run) has a yellow arrow
to its left (circled).*

Breakpoints

4. **Select the file with the script you wish to debug from the source menu (see Figure 15-6).**

    It's common to have scripts placed in different files: the web page itself, or one or more external JavaScript files. If your page uses scripts from multiple files, you need to select the file containing the script you wish to debug.

5. **Add breakpoints.**

    To add a breakpoint, click to the left of the line's number. A red bullet appears indicating a breakpoint.

Note: Adding a breakpoint to a line that only contains a comment has no effect—the debugger won't stop on that line. Only add breakpoints to lines containing actual JavaScript code.

---

6. **Reload the web page.**

    Since you have to view your web page in Firefox in order to open Firebug and add breakpoints, the JavaScript you want to debug may have already run (before you added any breakpoints). In this case, you need to reload the page so you can start the JavaScript over again.

    If you added a break point in a function that responds to an event (for example, you want to debug the code that runs when you click a button or mouse over a link), then you need to trigger that event—click the button, mouse over the link, or whatever—to reach the breakpoint and start the debugging process.

After the script begins to run, as soon as a breakpoint is reached, the script stops. The program is frozen in time, waiting to execute the line from the first breakpoint.

7. **Use Firebug's controls to step through the execution of the program.**

Firebug provides four controls (see Figure 15-6) that dictate how the program runs after stopping at the breakpoint. You can read about these controls in the next section.

8. **Monitor program conditions in the Watch list (see Figure 15-6).**

The point of stepping through a program is to see what's going on inside the script at any particular line. The Watch list provides basic information about the program's condition and lets you add additional variables you want to watch. For example, if you wanted to track the value of the variable score as the script runs, you can do that in the Watch list. You'll find out how to use the Watch list on page 488.

9. **Fix your script in a text editor.**

Hopefully, in stepping through your script you'll find out what's going wrong—for example, why the value of a particular variable never changes, or why a conditional statement never evaluates to false. With that information, you can then jump to your text editor and modify your script (you'll run through an example of fixing a script in the tutorial on page 489).

10. **Test the page in Firefox, and, if necessary, repeat the above steps to keep debugging your script.**

Controlling your script with the debugger

Once you've added breakpoints to the script and reloaded the page, you're ready to step through the script line by line. If you added a breakpoint to part of the script that runs when the page loads, the script will stop at the breakpoint; if you added a breakpoint to a line that only runs after an event (like clicking a link), you need to trigger that event before you can get to the breakpoint.

When the debugger stops the program at a breakpoint, it doesn't run that line of code; it stops just *before* running it. You can then click one of the four buttons on the debugger to control what the debugger does next (see Figure 15-6):

- **Play**. The Play button simply starts the script running. The script won't stop again until the JavaScript interpreter encounters another breakpoint, or until the script has finished running. If there's another breakpoint, the script stops again and waits for you to click one of the four debugger controls.

  Use the Play button if you just want run the program through or skip to the next breakpoint.

- **Step Over**. This useful option runs the current line of code, then stops at the next line in the script. It's named Step Over because if the current line of code includes a call to a function, it won't enter the function—it steps over the function and stops at the next line of code. This option is great if you know the function that's being called works flawlessly. For example, if your script calls a jQuery function, you'll want to step over the call to that function—otherwise, you'll be spending a lot of time viewing the scary jQuery programming line by line. You'll choose the Step Over option, unless you're at a line of code that calls a function you've created—then you'll want to see what happens inside that function using the Step Into option described next.

- **Step Into**. Step Into takes the debugger into a function call. That is, if you're on a line that includes a call to a function, the debugger enters the function and stops at the first line of that function. This option is the way to go when you're not sure if the problem is in the main script or within a function you wrote.

  Skip this option if you're sure that the function being called works—for example, if the function is one you've used dozens of times before. You also want to use Step Over instead of Step Into when you're debugging a line of code that includes a jQuery selector or command. For example, *$('#button')* is a jQuery way to select an element on the page. However, it's also a function of the jQuery library, so if you click the Step Into button when you encounter a jQuery function, you'll jump into the complex world of the jQuery library. (And if that happens, you'll know because the script tab will change to show all of the JavaScript code for the *jQuery* file.)

  If, when using the debugger, you find yourself lost within a function, or in the code of a JavaScript library like jQuery, you can use the control described next to get out.

- **Step Out**. The Step Out button gets the debugger out of a function call. You'll usually use it after using Step Into. When you do, the function runs as normal, but you won't stop at each line of the function as you would if you clicked the Step Over or Step Into buttons. When you click this button, the debugger returns to the line where the function was originally called and then stops.

Watching your script

While the buttons at the top of the debugger let you control how the script executes, the whole point of a debugger is to see what's going on inside the script. That's where the Watch list comes in (see Figure 15-7). The Watch list provides a listing of variables and functions within the context of the current executing line of code. All that means is if you put a breakpoint within a function, you'll see a list of all of the variables that are defined within that function; if you put a breakpoint in the main body of your script, you'll see a list of all variables that are defined there. You'll also see any functions that you've created listed in the Watch list.

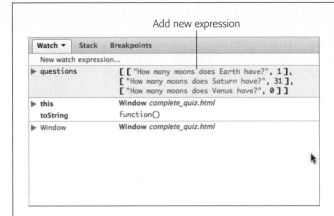

Add new expression

Figure 15-7:
Firebug's Watch list shows the value of different variables as the program runs. You can add your own expressions to the list, which appear as grey stripes at the top of the window.

You can add your own variables and expressions using the yellow bar with the label "New watch expression…". Just click the yellow bar, and a text field appears. Type the name of a variable you'd like to track, or even a JavaScript statement you'd like to execute. For example, since the debugger doesn't keep track of a counter variable in a *for* loop (page 97), you can add this variable, and as you go step by step through the loop, you can see how the counter changes each time through the loop.

You can think of this Watch list as a kind of a continual *console.log()* command. It prints out the value of a particular variable or expression at the time a particular line of code is run.

The Watch list offers valuable insight into your program, providing a kind of freeze-frame effect so you can find exactly where in your script an error occurs. For example, if you know that a particular variable holds a number value, you can go step by step through the script and see what value gets stored in the variable when it's first created and see how its value gets modified as the program runs. If, after you click the Step Through or Step Into buttons, you see the variable's value change to something you didn't expect, then you've probably found the line where the error is introduced.

Debugging Tutorial

In this tutorial, you'll use Firebug to debug a file that's filled with various types of errors (syntax errors, runtime errors, and logic errors). The page is a simple quiz program that poses three questions and prints quiz results. (Open the *complete_debugger.html* file in the *chapter15* folder in any web browser to see how the page is supposed to work.)

Note: See the note on page 29 for information on how to download the tutorial files.

To complete this tutorial, you'll need run the Firefox web browser and have the Firebug extension installed and turned on—see page 477 for instructions.

1. **Start Firefox and open the file** *debugger.html* **from the** *chapter15* **tutorials folder.**

   In the top, right of the browser window, Firebug indicates that there is 1 error (see Figure 15-8). You must open the Firebug console to find out what's wrong.

2. **Click the Firebug icon in the top right of the browser to open Firebug, and select the Console tab.**

   You should see the error message in Figure 15-8: "Missing] after element list." Square brackets are used for creating arrays (see page 60), so it appears that one of an array's closing brackets is missing. This omission is a syntax error (see the box on page 471) because it represents a "grammatical error" in the code (like a sentence missing a period). You'll notice that to the right of the error message, Firebug lets you know that this error occurred in line 15.

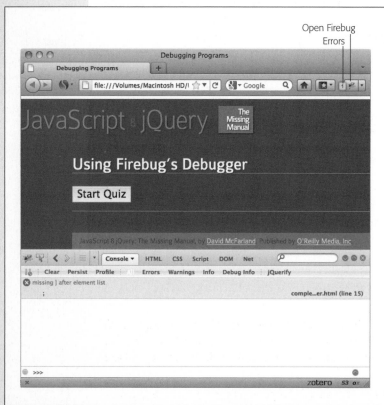

Open Firebug
Errors

Figure 15-8:
The Firebug console is the first stop for tracking down syntax and runtime errors that bring a script to its knees.

3. **Launch your text editor and open the file** *debugger.html.* **Locate line 15 (it's a single ; on a line by itself). Type a closing square bracket before the ; so the line looks like this:**

```
];
```

This bracket ended a nested array (page 110) that contained all of the questions and answers for the quiz.

4. **Save the file; return to Firefox, and reload the page.**

Another error! This time the error console says "$ is not defined" and points to line 10 containing jQuery's *$(document).ready()* function. When Firefox reports that something's "not defined," it means the code is referring to something that doesn't exist, which could be the name of a variable or a function that hasn't yet been created. Or you might just have a typo in the code. In this case, the code looks OK. The culprit is actually earlier on the page, in this code:

```
<script src="_js/jquery-1.6.3.min.js"></script>
```

A common problem when working with external scripts is accidentally typing the wrong path to the script. In this case, the *jquery-1.6.2min.js* file is located inside a folder named *_js* that's *outside* this file's folder. The code here says that the file should be inside the same folder as this web page; because Firefox can't find the *jquery-1.6.3.min.js* file (where jQuery's special *$()* function is defined), it spits out an error.

5. **Change the <script> tag to read:**

```
<script  src="../_js/jquery-1.6.3.min.js"></script>
```

The ../ indicates that the *js* folder is outside this folder, and the path is now correctly pointing to the jQuery file. What else could be wrong with this program?

6. **Save the file; return to Firefox and reload the page.**

No errors! Looks like the page is fixed…or is it?

7. **Click the Start Quiz button on the web page.**

Bam! Another error. This time the console reports that "askQuestions is not defined" and points to line 69 near the end of the script. Since this error only appears while the program is running, it's called a runtime error (see the box on page 471). The problem appears toward the end of the script, within this conditional statement:

```
if (quiz.length>0) {
  askQuestions();
  } else {
    giveResults();
  }
```

By now it's probably dawning on you that when something's not defined, it's often just because of a simple typo. In this case, *askQuestions()* is a call to a function, so take a moment now to look through the code and try to find this function.

Did you find it? While there isn't an *askQuestions()* function, you should have noticed an *askQuestion()* function (without an *s*).

8. **Return to your text editor, and then remove the last *s* from *askQuestions()* in line 70 (near the end of the script). Save the file, reload it in Firefox, and then click the Start Quiz button again.**

   Now, a quiz question appears along with five multiple-choice options. Unfortunately, the last option has a label of *undefined*. Smells like an error. However, the Firebug console is empty, so technically there's no JavaScript error. Something must be wrong with the program's *logic*. To get to the bottom of the trouble, you'll need to use Firebug's debugger.

9. **In Firebug, click the Script tab and select *debugger.html* from the source menu directly above the Script tab (see Figure 15-9).**

   The Script tab gives you access to the page's JavaScript. If the page includes JavaScript and you've linked to other external JavaScript files, the Source menu lets you choose which JavaScript code you wish to debug.

   Because the "undefined" radio button seems to be out of place, the code that creates the radio buttons is a good place to start looking for this bug. If you had written this script, you'd probably know just where to look in your code; however, if you were just handed this buggy script, you'd have to hunt around until you found that part of the script.

   In this case, the radio buttons are created within a function named *buildAnswers()*, whose purpose is to build a series of multiple choice options represented by radio buttons. That function is passed an array that includes a list of values for each radio button. When the function is done, it returns a string containing the HTML for the radio buttons. So this function's a good place to start debugging.

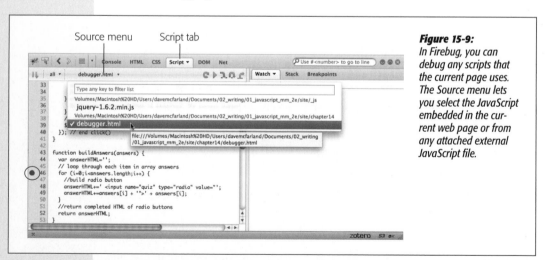

Figure 15-9:
In Firebug, you can debug any scripts that the current page uses. The Source menu lets you select the JavaScript embedded in the current web page or from any attached external JavaScript file.

10. **In Firebug's Script tab, scroll down until you see line 47. Click to the left of 46 to insert a breakpoint (circled in Figure 15-9).**

A red dot appears to the left of line 46. The dot indicates a breakpoint, or a spot in the code, where the JavaScript interpreter stops running the script. In other words, when this script runs again, the moment the JavaScript interpreter hits that line, it stops, and you'll be able to step line by line through the code to see what's happening under the hood.

The debugger also lets you look at the values of variables as the program runs, much as you used the *console.log()* function on page 479. You'll tell Firebug what variables you want to track next.

11. **In the right side of the Firebug window, click the New Watch Expression bar, type *i*, and then press the Return (or Enter) key.**

    This step adds the variable *i* to the Watch list. That variable is used in the *for* loop as a counter to track how many times the loop runs (see page 97 for more on for loops). As the script runs, you'll be able to see how that value changes. Next, you'll add another variable to watch.

12. **Click the New Watch Expression bar again, type *answers.length*, and then hit Return.**

    Don't worry about the value Firebug displays at this point (it probably says "answers is not defined"). You can't track the values of many variables until you're actually running the debugger and are inside the function where the variable lives. Now it's time to take a look inside the script.

13. **Click Firefox's Reload button or press Ctrl+R (⌘-R). When the page reloads, click the Start Quiz button on the web page.**

    The script starts, and the first question is written to the web page. But when it comes time to create the radio buttons, the debugger stops at line 46 (see the top image in Figure 14-10). Notice that in the Watch tab, the value for *i* is *not defined*. That's because the breakpoint stops the program just before the line is executed. In other words, the loop hasn't started, and the *i* variable hasn't yet been created.

    However, the value of *answers.length* is set to 4. The array *answers* is an array of answers that was passed to the function (you can see the array elements listed lower down in the Watch list). An array's *length* property indicates the number of items in the array; in this case there are four, so you should get four radio buttons when the function's completed.

14. **Click the Step Over button (see Figure 15-10).**

    This button takes you to the next line in the program. Now you can see that *i* is set to 0. You'll keep clicking through this loop.

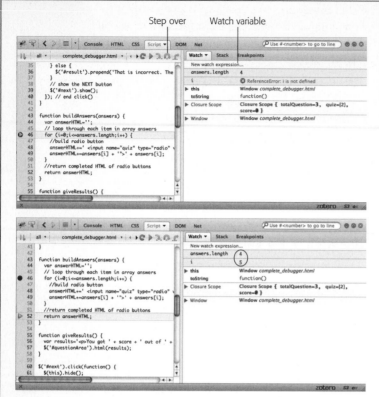

Figure 15-10:
When you step through a program using Firebug, red circles to the right of a line number indicate a break point, while yellow arrows indicate the line of code that the JavaScript interpreter is currently stopped at. Click Step Over (or Step Into) to run that line of code and stop at the next line.

15. **Click the Step Over button until you see the value of *i* change to *5* in the Watch list (bottom image in Figure 15-10).**

Although there are only four items in the *answers* array, you can see that the *for* loop is actually running five times (the value of *i*). So something's funny about how the loop is terminated. Remember that in a *for* loop, the middle statement in the *for* statement is the condition that must be true for the loop to run (see page 97). In this case, the condition is *i<=answers.length;*. In other words, the loop starts out with *i* containing 0 and continues to run as long as *i* is less than or equal to the number of items in the *answers* array. In other words, *i* will be 0, 1, 2, 3, and 4 before it terminates—that's five times. However, since there's only four items in the answers array, the fifth time through the loop there are no more answers to print: "undefined" is printed because there is no fifth item in the answers array.

16. **Return to your text editor, and change the for loop at line 46 to read:**

    ```
    for (i=0;i<answers.length;i++) {
    ```

    Now the loop only runs for the number of items in the answers array, creating one radio button for each possible answer.

17. **Save the file, and preview it in Firefox.**

    You can turn off the breakpoint by clicking its red dot in the firebug script window to see the finished page run without interruption.

The page *complete_debugger.html* contains the completed version of this tutorial. As you can see, finding bugs in a program can take a lot of work. But a debugging tool like Firebug makes it a lot easier to see inside a program's "guts" and find out what's going wrong.

JavaScript Resources

This book provides enough information and real-world techniques to get your JavaScript career off to a great start. But no one book can answer all of your JavaScript or jQuery questions. There's plenty to learn when it comes to JavaScript programming, and this appendix gives you taking-off points for further research and learning.

References

Sometimes you need a dictionary to read a book. When programming in JavaScript, it's great to have a complete reference to the various keywords, terms, methods, and other assorted bits of JavaScript syntax. You can find references both in online and book form.

Websites

- **Mozilla Developer Center Core JavaScript Reference** (*https://developer.mozilla .org/en/JavaScript/Reference*) provides a complete reference to JavaScript. It's very detailed, but sometimes hard to understand since it's aimed at a technical audience.

- **JavaScript Quick Reference from DevGuru** (*www.devguru.com/technologies/ javascript*) is a straightforward listing or JavaScript keywords and methods. Click a term, and a page explaining the keyword or method appears.

- **Google Doctype** (*http://code.google.com/doctype*) covers JavaScript, DOM, and CSS and tells you which features are supported by each browser. It's a kind of encyclopedia for Web developers.

- MSDN JavaScript Language Reference (*http://msdn.microsoft.com/en-us/library/yek4tbz0(v=VS.94).aspx*) from Microsoft is an excellent resource if you're developing with Internet Explorer. While it provides technical information on the JavaScript used in other browsers, this resources provides a lot of IE-only information.

Books

- **JavaScript: The Definitive Guide** by David Flanagan (O'Reilly) is the most thorough printed encyclopedia on JavaScript. It's a dense, heavy tome, but it has all the details you need to thoroughly understand JavaScript.

Basic JavaScript

JavaScript isn't easy to learn, and it never hurts to use as many resources as possible to learn the ins and outs of programming for the Web. The following resources provide help with the basics of the JavaScript language (which can sometimes be quite difficult).

Articles and Presentations

- **A (Re)-Introduction to JavaScript** by Simon Willison (*www.slideshare.net/simon/a-reintroduction-to-javascript*). This entertaining presentation provides a slide-based overview of the JavaScript language.

Websites

- **The W3 Schools JavaScript tutorial** (*www.w3schools.com/js*) is a thorough (though not always thoroughly explained) tutorial that covers most aspects of JavaScript programming.

- **An Introduction to JavaScript** from howtocreate.co.uk (*www.howtocreate.co.uk/tutorials/javascript/introduction*) provides a free, detailed discussion of JavaScript. Of course, since you're using jQuery you won't need a lot of the information on this site, since it covers much of the traditional methods of selecting and manipulating DOM elements.

Books

- **Head First JavaScript** by Michael Morrison (O'Reilly) is a lively, highly illustrated introduction to JavaScript programming. It provides lots of information on how JavaScript works and how to program with it, but doesn't provide much in the way of immediately useful web page examples.

jQuery

Much of this book covered the jQuery JavaScript library, but there's still lots to learn about this powerful, timesaving, and fun programming library.

Articles and Presentations

- **jQuery Essentials** by Marc Grabanski (*www.slideshare.net/1Marc/jquery-essentials*) is a fun and thorough slideshow covering the basics of jQuery. Highly recommended.

- **jQuery Tutorials for Designers** (*www.webdesignerwall.com/tutorials/jquery-tutorials-for-designers*) is an article from the well-known web design blog, Web-Designer Wall, that includes 10 cool, simple things you can do with jQuery.

- **jQuery Cheatsheet** (*http://woorkup.com/2011/05/12/jquery-visual-cheat-sheet-1-6/*) is a downloadable PDF that puts all of jQuery's functions on a single, printable page.

Websites

- **jQuery.com**, the home of the wonderful jQuery JavaScript library, provides access to discussion groups, documentation, plug-ins, and downloads.

- **jQuery's documentation** is provided via a user-generated Wiki (*http://docs.jquery.com*). Anyone's free to add or edit the descriptions of jQuery's many features on this site, but a core group of people handles most of the documentation. It's the number one place for complete information on jQuery.

- **jQuery for Designers** (*http://jqueryfordesigners.com*) is a site that includes written and video tutorials for creating interesting visual effects, useful interfaces, and generally improving websites using jQuery.

- **Learning jQuery** (*www.learningjquery.com*) provides information from some of jQuery's lead developers.

- **Script Junkie** (*http://msdn.microsoft.com/en-us/scriptjunkie*) is a Microsoft site aimed at web developers. It includes great articles on HTML, CSS, and JavaScript (with an emphasis on jQUery).

Books

- **jQuery in Action** by Bear Bibeault and Yehuda Katz (Manning) covers jQuery thoroughly with lots of example programming. It assumes some JavaScript and programming knowledge.

- **jQuery Cookbook** (O'Reilly) features tons of "recipes" for some of the most common tasks and problems you'll face as a programmer. It's written by a cast of characters, many of them the brilliant minds behind jQuery.

- **jQuery: Novice to Ninja** by Earle Casteldine and Craig Sharkie (Sitepoint) provides lots of instructions in using jQuery as many hands-on examples that show how to tackle common user-interface needs.

Ajax

Ajax brings together your Web browser, JavaScript, and server-side programming, for triple the fun (and three times the headache). Fortunately, there are plenty of resources to turn to for learning how to use Ajax.

Websites

- **Ajaxian** (*http://ajaxian.com*) is a great source for the latest news concerning Ajax, JavaScript frameworks, and useful web services. The site is aimed at professional JavaScript programmers but is also full of news, tidbits, and often highlights sites that use Ajax in creative ways.

Books

- **Head Rush Ajax** by Brett McLaughlin (O'Reilly) is probably the best introduction to Ajax for those new to both JavaScript and server-side programming. Its playful approach and graphical layout make all of the basic concepts and techniques of Ajax easily understandable.

Advanced JavaScript

Oh yes, JavaScript is even *more* complicated than this book leads you to believe. Once you become proficient in JavaScript programming, you may want to expand your understanding of this complex language.

Articles and Presentations

- **Show Love to the Object Literal** by Chris Heilman (*www.wait-till-i.com/2006/02/16/show-love-to-the-object-literal*) is a short blog post that explains good uses for JavaScript object literals.

- **Do Object Oriented Programming with JavaScript** by Chris Pels (*http://msdn.microsoft.com/en-us/scriptjunkie/ff698282.aspx*) provides a short video introduction to a complex topic. It's a good place to start learning object-oriented programming with JavaScript.

- **Sorting a JavaScript array using** *array.sort()* (*www.javascriptkit.com/javatutors/arraysort.shtml*) provides a useful information on how to sort the contents of arrays, including a quick method of randomizing and array (think shuffling a deck of cards).

Websites

- **Eloquent JavaScript** (*http://eloquentjavascript.net*) is a JavaScript tutorial site. It's organized well, with creative ways of teaching lessons. Although it's supposed to be a beginner JavaScript tutorial site, the author writes as though he's talking to a bunch of computer scientists, so it's not the best place to start if you're new to JavaScript or programming. It's also available as a print book.

- **Unobtrusive JavaScript** (*www.onlinetools.org/articles/unobtrusivejavascript/index.html*) from Christian Heilmann is a mini-site dedicated to explaining the concept of *unobtrusive JavaScript*—specifically, how to make a website accessible to everyone (even those whose browsers don't have JavaScript enabled).

- **The JavaScript section of Douglas Crockfords' World Wide Web** (*http://javascript.crockford.com*) provides a lot of (complex) information about JavaScript. There's a lot of information on the site, some of it requiring a computer science degree just to understand.

- **Yahoo's JavaScript Developer Center** (*http://developer.yahoo.com/javascript*) has more information on JavaScript than nearly any other site on the Web. Much of the information is geared toward Yahoo's own JavaScript library, YUI, as well as the many Web services Yahoo offers (like Yahoo Maps).

- **Mozilla Developers Network JavaScript section** (*https://developer.mozilla.org/en/javascript*) contains tons of JavaScript information including the JavaScript reference mentioned at the beginning of this appendix, but also a detailed guide (*https://developer.mozilla.org/en/JavaScript/Guide*) that covers the different versions of JavaScript as well as detailed examples of JavaScript concepts in action.

Books

- **JavaScript Patterns** by Stoyan Stefanov (O'Reilly). When you really want to push your JavaScript programming forward, this book provides programming "patterns" that solve common tasks including how best to work with object literals, JSON, and arrays. Heavy duty programming; not for beginners.

- **JavaScript: The Good Parts** by Douglas Crockford (O'Reilly) uncovers the most useful parts of JavaScript, sidestepping bad programming techniques. Douglas should know what he's talking about, since he's a Senior JavaScript Architect at Yahoo. The book is short and dense, but contains a lot of wisdom about how to use JavaScript well.

CSS

If you're tackling this book, you're probably already pretty comfortable with CSS. JavaScript can really take advantage of the formatting power of CSS to control not only the look of elements, but even to animate them across the screen. If you need a CSS refresher, here are a few helpful resources.

Websites

- **The Complete CSS Guide** from WestCiv (*www.westciv.com/style_master/ academy/css_tutorial*) covers pretty much every part of Cascading Style Sheets. You won't learn a lot of different techniques here, but the basics of what CSS is and how to create styles and style sheets are thoroughly covered.

- **The SitePoint CSS Reference** (*http://reference.sitepoint.com/css*) is another online CSS reference that's easy to use and has a search engine.

- **Selectutorial** (*http://css.maxdesign.com.au/selectutorial*) is a great way to learn CSS selector syntax. Since jQuery is pretty much founded on the idea of using CSS selectors to manipulate the HTML of a page, it pays to have a very good understanding of this concept.

Books

- **CSS: The Missing Manual 2nd Edition**, by David Sawyer McFarland (O'Reilly) is a thorough, tutorial-driven book on Cascading Style Sheets. It includes in-depth coverage of CSS as well as real-world examples and troubleshooting tips for making sure your CSS works in a cross-browser world.

- **CSS: The Definitive Guide** by Eric Meyer (O'Reilly). The name says it all; this book covers CSS in such detail that your brain will definitely hurt if you try to read it all in one sitting.

- **Stunning CSS3** by Zoe Mickley Gillenwater (New Riders) is a well-designed book that covers many aspects of the new CSS3 standard and demonstrates sophisticated CSS3-based designs, as well as many techniques for working effectively with CSS3.

Index

Symbols

& (ampersand)
&& logical AND operator, 86
<...> (angle brackets), enclosing HTML tags, 6
* (asterisk)
in regular expressions, 435
multiplication operator, 50
*= multiply and assign operator, 54
\ (backslash), in regular expressions, 432
{...} (braces)
in CSS styles, 9
in function, 100
in if statement, 79, 89
in regular expressions, 435–436
syntax errors involving, 469–470
[...] (brackets)
in array declaration, 61
in regular expressions, 432–433
^ (caret), in regular expressions, 432
: (colon), in jQuery filters, 135
$ (dollar sign)
preceding jQuery object, 129, 403–404
in regular expressions, 432
= (equal sign)
assignment operator, 48
syntax errors involving, 473
== equality operator, 80–81, 89
=== strict equality operator, 80
! (exclamation point)
NOT operator, 87–88
!= inequality operator, 80–81
!== strict inequality operator, 80
/ (forward slash)
division operator, 50
in HTML tags, 6
/= divide and assign operator, 54
/*...*/ enclosing comments, 73
/.../ enclosing regular expressions, 431
// preceding comments, 73–74
- (hyphen), in CSS properties, 193
< (left angle bracket)
less than operator, 80
<= less than or equal to operator, 80

- (minus sign)
subtraction operator, 50
-- subtract 1 operator, 54
-= subtract and assign operator, 54
(...) (parentheses)
following function name, 42, 100, 102
grouping operations, 51
in if statement, 79
syntax errors involving, 468
. (period)
preceding class selectors, 132
preceding jQuery functions, 138
preceding object properties or methods, 63, 64, 71
in regular expressions, 432
| (pipe character)
|| logical OR operator, 86
+ (plus sign)
addition operator, 50
concatenation operator, 51
in regular expressions, 435
++ add 1 operator, 54
+= add and assign operator, 54
+= concatenate and assign operator, 55
 # (pound sign), in ID selectors, 130
? (question mark)
in regular expressions, 435
? : ternary operator, 461–462
"..." or '...' (quotes)
enclosing strings, 43–44
syntax errors involving, 469, 472
> (right angle bracket)
greater than operator, 80
>= greater than or equal to operator, 80
; (semicolon), ending JavaScript statements, 41–42

A

a tag, HTML. *See* **links**
absolute path URL, 28
absolute positioning, 189
add 1 operator (++), 54
add and assign operator (+=), 54

addClass() function, jQuery, 142
addition operator (+), 50
adjacent sibling selectors, 133
after() function, jQuery, 139–140, 419
Ajax (Asynchronous JavaScript and XML), 23,
    341–349
    error handling, 364
    JavaScript for, 345
    jQuery functions for
        error() function, 364
        get() function, 356–357, 358, 365–370
        getJSON() function, 371–376, 378, 381
        load() function, 349–356
        post() function, 356–357, 358
        serialize() function, 360
    jQuery plug-ins for, 388
    receiving data from web server
        from Flickr, 378–383
        get() function for, 356
        from Google Maps, 387–400
        JSON format for, 370–376
        JSONP format for, 377–378
        loading HTML file content from, 349–352
        post() function for, 356
        processing data, callback function
            for, 360–364
        XML format for, 365
    resources for, 410, 500
    sending data to web server
        formatting data, 357–360
        get() and post() functions for, 356–357
    tutorials for, 352–356, 365–370, 383–387,
        397–400
    uses of, 342–343
    XMLHttpRequest object for, 344–345,
        346–349
Ajax File Upload plug-in, 388
Ajaxian (web site), 500
Alert box, displaying, 30–31
alert() function, JavaScript, 30, 42
AMP (Apache, MySQL, and PHP), 346
ampersand (&)
    && logical AND operator, 86
AND operator, logical (&&), 86
angle brackets (<...>)
    enclosing HTML tags, 6
    left angle bracket (<)
        less than operator, 80
        <= less than or equal to operator, 80
    right angle bracket (>)
        greater than operator, 80
        >= greater than or equal to operator, 80
animated navigation bar, 249–256
animate() function, jQuery, 192–194

animations, jQuery, 192–196
    callback function for, 196–198
    of color, 192
    completion of, performing actions after, 196–
        198
    speed of (easing), 194–196
    tutorials for, 198–204
anonymous functions, 148–149, 171–172
AnythingSlider plug-in, 312–319
API (Application Programming Interface),
    jQuery, 407–413
append() function, jQuery, 139, 405–406, 419
application server, 345
Aptana Studio, 10
arguments, for functions, 103–104
array notation, for JSON data, 372–373
arrays, 59–66
    accessing items in, 62–63, 67–69
    adding items to, 63–65, 69
    assigning values to, 61, 62, 67
    counters for, in loops, 96, 97–98
    data types in, 61
    declaring, 60–61, 67
    deleting items from, 65, 66
    empty, 61
    index for, 62–63
    length of, 63, 65
    looping through items in, 95–99
    queues created from, 65
    selecting random elements of, 450
    tutorials for, 66–70
arrows, as used in this book, 15
assignment operator (=), 48
asterisk (*)
    in regular expressions, 435
    multiplication operator, 50
    *= multiply and assign operator, 54
Asynchronous JavaScript and XML. See Ajax
attr() function, jQuery, 146–147, 208, 236
attributes, of HTML tags, 6
    manipulating, 146–147, 409
    selectors for, in jQuery, 133–134, 239
Autocomplete plug-in, 388
automatic loops, for jQuery selections, 136–
    137
automatic type conversion, 53

B

\b symbol, in regular expressions, 432
backslash (\), in regular expressions, 432
BBEdit, 11
before() function, jQuery, 139–140, 419
behavioral layer, 4. See also JavaScript
Bibeault, Bear (author)
    jQuery in Action (Manning), 499

bind() function, jQuery, 177–179, 421–422
blur event, 161, 266
blur() function, jQuery, 266
blur() method, window object, 244
body tag, HTML, 6
books and publications
    CSS: The Definitive Guide (O'Reilly), 502
    CSS: The Missing Manual 2nd Edition
      (O'Reilly), 4, 132, 502
    Head First HTML with CSS and XHTML
      (O'Reilly), 4
    Head First JavaScript (O'Reilly), 498
    Head First PHP & MySQL (O'Reilly), 351
    Head Rush Ajax (O'Reilly), 500
    HTML5: The Missing Manual (O'Reilly), 5
    JavaScript Patterns (O'Reilly), 501
    JavaScript: The Definitive Guide
      (O'Reilly), 498
    JavaScript: The Good Parts (O'Reilly), 501
    jQuery Cookbook (O'Reilly), 499
    jQuery in Action (Manning), 499
    jQuery: Novice to Ninja (Sitepoint), 500
    Learning PHP, MySQL, and JavaScript
      (O'Reilly), 351
    PHP Solutions:Dynamic Web Design Made
      Easy (Friends of Ed), 351
    Stunning CSS3 (New Riders), 502
booleans, 44–45, 82
braces ({...})
    in CSS styles, 9
    in function, 100
    in if statement, 79, 89
    in regular expressions, 435–436
    syntax errors involving, 469–470
brackets ([...])
    in array declaration, 61
    in regular expressions, 432–433
breakpoints in scripts, 485–489
browsers. See also specific browsers
    incompatibilities between, 2–3
      DOM handling, 129
      jQuery handling, 4
    JavaScript interpreter in, 25
    layout/rendering engine in, 25
    View Source command in, 141
browser window. See window object
built-in functions, 42. See also window object,
    methods for
    alert() function, 30, 42
    isNaN() function, 42, 92, 447–448
    Number() function, 53, 446
    parseFloat() function, 447
    parseInt() function, 446–447
    prompt() function, 57–58
:button selector, 260

C

calendar. See Datepicker plug-in
callback function
    for effects and animations, 196–198
    for processing data from Ajax, 360–364
caret (^), in regular expressions, 432
carriage returns, in JavaScript, 49
Cascading Style Sheets. See CSS (Cascading
    Style Sheets)
case, of strings, 426–427
case-sensitivity of JavaScript, 473–474
Casteldine, Earle (author)
    jQuery: Novice to Ninja (Sitepoint), 500
CDN (content distribution network), for
    jQuery, 119–120
chaining functions, jQuery, 137–138, 146
change event, 161, 267–268
change() function, jQuery, 267
changeSpeed option, FancyBox, 227
checkboxes
    selecting, 260–261
    status of, determining, 262–263
    validating, 297–299
:checkbox selector, 260
:checked filter, 260–261
children() function, 415
child selectors, 133
Chrome
    Developer Tools in, 141
    JavaScript Console in, 38–39
classes, CSS, 142–143
class selectors, 131–132
click event, 159
    for forms, 266–267
    to open a new window, 245
click() function, jQuery, 267
clicking, 14
client-side languages, 23
close() method, window object, 243
closest() function, 416
code examples. See online resources
CoffeeCup, 11
CoffeeCup Free HTML Editor, 10
colon (:), in jQuery filters, 135
color, animating, 192
Color plug-in, 192
combining strings. See concatenating strings
comments, 72–76, 124
comparison operators, 80
compiled languages, 25
The Complete CSS Guide (web site), 502
compressing external JavaScript files, 465–466
concatenate and assign operator (+=), 55
concatenating strings, 51–52, 55, 56

concatenation operator (+), 51
condition
    in do/while loop, 98
    in for loop, 97
    in if statement, 79–81
        combining, 86–88
        negating, 87–88
    setting variables based on, 461–462
    in while loop, 93–95
conditional statements, 77–89
    conditions in, 79–81
        combining, 86–88
        negating, 87–88
    else clause in, 82–83
    else if statement, 83–85
    if statement, 79–82
    indentation in, 89
    nesting if statements, 88–89
    switch statement, 462–465
    troubleshooting, 89
    tutorials for, 89–92
console.log() function, Firebug, 479–480
:contains filter, 136
content distribution network (CDN), for
        jQuery, 119–120
content slider, 312–319
    arrows in, 316, 317–318
    autoplay for, 318
    borders for, 317
    creating, 313–316
    dimensions of, 316–317
    labels for, 318
    navigation buttons, 317
    orientation of, 318
    slides of variable sizes, 319
controls. See fields in forms
conventions used in this book, 14–15, 74
conversions between data types
    automatic type conversion, 53
    converting strings to numbers, 445–447
counters, in loops, 96, 97–98
creditcard validation rule, 282
Crockford, Douglas (author)
    Douglas Crockford's World Wide Web,
        JavaScript section (web site), 501
    JavaScript: The Good Parts (O'Reilly), 501
CSS (Cascading Style Sheets), 4, 7–9
    absolute positioning, 189
    applying to HTML elements, 124–127
    classes, manipulating, 142–143
    location of stylesheets, relative to scripts, 124
    object literals for, 145–146
    properties, manipulating, 143–146
    resources for, 132, 409, 501–502
    selectors. See selectors
    for tabbed panels, 304–306

css() function, jQuery, 143–146
CSS sprites
    in content slider, 316
    FancyBox using, 228
CSS: The Definitive Guide (O'Reilly), 502
CSS: The Missing Manual 2nd Edition
        (O'Reilly), 4, 132, 502
curly brackets ({...}). See braces
currency, formatting, 448–449
cyclic option, FancyBox, 228

D

\d symbol, in regular expressions, 432
\D symbol, in regular expressions, 432
dashboard tutorial, 198–204
database, browsing, 343
database server, 345
data property, event object, 174
data types, 42–45. See also booleans; numbers;
        strings
    in arrays, 61
    automatic type conversion, 53
    determining for an object, 72
Date() method, 450–451, 456–457
Date object, 450–451, 453
Datepicker plug-in, 125, 276
dates
    creating, 456–457
    functions for, 450–457
    regular expressions for, 439
    users selecting, plug-in for, 125, 276
    validating, in a form, 282
date validation rule, 282
dblclick event, 159
DDMegaMenu plug-in, 256
debugging, 477–489. See also troubleshooting
    installing Firebug for, 477–478
    stepping through scripts with
        breakpoints, 485–489
    tracking scripts, 479–480
    tutorials for, 481–484, 489–496
    viewing errors, 478–479
decision making statements. See conditional
        statements
declaration blocks, CSS styles, 8, 9
declarations, CSS styles, 9
delay() function, jQuery, 198
delegate() function, 422–423
descendent selectors, 133
development server, 346
dialog boxes
    alert message in, 42
    prompt in, 57–58
digits validation rule, 282

dimensions
  of browser window, 319–320
  of content slider, 316–317
  of document, 320
  of web page elements, 319–322
disabling form fields, 269–271, 273–276
divide and assign operator (/=), 54
division operator (/), 50
div tag, HTML
  for tabbed panels, 302, 303–304
  for tooltips, 326–327
doctype declaration, HTML, 5
document
  dimensions of, determining, 320
  events for, 160
document.getElementById() method,
  JavaScript, 128
document.getElementsByTagName() method,
  JavaScript, 128
Document Object Model. *See* DOM
$(document).ready() function, 123, 124,
  170–171, 458
document-relative path URL, 28
document.write() method, JavaScript, 31–32,
  56
Dojo Toolkit library, 119
dollar sign ($)
  in regular expressions, 432
  preceding jQuery object, 129, 403–404
DOM (Document Object Model), 127–129
  compared to jQuery selections, 136–138
  finding elements in, 413–418
Do Object Oriented Programming with
  JavaScript (web site video), 500
dot syntax
  for JSON data, 372–373
  for object properties or methods, 71
Douglas Crockford's World Wide Web,
  JavaScript section (web site), 501
do/while loops, 98–99
Dreamweaver, 11

E

each() function, jQuery, 147–150
easingIn option, FancyBox, 227
easingOut option, FancyBox, 227
easing (speed) of effects and animations, 185,
  194–196, 227
Eclipse, 10
editors, 10–11
EditPlus, 11
effects, jQuery, 185–189. *See also* FancyBox
  plug-in
  callback function for, 196–198

  completion of, performing actions after, 196–
    198
  fading elements in and out, 187–188
  resources for, 409
  sliding elements, 188–189
  speed of, 185, 194–196
  tutorials for, 190–192, 216–222
  visibility of elements, 187
element selectors, 131
Eloquent JavaScript (web site), 501
else clause, conditional statements, 82–83
else if statement, 83–85
email addresses, regular expression for, 438–
  439
email validation rule, 282
empty array, 61
empty() function, 421
empty string, 58
enabling form fields, 269–271
end() function, 418
equality operator (==), 80–81, 89
equal sign (=)
  assignment operator, 48
  syntax errors involving, 473
  == equality operator, 80–81, 89
  === strict equality operator, 80
equalTo validation rule, 288
error() function, jQuery, 364
errors. *See also* **debugging; troubleshooting**
  for form validation, 283–284, 288–291,
    299–300
  in Internet Explorer, blocked content, 31
  preventing, 477
  syntax errors, 31, 36–37, 467–477
  types of, 471
  viewing in Firebug, 478–479
  from web server, with Ajax, 364
:even filter, 135
event bubbling, 176
event object, 173–175
events, 157–162, 421–424
  applying to new elements, 422–423
  assigning to selections, 163–164
  document/window events, 160
  form events, 161, 263–268
  keyboard events, 162
  mouse events, 159–160, 171–173
  multiple, using the same function, 179
  passing data to, 177–179
  passing functions to, 163–164
  removing, 175–176
  resources for, 409
  stopping normal behavior of, 175
  tutorials for, 165–169, 180–184

examples. *See* online resources; tutorials
exclamation point (!)
  NOT operator, 87–88
  != inequality operator, 80–81
  !== strict inequality operator, 80
Expression Web Designer, 11
external HTML files, loading into web
    page, 349–356
external JavaScript files, 27–29, 457–459
  attaching to web pages, 27–29, 33–34
  compressing, 465–466
  location of, 29
  multiple, order of, 29
  path errors involving, 474–476
external links, opening in new window, 238–
    240

F

fadeIn() function, jQuery, 34, 187
fadeOut() function, jQuery, 147, 187
fadeTo() function, jQuery, 188, 414
fadeToggle() function, jQuery, 187
false value. *See* booleans
FancyBox plug-in, 222–234
  CSS sprites used by, 228
  customizing, 226–231
  downloading files for, 224–225
  gallery page for, setting up, 223–225
  opening a page within a page, 246–249
fancybox.png file, 228
FAQ (Frequently Asked Questions)
    tutorial, 180–184
fields in forms, 273. *See also* forms; specific
    fields
  changing value of, 267
  checking status of, 262–263
  clicking, 266–267
  disabling, 269–271, 273–276
  enabling, 269–271
  focus on, 161, 264–265, 268–269, 273
  getting value of, 261–262
  hiding, 271–272, 276–278
  leaving, 266
  selecting, 259–261
  setting value of, 261–262
  showing, 271–272
  tags for, 258–259
  validating, 278–291
    error messages for, 283–284, 288–291,
        299–300
    plug-in for, setting up, 280–281
    on server, 289
    tutorial for, 291–300
    validation rules for, 281–283, 284–288

:file selector, 260
files, external. *See* external JavaScript files
filters for selectors, 135–136, 260–261
find() function, jQuery, 365, 407, 413, 414–415
Firebug plug-in, 37, 141, 477–489
  installing, 477–478
  stepping through scripts with
      breakpoints, 485–489
  tracking scripts, 479–480
  tutorials for, 481–484, 489–496
  viewing errors, 478–479
Firefox
  JavaScript console in, 35–37
  plug-ins for. *See* Firebug plug-in; HTML
      Validator plug-in
:first filter, 135
flags, boolean data type used for, 82
Flanagan, David (author)
  JavaScript: The Definitive Guide
      (O'Reilly), 498
Flash, 23
Flickr
  images from, adding to web page, 378–383
  tutorials for, 383–387
floor() method, Match object, 449
focus event, 161, 264–265
focus for form fields, 161, 264–265, 268–269,
    273
focus() function, jQuery, 265, 269, 273
focus() method, window object, 244
for loops, 97–98
Form plug-in, 388
forms, 257–268
  events for, 161, 263–268
  fields in
    checking status of, 262–263
    clicking, 266–267
    disabling, 269–271, 273–276
    enabling, 269–271
    focus on, 161, 264–265, 268–269, 273
    getting values of, 261–262
    hiding, 271–272, 276–278
    leaving, 266
    selecting, 259–261
    setting values of, 261–262
    showing, 271–272
    tags for, 258–259
  in HTML5, 22
  resources for, 410
  submitting, 161, 263–264
    multiple times, preventing, 271
    without reloading page, 343, 347–348,
        365–370
  tutorials for, 272–278

validating, 278–291
    error messages for, 283–284, 288–291,
        299–300
    plug-in for, setting up, 280–281
    on server, 289
    tutorial for, 291–300
    validation rules for, 281–283, 284–288
form tag, HTML, 257–259
forward slash (/)
    division operator, 50
    in HTML tags, 6
    /= divide and assign operator, 54
    /*...*/ enclosing comments, 73
    /.../ enclosing regular expressions, 431
    // preceding comments, 73–74
Freeman, Elisabeth (author)
    Head First HTML with CSS and XHTML
        (O'Reilly), 4
Freeman, Eric (author)
    Head First HTML with CSS and XHTML
        (O'Reilly), 4
Frequently Asked Questions (FAQ)
    tutorial, 180–184
functions, built-in to JavaScript. *See* **built-in**
    functions
functions, jQuery. *See also* **specific functions**
    anonymous, 148–149, 171–172
    chaining, 137–138, 146
    passing to events, 163–164
functions, user-defined in JavaScript, 100–108
    calling, 101
    creating, 100–101
    libraries of. *See* libraries
    location of, 101
    naming, 100
    parameters for, 102–104
    for random numbers, 450
    returning a value from, 104–105
    scope of variables in, 105–108
    tutorials for, 101–102, 108–114
    undefined errors involving, 476

G

getDate() method, Date object, 451
getDay() method, Date object, 451, 452
getElementById() method, document
    object, 128
getElementsByTagName() method, document
    object, 128
getFullYear() method, Date object, 451
get() function, jQuery, 356–357, 358, 365–370
getHours() method, Date object, 451, 452–456
getJSON() function, jQuery, 371–376, 378, 381
getMinutes() method, Date object, 451,
    452–456

getMonth() method, Date object, 451, 451–452
getSeconds() method, Date object, 451,
    452–456
getTime() method, Date object, 451
global variables, 107–108
GoMap plug-in, 387–400
    information windows, adding, 397
    map location, setting, 390–391
    markers in map, adding, 393–396
    navigation controls, removing, 392
    scale of
        marker for, adding, 392
        setting, 391
    tutorials for, 397–400
    type of map
        setting, 391–392
        switching between, 392–393
    using, 388–389
Google Chrome. *See* **Chrome**
Google Docs (web site), 2
Google Doctype (web site), 497
Google Maps (web site)
    adding to web page, 387–400
    as example of JavaScript, 2, 23, 124
grammatical errors. *See* **syntax errors**
graphics. *See* **images**
greater than operator (>), 80
greater than or equal to operator (>=), 80

H

h1 tag, HTML, 7
h2 tag, HTML, 7
:has filter, 135
Head First HTML with CSS and XHTML
    (O'Reilly), 4
Head First JavaScript (O'Reilly), 498
Head First PHP & MySQL (O'Reilly), 351
Head Rush Ajax (O'Reilly), 500
head tag, HTML, 6
height. *See* **dimensions**
height() function, jQuery, 319–322
height property, windows, 242
Heilman, Chris (author)
    Show Love to the Object Literal (blog
        post), 500
:hidden filter, 136
:hidden selector, 260
hide() function, jQuery, 34, 187
hiding elements. *See* **visibility of elements**
hover event, 171–172, 210–211
href attribute, links, 236
HTML5: The Missing Manual (O'Reilly), 5
html() function, jQuery, 138, 405–406, 419

HTML (Hypertext Markup Language), 4–7. *See also* web pages; specific tags
  effects for. *See* effects, jQuery
  loading in web page from external file, 349–352
  manipulating, 124–127, 138–141, 146–147, 419–421
  model of, for a web page. *See* DOM
  rendered, viewing source for, 141
  selecting tags in
    with JavaScript, 128–129
    with jQuery. *See* selectors
  tags, 5–7
  types/versions of, 5, 22
  validating, 7
HTML-Kit, 10
html tag, HTML, 6
HTML Validator plug-in, 7
hyperlinks. *See* links
Hypertext Transfer Protocol. *See* HTML
hyphen (-), in CSS properties, 193. *See also* minus sign (-)

I

ID
  selecting tags by, in JavaScript, 128
  selectors for, in jQuery, 130–131, 406
iframe tag, HTML, 245–249
if statement, 79–82, 89–92
  combining conditions in, 86–88
  condition in, 79–81
  else clause in, 82–83
  else if statement with, 83–85
  indentation in, 89
  negating conditions, 87–88
  nesting, 88–89
  troubleshooting, 89
images
  from Flickr, adding to web page, 378–383
  photo gallery of
    with effects, 216–222
    with FancyBox. *See* FancyBox plug-in
  preloading, 209–210
  rollover images, 210–216
  src attribute, changing, 208–209
  swapping, 207–211
  tutorials for, 211–216, 216–222, 231–234
:image selector, 260
index, for array, 62–63
indexOf() method, strings, 427–428
inequality operator (!=), 80–81
infinite loops, 94
innerHeight() function, jQuery, 321
innerWidth() function, jQuery, 321
:input selector, 260

input tag, HTML, 258–259, 260
instances of objects, 71
Internet Explorer
  blocked JavaScript content, 31
  Console in, 37–38
  developer tools in, 141
interpreters, 25
An Introduction to JavaScript (web site), 498
isNaN() function, JavaScript, 42, 92, 447–448

J

Java applets, 23
Java, compared to JavaScript, 2
JavaScript, 1–3
  adding to web page, 25–29
  arrays. *See* arrays
  case-sensitivity of, 473–474
  as client-side language, 23
  comments, 72–76, 124
  compared to Java, 2
  conditional statements. *See* conditional statements
  data types, 42–45. *See also* specific data types
  debugging. *See* debugging
  editors for, 10–11
  in external files. *See* external JavaScript files
  functions, built-in. *See* built-in functions
  functions, user-defined, 100–108
  history of, 2–3
  libraries for, 33, 117–119. *See also* jQuery
  loops. *See* loops
  math operations, 50–51, 54–55
  objects, 70–72
  online examples using, 2, 23, 124
  other software using, 3
  resources for, 11, 497–498, 500–501
  as scripting language, 25
  statements, 41–42
  variables. *See* variables
JavaScript interpreter, 25
JavaScript Object Notation. *See* JSON (JavaScript Object Notation)
JavaScript Patterns (O'Reilly), 501
JavaScript Quick Reference from DevGuru (web site), 497
JavaScript: The Definitive Guide (O'Reilly), 498
JavaScript: The Good Parts (O'Reilly), 501
jqDock plug-in, 256
jQuery, 3–4, 117
  Ajax, functions for
    error() function, 364
    get() function, 356–357, 358, 365–370
    getJSON() function, 371–376, 378, 381
    load() function, 349–352, 352–356

post() function, 356–357, 358
serialize() function, 360
animations, 192–198
attaching to a web page, 122–124
CSS classes, manipulating, 142–143
CSS properties, manipulating, 143–146
DOM, traversing, 413–418
downloading, 120–121
effects. *See* effects
events. *See* events
filters, 135–136, 260–261
forms. *See* forms
functions. *See also* specific functions
anonymous, 148–149, 171–172
chaining, 137–138, 146
passing to events, 163–164
HTML manipulation, 124–127, 138–141,
146–147, 419–421
image manipulation. *See* images
linking to CDN version of, 119–120
navigation. *See* navigation
online examples using, 4
performance of, 407
plug-ins for. *See* plug-ins, for jQuery
resources for, 12, 312, 407–413, 499–500
selectors. *See* selectors
versions of, 122
**jQuery API (Application Programming
Interface),** 407–413
jQuery Cheatsheet (web site article), 499
jQuery.com (web site), 499
jQuery Cookbook (O'Reilly), 499
jQuery Essentials (web site presentation), 499
jQuery for Designers (web site), 499
jQuery() function, 403–404, 408
jQuery in Action (Manning), 499
jQuery: Novice to Ninja (Sitepoint), 500
jQuery objects, 129, 403–404
jQuery Tools Tooltip plug-in, 338
**jQuery Tutorials for Designers (web site
article),** 499
jQuery UI project, 312
jQuery UI Tooltip plug-in, 338
.js file extension, 27, 33
js folder, 29
JSON (JavaScript Object Notation), 370–376
accessing data formatted as, 372–373
nested JSON objects, 373–376
receiving data formatted as, 370–372
JSONP (JSON with padding), 377–378

K

Katz, Yehuda (author)
jQuery in Action (Manning), 499
keyboard events, 162
keyboard shortcuts, 14
keydown event, 162
keypress event, 162
keyup event, 162
keywords (reserved words), 46–47, 472–473

L

label tag, HTML, 259
:last filter, 135
layers of a web page, 4
behavioral. *See* JavaScript
presentational. *See* CSS (Cascading Style
Sheets)
structural. *See* HTML (Hypertext Markup
Language)
layout of web pages
content slider. *See* content slider
dimensions of elements, determining, 319–
322
position of elements, determing, 322–324
scrolling position, determing, 324–325
tabbed panels. *See* tabbed panels
layout/rendering engine, 25
Learning jQuery (web site), 499
**Learning PHP, MySQL, and JavaScript
(O'Reilly),** 351
left angle bracket (<)
less than operator, 80
<= less than or equal to operator, 80
left property, windows, 242
length property
arrays, 63, 65
strings, 425–426
less than operator (<), 80
less than or equal to operator (<=), 80
libraries, 33, 117–119. *See also* external
JavaScript files; jQuery
libs folder, 29
Lightbox, 222
linear easing method, 194
links, 235–238
a tag for, 6
destination of
determining, 236–237
preventing from going to, 237–238
external, opening in new window, 238–240
HTML syntax for, 6
selecting, 235–236
for tabs in tabbed panels, 304–305

li tag, HTML, for navigation menu, 250–252
load event, 160
load() function, jQuery, 349–356
local variables, 107–108
location property, windows, 243
logging in without leaving web page, 343
logical AND operator (&&), 86
logical OR operator (||), 86
logic errors, 471
login slider tutorial, 190–192
loops, 93–99
    automatic, for jQuery selections, 136–137
    do/while loops, 98–99
    for loops, 97–98
    infinite loops, 94
    traversing arrays using, 95–99
    tutorials using, 108–114
    while loops, 93–95

M

MacDonald, Matthew (author)
    HTML5: The Missing Manual (O'Reilly), 5
MAMP, 346
maps. See GoMap plug-in; Google Maps (web
    site)
match() method, strings, 441–443
math operations, 50–51, 54–55
maxlength validation rule, 287
max validation rule, 287
McLaughlin, Brett (author)
    Head Rush Ajax (O'Reilly), 500
menubar property, windows, 243
menus, 14
methods, 71
Meyer, Eric (author)
    CSS: The Definitive Guide (O'Reilly), 502
Mickley Gillenwater, Zoe (author)
    Stunning CSS3 (New Riders), 502
.min file extension, 33, 121
minified files, 121
minlength validation rule, 287
minus sign (-). See also hyphen (-), in CSS
    properties
    subtraction operator, 50
    -- subtract 1 operator, 54
    -= subtract and assign operator, 54
min validation rule, 287
Mootools library, 119
Morrison, Michael (author)
    Head First JavaScript (O'Reilly), 498
mousedown event, 159
mouse events, 159–160, 171–173
mousemove event, 159
mouseout event, 159, 329
mouseover event, 159, 210–211, 329, 330–338

mouseup event, 159
moveBy() method, window object, 244
moveTo() method, window object, 244
Mozilla Developer Center Core JavaScript
    Reference (web site), 497
Mozilla Developers Network, JavaScript
    section (web site), 501
MSDN JavaScript Language Reference (web
    site), 498
multiplication operator (*), 50
multiply and assign operator (*=), 54

N

navigation
    animated navigation bar, 249–256
    links. See links
    opening a new window, 240–245
    opening a window within a page, 245–249
Navigation plug-in, 252–253
nesting
    if statements, 88–89
    JSON objects, 373–376
Netflix (web site), 124
next() function, 417
Notepad++, 10
:not filter, 135
NOT operator (!), 87–88
Number() function, JavaScript, 53, 446
numbers, 43
    combining with strings, 52–53
    converting strings to, 445–447
    currency, formatting, 448–449
    random numbers, creating, 449–451
    rounding, 448
    testing for, 447–448
number validation rule, 282

O

object literals
    for CSS, 145–146
    for data to send to server, 359–360
    for JSON, 371
objects, 70–72
:odd filter, 135
offset() function, jQuery, 322
online resources
    Ajax, 500
    CSS, 132, 502
    easing methods, 195
    editors, 10–11
    for this book, 15–18, 16, 29
    HTML5, 5
    HTML types, templates for, 5
    iframes, 246
    JavaScript, 11, 497–498, 500–501

examples using, 2, 23, 124
libraries for, 119
jQuery, 12, 499
    documentation for, 407–413
    examples using, 4
    performance of, 407
    plug-ins for, 256
    UI project, 312
PHP, 351
open() method, window object, 240–241
order of operations, 51
OR operator, logical (||), 86
outerHeight() function, jQuery, 321
outerWidth() function, jQuery, 321
overlayColor option, FancyBox, 227
overlayOpacity option, FancyBox, 227

P

padding option, FancyBox, 227
pageX property, event object, 174
pageY property, event object, 174
parameters, for functions, 102–104
parent() function, 415–416
parentheses (())
    following function name, 42, 100, 102
    grouping operations, 51
    in if statement, 79
    syntax errors involving, 468
parseFloat() function, JavaScript, 447
parseInt() function, JavaScript, 446–447
:password selector, 260
patterns in strings, 430–445
    for dates, 439
    for email addresses, 438–439
    match() method for, 441–443
    regular expressions, creating, 431–436
    replacing, 443–444
    search() method for, 431
    for U.S. phone numbers, 437–438
    for U.S. Zip codes, 436
    for web addresses, 440–441
Pels, Chris (author)
    Do Object Oriented Programming with
        JavaScript (web site video), 500
performance. *See also* **speed (easing) of effects**
    and animations
    chaining functions, 146
    changing page content, 405–406
    compressing external JavaScript files, 465–
        466
    ID selectors, 406
    of jQuery, 407
    resources regarding, 407

period (.)
    any one character, in regular expressions, 432
    preceding class selectors, 132
    preceding jQuery functions, 138
    preceding object properties or methods, 63,
        64, 71
phone numbers, regular expression for, 437–
    438
photo gallery
    with effects, 216–222
    with FancyBox. *See* FancyBox plug-in
PHP, 351
PHP Solutions:Dynamic Web Design Made
    Easy (Friends of Ed), 351
pipe character (|)
    || logical OR operator, 86
plug-ins
    for Firefox
        Firebug. *See* Firebug plug-in
        HTML Validator, 7
    for jQuery, 118
        for Ajax, 388
        AnythingSlider, 312–319
        Color, 192
        Datepicker, 125, 276
        DDMegaMenu, 256
        FancyBox. *See* FancyBox plug-in
        GoMap, 387–400
        jqDock, 256
        Navigation, 252–253
        for tooltips, 338
        Validation, 280–291
    for Safari
        Safari Validator, 7
plus sign (+)
    addition operator, 50
    concatenation operator, 51
    in regular expressions, 435
    ++ add 1 operator, 54
    += add and assign operator, 54
    += concatenate and assign operator, 55
pop() method, arrays, 65, 66
pop-up windows. *See* **dialog boxes; tooltips**
position
    absolute positioning, 189
    scrolling position of web page, 324–325
    of web page elements, 322–324
position() function, jQuery, 323
postal codes, regular expressions for, 436
post() function, jQuery, 356–357, 358
pound sign (#), in ID selectors, 130
prepend() function, jQuery, 139, 405–406, 419
presentational layer, 4. *See also* CSS (Cascading
    Style Sheets)

preventDefault() function, jQuery, 175, 237–238

prev() function, 417

processContacts() function, jQuery, 372

programming, 22–25

prompt() function, JavaScript, 57–58

properties, CSS, 9
 hyphens in, handling in JavaScript, 193
 manipulating, 143–146

properties, JavaScript, 71

Prototype library, 119

p tag, HTML, 6, 7

pull quotes, tutorial for, 150–156

punctuation errors, 31, 36–37, 467–472

push() method, arrays, 64, 65

Q

qTip2 plug-in, 338

query strings, 357–359

question mark (?)
 in regular expressions, 435
 ? : ternary operator, 461–462

queues, creating, 65

quiz, tutorial for, 108–114

quotes ("..." or '...')
 enclosing strings, 43–44
 syntax errors involving, 469, 472

R

radio buttons
 selecting, 260
 status of, determing, 262–263
 validating, 297–299

:radio selector, 260

random() method, JavaScript, 449–451

rangelength validation rule, 287

range validation rule, 288

ready() function. *See* $(document).ready()
 function

regex. *See* regular expressions

regular expressions, 430–445
 creating, 431–436
 for dates, 439
 for email addresses, 438–439
 match() method using, 441–443
 replace() method using, 443–444
 search() method using, 431
 subpatterns in, 435–436, 437, 438, 444
 for U.S. phone numbers, 437–438
 for U.S. Zip codes, 436
 for web addresses, 440–441

A (Re)-Introduction to JavaScript (web site
 presentation), 498

remote validation, 289

removeAttr() function, jQuery, 147

removeClass() function, jQeury, 142

remove() function, jQuery, 140, 419

rendering engine. *See* layout/rendering engine

replace() function, jQuery, 140

replace() method, strings, 443–444

replaceWith() function, 419

required validation rule, 282

reserved words (keywords), 46–47, 472–473

reset event, 161

:reset selector, 260

resizeBy() method, window object, 244

resize event, 160

resizeTo() method, window object, 244

resources. *See* books and publications; online
 resources

return value, of function, 104–105

right angle bracket (>)
 greater than operator, 80
 >= greater than or equal to operator, 80

rollover images, 210–216

root-relative path URL, 28

round() method, Math object, 448

rules, CSS. *See* styles, CSS

runtime errors, 471

S

\s symbol, in regular expressions, 432

\S symbol, in regular expressions, 432

Safari
 Develop menu in, 141
 Error Console in, 39–40

Safari Validator plug-in, 7

Sawyer McFarland, David (author)
 CSS: The Missing Manual 2nd Edition
 (O'Reilly), 4, 132, 502

scope of variables, 105–108

screenX property, event object, 174

screenY property, event object, 174

scripting languages, 25

Script Junkie (web site), 499

scripts. *See also* JavaScript; jQuery
 embedding in web page, 25–27, 124
 external. *See* external JavaScript files
 order executed, 31

script tag, HTML, 25–27
 src attribute, 27–29, 33–34
 type attribute, 26

scrollbars property, windows, 242

scrollBy() method, window object, 244

scroll event, 160

scrolling position of page, 324–325

scrollLeft() function, jQuery, 325

scrollTo() method, window object, 244

scrollTop() function, jQuery, 325

searching DOM, 413–418

searching selections, 365, 407, 413, 414–415
searching strings
    for exact strings, 427–428
    for patterns. *See* patterns in strings
search() method, strings, 431
:selected filter, 261
selectors, 8, 129–138
    acting on each element of, 147–150
    adjacent sibling selectors, 133
    assigning events to, 163–164
    attribute selectors, 133–134, 239
    automatic loops for, 136–137
    chaining functions for, 137–138
    child selectors, 133
    class selectors, 131–132
    compared to DOM, 136–138
    descendent selectors, 133
    effects applied to, 185–186
    element selectors, 131
    filters for, 135–136, 260–261
    for form elements, 259–261
    ID selectors, 130–131, 406
    for links, 235–236
    optimizing performance of, 406–407
    resources for, 409
    saving into variables, 404–405
    searching selections, 365, 407, 413, 414–415
    tutorials for, 150–156
select tag, HTML, 258–259, 260, 261
Selectutorial (web site), 502
semicolon (;), ending JavaScript
    statements, 41–42
serialize() function, jQuery, 360
server
    application server, 345
    database server, 345
    development server, 346
    web server, Ajax communication with,
    343–349
server-side languages, 23
server side programming, 351
Sharkie, Craig (author)
    jQuery: Novice to Ninja (Sitepoint), 500
shiftKey property, event object, 174
shift() method, arrays, 65, 66
show() function, jQuery, 187
showing elements. *See* visibility of elements
Show Love to the Object Literal (blog
    post), 500
siblings() function, 416–417
The SitePoint CSS Reference (web site), 502
slash. *See* backslash (\); forward slash (/)
slice() method, strings, 428–430
slideDown() function, jQuery, 188

slideshow of web page content. *See* content
    slider
slideToggle() function, jQuery, 188
slideUp() function, jQuery, 188
sliding elements, 188–189, 190–192
software
    editors, 10–11
    plug-ins. *See* plug-ins
Sorting a JavaScript Array (web site
    article), 500
spaces, in JavaScript, 49
speed (easing) of effects and animations, 185,
    194–196, 227. *See also* performance
spelling errors. *See* syntax errors
sprites, CSS
    in content slider, 316
    FancyBox using, 228
square brackets ([...]). *See* brackets ([...])
src attribute
    image tag, 208–209
    script tag, 27–29, 33–34
star-rating widget, 343
statements, 41–42
status property, windows, 242
Stefanov, Stoyan (author)
    JavaScript Patterns (O'Reilly), 501
stepping through scripts in debugger, 485–489
stopPropagation() function, jQuery, 176
strict equality operator (===), 80
strict inequality operator (!==), 80
strings, 43–44, 425–430
    case of, 426–427
    combining with numbers, 52–53
    concatenating strings, 51–52, 55, 56
    converting to numbers, 445–447
    empty string, 58
    extracting part of, 428–430
    length of, 425–426
    searching for exact strings in, 427–428
    searching for patterns in, 430–445
        dates, 439
        email addresses, 438–439
        match() method for, 441–443
        regular expressions, creating, 431–436
        replacing text using, 443–444
        search() method for, 431
        U.S. phone numbers, 437–438
        U.S. Zip codes, 436
        web addresses, 440–441
strong tag, HTML, 6
structural layer, 4. *See also* HTML (Hypertext
    Markup Language)
Stunning CSS3 (New Riders), 502
styles, CSS, 7–9. *See also* CSS (Cascading Style
    Sheets)

submit event, 161, 263–264
submit() function, jQuery, 263–264, 271
:submit selector, 260
submitting forms, 161, 263–264
    multiple times, preventing, 271
    without reloading page, 343, 347–348,
        365–370
subpatterns, in regular expressions, 437, 438,
    444
subtract 1 operator (--), 54
subtract and assign operator (-=), 54
subtraction operator (-), 50
swing easing method, 194
switch statement, 462–465
syntax errors, 31, 37
    with case-sensitivity, 473
    with paths, 474–476
    with punctuation, 31, 36–37, 467–473
    with reserved words, 472–473
    with undefined elements, 37, 476–477

T

tabbed panels, 301–312
    CSS elements for, 304–306
    HTML elements for, 302–304
    JavaScript for, 306–307
    jQuery UI project for, 312
    tutorials for, 307–312
tab characters, in JavaScript, 49
Taconite plug-in, 388
tags, HTML, 5–7
target attribute, links, 238–240
target property, event object, 174
ternary operator (? :), 461–462
textarea tag, HTML, 258, 260
text() function, jQuery, 139, 405–406, 419
textMate, 11
:text selector, 260
TextWrangler, 10
$(this) variable, 149–150, 405
times, functions for, 450–457
titlePosition option, FancyBox, 228
toFixed() method, JavaScript, 448–449
toggleClass() function, jQuery, 143
toggle event, 173
toggle() function, jQuery, 187
toLowerCase() method, strings, 426–427
toolbar property, windows, 243
tooltips, 326–338
    CSS styles for, 328
    div tag for, 326–327, 329
    hiding when page loads, 328–329, 330
    mouseout event for, 329
    mouseover event for, 329, 330–338
    plug-ins for, 338

trigger for, 326–327, 330
    tutorial for, 329–338
top property, windows, 242
toUpperCase() method, strings, 426–427
transitionIn option, FancyBox, 227
transitionOut option, FancyBox, 227
trigger, for tooltip, 326–327, 330
troubleshooting, 34–40, 467–477. See
    also debugging
    Chrome JavaScript Console for, 38–39
    conditional statements, 89
    Firefox JavaScript Console for, 35–37
    Internet Explorer 9 Console for, 37–38
    logic errors, 471
    runtime errors, 471
    Safari Error Console for, 39–40
    syntax errors, 31, 37
        with case-sensitivity, 473
        with paths, 474–476
        with punctuation, 31, 36–37, 467–473
        with reserved words, 472–473
        with undefined elements, 37, 476–477
true value. See booleans
tutorials
    Ajax, 352–356, 365–370, 383–387, 397–400
    animated dashboard, 198–204
    animated navigation bar, 249–256
    AnythingSlider plug-in, 314–316
    arrays, 66–70
    conditional statements, 89–92
    CSS selectors, 150–156
    debugging, 481–484, 489–496
    effects, 190–192, 216–222
    events, 165–169, 180–184
    FAQ (Frequently Asked Questions), 180–184
    Flickr, 383–387
    forms, 272–278
    form validation, 291–300
    functions, 101–102, 108–114
    GoMap plug-in, 397–400
    images, 211–216, 216–222, 231–234
    login slider, 190–192
    loops, 108–114
    opening a page within a page, 248–249
    photo gallery
        with effects, 216–222
        with FancyBox, 231–234
    pull quotes, 150–156
    quiz, 108–114
    rollover images, 211–216
    tabbed panels, 307–312
    tooltips, 329–338
    variables, 55–59
Twitter plug-in, 388
type attribute, script tag, 26

typeof operator, 72
typing errors. *See* syntax errors

U

ul tag, HTML, 7
    for navigation menu, 250–252
    for tabs in tabbed panels, 302–303, 304
unbind() function, jQuery, 175–176
Uniform Resource Locator. *See* URL
unload event, 160
Unobtrusive JavaScript (web site), 501
unshift() method, arrays, 64, 65
unwrap() function, 421
URL (Uniform Resource Locator)
    for Flickr feeds, constructing, 379–381
    in links, 6
    for src attribute, script tag, 28
    types of, 28
    validating user input for, 282
url validation rule, 282
U.S. phone numbers, regular expression
    for, 437–438
U.S. Zip codes, regular expression for, 436

V

val() function, jQuery, 261–262
validate() function, jQuery, 281, 284–288,
    294–297
validating forms, 278–291
    error messages for, 283–284, 288–291,
        299–300
    plug-in for, setting up, 280–281
    on server, 289
    tutorial for, 291–300
    validation rules for, 281–283, 284–288
validating web pages, 7
Validation plug-in, 280–291
variables, 45–49. *See also* parameters
    accessing values in, 48
    assigning values to, 48, 55
    changing value of, 53–55
    declaring, 45, 55
    global variables, 107–108
    increasing flexibility of code, 460–461
    local variables, 107–108
    naming, 45–48, 404
    as objects, 72
    saving selections into, 404–405
    scope of, 105–108
    setting based on a condition, 461–462
    tutorials for, 55–59
    undefined errors involving, 476
var keyword, 45, 49, 61, 107
vertical bar (|). *See* pipe character (|)
View Source command, in browsers, 141

visibility of elements, 187
    form fields, 271–272, 276–278
    :hidden filter for, 136
    :hidden selector for, 260
    tooltips, 328–329, 330
    :visible filter for, 136

W

\w symbol, in regular expressions, 432
\W symbol, in regular expressions, 432
The W3 Schools JavaScript tutorial (web
    site), 498
WAMP, 346
web addresses, regular expressions for, 440–
    441
web pages. *See also* HTML (Hypertext Markup
    Language)
    adding content to, 31–32, 66–70, 138–141,
        405–406
    adding JavaScript to, 25–29
    adding jQuery to, 122–124
    applying CSS styles to, 124–127
    forms in. *See* forms
    images in. *See* images
    layers of, 4
    layout of
        content slider. *See* content slider
        dimensions of elements,
            determining, 319–322
        position of elements, determing, 322–324
        scrolling position, determing, 324–325
        tabbed panels. *See* tabbed panels
    model of HTML elements in. *See* DOM
    modifying, 124–127, 146–147, 419–421
    navigation for. *See* navigation
    tooltips for, 326–338
    updating content without reloading. *See* Ajax
        (Asynchronous JavaScript and XML)
    validating, 7
    waiting to download before running
        scripts, 123, 169–171
web server, Ajax communication with, 343–
    349
web site resources. *See* online resources
which property, event object, 174
while loops, 93–95
white space, in JavaScript, 49
width. *See* dimensions
width() function, jQuery, 319–322
width property, windows, 242
Willison, Simon (author)
    A (Re)-Introduction to JavaScript (web site
        presentation), 498

window object (browser window), 72. *See also* dialog boxes
   closing, 243
   events for, 160
   focus of, setting, 244
   methods for, 240–241, 243–245. *See also* built-in functions
   moving, 244
   new
      creating, 240–245
      creating within an iframe, 245–249
      opening external links in, 238–240
   properties of, 241–243
   resizing, 244
   scrolling, 244
wrap() function, 420
wrapInner() function, 420–421
wrapping. *See* **text wrapping**
write() method, document object, 31–32, 56

X

XHR object. *See* **XMLHttpRequest object**
XHTML, 5
XMLHttpRequest (XHR) object, 344–345, 346–349
XML, receiving from web server, 365

Y

Yahoo's JavaScript Developer Center (web site), 501
Yahoo User Interface (YUI) library, 119

Z

Zip codes, regular expression for, 436

Colophon

This book was composited in Adobe InDesign CS4 by Newgen North America. Rebecca Demarest provided production assistance.

The cover of this book is based on a series design originally created by David Freedman and modified by Mike Kohnke, Karen Montgomery, and Fitch (*www.fitch.com*). Back cover design, dog illustration, and color selection by Fitch.

David Futato designed the interior layout, based on a series design by Phil Simpson. The text font is Adobe Minion; the heading font is Adobe Formata Condensed; and the code font is LucasFont's TheSansMonoCondensed. The illustrations that appear in the book were produced by Robert Romano using Adobe Photoshop and Illustrator CS5.5.

Get even more for your money.

Join the O'Reilly Community, and register the O'Reilly books you own. It's free, and you'll get:

- $4.99 ebook upgrade offer
- 40% upgrade offer on O'Reilly print books
- Membership discounts on books and events
- Free lifetime updates to ebooks and videos
- Multiple ebook formats, DRM FREE
- Participation in the O'Reilly community
- Newsletters
- Account management
- 100% Satisfaction Guarantee

Signing up is easy:

1. Go to: oreilly.com/go/register
2. Create an O'Reilly login.
3. Provide your address.
4. Register your books.

Note: English-language books only

To order books online:

oreilly.com/store

For questions about products or an order:

orders@oreilly.com

To sign up to get topic-specific email announcements and/or news about upcoming books, conferences, special offers, and new technologies:

elists@oreilly.com

For technical questions about book content:

booktech@oreilly.com

To submit new book proposals to our editors:

proposals@oreilly.com

O'Reilly books are available in multiple DRM-free ebook formats. For more information:

oreilly.com/ebooks

O'REILLY®

Spreading the knowledge of innovators   oreilly.com